WORLD WAR II
CHRONICLE

PRIMARY CONSULTANTS
Gerhard L. Weinberg, Ph.D.
Mark R. Peattie, Ph.D.

ESSAYIST AND CONSULTANT
Richard Overy, Ph.D.

WRITER AND CONSULTANT
David J. A. Stone

CONTRIBUTING WRITERS
Wim Coleman
Martin F. Graham
James H. Hallas
Mark Johnston, Ph.D.
Christy Nadalin, M.A.
Pat Perrin
Peter Stanley, Ph.D.

FOREWORD
John S. D. Eisenhower

PREFACE
U.S. Senator Daniel K. Inouye

LEGACY

Publisher & CEO
Louis Weber

Editor-in-Chief
David J. Hogan

Editor
David Aretha

Art Director
James Slate

Creative Director
Marissa Conner

Acquisitions Editor
Robert A. Rodriguez

Director of Acquisitions & Visual Resources
Doug Brooks

Manager of Acquisitions
Jamie Santoro

Administrative Coordinator
Kathline Jones

Special Projects Editor
Valerie A. Iglar-Mobley

Production Director
Steven Grundt

Digital Publishing Programmer
Michael A. Anderson

Visual Resources Specialists
Rebecca Gizicki
Angela Ogle

Legacy Logo Designer
James Schlottman

Contract Manager
Renee G. Haring

Editorial Assistant
Mariel Demler

Publications Coordinator
Julie L. Greene

Prepress Manufacturing Director
Dave Darian

Prepress Coordinator
Timothy Griffin

Imaging Development Manager
Paul Fromberg

Imaging Technician
Sherese Hopkins

Imaging Assistant
Jacob Strickann

Vice President, Purchasing and Manufacturing
Rocky Wu

Manufacturing Manager
Jared Svoboda

Legal Adviser
Dorothy Weber

Front cover images

Top row, left to right: Adolf Hitler, June 6, 1939; U.S. Army Air Force WASP Elizabeth L. Gardner and B-26 bomber, Harlingen Air Force Base, Harlingen, Texas, c. 1943; Soviet troops in Berlin, May 1945; Hiroshima survivors, mother and child, December 1945; Benito Mussolini, 1938.

Middle row, left to right: V-J Day celebrants, New York City, August 14, 1945; Royal Air Force Bristol Blenheim bomber, 1942; 40mm twin-mount antiaircraft guns in action, USS *Independence*, 1942; U.S. war worker, c. 1943; child survivors of Auschwitz, January 27, 1945.

Bottom row, left to right: British soldier kisses his daughter goodbye, September 21, 1939; General MacArthur and staff wade ashore at Leyte, the Philippines, October 20, 1944; Yalta Conference of Allied leaders (from left, Winston Churchill, Franklin D. Roosevelt, Joseph Stalin), the Crimea, February 1945; U.S. Marines raise the Stars and Stripes atop Mt. Suribachi, Iwo Jima, February 23, 1945; mushroom cloud of "Fat Man" atomic bomb over Nagasaki, Japan, August 9, 1945.

Back cover images

Background image: U.S. Coast Guard amphibious maneuvers, c. 1944.

Inset image: National World War II Memorial, Washington, D.C., April 2005.

Library of Congress Cataloging-in-Publication Data

World War II chronicle / primary consultants, Gerhard L. Weinberg, Mark R. Peattie ; essayist and consultant, Richard Overy ; writers, Wim Coleman ... [et al.] ; foreword, John S. D. Eisenhower ; preface, Daniel Inouye.
    p. cm.
Includes index.
ISBN-13: 978-1-4127-1378-8
ISBN-10: 1-4127-1378-1
1. World War, 1939-1945—Chronology. 2. History, Modern—20th century—Chronology. I. Weinberg, Gerhard L. II. Peattie, Mark R., 1930- III. Overy, R. J. IV. Coleman, Wim. V. Title: World War Two chronicle. VI. Title: World War 2 chronicle.
D743.W6665 2007
940.5302'02—dc22
                    2007015187

Contributors

Foreword Author

John S. D. Eisenhower is a retired U.S. military officer and the author of several books on military history. The son of U.S. Army general and U.S. president Dwight D. Eisenhower, he served in the Army during World War II and the Korean War. He later attained the rank of brigadier general in the U.S. Army Reserve. From 1969 to '71, he served as the U.S. ambassador to Belgium. A self-described "storyteller," his works include *The Bitter Woods*, *General Ike*, and *They Fought at Anzio*.

Preface Author

Senator Daniel K. Inouye has served as U.S. senator from Hawaii since 1963. The son of Japanese immigrants, he administered medical aid during the attack on Pearl Harbor. He enlisted at age 19 and served with the legendary "Go for Broke" 442nd Regimental Combat Team in Italy during World War II. For "extraordinary heroism" in battle, he was awarded the Bronze Star as well as the Distinguished Service Cross, which was later upgraded to the Medal of Honor. His book *Journey to Washington* was published in 1967.

Primary Consultants

Gerhard L. Weinberg, Ph.D., served in the U.S. Army in 1946-47, took a history Ph.D. at the University of Chicago, worked on Columbia University's War Documentation Project, and established the program for microfilming the captured German documents. He taught at the Universities of Chicago, Kentucky, Michigan, and North Carolina, and has served on several U.S. government advisory committees. He is the author or editor of 10 books, including *World in the Balance: Behind the Scenes of World War II*; *Hitler's Foreign Policy 1933-1939: The Road to World War II*; *A World at Arms: A Global History of World War II*; and *Visions of Victory: The Hopes of Eight World War II Leaders*. He also has written more than 100 chapters, articles, guides to archives, and other publications.

Mark R. Peattie, Ph.D., is a research fellow at the Hoover Institution on War, Revolution, and Peace at Stanford University, and is a visiting scholar at the Shorenstein Asia-Pacific Research Center on the same campus. A former Foreign Service officer with extensive experience in Japan, Peattie holds a doctoral degree in modern Japanese history from Princeton University. He has taught at The Pennsylvania State University, the University of California at Los Angeles, and the University of Massachusetts at Boston. He is the author of a number of books on modern Japanese imperial, military, and naval history, most notably *Ishiwara Kanji and Japan's Confrontation with the West*; *Nan'yô: The Rise and Fall of the Japanese in Micronesia, 1885-1945*; and *Kaigun: Strategy, Tactics, and Technology in the Imperial Japanese Navy, 1887-1941*.

Essayist and Consultant

Richard Overy, Ph.D., (essayist for chapters 1-11, 13, and 14) is professor of history at the University of Exeter, UK. He was previously professor of modern history at King's College London, where he taught for 25 years. He has written extensively on World War II and the European dictatorships, including *The Air War 1939-1945*; *The Battle of Britain*; *Why the Allies Won*; and *Russia's War*. His *Dictators: Hitler's Germany and Stalin's Russia* won the 2004 Wolfson Prize for History. He was elected a fellow of the British Academy in 2000.

Writer and Consultant

David J. A. Stone is a former British Army officer whose military service included the command of his regiment and various command, staff, and other assignments throughout the world. He is a graduate of the Royal Military Academy Sandhurst, the UK Army Staff College, and the U.S. Army John F. Kennedy Special Warfare Center. He became a freelance military historian and writer in 2002, and now lives in Devon, England. One of his particular areas of expertise is the history and development of the German army from the 17th century to the present day. His published works include *Cold War Warriors*; *'First Reich'*; *Dien Bien Phu*; *Wars of the Cold War*; *War Summits*; and *Fighting for the Fatherland*.

Contributing Writers

Wim Coleman has written books, plays, and articles about U.S. history for READ, Appleseeds, Greenhaven, Perfection Learning, Discovery Enterprises, Portable Press, and Enslow. He also contributed to *American West Chronicle*.

Martin F. Graham is a contributor to *World War II Magazine*. He also has worked closely with veterans of the 463rd Parachute Field Artillery Battalion, chronicling their service throughout North Africa and Europe. In addition, he has authored several Civil War books, including *Civil War Chronicle*

James H. Hallas is a graduate of Syracuse University's Newhouse School of Communications. A military historian, he has penned a pair of World War II histories that focus on U.S. Marine Corps campaigns: *The Devil's Anvil: The Assault on Peleliu* and *Killing Ground on Okinawa: The Battle for Sugar Loaf Hill*. He also wrote *Doughboy War: The American Expeditionary Force in World War I*.

Mark Johnston, Ph.D., is head of history at Scotch College in Melbourne, Australia. He has authored six books on World War II, including *Fighting the Enemy: Australian Soldiers and Their Adversaries in World War II* and (with Peter Stanley) *Alamein: The Australian Story*. He has edited four books on the German armed forces.

Christy Nadalin, M.A., is a freelance writer, editorial researcher, and documentary television producer whose work has appeared in publications and productions by the National Geographic Society, the Discovery Channel, A&E Television Networks, and Time Life Books. She also contributed to *Civil Rights Chronicle*, *The Sixties Chronicle*, *The Fifties Chronicle*, and *American West Chronicle*.

Pat Perrin has authored U.S. history books, plays, articles, and stories for Greenhaven, Perfection Learning, Discovery Enterprises, Portable Press, ETS, Appleseeds, and Enslow. She also contributed to *American West Chronicle*.

Peter Stanley, Ph.D., is the principal historian at the Australian War Memorial, and appears regularly at conferences and on television. In 2006 he received a Flagship Fellowship by the Eleanor Dark Foundation. He has authored 18 books, including *Alamein: The Australian Story* (with Mark Johnston) and *Quinn's Post, Anzac, Gallipoli*.

Factual Verification and Research

Marci McGrath, M.A., (fact-checker) holds a master's degree in history from the University of New Orleans. She has taught history at the secondary school level.

Christy Nadalin, M.A., (fact-checker; professional information above)

Richard A. Sauers, Ph.D., (researcher) is the author of more than two dozen books and a contributor to *American West Chronicle*. He is director of the Packwood House Museum in Lewisburg, Pennsylvania.

Chris Smith (fact-checker) is a New Orleans-based writer and researcher.

National Archives photo research by **Jane Martin**

Maps by **Chris Bowden**

Index by **Ina Gravitz**

CONTENTS

November 1918–August 1931 The redrawn Europe of 1918 provoked resentment, political agitation, and an ambitious politican named Adolf Hitler, who found his voice in Germany's democratic process.

January 1931–August 1939 Japan's imperial ambitions were matched by Germany's desire for "living space," and Italy's dreams of glory. Britain's appeasement encouraged Hitler's schemes, while the USA remained sunk in isolationism.

September 1939–March 1940 On September 1, 1939, German forces moved against Poland. Treaty obligations forced England and France to declare war on Germany. For the second time in barely more than 20 years, Europe was at war.

April 1940–June 1941 In 1940 the Nazi war machine conquered much of Western Europe, including France. Britain battled back with great courage. And then came Hitler's most audacious campaign: Barbarossa.

July 1941–December 1941 Hitler's forces cut across Russia like a scythe, and were not halted until at the gates of Moscow. In the Pacific, Japan sent planes to Pearl Harbor, Hawaii, to strike the U.S. fleet that blocked Japan's access to oil. America was in the war.

January 1942–July 1942 The high point of Axis conquest came in 1942. Ironically, though, the U.S. Navy had already forced Japan into a defensive posture, and Germany would find it increasingly difficult to mount sustained offensives.

August 1942–January 1943 A renewed offensive by the Germans in Russia was a seesaw affair that ended in complete disaster for Germany at Stalingrad. In the Pacific, Allied forces advanced on the Japanese homeland, one outlying island at a time.

FOREWORD

ON THE EVENING of September 3, 1939, I sat with my parents in the Manila Hotel as we strained our ears over a shortwave radio. We were listening to an address being delivered by British prime minister Neville Chamberlain, speaking from London, half a world away. It was a moment I shall never forget, especially when he uttered the dreaded words, "Now Great Britain is at war with Germany."

John S. D. Eisenhower

The awful message was not unexpected. Two days earlier, German dictator Adolf Hitler's panzers had rolled across the border into Poland. Britain, as Poland's ally, had no choice but to come to Poland's aid.

Like millions everywhere, my parents and I clung to the hope that this war was not for real, that somehow this could be a limited war, quickly negotiated. For a while it appeared that this wish might come true. Once Germany (and Russia) had subdued Poland, an eerie peace settled down in Western Europe, and perhaps some accommodation might be reached that would avoid a repetition of the horrors of the First World War, which had ended only 21 years earlier. That slaughter needed to be avoided at all costs.

It was not to be. In the spring of 1940, Hitler's forces overran Western Europe, including Norway and Denmark. France surrendered, and the British stood alone. As the years ground on, the Second World War turned out to be more destructive in lives and treasure than the first. In the 1914–18 war, civilians were largely spared. In the second war, millions upon millions would die, civilians as well as soldiers, thus making this conflict many times more horrible than its predecessor.

Despite these grim facts, the Second World War has often been described as "the last good war," usually half in jest. The reason for such an outlandish thought comes from nostalgia based on the memory of a national unity that existed to a degree almost unparalleled in our history. Further, with rare exceptions such as the American Revolution, this country has fought few "necessary" wars. In that, however, World War II stands paramount. It was our most "necessary" war. Even the more costly American Civil War, it can be argued, might possibly have been avoided.

And yet, despite the catastrophe to the world that would accompany a complete Nazi victory, the United States refused, as long as was possible, to enter on the side of the Allies. For more than two years—27 months—America stood on the sidelines, strong in its sympathies for the British, French, and later the Russians but refusing to join them. Fortunately, however, President Franklin D. Roosevelt recognized the need for an Allied victory much sooner than did the majority of his countrymen, and America moved slowly but inexorably toward active participation. Thus, by the time the Japanese Imperial Navy attacked our Pacific Fleet at Pearl Harbor, Hawaii, on December 7, 1941, the reaction was shock, anger, and determination but not complete surprise.

As a quirk of history, it is interesting that America's entry into the Second World War was triggered not by an incident in Europe, from which direction lay our greatest danger, but from the East. The overt attack against our armed forces—combined, it must be admitted, by a touch of racism—engendered a thirst for revenge against Japan, not against Hitler.

From a strategic viewpoint, however, it was logical that Germany be defeated first. Not only was Hitler our greatest threat, but Europe was the only area where the armed might of all three major Allied nations—Britain, America, and Russia—could be concentrated. But given the hatred of our people against the Japanese, it required all the authority and persuasiveness that President Roosevelt could muster to support the "Europe First" strategy. It was the supreme test of Roosevelt's leadership in the war.

The strategies followed by the Allies and Axis will be described throughout this book. From the Allied viewpoint, the formulation of these strategies was extremely difficult, largely because of the somewhat different war aims of the Americans and British. The Americans had no interest other than the defeat of the Axis. The British viewpoint was less simple: the destruction of Hitler, yes, but also the preservation of what was left of the British Empire. In the course of studying strategy, however, the reader will be enlightened to read of the various personalities of the war—colorful, strong, and independent but all dedicated to the common cause of victory. In the background will loom the vast loss of civilian life, including the victims of the Nazi Holocaust.

Personally, one incident at the end of the war in Europe is etched in my memory. I was a lieutenant in the First Army, which was dashing eastward across Thuringia, Germany, toward the Elbe River. One morning—Friday, April 13 in Europe—I rolled out of my sleeping bag on the floor of a German farmhouse to be greeted with the news that President Roosevelt had died the day before at Warm Springs, Georgia. I can still remember the shock. No concern about winning the war—that was now a foregone conclusion. But though his successor, President Harry Truman, would conduct the rest of the war competently, it seemed unjust that one of the principal architects of victory, President Roosevelt, should not live to see his handiwork come to fruition.

As with any other such cataclysmic event, the six years of the Second World War have left a deep imprint. Part of the legacy of the war, tragically, was the degeneration of relationships among the victors, which led to a so-called "Cold War" between the West and its previous ally, Russia, exacerbated by the invention of the atomic and later thermonuclear bombs. It is no wonder that Winston Churchill named the last volume of his World War Two memoirs *Triumph and Tragedy*.

This book does not confine itself to the largely military considerations I have described. Life goes on at home, even in wartime. And no military operation can long be sustained without the support of the people. *World War II Chronicle* will make those years vivid. After all, nobody should be uninformed of the most dramatic moment of our time.

John S. D. Eisenhower

John S. D. Eisenhower, retired brigadier general, USAR, served as U.S. ambassador to Belgium during the Nixon administration. He is an acclaimed military historian whose books include The Bitter Woods: The Battle of the Bulge.

PREFACE

ON THE MORNING of December 7, 1941, I was preparing to go to church with my family. As I was buttoning my shirt, the voice from my bedside radio suddenly blared: "Pearl Harbor is being bombed by the Japanese! I repeat: This is not a test or a maneuver! Japanese planes are attacking Oahu!"

My father and I rushed outside of our home, and we stared toward Pearl Harbor. We saw the black puffs of smoke from anti-aircraft fire, the dirty gray smoke of fires billowing over Pearl, and the Japanese fighter planes that soared overhead.

Since I had medical-aid training, I was quickly called into service as the head of a Red Cross first-aid team. In the chaos of that Sunday morning, as I helped the injured and dying in my Honolulu neighborhood, I soon realized that my country, the United States of America, had been thrust into World War II. I was 17 years old, and the war would soon become the defining experience for me and my generation.

The men in multiethnic Hawaii, then a U.S. territory, were no different from the men on the U.S. mainland. We were outraged by the attack. We wanted to serve, and we wanted to defend our nation and its democratic ideals. But shortly after the attack on Pearl Harbor, the U.S. government declared that all Japanese Americans

Senator Daniel K. Inouye

were "enemy aliens." That meant Japanese Americans could not serve in the uniform of our country. We could not volunteer or be drafted. We were just 4-C—"enemy aliens."

In the aftermath of Pearl Harbor, Executive Order No. 9066 was also issued. It established 10 internment camps in desolate parts of the country, and 120,000 Americans of Japanese ancestry were rounded up and herded into these camps. The mass incarceration of Japanese Americans was unconstitutional. It was done without the filing of charges, and no trials were held. In the end, not one Japanese American was ever found guilty of espionage or any treasonous act.

On February 1, 1943, nearly 14 months after Pearl Harbor, the opportunity to serve was finally offered to Japanese Americans when President Franklin D. Roosevelt authorized the formation of a Japanese American combat team. When he made his announcement, President Roosevelt declared, "Americanism is a matter of mind and heart; Americanism is not and, never was, a matter of race or color."

In Hawaii, the response to the call to arms was dramatic. The original plan called for 1,500 Nisei—second-generation Americans of Japanese ancestry—to serve in the 442nd Regimental Combat Team. But nearly 10,000 volunteered, roughly 80 percent of the eligible men. I was among the more than 2,600 who were accepted. Later, we would train and serve alongside mainland Japanese Americans who had also volunteered for service in the 442nd.

The day I reported for my induction, my father, who had immigrated to Hawaii, escorted me to the recruiting station, where trucks were waiting to take recruits to Schofield Barracks. He didn't say a word in the streetcar until we finally reached the recruiting station. He looked at me and said: "This country has been good to us. Whatever you do, do not dishonor this country, and do not dishonor the family. If you must die, die with honor." My father's words were very profound, and they have always stayed with me.

When the 442nd was training at Camp Shelby, Mississippi, I learned of the internment camps, and that the 442nd's mainland Nisei—who comprised one-third of the unit—had volunteered while confined in the camps. To this day, I ask myself: Would I have volunteered if I were behind barbed wire with my family members? It didn't take much courage for us from Hawaii to enlist because we believed it was the right thing to do. For the mainland Nisei, they were willing to fight for—and die for—their country, even though it had unjustly spurned them when it abandoned its democratic ideals.

For the men of the 442nd, the war was a costly demonstration of our citizenship. The combat team numbered 4,500 soldiers, but it would take more than 12,000 men to sustain that 4,500 number because of the unit's high casualty rate. The blood we spilled, however, resulted in more than 18,000 individual decorations, including 21 Medals of Honor, our nation's highest award for military valor. Many of the decorations were awarded posthumously for acts of extraordinary bravery and courage shown on the battlefield. Because of the valor of the 442nd and other segregated units, the courage and patriotism of minority Americans could no longer be questioned.

The bravery of Japanese Americans, African Americans, and other minorities who wore the uniform of our nation during World War II moved President Harry Truman to issue the order desegregating the armed forces of the United States. So not only did we triumph over the enemy abroad, we also won a crucial battle at home—against prejudice in America. When we came home, we were determined to transform Hawaii and our nation into a society in which we and our families were no longer second-class citizens. We wanted a country that, indeed, stood for justice for all.

Aloha,

Daniel K. Inouye
United States Senator

Daniel K. Inouye, the first American of Japanese ancestry to serve in the Congress, is a recipient of the Medal of Honor.

INTRODUCTION

WORLD WAR II IS THE Janus event of the 20th century: a dual-natured homunculus that created even as it destroyed, gave even as it stole—though what it was giving was far less apparent at the time than what it was taking. Its horrors were almost literally unimaginable, its scope breathtaking. It presented clear demarcations between ideologies, and while soldiers, civilians, and functionaries argued the finer points, more than 50 million people perished.

The conflict built upon festering resentments left over from the Great War of 1914–18, and brewed in the 1920s, the century's first "modern" decade of personal mobility, mass communication, assembly-line production, large-scale agriculture, and increasing urbanization. Although the jolly economic ride enjoyed by the developed world crashed in the 1930s, the engine that would propel future developments had been put into motion.

The improved working conditions, healthier diets, and better pay of the interwar years freed individuals and whole cultures from energy-sapping searches for food, clothing, and shelter. With full bellies and a warm hearth, people in America, Europe, and parts of Asia had the leisure to think superficially about weighty topics, such as politics, nationalism, a bigger and better military, the religions that rubbed them the wrong way, that bothersome country next door.

Hitler, Stalin, Mussolini, and other, lesser European lights pulled the neat trick of exploiting horrific memories of the Great War in the name of national pride and

Monte Cassino, Italy, after heavy fighting

progress while simultaneously inducing a sort of amnesia, whereby far too many of Europe's citizens became hazy about the destructiveness of combat, and thus were primed for another, bigger war.

Elsewhere, a mutual, cross-oceanic disdain shared by the West and Asia helped contribute to the rise of militarism in Japan, a nation that had pummeled Russia during a little war in 1904–05, and thereafter resolved to be neither technologically backward nor ignored. Like the terror regimes of Europe, Japan craved empire.

Expansionist schemes were encouraged by the staunch isolationism of the United States, which had entered the Great War late and whose shores were never physically touched by battle, but which nevertheless saw enough to know that it didn't want to see any more.

If the global political landscape was ripe for war, so was the physical landscape. The increasing urbanization conveniently placed enormous populations and industry in small geographic areas. This would turn out to be handy for bombers sent by the enemy, and for ground troops who could conquer a nation by subduing a capital city and the roadways and rail lines that serviced it.

New philosophies of ground combat and, more strikingly, air assault involved civilians in battle on scales previously unimagined. Because technology encouraged speedier and more expansive ground mobility during World War II than in the Great War, noncombatants across vast areas of Europe and Asia were rolled up by advancing armies, or swept beneath the wheels of their own forces in retreat. Invading troops, often frustrated by great physical remove from adequate supply, and full of propaganda-fed contempt for enemy civilians, committed atrocities freely; women and children were particularly noticeable in victims' roles.

Area bombing—a polite term for terror bombing of nonmilitary targets—was adopted by Axis and Allied powers alike. No potential target was considered off-limits. High-explosive ordnance was joined by fiendishly effective incendiaries that reduced residential areas, and people, to ash.

If there is a signature event of World War II it is the Holocaust—the German-engineered "Final Solution" to the Jewish "problem," by which some six million Jews were kidnapped, interned, tortured, and murdered. It is the Holocaust, above all, that gives World War II its peculiarly unsavory luster.

Looking back on the war more than 60 years later does suggest some positive outcomes. The conflict sparked greatly improved medical care, improved transport, impressive industrial efficiencies, and sophisticated communication. It brought democracy to Germany and Japan, and encouraged the creation of Israel. The conflict ushered in some 30 years of uninterrupted world economic growth, and planted the seeds for the 1991 demise of the Soviet Union.

Most significantly, World War II revealed itself as the last of its breed, for with the advent of atomic weapons, war on such a scale became an impossibility. The next world war, if it came, could begin and end within hours. Although countless local and regional conflicts flared after 1945, humanity did not lose its mind and reduce the planet to a cinder.

The greatest gift of World War II, then, is the brutal epiphany it delivered: Next time will be worse, so "next time" must never come.

BEYOND THE GREAT WAR

NOVEMBER 1918–AUGUST 1931

"I can predict with absolute certainty that within another generation there will be another world war if the nations of the world do not concert the method by which to prevent it."

—U.S. PRESIDENT WOODROW WILSON

ON MAY 7, 1919, in a room in the grand Versailles Palace outside Paris, German foreign minister Count Ulrich von Brockdorff-Rantzau arrived at the head of a delegation of diplomats. They came to negotiate with representatives of the major Allied powers—Britain, France, Italy, Japan, and the United States—following the armistice that had ended hostilities in Europe. Instead of finding seats laid out for his delegation, Brockdorff-Rantzau and his colleagues, dressed stiffly in frock coats and wing collars, were made to stand like so many errant schoolboys. This was the first of many humiliations imposed on the Germans.

The Allied powers thought they had won the war and that Germany had been the architect of its outbreak. The German view that an armistice was really a truce, rather than surrender, was ignored.

The origins of this humiliation lay five years before, in the crisis that led to the outbreak of what became known as the Great War. The victorious Allies blamed Germany and Austria-Hungary for causing that war, but the explanation is more complex. Before 1914 Europe had entered a new phase in its history with the emergence of a group of powerful, industrialized, and heavily armed states, each of which had imperial interests to defend. National competition became the key characteristic of the age.

Earlier, in the 19th century, these states had collaborated to keep the peace, because the kings and aristocrats who dominated the political scene had a strong interest in avoiding conflict. But by the turn of the 20th cen-

Punch magazine weighed in on the practicality of the new League of Nations with this cartoon, published in 1919. It shows an idealistic Woodrow Wilson, the American president, presenting an impossibly heavy olive branch to the Dove of Peace. Formed to preserve world peace, the League faced too many national resentments and ambitions to live up to its idealistic purpose.

tury, the old regimes were in retreat and modern political movements—many of them strongly nationalist in outlook—had begun to emerge. The new working classes, thrown up by rapid industrialization, offered a different kind of threat, though many of them could be won over to a patriotic cause. Throughout Eastern and Southern Europe, where there existed a mixture of nationalities under imperial Prussian or Austrian or Russian rule, mass politics led to agitation for national self-determination. This issue was at its most acute in the Habsburg Empire, whose capital was in Vienna. Its rulers maintained a precarious hold on a territory that comprised a dozen nationalities, many of them eager for autonomy.

U.S. doughboys fire on German troops with a 37mm gun in the Meuse-Argonne campaign in late 1918. The American entry into the European conflict ensured an Allied victory in World War I. Unfortunately, despite great hopes, the United States was unable to engineer a lasting peace once the "War to End All Wars" was won.

It is no accident that it was there, in the national patchwork of the Habsburg Empire, that the immediate origins of the war of 1914–18 are found. The empire seethed with conflicts—between rival nationalities, between different classes, and between the new democratic parties and the authoritarian monarchy that ran the system. Most acute of all was the crisis with the southern Slav populations of the monarchy. Backed by the independent state of Serbia, Slav nationalists in the empire looked for a southern Slav state (Yugoslavia). In Vienna, fears arose that the Serbs would provoke the breakup of the old order.

On June 28, 1914, on an official visit to Sarajevo (capital of the recently annexed province of Bosnia), the heir to the Habsburg throne, Archduke Franz Ferdinand, together with his wife Sophie, were assassinated by a young Bosnian terrorist named Gavrilo Princip. The Austrian authorities demanded action. They blamed Serbia for encouraging the Black Hand society to which Princip belonged, and demanded that Serbia accept Austrian interference in their internal investigation of the murder. The Serbs accepted parts of Austria's ultimatum but balked at other portions. This was the trigger for Austria's declaration of war.

None of the other European powers had expected or planned for war in 1914, but it was a fear that each of them had harbored. In the 10 years before 1914, many such crises had arisen. Each power's fear of the other powers fueled an arms race that produced large armies and navies with little to do but plan ways of outmaneuvering perceived enemies. Armaments did not cause war, as many believed at the time, but they contributed to a growing sense of instability and antagonism, and lessened the capacity of states to restrain the military when crisis beckoned.

This is what happened in 1914. Austria was prepared to go to war with Serbia without the other powers intervening, but it needed the support of Germany, its ally, and the neutralization of any threat from Russia. Austria got full support from Berlin, but Russia—fearful that Austria would use the crisis to dominate the Slavic Balkans and stall Russian imperial ambitions in the region—backed up Serbia and began to mobilize.

This decision produced a domino effect. In Berlin, it was assumed that Russian mobilization was the result of French and British encouragement. The German military persuaded the German emperor to let them carry out the so-called Schlieffen Plan, to attack France first and then to turn and defeat Russia. When Austria finally invaded Serbia, Germany prepared to attack France. Britain sided with France when the Germans invaded Belgium, which was in violation of the agreement to respect its neutrality. By August 4, 1914, all the major powers of Europe were at war.

The German delegation (*left*) arrives on November 11, 1918, to sign the armistice agreement that ended the Great War. Germany was forced to sign a "guilt clause" accepting responsibility for the war, and was saddled with huge reparations payments.

The remarkable fact is that few of the powers that entered the war really understood what form it would take. The prevailing thought was that the conflict might be resolved by a few large set-piece battles and be "over by Christmas." The war that developed could not have been more different. A stalemate developed on the Western Front, while there was much movement back and forth on the Eastern Front. Combat was dominated by artillery and the newly developed machine gun. Warfare stagnated into a terrible contest of attrition in which both sides sustained losses on scales unimaginable before 1914.

The conflict was presented as a life-and-death struggle for national survival. The Turkish Empire joined the conflict in 1914, siding with Germany and Austria. Italy entered in 1915, siding with the Western Allies. In 1917 the United States, entirely distant from the conflict when it broke out, moved to belligerency in response to Germany's unrestricted use of submarines against American shipping. In three years, the war between Austria and Serbia had become global.

To win the war, the major combatants found themselves facing an unprecedented task. It became necessary for the states to control their economies, to regiment agriculture, to direct trade, and to conscript labor (and to draw in an army of female workers). Production was directed more and more to armaments. The inflated demands of this new form of national conflict came to be known as "total war," a term coined by German general Erich von Ludendorff in 1919 to describe the mobilization of the entire economic, social, and moral energies of the nation. In the end, the economic resources of the Allied powers proved greater than those of Germany and its allies. Tanks and aircraft began to change the nature of war, and the Allies had more of both. With its allies having already been defeated and its own army beaten, Germany sought an armistice, which was signed on November 11, 1918.

The cost of the conflict in terms of human losses was colossal. More than nine million soldiers were killed, millions were permanently maimed, and an unknown number of civilians died from malnutrition, disease, and combat. In 1918 and 1919, an influenza epidemic wiped out millions more from a population debilitated by four years of growing privation.

It is against this background that the decision to blame the Central Powers for the war must be understood. When the Treaty of Peace was drawn up in the spring of 1919, a clause was inserted that made clear the responsibility of the Central Powers for reparation. Clause 231, the "War Guilt" clause, was signed by the German delegation, under protest, on June 28, 1919.

A crowd flees a street confrontation with government forces during the Russian Revolution in 1917. The First World War transformed the political geography of Europe, prompting the fall of Czarist Russia, the Austro-Hungarian Empire, and the Ottoman Empire. The numerous small states and territorial squabbles that resulted would lead to war again within 20 years.

The Germans believed that the conditions imposed on them were exceptionally harsh. The German armed forces and fortifications were to be disbanded, and Germany was allowed to retain only a rump 100,000-man army to keep domestic peace. Germany was denied the right to possess aircraft, submarines, and most forms of heavy army weapons. All German colonies were taken and distributed as mandates to the victorious powers. Territory taken by Prussia or Germany in the past was returned to Germany's neighbors. France took back Alsace-Lorraine, seized by Germany in 1870, while the restored Polish state was awarded the rich coal and steel region of Silesia. To compensate for damages caused by the war, Germany was eventually required to pay 132 billion gold marks, in installments, up to the year 1988.

No other issue so united Germans in their resentment of the victors than the question of reparations. Though Germany managed to avoid paying much of what it was supposed to pay, and borrowed and then repudiated vast sums, the important point is that ordinary Germans perceived reparations to be a punitive sanction. They were determined to overturn the *Diktat* (dictated peace).

The final year of war had ushered in a period of momentous transformation worldwide. In 1917 the Russian war effort collapsed and the emperor, Nicholas II, was forced to abdicate. The revolutionary regime tried to continue the fight, but economic conditions and military capability deteriorated sharply. In October 1917, Lenin's Bolshevik Party—the most radical wing of the Russian revolutionary movement—seized power in Petrograd (St. Petersburg), and declared a Communist regime. Bolshevik leaders expected that their revolt would herald the onset of worldwide revolution. After three years of bitter civil war, Bolshevik rule was secured by 1921 but world revolution did not follow. Short Communist revolts erupted in Hungary and Germany in 1919, and violent confrontations occurred between workers and the state in Italy and Spain in the immediate postwar years, but no other European society saw a Communist takeover. The Communist movement outside Russia was violently suppressed, and many of its leaders were murdered or imprisoned.

The end of the war transformed the political geography of Europe and the Middle East. After the fall of the Russian Empire, the German, Austrian, and Ottoman Turkish empires also disappeared. They were replaced by new, small states from the Baltic Sea to the Suez Canal. The former Turkish provinces in Iraq, Syria, Lebanon, and Palestine were handed over as mandates to Britain and France.

The former imperial territories in Europe held by Russia, Austria, and Germany all became independent national states. This was consistent with the demand expressed by U.S. president Woodrow Wilson that the peoples of Europe should be allowed national "self-determination." From 1919 to 1921, more treaties were drawn up and signed with Germany's allies—Austria, Hungary, Bulgaria, and Turkey—which confirmed the new shape of the continent. In every case, the national settlements were messy. Small national fractions were isolated in the territory of other states.

The end of the war produced a paradox of crisis coexisting with a mood of optimism about the future. Parliamentary democracy was introduced everywhere in the areas dominated by the prewar monarchies (except for Russia), and in 1920 almost every European state was, in formal terms, demo-

The figure of "Peace" stands beside an honor roll that includes a list of names representing the different national origins of Americans who died in the Great War. President Woodrow Wilson hoped that the solidarity demonstrated by Americans of different origins during the war could be emulated by the nations of the world in a quest for lasting peace.

cratic, even though millions of women still lacked the vote. The settlement in 1919 was supposed to pave the way for a new world order based on collaboration and mutual respect. At Versailles, the foundations were laid for the League of Nations, which was committed to isolating international aggression and providing a framework for the peaceful resolution of conflicts.

In 1920 the League of Nations finally met in session in the Swiss city of Geneva, chosen because of Switzerland's long tradition of neutrality. The League reflected a widespread revulsion against war. The Covenant of the League of Nations committed all its members to work toward universal disarmament.

As the terrible human costs of the war were inscribed on thousands of monuments to the war dead across Europe, the popular mood echoed the slogan that the Great War had really been "The War to End All Wars." In 1928 German author Erich Maria Remarque published his classic account of the war, *All Quiet on the Western Front.* The novel was immediately translated into other languages. The book's vivid descriptions of death and mutilation reminded Europeans of the futility of war.

German workers dismantle a tank outside Berlin following the armistice. Under the terms of the Treaty of Versailles, Germany was forbidden to possess aircraft, submarines, and most heavy weapons. The army was limited to 100,000 men, solely to keep domestic peace. The harsh peace terms only fueled German anger.

From the start, it was difficult to operate the new postwar order on the idealistic terms in which it had been constructed. The peace settlement sparked a wide range of grievances for those states that regarded themselves as victims. Even the victors were not entirely happy. Italy got little out of the territorial readjustments, and Italian nationalists condemned what they called "the mutilated peace." Japan was resentful at what it regarded as the race prejudice of the other victorious states. In Britain, the peace was viewed as unnecessarily harsh. In the United States, whose president had been the main architect of the new order, the peace settlement was rejected by Congress as the result of a growing backlash against the European Allies, who were seen as self-interested imperial states exploiting American assistance for their own ambitions. The United States abandoned the League and the peace settlement altogether. It refused to ratify the treaty with France intended to ensure that the French would not detach the left bank of the Rhine from battered Germany.

The Soviet Union regarded the new order as a mask to cover the interests of imperialist capitalism. It was excluded from the League because of the prevailing hostility toward communism. As the principal former enemy, Germany was also excluded from the League until 1926. This placed the three potentially most powerful economic and military states outside the prevailing order. The situation only enhanced the opinion that the League really was a Franco-British puppet designed, in the words of American "radio priest" Father Charles Coughlin, "to make the world safe for hypocrisy."

The system was also weakened by economic crisis. The pre-1914 world trading economy could not be fully revived, and during the 1920s widespread unemployment and poverty existed across much of Europe. From 1919 to 1924, currency collapsed completely in Russia, France, Germany, Austria, and Hungary. Bank accounts and paper assets became worthless. The result was the dispossession of broad sections of the European middle class, leaving behind a legacy of bitterness that fueled the growth of radical right-wing politics.

The development of sharp ideological divisions in European politics can be explained not only by the rise of communism and socialism but also by the collapse of the established conservative order in much of Europe and the emergence of mass nationalism. Many ex-soldiers returned home angry at failure in the war and resentful of the workers and wealthy who had stayed behind. They preached a new kind of nationalism that was hostile to the old order and fanatically anti-Communist. They were attracted to new forms of authoritarian and collectivist rule. The first evidence of what this new politics meant was seen in Italy, where a young, militant veteran, Benito Mussolini, established the Italian Fascist movement in 1919.

Benito Mussolini (pictured with his pet lion) returned from the war to establish the Italian Fascist movement in 1919. The new political philosophy combined radical nationalism and social policy under authoritarian rule. The movement would be eagerly embraced by populations tired of economic and social strife, and desperate for order.

Fascism took its name from the arrangement of rods and axes—the *fasces*—that had been a symbol of authority in ancient Rome. Soon the term "Fascist" became shorthand for any political group that combined a radical nationalist and social policy and called for dictatorial rule. In Munich in southern Germany, another veteran—young Austrian agitator Adolf Hitler—assumed leadership in 1921 of a small political party, the National Socialist German Workers' Party. Its name made clear a joint commitment to national revival and radical social change.

If fascism had just remained a small fringe movement, the history of the post-Great War years would have been very different. But Mussolini's new party, through a combination of effective propaganda and street violence, soon became a contender for power. In October 1922, after threatening a march on Rome, Mussolini was offered the premiership. Within four years, he had subverted parliamentary rule, destroyed the Italian left, and established a one-party state with himself as *Il Duce* (The Leader).

Fascism was imitated in every European state. It traded on each country's grievances but also promised a bright utopian future. Militarism was a central feature of Fascist appeal, and thousands of young Europeans flocked into the movements and their paramilitary organizations.

In 1923, at the height of the European inflationary crisis, Hitler moved to imitate Mussolini. In addition to planning a march on Berlin, he staged a coup in Munich on November 8–9 as a prelude to a national seizure of power. His *putsch* was suppressed, and Hitler was imprisoned. However, he emerged a year later, reestablished his leadership of the National Socialist movement, and launched a campaign of violent anti-Marxism side-by-side with a struggle for parliamentary seats. Both Mussolini and Hitler were unwilling to accept the postwar settlement. Their rhetoric suggested that a "new order" was needed to replace a liberal international system that they regarded as decadent.

German soldiers cluster around a tank on a Berlin street during a troubled period of the Weimar Republic. The fledgling democracy faced growing social unrest, as unemployment and the collapse of the German currency thrust the nation deeper into poverty following the war. The bleak outlook encouraged the rise of extreme nationalist movements.

The threat posed by fascism lay in the future. In the 1920s, the international order was dominated by the interests of Britain and France, and there was little to menace it. In 1925 a pact was signed at Locarno between Britain, France, Italy, Germany, and other European countries that gave a mutual guarantee of the frontiers agreed upon in 1919. In 1926, thanks to the efforts of German foreign minister Gustav Stresemann, Germany was admitted to the League with a permanent seat on the Council. The willingness of the United States, despite the failure to join the League, to shore up the European economy with generous credits helped to produce a brief period of economic stability from 1924 to 1928.

The high point of the postwar decade was reached in 1928, when U.S. secretary of state Frank Kellogg and French foreign minister Aristide Briand invited the states of the world to Paris to sign a solemn declaration that they would never again resort to war as a means of settling disputes between them. The Pact of Paris was signed by more than 60 states, including the representatives of Italy, Germany, Japan, and the Soviet Union (each of which would launch wars of aggression in the 1930s).

The fragility of the existing order was exposed suddenly in 1929 by a severe economic crisis. The world economy had never returned to full health after 1919, but the buoyant American boom of the 1920s, fueled by expectations of a secure trading future, had masked the underlying problems. When the speculative share bubble broke on Wall Street in October 1929, the impact was catastrophic. Desperate American lenders tried to recall their money at home and abroad, provoking a wave of bankruptcies and widespread unemployment. The economic orthodoxy of the time preached retrenchment and cuts on spending at points of crisis. As governments tried to balance their budgets and the balance of payments, a further wave of economic crisis followed.

The downward spiral was not halted for some time. World trade fell by 60 percent from 1928 to 1932, and unemployment worldwide reached an estimated 40 million workers. The weaker economies, already hit by wartime losses and the inflation crisis, suffered most. In Germany, 30 percent of the workforce was unemployed by 1932 and industrial output was halved. Unwilling to honor debts abroad, Germany faced serious problems. It was rescued only by the American decision to suspend debt repayments for a year. By that stage, the United States faced a business-cycle crisis so severe that many observers assumed that Marx must have been right to predict that overheated capitalism was destined to collapse in revolution.

Adolf Hitler emerged from the trenches of the Western Front embittered by defeat and the harsh conditions imposed upon Germany by the Allies. He found a ready audience for his message (conveyed in his book *Mein Kampf*), which offered hope and a new order through National Socialism.

The political fallout from the economic slump was equally severe. International collaboration to avert disaster evaporated. National economies were protected by new protective walls. In the U.S. in 1930, the Hawley-Smoot Tariff Act (named after the two congressmen who introduced it) placed severe limits on imports. Two years later, Britain adopted a system of Imperial Preference, giving a privileged position to empire traders. Thus, the two largest trading economies in the world became committed to saving their own interests first in order to avoid further risk of domestic political crisis.

In Germany, politics was polarized between extreme right and left. In the 1930 parliamentary elections, both German Communists and National Socialists made substantial gains, taking almost one-third of the popular vote between them. All parties became united in hostility to the major Western countries. The economic slump inflamed existing resentments and ignited new ones. The mood of cautious optimism that had characterized the brief period of stability in the 1920s was replaced with an overwhelming sense of foreboding.

BUILDUP TO WAR

JANUARY 1931–AUGUST 1939

> **"Whoever wants to live has to fight, and whoever refuses to fight in this world of eternal challenge has no right to live."**
>
> —Adolf Hitler, quoted in a German children's schoolbook, c. 1937

O<small>N</small> S<small>EPTEMBER</small> 18, 1931, a group of Japanese soldiers stationed in the northern Chinese province of Manchuria, masquerading as Chinese bandits, blew up a few feet of the Japanese-controlled South Manchurian Railway. The clumsily orchestrated incident was used as a pretext to launch an attack by the Kwantung Army (Japan's field army in China), which aimed to occupy the whole of the province and bring its rich resources under Japanese control. This was the start of a decade of escalating violence that would culminate in the German assault on Poland and the start of the Second World War.

Within months of the Japanese seizure of Manchuria, the fragile international order of the 1920s was in tatters. The League of Nations did little to protect China from Japanese aggression, and in February 1933 Japan left the League altogether. Japanese statesmen and military leaders had grown frustrated by an international political and economic order that they thought gave them a second-rate status. The global economic slump hit Japan hard, and its goods were excluded from some markets. The world order seemed set to benefit big imperial powers rather than what were called the "have not" powers—those with poor supplies of raw materials, a modest colonial empire, and an alleged imbalance between population and territory.

Japan was only the first of the powers that acted in defiance of the existing order. Italian dictator Benito Mussolini wanted an international revolution by what he called the "proletarian states" against the "plutocratic powers,"

The malevolent but compelling influence of Nazi Germany's messianic leader, Adolf Hitler, dominated international events from 1933 to '39—and Germany's war policies and strategies thereafter. Hitler was the principal instigator of the Second World War in the West, and was therefore directly responsible for most of the global devastation, death, and human misery that ensued from 1939 to '45.

namely Britain, France, and the United States. From 1932 he hatched plans to conquer the independent African state of Abyssinia (present-day Ethiopia), and in October 1935 Italian forces invaded the kingdom, which they conquered by the following May. This time the League imposed half-hearted economic sanctions. In December 1937, Italy also left the League.

For the long-term stability of the international order, the most dangerous development was the rise to power in Germany of Adolf Hitler and his movement of fanatical nationalists. The National Socialist Party rejected the Versailles settlement, repudiated the international economy (which they associated with Jewish financial power), and called for the rearmament of Germany to conquer the globe. On January 30, 1933, Hitler was appointed chancellor. Over the next six years, he was the driving force behind public repudiation of the peace settlement and the expansion of German political and economic influence over Europe.

Hitler was convinced that Germany was a "have not" power. He adopted the popular idea of *Lebensraum* (living space) as a justification for German territorial expansion and the seizure of new economic resources. He also was convinced that Germany represented a superior culture and was destined to dominate lesser races. He attributed Germany's current weakness to the malign influence of international Jews, whom he felt had stifled German economic growth, enfeebled the German people, and undermined German cultural heritage. This potent mix of prejudices and grievances became the basis of German foreign policy.

In early 1935, Hitler publicly announced a secret rearmament that had been going on since the late 1920s. In March 1936, he ordered German forces to remilitarize the Rhineland region in defiance of the Treaty of Locarno. On November 5, 1937, he announced to his military commanders his intention of uniting Austria with Germany and destroying the Czechoslovakian state (set up in 1919) as the preliminary to a wider war. On March 12, 1938, German forces entered Vienna amid scenes of hysterical enthusiasm. The rest of the world did nothing, as it had done nothing over Manchuria and Abyssinia.

By the mid-1930s, a gulf separated the three revisionist powers—Germany, Italy, and Japan—from the major democracies that had dominated the world order in the 1920s. In November 1936, Germany and Japan signed the

Japanese troops advance on Shanghai, China, in March 1932. Japan's assault on Manchuria in 1931 marked the start of a series of international events that eventually culminated in the outbreak of World War II in the East. Later, the atrocities committed by Japanese forces against Chinese civilians exemplified the dehumanized nature of the growing global conflict.

Anti-Comintern Pact, which was directed at the international struggle against communism; a year later, Mussolini signed up to it as well. These three nations wanted to alert the Western powers that they saw themselves as a Fascist bloc increasingly opposed not just to communism, but to Western liberal democracy as well. This division was made explicit with the outbreak of civil war in Spain in July 1936. Germany and Italy both committed forces to help the nationalist rebels under General Francisco Franco. Britain and France led a noninterventionist movement that weakened the cause of the legitimate republican government and exposed the weakness and uncertainty of the West.

For Britain, France, and the United States, the main architects of the post-WWI international order, it was difficult to find ways of containing the sudden crisis. None of the three wanted to risk a major war so soon after the last, but none of them wanted to let the world order slide into chaos. There were powerful pressures against an active foreign policy. The British and French empires were menaced by anticolonial nationalism in India, Indochina, the Middle East, and Africa. In Palestine, Britain was forced to deploy troops in large numbers to keep the peace between the Arab majority and the Jewish population, which had been promised a Jewish homeland at the end of World War I. In India, the so-called jewel in Britain's imperial crown, popular nationalism—inspired by the apostle of nonviolent resistance, Mohandas Gandhi—forced the British government to grant limited self-government with the India Act of 1935. The United States had abandoned the settlement it had helped write.

Even if British and French leaders had taken a more active line, powerful domestic lobbies pushed for pacifism. When a center-left government was elected in France in 1936 under the slogan of the Popular Front, a million Frenchmen marched through Paris demanding peace. In 1934 British citizens founded the Peace Pledge Union, which over the next five years became a mass movement that campaigned against war. Not until Germany seemed a very real threat in 1939 did public opinion swing more clearly in favor of confronting fascism by violent means.

A second major issue was the attitude of the two potential economic and military giants of the 1930s, the United States and the USSR. Only a decade later, these two states would be the world's superpowers. Yet in the 1930s, they played a more limited role, and their military power was more potential than real. In the United States, the impact of the Great Depression after 1929

Overcome with emotion, a woman greets German troops with the Nazi salute during the occupation of the Sudetenland in the fall of 1938. While the ethnic Germans in the region celebrated the annexation, the Czechs of Sudetenland rightfully worried about their future.

encouraged a mood of isolationism. When Democrat Franklin D. Roosevelt was elected president in 1932, he promised a "New Deal" for America's impoverished population. His priority was to heal America first and to avoid any international policies that compromised that priority.

Congress adopted the provisional Neutrality Law in 1935, then passed permanent legislation in 1937 designed to prevent the United States from giving money, economic aid, or arms to any combatant state. Though American statesmen remained anxious about Japanese ambitions in the Pacific, and sympathized instinctively with Chinese resistance, Americans did nothing to inhibit Japanese aggression. Roosevelt was personally hostile to Germany and to fascism, but he felt too constrained by the economic crisis at home to risk persuading the American people that involvement in European affairs was necessary for American security.

The Soviet Union was an unknown and potentially dangerous power. Though the Communist threat was just brewing by the 1930s, Western states were aware that Communists were committed to the long-term subversion of the West's social and political systems. In the 1930s, the USSR began a program of massive industrialization and rearmament, which made Russia the third largest industrial economy by 1939 and, on paper, the world's biggest military power. Yet Soviet leader Joseph Stalin concentrated on building up the new Soviet system and defeating the remaining domestic "enemies" of the revolution rather than act more forcefully in international affairs. The Soviets did not want war, and hoped to minimize its risks.

In September 1934, the Soviet Union was admitted to the League. However, Communists distrusted the democratic leaders as much as the Fascists, seeing both as varieties of capitalist politics. Britain and France were wary throughout the 1930s of any commitment to the Soviet Union. Although a pact of mutual assistance was signed between France and the USSR in May 1935, it was never turned into a military alliance.

The result of all these many pressures was a confused Anglo-French response—a mix of inaction, mild protest, and concession that is normally described by the term "appeasement." Efforts were made to find ways to keep Germany, Italy, and Japan within the existing power structure. In 1935 Britain and Germany signed the Anglo-German Naval Agreement, which

The Munich Agreement of September 30, 1938, epitomized the Anglo-French policy of appeasing Hitler during the late 1930s. The document waved so triumphantly by British prime minister Neville Chamberlain was described by him as having achieved "peace in our time." In reality, it ultimately became Czechoslovakia's death warrant, though Hitler regretted not going to war in 1938.

legitimized German naval rearmament, although it was broken by Germany the year it was signed. Neither Britain nor France risked confronting the Fascist states regarding intervention in Spain. Japan was left alone in the Far East, with only minimal aid provided to China. Nevertheless, both Britain and France realized that war was a strong possibility, and fear of war was a central element in the popular political culture of these nations in the 1930s. From 1936 both states began a program of rearmament.

Evidence of Western hesitancy encouraged the revisionist powers to press on. Japan began full-scale war with China in 1937 and conquered much of China's eastern seaboard by 1938. In Europe, Hitler ordered his generals in May 1938 to plan an autumn war against Czechoslovakia on the pretext of freeing the German-speaking peoples of the Sudetenland from Czech domination. But when German pressure reached a peak in the summer, Britain and France intervened. Neville Chamberlain, Britain's prime minister, flew to Germany to meet Hitler and broker a deal. The result was the Munich Agreement signed on September 30, 1938. The Sudetenland was given to Germany, but war was averted. In addition, Hitler was forced to back down from the destruction of Czech independence, which had been his aim.

Stalin and Ribbentrop seal a fait accompli

On August 23, 1939, Germany and the Soviet Union shocked the world by concluding a strategically pragmatic non-aggression pact. The Hitler-Stalin pact (negotiated by Joachim von Ribbentrop and Vyacheslav Molotov) subsequently enabled the invasion and partition of Poland, and thus precipitated the outbreak of the war in Europe.

Unhappy that he had not gone to war with the Czechs in 1938, Hitler added Britain and France to his list of potential enemies. But he turned first to the east, annexing a large part of Czechoslovakia in March 1939, before insisting that Lithuania and Poland cede Memel and Danzig and come into the German orbit. Only Poland refused to subordinate itself to Berlin, so Hitler decided to attack that country either by itself or alongside France and Britain if those states intervened. Under these circumstances, he responded to soundings from Moscow that he had earlier rejected. In a secret agreement with the Soviet Union, he agreed to partition Eastern Europe on the assumption that he would conquer it all after defeating the Western powers.

In the winter of 1938–39, the British and French decided that if the Germans attacked any country that defended itself, they would join in its defense. In the hope that this might deter Germany, they publicly promised to defend Romania, Poland, and Greece, but Germany went ahead anyway.

On August 31, despite mounting evidence of Western firmness, Hitler ordered the campaign to begin the next day. Heinrich Himmler, his security chief, repeated what Japanese soldiers had done in Manchuria in 1931 by staging a fake act of provocation. In alleged retaliation, German forces advanced on a broad front into Poland on the morning of September 1, 1939.

1931-33

1931: Japan invades Manchuria in northern China. It will establish a puppet state that it will rename Manchukuo.

1932: The stress of the Great Depression, combined with unwillingness to accept defeat in the Great War and reparation obligations for that war, has left Germany in economic ruins and susceptible to extreme nationalism. It is in this political climate that Adolf Hitler's Nazi Party becomes the largest in Germany.

January 9, 1932: Germany defaults on its Great War reparations payments, which were mandated by the Treaty of Versailles. • A failed assassination attempt by a Korean nationalist on Emperor Hirohito inflames anti-Chinese sentiment in Japan, especially after the official paper of the Chinese *Kuomintang* publicly laments Hirohito's survival.

January 29, 1932: Thousands die when Japanese bombers level Chapei, in northern Shanghai. This marks the first of Japan's so-called terror bombings of civilians that will become standard policy during World War II.

June 16, 1932: The Lausanne Conference opens in Lausanne, Switzerland, with representatives from Britain, Germany, and France in attendance. The three nations agree to end the Great War reparations payments established by Versailles in 1919.

November 8, 1932: Democrat Franklin Delano Roosevelt is resoundingly elected the 32nd U.S. president.

1933: Albert Einstein flees Germany for the United States. He vows never to return, asserting that he "shall live only in a country where civil liberty, tolerance, and equality . . . prevail."

> ## "His gift of foreseeing what the future will bring places him high above all other world leaders. He towers above them, not only by his genius and political instinct, but also by his knowledge, character, and willpower."
>
> —Joseph Goebbels, Germany's minister of propaganda, describing Hitler

Hindenburg transfers power

Weimar Republic president Paul von Hindenburg (*right*) appoints Nazi leader Adolf Hitler to the position of chancellor on January 30, 1933. Hindenberg, elected in 1925, had been unable to relieve the nation's political turmoil and economic depression. By the 1930s, he was also battling senility. As the Nazi Party gained power, Hitler repeatedly demanded the position of chancellor in return for Nazi support of any government. Hindenburg resisted appointing "this Austrian corporal," but he gave in to advisers who believed that Hitler could be controlled since few Nazis held political positions at the time.

Japan takes Manchuria Early in 1932, the Japanese Kwangtung Army occupied the Chinese area of Manchuria and changed its name to Manchukuo. Here, representatives of Japan (*left*) and Manchukuo (*right*) make it official. Germany and Italy recognized Manchukuo, but the League of Nations condemned the Japanese occupation. Control of this puppet state provided Japan with a portion of the mineral and industrial resources it needed to support its Pacific war with the Allied nations.

Hitler's Rise to Power

DESTINED TO BECOME one of the most infamous figures of the 20th century, Adolf Hitler was born to Alois and Kara Hitler on April 20, 1889, in Braunau, Austria. As a youth, Hitler was unfocused and had emotional problems. However, as a soldier in the 1914–18 conflict, he found meaning, direction, and purpose. He also learned the efficacy of violence, and in 1918 he was awarded the Iron Cross First Class.

Hitler shared a view with many veterans: that the war had been lost not by the German field army but by the politicians in Berlin, abetted by the Jews. In 1919 he joined like-minded individuals in a fledgling party that in 1920 would be renamed the *Nationalsozialistische Deutsche Arbeiterpartei* (National Socialist German Workers Party, *aka* the NSDAP and the Nazi Party). Hitler became chairman of this nationalistic, anti-Semitic party on July 28, 1921. The German people's widespread resentment over the punitive terms of the Treaty of Versailles, accompanied by several outbreaks of serious civil disorder—all exacerbated by the 1929 Wall Street Crash—provided a cocktail of discontent, economic collapse, and insecurity across the nation. These circumstances enabled the Nazis to rise to political prominence, then to gain legitimacy, and finally to win power.

While undergoing a short prison sentence following an abortive coup in 1923, Hitler wrote the first part of *Mein Kampf* (*My Struggle*). The book laid out his political philosophy and his plans for the resurgence and expansion of Germany, while also highlighting his condemnation of Jews, Communists, liberals, and others. *Mein Kampf* exposed his dangerously irrational and obsessive ideas, but in 1920s Germany even irrational ideas could appear credible. Although physically rather ordinary, colorless, and lacking some intellectual qualities, Hitler nevertheless possessed an uncanny ability to relate to, enthuse, and motivate the masses. He sensed precisely what people wanted to hear, and he reflected this in speeches that were often long and repetitive but always perfectly pitched—whether unifying, divisive, coercive, or blatantly seductive. (Witness his promise to restore German military primacy, which led many senior officers to overlook his less edifying policies.)

Hitler feted in Nuremberg, Germany, 1933

In 1934 Hitler demonstrated his ruthlessness when he used the SS to purge the *Sturmabteilung* (SA). His order meant that many of his original Nazi supporters would be murdered. Hitler declared that he embodied the very essence of Germany. As *Führer* (chancellor and president), his personal views on every aspect of German life—art, culture, the role of German women, the family, genetics, Social Darwinism, politics, economics, foreign policy, and strategy—were rigorously imposed upon a largely acquiescent nation.

Some fortuitous successes early in the war established Hitler's undeserved reputation as a competent strategist, rather than an irresponsible risk-taker. His greatest military adventure—the 1941 attack on Russia, which forced Germany to fight on two fronts simultaneously—finally ensured Germany's defeat in 1945. Although at the time many Germans realized how fatally flawed Hitler's policies and leadership really were, it was all too late and his position was unassailable.

Hitler committed suicide on April 30, 1945, while still convinced of his own infallibility. To the end, he blamed Germany's imminent catastrophic defeat upon the failure of its people to rise to the historic challenge he had set for them when he initiated the Third Reich in 1933.

1933

January 30, 1933: Hitler becomes chancellor of Germany.

February 4, 1933: Hitler tightens his absolute power in Germany with the decree "For the Protection of the German People," which gives the Nazis the authority to censor publications and ban political agitating.

February 27, 1933: The *Reichstag* building in Berlin is set afire. Hitler's government accuses Communists of arson, triggering an anti-Communist crackdown throughout Germany.

March 20, 1933: SS chief Heinrich Himmler announces the establishment of Dachau, the first Nazi concentration camp. The camp will receive its first inmates, political prisoners, within the next few days.

March 23, 1933: Germany's *Reichstag* passes the Enabling Act, affording Hitler total dictatorial powers.

March 27, 1933: Japan announces that it will no longer be part of the seemingly impotent League of Nations.

April 1, 1933: Hitler orders a boycott of all Jewish-owned businesses in Germany. The boycott itself fails when most German citizens ignore it, but Hitler will follow with a series of laws that effectively strangle the civil liberties of German Jews.

April 7, 1933: With the passage of the Aryan Law, any German who is one-quarter or more Jewish is barred from civil service employment.

July 14, 1933: All German political parties except the Nazi Party are outlawed.

October 14, 1933: Germany announces that it intends to follow Japan's lead and withdraw from the beleaguered League of Nations.

The *Reichstag* fire Less than a month after Hitler was appointed chancellor, arson gave the Nazis an excuse to suspend civil liberties and crack down on their political enemies. On February 27, 1933, the *Reichstag* (parliament) building in Berlin went up in flames, and a Dutch Communist found at the scene was charged with the crime. Claiming that acts of terrorism were about to break out all over Germany, the Nazis imposed martial law, made mass arrests, and carried out summary executions. Many historians believe that the Nazis set the fire themselves.

Fighting along the Great Wall Once the Japanese established the puppet government of Manchukuo, the Kwangtung Army turned its attention to the northeast provinces of China. It achieved its first objective, the capture of Shanhai Pass—the easternmost stronghold of the Great Wall—on January 3, 1933. After Japan took the Chinese province of Jehol on March 1, Chinese troops attempted to make a stand along the Great Wall, but Japan drove them from the Wall by May 12. Representatives of both countries signed the Tanggu Truce on May 22, the provisions of which entirely favored the Japanese. China relinquished Jehol and agreed to a 100-mile-wide demilitarized zone south of the Great Wall.

Evolution of the Japanese Government

THE ARRIVAL OF U.S. COMMODORE Matthew Perry in 1853 during a time of fear of Western colonization inspired a radical change in Japan's government structure. For more than 260 years, power had been vested in the decentralized Tokugawa shogunate, while the Imperial Court in Kyoto had remained mostly symbolic.

Recognizing that Japan's continued autonomy depended on a unified nation and a centralized government, a cadre of nobles and former samurai forced the collapse of the much-weakened Tokugawa shogunate in 1868. Nominal authority was returned to the emperor in what became known as the Meiji Restoration, though real power remained in the hands of the samurai activists who had overthrown the Tokugawa shogunate and seized control of the new government.

The new government forced the dissolution of some 250 semi-autonomous domains, and brought all territory under central control. Reform continued in 1889 when the Meiji Constitution established a rather ineffective two-house legislature (the Diet) and a politically powerful cabinet of ministers under the emperor. The system suffered from fundamental weaknesses in that the ministers did not have to answer to the Diet. As before, real power remained with the ruling clique of insiders.

During the period of Emperor Taisho (1912–26), a democratic movement briefly shifted influence to the parliament and democratic parties. However, economic depression in the 1920s and the rising assertiveness of the military soon stifled that movement.

The army and navy already exerted great political influence through their own cabinet ministers. Moreover, the emperor's passive role in government allowed the militarists to flourish. The military also claimed immunity from civilian control on grounds that only the emperor was commander-in-chief of the armed forces. Political leaders who opposed the militarist agenda were targeted for assassination by radical young officers.

The military demonstrated its disdain for civilian control in 1931 when the Kwangtung Army seized Manchuria without even consulting its own government. By 1941, when General Tojo was named prime minister, Japan was essentially a military autocracy.

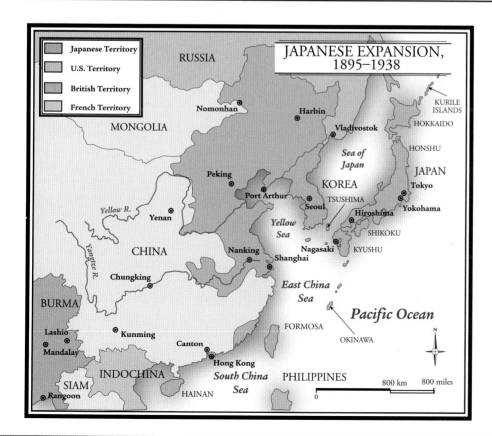

JAPANESE EXPANSION, 1895–1938

Legend:
- Japanese Territory
- U.S. Territory
- British Territory
- French Territory

RUSSIA • MONGOLIA • Nomonhan • Harbin • Vladivostok • KURILE ISLANDS • HOKKAIDO • HONSHU • Sea of Japan • JAPAN • Tokyo • Peking • Port Arthur • KOREA • TSUSHIMA • Seoul • Hiroshima • Yokohama • Yenan • Yellow R. • Yellow Sea • SHIKOKU • CHINA • Nanking • Nagasaki • KYUSHU • Shanghai • Chungking • East China Sea • Yangtze R. • BURMA • FORMOSA • Pacific Ocean • Lashio • Kunming • OKINAWA • Mandalay • Canton • Hong Kong • INDOCHINA • South China Sea • PHILIPPINES • SIAM • HAINAN • Rangoon

800 km   800 miles
0

Japan's ambitions The Russo-Japanese war of 1904–05 demonstrated Japan's emergence as a significant 20th century power. Its successful surprise attack against Port Arthur in 1904—without any declaration of war—and the destruction of the Russian fleet at Tsushima in 1905 also indicated the way that Japan might conduct itself strategically and diplomatically in the future. By the 1930s, the leadership of an increasingly militaristic and radicalized country felt strategically isolated and economically threatened by Anglo-French-U.S. encroachments within the region and by Japan's lack of raw materials. These fears eventually precipitated Japan's campaigns in Manchuria and China from 1931. Its military successes fueled its future imperial ambitions in the Pacific and Southeast Asia areas.

1933-34

November 16, 1933: Washington normalizes diplomatic relations with Moscow, with the understanding that Moscow will not sponsor Communist propaganda within the United States.

January 1, 1934: In a year that will see massive buildup of all branches of the German military, officials order some 4,000 new aircraft for the *Luftwaffe.*

May 5, 1934: The Soviet Union and Poland reaffirm their mutual nonaggression pact, strengthening the geographical buffer zone between Russia and Germany.

June 14–15, 1934: Hitler and Italian dictator Benito Mussolini rendezvous in Venice and leave their first face-to-face meeting mutually unimpressed, with Mussolini whispering "I don't like him" to his staff.

June 30, 1934: At least 77, and perhaps as many as 400, are killed during Germany's "Night of the Long Knives," a purge of Nazi Party and other enemies ordered by Hitler that will secure his ascendancy in the state.

July 25, 1934: Austrian Nazis murder Chancellor Engelbert Dollfuss in a coup attempt. He will be succeeded by Kurt von Schuschnigg.

August 1934: Hitler officially becomes *Der Führer,* a combination of chancellor and president, when the German army swears him allegiance upon the death of President von Hindenburg.

August 19–September 1934: Chinese Nationalist troops launch an aggressive campaign to eject Chinese Communists from their occupied territory south of the Yangtze River.

September 18, 1934: The Soviets belatedly join the League of Nations.

December 1934: A buildup of the Italian military follows Mussolini's order for the conquest of Abyssinia (present-day Ethiopia).

Raising Nazi children German children parrot their teacher's Nazi salute. The Third Reich carefully subverted the educational system in order to mold children into loyal adult Nazis. School curricula reflected the Nazi line, blaming Jews and Marxists for Germany's woes. Biology courses taught the "reality" of Aryan racial superiority, while science courses focused on military themes. To ensure compliancy, teachers were vetted by local Nazi officials; 97 percent joined the Nazi Teachers Association.

Anti-Nazi sentiment in Britain British views on Hitler and the rise of the Nazis during the 1930s were often ambivalent. Many underestimated the Nazis or thought them irrelevant, while others actually admired Hitler's achievements in Germany. However, some of those who understood the Nazi policies resorted to direct protests in a vain attempt to expose the growing peril. In 1933 three men and one woman were convicted for damaging this wax figure of Hitler at Madame Tussauds, a wax museum in London.

Roosevelt takes office Newly elected, President Franklin Delano Roosevelt (*left*) and Vice President John Nance Garner (*right*) took office in March 1933. During his campaign, Roosevelt had proposed ways to pull the country out of the Depression. Although his sophisticated education included a background in international affairs, Roosevelt's foreign agenda seemed compatible with the nation's isolationism. However, at the 1936 Democratic National Convention, he stated that all was not well with the world, warning that "clouds of suspicion, tides of ill-will and intolerance gather darkly in many places." FDR would initiate naval and air rearmament in 1936 and 1938, respectively, and put the U.S. on a war footing in 1939.

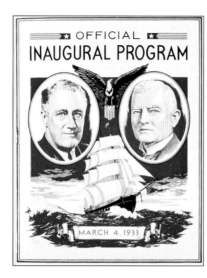

Germany's economic mastermind Hjalmar Schacht was a brilliant German financier who believed in "a sound economy in a strong state" and that "the basic ideas of National Socialism contain a great deal of truth." During the 1920s and '30s, Schacht utilized his mastery of economics and the correlation between the state, industry, and commerce to help Hitler. As president of the *Reichsbank* and minister of economics, he established the financial trickery that enabled German rearmament.

"They that start by burning books will end by burning men."

—German Jewish poet Heinrich Heine, 1821

The Dachau camp Prisoners march to the kitchen with mess kits for a meal at the Dachau, Germany, concentration camp, which opened in March 1933 as a prison for opponents of the Nazi regime. Political prisoners were soon joined by Gypsies, Jehovah's Witnesses, homosexuals, clergy, and repeat criminals. Gradually, the number of Jews increased at Dachau, especially after *Kristallnacht* in 1938. Selections for extermination began at Dachau in 1941. In all, the camp held nearly 200,000 prisoners, and about 30,000 were killed. Thousands more died from medical experiments, forced labor, and horrific living conditions. The Nazis, who considered Dachau an ideal concentration camp, modeled others after it.

Nazi book burnings On May 10, 1933, Nazi Brownshirts ransacked libraries, public buildings, private offices, and even private homes for materials deemed un-German. Chanting scripted slogans, students and Storm Troopers threw more than 20,000 books into roaring bonfires. Bands played and officials gave speeches. In Berlin, Propaganda Minister Joseph Goebbels announced, "The future German man will not just be a man of books, but a man of character."

1934-35

December 1, 1934: Soviet official Serge Kirov, an associate of Soviet premier Joseph Stalin, is assassinated. Stalin will use Kirov's death as a pretext to purge Leningrad of 2,000 party officials.

January 7, 1935: France undercuts international efforts to censure Italy for its actions in Abyssinia when it enters into a treaty with Rome. France thinks it is buffering itself against Hitler's aggression, but it is actually giving also-dangerous Mussolini carte blanche in Northeast Africa.

March 1935: Hitler publicly repudiates the Treaty of Versailles, announcing that he will not adhere to the limits on the German military imposed by the treaty.

May 2, 1935: Berlin is incensed by a mutual assistance treaty signed between Russia and France that would serve to force Germany into a two-front war. Russia will enter into a similar agreement with Czechoslovakia within the month.

July 28, 1935: Boeing's B-17 Flying Fortress, a heavy bomber that will become the workhorse of the war's signature European bombing raids, makes its maiden voyage.

August 31, 1935: President Roosevelt signs the U.S. Neutrality Act, prohibiting material support for any side in a European war. FDR famously predicts that the act "might drag us into war instead of keeping us out."

September 1935: Germany adopts the swastika, an ancient symbol representing life, power, and luck, for its national flag. The Nazi Party had already co-opted the swastika in the 1920s, radically altering its symbolism.

September 15, 1935: The Nuremberg Laws, which impose strict limits on citizenship and civil rights for German Jews, are adopted.

Anti-Semitic propaganda
At a 1934 Nuremberg rally, Joseph Goebbels advocated mass-media propaganda to influence the public to follow "superior leadership." With the Nazis in power, many newspapers and radio broadcasts turned anti-Semitic. The political newspaper *Der Stürmer* (*The Attacker*) repeated the slogan "The Jews are Our Misfortune." Edited by Nazi politician Julius Streicher, the popular sheet featured cartoons by Fips (Philip Rupprecht) that portrayed Jews as swindling, money-hoarding sexual perverts. This 1934 special edition accused Jews of ritual murders of Christian children.

Hitler and the Brownshirts Hitler leads senior officers of the *Sturmabteilung* (SA; Storm Troopers), who were also known as the "Brownshirts." This often-brutal force of roughly two million men, headed by Ernst Röhm (*center*), helped bring Hitler to power. When his position became more secure, Hitler looked to weed out potential threats within the SA. Röhm's homosexuality—long overlooked by Hitler in spite of strict Nazi bans against gays—suddenly became an issue. During the June 30–July 1, 1934, purge that Hitler called the "Night of the Long Knives," hundreds of SA officers were arrested. Many, including Röhm, were executed.

The Dollfuss assassination A wounded Nazi is removed from the Vienna Broadcasting Station on July 27, 1934. In February, in a bid to prevent a German takeover of Austria, Chancellor Engelbert Dollfuss abandoned parliamentary government and established a dictatorship. Dollfuss used Austrian troops and Fascist militias to suppress the Social Democrats, which resulted in more than 1,000 deaths. Austrian Nazis supported by Berlin launched a sabotage and terror campaign across Austria. At Hitler's orders, on July 25, eight Austrian Nazis attacked the Federal Chancellery and murdered Dollfuss. Alarmed by these events, the Italians mobilized four divisions at the Brenner Pass, prompting the postponement of Hitler's planned *Anschluss* until 1938.

TIN SOLDIERS IN THE STREETS

THE SA TAVERN was only a short distance away. The SA members often left there late and drunk and came over to our clubhouse to raise hell. But they were usually driven off with table and chair legs. My father usually led the counterattack.

I got my first impression of National Socialism as a child, when I saw SA model soldiers in a store window. There was also a tin Hitler with a moveable arm. A few days later these tin soldiers were parading through the streets in the flesh. They always carried the party flag right up front, and everyone had to greet them with a tip of the hat or a raised arm, just like that tin Hitler in the showcase.

—PETER HERZ, SON OF AN ANTI-NAZI SOCIALIST

Triumph of the Will "It is a documentary, not propaganda," German director Leni Riefenstahl declared after the war in defense of her most famous work, *Triumph of the Will.* Hitler had personally chosen Riefenstahl (*pictured*) to film the German Nationalist Socialist Party conferences in Nuremberg in 1933 and 1934. She won numerous awards for *Triumph,* but had to defend her work to those who claimed it was the most insidious propaganda film ever made. Heavily choreographed, it opened with a sequence portraying Hitler as a god emerging from the clouds to address his followers.

A German Communist's perspective *The Thousand-Year Reich* (1938), depicting the fundamental flaws in the Nazi state, was Hans Grundig's greatest masterpiece. The native German and his wife, Lea, were ardent Communists and critics of the Nazi regime. Lea escaped to Palestine in 1939, but in 1940 Hans was committed to the Sachsenhausen concentration camp. After the war, they returned to Dresden. There they were officially recognized for their art and as acclaimed political campaigners against fascism and repression.

1935-36

October 1935: Mussolini orders his troops into Abyssinia. The League of Nations will call for economic sanctions against Italy, but in the absence of French and British enforcement, the sanctions will be meaningless.

December 1935: Samuel Hoare of Britain and Pierre Laval of France create the Hoare-Laval Pact. According to this proposal, France and Britain would give Italy a part of Abyssinia and would give that African nation a guaranteed corridor to the ocean. The plan will be scrapped because of public uproar in England.

February 10, 1936: SS and Gestapo chief Heinrich Himmler gains total control of German internal security when the *Reichstag* declares the Gestapo a "Supreme Reich Agency."

March 7, 1936: On Hitler's orders, German troops enter the demilitarized Rhineland. A clear violation of the Treaties of Versailles and Locarno, this maneuver also deals a blow to collective security because Britain and Italy, who pledged aid to France in the 1925 Locarno Pact, do nothing.

May 2, 1936: With his country largely overrun by Italian troops, Abyssinian leader Haile Selassie flees the capital of Addis Ababa.

May 12, 1936: Like Japan and Germany before it, Italy informs the League of Nations that it intends to renounce its membership.

July 17, 1936: A coup attempt led by General Francisco Franco against the Popular Front government launches the Spanish Civil War. The rebellion spreads like wildfire throughout Spain. Hitler and Mussolini send planes to fly Franco's troops from Spanish Morocco to Spain. They will later send planes and soldiers to help Franco fight the Spanish Republic.

A thorn in the Nazis' side In 1924 freelance correspondent Dorothy Thompson became head of the *Philadelphia Public Ledger*'s Berlin news bureau. Thompson irritated both Nazi politicians and American isolationists, calling the Nazi rise to power "the most world disturbing event of the century and perhaps of many centuries." Expelled from Germany in 1934, Thompson continued her crusade against dictatorships in books, articles, her syndicated column "On the Record" (1936–41), and broadcasts on NBC. In 1939 *Time* magazine ran a cover story naming Thompson and Eleanor Roosevelt two of the most influential women in the country.

British Fascists Sir Oswald Mosley was the leader of the British Union of Fascists from its formation in 1932. Throughout the decade, Mosley exploited British anti-Semitism and anti-bolshevism while creating positive perceptions of Hitler's regime in Germany. The union's membership rose to as much as 50,000 in 1934. Of the Axis powers, only Italy provided any financial support for Mosley's British Union. Mosley, his wife (the former Diana Mitford), and others in the union were interned from May 1940 to November 1943.

Himmler and the SS

THE *SCHUTZSTAFFEL* (SS) WAS the most infamous and feared organization of the Third Reich. At its head from 1929 was Heinrich Himmler—a former Bavarian farmer, an effective organizer, and a close associate of Hitler.

The SS, which developed from Hitler's 280-strong "Black Guard" (bodyguard), coexisted alongside the much larger *Sturmabteilung* (SA) organization. However, by 1933 Himmler had increased the strength of the SS to more than 50,000. On June 30, 1934, the SS was used by Hitler and equipped by the German army to behead the SA in the "Night of the Long Knives," during which hundreds of prominent SA and lesser NSDAP members were murdered.

In 1936 Himmler was appointed *Reichsführer-SS*. He headed the SS, the Gestapo, and all of the Third Reich's police and security forces, making him the second most powerful man in Germany. The principal components of the SS were the *Allgemeine-SS* (General-SS), the *Waffen-SS* (Armed-SS, which engaged in combat), and the *Sicherheitsdienst* (Security Service). Together they followed the National Socialist dogma, pursued a fanciful reinterpretation of Germany's Teutonic heritage, and indulged in ritualism that verged on the occult. Officially, all SS candidates had to be NSDAP members, exceptionally fit physically, and possess an Aryan bloodline traceable through several generations. However, these requirements were necessarily relaxed as the war progressed.

The SS was prominently engaged in the administration and operation of the concentration and extermination camps, the persecution of Jews and others, the management of the slave labor force, and the security of strategically vital sites (such as the V-weapons factories). They also engaged in wider policing as well as disciplinary and security operations—both within Germany and throughout Germany's newly occupied territories.

At Nuremberg, the International Military Tribunal formally declared the SS to be a criminal organization. Himmler, however, would never make it to trial. He committed suicide on May 23, 1945, shortly after his capture by the British.

Breeding a "super race" The *Lebensborn* (source of life) program was developed in 1935 by *Reichsführer-SS* Heinrich Himmler to produce a German "super race" by selective breeding. Suitable young German women—those displaying the Aryan characteristics idealized by Himmler in his perverted views of Germany's heritage and culture—were encouraged to become pregnant by SS officers, all of whom were considered to be politically sound and "racially pure." Once the women were pregnant, special SS-administered medical centers pro-

vided them with exemplary maternity care. The young woman seen here was a resident of the *Lebensborn* home on Swan Isle, a small residential island in Lake Wannsee, near Berlin. (Goebbels and other top Nazis owned homes there.) The cradle room (*right*) was in the *Lebensborn* home in Steinhoring.

1936-37

November 1, 1936: Speaking to a crowd in Milan, Mussolini coins the name "Axis" for Italy and its allies when he states that the "line between Rome and Berlin is not a partition but rather an axis around which all European states . . . can also collaborate."

November 18, 1936: General Franco's new Spanish government gains formal recognition from Italy and Germany.

November 25, 1936: The Anti-Comintern Pact is signed by Germany and Japan against the International Comintern but not against the Soviet Union.

December 1936: Chinese Nationalist leader Chiang Kai-shek is kidnapped by General Chang Hsueh-liang in order to force Chiang to devote more time and energy to confronting the Japanese, and not the Chinese Communists.

December 11, 1936: George VI is crowned king of England following the abdication of his brother, Edward VIII, who married Wallis Simpson, an American divorcée.

April 27, 1937: In support of Franco, the German air force in Spain carries out a bombing raid that destroys the Basque city of Guernica.

May 28, 1937: Neville Chamberlain becomes Britain's prime minister.

June 25, 1937: Chamberlain, in his first speech as Britain's prime minister, inexplicably congratulates Germany for its supposed military restraint.

July 7, 1937: Japanese troops meet resistance in China when they demand access to the town of Wanping, near Peiping. A skirmish ensues at the Marco Polo Bridge on the edge of town, providing the spark that will ignite the Second Sino-Japanese War.

Chinese propaganda For centuries, Chinese rulers expressed their beliefs to their peasant population through propaganda posters. With pictures posted on walls, billboards, and other surfaces, the government was able to communicate to a population that was mostly illiterate. This picture is a characterization of good (China) versus evil (Japan). In stark contrast to the posters, however, is the emaciated man squatting underneath them. To the vast majority of the 500 million Chinese, there was little concern about the ultimate result of the war. Their daily struggle for survival would continue no matter who was running the country.

Italy attacks Abyssinia On October 3, 1935, in his fervor for empire, Italian dictator Benito Mussolini attacked the African nation of Abyssinia (present-day Ethiopia), which had successfully resisted Italian colonialism in 1889. Italian planes strafed rifle-bearing tribesmen with machine-gun fire and bombed mud-hut villages. Mussolini's son proudly commented that the victims blew up like "a budding rose unfolding." The air attack was followed by Italian artillery (*pictured*), infantry, and the use of mustard gas. After a little more than seven months of fighting, Mussolini's forces prevailed.

Germans occupy the Rhineland In March 1936, Hitler ordered the army to occupy the demilitarized Rhineland, located in the west of Germany. There, the troops received an enthusiastic reception from the population. In practice, this was a risk by Hitler, as Germany was still ill-prepared for war. Britain and France hardly objected to this provocative military action, although France did move 13 divisions to the border area. This remarkable success enhanced Hitler's wider standing in Germany. Construction of Germany's West Wall defenses now could be initiated.

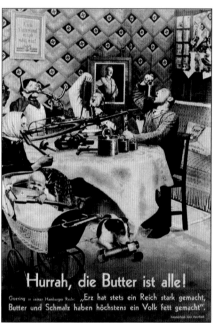

Heartfield's biting criticism German artist John Heartfield used politically charged images in works of political criticism. During WWI, he changed his name from Helmut Herzfeld to protest Germans' anti-British sentiment. After the Nazis rose to power, Heartfield exiled himself to Czechoslovakia and later to England. He put swastikas and other Nazi symbols to ironic use in his photomontages, such as *Hurrah, die Butter ist alle!* (*Hurrah, the Butter Is All Gone!*). Quoting Hermann Göring's statement about iron making people strong (and butter only making them fat), Heartfield showed a family consuming pieces of metal.

Hitler's Games In May 1931, the International Olympic Committee awarded the 1936 Summer Olympics to Berlin. The Nazis schemed to exploit the Olympics by portraying Germany as a peaceful member of the international community. Prior to the Summer Games, Hitler ordered the removal of vicious anti-Jewish signs throughout Berlin, such as "Jews are not wanted in this place." As a token, he allowed one German Jewish athlete to participate. Through the veneer, many saw the ugliness of Nazi racism. One German official groused that the Americans were letting "non-humans, like [sprinter Jesse] Owens and other Negro athletes," compete.

1937-38

July 29, 1937: Japanese forces occupy Peiping.

September 7, 1937: In a speech underscoring a perceived need for *Lebensraum* (living space), Hitler claims that Germany "is too small to guarantee an undisturbed, assured, and permanent food supply."

December 1937: Japanese troops pillage the Chinese Nationalist capital of Nanking, murdering tens of thousands of civilians, in what will become known as the "Rape of Nanking."

February 1938: Hitler calls Austrian Chancellor Kurt von Schuschnigg to Berchtesgaden, Germany, and bullies him into giving the Nazis complete control of Austria's interior ministry.

February 4, 1938: Hitler becomes commander-in-chief of the *Wehrmacht* (German armed forces) as well as German war minister.

March 12, 1938: The *Anschluss,* the annexation of Austria into Greater Germany, begins as a large contingent of German troops enters Austria. The *Anschluss* ostensibly reunites the ethnically similar cultures, and many Austrians welcome the German soldiers.

March 24–April 7, 1938: Approximately 16,000 Japanese soldiers die at the hands of Chinese during the two-week Battle of Taierzhuang, Japan's first military defeat in modern history.

June 1938: In a remarkably ill-advised attempt to bog down invading Japanese forces, Chiang Kai-shek orders the destruction of dikes along the Yellow River. The ensuing flood leaves two million homeless; destroys more than 4,000 cities, towns, and villages; and leads to a devastating famine.

August 1938: The German government decrees that all Jews must add Israel or Sara to their first names for ease of identification.

German military brass Many German senior officers (here, from left, Field Marshal Werner von Blomberg, Colonel General Werner von Fritsch, and Admiral Erich Raeder) enthusiastically supported Hitler's rearmament program in order to redress the terms imposed by the Versailles Treaty of 1919. Blomberg was forced to resign in 1938 after it became known that his new wife had a promiscuous background. Meanwhile, Fritsch's own resignation followed accusations that he was homosexual.

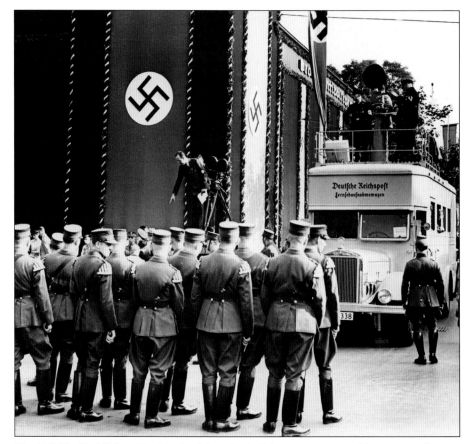

Nazi TV hails Hitler The Nazis claimed television as a great achievement of German technology. In March 1935, Reich director of broadcasting Eugen Hadamovsky described its mission: "to plant the image of the *Führer* indelibly in all German hearts." In 1936, 150,000 Berliners paid one *Reichsmark* each to enter special viewing halls for up to eight hours of TV. Later programming included a broadcast of the Nuremberg Rally, being filmed here. During the war, TV sets in military field hospitals provided cabaret and newsreels for wounded soldiers.

Forces behind the *Luftwaffe*
In violation of the Treaty of Versailles, Erhard Milch (*right*) worked secretly with Hermann Göring to build German planes and train pilots. Milch's practical skills contributed to the powerful *Luftwaffe*, which devastated European cities at the beginning of the war. To conceal that his father was Jewish, Milch produced an affidavit by his mother that she had committed adultery. Seen with Milch is one of America's staunchest isolationists, the famed aviator Charles Lindbergh, who considered the *Luftwaffe* invincible.

"Degenerate" art In a 1935 Party Day speech, Hitler praised artworks that bore "the cultural stamp of the Germanic race." His favorite artists either realistically depicted healthy, handsome Aryans or disparaged Jews. The Nazis cleansed German museums of "inferior" modern styles. Their 1937 *Entartete Kunst* (*Degenerate Exhibit*) of unacceptable art—which included *Large Kneeling Woman* (*pictured*) by Wilhelm Lehmbruck along with works by Chagall, Kandinsky, Klee, Mondrian, Munch, and others—opened in Munich and traveled to 11 other German and Austrian cities. It was a hit, drawing more than three million visitors.

A trial run for German military
German Condor Legion soldiers move an artillery piece in Spain. German intervention in Spain's civil war in 1936 ensured Franco's nationalist victory, and thus provided Hitler with an important and supportive—if generally passive—Fascist ally. Additionally, German intervention facilitated battle-testing of a whole range of the *Wehrmacht*'s new weapons, vehicles, and tactics. The *Luftwaffe*'s capability was demonstrated most dramatically when waves of the Condor Legion's Heinkel, Junkers, and Messerschmitt bombers and fighters devastated Guernica—a Basque town without any air defenses. Some tanks of Germany's new panzer divisions were also given successful trials in Spain.

1938-39

September 15, 1938: Hitler meets with Chamberlain and states his demand that Czechoslovakia yield the Sudetenland, a region of Czechoslovakia with a large German population, to Germany.

September 29–30, 1938: Leaders of Britain, France, Germany, and Italy meet at the Munich Convention. In a profound act of capitulation, the delegates deliver the Sudetenland into Hitler's hands. Neither Russia nor Czechoslovakia are invited to Munich. Chamberlain returns to England following his role in the disastrous Munich Agreement claiming to have achieved "peace in our time."

October 1, 1938: German troops march into the Sudetenland. Without the support of their alleged allies, France and Britain, the Czechoslovakians are powerless against Hitler's army.

November 9–10, 1938: Nazi-led mobs engage in a night of terror against Germany's and Austria's Jewish population, destroying more than 1,000 shops and synagogues, arresting 30,000, and killing nearly 40. The action will become known as *Kristallnacht* (Night of Broken Glass).

December 1938–September 1939: The British Cabinet allows 10,000 unaccompanied Jewish children into Britain in an action called the *Kindertransport*.

January 1, 1939: Nearly 320,000 of a total population of 500,000 German Jews have fled the nation in the face of Nazi hostility.

January 5, 1939: Hitler pressures Poland to return its principal port of Gdansk (called Danzig in German), a free state run by the Nazis under the auspices of the League of Nations, to Germany. Hitler insists that the city will "sooner or later return to Germany."

Nazi pageantry In parades in Nuremberg (*pictured*) and other cities, the Nazis mesmerized their audiences with well-organized rituals, operatic staging, brightly colored flags, and other elements chosen for their nationalistic, mystical, and religious connotations. The settings were often illuminated by giant kleig lights and accompanied by classical music or military marches. This nighttime march features torchlight. William L. Shirer, foreign correspondent for CBS during the 1930s, wrote in his *Berlin Diary* that he was beginning to comprehend some of the reasons for Hitler's astounding success: "He is restoring pageantry and colour and mysticism to the drab lives of twentieth-century Germans."

The Hitler-Mussolini alliance In 1937, a year after the emergence of the Berlin-Rome axis, Hitler and Italian dictator Benito Mussolini together attended *Wehrmacht* maneuvers. Although Italy had frustrated Hitler's ambitions in Austria in 1934, and Hitler generally regarded Mussolini as a lesser leader, the *Führer* still needed a like-minded European ally to offset the two-front threat to Germany. He also

needed Italian acquiescence for the *Anschluss* in 1938 as well as Mussolini's support for his expansionist plans for Eastern Europe. However, despite their shared Fascist ideologies, the later inadequacies and unreliability of Italy's military forces eventually all but negated Mussolini's value as Hitler's ally.

Japan's War with China

JAPAN SEIZED THE CHINESE province of Manchuria in 1931, but its expansionist ambitions had begun decades earlier. Japan had first gained a foothold in this resource-rich province following the 1904–05 Russo-Japanese War, when it took control of the South Manchuria Railroad Company. Troops were brought in to protect company property—an excuse the Japanese military eventually used to create a *de facto* occupation force, the Kwangtung Army.

In 1931 the Kwangtung Army put pretense aside and seized the entire province, claiming that Chinese saboteurs had attempted to blow up the railroad. The weak Chinese government had little choice but to acquiesce. Following this so-called "Manchurian Incident," the Japanese established the puppet state of Manchukuo.

Following the Japanese conquest of Manchuria, the Kwangtung Army and other Japanese forces in China spent the next five years trying to detach the provinces of north China from Nationalist control through relentless military pressure and diplomatic bullying. But in 1936, the Chinese Nationalists decided to resist. In July 1937, at the Marco Polo Bridge outside Peiping, fighting broke out between Chinese Nationalist forces and a local Japanese garrison. In August, the conflict spread to Shanghai, and an "incident" exploded into a full-scale war.

In this combat, Japanese troops responded with unimaginable cruelty. Tens of thousands of Chinese civilians were killed out of hand: shot, decapitated, or bayoneted. This barbarism culminated with the fall of the

Two Chinese men held captive by Japanese troops, 1931

capital city, Nanking, in December 1937, when Japanese soldiers embarked on a six-week orgy of murder, rape, mutilation, and torture. Tens of thousands of Chinese civilians died.

Despite these defeats and a retreat into the country's interior, the Chinese stubbornly continued to resist. Tens of thousands of Japanese troops were killed from 1937 to 1941 alone. Chinese civilian and military deaths numbered in the millions. The stalemate would drag on for eight years until the downfall of Japan in 1945. In the interim, the Japanese set up a collaboration government in Nanking. However, it never managed to establish dominance over China or compel the Chinese Nationalist government to surrender or even to negotiate.

War erupts in China A minor skirmish between Chinese and Japanese troops at the Marco Polo Bridge near Peiping, China, on July 7, 1937, quickly escalated into the Second Sino-Japanese War (1937–45). Unprepared for a sustained conflict, the Chinese army (*pictured*) could do little to stop the Japanese advance. In less than a year, the invaders destroyed China's best fighting units and controlled northern China, the industrial center of the country. Initially, Japan's objective was the overthrow of the Nationalist government of Chiang Kai-shek, but its advance stalled as China's resistance stiffened.

1939

January 12, 1939: In a speech before Congress, President Roosevelt details his $552 million defense plan.

January 24, 1939: Hermann Göring establishes the National Central Office for Jewish Emigration, and orders the SS leadership to step up the evacuation of German Jews.

March 15, 1939: German troops occupy the rest of Czechoslovakia: Bohemia and Moravia.

March 17, 1939: In the company of the White House press corps, President Roosevelt underscores the importance of amending the U.S. Neutrality Act.

March 22, 1939: Germany strong-arms Lithuania into returning the Memel District to Germany.

March 25, 1939: Because the Polish government will not subordinate the country to Germany, Hitler directs his generals to develop plans for war.

March 28, 1939: General Francisco Franco captures Madrid, ending hostilities in the Spanish Civil War. Franco will declare the war officially over on April 1.

March 29, 1939: In a response to Germany's posturing over Danzig, Warsaw announces that the Polish army would retaliate against any attempt to take the port.

April 3, 1939: *Fall Weiss* (Case White), the Nazi war plan for the invasion of Poland, is completed. The plan, scheduled to be implemented on September 1, calls for a three-front attack that would end with the capture of Warsaw.

April 7, 1939: Italy invades the small Adriatic nation of Albania. The Italians will capture the capital of Tiranë within a day. • Spain signs the Anti-Comintern Pact, aligning itself with Japan, Germany, and Italy.

Japanese take Peiping The Chinese city of Peiping fell to Japanese troops on July 29, 1937, only 22 days after the start of the Second Sino-Japanese War. Chinese defenders offered little resistance as the enemy closed in on the major cities of Peiping and Tientsin. The former had been the capital of China until the government moved to Nanking in 1928. During the Japanese occupation, Peiping's name was changed to Beijing and was made the capital of the provisional government of the Republic of China. A puppet regime ruled northern China until the Japanese abandoned Beijing in 1945.

Mass killings in Chinese capital Although outnumbered by almost two to one, the Japanese Imperial Army captured the Chinese capital of Nanking on December 13, 1937. They entered the city with orders to "kill all captives." Because they were trained to fight until death, Japanese soldiers saw surrender as an act of cowardice and therefore treated the surrendering Chinese soldiers with contempt. Moreover, as representatives of the emperor, Japanese soldiers believed that the citizens of the nations they conquered were less than human and deserved rape, torture, and death. Within six weeks, tens of thousands of Chinese soldiers and civilians in Nanking were killed, with many buried alive (*pictured*).

The Rape of Nanking As Japanese soldiers overtook Nanking, they trucked Chinese prisoners of war to the outskirts of the city. Japanese officers ordered their men to torture and kill these prisoners so as to banish any feelings of humanity that a Japanese soldier may still hold for his captives. Many photos, such as this one of prisoners being killed during a bayonet drill, were taken of the slaughter. Very few Japanese soldiers refused to carry out the barbaric orders. Failure to do so meant immediate death.

"MURDERING DEMONS"

A NEW CONSCRIPT became a full-fledged soldier in three months in the battle area. We planned exercises for these men. As the last stage of their training, we made them bayonet a living human. When I was a company commander, this was used as a finishing touch to training for the men and a trial of courage for the officers. Prisoners were blindfolded and tied to poles. The soldiers dashed forward to bayonet their target at the shout of "Charge!" Some stopped on their way. We kicked them and made them do it. After that, a man could do anything easily. The army created men capable of combat. The thing of supreme importance was to make them fight. It didn't matter whether they were bright or sincere. Men useless in action were worthless. Good soldiers were those who were able to kill, however uncouth they were. We made them like this. Good sons, good daddies, good elder brothers at home were brought to the front to kill.... Human beings turned into murdering demons. Everyone became a demon within three months.

—TOMINAGA SHOZO, 232ND REGIMENT, 39TH HIROSHIMA DIVISION, STATIONED IN YANGTZE VALLEY NEAR CHUNGKING, CHINA

Poisoning young minds
"The Jew is the most dangerous poison mushroom in existence," a pious mother teaches her son in this 1938 children's book, which was illustrated by the anti-Semitic cartoonist "Fips" (Philip Rupprecht). The success of Julius Streicher's political newspaper allowed him to publish such books as *Der Giftpilz* (*The Poisonous Mushroom*) to educate German

youngsters in proper Nazi attitudes. Determined to have children well-indoctrinated before adulthood, the Nazis built propaganda into the school curriculum, screened teachers for adherence to the party line, and shaped science programs around their notions of "blood purity."

Nazis press for union with Austria Following the assassination of Austrian chancellor Engelbert Dollfuss by the Nazis in 1934, the new chancellor, Kurt von Schuschnigg, tried to maintain Austria's independence and constitutional government. Within Austria, Nazi pressure for union with Germany escalated, and was reinforced by a relentless propaganda campaign (*pictured*) that pushed for a "yes" vote on union. Eventually, in 1938, the *Anschluss* preempted a democratic outcome when Arthur Seyss-Inquart—the pro-Nazi interior minister—"requested" the German invasion. Subsequently, Seyss-Inquart supplanted Schuschnigg as Reich governor of Austria.

1939

April 11, 1939: Following the lead of an increasingly influential Berlin, Hungary withdraws from the failing League of Nations.

April 13, 1939: France and Britain pledge that they will support Greece and Romania if attacked.

April 28, 1939: Hitler announces he will no longer honor the nonaggression pact Germany signed with Poland in 1934, prompting Polish authorities to negotiate an alliance with London.

May 3, 1939: Maxim Litvinov, the Soviet Union's people's commissar for foreign affairs and a staunch supporter of collective security, is replaced by Vyacheslav Molotov. This move will pave the way for a Soviet-German alliance later in the year. • State-sanctioned persecution of Hungarian Jews begins with a series of laws that restricts civil liberties.

May 5, 1939: In another step toward war, Poland reiterates its refusal to capitulate to Germany's demand to annex Danzig and the Polish Corridor.

May 11, 1939: No longer content with Manchukuo, its puppet state of Manchuria, Japan eyes Soviet territory, kicking off a series of border skirmishes that will continue through August.

May 17, 1939: Norway, Sweden, and Finland reject Germany's offer of a nonaggression pact.

May 22, 1939: Galeazzo Ciano, Mussolini's foreign minister (and son-in-law), reluctantly signs the Pact of Steel with German representatives in Berlin.

May 27, 1939: U.S. secretary of state Cordell Hull pens a letter to the Senate Foreign Relations Committee urging an end to the arms embargo provision of the U.S. Neutrality Act.

The *Anschluss* The political union (*Anschluss*) of Austria and Germany was a key element of Austrian-born Hitler's foreign policy, but it was forbidden by the 1919 Treaty of Versailles. Generally, both countries favored an economic and customs union, but in 1931 this was denounced by France and others and prevented by the International Court of Justice. Then, beginning in 1933, the Nazis revived the issue. They supported an abortive coup attempt in 1934 and annexed Austria by an unopposed invasion in 1938. Apart from the Jewish population, most Austrians, including those pictured, welcomed the German army enthusiastically and applauded Austria's union with Germany.

Puppet president With the international abandonment and impending dismemberment of his country, Czechoslovakian president Edvard Benes resigned in protest in 1938. Emil Hácha (*pictured*) was chosen as his successor. With the German invasion imminent and aware of Hitler's threat to bomb Prague, Hácha capitulated, signing a declaration surrendering Czechoslovakia and incorporating it into the Third Reich. Subsequently, Hácha became the Nazis' puppet president of the Reich Protectorate of Bohemia and Moravia and urged the Czechs not to resist. He died in prison in 1945 while awaiting trial for high treason.

> ## "My good friends, this is the second time in our history that there has come back from Germany to Downing Street peace with honor. I believe it is peace in our time."
>
> —British prime minister Neville Chamberlain, September 30, 1938

Chamberlain: "Peace in our time" The Munich Agreement between Germany, France, Britain, and Italy made Hitler master of Central Europe. It eliminated Czechoslovakia's defensive capability, highlighted the military weakness of Britain and France, and provided all concerned with more time to prepare for war. Meanwhile, while stating he achieved "peace in our time," Neville Chamberlain received a hero's welcome in Britain, where—for much of the population—fears of yet another European war far exceeded any concerns for distant Czechoslovakia. However, war would ensue in 1939. When Germany attacked Norway in April 1940, Chamberlain's parliamentary support finally collapsed, and Churchill replaced him soon after.

Tensions rise in Sudetenland The Sudetenland, the mountainous region of northeastern Bohemia and northern Moravia, was placed within Czechoslovakia by the 1919 Versailles settlement primarily for historical and economic reasons. However, many of the three

million ethnic Germans living in the Sudetenland believed that the Czech central government's policies discriminated against them—a perception enhanced by pro-German agitator Konrad Heinlein in the 1930s. This volatile situation was subsequently exploited by Hitler, and regional tension increased significantly. With conflict clearly looming, this Sudeten-German woman and her twin sons sought safety in the German border village of Friedland during September 1938.

Hitler leans hard on Britain Franco-British apathy over the *Anschluss* encouraged Hitler to proceed with his plans to destroy Czechoslovakia. By doing so, he hoped to eliminate Czechoslovakia as a separate state while gaining access to its burgeoning steel and armaments industries. During three meetings with Hitler, Prime Minister Neville Chamberlain (*left*) was presented with ever-greater territorial demands. Eventually, at the Munich meeting of September 29–30, 1938 (*pictured*), appeasement triumphed, and Czechoslovakia was effectively sacrificed. The cession of the Sudetenland to Germany provided Hitler with yet another strategic victory achieved through coercion rather than war. However, he bitterly regretted pulling back from war in the face of Britain's threat to fight if he went further.

Sudeten Germans welcome occupiers Most of the population of the Sudetenland (northeastern Bohemia and northern Moravia) was ethnically German, although Czechs comprised the majority in the two provinces overall. This potentially volatile ethnic mix was exploited by pro-Nazi agitator Konrad Heinlein during the 1930s. In early October 1938, the Sudeten Germans finally realized their aspirations with their annexation by the Third Reich. Those pictured welcomed the Germans enthusiastically.

1939

May 31, 1939: In a move that emboldens Hitler, Vyacheslav Molotov addresses the Supreme Soviet and denies that the Soviet Union is aligning itself with the Western powers against Germany. • Germany signs a nonaggression pact with Denmark.

June 2, 1939: Just two days after Molotov's denial that the Soviets had picked sides, Soviet authorities attempt to create a mutual assistance pact with France and Britain.

July 9, 1939: Realizing that Britain could not successfully defend Poland against German aggression, British Parliament member Winston Churchill calls for a British-Russian alliance. Having imperialist designs of his own on Poland, Stalin will decline.

July 26, 1939: Secretary of State Cordell Hull informs the Japanese ambassador that the United States will not extend the 1911 commercial treaty between the two nations.

August 1939: Despite pressure from the West and his own dire assessment of the German threat, Polish General Edward Smigly-Rydz declares that allowing the Soviets passage through Poland would be a mistake, claiming that once the Red Army enters Polish territory, "they will never leave it." • The Nazi SS obtains 150 concentration camp prisoners, dresses them in Polish army uniforms, and shoots them. Their bodies are used as planted evidence of Polish aggression along the German border, and Hitler uses the fictional skirmish as a pretext for war.

August 2, 1939: Physicist Albert Einstein signs a letter to President Roosevelt stating that scientists have discovered how to create a nuclear chain reaction, which could lead to "extremely powerful bombs of a new type." This will be a key factor in Roosevelt's pushing for the U.S. atomic bomb project.

Night of Broken Glass Jews in Berlin clean up after *Kristallnacht* (Night of Broken Glass), which raged on November 9 and 10, 1938. After a Jewish teenager shot a German diplomat in Paris, Nazi propaganda minister Joseph Goebbels organized a pogrom against German Jews. Citizens joined Storm Troopers in destroying and looting Jewish homes, stores, and synagogues, and killing nearly 40 Jews. Some 30,000 Jewish men were taken to concentration camps. In addition, Hermann Göring levied an "atonement fine" to pay for all the damage. *Kristallnacht* signaled many more Nazi cruelties to come.

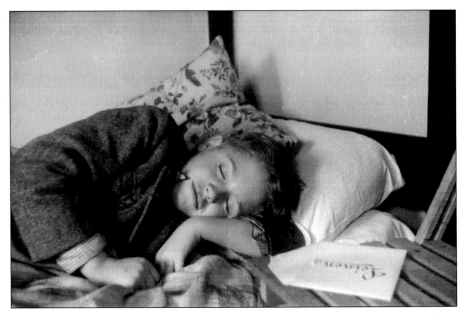

Saving the children A Jewish child rests following a *Kindertransport* journey. After *Kristallnacht,* the British government agreed to receive Jewish children under age 17 from Nazi Germany and its occupied territories. Jewish organizations selected children—generally orphaned, impoverished, in danger of arrest, or with parents in concentration camps—and financially guaranteed each child's care and eventual re-emigration. From December 1938 to September 1939, about 10,000 children traveled by train and ferry to Great Britain, where they lived in foster families, in group homes, or on farms. Most of the refugees never saw their parents again.

The Youth Aliyah Jewish students sing at the Youth Aliyah school in Berlin. Before the war, the Youth Aliyah organization prepared Jewish children for a future life in Palestine. When other Jewish youth groups were banned by the Nazis, the Youth Aliyah was allowed to continue because it encouraged Jewish emigration. The organization helped as many as 22,000 Jewish children reach Palestine and other countries. In 1941 the Nazis prohibited all Jewish emigration and closed the Berlin school, but many former Youth Aliyah students would play key roles in the establishment of Israel.

Germany takes control of Prague The German annexation of Bohemia and Moravia occurred soon after President Hácha's capitulation. The Germans occupied Prague (*pictured*) on March 15, 1939, and seized the Czech armaments industry and tank production lines. The Czech army was disbanded, with much of its excellent equipment adopted by the Germans—including 469 tanks. Politically, the annexation furthered Hitler's policy of developing *Lebensraum* (living space) for Germany in the east. It also delivered some 120,000 Czech and refugee German Jews into the hands of the SS.

Britain institutes conscription Because Great Britain had only a small professional army, in April 1939 men ages 20 and 21 were required to register for six months of military training. This was the first peacetime conscription in British history, and all Labour and Liberal members of Parliament voted against it. By 1941 conscription was extended to men ages 18 to 41 (single men were inducted before married men) and to unmarried women.

Jews not welcomed
Twins Renate and Innes Spanier gaze out of a porthole on the ship *St. Louis*. In May 1939, more than 900 Jewish refugees booked passage on the liner, hoping to escape Nazi Germany. However, Cuba, the United States, and Canada all denied permission for the ship to dock. After fruitlessly sailing up and down the North American coast, the *St. Louis* returned to Europe. Most passengers had to disembark in countries that were later overrun by Nazi Germany. Many died in concentration camps, though the Spaniers survived in Holland and eventually immigrated to the U.S.

1939

August 4, 1939: General Francisco Franco establishes authoritarian rule in Spain. He titles himself *El Caudillo* (The Leader) and asserts that he will answer only "to God and to history."

August 12, 1939: Military representatives from the Soviet Union, France, and Britain meet in Moscow to discuss an alliance. Talks will adjourn on the 19th without resolution, as Russia prefers an agreement with Germany.

August 12–13, 1939: Italian foreign minister Galeazzo Ciano informs Hitler that the Italian military would not be sufficiently rebuilt to fight alongside the Germans for another two years.

August 15, 1939: In a letter to French foreign minister Georges Bonnet, the French ambassador to Berlin describes a meeting with German officials in which he expressed the certainty that Britain, Poland, and France would go to war "automatically in case of aggression against any one of them."

August 20–31, 1939: In one of the largest battles since the Great War, the Soviets attack Japanese army units along Mongolia's Khalka River. Some 45,000 Japanese soldiers are killed, while 17,000 Soviets lose their lives.

August 22, 1939: Hitler calls a meeting of his military leadership at Obersalzberg and, in a chilling speech, leaves no doubt that he intends to "kill without pity or mercy all men, women, and children of the Polish race or language."

August 23, 1939: Germany's Axis ally, Japan, is stunned by the signing of the German-Soviet nonaggression agreement, known as the Molotov-Ribbentrop Pact. War is all but unavoidable, as the two powers agree to carve Poland in half.

Hitler's last peace-time speech Hitler (*at lower podium*) makes his last peace-time public speech—a two-hour rant to the *Reichstag*—on April 28, 1939. Claiming to be a pacifist, Hitler spoke scornfully of President Roosevelt, presented Germany as the victim of injustice, rejected the 1934 German-Polish nonaggression pact, and denounced the 1935 Anglo-German Naval Treaty (which supposedly restricted the size of the German navy). Broadcast to the world, the speech generated no surprise in Poland and elsewhere.

Soviets rout invading Japanese After a series of probes along the Mongolian border met with mixed results in 1937 and '38, Japanese troops invaded Outer Mongolia and set up a defensive position in the Khalkin Gol mountains. Concerned for the security of the Trans-Siberian Railroad, Soviet leader Joseph Stalin sent his best commander, Lieutenant General Georgi Zhukov, to stabilize the region. Zhukov launched a swift and unexpected attack, using ground and air forces, on August 20, 1939, against the enemy position at Khalkin Gol. When the battle ended 11 days later, the Soviets had achieved a strategic victory, celebrated by these Russian soldiers. The Japanese 23rd Division was wiped out, with 18,000 dead.

The German-American Bund

ON FEBRUARY 20, 1939, 22,000 people packed Madison Square Garden in New York City. They anxiously awaited the appearance of Fritz Kuhn, a German-born engineer and leader of the German-American Bund, a political group of anti-Semitic Nazi sympathizers. It was two days before George Washington's birthday, and a 30-foot-high portrait of the first president (called the first Fascist by the group) hung behind the podium, which was bordered by Nazi flags and swastikas. Kuhn was ushered into the arena by 3,000 Nazi uniformed guards. This was the greatest moment in the history of the Bund. It would also prove to be its last.

Bund members advanced their anti-Semitic and anti-Communist beliefs through newspapers, magazines, and demonstrations in American cities. The group also ran a number of social clubs and youth camps, which were modeled after the Nazi youth camps in Germany. With Hitler's support, Fritz Kuhn—an American citizen—was named leader of the organization in 1936. He carried the Bund's message across America through appearances, film strips, and support of other anti-Semitic groups, including the one led by popular Catholic priest Father Charles Coughlin.

A meeting in New York City, March 1937

Following his appearance at Madison Square Garden, Kuhn became a target for prosecution by government officials. He was convicted of embezzling money from the proceeds of the February 1939 rally and was sent to Sing Sing Prison that same year. Never reaching more than 25,000 members, the German-American Bund virtually disappeared after America entered the war.

The significance of Danzig The Free City of Danzig was created by the Versailles settlement of 1919. Despite being a major port on Poland's littoral, it was placed under the direct supervision of the League of Nations. However, Danzig's population of 400,000 was overwhelmingly German; less than six percent was Polish. The Germans refused a Polish plan to partition the territory of the Free City that would give Germany the city itself. The Germans wanted war.

Germans, Soviets agree to split Poland One of the great politico-strategic surprises of the war was the signing of the non-aggression pact between Germany and the Soviet Union on August 23, 1939. These two states' respective political ideologies, fascism and communism, had been considered entirely irreconcilable. The treaty was signed by Reich minister for foreign affairs Joachim von Ribbentrop (*top left*) and Soviet foreign minister Vyacheslav Molotov (*bottom left*) in the presence of Soviet leader Joseph Stalin. This unlikely but undeniably pragmatic agreement provided for the German-Soviet partition of Poland.

1939

August 24, 1939: In a last-ditch effort to avoid war, President Roosevelt sends a personal appeal to Hitler, asking him to address the Polish issue through diplomatic channels.

August 25, 1939: Poland and Britain sign a treaty in which they promise mutual assistance.

August 27, 1939: In a major conscription push, Britain calls for the enlistment of all men ages 20 and 21. • The German Heinkel He 178, the world's first jet aircraft, makes its maiden voyage, reaching a top speed of 403 mph.

August 29, 1939: Hitler agrees to sit down at the bargaining table with Polish leaders, but the next day Warsaw will send word that it will not be sending a delegation to Berlin. • The noose tightens further still around Poland with the Nazi occupation of Slovakia.

August 31, 1939: Germany insists that the time for negotiation with Warsaw has now passed, claiming that it has been "put off by the Polish side with feeble subterfuges and empty declarations." • With war imminent, Britain begins to evacuate large numbers of people from cities and towns and disperse them in the countryside. Britain mobilizes the Royal Navy and calls up naval reservists. • With the code words "Canned Goods" as the trigger, German operatives seize a radio station in Gleiwitz, Germany, and broadcast a message telling all Poles to attack Germans. The operation goes off smoothly, leaving the impression that insurgents were attacking Germans, and giving Hitler one more contrived pretext for war.

Europe before the war Throughout the summer of 1939, Europe teetered on the brink of war, while from 1933 Hitler and the Nazis—and therefore a resurgent and militarily reinvigorated Germany—became increasingly more powerful. In 1935 Germany regained control of the Saar Basin; in 1936 it remilitarized the Rhineland; in 1938 the *Anschluss* subsumed Austria into Greater Germany. Germany also annexed the Sudetenland in 1938 and Memel in 1939. Meanwhile, Germany's 1939 "Pact of Steel" with Italy and its nonaggression pact with Soviet Russia ensured the security of its southern and eastern borders in the event of war. Elsewhere, Franco's German-supported nationalists were finally triumphant in Spain's three-year civil war.

Japan pushes its luck with Soviets Following Japan's victory over Russia in 1905, the latter had to make a number of concessions. The Russians withdrew troops from Manchuria and recognized that Korea was in the Japanese sphere of influence. As Japan pursued its policy of expansion into Asia in the 1930s, its leaders underestimated the military strength of the USSR. This belief was reinforced when the Soviets offered little resistance to Japanese probes along its borders. Japan would soon suffer severe setbacks, however, at the hands of a revitalized Soviet army. Here, Soviet troops and armor go on the attack in the summer of 1939.

The Emperor in Japanese Society

THE EXTENT OF EMPEROR Hirohito's involvement in the outbreak and conduct of World War II is highly debated. One school charges that the emperor was deeply involved in the prosecution of Japanese war aims and took an active part in events. Others maintain that Hirohito was a figurehead who could only react to policies and events crafted by militants in the army and government.

As emperor, Hirohito was considered a divinity. His subjects were forbidden to look at his face, address him by name, or speak to him from a greater height. His divine authority was unquestioned, though his constitutional authority to act was limited.

Emperor Hirohito

However, being a divine figure had its drawbacks. By tradition and by the constitution, it was difficult for him to become involved in the give-and-take of political or strategic discussions. Japanese emperors were not without influence, but that influence traditionally tended to be more in the form of insinuation than directive. Moreover, Hirohito was personally disinclined to taking direct action. He was introspective and somewhat passive by nature. His greatest pleasure was the study of marine biology.

Nevertheless, Hirohito was not uninformed. Officials kept him abreast of negotiations before the war as well as developing plans to confront the United States. It appears that the emperor urged continued negotiation but did not exert his "divine" influence to avert war. Once war came, he followed events avidly, apparently hoping for a decisive battlefield win that would force the Allies to a negotiated peace. However, the extent of his influence on policy remains ambiguous.

In 1945, with his nation facing extinction, Hirohito finally insisted upon an end to the war, and he directly addressed the Japanese people. Some consider this his finest moment, while others observe that he had little choice if he hoped to preserve the imperial line.

The Allies subsequently ignored calls to try the emperor as a war criminal, as they realized that the occupation of Japan would be virtually impossible without his authority. Though he renounced his "divinity" after the war, Hirohito remained on the throne until his death at age 87 in 1989.

Poland not prepared Although Poland had the fifth largest armed forces in Europe, including an army of a million men with almost 500 tanks, it was unprepared for a modern war of maneuver. In fact, it still included many horse-mounted fighting units (*pictured*). Despite the inevitability of war, Poland mobilized late to avoid being blamed for an outbreak of war. Only 17 of 30 mobilized divisions were fully deployed by August 31. Finally, despite having well-prepared defensive positions, these were dispersed too widely to present a cohesive and viable defense against a mobile fighting force—especially the powerful *Wehrmacht*.

GERMANY MAKES ITS MOVE

SEPTEMBER 1939–MARCH 1940

> **"Kill without mercy all men, women, and children of Polish descent or language. Only in this way can we obtain the living space we need."**
>
> —ADOLF HITLER, INSTRUCTING SUBORDINATES ON THE CONDUCT OF GERMANY'S POLISH CAMPAIGN

O N SEPTEMBER 1, 1939, Zygmunt Klukowski, a young Polish doctor, confided in his diary that everyone was talking about war. "Everybody," he continued, "is sure that we will win." The reality was startlingly different.

Germany's war with Poland, begun on September 1, was an uneven contest. Five German armies with 1.5 million men, 2,000 tanks, and 1,900 modern aircraft faced fewer than a million Polish troops with less than 500 aircraft and a small number of armored vehicles. In addition, German planning and technical support—and German understanding of the importance of modern tactical airpower—gave the aggressor great advantages.

Within five days, German forces occupied all of the frontier zones. By September 7, forward units were only 25 miles from Warsaw, the Polish capital. Polish air forces were eliminated, and the Polish army was split and encircled. By September 17, the war was virtually over. Ten days later, after a devastating air assault, Warsaw surrendered. "We were not yet ready," wrote Dr. Klukowski two weeks later, "to discuss the causes of our defeat.... This is a fact, but we just can't believe it."

This was the war Hitler had hoped for in 1939. But in addition to the localized conflict with Poland, the German invasion provoked a global con-

The *Wehrmacht*'s armor and aircraft spearheaded the *Blitzkrieg* onslaught that fell upon Poland in September 1939. However, it was ultimately the German infantrymen—such as these *panzergrenadiers*—who secured the final victory. Superbly trained and equipped, well led and motivated, these men were truly the advance guard of Hitler's "Thousand-Year Reich."

flict. Britain and France declared war on Germany on September 3 when it became clear that negotiating a German withdrawal was hopeless. In Britain and France, the populations had braced themselves for war in the closing weeks of the summer. There was little popular enthusiasm for war, but a strong wave of anti-German and anti-Fascist sentiment produced a resigned recognition that Hitler would only stop if he was faced by force.

Almost immediately, the British and French empires (except for Ireland) joined the contest, turning it into a worldwide war, fought not only in Europe but across the oceans. German invasion also triggered Soviet intervention. The terms of the German-Soviet pact, signed in August 1939, gave Stalin a sphere of influence in eastern Poland. On September 17, once it was clear that Poland was close to defeat, Red Army units moved into Poland and met up with victorious German troops along a prearranged frontier. On September 28, the two dictatorships signed another treaty, which divided Poland between them.

For the Western powers, this provoked fears of a totalitarian alliance against them. For Poland, dismemberment and harsh totalitarian rule was the reality. Britain and France did nothing to help their smaller ally. Their military staffs had drawn up a "war plan" during the summer of 1939 in which the loss of Poland was accepted as inevitable. The core of the plan was to blockade and contain Germany until the war of attrition forced the Germans to abandon the contest as they had done in 1918. Britain and France expected a war of at least three years. This explains why for the first six months of the war the Western states did very little. The lull was nicknamed the "Phony War"—a war with no fighting.

The Western powers had failed them, and their armed forces had proved incapable of defending them. In September 1939, a group of Polish Catholic women in Warsaw sought a more spiritual form of support and comfort, praying before the crucifix at a church partially destroyed by German bombing the previous day.

A small amount of naval activity did occur, which gave citizens on both sides something to cheer about. In December 1939, Britain's Royal Navy so damaged the German pocket battleship *Graf Spee* that it was scuttled in the South Atlantic. Conversely, German submarines began to sink Allied merchant ships. On October 14, 1939, a German submarine managed to penetrate the defenses of the main British naval base at Scapa Flow in the Orkney Islands, and there sank the battleship *Royal Oak*. The Germans bombed Polish citizens mercilessly, but for a while refrained from bombing cities in the West. The British only dropped leaflets on German cities.

The chief beneficiary of the war in Poland was the Soviet Union. Suffering almost no casualties, the Red Army took parts of Poland that had been seized by Russia and Austria back in the 18th century but returned to Poland after World War I. The region was integrated at once into the Soviet system. More than one million Poles, those regarded as a threat to the Communist order, were deported to labor camps in the Soviet Union. The three Baltic States—Latvia, Lithuania, and Estonia—had been assigned to the Soviet sphere by the August and September agreements. They were compelled by Soviet pressure to accept Soviet military garrisons and political advisers on their soil.

In the fall of 1939, the USSR demanded that the Finnish government cede some territory and allow bases on Finnish soil. Stalin had, in fact, already drawn up plans for a Communist Finland, and he expected the same response as the Baltic States had given. Instead, Finland rejected the Soviet demands, and on November 30 Soviet forces invaded along the entire Finnish frontier. Finland's army of 200,000 mounted a spirited defense. Only after the mobilization of further Soviet forces in February 1940 did Finnish resistance wear down. Finland sought an armistice on March 6, and a week later it conceded all the territory and a base that had been originally demanded.

For Hitler, the Soviet advance in Eastern Europe and the spread of Communist influence were prices he had to pay for securing the German rear while Germany attacked Britain and France. But it was a dangerous situation. In October 1939, he hinted to his military staff that he would settle with the USSR as soon as he could. He hoped the West might seek terms, but when it became clear they were serious about war, he planned to attack the French front in November 1939. Poor weather prevented it, and Hitler reluctantly accepted a postponement until spring.

Urged forward by the German navy, Hitler decided to seize Norway and Denmark for the naval war against British trade supplies from America. What had begun as a war to extend German power in Eastern Europe had become an open and unpredictable conflict with the intervention of Britain and France. Only in Poland was the war really over. Dr. Klukowski watched in dismay as German troops looted shops and churches and forced Jews to give up their valuables and clean the streets. As he wrote late in 1939, "It is really hard to live in slavery."

A political cartoon published in the London magazine *Punch* in 1939 vividly portrayed a widely held British view of Hitler and Stalin—of their duplicitous, avaricious, and evil natures. The cartoon also reveals the disastrous consequences of the German-Soviet nonaggression pact for the countries of Eastern Europe, including the division of Poland.

1939

September 1: World War II begins as the Germans invade Poland with a three-front *Blitzkrieg*. They attack the Polish army with an overwhelming force of 1.5 million troops backed by tactical aircraft in the sky and mobile armor on the ground.

September 2: Poland pleads for assistance from sworn allies Britain and France. They respond the following day by demanding Germany's withdrawal and declaring war against the Nazi regime. India, Canada, Australia, and New Zealand (and soon South Africa) issue their own declarations of war.

September 3: Conservative parliamentarian Winston Churchill is named first lord of the admiralty. • Britain's Royal Air Force (RAF) carries out the first propaganda air raid of the war, salting northern Germany with six million pamphlets. • Without warning, a German U-boat torpedoes the *Athenia,* a British passenger ship carrying 1,400 civilians from England to Canada, killing 118.

September 4: The first RAF air assault is a disaster, with only eight of 29 bombers striking German naval bases. Ten of the RAF bombers get lost, seven are shot down, three attack one of Britain's own ships, and one attacks neutral Denmark. • Spain's General Franco offers his support to the Axis while publicly declaring neutrality.

September 5: The Nazis occupy the medieval Polish city of Kraków. • The United States officially declares its neutrality.

September 6: RAF Hurricanes and Spitfires that scramble during a false air raid alert end up shooting at each other, with the Spitfires downing the Hurricanes.

German forces storm Poland At dawn on September 1, 1939, the *Wehrmacht*'s armored spearhead swept into Poland. Four light, six panzer, and four motorized divisions cut through the sizeable but thinly spread Polish forces. In a foretaste of *Blitzkriegs* to come, armor, infantry, and artillery fought as a closely coordinated team, while the *Luftwaffe* rained death from the skies. General von Bock's Army Group North struck into Poland from Pomerania and East Prussia. Simultaneously, General Rundstedt's Army Group South surged northeast from Slovakia and Silesia. Behind the German armored divisions, some 40 infantry divisions stood ready to exploit the panzers' successes. Everywhere, the woefully unprepared Polish forces were shocked by the speed, scale, and ferocity of the German onslaught.

Poland has no chance As commander-in-chief of the Polish forces, Marshal Edward Smigly-Rydz (*pictured, front*) had the all-but-impossible task of countering the German invasion with outdated and largely static defense forces. Poland's borders, set in 1920, were generally indefensible because of the lack of rivers and mountains. With such constraints, as well as a dispersed force deployment, Poland's demise was inevitable. All hopes of holding out through winter in the woods and marshes of eastern Poland were destroyed by the Soviet invasion in mid-September.

The terrifying Stukas Close air support was a prerequisite for the success of the *Wehrmacht*'s *Blitzkrieg* operations. In 1939 and early 1940, the gull-winged, single-engine Junkers Ju-87 (Stuka)—with its three machine guns and a maximum bomb load of 1,540 pounds—was vital to such operations. The terror sirens of these diving aircraft struck fear into those on the ground below, while their bombs and guns amplified this terror with death and destruction. However, once opposed by more modern fighter aircraft—such as the British RAF's Spitfires and Hurricanes beginning in 1940—the Ju-87s proved vulnerable. They were subsequently utilized only occasionally in support of front-line offensive operations.

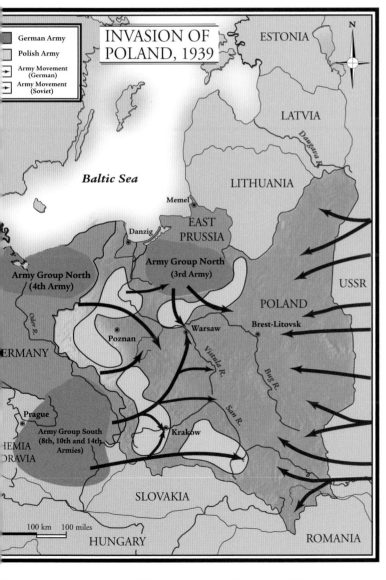

INVASION OF POLAND, 1939

Legend:
- German Army
- Polish Army
- Army Movement (German)
- Army Movement (Soviet)

ESTONIA
LATVIA
LITHUANIA
Baltic Sea
Memel
Danzig
EAST PRUSSIA
Army Group North (4th Army)
Army Group North (3rd Army)
USSR
POLAND
Warsaw
Brest-Litovsk
Poznan
Oder R.
ERMANY
Vistula R.
Bug R.
San R.
Prague
Army Group South (8th, 10th and 14th Armies)
Kraków
HEMIA ORAVIA
SLOVAKIA
100 km   100 miles
HUNGARY
ROMANIA
Daugava R.

Tops in the field German general Fedor von Bock was a distinguished old-style Prussian officer who commanded the German *Anschluss* forces in 1938. In 1939 he commanded Army Group North during the Polish campaign and, in 1940, Army Group B during the *Blitzkrieg* that speedily overran the Low Countries and defeated France. Later, Bock was twice relieved of commands in Russia: first in 1941 following a failed offensive against Moscow, and subsequently in 1942 after disagreements with Hitler over operational decisions. Having survived both those campaigns and Hitler's displeasure, he was killed in an Allied air raid on May 4, 1945.

Poland succumbs The event that finally destroyed any residual hopes in London or Paris that appeasement might yet succeed was Hitler's invasion of Poland. At dawn on September 1, 1939, successive waves of bombers and fighter-bombers raided deep into Poland. Simultaneously, the tanks, artillery, and infantry of two German army groups, comprised of five separate armies, launched devastating attacks against the sizeable but outdated and poorly deployed Polish forces. Warsaw finally fell on September 27, the effectiveness of Germany's *Wehrmacht,* had been validated, and the *Blitzkrieg* concept of warfare was born.

1939

September 7: Wary of inflaming public sentiment and pulling the United States into the war, Hitler warns his military leaders against attacking passenger vessels.

September 8: President Roosevelt calls for a strengthening of the U.S. military and begins to use his constitutional power to call up the reserves, as the war in Europe has created a state of "limited national emergency."

September 13: Claiming that Polish civilians are attacking their troops, German military leadership vows to target Polish noncombatants, of whom thousands have already been murdered.

September 14: Germany loses its first ship of the war when a U-boat is depth-charged and sunk by British destroyers.

September 17: The Soviet Union invades Poland with 40 divisions, many waving white flags at a perplexed Polish population. Already beaten by the Nazis, Poland's army is unable to put up much of a fight, and the following day Russia will easily claim the territory it was promised by Germany when the two nations signed the Molotov-Ribbentrop Pact.
• Five hundred die when the British Navy loses its first ship, the *Courageous*, which is sunk by a U-boat off Ireland.

September 18: Armed with inside knowledge of the German Enigma code, members of the Polish Cipher Bureau escape from Poland with two of the Enigma machines. They will arrive in Paris on October 1.

September 20: The *Luftwaffe* and the RAF clash for the first time, in the skies over the border between Germany and France, when German Me109s attack Fairey Battle bombers. The RAF loses two aircraft, while the Germans lose one.

Poland's tanks The Polish army fielded some 500 tanks of various types. Their capabilities of firepower, mobility, and armored protection ranged from very good to patently obsolescent. The army's tactical doctrine emphasized the importance of maneuver, concentration of force, and economy of effort. In 1939, however, the lengthy process of converting the horse-mounted cavalry into armored units was still at an early stage. Also, despite the undoubted bravery, élan, and high training standards of many tank crewmen and junior commanders, some senior commanders held an outdated belief that tanks were merely fire support for the infantry, rather than the leading edge of aggressive advances.

British take cover On September 3, 1939, civilians hurry to a London air-raid shelter just 20 minutes after Prime Minister Neville Chamberlain told Britain that it was at war with Germany. Prior to the war, British officials had feared that bombing would take a terrible toll on life and property, so thousands of makeshift coffins were prepared and gas masks issued. Air Raid Precautions committees already existed; an ARP warden is visible in a helmet here. Ominous though it was, this air raid warning proved to be a false alarm, triggered by a lone French aircraft. London would suffer its first raid in July 1940.

Lord Haw-Haw Believing that the British Union of Fascists was too soft on Jews, William Joyce in 1937 cofounded the National Socialist League, which was based on the policies of Nazi Germany. Two years later, Joyce fled to Germany, where—as "Lord Haw-Haw"— he broadcast the English-language Nazi propaganda program *Germany Calling*. Joyce was drunk when he made his final broadcast from Hamburg on April 30, 1945, as British troops entered the city. Captured by the British, Joyce was tried for treason, found guilty, and hanged.

London prepares for blackout In expectation of aerial assaults, the British mobilized civilians as well as the military. In 1940, after the defeat of France, other measures were needed. Air Raid Precautions organizations and air-raid wardens designated public shelters and advised citizens how to prepare their homes for possible bombardment. Here, workers paint a London curb to make it visible during a blackout.

HITLER HEARS FROM BRITAIN

WHEN I ENTERED the next room Hitler was sitting at his desk and Ribbentrop stood by the window. Both looked up expectantly as I came in. I stopped at some distance from Hitler's desk, and then slowly translated the British Government's ultimatum. When I finished, there was complete silence.

Hitler sat immobile, gazing before him. He was not at a loss, as was afterwards stated, nor did he rage as others allege. He sat completely silent and unmoving.

After an interval which seemed an age, he turned to Ribbentrop, who had remained standing by the window. "What now?" asked Hitler with a savage look, as though implying that his Foreign Minister had misled him about England's probable reaction.

—PAUL SCHMIDT, TRANSLATOR IN THE GERMAN FOREIGN MINISTRY, AFTER INFORMING HITLER THAT BRITAIN HAD JUST DECLARED WAR ON GERMANY, SEPTEMBER 3, 1939

British women join the fight Women gather at the recruitment office of Britain's Auxiliary Territorial Service (ATS), reformed in 1938 from the Women's Army Auxiliary Corps (WAACS) of World War I. By 1939 British women also could join the Women's Auxiliary Air Force (WAAF), the Women's Royal Naval Service (WRNS), and other military units. In December 1941, a British National Service Act began the conscription of childless widows and single women ages 20 to 30. British military women filled clerical, domestic, and medical positions; drove and maintained vehicles; manned antiaircraft guns, barrage balloons, and radar stations; ferried aircraft; deciphered coded messages; and served as spies.

1939

September 21: Pro-Nazi Iron Guardsmen assassinate Romanian prime minister Armand Calinescu, ostensibly because he was conspiring to blow up Romanian oil fields to keep them out of German hands.

September 22: Wartime shortages settle in as Britain begins rationing gas. Three days later, Germany will begin rationing bread and flour.

September 25: Warsaw is bombed into utter submission by the *Luftwaffe*. The city will surrender to the Nazis on the 27th.

October 5: The last of the Polish army lays down its guns. Of the more than half-million troops that faced the Nazis in the preceding month, most were taken prisoner while roughly 100,000 died in the fighting or fled the country.

October 6: While addressing the *Reichstag* in Berlin, Hitler accuses Poland of initiating hostilities. He insists that he has no territorial ambitions toward England, France, Belgium, Holland, and several others that he will attempt to occupy in the upcoming months and years.

October 7: Hitler moves forward with his plan to evict or kill Poles and annex their territory. He calls for the "elimination of the harmful influence of nationally alien populations, which constitute a danger to the Reich."

October 9: The U.S. Neutrality Act suffers a public relations setback when the German battleship *Deutschland* captures the *City of Flint,* an American cargo ship carrying farming supplies to England.

October 12: Rejecting Hitler's insincere peace proposals, British prime minister Neville Chamberlain asserts that "no reliance can be placed upon the promises of the present German government."

"Please talk to me! What will become of me without you?"

—10-YEAR-OLD KAZIMIERA MIKA TO HER OLDER SISTER
AFTER THE LATTER WAS GUNNED DOWN BY A NAZI FLIER

Murder of the defenseless Kazimiera Mika, a 10-year-old Polish girl, stoops over the body of her older sister. The elder Mika girl and six other women, desperate for food, had been digging for potatoes in a field in besieged Warsaw when the *Luftwaffe* struck. Nazi fliers swooped down to within 200 feet of the ground and attacked the group with machine-gun fire. Two were killed. As the aircraft left, the 10-year-old Kazimiera ran to her fallen sibling. This was Kazimiera's first experience with the finality of death, and she was unable to understand why her sister could no longer speak to her.

Warsaw puts up a fight The German capture of Warsaw, Poland, seen here with its buildings burning on the horizon, proved costly for Germans and Poles alike. On September 9, the Fourth Panzer Division lost 57 of 120 tanks in early street fighting for the city, and the panzer commanders learned many hard lessons from this clash. However, after more than two weeks of intensive air bombardment and ground combat, characterized by a succession of closely coordinated ground and air assaults and artillery bombardments, the city finally fell on September 27.

Hermann Göring

On September 1, 1939, Hitler designated Hermann Göring as his successor. Since 1933 Hitler had entrusted Göring with diverse roles, including president of the *Reichstag*, Reich minister for aviation, supreme commander of the *Luftwaffe*, and deputy for the Four-Year Plan.

Göring's upbringing in an upper-class family and his distinguished Great War career, in which he earned the *Pour le Mérite* and succeeded Manfred von Richthofen as commander of the Flying Circus, were atypical of Nazi leaders. His comically elaborate outfits and outward joviality hid brutality and unscrupulousness. His contemporaries called him the "Iron Man" and "Hermann the Terrible."

Göring, who joined the NSDAP as early as 1922, became a committed, if rather cynical, Nazi. During the Polish crisis of 1939, he sought to avert war but benefited from the early victories. As reflected in the unique title of *Reichsmarschall* (marshal of the empire), bestowed upon him in July 1940, he earned credit for the *Luftwaffe*'s vital contribution to the *Blitzkrieg* successes. However, he was also chiefly responsible for the German failure to win decisive victories at Dunkirk and in the Battle of Britain. His unrealistic promise to sustain the troops encircled in Stalingrad in 1942 set his star on the wane. The incessant bombing of Germany from 1943 on helped render him increasingly irrelevant even within the military and economic spheres.

Göring lost interest in all but his grotesque appetites for morphine, plundered art, and luxury homes. In April 1945, Hitler stripped Göring of his powers after he asked to be given the helm of the sinking ship. Yet at the Nuremberg Trials, a drug-free Göring offered a spirited defense of the indefensible. He was convicted of war crimes, including authorizing the Final Solution. On October 15, using smuggled cyanide in his prison cell, he followed his master's example by taking his own life—just before he was to be executed.

Fully equipped Messerschmitt
Flying at 350 mph with a range of 565 miles, the German Messerschmitt Me 110 fighter bomber accommodated a two-man crew, carried 2,000 pounds of bombs or four air-to-air rockets, and was armed with two 20mm cannons and five machine guns. The first twin-engine fighter to enter operational service during the war, the Me 110 was highly successful during the 1939 *Blitzkrieg* against Poland. However, it was outclassed by the RAF Hurricanes and Spitfires during the Battle of Britain in 1940, proving to be both slower and less maneuverable. It later enjoyed a renaissance as a night fighter.

Displaced Poles Due mainly to the short duration of the Polish campaign, the numbers of civilians displaced as a direct result of the German bombing campaign were not particularly great—although this child's home lay in ruins. Meanwhile, an existing international perception that the *Luftwaffe* routinely used the terror bombing of civilians as a deliberate strategy was undoubtedly reinforced by the campaign.

Soviets take their half of Poland The notorious Nazi-Soviet nonaggression pact of August 1939 contained a secret protocol that called for Germany to take the western half of Poland and the USSR the eastern half. Hitler began his invasion of Poland on September 1. On the 17th, the Soviet government bluntly told the Polish ambassador in Moscow that Poland no longer existed as a nation. That very day, the Soviets began their effortless invasion of eastern Poland. Germany and the USSR completed their conquest of the country later that month. Here, a Soviet tank passes through the Polish town of Rakov.

The capital in ruins When the first assaults against the Polish capital proved unsuccessful, the Germans besieged Warsaw. They systematically bombed and shelled the city, causing extensive destruction and loss of life. The city's own air defenses were overwhelmed by the tempo of the *Luftwaffe* onslaught, while the outclassed Polish air force was effectively neutralized by September 17. Much of Warsaw's industrial and commercial heart—including its great complex of flour mills—was set ablaze, and its system of water-pumping stations and filtration plants was extensively damaged.

A POPULAR WAR

I HAVE STILL TO FIND A GERMAN, even among those who don't like the regime, who sees anything wrong in the German destruction of Poland. All the moral attitudes of the outside world regarding the aggression against Poland find little echo among the people here. People of all classes, women as well as men, have gathered in front of the windows in Berlin for a fortnight and approvingly gazed at the maps in which little red pins showed the victorious advance of the German troops in Poland. As long as the Germans are successful and do not have to pull in their belts too much, this will not be an unpopular war.

—AMERICAN JOURNALIST WILLIAM SHIRER, *BERLIN DIARY*

Jews must dig their own graves Soon after the German victory, the SS death squads in Poland began their work of dealing with what the Nazis termed the "Jewish question." These two Polish Jews are about to be murdered once they have completed digging their own graves. Such denigration contributed directly to a victim's dehumanization, and consequently to a perverse legitimization by the Nazis of such atrocities. Of the approximately six million European Jews murdered during the Holocaust, 2.9 million were Polish.

British children evacuated In Great Britain's "Pied Piper" evacuation, nearly three million people moved from London and other cities to rural locations that were considered safe from German air attacks. Most were schoolchildren—often from poor neighborhoods—who had never met the families they would live with during the war. Pictured are some of the young evacuees. Some parents, including the Royal Family, kept their children in town with them as a patriotic gesture.

Rundstedt carries out Hitler's wishes General Karl Rudolf Gerd von Rundstedt mounted the coup that destroyed the last legal government of Prussia in 1932. Despite being removed (together with other senior army officers) by Hitler in 1938 during the Blomberg-Fritsch crisis, Rundstedt was recalled to duty in August 1939 to lead the Polish invasion. He commanded Army Group South throughout that

campaign. His undoubted talents as a field commander and staff officer were employed against France in 1940, and subsequently elsewhere. Rundstedt always served within or close to the high command. He was enthusiastic about the mass killing of Jews, and accepted huge bribes from Hitler.

Hitler stands tall in Poland A conquering Hitler visits the area to the west of Warsaw shortly before the Polish capital fell. On the left is Hitler's long-standing and loyal comrade, SS-*Oberstgruppenführer* Josef "Sepp" Dietrich, the commander of the elite *Leibstandarte Adolf Hitler* regiment. From Hitler's standpoint, the total success of Germany's campaign in Poland finally and indisputably proved the validity of his *Blitzkrieg* strategy as well as his National Socialist policies.

1939

October 12: The Nazis begin to consolidate the Jewish population in Germany's occupied territories. They send Austrian and Czechoslovakian Jews to Poland. • The Soviet Union sends Finland a list of territorial demands, which include a land exchange and the right to establish military bases. Finland will reply with its own acceptable terms on the 14th, but Russia will stand by its initial demands.

October 14: More than 800 sailors die when a German submarine torpedoes the *Royal Oak,* a British battleship.

October 26: Nazi Hans Frank is appointed governor general of a portion of German-occupied Poland, with his headquarters in Kraków.

October 28: A motion to amend the U.S. Neutrality Act to allow the sale of arms to besieged allies passes the Senate. It will clear the House and be signed by President Roosevelt on November 4. The change is contingent on the requirement that arms are not transported by American ships.

October 31: The SS imposes a series of arbitrary and highly restrictive laws on the Poles, including prohibitions against using phone booths and wearing felt hats. Violators can be given the death penalty.

November: In just one week, some 60,000 tons of supplies destined for the Allied cause are lost to German magnetic mines.

November 1: Western Poland officially becomes part of the Reich. Eastern Poland will become part of the Soviet Union two days later.

November 4: An anonymous person who signed himself "German scientist who wishes you well" leaves German weapons research secrets and a mine fuse on the windowsill of the British attaché in Oslo, Norway. • Warsaw's Jews are all herded into a ghetto.

Polish Jews rounded up The Germans arrived at Plonsk, Poland—with its 6,000-strong Jewish community—on September 5, 1939, then established a *Judenrat* (Jewish council) the following July and a ghetto that September. Here, German troops assemble the Jews soon after the town's capture. During the next two years, as many as 12,000 Jews from Plonsk and the surrounding area passed through the ghetto. It was eventually emptied in November 1942 when its remaining inhabitants were consigned to Auschwitz for extermination.

Death tolls By the end of the four-week campaign in Poland, 50,000 German soldiers were dead, wounded, or missing. Polish losses amounted to some 70,000 soldiers killed and 130,000 wounded. Another 90,000 Polish soldiers escaped to Hungary, Lithuania, Romania, and Latvia; many of them later made their way to Allied lines. Initially, the *Wehrmacht*'s treatment of its 694,000 Polish prisoners was generally appropriate, although many civilians, a large proportion of them Jewish, were murdered. The SS and SD soon established themselves in German-occupied Poland, which was now regarded as a "nonexistent" state. Thereafter, the civilian population, especially Jews, suffered increasing oppression and persecution.

The *Waffen-SS*

THE *WAFFEN-SS* (ARMED SS) evolved directly from the three original *SS-Verfügungstruppe* (Emergency Force) regiments—*Deutschland, Germania,* and *Der Führer*—within the *Allgemeine-SS* (General-SS). Many of the elite *Waffen-SS* units that were created attracted widespread notoriety. Warriors fought with a dedication, professionalism, loyalty, cruelty, and self-sacrifice that stemmed directly from their commitment to Nazi ideology and an absolute belief in Hitler.

Among the better known of the 39 *Waffen-SS* divisions (all of which had nationalistic or Teutonic titles) were *Leibstandarte Adolf Hitler, Das Reich, Totenkopf, Wiking, Prinz Eugen, Hohenstaufen, Nordland,* and *Hitlerjugend.* Generally, the *Waffen-SS* divisions had some of the best weapons and equipment available, and their achievements in combat were regularly prodigious. Their ideological faith in the Nazi cause and its political imperatives led various *Waffen-SS* units to commit a litany of atrocities and war crimes against military personnel and civilians alike—especially on the Eastern Front.

WAFFEN-SS
EINTRITT NACH VOLLENDETEM 17. LEBENSJAHR

Recruitment for the *Waffen-SS* was initially voluntary, with superlative fitness, Aryan antecedents, and NSDAP membership the basic prerequisites for all applicants. However, as the war continued, groups such as the *Hitlerjugend* (Hitler Youth) were increasingly pressuring recruits into "volunteering." Similarly, fitness requirements were relaxed over time—notwithstanding an often harsh training regimen that demanded unquestioning obedience, was physically rigorous, and routinely included exercises that utilized live ammunition.

From 1941 on, the *Waffen-SS* was expanded significantly to enable the raising of "foreign legions." Heinrich Himmler depicted this as the creation of a "European army" to fight the "great crusade against Bolshevism." These foreign units varied widely in quality and were recruited from countries as diverse as Latvia, Estonia, Lithuania, Croatia, Norway, Denmark, Holland, France, Belgium, Italy, Russia, Galicia, Albania, Finland, and India. A 60-strong *Britisches Freikorps* was even recruited from disaffected British POWs.

The Kielce Ghetto Kielce, Poland, fell to the Germans on September 4. This was quickly followed by the deliberate persecution of its Jewish community, with expropriations, deportations (*pictured*), fines, hostage-takings, beatings, and killings. A Jewish supervising council—the *Judenrat*—was established, headed by Dr. Moses Pelc, but he was later dispatched to the Auschwitz extermination camp for failing to cooperate with the SS authorities. A formal ghetto was set up in Kielce in April 1941, and by 1942 it held 27,000 inhabitants. Thereafter, the Kielce Ghetto's Jews were systematically murdered—either in place or via the extermination camps—with the last 45 Jewish children being killed in August 1944.

1939

November 8: Nine die when a concealed bomb detonates in a Munich beer hall 20 minutes after the departure of Hitler, the bomb's intended target.

November 13: Stalin orders the drafting of war plans against Finland following a breakdown in negotiations.

November 16: In Prague, Czechoslovakia, Nazi occupation forces violently suppress an uprising by students and dissidents.

November 23: Effective today, all Jews over age 10 living in Nazi-occupied Poland must wear the Star of David.

November 30: The Winter War begins with a Soviet invasion of Finland. In December, the Soviet Union will be expelled from the League of Nations for its aggression.

December: The upper age limit of British conscription is expanded twice this month. Initially, all men ages 19 to 41 are registered, and ultimately men as old as 60 and women ages 20 to 30 will be pressed into some level of service.

December 13–17: The Royal Navy engages the *Graf Spee,* a German warship, off the coast of Uruguay. After a protracted battle, the *Graf Spee* captain scuttles the ship near Montevideo.

December 17: Canada sends more than 7,000 troops to Britain to assist the Allies.

December 19: British scientists develop a technique, known as "degaussing," to suppress the trigger that trips Germany's magnetic mines.

December 20: The United States unveils a new policy in which it embargoes supplies to nations that target civilians and violate other rules of engagement in what will become known as a "moral embargo."

Canaris turns against Hitler Admiral Wilhelm Canaris was director of the *Abwehr,* the counterintelligence department of the high command of the German armed forces (OKW). Described as a humane man who hated violence, he was appalled by the atrocities of the SS in Poland in 1939. As the war unfolded, Reinhard Heydrich kept a close eye on Canaris, sensing correctly that the *Abwehr* chief was working with others to bring down the *Führer.* Hitler dismissed Canaris in February 1944, and weeks later he was placed under house arrest. After the July 1944 bomb plot against Hitler, Canaris was arrested. He was hanged by the Nazi regime in April 1945.

Germans, Soviets celebrate On September 17, 1939, after succumbing to invasions by Germany and the Soviet Union, the Polish government went into exile without surrendering. A remnant of Poland's army continued fighting into October, and guerrillas resisted into the winter. Nevertheless, on September 28 the nation was divided between the two conquering powers along the Bug River. Germany controlled about 73,000 square miles of Poland; the USSR about 78,000. Here, German and Soviet military forces hold a joint parade in Brest-Litovsk in October to celebrate Poland's destruction.

Joseph Stalin

By 1929 JOSEPH STALIN emerged as the undisputed leader of the Soviet Union. In the succeeding decade, he killed many millions of his compatriots, including all real and imagined potential rivals. Through force and persuasion, "Comrade Stalin" achieved the status of an infallible demigod.

Decisions that Stalin made in the 1930s would have momentous wartime consequences. His policy of accelerating industrialization boosted the USSR's war-making potential enormously. However, his armed forces were initially stronger on paper than in reality, and his political purging of more than 35,000 military officers in 1937–38 left Soviet forces drastically weakened when the Germans invaded in June 1941. So, too, did Stalin's uncharacteristic trust in Hitler in the preceding months.

The nonaggression pact that the Soviets and Germans signed in August 1939 reflected Stalin's pragmatism in foreign affairs, as it gave the USSR more territory and more time to prepare for war. However, his naive faith in the pact backfired on him. Stalin got the worst of the deal, accepting the port city of Riga when Hitler claimed Rotterdam, and enjoying nothing as splendiferous as Paris, which became one of Hitler's prizes. Stalin was so shocked by the invasion that he disappeared from government for several days. He recovered his nerve and, when Moscow seemed doomed in late 1941, steadied morale by remaining in the city.

As supreme commander and chairman of an all-powerful State Committee of Defense, Stalin oversaw the nation's complete and ruthless mobilization for war. He temporarily moderated his divisive viciousness by appealing to the unifying qualities of patriotism, religion, and tradition. He relaxed suppression of the church and artistic expression. Yet his brutality and homicidal paranoia never disappeared. He pushed his generals ruthlessly and used their subordinates as cannon fodder. Mere incompetence of a member of the general staff or government could bring anything from humiliating public censure to dismissal, torture, or years in prison. And heaven help the high-ranking soldier or government minister whom Stalin suspected of less than complete personal or philosophical fealty. In these cases, torture of a particularly prolonged and hideous nature was a virtual certainty, and often climaxed in execution or slow death in Siberia.

Stalin's limited personal experience of command in the Russian Civil War (1917–22) had included the defense of Tsaritsyn, which in 1942–43, as Stalingrad, became the site of an epic battle. Stalin felt qualified to pontificate on military affairs, and he made the final decision on every major wartime matter. He insisted on the successful December 1941 counteroffensive, but also gave disastrous orders at Kiev in 1941 and Kharkov in 1942. He learned from these mistakes and, although his vanity extended to taking the titles marshal (1943) and generalissimo (1945), he increasingly gave his generals considerable initiative and even the right to put forward alternative strategies.

Once Stalin found able generals—such as Zhukov, Rokossovsky, and Konev—he stuck with them, although he refrained from personal attachment. He even refused a German offer to exchange his captured son, Yakov, who subsequently died in captivity. Stalin officially deemed as traitors all Soviet POWs as well as entire ethnic groups within the USSR. His Order 227, issued in July 1942 when the Germans advanced again, demanded that Soviets fight to the death and that cowards be severely punished.

From 1941 on, Stalin urged his allies to open a second front and relieve the pressure on the USSR. He proved a cunning diplomat at conferences with Roosevelt and Churchill. The British prime minister developed a relatively good relationship with Stalin, but American officials later were alarmed when "Uncle Joe" reneged on promises to democratize liberated Eastern Europe. Though Stalin enjoyed wartime popularity in the West, he would be demonized during the Cold War.

1940

January: Temperatures plunge throughout Europe during one of the coldest winters on record. • As many as 70 Jews succumb to starvation and other ills each day in the Warsaw Ghetto. • A study reveals that, in the four months since Britain instituted its policy of nighttime blackouts, traffic deaths have increased nearly sevenfold, with pedestrians comprising the majority of the fatalities. • China mines the Yangtze and Whangpoo rivers in a moderately successful effort to impede shipping by the occupying Japanese forces.

January 2: The Soviet army launches a major offensive against Finland on the Karelian Isthmus.

January 3: Despite the U.S. policy of neutrality, President Roosevelt's annual budget request to Congress includes $1.8 billion in defense spending.

January 4: Hitler hands control of all German means of war materiel production to his trusted aide, Hermann Göring.

January 5: Unable to agree with military generals on Britain's war strategy, Leslie Hore-Belisha resigns from government following his removal as war secretary by Prime Minister Neville Chamberlain.

January 8: In a dramatic turnaround, Finnish forces annihilate the Russian army's 44th Division. • Rationing is imposed in Britain on such dietary staples as bacon, sugar, and butter.

January 9: Richard Hildebrandt, the SS chief of Danzig and West Prussia, tells SS *Reichsführer* Heinrich Himmler that he had instructed his troops to execute more than 4,000 mentally ill Polish citizens. • More than 150 die when the massive British liner *Dunbar Castle* founders off the English coast after hitting a German mine.

Khrushchev rises through the ranks Nikita Khrushchev (*right, with Stalin*) became a Communist Party member in 1918 following wartime service in the army. His rapid political rise thereafter included membership in the Central Committee of the CPSU in 1934 and a place within the all-powerful *Politburo* in 1939. He was directly involved in the Soviet annexation of eastern Poland in autumn 1939, and later served in important military-political commissar positions in Kiev, Kursk, and Stalingrad. After Stalin's death in 1953 and Georgy Malenkov's six-month rule, Khrushchev vied for and achieved leadership of the Soviet Union.

Street shelters These partially constructed "public air raid shelters" were built along the center of a South London street. They were to be used by those caught out on the streets by an air raid alert but unable to reach one of the main shelters underground or in a building in time. The staggered entrances at each end were designed to reduce the effects of a blast, and space was left for traffic (including emergency vehicles) to pass along both sides. By early 1940, such shelters were complemented by increasing numbers of underground household and community shelters.

"Degenerate music" In 1938 the Third Reich's respected "culture, art, and theater specialist," Hans Severus Ziegler, organized an exhibition called *Entartete Musik* (Degenerate Music). The poster seen here—with its stereotypical Negro playing jazz while wearing a Star of David on his lapel—crams as many symbols of supposed cultural

decay as possible into a single image. The avant-garde music of modern composers, such as Arnold Schoenberg and Paul Hindemith, was regarded as especially pernicious and un-Germanic by Nazi cultural authorities. Of course, if a composer had so much as one Jewish grandparent, any music he chose to write was labeled "degenerate."

Hitler calls for peace At the *Reichstag* on October 6, 1939, Hitler thanked God for blessing the German struggle and prayed that "all Europe may once more be granted the blessing of peace." The *Führer* denied any desire for further war, and called on Britain and France to cease hostilities. In secret soundings, the British and French insisted that peace could come only if Poland and Czechoslovakia had their independence restored, which Hitler, of course, rejected.

Chinese Nationalist leader Chiang Kai-shek emerged as commander-in-chief of the Chinese Nationalist forces following the death of Sun Yat-sen in 1925. During the war with Japan, Chiang and his third wife, "Madame Chiang" (*pictured*), were viewed in the West as symbols of Chinese democracy and heroic resistance to Japanese aggression. Yet Chiang, who faced civil war with the Chinese Communists, was neither pro-democracy nor eager to fight the Japanese. He hoped to rebuild and modernize China, and came to be its key military leader after July 1937. His stature at home declined due to rampant corruption in his government. Following the war, the Communists succeeded in driving Chiang from the mainland. He withdrew his government to Taiwan, where he died in 1975.

A fan of fascism Adolf Hitler called tall, strapping British socialite Unity Mitford "a perfect specimen of Aryan womanhood." An ardent admirer of fascism, Mitford visited Hitler in Germany. Appalled when Britain declared war on Germany, Mitford made a failed attempt at suicide. Other well-born British were attracted to fascism as the best way to solve social problems. In fact, Unity's sister, Diana, married Oswald Mosley, leader of the British Union of Fascists.

1940

January 10: A German officer crashes his plane in Belgium, and proceeds to intentionally ignite a set of war plans in full view of Allied soldiers. The salvaged, partially charred papers reveal Hitler's plan for a January 14 invasion of Holland and Belgium.

January 13: As Germany continues its aggressive posturing against the lowland nations, Holland and Belgium begin the process of moving their respective armies to a war footing.

January 15: France and Britain are rebuffed in their efforts to gain permission to cross Belgian territory in their defense against German aggression.

January 16: Reports of Nazi crimes committed against the civilian population of occupied Poland reach France, where the Polish government-in-exile is established.

January 18: Five people die in a munitions plant explosion in Essex, England. Authorities suspect enemy sabotage.

January 20: In a speech admonishing neutral nations to support the Allied cause, Winston Churchill, Britain's first lord of the admiralty, claims, "Each one hopes that if he feeds the crocodile enough, the crocodile will eat him last." Churchill also denounces Russia's invasion of Finland.

January 21: Torpedoed by a German U-boat, the British destroyer *Exmouth* goes down with its 175-man crew.

January 22: The British government imposes a level of censorship on the media. It requires Ministry of Information approval of newsreels before release.

January 23: Allies France and Britain announce that they will no longer recognize the neutrality of the waters off the Americas, and that German ships operating in the area are subject to attack.

"The idea is unbearable to me that the best, the flower of our youth must lose its life at the front in order that feebleminded and irresponsible asocial elements can have a secure existence in the asylum."

—Dr. Hermann Pfannmüller, a strong advocate of the Nazi "euthanasia" program

Nazis "euthanize" the handicapped
In October 1939, Hitler signed this letter (backdated to September 1) authorizing *Reichsleiter* Philipp Bouhler and Dr. Karl Brandt to begin "euthanizing" physically and mentally handicapped people. Under the program *Aktion T4,* doctors could identify individuals as unsound and incurable, then put them to death. Neither patient nor family consent was required. Based on Nazi concepts of "racial hygiene" and supported by a desire to limit the costs of patient care, T4 systematically destroyed as many as 100,000 human beings. It was another demonstration of Nazi policies designed to eliminate those they considered unworthy of life.

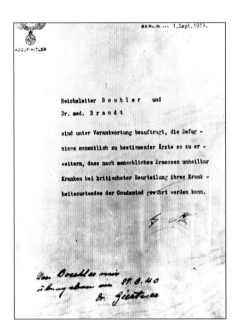

British prepare for gas bombs Poison gas had been a frightful weapon used by both sides, to devastating effect, during World War I. Given this history, and the advancements in airpower during the interwar years, Britain feared that Germany might drop gas bombs from the air. By 1940 the British government issued 38 million gas masks to civilians. Adults wore black masks while infants up to age two were placed inside sealed helmets. The helmets' canvas bottoms wrapped and fastened like a diaper, and an adult used a bellows to pump air in to the baby. "Mickey Mouse" gas masks for older children had brightly colored trim.

U.S. ends arms embargo President Franklin Roosevelt addresses the American people via radio in the fall of 1939. Beginning in 1935, a series of American neutrality acts and extensions banned arms shipments, loans, and other aid to belligerent countries, including Great Britain. Roosevelt came to regret signing the 1935 act. On September 21, 1939, he urged an end to the arms embargo. In November, Congress repealed the embargo and passed a "cash and carry" policy for Allied purchases, though other bans remained in effect.

Germany destroys the *Royal Oak* The HMS *Royal Oak* was one of five British *Revenge*-class WWI ships that were refitted for WWII. These relatively small battleships featured a "torpedo bulge" of protective armor. Even so, on October 14, 1939, the anchored battleship sank when the German submarine *U-47* slipped through British naval base defenses at Scapa Flow and struck with four torpedoes. The *Royal Oak* became the first major British ship to be destroyed in World War II. More than 800 crew members perished.

Assassination plots Hitler (*left photo*) speaks at a Munich beer hall on November 8, 1939, to commemorate the Nazi Party's failed coup of 1923. The *Führer* ended his speech earlier than expected. Minutes after he left the hall, an explosion buried the speaking platform under debris (*above*). Johann Georg Elser, a carpenter, had set the timer and planted the bomb. Elser was arrested and later executed. From 1939 to 1945, at least 17 other attempts to assassinate Hitler were made. Most were planned by officers who despised his military policies.

1940

January 24: Reinhard Heydrich, the chief of the Nazi Gestapo, is charged with overseeing the evacuation of all Jews from the Reich.

February 3: For the first time since the First World War, a German plane is shot down over England.

February 4: The Soviets attack Finland from the sky, killing 14 in the capital city of Helsinki.

February 5: France and England commit to providing the Finns with military aid to help them fend off the Soviets.

February 6: Britain launches a new poster campaign admonishing citizens not to discuss sensitive war information in public. The posters feature comical images of an eavesdropping Hitler and the slogan "Careless Talk Costs Lives."

February 9: U.S. undersecretary of state Sumner Welles leaves Washington on a futile mission to examine the possibility of a peace settlement in Europe.

February 10: The Soviet Union and Germany agree to strengthen their alliance through increased trading of war material. • President Roosevelt expresses American support for Finland in the face of Russian aggression. • Two British ships, *Salve* and *Servitor,* successfully sweep a German magnetic mine for the first time. • The occupying Nazis in Czechoslovakia place restraints on Jewish-owned businesses. They prohibit Jews from selling art, jewels, and precious metals, and force the closure of Jewish-owned textile and leather shops.

February 11: Some 140,000 Soviet troops attack Finnish defenses on the Karelian Isthmus in a bid to break Finnish resistance. This assault will prove successful for the Soviets, who will overwhelm the Finns with their sheer numbers.

Soviets battle ferocious Finns The Soviet Union's successful invasion of eastern Poland emboldened Stalin to attack Finland on November 30, 1939, beginning what was called the Winter War. But Stalin's purges of his officers and poor training had left his army largely ineffective. Moreover, Finland's outnumbered army fought back with surprising ferocity. Seen here are Finnish infantry on skis (*above*) and soldiers throwing hand grenades at a Soviet tank (*left*). Ill-equipped but innovative Finnish fighters also used "Molotov cocktails," glass jars filled with flammable fluid, to fight Stalin's troops. By March 1941, the Soviets had achieved a military victory, gaining considerable Finnish territory but at the cost of some 125,000 dead.

The Russo-Finnish War

BY THE TERMS OF THE Molotov-Ribbentrop Pact of 1939, Finland was assigned to the Soviet sphere of influence. That October, Stalin demanded that the Finns cede to him the Karelian Isthmus (north of Leningrad) and the city of Hangö (at the mouth of the Baltic). Though offered Soviet territory in Karelia in return, Finland refused. Stalin then disavowed the Soviet-Finnish nonaggression treaty and planned to incorporate Finland into the USSR by force. He established a Communist government for Finland, but abandoned it when Finnish resistance made its establishment in Helsinki too difficult.

The Red Army's initial performance was courageous but inept. Soviets outnumbered Finns about four to one at the front, but the fieldworks and bunkers of the Mannerheim Line (named after Marshal Mannerheim, the Finnish commander) proved too strong. The Finns submerged political and social divisions for the national good. As many as 125,000 Soviet troops were killed in four months of fighting, which revealed deficiencies in training, equipment, supplies, tactics, and a leadership decimated by Stalin's purges. The Finnish army was also ill-equipped, but its men were well trained and highly motivated, and its snipers and ski troops inflicted heavy casualties.

The arrival of Marshal Timoshenko, 27 new divisions, and armored support enabled the Soviets to breach the Mannerheim Line on February 11, 1940. Not long after, the Finns accepted a Soviet peace offer, which was formalized

Finnish civilians taking cover during hostilities

in the Peace of Moscow on March 12. Finland had to surrender the territory demanded in October 1939, although it was allowed to keep its independence and most of the Finnish territory in the north occupied by the Red Army during hostilities.

For its aggression in this "Winter War," the USSR was expelled from the League of Nations. Kliment Voroshilov, Stalin's old crony, was dismissed as defense commissar for his complacency and incompetence in the campaign. Timoshenko, his replacement, introduced urgently needed reforms. In Finland, bitterness at the Peace of Moscow contributed to the nation's decision to join Germany's Operation Barbarossa in 1941.

Convoys cross the Atlantic To reduce its loss of cargo ships, Britain used convoys—groups of merchant or troop ships that traveled with armed support. By summer 1941, British, Canadian, and American warships (in spite of U.S. neutrality) protected Atlantic convoys. German U-boat wolf packs fanned out to hunt them, then relayed messages for submarines, battleships, and bombers to converge on a detected convoy. English journalist Alexander Werth described an air strike on his merchant ship during the dangerous Murmansk Run to Russia: "For forty long minutes they attacked, usually in twos and threes, usually coming straight out of the sun, some diving low, others dropping their bombs from two hundred feet." Convoys lost ships, but the tactic proved safer than sailing alone.

1940

February 12: With paper in short supply, Britain adds it to the growing list of commodities subject to rationing.

February 14: Not immune to the troubles in the rest of Europe, the Vatican institutes a rationing program.

February 15: One day after Britain declares it is outfitting its merchant vessels with guns, Germany announces that it will henceforth treat all British merchant ships as hostile combatants.

February 16: After an exhaustive search, the British Navy locates, detains, and boards the German ship *Altmark* in Norwegian waters. The Nazis had been using *Altmark* as a prison ship, and the boarding party quickly secures the release of 299 British prisoners taken by Germans from Allied ships.

February 17: Despite the danger of a defeat of Finland by the Soviets, the Finns' request for aid from their supposed ally Sweden is rebuffed.

February 18: The "moral embargo," America's refusal to deal with imperialist belligerents in Europe, is extended to the Soviet Union.

February 27: In an effort to boost morale, Winston Churchill wildly overstates Britain's success on the seas, claiming that half of Germany's feared U-boats have been sunk by the Allies.

February 28: Parts of the Enigma cipher machine are recovered from the wreckage of a German U-boat, adding to the Polish-supplied information on the Enigma puzzle in the hands of the Allies.

February 29: Food and gas rationing begins in France.

Romania's Iron Guard Led by Corneliu Codreanu, Romania's Fascist Iron Guard was the paramilitary arm of the Legion of the Archangel Michael, which had been formed in 1927. Drawing popular support from the peasants and workers during the Depression years, the Legion was the country's third largest political party by 1937. Fearing its growing power, King Carol suspended parliament in 1938 and imposed a right-wing dictatorship. Widespread violence ensued. Codreanu was murdered, the premier was assassinated, and many Legionaries were executed as traitors. Subsequently, however, the Guard enjoyed a brief political renaissance within General Ion Antonescu's pro-Axis dictatorship. Seen here, the Iron Guard forms a stolid line in front of the podium where Antonescu delivers a speech. The Guard's excesses provoked its final suppression in 1941.

McCormick champions isolationism Robert R. McCormick, newspaper baron and owner of the *Chicago Tribune,* expressed contempt for all things foreign—which to him included the northeastern United States. Historian David M. Kennedy characterized McCormick as a man with "fixed, taproot convictions impermeable to evidence or reason." Nevertheless, by advocating isolationism and opposing U.S. entry into WWII, the *Chicago Tribune* gained popularity and garnered the largest circulation of any standard-sized American newspaper at the time.

Chronicling the war In September 1939, British citizens saw the rebirth of *The War Illustrated,* a magazine that had been popular during WWI. Promising to publish a photographic record of the "Second Great War" as it happened, the magazine covered both the war and the home front. Issue 5 featured photos showing U.S. reactions to the Nazi invasion

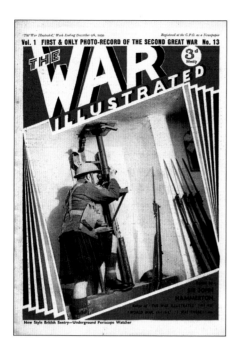

of Poland. Issue 13 (*pictured*) shows an underground sentry from a Scottish regiment keeping watch through a periscope.

The *Graf Spee* goes down The German pocket battleship *Graf Spee* explodes off Montevideo, Uruguay, on December 17, 1939. Built small, the ship was fast and heavily armed. That fall, the *Graf Spee* intercepted and sunk nine cargo ships. British warships mounted a hunt, and cruisers *Exeter, Ajax,* and *Achilles* engaged the *Graf Spee* at the mouth of Argentina's River Plate. Both the *Exeter* and the German ship were severely damaged. The *Graf Spee*'s captain, Hans Langsdorff, was unable to repair the ship in the time dictated by international law. When the neutral Uruguayans refused him extra time, Langsdorff scuttled his ship rather than let it be sunk by British warships. He committed suicide three days later.

Egypt lets Britain do the fighting Although independent since 1922, Egypt still depended upon Britain to defend its land and the Suez Canal. In 1939–40, anti-British and pro-Axis sentiments were widespread, so British forces occupied Egypt in strength. Meanwhile, the embryonic Egyptian army of 11 infantry battalions (*pictured*) and two other regiments was of little military significance. Even when Italy invaded Egypt in September 1940, its government declared nonbelligerent status, leaving the British to eject the invaders.

Canada commits to the war effort Men of the First Squadron of the Royal Canadian Air Force wait to disembark at a British port in February 1940. Originally, Canada supported appeasement of the Nazi regime. However, soon after Germany invaded Poland, the Canadian Parliament approved entry into the war. Canada began sending troops to Britain in December 1939, although those men did not see action for several years. Starting with a small military, Canada raised substantial armed forces and had one of the world's largest militaries by war's end.

1940

March: According to the BBC, two out of three British citizens listen to "Lord Haw-Haw," the "omniscient," traitorous announcer of the German propaganda radio show *Germany Calling*.

March 1: Facing shortages of darker dyes for servicemen's uniforms, British women are asked to wear only light-colored clothing. • Hitler orders his generals to create a plan for the invasion of Norway and Denmark.

March 2: The Allies ask Sweden and Norway for the right to cross their territory for the purpose of sending troops to reinforce a flagging Finnish force, but are refused.

March 6: A delegation leaves Helsinki for Moscow to negotiate the terms of Finland's surrender to the Soviets.

March 7: The *Queen Elizabeth*, the new flagship of Cunard's luxury liner fleet, arrives in New York at the end of a daring high-speed crossing of the German U-boat-infested Atlantic.

March 9: A belated offer of troops and material support from the Allies is relayed to Helsinki.

March 11: The United States has relaxed its arms embargo for its once and future allies, selling several P-40 fighters to Britain and France.

March 12: Marched for some 18 hours in a blizzard, 72 of 1,000 German Jewish deportees succumb to the elements in Lublin, Poland. • The Soviet Union and Finland sign a peace treaty in which Finland surrenders substantial strategic territory, including the city of Viipuri and the port of Hangö. The new order comes at a cost of some 25,000 Finnish lives and the deaths of nearly 70,000 Soviets.

March 14: Some half-million Finns pour out of the Soviet-occupied territory shortly after the cessation of hostilities.

The *Altmark* rescue The German supply ship *Altmark* supported the *Graf Spee*'s cargo ship raids. After the *Graf Spee* was scuttled, the *Altmark* headed back for Germany, carrying some 300 British merchant sailors as prisoners. Pursued by the British destroyer *Cossack*, the *Altmark* steamed around the northern coast of Great Britain and into a Norwegian fjord in violation of Norway's neutrality. On February 16, 1940, the *Cossack* pulled alongside the *Altmark* and mounted a boarding party. Fighting hand-to-hand with bayonets and yelling "the navy's here," British sailors rescued the prisoners.

The British-Australian alliance This piece of Allied propaganda, which emphasizes a cooperative effort against Japan by Australian and British forces, is not entirely accurate. Australia entered the war against Germany in 1939, sending troops to

the Middle East in accordance with British strategy. Volunteer Australian soldiers proved to be top-notch, despite the impact of prewar monetary cuts on military preparedness. However, Australian strategy changed with Japan's entry into the war in 1941 and the potential invasion of Australia itself. Preoccupied with the German threat, Britain was not able to guarantee support, and Australia turned to the United States instead.

Sweden's "Neutrality"

WHEN WAR BROKE OUT in September 1939, Sweden declared its neutrality as it had in every European conflict since 1814. Swedes opened their doors to those at risk of capture and imprisonment by Nazis. They sheltered almost 8,000 Jewish refugees in 1943, protected 44,000 Norwegians fleeing from German occupation, and sent one of the true heroes of the war, Raoul Wallenberg, to Hungary to save the lives of thousands of Jews. While Swedish citizens took pride in their humanitarian efforts, most of them did not know that their government was also providing important resources to the Nazis.

Sweden remained neutral when the Germans invaded Denmark and Norway in April 1940, and the nation resisted Germany's request to allow its troops to travel along the Swedish railroad. However, this resolve weakened as the war progressed and when it looked like no nation could stop the Nazi conquest. The Swedish government permitted German troops to travel its railroads to Norway in June 1940, and to transport a whole division from Norway to Finland for its invasion of the Soviet Union.

Swedish cooperation with the Nazis did not end with transportation. The Swedes supplied Germany with about

Crew members of a Swedish ship

30 percent of the iron ore the Germans used to manufacture weapons. Sweden also provided credit to the Germans, who repaid their debt with gold, including 13 tons of gold that the Nazis had stolen from Belgium and the Netherlands. Sweden's support continued until it became apparent that an Allied victory was inevitable.

Finland's strategic port A Finnish woman weeps as she leaves her home in Hangö. The small Finnish port city, strategically situated on the Baltic Sea, was much coveted by the Soviet Union before the Winter War of 1939–40. After its costly victory, the USSR established a naval base there under the peace treaty with Finland of March 1940.

Daladier's demise As the French premier, Édouard Daladier was a cosignatory of the agreement that Hitler, Mussolini, and Chamberlain negotiated in Munich on September 29–30, 1938. As such, he supported what proved to be the ill-judged

Anglo-French policy of appeasement that finally sealed Czechoslovakia's fate. In September 1939, he led a reluctant France into war with Germany. In March 1940, Daladier resigned after the defeat of the Finns in the Soviet-Finnish war. He subsequently held other ministerial appointments until his internment by the Vichy authorities in August 1940. In 1942 he was imprisoned and arraigned for being responsible for the defeat of France.

1940

March 14: The Polish government, operating in exile in France, reveals that Hitler attempted to persuade Poland to join him in an invasion of the Ukraine. • Nazi *Reichsmarschall* Hermann Göring orders all German citizens to surrender any metal that may be recycled into war materiel. • Japan's new Zero fighter planes prove formidable when 12 return from an encounter with Chinese fighters over Chengtu, having destroyed 27 of 30 Chinese planes with no casualties of their own.

March 16: James Isbister, of the Scottish village Bridge of Waithe, becomes the first United Kingdom civilian killed in an air raid since the First World War.

March 18: Hitler meets with Italian dictator Benito Mussolini to discuss Italy's entry into the war. It is determined that Mussolini's troops will attack France.

March 19: Avenging Germany's March 16 attack on Scapa Flow, 50 RAF bombers attack a seaplane base at Sylt, a German island in the North Sea.

March 20: Finance Minister Paul Reynaud succeeds Édouard Daladier as prime minister of France. • Having failed in his bid to convince Europe's belligerents to lay down their weapons, U.S. undersecretary of state Sumner Welles departs Genoa, Italy, for his return voyage to the United States.

March 27: As diplomatic relations between the Allies and Russia become difficult because of Soviet aid to Germany, Paris requests the removal of the Soviet ambassador.

March 28: Britain and France agree to not act independently in establishing treaties with any third nation.

March 30: Japan establishes a Chinese puppet government in Nanking, which the United States refuses to recognize.

Heavy-duty British bomber The twin-engine Wellington was one of the most famous bombers of the war—carrying up to 4,500 pounds of bombs, including the massive 4,000-pound "Blockbuster." The Wellington first entered squadron service with the RAF Bomber Command in 1938, and some 11,460 were eventually built. The aircraft was the RAF's principal night bomber from September 1939 until 1942. The amount of battle damage that Wellingtons could safely absorb was particularly appreciated by its five-man crews.

Eicke heads the camps and *Totenkopf* **units** Theodor Eicke joined the NSDAP in 1928. As the Nazis rose to power, Eicke was appointed commandant of the Dachau camp in 1933. His brutal actions there impressed Heinrich Himmler so much that he was appointed inspector of concentration camps and SS guard formations in 1934. From 1939 until his death in combat in 1943, Eicke commanded the *Waffen-SS Totenkopf* ("Death's Head") division in the Polish, French, and Russian campaigns. The *Totenkopf* division committed numerous atrocities, such as machine-gunning 99 British soldiers who had surrendered to them at Dunkirk.

Nazi Aesthetics

ADOLF HITLER HAD PARTICULARLY strong views about which forms of art were acceptable in the Third Reich, and which artistic imagery should be used as propaganda. Accordingly, Hitler in 1933 established the Reich Chamber of Culture under Joseph Goebbels, minister of propaganda. Goebbels and the Chamber of Culture would implement Nazi policies in all areas of the arts and media.

During Hitler's reign, paintings featured idealized images of a strong, peaceful, and pastoral Germany; of the Teutonic chivalry and military heroism of former times; and of the myths and legends of the Rhine. These concepts were fused with the physical strength, athleticism, and beauty thought to be exemplified by the Aryan man and woman, frequently pictured nude. Such emotive imagery generated sentiments and reactions ranging from selfless patriotism to blatant anti-Semitism and racism, from national pride to rampant militarism. Simplicity, realism, and heroism superseded all forms of modernism, such as impressionism, cubism, and Dada. Similar standards applied to German sculpture as well as to the architectural designs developed by Albert Speer for the

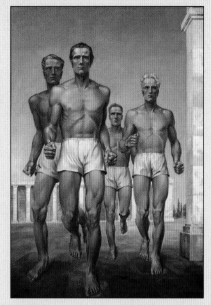

Gymnasts, by Gerhard Keil

grandiose new buildings of the Reich's capital.

The art that depicted "the true Germanic spirit" was set against the *Entartete Kunst* (degenerate art) of "lesser" cultures and peoples. The contrast reinforced the Nazi political and racist philosophy while simultaneously emphasizing Germany's heroic heritage. Nazi artwork contributed to the pageantry and martial spectacle for such events as the Nuremberg rallies of the 1930s.

In 1936 a German tribunal was established to purge the country of all *Entartete Kunst.* However, the Nazis' declared abhorrence of such works did not prevent them from looting many examples of it from the major galleries and museums of occupied Europe. More than 5,000 paintings—including many by Goya, Rembrandt, and Rubens—were transported to Germany along with thousands of other works of art. Hermann Göring and other senior Nazi officials accumulated personal art collections of immense value. While many of these items were recovered after the war, it was difficult to determine ownership and provenance. Disputes continued into the 21st century.

Quisling, as in "traitor" Vidkun Quisling (*left*), the man whose very name came to mean "traitorous collaborator," rides with SS head Heinrich Himmler, likely during Quisling's visit to see Hitler in December 1939. Quisling was a Norwegian military officer who helped form a Fascist political party in 1933, with himself as *Fører* (leader, comparable to *Führer*). When Germany invaded Norway in April 1940, Quisling made a radio news announcement declaring himself prime minister on behalf of the Nazis. Five days later, the Nazis threw Quisling out of power. However, in need of a Norwegian puppet, they reinstated him in 1942. After the war, Quisling was convicted of treason and executed.

THE WAR AGAINST THE WEST

APRIL 1940–JUNE 1941

> "My *Luftwaffe* is invincible.... And so now we turn to England. How long will this one last— two, three weeks?"
>
> —HERMANN GÖRING, AFTER THE FALL OF FRANCE

THE "PHONY WAR" began and ended with the German invasion of neighboring states—Poland first, in September 1939, and then Denmark and Norway in April 1940. Here, the similarity ended. Germany invaded Scandinavia in 1940 due to Germany's naval war against the British and their American suppliers, and to protect the winter route for iron from Sweden. And unlike the invasion of Poland, the attacks on Denmark and Norway launched a permanent state of fighting in Europe that lasted right down to German defeat in May 1945.

The brief northern campaign was one of the most successful of Hitler's gambles. On April 9, German forces entered Denmark and occupied the peninsula without serious resistance. A seaborne and airborne force, covered by a German air screen, then invaded Norway. Despite stubborn Norwegian resistance, and the landing of British and French troops in support in northern Norway, the Norwegian government agreed to an armistice on June 9. However, many German warships were sunk or damaged in this operation.

On May 10, Hitler had his forces in the West—after months of patient preparation—launch the attack on France through the Low Countries and the Ardennes Forest farther to the south, which the Allies had thought impassable by a modern army. A few hours after German troops crossed the

Images of victorious German troops marching into Paris on June 14, 1940, gladdened the hearts of most Germans—Nazis and non-Nazis alike. France, Germany's traditional enemy, had been defeated and humiliated—and Hitler's foreign policy direction apparently vindicated. Four years of German occupation began.

Dutch border, an act of long-term significance took place in London when Winston Churchill succeeded Neville Chamberlain as British prime minister. At that moment, Churchill later wrote, "I felt as if I was walking with destiny."

The first weeks of Churchill's premiership proved disastrous for the Allies. German plans to push heavily armored divisions along forested terrain, supported by waves of aircraft, succeeded well beyond the expectations of many German generals. The French defensive line was pierced, and within days a gap burst open in the Allied front that could not be closed. The British Expeditionary Force was pushed back toward the sea around the port of Dunkirk, France, and faced annihilation—until General Rundstedt and Hitler ordered German forces to stop on May 24 to refit and prepare to break the new French defense line further south. By the time the attacks began again on May 26, the British had planned a hasty marine retreat. By June 4, 338,000 troops, one-third of them French, had been evacuated.

Though the "miracle of Dunkirk" has long been celebrated in Britain, it represented an ignominious defeat. The surviving French resistance slowly crumbled. On June 14, German forces entered Paris; on June 22, the French sued for an armistice, and German victory was complete. While a similar campaign during World War I had lasted four years and cost the lives of 1.5 million Germans, this campaign was over in six weeks. This time, Germany lost 30,000 men.

The reasons for the rapid German victory have been debated often. The Allies, including Dutch and Belgian forces, had a clear advantage in number of army divisions, tanks, and armored vehicles. Airpower favored the Germans, but only because German air forces were concentrated in an aerial spearhead that pushed forward in coordination with the armored divisions on the ground. Military competence and strategic daring counted for something on the German side. The central problem for the Allies was the dispersal of their troops. Because French commander Maurice Gamelin had sent his reserve army northward, it could not plug the Ardennes gap. Aircraft were stationed all over France and Britain, but were not concentrated at the front; and the system of communications on the western side worked poorly. The argument that French soldiers lacked stomach for the fight because French society was in some sense "decadent" is difficult to prove. Their morale was poor because they sensed that they were poorly led.

The Germans began their western offensive in early April 1940, attacking both Denmark and Norway. The Danes surrendered a day after invasion, while the Norwegians—with Allied support— held out for several weeks. Here, German troops advance along Norway's rugged, snow-covered terrain.

German victory in June 1940 had profound consequences. For the British and French, it was the worst possible outcome. France was defeated, its northern half as well as its Atlantic coast occupied by German forces. Britain was isolated from Continental Europe and had no prospect of reentering it to dislodge Hitler without the help of powerful allies (i.e., the United States and Soviet Union). France was now ruled by the authoritarian Marshal Philippe Pétain, who set up a new government center at Vichy, where his regime pursued policies that mimicked those of other Fascist states.

On June 10, 1940, Mussolini's Italy declared war on Britain and France. Thus, a powerful enemy lay across Britain's main route in the Mediterranean to its eastern empire. Hitler was faced with the pleasing but unexpected prospect of German domination of Europe. On July 19, he announced before the *Reichstag* proposals for a European peace if Britain would accept the reality of German dominance and end hostilities. Churchill's government rejected it. British society braced itself for a possible invasion.

Hitler faced a critical dilemma in the summer of 1940. Successful beyond his expectations, he wanted to subordinate Britain in order to prepare for conflicts with the Soviet Union and the United States. When Britain refused to accept a German peace, Hitler ordered his forces to prepare to invade. The *Luftwaffe* (air force) was given the task of softening British resistance.

On July 31, a few days before the air attacks began in earnest, Hitler called his commanders together and told them that he had abandoned his and their hopes of invading the Soviet Union in the fall of 1940, and instead would begin that operation in the spring of 1941. German troops were sent into Romania and military arrangements were made with Finland since these two countries were to join Germany in invading the Soviet Union.

While the invasion of Britain (Operation Sealion) was being prepared, the *Luftwaffe* began its assault. This was the start of what would become known as the Battle of Britain. Waves of bombers, strongly supported by fighter aircraft, first attacked British air fields and sources of air supply. In September, they attacked the whole military and urban infrastructure within range of German fighters. The Germans' goal was to create conditions for landing an invasion force on the coast of southern England. The air battle was regarded as decisive only because the failure to eliminate the RAF would force the postponement of what the Germans considered a risky operation.

The defending British fighter force had difficulty preventing German bombing, but it was able to inflict high levels of attrition on the attacking

Hitler visited Paris only once following the defeat of France in 1940. This image of the victorious German warlord at the very heart of the French capital symbolized the fulfillment of his National Socialist ambitions, as well as the apparent success of his European foreign policy and military strategy.

force thanks to the first successful use of radar detection. From July to the end of October, the RAF lost 915 aircraft while the Germans lost 1,733. The number of fighter pilots and fighter aircraft on the British side remained at roughly the same level as at the start of the battle, but German numbers declined. By mid-September, it was evident that the *Luftwaffe* was making little headway, and the first phase of the Battle of Britain was over.

The second phase was more deadly and more prolonged. On September 17, Hitler postponed Sealion, and the *Luftwaffe* was given the task of knocking Britain out of the war by bombing alone. Heavy raids were directed at military and economic targets as well as urban areas, and civilian casualties were heavy. More than 40,000 British citizens were killed during the course of the "Blitz," which came to be directed at all major ports and industrial and commercial centers.

By December 1940, the German leadership expected Britain to surrender. "When will Churchill capitulate?" Joseph Goebbels wrote in his diary. Bombing did produce widespread disruption and local panic, but at no point did the British government consider surrender. Gold and foreign exchange reserves were moved to Canada, and preparations were made for guerrilla activities in any portion of the country occupied by the Germans. The public was heartened by news of British victories in East Africa and Libya against Italian-led forces, and the knowledge that British bombers were regularly attacking German cities in return.

Hitler gambled on forcing a British surrender, but his thoughts turned increasingly to the prospect of the invasion of the Soviet Union. His fanatical anticommunism was certainly one reason. He was also attracted by the oil and raw-material resources of the Soviet area—as well as the region's vast wheat lands, which had long been regarded in Germany as a potential area for colonization, or "living space." Strategic calculation also pushed him toward war. On the one hand, defeat of the Soviet Union, he believed, would eliminate the last prospect that Britain had for creating an anti-German alliance, and thus would hasten British surrender. Defeat of the Soviet Union would also free Japan to move in the Pacific. Thus, there was not one cause but many for Hitler's directive to "crush Soviet Russia in a rapid campaign."

While Germany was fighting in the West, the Soviet Union took advantage of the situation. In June 1940, the three Baltic States were incorporated formally into the Soviet Union, just as eastern Poland had been. In addition, the Soviets forced Romania to hand over the territories of Bessarabia and

Following the defeat of France, the *Luftwaffe* strove unsuccessfully to bomb Britain into submission during the Blitz. Here, a London milkman, apparently unaffected by the wholesale devastation about him, delivers the milk as usual on the morning after a German raid in October 1940.

northern Bukovina. In all of these areas, social and political opponents of the Soviet Union were rounded up and deported or murdered. In the Katyn Forest and two other sites, thousands of captured Polish officers were liquidated, their bodies buried in huge mass graves, each with a bullet hole in the back of the neck.

Stalin's ambitions continued to expand. The Soviets pressured Bulgaria to concede Soviet bases, and they urged Turkey to concede rights over the straits that separated the Black Sea from the Mediterranean. In October 1940, Mussolini launched a war against Greece. On September 27, Germany, Italy, and Japan signed the Tripartite Pact, dividing the world into spheres in which they could each establish a "new order."

In November, Soviet foreign minister Vyacheslav Molotov was invited to Berlin to discuss prospects for a further German-Soviet agreement. Molotov laid down terms for Soviet influence in Bulgaria and Turkey. Joachim von Ribbentrop, the German foreign minister, agreed to nothing and urged the Soviet Union to turn toward India as a sphere of expansion. Three weeks later, Hitler approved the operational plans for invasion of the Soviet Union, and on December 18 he signed War Directive 21 for Operation Barbarossa.

The plan called for launching the attack in May 1941, but transportation and supply problems forced postponement into June. Using bases in Hungary, Bulgaria, and Romania—all states that had now come into the German orbit—Hitler planned to rescue his Italian ally, whose troops were bogged down in the conflict with Greece. When Hitler demanded transit rights through Yugoslavia, anti-German elements launched a coup in Belgrade. German forces attacked Yugoslavia on April 6, and by April 30 the whole of the Balkan peninsula was in German hands.

The Germans maintained utmost secrecy regarding their preparations, but intelligence sources alerted Moscow. Stalin, anxious that nothing should provoke war, refused to accept the warnings and made every effort to appease the Germans. Though some Soviet reserves were moved to the frontier in May and June, nothing could stop the massive assault by more than three million German, Romanian, Finnish, and other forces along the whole Soviet line in the West. In the early hours of June 22, 1941, they launched the largest invasion in world history.

With Germany's victory in the West apparently assured, Hitler and his senior military commanders turned their eyes to Soviet Russia. Much of the strategic planning for Operation Barbarossa was carried out at Hitler's Alpine retreat—the Berghof—during high-level conferences such as this one, pictured in July 1940.

1940

April 2: Chinese Nationalists score a victory when they reoccupy the city of Wuyuan after successfully ambushing some 3,000 Japanese troops.

April 5: In what will become known as the Katyn Forest Massacre, Soviet secret police murder more than 4,000 Polish prisoners of war. The Soviet government will deny culpability until 1989. Around the same time as Katyn, more than 15,000 other Polish POWs are killed at other locations.

April 8: Despite Norway's neutrality, the Allies mine coastal waters in the region in an effort to impede German activity.

April 9: Germany attacks Norway and Denmark on the pretext that occupation is necessary to preserve their neutrality. Norwegian Fascist leader Vidkun Quisling quickly moves to create a pro-Nazi government. As a result, his surname will become synonymous with *traitor.*

April 10: Denmark surrenders to Germany. • Wary of abandoning its neutrality, Belgium declines the Allies' offer of "preventative aid." • The German cruiser *Königsberg* is sunk by British warplanes, marking the first time in history that a large warship is sunk by an aerial assault.

April 14: Allied troops arrive in Norway to counter the German invasion force.

April 15: MI6, Britain's secret intelligence service, unravels the Enigma code used by the *Wehrmacht* during the Norwegian campaign.

April 18: The Allies occupy Norway's Faeroe Islands to prevent the strategically important region from falling into Nazi hands.

The Maginot Line Soon after World War I, under the direction of Minister of War André Maginot, France constructed formidable concrete obstacles (*above*), machine gun posts, and forts along its borders with Germany, Italy, and later Belgium. In 1939–40, France hurried to improve the secret fortifications. Underground bunkers that could house thousands of men included such amenities as a wine cellar, morgue, chapel, hospital, and dental clinic. Illustrators often depicted the constructions as compact (*below*), but they were actually spread out and connected with tunnels through which trolleys carried troops and weapons. These preparations gave the French military a false sense of security. Invading German forces simply maneuvered around the Maginot Line.

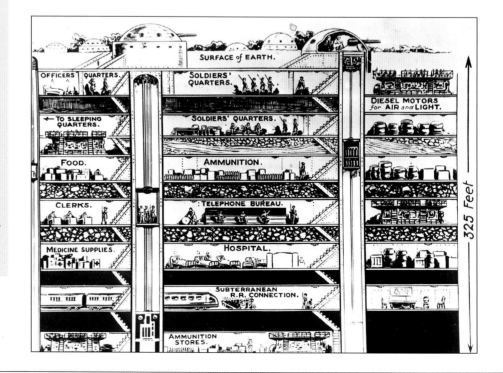

Plane spotters A Royal Observer Corps (ROC) plane spotter watches for enemy aircraft. Back in 1925, the ROC was formed to provide a system for detecting, tracking, and reporting aircraft over Britain. Plane spotters learned to recognize aircraft by their silhouette, and often by the sound of their engines. In the U.S., Civil Defense workers and WAACS (Women's Army Auxiliary Corps) maintained spotting stations, and in Germany the *Reichsluftschutzbund* (National Air Defense League) had a similar mission.

Norway forced into war Norwegian houses burn in Narvik during the spring 1940 German invasion. After the British rescue of *Altmark* prisoners and other actions in Norwegian waters, Hitler feared losing the neutral country's ports of Narvik, which were essential for shipping Scandinavian iron ore to Germany. Hitler attacked Norway by land, air, and sea, overrunning resistance. In mid-April, British, Polish, and French forces landed to aid the Norwegians and took Narvik. The British sank 10 German destroyers—half of the entire fleet. However, with France near collapse, the Allies withdrew on June 8, leaving Narvik to German occupation. The Norwegian conflict included the first paratrooper attack (by Germany) in history, and Britain's first major amphibious landing of the war (at Narvik).

Norwegians refuse to surrender When the Germans occupied Norway in April 1940, they showed off these three experimental tanks (never put into production) in the streets of Oslo. Germany had trouble taking Norway due to bad weather, strong fortifications, and tenacious Norwegian resistance. The royal family and members of Parliament had time to escape to the north. Although the Germans set up a puppet government under Nazi supporter Vidkun Quisling, Norway's King Haakon never surrendered. When the Allies evacuated Norway, the Norwegian government moved to Britain and operated in exile. It controlled its own merchant navy and built a new military to support the Allies.

1940

April 27: SS *Reichsführer* Heinrich Himmler orders the construction of a concentration camp in Oświecim, Poland. Known as Auschwitz in German, the facility will play a central role in the Nazi plan to exterminate Europe's Jews. • The Reich issues an official declaration of war against neutral Norway.

April 29: President Roosevelt sends a personal message to Mussolini in which he beseeches him to work for peace.

April 30: Carnegie Institute president Samuel Harden Church publishes a letter in *The New York Times* offering a $1 million reward to whomever can capture Hitler alive. • The Allies make a hasty retreat from Norway under the pressure of an intense German aerial assault. • The Nazis establish a Jewish ghetto in Łódź, Poland. • Hitler warns his generals to be prepared to invade Western Europe within 24 hours of receiving his orders on any date after May 5.

May 2: Mussolini contacts Roosevelt. He suggests that Italy's continued recognition of the Monroe Doctrine is contingent on America's continued neutrality in the European war.

May 7: President Roosevelt directs the Navy's Pacific Fleet to remain at the ready off the coast of Hawaii.

May 10: Asserting that the Allies are planning to use neutral nations Belgium, Luxembourg, and the Netherlands as a staging area for an attack on Germany, Hitler invades the Low Countries. • Winston Churchill becomes Britain's prime minister when Neville Chamberlain, who was losing support in Parliament, resigns. • Communication centers are targeted in the first RAF bombing raid over Germany.

Britain's flying boat The British Short Sunderland flying boat saw wide service during World War II, proving especially valuable in antisubmarine operations. Crewed by seven to 11 men and carrying machine guns, bombs, or depth charges, the Sunderland could remain in the air for as long as 11 hours searching for U-boats with its radar. The patrol bomber became such an effective sub killer that German admiral Karl Dönitz suspected that spies were tipping off the Allies about U-boat movements. The Sunderlands also proved useful for reconnaissance and water rescue missions. Total production was 749 aircraft.

Bomb shelters The Anderson garden shelter (*pictured*) became ubiquitous throughout Britain. Comprised of two curved galvanized steel plates, it was dug into a three-foot pit and covered with earth. Two million were issued free early in the war, until steel shortages halted further issues. The Morrison, designed to protect the family within the home, was simply a steel plate on legs, fitted with mesh sides. These shelters were provided free to families with low incomes and were sold to all others.

Francisco Franco

FOLLOWING HITLER'S ONE and only meeting with Fascist Spanish dictator Francisco Franco, in October 1940, he told his aides that he would just "as soon have three or four teeth pulled out" than have to bargain with Franco again. Hitler met with the Spanish dictator for nine hours with the hope that he could gain Franco's permission to march the German army through Spain to support an assault on Gibraltar. Capture of this British-controlled peninsula would give Hitler a stepping stone to North Africa.

The German leader found Franco's price too high, however. Franco demanded military and financial assistance as well as control of portions of France's holdings in northwest Africa. Hitler was agreeable to the colonial demands, but insisted on German ownership of bases on the coast and islands off Northwest Africa. Over this issue, Franco withdrew his offer to join Germany in war against Britain.

After the Spanish monarchy fell in 1931, conservative and radical parties alternately assumed power in Spain. During this time, Franco's military fortunes rose and fell. Following a bloody civil war, Franco assumed absolute power on April 1, 1939.

Both Hitler and Italian dictator Benito Mussolini sent aid to Franco during the civil war due to his Fascist leanings. When Hitler was rebuffed by the Spanish dictator, he did not take retaliatory action against Spain. Throughout the remainder of the war, however, Franco provided men, support for German U-boats, and valuable resources to the Germans while declaring Spain's neutrality.

Versatile German bomber The Ju-88 twin-engine medium bomber boasted a maximum speed of 269 mph, a ceiling of almost 30,000 feet, and a range of 1,112 miles. Carrying capacity was about 6,000 pounds of bombs. This fast, maneuverable, and versatile aircraft provided sterling service to the *Luftwaffe* throughout the war in bombing, occasional dive-bombing, close support, maritime torpedo, interceptor, and night-fighter roles. Some 14,676 Ju-88s were built, with about 9,000 used primarily as bombers.

Bletchley Park code-breakers
Alan Turing, a pioneer in the field of computing, was a leading member of the highly successful analysis and code-breaking team based at the top-secret signals intelligence center at Bletchley Park in England. With the assistance of material provided by Polish intelli-

gence, his team eventually broke the German operational and strategic Enigma encoding system. These code-breakers worked exceptionally long hours in cheerless office accommodations and excessively hot and noisy computer rooms. They included scientists, mathematicians, linguists, crossword experts, and others with diverse analytical skills.

1940

May 11: The Allies land in the Dutch West Indies to guard the oil resources of Aruba and Curaçao against German saboteurs. • Luxembourg falls to German troops.

May 11–12: In what is regarded as the Allies' first significant air raid against a civilian population, the RAF attacks Mönchengladbach, Germany, losing three planes in the process.

May 12: England and Scotland begin the practice of detaining German and Austrian men ages 16 to 60 in internment camps.

May 13: In his first speech before the House of Commons as prime minister, Winston Churchill delivers the famous line: "I have nothing to offer but blood, toil, tears, and sweat." • Northeast France is under heavy assault as several panzer divisions cross the Meuse River near the town of Sedan.

May 14: Rotterdam, Netherlands, capitulates after a heavy German bombing campaign devastates the city, claiming 980 lives and more than 20,000 buildings. • The Netherlands government flees The Hague. It will establish itself in exile in London. • The Royal Air Force suffers its greatest defeat to date in this conflict, losing 45 of 109 airplanes while attacking German troop positions in France.

May 15: The Nazi campaign in the Netherlands ends when the Dutch army surrenders to the *Wehrmacht*. • Concerned about Japan's activity in the Pacific Theater, Churchill asks Roosevelt for ships, planes, ammunition, and an American naval presence in Singapore and Ireland.

May 16: President Roosevelt asks Congress for a $1.2 billion increase in defense spending to mobilize the Army and Navy and procure an additional 50,000 planes a year.

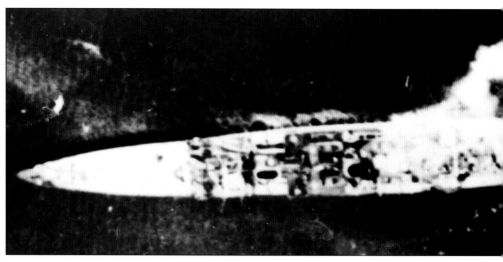

British dive-bombers prove effective Fires rage unchecked on the German light cruiser *Königsberg* after the first successful British air attack on a warship. On April 10, 1940, Blackburn Skua dive-bombers located the *Königsberg*—already damaged by Norwegian shore artillery—in Bergen Harbor, Norway. The Skuas dove out of the rising sun and dropped their 500-pound bombs from heights ranging from 3,000 feet to as low as 200 feet, proving the effectiveness of dive-bombing to a skeptical RAF establishment. The *Königsberg* lost electrical power and, unable to control the fires, sank within three hours.

Denmark no match for Germans When the Germans launched their invasion of Norway on April 9, 1940, they simultaneously invaded Denmark (*pictured*). German troops arrived by land across the Danish-German border and by sea at the capital city of Copenhagen, above which flew menacing German bombers. The small, ineffective Danish military put up some resistance, notably at Amalienborg Palace in Copenhagen, but was almost immediately overwhelmed. The Danish government promptly surrendered.

Nazi paratroopers succeed in Belgium German paratroopers who have just taken the "impregnable" Fort Eben-Emael in Belgium relax after their success. In history's first glider-borne assault, nine silent, engineless aircraft landed on the Eben-Emael roof on May 10, 1940. The gliders discharged 77 paratroopers, who quickly sealed in the fort's 650 defenders. Resistance was over in 30 minutes, and the entire garrison surrendered in 30 hours. These German special forces had practiced their attack on a similar fort. Additional troops from 10 other German gliders seized key bridges in the area.

Belgians face death, forced labor Belgian civilians hide from German soldiers. During the May 1940 *Blitzkrieg*, planes strafed and bombed Belgian military personnel and nonmilitary citizens alike, killing some 30,000 civilians. After Belgium surrendered, many of the nation's highly skilled workers were forced into German industrial jobs—including positions at arms factories. These *Westarbeiter* (workers from the West) in the *Arbeitseinsatz* (labor deployment) program faced severe penalties if they refused to work in Germany.

Germans storm France, Low Countries On May 10, 1940, German tanks, troops, and bombers smashed into France and the Low Countries in a *Blitzkrieg*—a swift attack with combined air and mobile land forces—that was totally unexpected by the Allies. Belgium, Luxembourg, and the Netherlands fell quickly. Hitler's tanks charged through the Ardennes forests, bypassed the static French defenses, and drove westward across northern France to the English Channel. By May 21, the Germans had split the Allied forces in two. Here, a French tank crewman surrenders to German forces.

BREEZING INTO FRANCE

THE PEOPLE IN the houses were rudely awakened by the din of our tanks, the clatter and roar of tracks and engines. [German] troops lay bivouacked beside the road, military vehicles stood parked in farmyards and in some places on the road itself. Civilians and French troops, their faces distorted with terror, lay huddled in the ditches, alongside hedges and in every hollow beside the road. We passed refugee columns, the carts abandoned by their owners, who had fled in panic into the fields. On we went, at a steady speed, towards our objective.... The flat countryside lay spread out around us under the cold light of the moon. We were through the Maginot Line!

—MAJOR GENERAL ERWIN ROMMEL,
COMMANDER OF THE SEVENTH PANZER DIVISION

1940

May 17: A Nazi occupying force marches into Brussels, Belgium. Antwerp, Belgium, will capitulate the next day.

May 21: According to reports out of Berlin, the French Ninth Army has been completely destroyed.

May 22: The Emergency Powers Act passes in Britain. It grants Churchill total control of the resources needed to run the nation's war machine.

May 24: London decides to pull its troops out of a defeated Norway.

May 26: The Allies launch Operation Dynamo, a massive rescue operation to save troops surrounded by the Axis in Dunkirk, France. In just one week, nearly 350,000 British, French, and Belgian soldiers will be evacuated while *Luftwaffe* planes try to hinder the operation.

May 27: Germany takes the port city of Calais, France—a mere 26 miles across the Channel from Dover, England.

May 28: King Leopold III orders the surrender of the 500,000-man Belgian Army, an order that will lead to his deposition at the hands of the Belgian government, which is in exile in France.

June 3: More than 250 Parisians lose their lives when the city endures an air assault by some 200 *Luftwaffe* planes.

June 4: Churchill delivers the memorable "fight on the beaches" speech before the House of Commons, claiming, "We shall never surrender."

June 5: The French capture *Luftwaffe* pilot Werner Mölders. He will be liberated at the armistice near the end of the month, resume flying, and ultimately be credited with more than 100 victories before being killed in an accident.

The Netherlands capitulates Initially, Hitler assured the Dutch that their neutrality would be respected—but this was another false promise. Pictured in May 1940 is the city of Rotterdam, Netherlands, which had been devastated by the *Luftwaffe* to force its speedy capitulation. It was an unnecessary air raid, in fact, as surrender negotiations were already in train, but the message to abort was not received before the city center had been destroyed, with 800 to 1,000 civilians killed.

Bad strategy dooms the Dutch The Netherlands was woefully unprepared for Germany's ground and air *Blitzkrieg* in May 1940. Dutch strategic planning had been shaped by an underestimation of Germany, strong pacifist influences, appeasement policies, refusal to coordinate with Britain and France, and a dependence upon defensive strong-points (such as this steel-gated bridge over the Maas River) and obstacles—including flooding large areas of Holland. Consequently, the Germans quickly overwhelmed the sizable but outdated, ill-equipped, and largely immobile Dutch army. While some Dutch citizens formed an effective resistance movement beginning in 1942, anti-Semitism and pro-German collaboration were also in evidence.

Germans slaughter French civilians French civilians lie dead, victims of the Nazi assault. As German troops drove into France, they shelled farmhouses as well as cities and towns. Soon, fleeing French citizens clogged all roads. A young British soldier reported seeing "whole families, mums with prams and mostly women pulling two-wheeled carts. Sometimes they'd have a goat or a cow tied to the back." During the German onslaught, many civilians were killed in their homes, and refugees were pushed from the roads and slaughtered. The total civilian dead from the Battle of France has been estimated at 92,000.

The "Schmeisser" The MP40 *Maschinenpistole* was known universally but inaccurately as the "Schmeisser" after weapons designer Hugo Schmeisser, who did not design this submachine gun. However, this was one of the iconic weapons of the war, with both Allied and German troops recognizing it as the best weapon of its class. Conceived originally as a weapon for paratroops, it quickly became the *Wehrmacht*'s principal submachine gun. It had a caliber of 9mm, a magazine that held 32 rounds, and a rate of fire of 500 rounds per minute. It was accurate up to 200 meters. Moreover, its all-metal stamped construction made it both cheap and easy to mass-produce.

French general fails his country French general Maurice Gustave Gamelin, a respected World War I military commander, brought outmoded strategies to WWII. He delayed attacking German forces, then took his troops too far north beyond France's border defense. The French and British were cut off and defeated, wrecking Allied defense plans for the continent. During the 1942–43 Riom Trial—in which the Vichy government charged that French politicians were responsible for both the war and the French defeat—Gamelin maintained complete silence. He was turned over to the Germans and held captive at the Buchenwald concentration camp for the rest of the war.

The MG 34 A German infantryman takes aim at the enemy with an MG 34 7.92mm light machine gun. While this version utilized a 50-round metal-link belt, the MG 34 could also be equipped with 50- and 75-round drum ammunition feeds. Although the MG 34 was expensive to produce, it was a highly effective weapon. It delivered a maximum rate of fire of 900 rpm to 600-800 yards (light role), and 300 rpm to 2,000-2,500 yards when mounted on a tripod in the heavy role. MG 34s were also fitted extensively to armored vehicles and trucks, and for antiaircraft defense.

1940

June 5: Marshal Philippe Pétain becomes prime minister of France, replacing Paul Reynaud.

June 7: Norwegian leadership flees the country and establishes a government-in-exile in London. • Berlin suffers its first bombing raid of the war when it is attacked by a single French aircraft, a four-engine Farman 223.

June 8: More than 1,500 British sailors perish when German ships sink the aircraft carrier *Glorious* and its escort of two destroyers.

June 9: A German panzer division crosses the Somme River and surrounds the French 10th Army.

June 10: After a lengthy delay, Italy enters the war with an invasion of a weakened France, already wounded by the German army. • With German troops only 50 miles from Paris, the French government relocates to Tours, France. • Mussolini declares war against both Britain and France, while Canada reciprocates by declaring war on Italy. South Africa, Australia, and New Zealand will join Canada the following day.

June 11–12: The RAF bombs Italy, losing one plane while scoring 10 hits on Turin and two on Genoa.

June 12: Italy launches its air war, dropping bombs on civilian targets on the British protectorate Island of Malta. • With Italy's entry into the war, President Roosevelt declares that the United States will offer material support to the Allies.

June 14: France asks the United States to intervene as the Nazis occupy Paris.

Calm before the storm First Lord of the Admiralty Winston Churchill congratulates sailors of HMS *Hardy* on April 19, 1940, for distinguishing themselves during the fighting in Norway. With the British Expeditionary Force in France and the German onslaught seemingly checked for the moment, Churchill had cause for guarded optimism. But the respite was brief. Within a few weeks, Norway, Denmark, and France would fall to the Germans. Elevated to prime minister in May after the resignation of Neville Chamberlain, Churchill faced a possible German invasion with a drastically weakened military and a Home Guard of boys and old men armed with everything from old rifles to pitchforks.

Barrage balloons
Throughout Britain, thousands of large hydrogen-filled barrage balloons were flown above many sites identified as likely targets for German air attack. The wire cables tethering them to the ground were a particularly effective deterrent against low-flying aircraft (seven German planes were downed by these balloons in February-March 1941 alone). All sides used barrage balloons, both for homeland defense and during certain tactical operations—including some of the Allies' major assault landings. Within the United Kingdom, the barrage balloon defenses were often managed and operated by female personnel of the RAF Balloon Command.

Winston Churchill

WINSTON SPENCER CHURCHILL did more than any other leader to attain Allied victory in World War II. On May 10, 1940, on the very day that Hitler unleashed his *Blitzkrieg* against the Low Countries, Churchill succeeded Neville Chamberlain as prime minister. As Britain endured the blows of Dunkirk, the fall of France, the Battle of Britain, and the Blitz, Churchill rallied the nation and the free world. It was his as well as Britain's "Finest Hour." His wartime speeches of defiance and hope inspired a nation facing seemingly imminent invasion.

The son of a British aristocrat and an American heiress, Churchill grew up in Blenheim Palace. A low achiever in school, he became a cavalry officer in frontier wars in India and Africa, finding adventure while discovering a knack for writing. During the Boer War, his daring escape from Boer captivity catapulted him into a parliamentary seat. The ambitious young politician rose swiftly, opportunistically switching from the Conservatives to the Liberals and back.

By 1914 the 39-year-old had become first lord of the admiralty, running the world's most powerful fleet. Churchill conceived the imaginative but inept invasion of Turkey on Gallipoli during World War I, which cost him power with its defeat and saddled him with a reputation as a dangerous strategic visionary. After serving as a battalion commander on the Western Front, Churchill returned to office as minister of munitions. Following the war, he helped to shape the modern Middle East, molding Arab national aspirations.

Between the world wars, Churchill established a reputation as a historian. He also held a parliamentary seat as well as several ministerial offices. Churchill quickly recognized the dangerous aggression of Hitler (and what he called "Nar-zees"). The outbreak of the war in 1939 saw him returned as first lord of the admiralty. The signal went around the fleet: "Winston's back!"

Churchill presided over a solid coalition government through defeats in the Mediterranean and a never-ending battle in the Atlantic. Though he was a determined conservative, in June 1941 he welcomed the Soviets as allies, knowing that Russian resistance weakened Germany. In 1941 Churchill and President Franklin Roosevelt drafted the Atlantic Charter, a stirring statement of what the Allies fought for, not what they opposed.

With the American entry into the war in December 1941, Britain's role as the mainstay of Allied power weakened. Churchill took part in a succession of conferences with Stalin and Roosevelt, helping to reshape Allied strategy worldwide.

Churchill's strategic vision was inspired but often flawed, and his military advisers worked hard to dissuade him from his wilder flights. Thinking that Italy represented a "soft underbelly" was perhaps his most startling mistake. He also has been damned in Canada for the bloody repulse at Dieppe and in Australia for the loss of Singapore.

Despite his flaws, Churchill's stamina, decisive leadership, and ability to inspire helped Britain achieve victory. In July 1945, Churchill's Conservatives lost office in the election, though he returned to power in extreme old age. His *History of the Second World War*, a racy mixture of memoir and on-the-spot history, still powerfully, and often mistakenly, shapes how we understand World War II.

1940

June 15: Despite pleas from both France and Britain, the U.S. Congress continues to refuse to intervene in Europe, with some legislators going so far as to suggest that England and France surrender to Hitler.

June 16: In an 11th hour rescue attempt, Britain offers to unite its empire with that of France. The following day, France will ask Germany for an armistice, requesting "peace with honor." • Italy sinks the British submarines *Grampus* and *Orpheus* in the first Mediterranean naval conflict of the war. • Prime Minister Eamon de Valera mobilizes the Irish military in preparation for an Axis invasion of nearby England.

June 17: About 2,500 British troops perish when five *Luftwaffe* bombers attack the *Lancastria*, a Cunard luxury liner being used to transport troops. • With most naval forces focused on the Pacific Fleet, the U.S. Navy asks Congress for $4 billion to build an equally strong Atlantic fleet.

June 18: The RAF pulls out of France, and the French military hastily retreats from the *Wehrmacht*. French general Charles de Gaulle, speaking from London, pleads with his countrymen to continue to resist Germany, claiming "France has lost a battle, but France has not lost the war." • In a meeting with Hitler in Munich, Mussolini is bitterly disappointed to find that he will not be granted large tracts of French territory. Hitler hopes that by offering France easy surrender terms, the French will be less likely to continue fighting from North Africa.

June 19: With the German conquest of France complete, the exiled governments of Poland and Belgium move to London.

"Down on the beach you immediately felt yourself surrounded by a deadly evil atmosphere. A horrible stench of blood and mutilated flesh pervaded the place. There was no escape from it."

—BRITISH INFANTRYMAN JOHN CHARLES AUSTIN, WHO WAS ON THE BEACH AT DUNKIRK IN JUNE 1940

The evacuation of Dunkirk Dunkirk evacuees escape by ship. In late May 1940, Hitler agreed with General Rundstedt to order a temporary halt. The reprieve lasted 48 hours and gave the British time to set up defenses and begin evacuation of 338,000 Allied troops. Hermann Göring promised that the *Luftwaffe* could destroy the Allied troops, but Dunkirk was too close to British air bases. The British evacuees included many highly experienced soldiers who were eager to return to the fight, but they had lost all of their equipment.

"Little Ships" save troops British soldiers wait for rescue on Dunkirk Beach. When the planned evacuation was announced to the British public on May 27, 1940, a fleet of fishing boats, pleasure craft, merchant marine vessels, and other small boats rushed across the English Channel to help. They retrieved the British, French, and Belgian troops from the bombed-out harbor, which the larger ships could not enter, and ferried those troops to the big ships. These "Little Ships" quickly gained legendary status, and the "Spirit of Dunkirk" became a British rallying cry.

The *Luftwaffe*

THROUGH THE EARLY YEARS of World War II, Nazi Germany's enemies feared the *Luftwaffe*, the most advanced and powerful air force in the world. This mighty force began (with Soviet assistance) as a clandestine program in the 1920s. After 1933 the *Luftwaffe* expanded to include 20,000 personnel and 1,888 aircraft. In 1936 the second generation of aircraft—including the Messerschmitt Bf 109 fighter, the Junkers 87 (Stuka) dive-bomber, and the Heinkel 111 bomber—were released. Most were trialed in 1937 during the Spanish Civil War.

The *Luftwaffe* was integral to the *Blitzkrieg* that swept away nearly all before it from 1939 to '41. Crucial was its tactical ground support, through dive-bombing, strafing, level bombing, and parachute operations. Its aircraft also sank 750,000 tons of Allied shipping in 1939 and more than four million tons in 1940. During the Battle of Britain, the Germans attempted to use the *Luftwaffe* to win a campaign on its own, as a strategic force. In failing, many of its best pilots were killed.

The *Luftwaffe* contributed substantially to victories in the Mediterranean and the USSR in 1941, but an agonizing decline followed. While the *Luftwaffe* responded effectively *initially* to the Anglo-American Combined Bomber Offensive of 1943, Hitler's preoccupation with retaliatory bombing hampered Germany's defense. Moreover, from late 1943, the Allies concentrated on destroying the *Luftwaffe*, targeting German fighters over the Reich, aircraft fac-

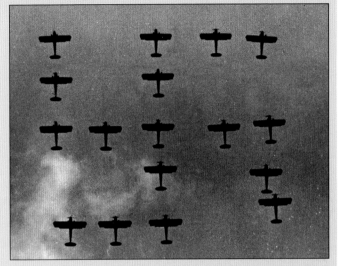

A *Luftwaffe* demonstration over Nuremberg, Germany

tories, and oil plants. The *Luftwaffe* was finished as an effective force by D-Day late in 1944, when only 170 aircraft faced 12,000 Allied planes in northern France.

From then until war's end, *Luftwaffe* fighters offered negligible aerial resistance. While Soviet armies were most responsible for the German army's defeat, Western air forces played a major role in crushing its aerial counterpart. The innovative last generation of German aircraft included jet and rocket fighters, but the quantity, fuel, and trained pilots needed to alter the war's course were simply not available.

Luftwaffe rains terror on France
Firemen turn their hoses on a Parisian building that has been reduced to a smoldering ruin by Nazi bombardment. Even as the Allies evacuated at Dunkirk, Göring directed his *Luftwaffe* bombers inland. On June 3, 1940, 200 planes struck airfields, industrial sites, and buildings in Paris. This successful German effort to damage France's economy, reduce its military, and create terror in its population had a devastating psychological effect. To keep government officials at their posts, the French minister of interior had to threaten dire penalties against any who fled.

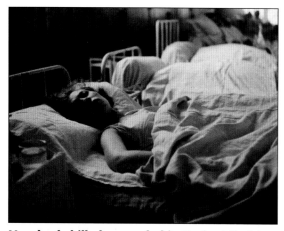

Hundreds killed, wounded in Paris A Parisian victim of German bombing raids lies in a hospital bed. The German bombardment of Paris inflicted some 900 casualties, including 254 dead. Most of the victims were civilians and many were schoolchildren. Designed to produce terror, the air attack had the desired effect. Fleeing civilians clogged all roads around Paris, where some were strafed by German planes.

Dunkirk goes up in flames French civilians flee danger and destruction during the aerial bombardment of Dunkirk, France. Heavy *Luftwaffe* attacks left the dead and wounded scattered among the burning wreckage of homes, vehicles, and military equipment. British Expeditionary Forces Captain Richard Austin wrote: "The whole front was one long continuous line of blazing buildings, a high wall of fire, roaring and darting in tongues of flame, with the smoke pouring upwards and disappearing in the blackness of the sky above the rooftops." Dunkirk was reduced to rubble.

Another 220,000 Allies evacuated British and French soldiers leave Cherbourg, France, on British ships bound for Southampton, England. After the successful evacuation at Dunkirk, the British rescued an additional 220,000 Allied troops that had been stranded in France. On June 10, Operation Cycle picked up evacuees at Le Havre. Beginning on June 15 at Cherbourg, in Operation Ariel, Allies spirited soldiers away from Saint-Malo, Brest, Saint-Nazaire, and other ports all the way down the French coast to the border with Spain. When the evacuations were complete on June 25, a total of 558,000 Allied troops had escaped the German invasion.

The fall of Paris "We watched the Germans, almost literally with their hands in their pockets, walk into Paris," wrote American war correspondent Demaree Bess. On the morning of June 14, 1940, German troops marched past the *Arc de Triumph* (*pictured*) and hung swastika flags on the arc, the Eiffel Tower, and other public buildings. The German army staged a ceremonial review in the *Place de la Concorde*, while German planes landed and delivered that morning's Berlin newspapers. Aware that the finest French troops had been cut off in Belgium and that the enemy had blasted through the Maginot Line, many Parisians had already abandoned the city. Defeatism gripped the French nation.

FALL OF FRANCE 1940

Legend:
- ▬▬▶ German Offensives
- ▬▬▶ Allied Forces Movement
- ▬▬ Maginot Line
- (44) Number of Divisions

North Sea

ENGLAND

NETHERLANDS

Zuider Zee

Rotterdam

Maas R.

Army Group B (29)

GERMANY

British Expeditionary Force (BEF)

Antwerp

Eben Emael

Dunkirk

Calais

Boulogne

Brussels

French 7th Army

BELGIUM

French 1st Army

Sambre R.

Ardennes Forest

Dinant

Army Group A (44)

Cambrai

Abbeville

Somme R.

French 9th Army

Sedan

LUXEMBOURG

Army Group C (19)

de Gaulle's Counterattack, May 18

French 2nd Army

Meuse R.

FRANCE

200 km   200 miles

The invasion of France On May 10, 1940, German general Bock's Army Group B struck into Belgium and the Low Countries. This was only a diversionary attack, as the main assault by General Rundstedt's Army Group A was launched from the Ardennes forests, while General Leeb's Army Group C secured the southern flank and pinned down some 30 French divisions. By June 25, France had fallen.

Vichy's minister of defense
French general Maxime Weygand served as Vichy Defense Minister from June to September 1940. In that burdensome role, he juggled Japanese demands for freedom of movement in northern Indochina against strong U.S. opposition to the idea.

Then as Vichy delegate to the French North African colonies, Weygand alternately protested and collaborated with Nazi policies. Heeding U.S. warnings, Weygand opposed German bases in Africa, though he had equipment delivered to Rommel's *Afrika Korps*. Weygand's semi-collaboration was insufficient for Hitler. Under Nazi pressure, Weygand was recalled in November 1941, arrested in 1942, and held by Germany for the duration of the war.

France's formal surrender The railway car in which French marshal Ferdinand Foch had dictated terms to Germany in 1918 was dragged out of its storage shed and returned to the same forest clearing near Rethondes. CBS war correspondent William Shirer noted in Hitler's expression "a sort of scornful, inner joy at being present at this great reversal of fate—a reversal he himself had wrought." On June 22, 1940, the Germans dictated armistice terms that left most of France occupied and set up Vichy France in the area that remained (roughly the southern third of the country).

101

1940

June 20: Japan coerces defeated France to allow landings of Japanese naval vessels in French Indochina. Japan also admonishes authorities in French Indochina to stop assisting the Nationalist Chinese.

June 21: Churchill calls for the outfitting and training of 5,000 paratroopers.

June 22: France surrenders to Germany, and will surrender to Italy on the 24th. A formal cease-fire will take hold on the 25th. • Britain uncovers the German *Knickebein* system when it locates a radio beam targeting the Rolls-Royce airplane engine factory and leading back to a transmitter in Germany. The system has been helping to guide *Luftwaffe* bombers to their targets.

June 23: Charles de Gaulle forms the French National Committee while exiled in London. Britain's government will recognize him as the French leader in exile on the 28th. • Hitler takes a brief, triumphant tour of Paris.

July 1: Churchill sends a letter to Moscow in which he requests a meeting to discuss German imperialism. Pleased with his agreement with Germany, Stalin maintains that Russia will avoid conflict with Hitler. • The French government moves to Vichy, France.

July 2: Hitler orders his generals to draft plans for Operation Sealion—the invasion of Britain.

July 3: With the Vichy regime running France, Britain takes measures to prevent the occupying Nazis from controlling the French navy. The British sink parts of France's fleet in Algeria and commandeer French ships in British ports.

Germans sink the *Lancastria* The Cunard liner *Lancastria*, refitted for military transport, helped evacuate British troops and civilians from France. On June 17, 1940, the loaded ship was struck by German Junker 88 airplanes near the port of St. Nazaire. The bombs—one of which is said to have gone down the ship's funnel—were fatal. The *Lancastria* rolled over and sank in minutes. Many who went into the water choked on spilled fuel oil or died when the oil slick caught fire. Of the estimated 4,000 to 9,000 on board, fewer than 2,500 survived.

British remove signs In mid-1940, many in Britain believed that a German invasion was all but inevitable. Throughout the country, and especially in southern England, numerous anti-invasion measures were implemented. Road signs were removed (*pictured*) so that parachutists would be disoriented; hundreds of concrete pillboxes were constructed in a series of east-west defensive lines; tall wooden posts were erected in open areas to disrupt parachute or glider-borne landings; hundreds of miles of barbed wire and thousands of mines were laid along the coastline; and detailed plans were made to defend every town and village. Meanwhile, the population everywhere was on the alert for spies, subversive agents, and enemy paratroopers.

Vichy's Philippe Pétain

MARSHAL PHILIPPE PÉTAIN became a French national hero in World War I, primarily because of his defense of Verdun. Between the wars, his posts included inspector general of the army, war minister, and ambassador to Spain.

In May 1940, French premier Paul Reynaud invited Pétain to become vice premier. After Paris fell, Pétain became head of state on June 16. French hopes for a repeat of Verdun proved misplaced. Now 84, Pétain cut a pathetic figure, apparently unable to raise enthusiasm for anything but minimizing French bloodshed. On June 22, 1940, he concluded an armistice with Germany.

At Vichy on July 10, the National Assembly appointed Pétain chief of the French State. Though many considered him above collaboration, he supervised it. Pétain sought to repatriate French POWs from Germany, but he did not protest the deportation of Jews to their death and did not protest the execution of hostages. He limited France's contribution to Hitler's war, but he promoted an anti-Bolshevik "volunteer legion" and ordered French troops to resist the Allied landings in North Africa in November 1942. Those landings prompted German occupation of Vichy

Pétain with Hitler

France, effectively ending Pétain's power. In 1944 he set up a government-in-exile in Germany.

Pétain surrendered to French authorities in April 1945 and was tried for treason in July and August. The judges and jury voted for death, but because of his advanced age he was instead imprisoned. He continued to assert that at Vichy, as at Verdun, he had saved France.

Head of aircraft production
Lord Beaverbrook (William Maxwell Aitken) was Britain's minister of aircraft production and a member of the War Cabinet from May 1940. His sometimes ruthless but invariably focused approach, coupled with his inspired leadership, produced remarkable results during 1940. More than 7,300 aircraft were built between January and August—just in time for the strategically vital Battle of Britain. He became minister of supply in 1941 and minister of production in 1942, while also dealing with the provision of Anglo-U.S. military aid to Russia. Soon thereafter, ill health forced the resignation of the man who Churchill said was "at his best when things were at their worst."

Reynaud stands up to Nazis Prior to the war, French lawyer and politician Paul Reynaud protested French and British appeasement, calling on France to remain united against the Nazis. Made premier in March 1940, Reynaud appointed Charles de Gaulle undersecretary of war. That June, *Time* magazine ran a cover story on Reynaud, quoting him: "Nothing has lowered our will to struggle for our land and liberty.... France cannot die." That same month, Reynaud refused to surrender to the Nazis, and resigned. He was arrested by the Vichy government and imprisoned for the duration of the war.

1940

July 4: Great Britain and France break off diplomatic relations.

July 5: Sweden allows the Nazis transit rights as Germany tries to get supplies and troops to and from Norway. • Romania announces its alliance with Germany and Italy, one day after King Carol oversees the installation of a pro-Axis government. • Vichy France attacks British Gibraltar with planes from its bases in French Morocco. • President Roosevelt launches a limited embargo against Japan, banning the shipment of materials that could be used to feed the Japanese war machine.

July 10: Berlin's Jewish Affairs Office proposes an emigration plan that would move as many as four million European Jews to Madagascar. • Roosevelt details his plans for an army of up to two million men, and asks Congress for the funds to make this plan a reality.

July 11: Germany installs Philippe Pétain as leader of unoccupied France.

July 13: Hitler orders the annihilation of the RAF, which he sees as a necessary first step to any invasion of the British mainland.

July 16: More than 20,000 French citizens are driven from Alsace-Lorraine when the Nazis annex the region. • Naturalized Jews are stripped of their French citizenship by France's Vichy government.

July 18: Britain acquiesces to Japan's demand that the Burma Road be closed to shipments of war materiel for three months, cutting off China's link to outside aid. • Germany begins propaganda broadcasts in the United Kingdom, agitating for Scottish separatism.

Bush launches atomic project In 1940 American research scientist Vannevar Bush proposed a National Defense Research Committee (NDRC) to coordinate the nation's scientific and military activities. Appointed NDRC chairman, Bush soon became convinced that an atomic bomb was feasible and started a research and development program. In March 1942, Bush wrote to President Roosevelt that an atomic bomb "might be determining in the war effort." With FDR's approval, Bush established the Military Policy Committee, which was granted oversight of the Manhattan Project.

U.S. Strategy in China

THE UNITED STATES' GOALS in China from 1941 to '45 were to keep the Chinese actively involved in war with Japan and to launch an attack on the Japanese home islands from China. The more the Japanese were preoccupied with China, the fewer resources the Japanese would have to battle other Allied forces.

Support for the Chinese war effort began even before Pearl Harbor. President Roosevelt approved $25 million in military aid in late 1940, followed by another $145 million in Lend-Lease funds in May 1941. Approval was also granted for an American volunteer group of U.S. civilian pilots—the so-called "Flying Tigers"—to fight alongside the Chinese.

After Pearl Harbor, Roosevelt appointed Lieutenant General Joseph Stilwell to command U.S. forces in the China-Burma-Indian theater and work with Nationalist leader Chiang Kai-shek to train and equip Chinese troop formations. Due to political and material complications, results were mixed.

Delivery of materiel also posed problems. Japanese forces controlled the coast, and in May 1942 they cut the tenuous Burma Road supply line. This forced supplies to travel by air over the Himalayas, known to U.S. flyers as "The Hump," which reduced the flow to Chinese units. Finally, Chinese needs ranked well down on the American priority list, after Europe and the Pacific.

But by mid-1944, Allied subs and air attacks destroyed Japan's ability to move troops by sea. At war's end, more than 600,000 Japanese—men who had been prevented from facing U.S. forces in the Pacific—surrendered in China.

British attack French ships The French battleship *Bretagne* burns in an Algerian port after being hit by British fire on July 3, 1940. Following the defeat of France, Britain moved to prevent French warships from falling into Nazi hands. A British ultimatum to the French commander in Algeria (where the substantial French fleet was of particular concern) demanded that the French ships either join with the British, sail under control to a British port, sail to a French port in the West Indies and be demilitarized, or be entrusted to the U.S. When no response came in six hours, Churchill gave the order to attack. In the ensuing Battle of Oran, the British damaged and destroyed several French warships, killing more than 1,200 French sailors.

The strategic importance of Sylt The Frisian island of Sylt, in the North Sea near the border of Denmark and Germany, was a strategic German position during World War II. Germany launched its first air raid against Great Britain from there on October 16, 1939, in a failed attempt to sink the HMS *Hood*. As the war continued, Germans built concrete bunkers beneath the island's sandy dunes. They also installed antiaircraft weapons, such as the ones pictured here, to protect the German coast from Allied bombers.

Hitler contemplates British invasion Hitler, Heinrich Himmler (*to Hitler's immediate left*), and staff officers view the English coastline from the cliff top at Calais while contemplating their plans for Operation Sealion. Hitler had assumed that Britain would submit once France had collapsed, but when it became clear that Britain would fight on he ordered the invasion plans to be finalized. Prerequisites for success were air supremacy, the clearance of mine-free channels, and the neutralization of the Royal Navy. However, the RAF's defeat of the *Luftwaffe* in September 1940 and the continuing British naval presence in the Channel resulted in the plan being postponed—and eventually abandoned.

1940

July 21: Estonia, Latvia, and Lithuania join the Soviet Union under duress.

July 22: Hitler's strings-attached "peace offer" is rejected by London.
• The Special Operations Executive is created by Britain's War Cabinet to carry out acts of sabotage against Nazi Germany in occupied countries.

July 24: Nearly 50 civilians are killed in an Italian air raid of Jerusalem.

August 1: Hitler orders increased bombing of strategic British targets in preparation for Operation Sealion, which he intends to launch on September 15.

August 3: East Africa's British Somaliland is overrun by a large contingent of Italian troops.

August 5: Hitler and Mussolini confer in Rome, with Mussolini assuring Hitler he will soon open the North African front with an assault into Egypt toward the Suez Canal.

August 8: In an effort to persuade India to take a more active role in promoting British interests in Southeast Asia, Britain promises its colony a new postwar constitution.

August 9: Due to greater needs on other fronts, British troops abandon Shanghai.

August 11: The U.S. Army announces plans to send 4,000 tanks to Britain.

August 15: Germany is dealt a major blow during the Battle of Britain. Intending to knock out the RAF, the *Luftwaffe* actually loses more than twice as many aircraft—75 compared to Britain's 32.

August 17: Germany blockades Britain, heavily mining its waters and vowing to attack all approaching ships, whether belligerent or neutral.

British submarines The HMS *Taku* (*pictured*) was one of the oceangoing T-class boats that formed the mainstay of the British submarine fleet. Royal Navy submarines operated in shallow waters that were heavily mined and well defended by antisubmarine forces. Of more than 50 deployed, nearly one out of three was destroyed, usually going down with all hands. Nevertheless, Royal Navy subs took a heavy toll on German ships in Norwegian waters. In the dangerously shallow and clear Mediterranean, British subs successfully interrupted German and Italian supply routes to Africa. British submarines also landed and picked up clandestine agents in various areas, and supported Allied efforts in the Malacca Straits and seas near Indonesia.

Germans train for Sealion
In this faked photo, a German armored vehicle is supposedly on the beach of Dover, England. In 1940 Operation Sealion was a high-risk undertaking; no invasion of Britain had succeeded since 1066. Nevertheless, German plans advanced throughout that summer. Thousands of troops of the Ninth and 16th Armies assembled and trained in the coastal region, horses were conditioned to travel on barges, and hundreds of troop-carrying vessels were collected in French and Belgian ports. However, all ultimately depended upon the *Luftwaffe* achieving overall air supremacy beforehand, and so the victory won by the RAF during September's Battle of Britain effectively made Sealion no longer viable.

Japan and French Indochina

THE FALL OF FRANCE and creation of the Vichy regime in 1940 benefited the Japanese in their war in China and their anticipated advance into Southeast Asia. The Japanese estimated that 41 percent of supplies reaching Chiang Kai-shek's Nationalist Chinese forces came through the port of Haiphong in French Indochina—which was comprised of the French colony of Cochinchina and the French protectorates of Cambodia, Laos, Annam, and Tonkin.

Using diplomacy and threats, as well as a "mistaken" incursion that killed more than 800 French troops, the Japanese forced the Vichy French regime to close the Yunnan railway in September 1940 and then to allow Japanese troops to occupy northern Indochina. There they consolidated their blockade of China and prepared for southward expansion. In July 1941, Japanese forces occupied southern Indochina, where they met no opposition. Vichy's accommodating responses to the Japanese demands of September 1940 and July 1941 contrasted sharply to its resistance to simultaneous demands from the British and Free French in Dakar and Syria.

Evacuation of French colonial forces in French Indochina

When the American government tried to avert war in late 1941, one of its key demands was that the Japanese evacuate French Indochina. Japan would have left the southern portion if the U.S. made concessions on the oil issue. That could not and did not happen. So, after Japan took Malaya in January 1942, Indochina sprouted Japanese air and naval bases, and became a valuable staging post for troops.

Japan eyes French Indochina Japanese troops work on a bridge in French Indochina in August 1940. The fall of France in 1940 left French Indochina defenseless before Japanese territorial ambitions. A pact between Vichy France and Japan, allowing the Japanese to station troops in northern Indochina, was ratified in September, though French agreement came only after the Japanese bombed Haiphong in a show of strength. The Matsuoka-Henry Pact of August 1940 supposedly recognized France's sovereignty over Indochina, but this was an empty gesture. The French were merely tolerated by the Japanese. In March 1945, even that pretense was abandoned when the Japanese moved to displace the French administration.

French resistance fighters After the fall of France in 1940, some Frenchmen fled to the *maquis* (wooded uplands). The word soon came to mean "armed resistance fighter." The *Maquis* harassed German and Vichy troops, found safe havens for Jewish children, aided downed Allied airmen, and helped fugitives evade the Nazis. In addition, some *Maquis* groups were guilty of raiding villages, torturing prisoners, and other atrocities. The *Maquis* members seen here inspect weapons parachuted to them from British planes.

The Blitz

"THE BOMBER," British prime minister Stanley Baldwin had told a somber Parliament in 1932, "will always get through." The examples of Guernica in Spain, as well as Japanese attacks in China, suggested that Baldwin had been correct. After Britain's declaration of war in September 1939, its citizens prepared for the anticipated German bombing Blitz (a contraction of *Blitzkrieg*). The British launched barrage balloons to force bombers to high altitudes, while antiaircraft batteries ringed industrial targets.

Since only a few bombs fell until mid-1940, Britain did have ample time to prepare. The government raised a dramatically resourceful civilian Auxiliary Fire Service. Moreover, it organized medical services and evacuated some three million women and children to the country. (Middle-class families hosting them learned appalling truths about the lives of the urban working class.) An efficient and dedicated Air Raid Precautions organization enforced civil defense measures, including a strict blackout, while many families built air raid shelters. In London especially, thousands sought protection in public shelters and famously in Underground stations, a sign of official unpreparedness as much as popular stoicism.

When the air strikes came in August 1940, German bombers attacked London by day and night. What happened in London was the defining experience of the Blitz, but most large English cities were attacked as well. The notorious raid on Coventry, for instance, destroyed the city's center and killed more than 500 people.

Children in an eastern suburb of London

The psychological basis of the attacks, that bombing would destroy a population's resolve, proved spectacularly wrong. "Britain Can Take It" became a popular motto, and though some cities approached panic at times, most people grew defiant rather than demoralized.

By mid-1941, when Germany's *Luftwaffe* joined the war against Russia, the sustained attacks against Britain largely ended. However, just days after the D-Day landing in June 1944, the first V-1 pilotless planes fell on London. In the fall of that year, V-2 ballistic missiles followed. Civilians wearied by five years of war were forced to endure a particularly terrifying weapon.

Some 70,000 British civilians died during the attacks of 1940–41 and 1944. But to this day, citizens still celebrate and romanticize the "spirit of the Blitz."

Two devastating nights On September 7, 1940, 300 *Luftwaffe* bombers and 600 fighters attacked London in the late afternoon, and a further 180 bombers continued the raid throughout the night. The resulting destruction and fires (*pictured*) were widespread; 430 civilians died and 1,600 were seriously wounded. Then, in full moonlight on October 15–16, 400 German bombers mounted attacks from 8:40 P.M. to 4:40 A.M. London's railway system, gas works, power stations, and water supply were all severely disrupted. Many houses were also destroyed, with more than 900 fires started. Although 41 RAF fighters were launched that night, only one German bomber was downed.

Antiaircraft guns defend London On September 7, 1940, only 92 antiaircraft (AA) guns were deployed about London, and the fire-control arrangements failed almost at once. Thus, the *Luftwaffe* enjoyed three nights with virtually no AA fire directed against it. However, by September 11, some 200 AA guns were put in place, together with supporting searchlights, so that a blaze of light and a curtain of fire (*pictured*) greeted the bombers that night. Few hits were claimed, but the guns and barrage balloons did force the bombers to fly much higher. In addition, this display of firepower boosted the morale of many Londoners.

CHURCHILL VOWS REVENGE

WINSTON STOOD ALONE in front, his dark blue boiler suit undone at the neck, a tin hat on his head, his hands folded on his stout stick in front of him, his chin thrust out, the long cigar in his mouth, and just across the other side of St. James's Park, Carlton House Terrace was ablaze: the boom of bombs exploding to the south, the crack and rattle of the AA guns and exploding shells, the red-white glow of the fire silhouetting the tall black trunks of the great trees in the park. It was a moment in history to remember, and above the noise came the angry voice of Winston Churchill: "By God, we will get the B's for this."

—ROYAL AIR FORCE INTELLIGENCE OFFICER F. W. WINTERBOTHAM, ON THE GERMAN BLITZ BOMBING OF LONDON

"The columns of smoke merged and became a monstrous curtain which blocked the sky; only the billows within it and the sudden shafts of flame which shot up hundreds of feet made one realize that it was a living thing and not just the backdrop of some nightmare opera."

—BRITISH PUBLISHER DESMOND FLOWER, DESCRIBING WHAT HE SAW AS A SOLDIER DURING THE GERMAN BOMBING OF THE LONDON DOCKS ON SEPTEMBER 7, 1940

Blitz bombing kills 43,000 From September to mid-November 1940, an average of 200 Axis aircraft bombed London on every night but one. Meanwhile, *Luftwaffe* fighter bombers and single bombers on precision bombing missions also attacked the capital by day. Regular air raids then continued until May. Destruction was widespread and severe. This massive crater was possibly caused by one of the *Luftwaffe*'s huge 2,500-kilogram "Max" *Sprengbombe Cylindrisch* bombs. Countrywide, from September 1940 to May 1941, the Blitz caused 43,000 civilian deaths and 139,000 serious injuries, as well as laying waste to many residential areas and industrial, dockland, and infrastructure facilities.

1940

August 20: Churchill offers Roosevelt the use of military bases in the West Indies and Newfoundland.

August 23–24: The *Luftwaffe* bombs London. Though oil facilities east of the city are targeted, London proper sustains most of the damage. The RAF will retaliate two nights later, attacking Berlin for the first time.

August 28: Liverpool, England, suffers its first bomb raid.

August 31: In the greatest one-day loss for the RAF to date, the *Luftwaffe* takes out 38 planes and critical airfields in southern Britain.

September 5: France's Vichy government severs diplomatic ties with Holland, Luxembourg, Belgium, and Norway. • As many as 4,000 German troops perish when the transport ship *Marion* founders after taking a direct hit from a British torpedo. • German authorities seize Jewish-owned businesses following Luxembourg's annexation by Germany and adoption of the Nuremberg Laws.

September 6: Fascist general Ion Antonescu and his Iron Guards take control of the Romanian government. Romania's King Carol is forced to abdicate after ceding much of Transylvania. • The U.S. Navy transfers the first eight of 50 destroyers promised to the Royal Navy in exchange for U.S. bases at Bermuda and other British possessions.

September 7: The *Luftwaffe* turns its attention from British military to civilian targets. This is part of what will be called the Blitz.

September 10: Italian troops stage themselves in Albania prior to their planned assault on Greece.

September 11: The *Luftwaffe* bombs London, inflicting heavy damage on St. Paul's Cathedral and Buckingham Palace.

Hurricanes, Spitfires defend Britain In 1937 the RAF's first monoplane fighter—the Hurricane Hurricane Mark I (*pictured*)—entered squadron service. It boasted a top speed of more than 300 mph, eight machine guns (replaced with cannons in late 1940), and an operating radius of up to 600 miles. This formidable aircraft, together with the Spitfire (introduced in 1938), proved to be the mainstay of RAF Fighter Command during the crucial Battle of Britain. Using radar to track the approaching German bombers, RAF headquarters sent these Hurricanes and Spitfires to intercept. They inflicted crippling losses upon the *Luftwaffe*, which helped prevent a German invasion.

Murrow reports from London When a German bomber bore down on London, American radio (CBS) reporter Edward R. Murrow stated, "We could see his exhaust trail like a pale ribbon stretched straight across the air." A canister with incendiary bombs was "like some giant had thrown a huge basket of flaming golden oranges high in the sky." Beginning in 1939, Murrow's vivid descriptions of the war brought radio news reporting to a new level of professionalism and popularity. Murrow accentuated the totalitarian threat with contrasts to democratic ideals, such as free speech.

Dowding thinks ahead

Air Chief Marshal Sir Hugh Dowding headed the RAF Fighter Command during the Battle of Britain, integrating radar, radio, and detailed plotting of raids. In 1940 he refused to send the greater portion of the RAF to assist France, which he considered a lost cause. When the *Luftwaffe* began attacking ships in the English Channel, Dowding resisted being drawn into a destructive confrontation. His tactics preserved the RAF for vital battles over Britain itself. Regardless, in November 1940 he was sacked for what was mistaken by some as a lack of aggressiveness.

ARP wardens often first to scene In addition to training for and carrying out such routine tasks as enforcing the blackout, fire watching, and bomb reporting, the British Air Raid Precautions (ARP) wardens were frequently involved in the harrowing task of rescuing survivors after an air raid, such as the rescue operation pictured. Being locally based, these wardens were often first to horrific scenes of death and destruction, with many blast victims identifiable only by their clothes or jewelry. Wardens often had to assist survivors who were severely burnt or traumatized in a state of deep shock.

Londoners sleep in Underground During the Blitz, thousands of Londoners endured a semi-troglodyte existence, sleeping in Underground (subway) stations. There, they were fairly well protected from the constant hail of high-explosive and incendiary bombs that fell upon the capital. Indeed, from September 7, 1940, London was bombed on all but one of 76 consecutive nights. Such extreme privation along with fear and their shared adversity during the Blitz shaped the uniquely resilient character of wartime Londoners.

The royal couple shows support Great Britain's King George VI and Queen Elizabeth talk with a workman in a bomb-damaged neighborhood of London in 1940. The royal couple often toured the sites of such destruction in London, and they also traveled via their royal train to other bombed cities. The king and queen even endured the bombing of Buckingham Palace (though no one was hurt). The queen's refusal to leave London during the *Luftwaffe* blitz served as an inspiration to ordinary Londoners who shared the same dangers.

1940

September 13: An anemic British force is pushed back when Italy embarks on its first significant assault on the North African front, marching five army divisions into Egypt from Libya. • The African war continues with a 20-mile incursion by Italian troops from occupied Ethiopia into British Kenya. • King George VI and Queen Elizabeth remain in London, despite narrowly missing being struck by bombs that tore through the roof of Buckingham Palace.

September 15: Canada conscripts its single men, ages 21 to 24. • Hitler postpones Operation Sealion after another botched air battle leaves the *Luftwaffe* with 60 planes lost while the RAF loses 26.

September 16: The U.S. Congress passes the Selective Training and Service Act, which will enable the registration and conscription of American males ages 21 to 35.

September 17: Seventy-seven British children, en route to Canada to escape the destruction of war, die when a U-boat sinks their ship, *City of Benares*.

September 21: Officials in London permit Londoners who do not have access to bomb shelters to use the Underground for that purpose. At one point, more than 170,000 people will be sleeping in the "Tube."

September 23: In a sign of horrors to come, SS chief Heinrich Himmler decrees that gold teeth should be removed from the mouths of dead concentration camp inmates.

September 25: American intelligence agents crack Japan's diplomatic code, known as "Purple." Along with Britain's deciphering of the German Enigma machine, this is a significant victory for Allied intelligence.

Fighting fires during the Blitz In 1940 and '41, Britain's fire services included full-time and part-time regular firefighters as well as part-time auxiliaries. The full-time firefighters worked shifts of 48 hours on duty followed by 24 hours off, and they were joined during the particularly busy night hours by the part-time auxiliaries. Here, firefighters battle a blaze in London. Initially, the firefighting response to major fires that involved operations across local authority boundaries was hampered by the fire service's localized and excessively parochial system of command and control. However, after the Blitz ended in May 1941, all of these semiautonomous forces were brought together to form the National Fire Service.

Britain's amateur firefighters Members of the Auxiliary Fire Service (AFS) add pins, probably representing the locations of pumps or fires, to a map of London on the wall of Fire Brigade Headquarters during the Blitz. The Auxiliary Fire Service had existed since 1937, and by September 1939 it had tens of thousands of male and female members. They were amateur firefighters recruited to work alongside regular fire brigades fighting fires started by enemy bombing. Incompatibility of the brigades' equipment hampered effectiveness, and in 1941 the AFS and regular brigades were merged into the National Fire Service. Churchill called the London firefighters "heroes with grimy faces." More than 900 firemen and women lost their lives during the war.

Carrier pigeons British, American, Canadian, and German forces all used homing pigeons, such as this one, to carry essential war-front messages. Dropped by parachute, pigeons also enabled communications from resistance fighters in France, Belgium, and Holland. One of the most famous birds was "GI Joe," a pigeon that raced to the U.S. Air Support Command with word that the Italian village of Colvi Vecchia had been taken by the British. The message arrived just in time to cancel a scheduled bombing, saving the lives of the villagers and 1,000 British troops.

Bush-baby preaches safety George the bush-baby, sitting in an enameled cup, shows off his own tiny air-raid helmet. George was a galago, a nocturnal tree-dwelling primate from sub-Saharan Africa. Because of the galagos's childlike cries, British explorers called them "bush-babies." The British Air Raid Precautions (ARP) organization—responsible for maintaining shelters and handing out protective equipment—used George's photo to help sell the public on using safety measures during air raids.

Extinguishing incendiary bombs The *Luftwaffe*'s small incendiary bombs were made of magnesium alloy and were ignited by a small impact fuse. They burned for 10 minutes or more, initially at a temperature sufficient to melt steel and discharge molten metal up to 50 feet. If caught in time, however, they could often be extinguished. Ways to do so included smothering them with sandbags or dirt, dousing them with water from stirrup pumps, and employing a "snuffer," which was sprayed inside and out with asbestos fiber. This woman simply uses a metal scoop and a hoe.

What to do with "dud" bombs The skillful but immensely hazardous task of disposing of unexploded bombs (UXB) or "duds" fell primarily to the British Army's Corps of Royal Engineers. Some 10 percent of the high-explosive bombs that were dropped failed to explode or had delayed-action fuses, and by the end of 1940 there were some 3,000 UXBs waiting to be defused. Whether still lying buried or clearly visible, these marked and cordoned (but still potentially deadly) devices would disrupt all movement and activity in the surrounding area. Here, Royal Engineers remove a deeply buried one-ton UXB near St. Paul's Cathedral in London. The huge bomb was safely exploded 30 minutes later.

1940

September 27: France's Vichy government orders all Jews to carry cards identifying them as such. • The Axis is sealed with the signing of the Tripartite Pact, an economic and military alliance among Germany, Italy, and Japan.

September 29: Luxembourg is formally incorporated into the Reich.

October 3: Warsaw's Jews are herded into the city's Jewish ghetto.

October 4: With Operation Sealion temporarily delayed, Hitler meets with Mussolini in an effort to enlist Italy to take on Britain on alternate fronts. • Fearing Japanese aggression in the Pacific, Churchill requests naval reinforcements from Roosevelt to defend Britain's colony of Singapore.

October 7: With Ion Antonescu's assent in Romania, Germany occupies that country on the pretext of protecting its oil fields from British saboteurs. • Japan formally voices its objection to the American ban on sales of fuel, scrap metal, and machine tools to Asia.

October 9: London's Cathedral of St. Paul sustains serious damage to the roof and altar when it is struck by a German bomb.

October 12: Hitler reschedules his invasion of Britain for April 4, 1941, leading Churchill to joke that Britain is "waiting for the long-promised invasion. So are the fishes." • In a speech that implies that the U.S. may be ready for a greater role in the war, Roosevelt claims that Americans "reject the doctrine of appeasement," calling it "a major weapon of the aggressor nations."

RAF begins targeted bombing In 1940 RAF bombers began trying to hit German oil refineries, factories, communications sites, and transportation lines, then increased attacks in 1941. In August 1940, the RAF made its first bombing raid on Berlin. Soviet premier Vyacheslav Molotov, in the German capital in November 1940, was told that Britain had lost the war. If so, Molotov reportedly asked, "why are we in this shelter, and whose are the bombs which fall?" This photo of an RAF

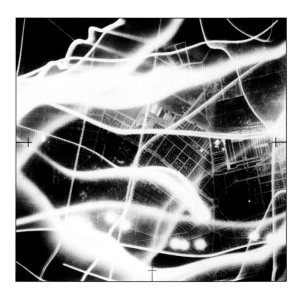

night raid on Berlin on October 7–8, 1940, shows German searchlights (broad, wavy lines) and tracks of antiaircraft fire. Exploding bombs show up as bright circles on the ground. According to later British assessments, few bombs hit their intended targets, and the bombing did little to diminish German morale.

The Importance of Radar

DURING THE WAR, combatants used radar to detect ships and planes far beyond the range of the human eye. In simple terms, radar (radio detecting and ranging) utilizes transmitters to bounce radio waves off distant objects, revealing the objects' location, speed, and distance.

The use of radio waves to detect distant or unseen metallic objects was first demonstrated by German scientist Christian Hulsmeyer in 1904. However, it was the British who first used radar for a military advantage, as they built a series of radar stations along the English coast in 1938 to detect approaching aircraft. Known as the Chain Home, this system subsequently played a crucial role in the victory over the *Luftwaffe* during the Battle of Britain.

The Axis powers had also dabbled with radar technology in the 1930s,

A radar scope

but they were slow to recognize its military potential, and never caught up with the Anglo-American technological edge.

Chaplin as Adenoid Hynkel Longstanding rumor holds that Hitler grew his trademark mustache to capitalize on his physical resemblance to the great film comedian Charlie Chaplin. Chaplin, who bitterly opposed Hitler's regime long before most Americans did, turned the tables by playing Adenoid Hynkel, a Hitler-inspired tyrant, in his 1940 comedy, *The Great Dictator*. Chaplin directed this masterpiece of slapstick comedy and penetrating satire. A high point of the film is a hilarious yet haunting sequence in which Hynkel dances with an inflatable globe, accompanied by a lyrical passage from Wagner's *Lohengrin*.

Food for the pigs "Daily we collected our potato peelings and scraps of left over vegetables," reported a British school-girl in 1946, "and together we carefully stowed them in a bucket" to take to the nearest "pig bin." Here, two women drop leftovers into a bin in Cheltenham, where the "Save Your Bacon" project—created to provide food for pigs to eat—started in September 1940. A local art school designed posters, and citizens participated enthusiastically. The 100 bins placed around town provided 10 tons of pig food each week. The program soon spread to other cities, including London.

Germany's mainstay bomber The Heinkel He 111 medium bomber, of which about 7,300 were built, was one of the few prewar aircraft to continue in full operational use through-out the war. Early versions of the He 111 were battle-tested by the Condor Legion during the Spanish Civil War. With a crew of five, a speed of 258 mph, and a range of 1,740 miles, it carried a bomb load of 5,500 pounds and was armed with a 20mm cannon and up to seven machine guns. Although this bomber became increasingly vulnerable, slow develop-ment of Germany's next generation of medium bombers necessitated the He 111's retention in service to 1945.

Bombsights key to accuracy During their strategic bomb-ing campaigns, the Allies needed to deliver bombs from high altitudes to specific targets from aircraft that were under heavy antiaircraft fire—and sometimes fighter attack as well. The bombardiers of the USAAF and RAF were skilled opera-tors of bombsights, which they hoped would help them drop bombs accurately. Bombsights included the USAAF's Nor-den (*pictured*) and the RAF equivalent—the Mark XIV Bomb-sight. By using electronic navigation aids and such advanced bombsights, the Allied bombers by 1945 occasionally achieved an accuracy range of just 80 yards from 20,000 feet.

1940

October 13: More than 150 people die when a London bomb shelter sustains a direct hit during an air raid. Another 64 will be killed on the 15th when bombs strike the Balham Underground Station. • Stalin sends Foreign Minister Molotov to Berlin to negotiate Soviet adherence to the Tripartite Pact.

October 15: London's primary water source, a pipeline that carries some 46 million gallons every day, is severely damaged in a bombing raid.

October 17: More than 1,500 British civilians have been killed in German bombing raids in the past week alone.

October 18: In defiance of Japan, Britain restores China's trade route to the West by reopening the Burma Road.

October 18–19: German U-boats attack two British convoys, sinking more than 30 ships.

October 22: The Nazis begin to deport Jews from parts of Germany to southern France.

October 23: Francisco Franco, Spain's Fascist leader, is unmoved by a nine-hour meeting with Hitler, and refuses to ally Spain with the Axis.

October 26: With more than 150,000 Italian troops at the ready, Mussolini attempts to justify his inevitable invasion of Greece by claiming that Greece has attacked Albania.

October 28: Mussolini sends Italian troops into Greece in an invasion attempt that will end in total disaster for the Italians.

November 3: British troops and RAF units land in Greece to help repel the invading Italian army.

Nazis ghettoize Warsaw's Jews Polish and Jewish laborers contribute to the construction of a 10-foot-high wall that will enclose the Jewish ghetto of Warsaw. After the 1939 German takeover of Poland, Gestapo chief Reinhard Heydrich ordered Jews into segregated living areas. In the fall of 1940, Heydrich used the pretext of a typhus outbreak in Jewish neighborhoods to force the city's Jews into a 3.5-square-mile section of town. Non-Jewish Poles were moved out of the area. That November, the ghetto wall's 22 gates were closed, sealing off 360,000 Jews (one-third of Warsaw's entire population) from the rest of the Polish capital.

U-boats feast on Allied ships In 1940 Germany had a small but effective fleet of submarines, such as the U-boat *Krieg* seen here. In addition to successful attacks on British warships, German U-boats proved especially deadly against Allied merchant shipping. The fall of France provided a 2,500-mile coast from which to unleash U-boat "wolf packs" against still-unescorted transatlantic merchant convoys. That fall, U-boats sank some 200 Allied ships. However, these early successes led Hitler to conclude that he had enough submarines and could shift to building surface ships for war with the U.S. He did not increase production until mid-1941, by which time Britain had acquired more destroyers and developed better defenses.

QUESTIONS FROM THE DEEP

WHAT DOES A [merchant] steamer look like after sinking six or eight thousand feet? What happens to boats like ours [submarines] when they can no longer be kept from drowning? Are the wrecks crushed into huge compact lumps? Or do the compartments and the ruptured pressure hull flood so quickly with water that the pressure outside and in is soon equalized? Do they therefore retain their shape as they sink onto the seabed? And what happens to the men sunk along with their ships? Do corpses gradually rot in the lower depths? Are there fish that far down, to gnaw the flesh off their bones? There's no one to talk to about such things, no one to provide hard information.

—GERMAN WAR CORRESPONDENT LOTHAR-GUNTHER BUCHHEIM, WHO WORKED ONBOARD THE NAZI SUB *U-96*

Battle of the Atlantic

FROM THE WAR'S FIRST HOURS (when the German sub *U-30* sank the liner *Athenia*) to its final days, Germany tried to cut Britain's vital seaborne supplies. Much of Britain's food and munitions and most of its fuel had to pass across the Atlantic, running the risk of attack by the *Kriegsmarine*'s U-boat (submarine) fleet. As in World War I, when analysis showed that ships sailing in convoy had much better chances of reaching safety, the Admiralty introduced a complex convoy system.

The "battle" to get materials and troops from Britain's empire and dominions, as well as products of America's industrial might, to Britain was really a continuous series of related campaigns, beginning in earnest in mid-1940 when Germany's European victories gave it strategically important Atlantic bases. While surface warships and armed merchant cruisers played a part in the war at sea, by 1942 the battle was between U-boats and escorting warships and aircraft. In the winter of 1940–41, the U-boats enjoyed their first so-called "happy time."

A British sailor signaling a merchant ship

British, Canadian, and (beginning in September 1941) United States escorts, at first pitifully few, faced aggressive and persistent U-boat activity. America's entry into the war increased the number and spread of targets, leading to a second "happy time." U-boats torpedoed ships off the American East Coast before the U.S. finally introduced a convoy system and ordered a coastal blackout.

Churchill confessed his fear that the U-boats might win. Only in the fall of 1943 did Allied shipbuilding exceed monthly losses. However, though they sank hundreds of ships, the submarines were too few in number to achieve real victory. Those hundreds of lost ships represented only a fraction of the Allied shipping available. But for tanker crews in midocean, the threat of a torpedo strike made the Battle of the Atlantic a terrifying ordeal.

Technological developments gave each side crucial and sometimes short-lived advantages, making scientists and technicians as vital as submarine and escort crews. German grand admiral Karl Dönitz directed the U-boats via high-frequency radio, transmitting orders using the Enigma code. Gradually, Allied "boffins" (scientific geniuses) gave the escorts a crucial technological edge in the battle against the U-boats. Asdic (a sonar system for submarines), High-frequency Direction Finding, airborne radar, and, above all, the breaking of the Enigma code gradually gave the Allies a decisive edge.

The Battle of the Atlantic, the war's most unremitting and crucial battle, formed the basis of the Allied victory in the European war. Control of the Atlantic enabled the Allies to hold Britain as a base for the liberation of Europe. Both sides paid a high price. Fifty thousand Allied merchant sailors died in battle, nearly matching the number of British aircrew who died bombing Germany. Successful U-boat commanders were exalted as "aces," though eventually they were likely to die. Eighty percent of Germany's 1,000 operational submarines were sunk, and two-thirds of their crews perished.

The battle inspired several powerful works of art, notably Nicholas Monsarrat's novel *The Cruel Sea* and Wolfgang Petersen's film *Das Boot*.

1940

November 5: The tremendously popular Franklin Roosevelt is elected to a third term, a break from the presidency's traditional, though not mandated, two-term limit.

November 7: The RAF bombs the Krupp munitions factory in Essen, Germany. • Irish prime minister Eamon de Valera denies Britain the use of Irish naval bases.

November 8: Hitler's annual observance of his 1923 coup attempt is interrupted by an RAF air raid on Munich.

November 9: Germany begins the process of expelling some 180,000 French citizens from Alsace-Lorraine, the partially ethnically German region in southern France.

November 11: In the first successful attack by carrier-based warplanes, a flight of 20 RAF biplanes bombs Taranto, destroying or damaging half the Italian fleet. • Fifty-five Polish intellectuals are murdered in the first of many mass executions at Dachau, the concentration camp outside of Munich.

November 12–14: Soviet foreign minister Molotov meets with Hitler to discuss possible Soviet adherence to the Tripartite Pact.

November 14: Much of the British city of Coventry, including its stunning medieval cathedral, is destroyed in a *Luftwaffe* raid in which 449 bombers attack the region. • In an embarrassing defeat for the Italian military, the Greek army pushes the Italians out of Greece and follows their retreat into Albania.

November 16: Hamburg, Germany, is blasted by RAF bombers.

French colonial troops Members of the First Battalion AEF (Afrique Equatoriale Française) charge across the desert. The French military had a long history of filling its ranks with colonial troops. Before the fall of France in 1940, more than 100,000 men had been recruited from West Africa alone. Following the armistice, the four territories of French Equatorial Africa—Gabon, Chad, and present-day Republic of the Congo and Central African Republic—sided with the Free French. About 100,000 Africans served with the Free French from 1943 to '45, participating in the fighting in North Africa, Italy, and southern France.

America's peacetime draft Colonel Charles R. Morris (*right*) adjusts a blindfold on Secretary of War Henry L. Stimson as Stimson prepares to pick an opaque blue capsule containing a draft number out of a large bowl. President Roosevelt (*left*) waits to read the selected number to the nation in a radio broadcast. This first U.S. peacetime conscription was inaugurated by the Selective Service Act of 1940, which required every American male citizen or resident alien from age 21 through 35 to register for a draft number.

> ## "We cannot escape danger, or the fear of danger, by crawling into bed and pulling the covers over our heads."
>
> —President Roosevelt, December 29, 1940

FDR and the Coming War

WHILE PRESIDENT FRANKLIN D. Roosevelt guided America through the Great Depression of the 1930s, Hitler and his fellow Axis leaders constructed military juggernauts with the mission to crush the democratic nations of the world. When war broke out in September 1939, Roosevelt's attempts to aid America's allies in Europe were blocked both by Congress and a majority of American citizens committed to the policy of neutrality and isolationism. America's experience in World War I had soured many on the idea of any more "European entanglements," if only because of the great monetary cost. The realities of the Depression had encouraged a shrinking of the American worldview; U.S. concerns, in the minds of many, overrode all others. FDR fought hard to break through this resistance because of a conviction that if the Axis powers were successful in their conquests, the United States would eventually become the only surviving democracy in the world, standing alone and outnumbered against well-armed enemies. And *that* reality could one day make the Depression seem like a picnic.

Roosevelt had to walk a fine line, however, avoiding any impression that he intended to thrust the country into the middle of this world war. During his campaign for an unprecedented third term, Roosevelt assured Americans that they would not go to war. "And while I am talking to you mothers and fathers," Roosevelt declared in a pre-election speech, "I give you one more assurance. . . . Your boys are not going to be sent into any foreign wars."

Early in his presidency, Roosevelt began a series of radio "fireside" chats as a means to talk directly to Americans on national and international issues. In a December 1940 broadcast, he introduced his vision of making the United States the "Arsenal of Democracy." "The people of Europe who are defending themselves do not ask us to do their fighting. They ask us for the implements of war . . . which will enable them to fight for their liberty and for our security. Emphatically we must get these weapons to them . . . so that we and our children will be saved the agony and suffering of war which others have had to endure."

Congress supported Roosevelt's "Arsenal of Democracy" and passed the Lend-Lease Act, which authorized the president to sell, exchange, or trade $50 billion in war materials to the Allied nations, principally Great Britain. Roosevelt hailed the passage of this act as a way to help other countries defeat Germany without direct U.S. participation. He continued, however, to be careful how his actions appeared to Americans. He feared that if he assumed a more aggressive approach to the war, he would fracture the country at a time when unity was essential.

While Americans believed that they could remain neutral observers of the events in Europe and the Pacific, Roosevelt and his advisers secretly developed several strategies they could follow if America was forced into the war. He favored the "Europe first" plan, in which America would join its allies in defeating Germany and Italy before turning its attention to Japan. However, the possibility of staying out of the war ended on December 7, 1941, with the attack on Pearl Harbor, "a day," Roosevelt declared, "that will live in infamy."

Americans rallied around their president as Congress declared war on Japan the next day. Germany and Italy declared war on the United States three days later. As American men rushed to enlistment centers, Roosevelt and his advisers planned for war on two fronts. America now faced its greatest challenge of the 20th century.

1940

November 20: Hungary signs the Tripartite Pact, joining Germany, Italy, and Japan in the Axis. • In what will become known as the "100th Regiment Offensive," Chinese Communists stage guerrilla raids against Japanese forces.

November 22: The Greeks overwhelm Italy's Ninth Army and occupy Korçë, an Albanian town strategically important to the Italians.

November 23: Romania follows Hungary's lead and signs the Tripartite Pact, joining the Axis. Slovakia will join the following day.

November 25: A wood-bodied De Havilland Mosquito prototype—a fast, light, and agile British fighter that will become known as the "Timber Terror"—takes to the air for its first flight. • Bulgaria postpones signing the Tripartite Pact.

November 26: Pierre Ryckmans, the governor general of the Belgian Congo, declares war on Italy. Italy will declare war on Belgium the following day. • Workers begin the construction of a 10-foot-high wall around the Jewish ghetto in Warsaw, Poland.

November 27: In an effort to bolster his power, Romanian dictator Ion Antonescu orders his Iron Guard to execute 64 officials who are loyal to the government of King Carol.

November 29: Plans for the Nazi invasion of the Soviet Union, dubbed Operation Barbarossa, are finalized.

December 1: Italy begins rationing its key staple: pasta.

December 6: A major upheaval in the Italian military command follows the disastrous invasion of Greece, as the army's chief of staff resigns. The chief of the Italian navy will resign on December 8.

U-48 **sinks more than 50 ships** On September 11, 1940, Herbert Schultze, commander of the German submarine *U-48* (*pictured*), sent a terse radio message to Winston Churchill, announcing that he had sunk the British steamer *Firby*. After giving the wreck's coordinates, Schultze added, "Save the crew, if you please." Fast, agile, and far-ranging, the *U-48* was commissioned on April 22, 1939, and proved herself the most successful German U-boat of the war, sinking more than 50 ships and damaging others during its 12 patrols. By June 1941, the *U-48*, already becoming obsolete, was relegated to training exercises.

Republican Willkie supports FDR Even though Republican lawyer and industrialist Wendell Willkie ran against President Roosevelt's 1940 bid for an unprecedented third term, he was no isolationist. He opposed the New Deal, but his foreign policies were very similar to the president's. After his loss, Willkie became a strong supporter of Roosevelt's Lend-Lease Act and urged unlimited aid to Britain. Appointed Roosevelt's personal representative, Willkie traveled to Britain, the Middle East, the USSR, and China.

Ambassador Kennedy Joseph Kennedy greets the British press on his return from a trip to the United States. FDR appointed Kennedy—an isolationist who believed that entry into the war would be far from America's best interests— ambassador to Britain in 1938. Kennedy expected Britain to be defeated, and some of his speeches even seemed to imply sympathy with Hitler. Forced to resign in November 1940, Kennedy was succeeded by John G. Winant, an advocate of the Lend-Lease program. Kennedy's eldest son, Joe, died in the war; son John would be elected U.S. president in 1960.

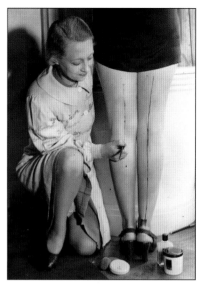

Fake stockings In the 1940s, stylish women wore nylon stockings with seams down the back. During the World War II embargo on Japanese silk, nylon was in demand for parachutes and stockings were hard to find. Women simply darkened their legs with makeup and drew "seams" with an eyebrow pencil to make it look like they were wearing stockings. Some resorted to professional help, such as the Max Factor beautician seen here applying fake stockings.

America first In rallies, publications, posters, and speeches, the America First Committee insisted that the way to preserve American democracy was to stay out of the European war. Formed at Yale University Law School in 1940, the powerful isolationist group soon had as many as 800,000 members in 650 chapters. Convinced that no foreign power could successfully attack a fully prepared America, the committee encouraged maintaining a strong national defense. Four days after the Japanese attacked Pearl Harbor on December 7, 1941, the America First Committee was dissolved.

Greece defends its soil Greek and Italian troops are portrayed in battle during the Greco-Italian War (1940–41). Embarrassed that his Italian forces had not achieved conquests comparable to Germany's, Mussolini decided that Greece would be an easy target for invasion. Boasting that Hitler "will find out from the papers that I have occupied Greece," Mussolini launched his attack from Italian-occupied Albania on October 28, 1940. The outnumbered and outgunned Greeks won an unexpected victory in the Pindus Mountains, then drove the Italians back into Albania. By mid-December, the Greeks had seized a third of Albania, including the strategic Ionian port of Sarandë. After the Italian defeat, a dismayed Hitler was forced to invade Greece.

1940

December 8: Desperately outmatched, Italy pleads with Germany for assistance with its campaign against Greece.

December 10: Hitler is forced to cancel a planned invasion of Gibraltar when Spain's General Francisco Franco refuses to assist. • In London, British officials hang Jose Waldberg and Carl Meier. Both are convicted spies for Nazi Germany.

December 11: Britain recaptures the Egyptian city of Sidi Barrani from Italy following a surprise offensive of 30,000 British soldiers against a larger Italian contingent.

December 18: Hitler approves the outline for plans for a massive German invasion of the Soviet Union.

December 20: The small Dutch navy escapes in its entirety across the English Channel to safety in Britain.

December 23: Jacques Bonsergent becomes the first French citizen executed by the Nazis in Paris, following an altercation with a German officer.

December 25: With Italian bombers threatening, the town of Bethlehem is blacked out on Christmas for the first time in memory.

December 27: The *Luftwaffe* begins its firebombing of London. Over the next several days, some 20,000 British firemen will struggle to extinguish the flames.

December 28: Resource-pinched Japan begins an alternate-fuel program by which private automobiles will be powered by charcoal.

December 29: Finally abandoning America's isolationist stance, Roosevelt publicly recommends a program of direct arms aid to Great Britain.

Bombs pummel Liverpool Citizens inspect a demolished school and damaged houses after a 1940 German bombing raid on Liverpool, England. That year, Liverpool was hit with more than 300 air attacks. In addition to the well-known London Blitz, German bombers struck at industrial cities and ports all over England, Scotland, and Wales. *Luftwaffe* planes flew from Scandinavia to targets in northeastern Great Britain. The fall of France provided the Germans with new bases, putting even the shipyards and aircraft factories of Belfast, Northern Ireland, within range.

Antiquated but deadly The Fairey Swordfish torpedo bomber entered service with the British Royal Fleet's Air Arm in 1936. Although limited by a slow speed of 138 mph and armed with just two machine guns, the carrier-launched biplane had much to offer. It was highly maneuverable, had a range of more than 500 miles, and could carry either a 1,620-pound torpedo or the equivalent weight of bombs, mines, or depth charges. It flew with a two- or three-man crew. On November 11, 1940, 21 of these aircraft neutralized the Italian fleet at Taranto, Italy, knocking three battleships out of commission and inflicting serious destruction in general. Later, on May 26–27, 1941, the Swordfish also played a crucial part in the sinking of the German battleship *Bismarck*.

Benito Mussolini

ITALY'S BENITO MUSSOLINI was a Socialist journalist until the Great War made him an ardent nationalist. In Milan, Italy, in 1919, he founded the *Fasci di combattimento* (Combat Groups), the basis of the Fascist Party. By 1922 it controlled the government, and in 1925 Mussolini assumed dictatorial powers.

In foreign policy, Mussolini sought to create a new Roman empire by employing the violence and threats that were central to his domestic program. However, he did not develop armed forces capable of fulfilling this fantasy, although in 1935–36 Italian troops conquered the African country of Abyssinia. This aggressive action brought domestic acclaim and ineffective sanctions by the League of Nations. The fateful Rome-Berlin Axis followed. Mussolini consolidated his alliance with Hitler by participating in the Spanish Civil War, accepting the *Anschluss*, and facilitating the Munich Conference. Regardless, in September 1939 he declared Italy's neutrality. Only when Germany's conquest of France was imminent did he join Germany.

The war proved disastrous for Mussolini. Though Hitler accepted *"Il Duce"* as an ally, he never consulted him. Mussolini's invasion of Egypt in September 1940 ended in a costly retreat before smaller British forces. Only German general Rommel's arrival saved the Italian colony of Libya. Mussolini's botched invasion of Greece was similarly salvaged with German help, but Abyssinia was soon lost. Mussolini's forces contributed substantially to Rommel's successes in North Africa, but his renewed imperial hopes evaporated at El Alamein in Egypt.

In addition, Mussolini's fleet was decimated at Taranto, Italy, and his army in Russia was virtually destroyed after the Battle of Stalingrad. Defeat in Tunisia was followed by the invasion of Sicily in July 1943, which led Italy's Fascist Grand Council to dismiss him.

Mussolini was arrested by order of King Vittorio Emanuele III, but German paratroops rescued him in September 1943. Because Italy had just surrendered to Germany and was under Nazi occupation, Mussolini was installed as puppet ruler of the Italian Socialist Republic. With defeat inevitable, he sought to flee Italy in 1945, but partisans found and executed him and his mistress on April 28. Their defiled bodies were hung upside down in Milan's Piazzale Loreto. Throughout Italy, his death was widely celebrated.

Fascist indoctrination In Fascist Italy, boys ages six to eight joined the organization Sons of the Wolf. As seen here, their caps bore an image of a wolf suckling the twins Romulus and Remus. (According to classic mythology, Romulus founded Rome.) Italian youth organizations, like those in Nazi Germany, provided athletics and gymnastics to keep young people strong and healthy for future military service. They also indoctrinated the children in the fundamentals of fascism to assure their party loyalty.

1941

January 1: A portion of Bremen, Germany, burns out of control when nearly 100 RAF planes hit the city with firebombs.

January 2: In an early indication of the dark days to come, all Jews in the Netherlands are required to register with the authorities.

January 3: After two straight days of air assaults by the RAF, Australian ground forces capture Libya's Italian-occupied town of Bardia. • The *Luftwaffe* arrives in Albania to aid Italy's counteroffensive against Greek forces. • In an effort to encourage Irish prime minister de Valera to continue to resist Allied requests to use neutral Ireland's military bases, Germany bombs Northern Ireland three times over the course of 24 hours.

January 6: In a congressional speech that features his principle of four freedoms—of speech, of religion, from want, and from fear—President Roosevelt promotes his lend-lease plan to "act as an arsenal" and provide material support to European allies.

January 7: Japanese admiral Yamamoto puts on paper Operation Z, a scheme to attack U.S. and British military positions in Hawaii, the Philippines, Java, the central Pacific islands, and elsewhere.

January 8: In his annual budget request to Congress, Roosevelt asks for an increase in defense spending to a total of $10.8 billion for 1942.

January 9: A prototype of the British-built Avro Lancaster long-range heavy bomber makes its maiden voyage.

January 10: Britain loses control of shipping in the central Mediterranean when the *Luftwaffe* cripples the carrier *Illustrious*, which had been escorting supply convoys to Malta. Shipping routes to North Africa are now laid open for the Germans.

The Sheffield blitz Sheffield was a key British armaments center that produced everything from bayonets to armor, including crucial components of the Spitfire aircraft. Inevitably, the "Steel City" became a target of German bombing, though not at the sustained level expected. The Sheffield blitz occurred on the nights of December 12 and 15, 1940, when more than 660 people were killed and nearly 80,000 buildings damaged. The bombs fell on the city center (*pictured*) rather than the steelworks, which remained largely untouched. Though many civilians took cover in Anderson shelters, some were killed while sheltering in basements, most tragically in the Marples Hotel.

U.S. military inductions New American draftees get simultaneous injections from medical officers at Fort Dix, New Jersey. After conscription, all inductees received a smallpox vaccination and an inoculation against typhoid. Subsequently, the men went on to training and eventually were mustered into the Army. The September 1940 Selective Service Act provided for the conscription of 1.2 million troops and 800,000 reservists for a period of one year, although not more than 900,000 men were to be in training at any one time. After America entered WWII, age and service limits were extended.

U.S. Armed Forces

THE U.S. ARMED FORCES were limited in their development in the 1920s and 1930s by isolationist sentiment, disarmament, and the Great Depression. The Navy, the nation's first line of defense, suffered until President Roosevelt revitalized shipbuilding in response to unemployment, the rise of Nazism, and Japanese expansionism. The Navy's priority was battleships—central to Plan Orange, which foresaw a decisive engagement with Japan—but aircraft carriers and submarines were also constructed. By 1940 the Navy had a force of 161,000 men, while the Marines boasted 28,000.

An Army paratrooper

The U.S. Army grew considerably after September 1939, but it was not well equipped or trained for war. The U.S. Army Air Corps was reorganized in June 1941 as the U.S. Army Air Forces (USAAF), but it remained subordinate to ground commanders. In December 1941, the USAAF had about 12,000 aircraft and 350,000 men. The war would make it independent and massive.

In 1940 Roosevelt initiated a $10 billion buildup of the military. A two-ocean navy was authorized, as was the first peacetime conscription in U.S. history. By June 1941, the Army was nearly 1.5 million strong. Yet Roosevelt still insisted that the U.S. would not join the fighting, remaining instead the "Arsenal of Democracy." The initial American response to Pearl Harbor would deplete the arsenal and necessitate great changes. Fortunately for the U.S., much of the framework for future growth was already in place.

Nazi film spews anti-Semitism

This poster promotes the 1940 German film *Der ewige Jude*, known in English as *The Eternal Jew*. A viciously inaccurate anti-Semitic pseudo-documentary, the film purports to recount the history of the Jewish people. It claims that Jews had a pernicious influence on art, science, politics,

finance, sexual morality, and many other aspects of contemporary life. Frequent images of rats symbolize the infestation of Jews throughout society. The film's climax features a speech by Hitler promising the annihilation of European Jewry. Actor Peter Lorre, though pictured on the poster's lower right, does not appear in *Der ewige Jude*.

Papagos drives out Italians

On October 28, 1940, Mussolini invaded Greece from Albania, declaring that Britain had violated Greek neutrality by pledging to maintain Greek independence. An inept Italian offensive was quickly halted by the Greek army, supported by British bombing. Immediately, the Greek commander, General Alexandros Papagos (*pictured*), launched a counteroffensive

before Italian reinforcements arrived, and by early 1941 he had successfully pushed the Italians back into Albania. However, diverging national strategic priorities caused Anglo-Greek relations to deteriorate significantly after January. Then, following the successful German invasion and resulting fall of Athens on April 27, General Papagos was detained and imprisoned at Dachau until his release in 1945.

1941

January 10: The Soviets spend about $7.5 million worth of gold for a small area of southern Lithuania that had been promised to Germany but was occupied by the Red Army. • After advancing over the Albanian border in pursuit of the retreating Italian army, Greece captures the town of Klisura, near the Greek-Albanian frontier.

January 13: Hitler demands that King Boris of Bulgaria sign the Tripartite Pact, fight alongside the other members of the Axis, and allow the Germans to attack Greece from Bulgarian soil. The unstated yet obvious result of a Bulgarian denial is invasion.

January 14: Germany puts Romania on notice that the time has come for it to begin fighting alongside the other members of the Axis.

January 15: Emperor Haile Selassie returns to Ethiopia five years after he was sent into exile by an Italian occupation force.

January 19: Italy retreats in the face of a British attack on forces in Eritrea and Ethiopia on the same day that Hitler and Mussolini discuss the ongoing difficulties on the North African and Albanian fronts. Hitler agrees to send German troop support to Libya.

January 19–21: Forces controlled by Romanian dictator Ion Antonescu brutally suppress a coup attempt by the leadership of the Iron Guard.

January 21: The United States suspends its "moral embargo" on exports destined for the Soviet Union.

January 22: The Allies occupy Tobruk, Libya, in a remarkably unbalanced battle that leaves the Italians short 25,000 soldiers at the expense of 400 Australian and British casualties.

January 24: The United States denies a Vichy French request to welcome German Jewish refugees to America.

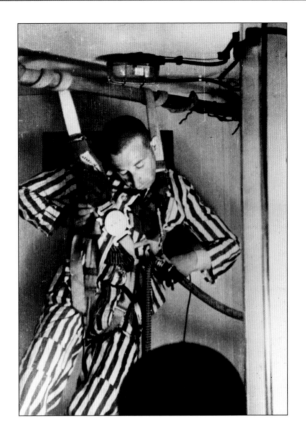

Inhumane experiments A prisoner is slumped unconscious in a harness after an experiment. Nazi doctors used concentration camp prisoners in often gruesome medical experiments, usually claiming that the results could be valuable (though most were scientifically useless). Their projects included freezing to test hypothermia treatments; testing antidotes to poisonous gases; using low-pressure chambers to determine the maximum altitude at which a human being might survive; and infecting subjects with diseases, such as malaria, to test immunizations, treatments, and the effects of diseases on different "races."

Half-tracked vehicles Engineers of half-tracked vehicles achieved mobility and agility by combining a conventional front-wheel steering system with the tracked rear drive. These vehicles were used in many roles by the Allies and the Axis, including weapon carriers, antiaircraft gun platforms, artillery prime-movers, armored personnel carriers, and recovery vehicles. The U.S. and Germany led the way in half-track development. Pictured is a U.S. M2A1 White carrier, many of which were supplied to America's allies through Lend-Lease. Meanwhile, Germany developed an extensive range of half-tracks, from the *Kettenkraftrad* motorcycle tractor to heavy-duty utility and fighting vehicles.

The still-effective Gladiator Although clearly dated, the Gladiator biplane was the RAF's principal fighter aircraft in 1938. However, its outstanding maneuverability and four machine guns could not compensate for its relatively slow maximum speed of about 250 mph. Spitfires and Hurricanes soon replaced the Gladiators in Europe, although the biplanes continued to operate in the Middle East, where they were particularly effective against the Italian air force. They also played a vital part in the defense of Malta in 1940–42.

Britain's standard-issue rifle Winston Churchill examines the .303-inch Lee-Enfield rifle, which was the standard issue rifle of the British and Commonwealth forces throughout the war. In many respects, it had changed little from its First World War predecessor. Robust, reliable, and extremely accurate—even at ranges beyond 1,000 yards—the magazine held 10 rounds of the same caliber as the British Army's Bren light machine gun and Vickers medium machine gun. Although the bolt had to be worked between shots, a trained soldier could fire 20 aimed shots per minute. The rifle's bayonet options included a traditional bladed type and a short spiked pattern.

Protectors of the homeland In Britain, Air Raid Precautions wardens (pictured during training) operated from local posts, with about 10 wardens per square mile in urban areas. They were responsible for blackout enforcement, bomb reporting, working with the emergency services, and acting as the "eyes and ears" of the Civil Defense organization. Meanwhile, the Home Guard (originally the Local Defense Volunteers) was formed in May 1940 from volunteers ineligible for regular military service. It was designed to help the regular army defeat a German invasion. It soon numbered about 1.5 million men. Although initially poorly armed and equipped, the Home Guard released regular troops from many mundane security duties, and so made a vital contribution to the nation's war effort.

Germany's need for oil In 1938 Germany was already naturally deficient in 20 of 26 strategic raw materials, including oil and crude petroleum—the lifeblood of modern warfare. Consequently (especially after imposition of the Allied blockade in 1939), the Axis depended upon supplies from the Soviet Union and Axis conquests to provide the natural resources essential to its war aims and industries. This image, dated January 28, 1941, apparently shows German soldiers using a pedal car in order "to save petrol." However, Germany did not suffer catastrophic fuel shortages until 1944, when the Allies heavily bombed Germany's oil producing and refining plants.

1941

January 26: Japan's imperialist plans are evident when Foreign Minister Yosuke Matsuoka calls for a "new order" in Asia.

January 27: Joseph Grew, the American ambassador in Tokyo, passes on to Washington a rumor that Japan is planning a surprise attack on the U.S. naval base at Pearl Harbor, Hawaii.

January 29: Representatives from the United States and Britain secretly meet in Washington to discuss joint military strategy if the U.S. is forced into war.

January 30: In an effort to cut the British supply chain, Germany threatens to torpedo any neutral ship carrying supplies to Allied troops.

January 31: The government of Turkey denies Churchill's request to station 10 squadrons of RAF planes and pilots on Turkish soil.

February 1: Recognizing a need to protect merchant ships in the Atlantic, the U.S. Navy creates the Atlantic Fleet, with Rear Admiral Ernest J. King commanding.

February 8: The Lend-Lease Bill, designed to provide a framework through which the United States can assist the Allies while maintaining neutrality, passes the House of Representatives. It will pass the Senate on March 8.

February 14: Roosevelt cautions Yugoslavia's Prince Paul against aligning with Germany on the same day that Hitler sends an ultimatum demanding cooperation.

February 15: The Nazi administration in Austria inaugurates its plan to deport Austrian Jews to Polish ghettos.

Park "wins" Battle of Britain
RAF Commander Keith Park led air protection and reconnaissance during the Dunkirk evacuation and during the Battle of Britain. In 1947 Lord Tedder, chief of the Royal Air Force, said of Park, "If any one man won the Battle of Britain, he did." Even though Park was rewarded for his service with the Order of Commander of the Bath, he was removed from command during rancorous debates about his conservative tactics. Beginning in July 1942, Sir Park saw action in Malta, Italy, and Sicily, and then as commander of Allied forces in the Middle East. Park is often referred to as the "Savior of Britain."

The *Bismarck* sinks the *Hood* The German battleship *Bismarck* fires toward the British battle cruiser *Hood* on May 24, 1941. According to Lieutenant Esmond Knight, who witnessed the attack while on the British *Prince of Wales*, "a great spouting explosion issued from the centre of the *Hood*, enormous reaching tongues of pale-red flame shot into the air, while dense clouds of whitish-yellow smoke burst upwards, gigantic pieces of brightly burning debris being hurled hundreds of feet in the air.... *Hood* had literally been blown to pieces." Of the *Hood*'s crew of more than 1,400 men, only three survived.

Sinking of the *Bismarck* After sinking the *Hood* on May 24, 1941, and seriously damaging the *Prince of Wales*, the German battleship *Bismarck* (*pictured*) slipped away. British crews eagerly tried to catch the *Bismarck*, but with their ships running low on fuel, the British despaired of catching Germany's magnificent menace. Then, on May 26, a Royal Air Force flying boat spotted the *Bismarck* heading for the French coast. British torpedo planes slowed the German ship down, but then lost it again. At last the *Bismarck*—damaged, unable to steer properly, and off course—was relocated. On the 27th, it was encircled by Royal Navy battleships and cruisers. In the battle that followed, the *Bismarck* was sunk.

British trounce Italy in North Africa Following their defeat at the hands of Britain's Western Desert Force in February 1941, 130,000 Italian troops were sent to POW camps. Although Italian general Berti's 10th Army was much larger than the British force when it set out to invade Egypt in September 1940, its divisions were ill-equipped and poorly trained for mobile armored warfare. Inevitably, a succession of telling defeats followed: Sidi Barrani in December, Bardia and Tobruk in January 1941, and Beda Fomm in February 1942. Only the arrival of German support presaged a change in Axis fortunes.

Germany's "Desert Fox" General Erwin Rommel (*left*) probably was the best-known German military commander of the war. Rommel, the "Desert Fox," was a highly professional and popular officer, widely admired throughout Germany and generally respected by most of the Allies who fought against him. Rommel's greatest successes were in North Africa, where from February 1941 his *Deutsches Afrika Korps* (DAK) pushed the British steadily eastward from Libya into Egypt. He won a succession of battles and famously captured Tobruk, Libya, on June 21, 1942—although he would be defeated at El Alamein later that year.

Italy's inept air force Despite possessing some reasonably capable combat aircraft, such as this Macchi C.200 fighter, Italy's air force was in a perilous state. Even with twice as many airplanes as the British, it was easily overwhelmed during the desert campaign in Cyrenaica in 1940. Endemic inefficiency, excessive bureaucracy, and the exclusion of air force officers and experts from the aircraft selection and development process all contributed to the failure of Italian airpower.

1941

February 19: Nomura Kichisaburo, the Japanese ambassador to the U.S., asserts that any war between Japan and the United States would occur only at America's discretion.

February 20: El Agheila, Libya, is the site of the first desert battle between the British and German armies.

February 22: Some 400 Jews a week perish of starvation in the Warsaw Ghetto, a grim figure that will not improve with the enforcement of the new daily bread ration of three ounces per adult.

February 24: Hitler reports great success in the Battle of the Atlantic, claiming that in the past 48 hours alone, Germany has sunk British cargo weighing more than 200,000 tons. • Despite British pleas, the United States will not be sending any ships to protect the territory of Singapore against Japanese aggression in the East.

February 25: Advocates for the Netherlands's Jews are silenced by the SS, which puts an end to public demonstrations objecting to Jewish persecution.

February 26: The Nazi occupation government in northern Holland declares martial law in the wake of a series of attacks on Germans—attacks that the Nazis claim were perpetrated by Jews.

February–March: British troops take a heavy toll on Italian forces at Cyrenaica, Ethiopia, and elsewhere in Africa.

March 1: Auschwitz commandant Rudolf Höss is informed that he will receive 130,000 prisoners for his new camp, 10,000 of whom will be forced into slave labor at the IG Farben company's synthetic rubber plant.

March 2: One day after Bulgaria's King Boris III is coerced into accepting Hitler's terms and joins the Axis, the German army marches into Bulgaria.

Germans score victories in Libya German general Rommel's preemptive strike into Cyrenaica, the eastern coastal region of Libya, in March 1941 was a strategic masterstroke. Although parts of his *Afrika Korps* were still forming, he had judged correctly that the British and Commonwealth forces were exhausted after their successful campaign against the Italians, and that they believed no German offensive was possible before May. Accordingly, within a week of arriving in North Africa in February, German troops (*pictured*) were reconnoitering their opponents' positions. The Libyan towns of El Agheila and Mersa Brega fell on March 24 and April 1, respectively, and Tobruk, Libya, was besieged. Meanwhile, Italian morale was restored and all the British successes of 1940–41 reversed.

Legendary U-boat commander German U-boat commander Otto Kretschmer perfected "silent running," slipping his submarine into the midst of a convoy before attacking. His refusal to radio his base annoyed his superiors, as did his reluctance to broadcast Nazi propaganda. In 1940 Kretschmer and his *U-99* famously needed just one torpedo for each target. He sank 47 Allied merchant ships (more than 270,000 tons). Captured by the British in March 1941, Kretschmer spent seven years as a POW. After the war, he served as a commanding officer in the newly formed German navy and as a chief of staff of a NATO command.

Bulgaria forced to join the Axis At the outset of World War II, the Balkan nation of Bulgaria was torn between its longtime friendship with Russia and threats from the Axis powers. Matters came to a head after Mussolini's ill-fated 1940 invasion of Greece, which lay along Bulgaria's southern border. In early March 1941, Bulgaria joined the Axis bloc and Germany launched its own invasion of Greece from the small country. In this photograph, Bulgarian villagers greet German forces.

Jews as animals Hitler predicted genetic catastrophe if Jews were allowed to marry non-Jews. The title of the children's book seen here, *Der Pudelmopsdack-elpinscher,* describes the genetically absurd poodle-pug-daschsund-pinscher mutt that adorns the cover. The title can be usefully translated as *The Mongrel.* As written by Ernst Hiemer (No. 2 man to

Der Stürmer publisher Julius Streicher) and illustrated by Willi Hofman, this collection of 11 fable-like vignettes about lazy, parasitic hyenas, serpents, locusts, tapeworms, and others links each creature, via supposedly scientific epilogues, to the innately pernicious Jews, who must be destroyed.

The Halifax heavy bomber In March 1941, the RAF employed the Handley Page Halifax heavy bomber on its first operational mission with a successful raid on Le Havre, France. Due to ever-improving Axis air defenses, the Halifaxes were later confined to night bombing. However, with its seven-man crew, five machine guns, a bomb load of more than 13,000 pounds, a maximum speed of 308 mph, and a range of 1,260 miles, the Halifax was a mainstay of the Allied strategic bombing campaign throughout the war.

Commandos raid Norwegian islands On March 4, 1941, a British commando raid on the Norwegian Lofoten Islands left behind burning fish-oil factories and smoldering oil dumps, as seen here from the destroyer HMS *Legion.* Landing in intense cold, the invaders met little resistance to their surprise attack, known as Operation Claymore. The commandos took some 200 German prisoners, recruited more than 300 Norwegian volunteers, captured encryption equipment and codebooks, and destroyed several enemy ships— and were ready to leave the island by midday. The success of this first major Special Forces operation raised the morale of the commandos and the British public alike.

1941

March 5: Britain breaks all diplomatic ties with Bulgaria.

March 6: In his Battle of the Atlantic Directive, Churchill underscores the importance of neutralizing U-boats and aerial assaults on British shipping. • British shipping in the Mediterranean faces a new obstacle, as Germany begins to pepper the Suez Canal with aircraft-delivered acoustic magnetic mines.

March 12: Roosevelt asks Congress for $7 billion in military credits to Britain under the new Lend-Lease law.

March 13: Realizing that success in Greece is dependent on an ability to move troops through Yugoslavia, Hitler steps up pressure on the Yugoslav government to join the Axis. • Glasgow, Scotland, is hit by its first significant air raid of the war. More than 230 *Luftwaffe* planes hit the Scottish city with hundreds of tons of explosives and tens of thousands of incendiary devices.

March 20: U.S. undersecretary of state Sumner Welles informs the Soviet ambassador of an intelligence report with the plan for the German attack on the Soviet Union.

March 23: German U-boats are dominating the Battle of the Atlantic, sinking more than 59,000 tons of British shipping in the past week alone.

March 25: In advance of any action in the Baltic States, some 60,000 ethnically German people from Latvia, Estonia, and Lithuania have been resettled on German territory. • Facing German occupation, Yugoslavia formally joins the Axis and agrees to the provisions of the Tripartite Pact.

March 27: Yugoslavia throws a wrench into Hitler's plans when military officers, demanding a neutral Yugoslavia, overthrow the government that capitulated to the Axis, and place a teenaged King Peter II on the throne.

Scotland takes heavy hits
Because Clydebank, Scotland, with its vast areas of dock-land, lay so far north, its citizens dared to hope that they were safely beyond the range of German bombers. However, on the nights of March 13–14 and 14–15, they were disabused of any such hopes when 400 bombers dropped more than 500 tons of high-explosive bombs and 2,400 incendiaries on Clyde-bank. In addition to devastating the docks, only eight of 12,000 houses escaped damage. Approximately 35,000 people became homeless and more than 1,000 were killed. The resulting fires were visible 100 miles away.

Battle of Cape Matapan A Royal Navy Fairey Fulmar flies air cover over the British fleet at the Battle of Cape Matapan off Crete on March 27–29, 1941. The combined force of British Royal Navy and Australian Navy ships protecting convoys bound for Greece engaged an Italian naval force. The heaviest fighting occurred after dark on March 28. Aided by radar, which the Italian ships lacked, British warships sent three enemy heavy cruisers and two destroyers to the bottom with heavy loss of life. Britain lost only a single torpedo bomber. After the battle, the Italians temporarily conceded the eastern Mediterranean to the British, who could now concentrate more on the fighting in North Africa.

Italy's Incursions in East Africa

IN 1935 ITALY INVADED and occupied the independent kingdom of Ethiopia, forcing Emperor Haile Selassie into exile in Britain. Italy's entry into World War II in June 1940 brought Italian East Africa into a theater of war.

That summer, the Italians attacked the British colonies of the Sudan and Kenya and occupied British Somaliland. British (mainly African and Indian) forces faced a larger and apparently better equipped Italian army, though the Italians were cut off from resupply because of Britain's hold on Egypt.

Late in 1940, British forces advanced into Abyssinia from eastern Sudan and from northern Kenya. Meanwhile, the "Gideon Force" (British, Sudanese, and Ethiopian soldiers) under the charismatic Orde Wingate fought a guerrilla war against the Italian occupation troops. Despite early setbacks (due largely to Italian air superiority), the British soon gained the initiative thanks to the code-breakers of Bletchley Park, who read Italian messages.

Italy's fortunes continued to wane. On the Red Sea coast, British naval forces from Aden retook British Soma-

The Italian Camel Corps, in Libya

liland. In March 1941, the Italians decisively lost the Battle of Keren in mountainous terrain in Eritrea. Also, Wingate's troops achieved striking success in central Abyssinia. In early April, a British-Indian-African and South African force advancing from Kenya entered the Abyssinian city of Addis Ababa. By the end of the year, the isolated Italian forces had to surrender.

Italy wins, loses Abyssinia In 1936 Benito Mussolini's expansionist ambitions resulted in Italy's defeat of Abyssinia (present-day Ethiopia) and the exile of Emperor Haile Selassie. A repressive Italian regime ensued, prompting increasing civil unrest. Meanwhile, beginning in 1940, Abyssinia provided a strategic base for Italy's successful operations against Sudan, Kenya, and British Somaliland. Accordingly, although heavily outnumbered, British and Commonwealth forces launched their East African Campaign in November 1940, decisively defeating the Italian occupiers by April 1941. Abyssinian troops (*pictured*) played an important part in the campaign.

1941

March 28: The Italian fleet is decimated and nearly 2,500 sailors die when the British sink three of its cruisers and two destroyers at the Battle of Cape Matapan. • The Eagle Squadron, comprised of American pilots operating under the British flag, is ready for battle. • Plutonium-239, a uranium isotope that will prove critical in the development of nuclear weapons, is discovered by a team of American physicists.

March 29: The Royal Navy traps Italian warships in waters between Greece and Crete. Three Italian cruisers are sunk and an important Italian battleship, *Vittorio Veneto*, is badly damaged.

March 30: The U.S. Navy commandeers ships flying the flags of Axis nations stationed in ports across the United States.

April 2–3: Count Teleki, the prime minister of Hungary, takes his own life because Hungary is joining Germany in an invasion of Yugoslavia, with which he had signed a non-aggression treaty.

April 3: Stafford Cripps, the British ambassador to Moscow, delivers a warning to Stalin from Churchill that an attack on the Soviet Union by Nazi Germany could happen any day.

April 4: Under pressure from the advancing Allies, the Italians abandon the Ethiopian capital of Addis Ababa. South African troops will occupy the city for the Allies on the 6th. • Hitler assures Japanese leaders that Germany will fight the United States if Japan attacks the U.S. in the Pacific.

April 5: The Soviet air force test-flies its new MiG-3 fighter for the first time. • The gulf between Hitler and Stalin grows when Yugoslavia signs a nonaggression treaty with the Soviets, drawing the ire of the Germans.

British unwelcome in Iraq Indian troops guard an Iraqi oil refinery in 1941. Iraq had been independent since 1932, but Britain retained privileges there. The British maintained air bases at Habbaniya and Basra, had the right to pass troops through Iraq, and held commercial interest in oil refineries. The wartime government was initially pro-British, but on April 3, 1941, pro-Axis Rashid Ali El-Ghailani became prime minister following a coup. Britain dispatched a brigade to Basra, but Rashid Ali refused entry to further brigades until it left. Iraqi troops surrounded Habbaniya, but British aircraft and the garrison defeated them by early May. British reinforcements arrived, and Rashid Ali fled to Germany.

Hitler turns rage toward Yugoslavia On March 25, 1941, Yugoslavia's regent, Prince Paul, signed an important treaty with Germany. But on March 27, Prince Paul's countrymen overthrew him and rejected the agreement. Hitler became enraged and decided to destroy Yugoslavia. On April 6, he launched a four-pronged land invasion of the Balkan nation, along with a merciless air attack against the country's nearly defenseless capital of Belgrade. Within 11 days, Yugoslavia had fallen. Hitler's brutality—including the slaughter of villagers like those seen here—inspired an effective Yugoslav guerrilla movement against Axis occupiers.

British Colonial Soldiers

COLONIAL SOLDIERS DEFENDED and extended the British Empire as early as the 18th century, with the volunteer, professional Indian Army proving its worth during the Great War. From the beginning to end of World War II, this combined force expanded from 200,000 men to 2.5 million.

Indian divisions served in the Middle East, North Africa, Italy, Malaya, and Singapore, and constituted the bulk of British forces in Burma. Increasingly mechanized and led by Indians at battalion level, they formed the basis of what would be the regular post-independence armies of India and Pakistan. Large numbers of Gurkhas (brave warriors from Nepal) and the traditional "martial races" volunteered, but the British Indian Army also recruited across India's ethnic spectrum.

Colonial troops generally remained loyal. However, the Burma Rifles proved unreliable, while gunners of the Ceylon Garrison Artillery mutinied on the Cocos Islands in 1942. Moreover, the Indian Army's rapid expansion in 1940–41 led to demoralization and disasters in Malaya. It also led to the loss of about 40,000 men who surrendered in Singapore to the Japanese, who subsequently assigned them to the Japanese-controlled Indian National Army. However, the Indian Army remained "loyal to its salt" despite defeats as well as famine and nationalist unrest in India itself.

Colonial troops from India and Africa

African soldiers from British colonial possessions served against the Italians in East Africa. From 1943, East and West African divisions fought the Japanese in Burma. Led by British officers, they gained a reputation for toughness. Military service gave African soldiers wider horizons, transforming the political expectations of Britain's African colonies. Within two decades, these colonies would gain independence.

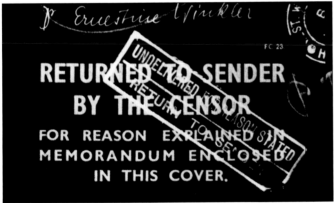

Censorship For national security reasons, this British document was returned to sender by the official censor. In Britain and its empire, censorship was applied to citizens' and servicemen's mail, as it was to the press, to eliminate references to military movements and other secrets that might help the enemy. American abhorrence of censorship ensured a milder approach, though Roosevelt established an Office of Censorship in 1941. The USSR and Axis states claimed a monopoly of information even before the war.

The formidable Indian Army In 1939 the British Empire's all-professional Indian army included about 200,000 Indian and British troops. Of its roughly 4,000 officers, some 400 were Indian. The army

included many tribal, cultural, and religious groupings, including Sikh machine-gunners (*pictured*). It was generally based upon the British model, albeit that of some years earlier. Consequently, its soldiers initially lacked some modern equipment and weaponry. By 1945 this army increased to 2.5 million men, with 8,300 Indian and 34,500 British officers. Its soldiers had provided exceptionally loyal and brave service in many theaters, including Southern Europe, Burma, and North Africa.

1941

April 5: General Rommel's *Afrika Korps* and Italian forces drive eastward against Libya, forcing a British retreat.

April 6: A four-front attack overwhelms Yugoslavia, as the German army storms the country from Bulgaria, Romania, Hungary, and Austria. Belgrade, the capital, is destroyed and thousands are killed when the Germans initiate their invasion with a Sunday attack.
• Germany attacks Greece by way of Bulgaria.

April 7: London severs all ties to Budapest, as Hungary is now wholly under the influence of Nazi Germany.
• Britain's plans to help defend Greece are complicated when *Luftwaffe* bombers blow up a ship packed with explosives in the port of Piraeus, damaging critical port infrastructure in the process.

April 9: Concerned that Berlin has designs on bases in Greenland, the United States obtains the rights to provide military protection to the remote but strategically located island.
• In Croatia, a pro-German region of Yugoslavia, Germany and Italy create a puppet state as German troops approach the Croatian capital of Zagreb.

April 9–10: Berlin is badly damaged and the State Opera House is gutted during a large RAF attack on the city.

April 10: Rommel begins a siege of Allied positions at Tobruk, Libya.
• The USS *Niblack*, a destroyer on a rescue mission off the coast of Iceland, drops depth charges near a German submarine. The incident is the first case of American hostile fire directed at a German ship.

April 12: A German panzer corps takes the Serbian capital of Belgrade, Yugoslavia, while the Croatian people of Zagreb welcome the German army invasion.

German troops storm Greece Hitler had no desire to conquer Greece in 1941. However, after Mussolini's imprudent invasion of the eastern Mediterranean nation failed early in 1941, the *Führer* had no choice but to come to his partner's rescue. On April 6, 1941, the Germans launched their invasion of Greece from Bulgaria, which had recently joined the Axis. Pictured here are German troops crossing the Pineios River in the Greek region of Thessaly, using boats and a makeshift bridge. By May 11, mainland Greece and all of its surrounding islands except Crete were fully under Axis occupation. Some 50,000 British troops were forced to hastily evacuate Greece.

Athens falls to Germany The Greek army, exhausted from fighting the Italians and struggling to control its newly seized areas in Albania, could not stand up against Hitler's forces. Here, German troops drive past government buildings in Athens after the city fell on April 27. Hitler's operation in Greece forced him to delay his planned invasion of the Soviet Union, leading to a fatally disastrous winter campaign there.

Conscientious Objectors

IN SEPTEMBER 1940, the U.S. Congress passed the Selective Service Act. The nation's first peacetime draft, it called for the registration of all male citizens from 21 to 35 years of age. The act also addressed the issue of conscientious objection. In order to qualify prior to the Second World War, one would have to prove to his local draft board that he belonged to a pacifist religious sect, such as the Mennonites or Quakers. With the passage of the 1940 law, the definition was broadened to include objections based on "religious training and belief." Most of the Allied nations used similar criteria.

In the U.S., those designated conscientious objectors (COs) were placed in one of three categories: those agreeing to enter the military in a noncombatant role, such as medics; those willing to join the Civilian Public Service; and those refusing to take part in any military or alternative service. About 25,000 COs agreed to serve as noncombatants, including Desmond Doss, who would win the Congressional Medal of Honor as a medic. About 12,000 worked in public projects during the war, and 6,000 were sent to prison for failure to cooperate with the draft board.

Smokejumpers (COs who battled forest fires)

The Soviet Union and the Axis nations did not acknowledge conscientious objection and publicly boasted that none of their countrymen opposed military service. Secretly, any dissenters were thrown into prison, where many were executed.

Germans take Crete

German paratroopers capture British soldiers on the Greek island of Crete. After its successful invasion of mainland Greece, Germany launched Operation Merkur, an airborne invasion of Crete, on May 20, 1941. Despite suffering horrific losses, German paratroopers seized the island's Maleme airfield, ensuring the invasion's success. Allied troops from Britain, Australia, and New Zealand were forced to evacuate Crete on June 1, 1941, leaving the island under Axis control. With almost 7,000 casualties, the German victory was so costly that Hitler chose never again to launch an airborne invasion.

1941

April 13: Confident that there will be no German invasion, Stalin shores up his eastern frontier with the signing of a Japanese-Soviet neutrality pact.

April 14: With supply lines stretched to the limit, Rommel's *Afrika Korps* is forced to halt its stunning advance across Libya, just beyond Tobruk.
• Egypt's King Farouk secretly tells Hitler that he would welcome a German invasion force and expulsion of the British.

April 16: Representatives of the United States and Japan meet in Washington to resolve their differences. Roosevelt opens the talks by laying out what he sees as four critical points in international relations: territorial integrity, noninterference, equal opportunity for commerce, and stability in the Pacific.

April 20: Greece surrenders to the Axis the day after Prime Minister Alexander Korizis commits suicide in despair.

April 22: Germany's newly formed *Afrika Korps*, comprised of two army divisions, arrives in Tripoli, Libya, to aid the foundering Italian army in North Africa.

April 26: Rommel's *Afrika Korps* advances, forcing the British to back out of Libya and into Egypt.

April 30: The Nazi Party bans the display of the crucifix in schools across Bavaria, inciting anger through this deeply Catholic region of southern Germany. The crucifixes will be restored.

May 1941: SS *Reichsführer* Heinrich Himmler decrees that writing one's name, simple arithmetic, and obedience to Germans is all the education needed for the non-German, eastern population of the conquered territories.

"If only he would drown in the North Sea! Then he would vanish without a trace, and we could work out some harmless explanation at our leisure."

—ADOLF HITLER, MAY 21, 1941, AFTER LEARNING OF THE UNAUTHORIZED "PEACE FLIGHT" TO GREAT BRITAIN OF HIS DEPUTY, RUDOLF HESS

Hess crashes in Scotland On May 10, 1941, German official Rudolf Hess (*right*) made an unauthorized visit to Britain. He was arrested after he broke his ankle in a parachute jump from his Messerschmitt, which crashed (*below*) just south of Glasgow, Scotland. Hess, whose German title of deputy *Führer* put him in charge of the Nazi Party apparatus, was on a solo mission. He said he wanted to negotiate a peace in which Britain would be safe from attack if it gave Germany a free hand in Europe. Dismissed as insane by the British and Hitler, Hess remained in Allied imprisonment until his death in 1987.

German magazine woos Europeans In March 1943, *Life* magazine declared, "The deadliest weapon in the vast Axis propaganda arsenal is *Signal* . . . a German twice-a-month picture magazine patterned after *LIFE*." *Signal* was a modern, attractive, oversized magazine that downplayed social and political differences among European nations, promoted their "common cause" against Bolshevism, and encouraged a new order referred to as *Pax Germanica*. Published from 1940 to 1945 in 25 languages, *Signal* reached a circulation of 2.5 million copies per issue—making it the most popular propaganda publication in wartime Europe.

Bombs destroy House of Commons Winston Churchill examines the remains of the House of Commons, destroyed by bombs dropped on the night of May 10, 1941. The raid was architecturally the most damaging to London. The Westminster Abbey and Lambeth Palace were also harmed. Westminster Palace, of which the Commons was part, was hit many times during the war, but remained in use throughout. The House of Commons continued to meet in the chamber of the House of Lords, while the lords met elsewhere.

Germany forced to ration food Even after war began in 1939, Hitler did not want to enforce rationing. He believed that shortages of food and other goods had contributed to the so-called "stab in the back," which he felt had caused Germany's loss of World War I. After invading Poland and other European countries, Germany ruthlessly exploited them to keep Germany well supplied. But after Germany began to experience military failures, especially the catastrophic 1941 invasion of the USSR, rationing became a necessity. Rationing cards such as these—which entitled bearers to meat, eggs, and bread—were complicated. Rationing efforts were far more successful in Britain than in Germany.

Britain takes control in Iraq In May 1941, British forces rolled into Baghdad to bring about regime change. For the rest of the war, Iraqi officials cooperated with the British. However, many historians believe that the easy British victory heightened both Arab nationalism and Islamic fundamentalism. Especially troubling to the British were the intrigues of Grand Mufti Muhammed Amin al-Husseini—a man of deceptively gentle manners and soothing voice. The grand mufti was a favorite of Hitler, for whom he recruited Muslim soldiers.

1941

May 2: The pro-Axis government of Iraq calls for German assistance as Britain occupies Basra and its surrounding oil fields.

May 5: Though apprised by Tokyo of the fact that Japan's secret Purple code is most likely compromised, the Japanese ambassador to the United States determines that is not the case, and makes no changes to the code.

May 7: Stalin is named Soviet premier by the *Politburo*. • The German vessel *München* is captured in the North Atlantic, with a complete cipher book on board. Two days later, Royal Navy divers will access a sunken German U-boat that includes an Enigma machine complete with rotor settings and another cipher book. These discoveries will lead the Allies to break the Enigma code and change the course of the Battle of the Atlantic for several months.

May 10: In a bizarre incident, third-ranking Nazi Rudolf Hess flies to Scotland solo and parachutes into British custody, claiming that he is there to negotiate peace with Britain. Hitler suggests that Hess has taken leave of his senses.

May 10–11: London is hit with its most intense *Luftwaffe* bombing raid of the war. Nearly 1,500 lives are lost, and landmarks such as the British Museum, House of Commons, and Westminster Abbey are badly damaged.

May 12: The British Army in North Africa, desperately short on materiel, is given a new lease on life when a British convoy reaches Alexandria, Egypt, with some 240 tanks and 40 Hurricanes.

May 14: Some 3,600 Jews are arrested and detained in Paris by the occupying Nazi Gestapo.

U.S. funds Soviet war effort Harry Hopkins, who was instrumental in developing the U.S. Lend-Lease program, was one of President Roosevelt's most trusted diplomatic advisers. In June 1941, Hopkins met with Winston Churchill, then went on a mission to Moscow. He carried a letter in which Roosevelt asked how the U.S. could most effectively "make available the assistance which the United States can render to your country in its magnificent resistance to the treacherous aggression by Hitlerite Germany. . . . " Following negotiations, FDR extended up to $1 billion lend-lease credit to the Soviet Union.

Panic in Chungking
Corpses litter the stairs to an air raid shelter in Chungking, China. The deceased were victims of a mass panic during a Japanese air raid in June 1941; more than 4,000 died after ventilators in the shelter broke down. Despite this tragedy, the provisional capital of Chungking was better prepared than most Chinese cities to survive enemy air attacks. Civilians there could take refuge in a network of caves and tunnels. Most other cities offered no protection from air attack. With little opposition in the skies, the Japanese repeatedly bombed Chinese cities, killing tens of thousands of civilians and leaving untold numbers homeless.

China's Eighth Route Army

CHINA'S EIGHTH ROUTE ARMY was the main fighting force of the Chinese Communist Party. Comprised of regular troops (as opposed to local forces and part-time militia), it served in North China as part of the so-called United Front of Communists and Nationalists.

Zhu De was the Eighth Route Army's military leader, while its political leader was Mao Zedong, who chaired the party's Military Affairs Committee. Though it was nominally part of the Chinese National Army, the Eighth Route Army's leaders never considered it bound by that force's orders. Moscow directed Eighth Army leaders to cooperate with Nationalist forces, but Mao and his subordinates disobeyed, and they continued their guerrilla war against the troops of anti-Communist Chiang Kai-shek. Chiang was unable to defeat the Eighth Route Army, but in 1941 he did crush the other major Communist force, the New Fourth Army, which was previously active in central China.

While the Eighth Route Army fought a guerrilla war against the Japanese, much of its energies were devoted to positioning itself against the Nationalist central army. Generally, its men had better training and higher morale

Chinese Communist troops, armed with American Thompson guns

than their Nationalist counterparts in the Central Army. However, they lacked heavy equipment and lived primarily off the land. Strictly enforced prohibitions on rapacious behavior helped the Communists' popular image. The army grew in size from 30,000 in 1937 to 600,000 in 1945.

China's Communist armies Zhu De (*left*), the Eighth Route Army's military leader, meets with that army's political leader, Mao Zedong. The New Fourth Army and the Eighth Route Army were the two most significant Chinese Communist forces during the war. The Fourth operated south of the Yangtze River; the Eighth operated in the northwest. The Fourth Army was supposed to represent a united front by Communists and Nationalists against Japan. This tenuous cooperation collapsed in 1940, and the Fourth Army suffered heavy losses fighting with the Nationalists. The Fourth was reorganized and remained in the war, and it later helped drive the Nationalists from the Chinese mainland.

1941

May 15: Sigmund Rascher, a doctor, *Luftwaffe* captain, and associate of Himmler, requests permission to use Dachau prisoners as test subjects for his medical experiments. He will become known especially for his hypothermia experiments, which will take 300 lives.

May 15: Roosevelt places 11 French ships in U.S. ports under U.S. jurisdiction due to Vichy France's compliance with the Nazis.

May 19: In gratitude, and as an incentive to continue its cooperation and collaboration, Germany releases 100,000 French prisoners and reduces the reparations payments it has demanded from the Vichy government.

May 20: In a spectacular but costly air assault on Crete, Germans drop nearly 23,000 paratroopers and glider soldiers onto its northwest coast. While succeeding in taking the island, the German death toll will be unacceptably high. • The Nazi central office of immigration forbids any future emigration of French Jews.

May 22: Fearing that Germany will attempt to seize the strategically critical Azores, Roosevelt calls for U.S. military occupation of these Atlantic islands.

May 24: The British battleship *Prince of Wales* and the cruiser *Hood* encounter the German battleship *Bismarck* and cruiser *Prinz Eugen* in the Denmark Strait. A ferocious, 20-minute gun battle ensues, ending with the sinking of the *Hood* and the deaths of 1,416 crewmen.

May 27: President Roosevelt, noting that the struggle in Europe has become a "war for world domination," suggests that any German occupation of either the Cape Verde Islands or the Azores would threaten U.S. security and draw a commensurate response.

America's helping hand The Lend-Lease program, promoted by President Roosevelt, is typically associated with America's provision of tanks, aircraft, trucks, and munitions to its allies. However, the program also encompassed a whole range of raw materials, agricultural products, foodstuffs, and related services, totaling about $50 billion by 1945. These children pictured in a northern English city during a lull in the Blitz eat sandwiches that contain cheese that came from the USA. Lend-Lease was a lifeline for a Britain under siege in 1940–41 and a significant public morale booster. It also demonstrated the practical benefits of the special Anglo-U.S. relationship.

U.S. arms the British Large quantities of U.S.-made Thompsons were purchased for the British Army in 1940–41, quickly filling the serious capability gap revealed during the *Blitzkrieg* of 1940. The Thompson M1 submachine gun—with a 20-round box magazine and a rate of fire of 700 rounds per minute—provided a useful short-range assault weapon for many combat and specialist troops. The M1 would be superseded by much lighter and cheaper submachine guns, including the American M3 "Grease Gun" and the British Sten Gun.

U.S. breaks Japan's Purple code This machine, constructed in 1940 by U.S. cryptanalysts, was used to read "Purple," the Japanese diplomatic code (not, it should be noted, the Japanese naval code). Purple offered millions of cipher combinations. The Japanese considered the system unbreakable, but they made the mistake of phasing it in gradually while still employing the previous "Red" code, which U.S. intelligence had been reading for some time. The overlap helped U.S. cryptanalysts break the Purple code and reproduce the machine, which employed telephone stepping switches rather than the more traditional rotor system. The cryptanalysts were hailed as "magicians," and the intelligence derived from reading Purple was known as "Magic."

Germany's recycling program Rearmament in the 1930s had depleted Germany's already low stocks of strategic resources, including most of the metals needed for weapons construction. Then, from 1939, the Allied sea blockade made Germany even more dependent upon acquiring raw and recycled materials from its newly conquered territories. Accordingly, the reclamation of metal from any available source, including this statue of French politician Marquis de Condorcet in Paris in 1941, was an important part of Germany's war effort.

American code-breaker Colonel William F. Friedman was the U.S. War Department's chief cryptanalyst, heading the team that broke the Japanese diplomatic ("Purple") code. Friedman was born in Russia, but his father immigrated to the United States to escape growing anti-Semitism when Friedman was still a child. A graduate of Cornell University, Friedman went to work for a Chicago research laboratory, where he became interested in codes and ciphers. He entered the Army in 1918 and is credited with introducing mathematical and scientific methodology to cryptology. His wife, Elizabeth, was also a gifted code-breaker and is buried next to him at Arlington National Cemetery.

Japanese barbarity Japanese troops execute Chinese civilians in a scene repeated countless times during the war. Japanese barbarity toward the Chinese stemmed from a sense of racial superiority, as well as frustration with persistent Chinese resistance to the occupation. Japanese soldiers commonly used live civilians, and Chinese and British prisoners of war, for bayonet practice. Officers decapitated prisoners for sport, even holding contests. One Japanese officer recalled that "if more than two weeks went by without my taking a head, I didn't feel right." An estimated 10 million Chinese civilians died at Japanese hands during the war.

1941

May 27: The battleship *Bismarck*, pride of the Nazi fleet, is sunk by British warships with most of its 2,000-man crew aboard.

May 31: Britain once again assumes control of Iraq following the implosion of its pro-Axis government.

June 1941: A series of attacks by Croatians against their Serbian countrymen in the newly created pro-Axis state of Croatia leaves hundreds dead.

June 1: Britain completes the evacuation of Crete.

June 2: Perhaps reevaluating his alliance with the inept Mussolini, Hitler declines to alert Mussolini of his plans to attack Russia when the two Fascist leaders meet at the Brenner Pass.

June 3: Hundreds of Jews are murdered, and their shops looted, in a series of riots in the streets of Baghdad.

June 6: Hitler issues his "Guidelines for the Conduct of the Troops in Russia." One provision, known as the *Kommissarbefehl*, calls for the execution of any captured Soviet commissars.

June 8–9: Free French and British forces drive deep into Syria.

June 11: Roosevelt agrees to send U.S. troops to man a British garrison in Iceland. The move will free a British division to be reassigned to a more critical war zone, without exposing U.S. troops to a combat situation.

June 12: In an agreement designed to strengthen the alliance, 14 Allied nations make a pact in which they agree to neither make nor honor separate treaties with any of the Axis nations.

June 14: Soviet foreign minister Molotov shrugs off intelligence indicating that Germany has Russia in its crosshairs, famously claiming that "only a fool would attack Russia."

"**Through the windscreen I could see fifteen German bombers approaching from the west. They were flying low, with provocative insolence, as though our sky belonged to them.**"

—SOVIET GENERAL IVAN BOLDIN, DESCRIBING GERMANY'S INVASION OF RUSSIA ON JUNE 22, 1941

German soldiers ready for action "The world will hold its breath and make no comment," declared Adolf Hitler as he ordered Operation Barbarossa. On June 22, 1941, German troops such as these—in top condition and high spirits—marched and rolled into Russia. Many Russian soldiers were killed or captured before they knew a war had started. Some, eager to escape Stalin's oppressive regime, actually welcomed capture. The jubilant Germans expected to capture Moscow, Leningrad, and the Caucasus very quickly and to destroy the Red Army within four months.

Wehrmacht overwhelms Red Army When Operation Barbarossa began, three separate German army groups—comprised of tanks, trucks, motorcycle troops, foot soldiers, and several hundred thousand horses—raced into Russia, attacking in the north, south, and central areas. They surrounded and captured masses of Red Army soldiers. *Wehrmacht* general Blumentritt described "great clouds of yellow dust kicked up by the Russian columns attempting to retreat and by our infantry hastening in pursuit." However, the general also commented, "The infantry had a hard time keeping up." A march of 25 miles a day was not unusual, and when panzers encountered rough or wooded terrain and superior Russian tanks, they had to stop and wait for the infantry to catch up to help clear the route.

Timoshenko can't prevent onslaught

Soviet Marshal Semyon Timoshenko was one of the few capable military commanders to survive Stalin's purges of the 1930s. When the Germans launched Operation Barbarossa, Stalin went into seclusion—some historians say into emotional collapse—for more than a week. In July 1941, Stalin appointed Timoshenko to replace Western Front commander D. G. Pavlov (who had been dismissed and executed). Although Timoshenko slowed the German offensive, he was unable to stop it. Stuck with the blame for the unpreparedness of Russian troops, Timoshenko was demoted from front-line command.

Stukas knock out Soviet tanks Puffs of smoke rise from Soviet tanks that were hit by German Stukas. Russia's large, well-equipped tank units were poorly maintained and usually operated by untrained crews. Since the Red Army artillery often lacked both ammunition and transportation to move their guns, ground air defenses were nearly nonexistent. In the early days of Germany's invasion, the *Luftwaffe* took a heavy toll on Russia's mechanized divisions. On the opening day of Operation Barbarossa, German planes also destroyed 2,000 Soviet aircraft, most of which were lined up on the ground in peacetime fashion, meaning neat, unprotected rows.

The fortitude of Soviet soldiers

When Germany attacked, the Soviet army infantry was badly equipped, poorly trained, and demoralized by purges of its leadership. Russian troops were so severely battered by a string of military disasters that many Western military experts expected them to last only a few weeks. On July 3, 1941, Stalin made an emotional radio broadcast imploring his people to defend the mother country. German victory seemed so inevitable that Hitler made plans for reducing his forces. However, Russian resistance actually increased as equipment and territory were lost, and as large numbers of their soldiers were taken prisoner or killed. In August, a Red Army counteroffensive took Yelnya. The Germans also suffered heavy losses. That winter, the Russians gained heart from their stand before Moscow, and became convinced that they could stop the German juggernaut.

Grim fate for civilians Soviet civilians flee as Germany invades the Soviet Union. Since combat often occurred near heavily populated areas, large numbers of Russian civilians were killed or displaced by military action on both sides. The defenders of threatened Russian cities gave little thought to evacuating noncombatants. In fact, local women and teenagers were generally put to work digging trenches and building fortifications. Facing enslavement or death at German hands, many Russian civilians tried to escape. By July 1941, the Nazis began shooting all the refugees they saw.

1941

June 15: German high command instructs its warships to destroy submarines belonging to Russia. If caught, the Germans are told to claim to have mistaken the Soviets for Brits.

June 16: Rudolf Hess, still in British custody after his solo parachute trip to Scotland, breaks his leg attempting suicide on a flight of stairs. • The U.S. announces the expulsion of all Italian and German tourist and consular personnel, effective July 10.

June 17: Operation Battleaxe, a major Allied push to relieve besieged troops at Tobruk, Libya, fails.

June 19: Germany and Italy shutter U.S. consulates and expel diplomats.

June 22: German sentries murder their counterparts at the Russian border at Brest-Litovsk, touching off Operation Barbarossa, the largest army attack in world history. Three million German troops march into Russia along the entire 1,800-mile frontier. Though outnumbered by the Soviets, the Germans have the element of surprise.

June 23: The commander of the Russian bomber group takes his own life when the Soviets come out on the losing end of a wildly unbalanced dogfight, losing 500 planes while downing about 10 *Luftwaffe* aircraft. By the end of the week, the Soviet air force, the world's largest, will be down 2,000 planes and all but destroyed.

June 25: Roosevelt authorizes arms shipments to the Soviet eastern port of Vladivostok.

June 26–28: Finland, Hungary, Croatia, and Slovakia declare war on the Soviet Union.

June 30: After a series of catastrophic failures, Stalin orders the execution of the military leadership on the Soviet Union's western front.

Lithuanians see Germans as liberators In late June 1941, Lithuanian women greet German troops with flowers. In the Baltic nations, as in other areas under Soviet rule, most people were eager to escape Stalinist oppression. Local citizens welcomed the Germans as liberators until they discovered that "Germanization" was even more brutal than "Sovietization." Some historians contend that if Hitler had understood the potential value of the initially enthusiastic civilian welcome, and encouraged it, he might have fomented rebellion against Stalin, and undercut Russia's ability to resist invasion.

***Einsatzgruppen* execute Jews** Observers from the *Waffen-SS* and the Reich Labor Service watch as a member of the *Einsatzgruppen*—a Nazi task force whose main duty was to eliminate Jews—executes a Jewish man at the edge of a mass grave. Following close behind the German army, the *Einsatzgruppen* and police units entered towns, rounded up Jews, and marched them to execution sites. In the Ukraine and other occupied territories, Nazis successfully recruited the help of local anti-Semites. Nazis and their collaborators killed some 600,000 Ukrainian Jews.

At first, Ukrainians welcome Nazis A Nazi soldier happily clutches bread given to him by Ukrainian children. During the early stages of Operation Barbarossa, Ukrainians expected the German invaders to free them from Soviet oppression. But like all good Nazis, Reich Commissar for the Ukraine Erich Koch considered even the lowliest

German worker "a thousand times more valuable than the population here." Ukrainian goodwill succumbed to the horrors of Nazi mistreatment. Scattered opposition—the poisoning of wells, wrecking of Nazi troop trains, and killing of individual German soldiers—would turn into a strong Ukrainian resistance movement.

Hitler's list of Eastern enemies "We have only to kick in the door and the whole rotten structure will come crashing down," Hitler claimed just before he launched Operation Barbarossa. He viewed the Ukraine as the *Lebensraum* (living space) that Germany needed, the Slavs as a subhuman race, and the "Bolshevik hordes" as a danger to civilized Europe. The Nazis were especially intent on wiping out Jews, non-Jewish Communists, and members of the Red Army. Here, Germans soldiers break down a door during their house-to-house search of a Russian village.

Flamethrowers All sides employed flame-throwing weapons, including those mounted on vehicles, such as the British Army's "Crocodile" Churchill tank. Other flame-throwing weapons were man-packed and operated by assault engineers or infantrymen, such as the *Wehrmacht*'s *Flammenwerfer* Model 35 (*pictured*). The weapon's principal elements included a pressurized fuel container, a tube projector and nozzle, and a system to ignite the jet of flammable fuel. Flamethrowers were particularly useful against strongly constructed bunkers, pillboxes, trench systems, and similar fortifications, where external access was often extremely limited—sometimes only through a single weapon slit or window. At close range, flamethrowers were also effective against tanks.

The "Stalin Organ" The Russian army's BM-13 Katyusha multiple rocket-launcher was nicknamed the "Stalin Organ." The massive weapon was comprised of 16 rocket-launch rails mounted on a truck chassis, from which salvos of 132mm solid-fuel high-explosive rockets could be fired against targets several miles away. The crew of six needed five to 10 minutes to reload. The Soviet army treated its multilaunch rocket systems as core weapons within its massive artillery organization. Accordingly, virtually every offensive was preceded by a protracted and overwhelmingly destructive and mind-numbing bombardment by its massed artillery. The heart of the fire plan invariably included numerous batteries of Katyushas.

AXIS ON THE ATTACK

JULY 1941–DECEMBER 1941

"We have only to kick in the door and the whole rotten structure will come crashing down."

—ADOLF HITLER, ON THE INVASION OF THE SOVIET UNION

ON JULY 3, 1941, a little more than a week after the German invasion of the Soviet Union, Joseph Stalin spoke for the first time to the Soviet people about the progress of the war. He called the citizens of his nation "brothers and sisters," a term he had never used before. It was an intimacy born of the terrible crisis they shared. Stalin admitted that the enemy had succeeded in breaking through, and he urged his compatriots to annihilate the intruders with every means possible. Many Soviet memoirs attest to the power of his words, which reached out to millions of citizens clustered around primitive radios or streetside loudspeakers. The Soviet people were urged to rouse themselves for what was to become the largest military contest of all time.

The Axis assault on June 22, 1941, had caught Soviet forces almost entirely unprepared. Finnish armies in the north, Romanian armies in the south, and a three-million strong German force between them drove forward at a relentless pace, encircling whole Soviet armies. On June 28, German forces reached the Belorussian capital of Minsk. Riga was captured three days later, and by the first week of July German armies were approaching the Ukrainian capital of Kiev. By late July, German bombers came within range of Moscow. By August 19, Leningrad—the Soviet Union's second largest city—was cut off by German and Finnish forces, though it could not be captured outright.

Soviet officers pushed their soldiers to make suicidal attacks on German positions, as Stalin insisted that death was better than surrender. Nonethe-

Nazi propaganda had ensured that the German troops who stormed into Soviet Russia at dawn on June 22, 1941, believed that Operation Barbarossa was absolutely essential to the future security of the Fatherland. German soldiers were supremely confident in themselves and in their *Führer*. They were well-prepared, aggressive, and certain of victory.

less, by September Axis troops had rounded up more than two million Soviet prisoners and destroyed much of the Red Army's tank and aircraft strength. By October 3, when Hitler flew back to Berlin to address the German people, he was confident that the Soviet dragon was killed "and would never rise again." German production plans for weapons were changed: Large numbers of aircraft and additional naval power were added for the coming confrontation with Britain and the United States. New models of tanks had, however, been ordered, as the Germans discovered that Soviet tanks were superior to their own.

Hitler's changing strategic vision was a reaction to the increasing collaboration between the two Anglo-Saxon powers. Though President Roosevelt was constrained by a public opinion that was not yet prepared for full-scale belligerency, the United States had begun to give the British Empire extensive assistance. In December 1940, Roosevelt had introduced a program of aid for Britain. It was called Lend-Lease to give the impression that something eventually would be given back. In March 1941, the plan passed through Congress. So relieved was Churchill that he described Lend-Lease as "tantamount to a declaration of war."

During the early weeks of Operation Barbarossa, the armored divisions of three *Wehrmacht* army groups overwhelmed and destroyed the surprised and disorganized western Soviet forces. By August, these German machine-gunners were fighting in the southwest Ukrainian port city of Mykolaiv, having already advanced some 400 miles into Russia.

At the same time, the U.S. Navy entered the great naval conflict in the Atlantic, where German submarines threatened the vital trade lifeline from North America to Britain. This conflict cost the Allies 5.6 million tons of shipping from September 1939 to March 1941. In April 1941, the U.S. Navy began to cover part of the western Atlantic Ocean, and in July it began antisubmarine air patrols from Newfoundland. Consequently, convoy shipping across the Atlantic became more successful.

The Anglo-American relationship was sealed in August 1941 when Churchill and Roosevelt met aboard the American cruiser *Augusta* at Placentia Bay off the coast of Newfoundland. There, Churchill sketched out a document, which would become known as the Atlantic Charter, for the two statesmen to sign. It was not an alliance, as Roosevelt neither wanted nor could make a formal commitment to American belligerency. Instead, it was a statement of common political intent made in the name of liberal democracy for the restoration of a world based on political freedoms, open trade, and the self-determination of peoples. In private, the two men also agreed to give all possible help to the Soviet Union, to warn Japan against further encroachments in the Far East, and to involve American forces more fully in the Atlantic battle.

The summer of 1941 marked the beginning of the mass murder of Europe's Jews. Between the outbreak of war and June 1941, Jewish populations under German control in Eastern Europe had been herded into ghettos, their valuables seized and their livelihoods destroyed. In occupied Western Europe, Jews were compelled to wear the distinctive yellow star, and their property was seized or handed over on unfavorable terms. But only with the invasion of the Soviet Union were Jews systematically murdered. Pre-1941 instructions to German security units, the *Einsatzgruppen*—and to units of the regular police—made it clear that they should kill all Jews. On the assumption that most partisan activity was Jewish-inspired, whole villages were destroyed and their inhabitants murdered by the German army as well as by the police and security units.

From June 1941, Nazi security forces in Russia did not spare Jewish women and children. At Babi Yar outside Kiev, more than 34,000 Jews were slaughtered. In Serbia and in western Poland, Jews were killed systematically. Hitler at last approved deportation for German Jews as well, and the first trainloads arrived in the East in October 1941. At some point, a decision was made to augment the continuing murder by police and security men with mass murder at extermination camps in occupied Poland.

The precise moment of this decision is unclear, but the camps were under construction beginning in autumn 1941 and the first gassing began at Chelmno in January 1942. In December 1941, Hitler told an assembly of party leaders in a closed session that global war signaled a final war to the death against the Jewish enemy. The mass killing that began in 1941 ended in 1945 with the estimated death of approximately six million European Jews. They were killed not only by German security forces, but by the *Wehrmacht*, locally recruited anti-Semitic militia, and the troops of Germany's allies.

Only some of this race war was evident to the West in 1941. The United States was much more concerned with the threat to security posed in East Asia and the west Pacific by the continued belligerence of Japan. This was a crisis brought on by the German victories in Europe. Japan had used the opportunity presented by the defeat of France and the Netherlands, and the

On August 14, 1941, U.S. president Franklin Roosevelt is welcomed aboard the *Prince of Wales* by British prime minister Winston Churchill at Placentia Bay, Newfoundland. There, the two leaders developed an Anglo-U.S. war strategy underlined by the principles of the Atlantic Charter, which eventually would become the United Nations Declaration.

German threat to Britain, to pressure western colonial possessions in Southeast Asia. Japan coveted this area because it contained large reserves of vital raw materials—oil, rubber, and tin in particular—which were essential for the Japanese war effort.

The American reaction to continued Japanese aggression in China had been to impose a partial trade embargo in September 1940, but that only heightened Japanese determination to seize further economic resources. Japanese leaders began to argue that war with the United States was almost inevitable. The driving force behind Japan's strategy of southward expansion was its huge navy, which relied heavily on oil. To secure the northern perimeter of the Japanese empire, Japan signed a nonaggression pact with the Soviet Union in April 1941. In July, Japanese forces moved into southern Indochina. When the United States. responded to this threat by tightening the embargo, the Japanese army and navy agreed that unless diplomatic pressure could undo the economic stranglehold that Tokyo had anticipated, they would attack the United States, the Dutch, and the British Empire.

In China, the long-running and ruthless Japanese campaign of conquest continued unabated. Here, Japanese troops assault Yichang on July 22, 1941. Japan's strategic successes in China subsequently enabled its forces to strike southwest into Indochina and south into the Pacific region.

The Japanese war was not inevitable. However, once Germany had invaded the Soviet Union and apparently removed the threat from Japan's northern frontier, the southward advance became an attractive option for the Japanese leadership. During all of 1941, the Germans viewed the idea that Japan would occupy the United States in the Pacific as a strategic bonus. The Germans, in fact, urged Japan to do so, promising the Japanese that they would join in war against the United States.

In September 1941, the Japanese armed forces presented Emperor Hirohito with a plan for war if the United States did not end the embargo through diplomatic agreement. The emperor favored a solution short of war, and for two more months negotiations continued between Japanese and American officials to find a formula for peace. American intelligence could read the Japanese diplomatic (but not naval) codes, and knew that war was a very strong possibility. When General Tojo Hideki became Japan's prime minister in October, he set a deadline of November 30 for negotiations. This deadline was intercepted and decoded by the Americans.

Meanwhile, the Japanese navy developed detailed operational plans to secure a Pacific perimeter to protect seizure of Malaya, the Philippines, and the Dutch East Indies. On November 26, U.S. secretary of state Cordell Hull sent a set of proposals to the Japanese negotiators that included the withdrawal of all Japanese forces from China and Indochina. Subsequently, it was suggested that if the Japanese would withdraw from southern French Indochina, they could buy all the oil they needed, but Japan insisted on war. A task force of six fleet aircraft carriers and accompanying warships approached the Hawaiian Islands. Undetected on the early morning of December 7, they attacked the U.S. Pacific Fleet stationed in Pearl Harbor, destroying or damaging more than 300 planes and eight battleships, and killing more than 2,000 men. Roosevelt summoned Congress, which voted to declare war that same day.

The opening of a second major theater of war meant that even more of the world was engulfed in the conflict. Japan fought to achieve an Asian and Pacific new order, as Germany and Italy fought for domination in Europe and the Mediterranean. On December 11, Hitler declared war on the United States. Having planned for war with the U.S. since the 1920s, but not yet having built the warships for that conflict, he now had a navy on his side. War meant that German submarines could attack U.S. shipping without restriction. It also meant that Germany—now aided by a powerfully armed Japan—could begin the contest for a world in which, in Hitler's warped mind, only German or Jew would triumph.

Any hopes by Americans that their nation would avoid war vanished with the Japanese attack on Pearl Harbor on December 7, 1941. The very next day, President Roosevelt called for a congressional declaration of war on Japan. On December 11, Germany and Italy declared war on the United States.

Hitler's ongoing war with the Soviet Union, however, was no sure thing. In December, Red Army divisions began a major offensive around Moscow to force back German armies that had been prevented from capturing the capital. Against German soldiers who were at the end of tired supply lines in cold weather—for which the Germans had not prepared—the Soviets made substantial progress. The German army had already been driven back at the southern end of the front in late November. Soon after the German defeat before Moscow, they also suffered a defeat at the northern part of the front.

This news thrilled Churchill, as did America's entry into the war. After Pearl Harbor, he telephoned Roosevelt, who told Churchill that Britain and America were "in the same boat now." His words were hauntingly ironic. A few days later, the British battleship *Prince of Wales*—which had transported Churchill to negotiate the Atlantic Charter—was sunk by Japanese naval bombers in the South China Sea.

1941

July 1: Riga, the capital of Latvia, is overwhelmed by a German occupation force.

July 2: The first member of the RAF's American Eagle Squadron to be killed in action dies in a midair collision over France. • The Japanese military bolsters its strength with a million-man draft.

July 2–3: German *Einsatzgruppen* (Special Action Groups), charged with the execution of Hitler's plan to exterminate Jews, murder 7,000 Jews in the Polish city of Lvov.

July 3: Stalin calls for a "scorched earth" defense, in which both the Red Army and ordinary Russian citizens would lay waste to the land as they retreat from the advancing Germans, leaving nothing to support the enemy troops.

July 5: Josip Broz Tito, Yugoslavia's Communist Party leader, calls for armed resistance against the German occupation.

July 6: Churchill sends a message to Stalin expressing the hope that the great powers can join forces to fight the German menace. • The occupying Nazis order the murder of 2,500 Jews in Kovno, Lithuania.

July 7: In relief of British troops, U.S. forces arrive in Iceland to defend the strategically located island.

July 7–8: More than 100 RAF Vickers Wellington bombers attack Cologne, Germany, causing widespread damage.

July 8: The RAF raids the German naval base of Wilhelmshaven. • The occupying Nazis decree that all Baltic Jews must wear identifying yellow Stars of David.

July 9: George Johnson Armstrong, a British naval engineer who offered his services as a spy to the Nazis while stationed in the United States, is executed for treason.

Massacres in Lvov Before the Germans reached Lvov, Poland, on June 30, 1941, the NKVD (*Narodnyi Komissariat Vnutrennikh Del;* Soviet Secret Police) murdered 5,000 Ukrainian and Polish nationalists, Jews, and political prisoners in the city's jails. Subsequently, the Germans capital-

ized on the atrocity by blaming it on Lvov's Jews. A three-day killing spree resulted that was conducted by German troops and an SS *Einsatzgruppe,* together with local Ukrainians and Poles. Some 4,000 Jews were killed, and a further 7,000 Jews and captured NKVD men were executed by the SS before the end of the year. By November 1943, virtually all 150,000 of Lvov's Jews would be dead.

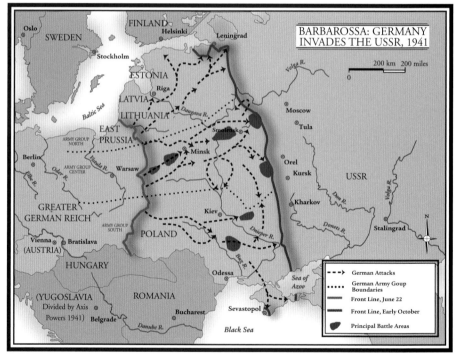

Operation Barbarossa At dawn on June 22, 1941, more than four million Axis soldiers (of whom at least three million were German), 3,360 tanks, and 7,000 artillery pieces—supported by 2,000 aircraft—stormed across the German-Soviet border. What Russia called the Great Patriotic War had begun. Initially, three German army groups—comprised of some 120 divisions—swiftly overwhelmed the Red Army's front-line defenses and struck deep into Soviet territory. However, despite the *Wehrmacht*'s early successes, Operation Barbarossa eventually proved to be Hitler's greatest strategic mistake, for he had badly underestimated the Soviet Union's military-industrial capability, its geography, and its environment.

> ### "Even the wives of the frontier guards were in the firing line, carrying water and ammunition, and taking care of the wounded. Some of the women were firing at the advancing Nazis...."
>
> —Soviet general I. I. Fedyuninsky, on the early weeks of the German invasion of the Soviet Union

The fate of Soviet POWs The Belorussian city of Minsk fell to the encircling advances of the Second and Third Panzer Groups on June 28, 1941, just six days after the start of Operation Barbarossa. During that week, panzer units captured more than 200,000 Soviets. Here, large numbers of those prisoners are transported in railway coal trucks from Minsk to Poland, where they would be interned or possibly moved on to camps further west. Thereafter, they probably would be used as slave labor while routinely experiencing deliberate maltreatment and appalling living conditions. Two-thirds of all Soviet POWs would be worked, starved, or shot to death.

The war's top tank Arguably, the Soviet T-34 was the best tank produced by any side during the war. T-34s first appeared on the battlefield in early July 1941, when their excellent cross-country performance, 33-mph top speed, and powerful 76.2mm guns completely outclassed the German panzers. Their well-sloped armor also proved impervious to anti-tank fire. T-34s were simple to operate and easily mass-produced (1,000 by 1941, with about 40,000 made during the war). Usually working closely with the infantry, who often rode into battle on the rear decks of the tanks, the T-34s were a highly important contributor to the eventual Soviet victory.

Fighting in the Ukraine In the Ukraine during the summer of 1941, Field Marshal Rundstedt's Army Group South had more difficulties than in the middle and north. The panzer groups fought their way across the sun-baked and seemingly endless Russian steppe. Soviet resistance held up the German advance. The Germans then struck behind the Red Army defending Kiev and surrounded them, capturing huge numbers of prisoners and equipment. Close-quarter fighting was typically carried out by the German infantry divisions. Assault engineer units that followed some days behind dealt with the many pockets of resistance that had been bypassed by the armored forces. German soldiers used flamethrowers (including this *Flammenwerfer* 35) extensively, particularly on bunkers and trench systems.

1941

July 10: In a shadowy case of "ethnic self-cleansing," some 1,600 Jewish villagers are tortured and murdered in Jedwabne, Poland. (The atrocity was blamed on the Nazis, but recent research indicates that Polish gentiles are to blame.) • Stalin demotes Marshal Timoshenko, the Red Army commander-in-chief, and assumes the position himself.

July 12: Representatives from Britain and the Soviet Union meet in Moscow to sign a mutual aid treaty.

July 16: About 600,000 Russians are trapped when the German army encircles the Soviet city of Smolensk.

July 21: The *Luftwaffe* suffers heavy losses in a bombing raid on Moscow.

July 22: With their supply lines stretched to the breaking point, German troops are forced to stop their progress through Russia for the first time in the campaign.

July 24: Nearly 4,500 Jews are murdered by Nazi *Einsatzgruppen* in the town of Lachowicze, Poland. • The Vichy French government hands southern Indochina over to the Japanese.

July 26: The British and American governments freeze hundreds of millions of dollars in Japanese assets in their respective nations. The Japanese will employ the same tactic in two days. • General Douglas MacArthur is called out of retirement by President Roosevelt to assume command of United States forces in the Far East.

July 31: In a memo to SS chief Reinhard Heydrich, Nazi *Reichsmarschall* Hermann Göring authorizes the "Final Solution" (complete annihilation) for Europe's Jews.

August 2: Roosevelt extends the Lend-Lease Act to allow for aid to the Soviet Union.

Japan's Need for Oil

JAPAN'S DESIRE FOR economic independence and the establishment of a commanding presence in East Asia required access to resources, particularly oil for the military machine. On July 24, 1941, the quest to conquer these resources prompted Japanese forces to enter southern Indochina.

With this incursion, Japanese military leaders knew they were courting war with the United States. Indeed, President Roosevelt reacted harshly, freezing Japanese assets and placing oil exports to Japan under restrictive licensing. This virtual embargo would be lifted only if the Japanese withdrew from China and Indochina and ended their pact with the Axis powers.

From the Japanese perspective, the situation was untenable. At least 65 percent of Japan's petroleum products came from American firms. The embargo would paralyze the country economically and leave the military with only 18 months of oil from reserve oil stocks. Without oil, the navy could not operate and Japan would become militarily impotent. Acquiescence to Roosevelt's conditions would not only entail an unacceptable loss of face, it would force an end to Japan's quest for regional dominance.

Japan's military demanded that the government either obtain a diplomatic settlement that would preserve Japanese interests or step down so a new government could prepare for war. Time was critical. Under the American restrictions, Japan would grow weaker as the Allies grew stronger. If diplomacy failed, Japan must fight. Of course in the end, diplomacy did fail. Japan attacked Pearl Harbor on December 7, 1941, and the U.S. declared war on Japan the next day.

U.S. deprives Japan of oil Oil barrels remain piled on the dock after President Franklin Roosevelt's declaration of an oil embargo on Japan in July 1941. The embargo, which followed similar restrictions on sales of iron and steel, was intended to persuade the Japanese to withdraw from Indochina, disavow the Tripartite Pact, and abandon the war in China. Instead, it only pushed energy-poor Japan, which depended on the United States for at least 65 percent of its petroleum products, closer to war with the West. Unwilling to abandon its ambitions in China and the Pacific, and with only 18 months of reserve stocks for the military, the Japanese armed services worked on their plans to seize the oil fields in the Dutch East Indies, even though that action risked war with the United States.

Long-distance relationships "And here in Ottawa we have little Polly and Geoffrey Carton, aged 8 and 5. Now...come in Mrs. Carton and say hello...." "Hello, Polly." "Hello, Mummy." "This is the nicest thing that's happened to me since you went away." This exchange took place on July 27, 1941, between the Cartons in Britain and their two children in Canada using a radio link-up similar to this. In summer 1940, it was expected that the Germans would soon invade England, so many parents sent their children oversees to family and friends in Canada, the United States, or any other safe haven. About 13,000 children were shipped to safety.

Wrens aid the Royal Navy "Wrens," members of the Women's Royal Naval Service (WRNS), move a torpedo for loading into a submarine at Portsmouth, England. Reactivated in 1939, the WRNS took over shore-based jobs, thereby freeing men for service at sea. Working at most naval shore establishments in Britain, the Wrens grew to number 74,620 in 1944. Many served on overseas bases in the Middle East and Far East. The Wrens did not serve on ships, but they crewed harbor launches and worked on tasks as diverse as signaling, driving, and welding.

Joubert takes charge of Coastal Command

British air marshal Sir Philip Joubert de la Ferté was one of the war's most influential airmen. As assistant chief of air staff in September 1939, he contributed significantly to the application of radar in the RAF. In June 1941, he became commander-in-chief of Coastal Command, which had lacked resources and had destroyed just two U-boats. It sank a further 27 during the following 20 months. Joubert centralized Coastal Command and narrowed the dangerous Atlantic Gap. He was appointed inspector-general of the RAF in 1943, and later that year joined Lord Mountbatten's South East Asia Command.

British put POWs to work These unidentified Axis prisoners of war, pictured in England, are almost certainly Italians, as very few Germans had been captured in 1940–41. It was not until July 1941 that POWs were used to support the Ministry of Agriculture's food-growing programs, when about 2,000 Italian POWs were transferred from North Africa specifically for that purpose. Despite some early hostility, the Italians often enjoyed remarkably amicable relations with the local British communities.

1941

August 5: German forces destroy Russia's 16th and 20th armies in the "Smolensk pocket." Germans capture more than 300,000 soldiers. • Romania kicks off the 73-day Siege of Odessa, which will end in October with the Romanian occupation of the Ukrainian city.

August 8: The Soviets suffer a crushing defeat at Roslavl, near Smolensk, as the Germans capture some 38,000 Russian prisoners of war.

August 10: Both Britain and the Soviet Union promise military aid to Turkey in the event that Germany pursues a policy of aggression against the Eurasian nation.

August 12: Roosevelt and Churchill announce the Atlantic Charter. • The Nazi occupation force in Romania requires all Jews to make themselves available for forced labor assignments.

August 13: Chungking, China, is largely in ruins after a week of bombing at the hands of the Japanese air force.

August 14: Josef Jakobs, a German spy, becomes the last person executed in Britain's legendary Tower of London.

August 16: Stalin accepts a joint proposal by the United States and Britain to meet in Moscow and develop a comprehensive plan on the aid that Britain and the U.S. will try to deliver to the Soviet Union.

August 17: Syracuse, Sicily, suffers an RAF bombing raid.

August 18: Hitler orders the remaining 76,000 Berlin Jews (out of an original 110,000) deported to Poland's ghettos.

August 24: In the Ukraine, Soviet forces mount an intense defense against German invaders.

America's Atlantic defense President Roosevelt considered Germany's naval threat to Atlantic shipping so serious that on May 27, 1941, he declared an Unlimited National Emergency. Here, New York harbor workers transport mines to a mine-planter in July. This vessel belonged to the Army Mine Planter Service, part of the Coast Artillery Corps. Responsibility for East Coast defense fell to a growing number of authorities, including the Coast Guard, Inshore Patrol, Ship Lane Patrol, and Coastal Picket Patrol.

Germans encircle Smolensk On July 15, 1941, a double breakthrough by Army Group Center's panzers cut off thousands of Soviet troops to the west of Smolensk and enabled the city's encirclement. Smolensk fell to an attack on July 16. Strong Soviet resistance continued in the pocket until August 5, by which time the Germans had captured some 310,000 prisoners, 3,205 tanks, and 3,120 guns. The fighting had been particularly intense, as evidenced in this photo by the weariness of the *Waffen-SS "Totenkopf"* (Death's Head) troops. Following their victory, the Germans paused for two weeks for reinforcement, regrouping, and maintenance.

The Atlantic Charter President Franklin Roosevelt and Prime Minister Winston Churchill meet aboard the ill-fated HMS *Prince of Wales* in Placentia Bay, off Newfoundland. Roosevelt had invited Churchill to the meeting, which lasted from August 10 to 15, 1941. Among many issues discussed were Japanese aggression, assistance for the USSR, and strategy (even though the U.S. was still officially neutral). At Roosevelt's suggestion, Churchill drafted a communiqué stating their common aims. In the eight points of this Atlantic Charter, the leaders emphasized that they made no territorial claims and favored self-determination, reduced restrictions on trade, collective security, and renunciation of force. The charter was endorsed by signatories of the Declaration of the United Nations on January 1, 1942.

***Wehrmacht* loses its momentum** A horse-drawn German supply train straggles across the vastness of the Russian steppes in this painting by Max Ohmayer. By August 1941, the *Wehrmacht*'s startling advance into Soviet territory had finally slowed. Overextended supply lines and the army's high dependence on mobility—involving fuel, ammunition, food, vehicle spares, and railway access—necessitated a period of regrouping and replenishment. But this pause also provided an opportunity for the badly battered Soviets to regroup. Now, some 30 Soviet Far Eastern divisions—men accustomed to the rigors of winter warfare—began to be deployed west from Siberia. The Red high command planned a major offensive, in the Moscow area, for early December.

Moscow spared from heavy bombing At the beginning of Barbarossa, Moscow was one of the more important German strategic objectives. Not only was it the nation's capital, but it was the center of the western Soviet Union's rail network and home to much of its industry. However, the *Luftwaffe*'s highest priority was to destroy the Soviet ground forces. Consequently, relatively few bombing raids (such as this one) struck the capital. Although probably exaggerated, a Soviet report stated that only 229 German aircraft appeared over Moscow from June to December 1941.

1941

August 24: In response to domestic discontent, Hitler orders a stop to his policy of exterminating the mentally ill. Since the beginning of the war, more than 70,000 such people have died at the hands of the Nazis. The policy will be continued in a decentralized manner, with another 100,000 dying by May 1945. Thousands also will be killed in German-occupied areas.

August 25: Spitsbergen, a remote Norwegian island best known as a historical whaling center, becomes a strategic war base with the arrival of British commandos. • The Allies occupy Iran on two fronts, with the British marching in from the south and the Red Army from the north.

August 26: In a stunning execution of the "scorched earth" war strategy, the Soviets will blow up their Dnieper Dam, the largest in the world. • The U.S. unveils plans to send a delegation to meet with Chiang Kai-shek's Nationalist Chinese government to determine what assistance they need to battle Japanese imperialism.

August 27: German submarine *U-570* is improbably captured by an RAF Hudson plane that drops four depth charges, which prompt the submarine's crew to surrender.

August 28: Vichy France's antiterrorist laws lead to the execution by guillotine of three members of the French Resistance. • The Japanese government sends a memo to Roosevelt offering disingenuous assurances that Japan has no imperialist designs on any foreign nation.

August 30: The last rail supply route to Leningrad is blocked when German troops occupy Mga, Russian.

September: "Potato Pete," a British food ministry creation, launches a campaign that urges citizens to eat plenty of unrationed potatoes.

The divisions of France After France capitulated to the Germans on June 22, 1940, France was divided. The elderly Marshal Philippe Pétain headed an authoritarian, nationalistic, anti-Semitic, and non-Republican Vichy regime that over time collaborated extensively with the Germans. The remaining French armed forces were divided between Vichy and Charles de Gaulle's Free French, with the latter exiled and commanded from England. Eventually, on November 11, 1942, the Germans and Italians violated the terms of the 1940 armistice by occupying the whole of France.

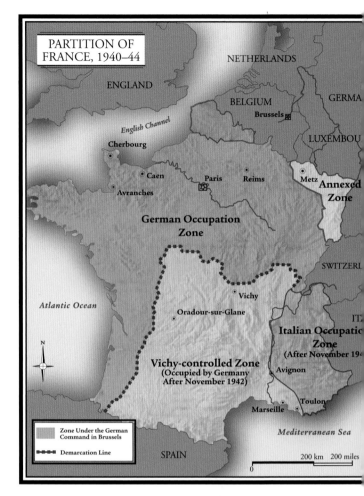

PARTITION OF FRANCE, 1940–44

NETHERLANDS
ENGLAND
BELGIUM
GERMA
Brussels
English Channel
LUXEMBOU
Cherbourg
Caen
Paris
Reims
Metz
Annexed
Avranches
Zone
German Occupation
Zone
SWITZERL
Atlantic Ocean
Vichy
Oradour-sur-Glane
IT
Italian Occupatio
Zone
(After November 19
N
Vichy-controlled Zone
Avignon
(Occupied by Germany
After November 1942)
Toulon
Marseille
Mediterranean Sea
Zone Under the German
Command in Brussels
Demarcation Line
SPAIN
200 km   200 miles
0

Lethal gas vans In September 1941, SS *Brigadeführer* Artur Nebe, commander of *Einsatzgruppe B* (a mobile killing squad), experimented with alternatives to shooting prisoners. He thought of a gas van, which could include a hermetically sealed cabin in which victims would be killed by carbon monoxide exhaust fumes. Reinhard Heydrich took up the idea, and by mid-1942 about 30 custom-built vans were made available. They were used from December 1941, especially by *Einsatzgruppen* and at the Chelmno death camp. Dozens of victims could be gassed at once. Altogether, many thousands of people were killed in the vans.

Brauchitsch toes the line Field Marshal Walther von Brauchitsch was commander-in-chief of the German army during its *Blitzkrieg* campaigns in Poland, the Low Countries, France, Yugoslavia, and Soviet Russia from 1939 to 1941. Increasingly, he fell under the *Führer's* thrall, agreeing to Hitler's strategies and policies. Meanwhile, Brauchitsch resisted many attempts to involve himself in the military conspiracy against Hitler. In December 1941, Hitler himself became commander of the German army, replacing Brauchitsch.

Hitler's favorite sculptor Arno Breker was a talented German sculptor who trained in Düsseldorf, Paris, and (in 1933) Rome. Although originally an abstract sculptor, his 1930s designs and output were particularly influenced by a deep appreciation of Roman "heroic sculpture." This formative influence coincided with the rise of Nazism, with its ideological and propaganda emphasis upon similar imagery to promote an idealized Germanic, Aryan, and Teutonic heritage. Consequently, Breker soon became Hitler's favorite sculptor. He received numerous state commissions, and was provided with vast studios and POW labor to assist him.

The Jew and France In September 1941, at the *Palais Berlitz* in Paris, French collaborationists staged a viciously anti-Semitic exhibition called *Le Juif et la France* (The Jew and France). Its advertising poster showed a monstrous Jewish man coiled around a globe, his sinister claws reaching toward France. Artworks displayed massive images of stereotypical Jewish features, including the hooked nose shown here. The exhibition pamphlet assured viewers that they would be "enlightened" concerning the Jews' "penetration into our country and the harm they have done here; you will therefore understand why so many Frenchmen are dead." About 200,000 French people paid to attend the exhibition.

Poet Pound trumpets fascism In the 1930s, expatriate American poet Ezra Pound became increasingly interested in sociopolitical issues. Disillusioned with Britain, he become enamored with Mussolini's ideals. In this photo, the stationery on which he is writing pro-Fascist commentaries displays Mussolini's motto: "Liberty is a duty, not a right." During the war, Pound made hundreds of anti-American radio broadcasts. He openly criticized the U.S. war effort and espoused anti-Semitic conspiracy theories. Arrested by American troops in 1945, he was imprisoned in Italy and, on return to the U.S., was pronounced mentally unfit to stand trial for treason.

Massacre at Babi Yar

O N SEPTEMBER 24, 1941, shortly after the Germans' successful 45-day battle for Kiev, Red Army engineers exploded a number of land mines that had been pre-positioned in key buildings in the city center. One of these was the Hotel Continental, in which the Germans had just established their headquarters. The devastation was enormous, with hundreds of German troops killed or severely injured and 25,000 Kiev residents left homeless.

Even though the attack had been carried out by Russian soldiers, the German high command blamed the city's Jewish community, and ordered it to assemble for "resettlement" on September 29. These Jews, together with a number of Gypsies, were then marched away in groups into the nearby forests by troops of *Sonderkommando 4a* of SS *Einsatzgruppe C* along with Ukrainian militiamen. Over a two-day period, the groups arrived at Babi Yar, a ravine. There they were summarily shot and then buried in a huge pit. In total, some 34,000 Jews died at Babi Yar. Subsequently, the Germans stated that they had solved Kiev's housing problem by evacuating an "adequate number of apartments."

Execution of Jews at Babi Yar

Far from condemning the atrocity, several non-SS senior officers applauded such actions. Among them was Field Marshal von Reichenau, commander of the German Sixth Army, who issued a directive emphasizing the need for his soldiers to "fully understand the need for severe but just atonement of the Jewish subhumans." While *Einsatzgruppen* would go on to execute hundreds of thousands of Jews during the war, Babi Yar was the largest individual massacre.

German forces seize Kiev
Prepared to defend Kiev on a street-by-street basis, the Soviets constructed an extensive system of trenches, bunkers, and roadblocks. However, when the panzers of Army Group South reached Kiev on July 11, they bypassed it to the south to avoid becoming embroiled in street fighting. On September 16, they joined with the southern arm of Army Group Center 120 miles east of Kiev— thereby encircling the city and Soviet general Mikhail Kirponos's armies. Stalin forbade Kirponos to break out, so his 665,000 men and much equipment fell into German hands. Meanwhile, Kiev's defenses were dismantled (*pictured*).

Sabotage and reprisals in Kiev After bombarding Kiev's defenses for six weeks, units of Army Group South entered the city on September 19. Five days later, massive explosions destroyed the German headquarters in the Hotel Continental, together with many other German-occupied buildings, including this one. Extensive fires were started and a large number of soldiers killed. The German military command blamed the Jewish population for this act of sabotage, and about 34,000 of Kiev's Jews were summarily executed in a reprisal action that became known as the Babi Yar massacre. In fact, the original explosions had almost certainly been caused by the Red Army's detonation of some 50 land mines.

Hull's important roles Cordell Hull, President Roosevelt's secretary of state from 1933 to 1944, played a major role in pushing Roosevelt's policy of lowering tariff barriers. When war began in Europe, he was instrumental in securing the neutrality of the Americas, and he also advanced FDR's interventionist policies regarding the Allies. Hull played a big part in Roosevelt's effort to keep the Japanese talking until they could see for themselves that the Axis might well lose the war. In 1945 Hull was awarded the Nobel Peace Prize for his efforts in creating the United Nations.

Shirer reports from Berlin From 1925 to 1932, William Shirer was the European correspondent for the *Chicago Tribune*. While chief of the Universal News Service's Berlin bureau from 1934, he worked for CBS radio and wrote a journal that would become a book, *Berlin Diary* (1941). Shirer's most famous CBS broadcast described the surrender of France to Hitler at Compiègne on June 21, 1940. Although eventually forced to leave Germany, he later returned to Europe on various reporting assignments, including the Nuremberg Trials. Shirer is best known for his book *The Rise and Fall of the Third Reich* (1960).

The German-occupied Channel Islands The only part of the United Kingdom occupied by the Germans during the war was the Channel Islands—Jersey, Guernsey, Alderney, and Sark—some 20 miles west of the Cherbourg Peninsula. Many of the islands' administrators collaborated with the Germans (*pictured*) and resistance was officially discouraged, although some ignored this directive. Meanwhile, life was harsh for the 60,000 ordinary people who had not been evacuated. Reprisals, internments, deportations, and heavy fines characterized the occupation, while near-starvation was pervasive. Informing, collaboration, and the black market flourished, and many women willingly consorted with German troops.

1941

September 1: The U.S. Navy's Atlantic Fleet assumes convoy protection in the North Atlantic from Iceland to Newfoundland. • Tokyo spars with Moscow over the inadvertent mining of a Japanese fishing boat off the coast of Vladivostok. The Japanese are enraged when Russia refuses to pay for the boat, insisting it would not have happened had the boat not been unacceptably close to Russia's shore.

September 3: Russian prisoners of war and Jews become the first victims of the poison gas Zyklon B, the newly preferred Nazi execution method, at Auschwitz.

September 5: The Soviet Union evacuates all children under age 12 from the capital of Moscow as German troops move toward the city.

September 7: French Resistance fighter Pierre Roche is executed by the Nazi occupation force.

September 7–8: Some 200 RAF planes mount the biggest air raid to date on Germany's capital of Berlin. The British will bomb the city for four solid hours overnight.

September 8: The German army places Leningrad in a state of siege. A desperate Stalin will ask Churchill for immediate military aid. The siege will last for 900 days. • Concerned that Russia may be harboring a homegrown population of Nazi sympathizers, Stalin exiles 600,000 Volga-area ethnic Germans to Siberia.

September 9: Iran surrenders to the Allies, agreeing, among other things, to deport Axis spies posing as diplomatic and tourist staff. Iran will order the "diplomats" and others out on the 13th.

Enigma machines
Regarded by the Germans as being entirely secure, the Enigma encoding and decoding machines were used in the major headquarters of all three services of the *Wehrmacht*, as well as by the SS, the *Abwehr*, and the *Reichsbahn* (the German state railways). Robust, portable, and relatively simple to operate even on the battlefield, these machines were also found in many operational headquarters and forward-command centers—including in the command vehicles of the panzer groups. Here, General Heinz Guderian, in his armored command vehicle, stands beside an early three-rotor Enigma machine.

Soviet partisans Soviet partisan groups were initially offshoots of the many Red Army units cut off by the German advance in 1941. However, being untrained in guerrilla warfare, they were very vulnerable. Moreover, their relentless suppression—often led by special SS counter-partisan units—was invariably brutal, usually culminating in collective reprisals and summary executions. However, such excesses actually boosted partisan recruitment. Beginning in 1942, the Soviet high command exerted better-coordinated political and military control over the partisans, whose operational significance increased from 1943. Although totalling as many as 700,000 and causing some 35,000 Axis casualties, their main impact was in the rear areas, where they disrupted communications, carried out raids and sabotage, gathered intelligence, and told the local population that the Soviet regime was coming back.

The Soviet *Stavka*

IN JUNE 1941, SHORTLY AFTER the Germans launched their invasion of Russia, a state defense committee—the *Gosudarstvennyi Komitet Oborony* (GKO)—of *Politburo* members was created as the headquarters of the supreme command. Stalin appointed himself commissar of defense and supreme commander of the Soviet armed forces. Simultaneously, the *Stavka* (the *Stavka Glavnovo Komandovaniya*, later the *Stavka Verhovnovo Komandovaniya*) was established as a general headquarters subordinate to the GKO and to Stalin himself.

The *Stavka* developed as the war progressed, but generally it included 12 to 20 senior officers. They represented all arms and services, including the chief of the general staff and the heads of the Soviet air force and maritime forces. Its political direction was assured because all GKO members had the right to sit as members of the *Stavka*. Its principal roles were to advise Stalin and to develop strategic plans, fusing Stalin's wishes with Soviet military activities in the field. It directed the high-level policy for manpower allocation as well as for combat, logistic, maritime, air, and administrative support.

Where necessary, the *Stavka* also directed retribution against those commanders whose performance fell short of Stalin's expectations. Despite an often obsessive centralization and the frequent divergence of its strategic functions and its political imperatives, the *Stavka* was nevertheless an indispensable contributor to the Soviets' final victory in 1945.

Hitler insists on autumn offensive On September 30, 1941, Field Marshal Rundstedt's Army Group South advanced to seize Kharkov, cross the lower Don, and reach the Caucasus oil fields. In agreement with army chief of staff general Franz Halder, Hitler ordered Army Group Center and Army Group North to launch coordinated thrusts against Moscow and Leningrad. Although the German offensive in the South initially made some progress (pictured are machine gunners in Kharkov), it was driven back at the end of November. In December, due to a disagreement with Hitler about the retreat in the South, Rundstedt was relieved of command.

Zhukov leads Soviet offensives In 1941 Stalin appointed Georgi Konstantinovich Zhukov chief of the general staff. In September, Zhukov assumed command of the Leningrad Front—just as the German advance halted. Then, as commander of the Western Front defending Moscow, he won a less ambiguous victory against Army Group Center, forcing a German withdrawal. He continued his offensive through the winter. Later, as deputy supreme commander to Stalin, Zhukov helped to oversee the Soviet battle for Stalingrad (1942–43), seized the strategic initiative at Kursk (1943), and directed part of the 1944–45 offensives into Poland and Germany—including the hard-fought capture of Berlin.

1941

September 11: A shoot-on-sight order is handed down to U.S. Navy ships running convoy protection operations on the seas. • Aviator and isolationist Charles Lindbergh delivers a speech in Des Moines, Iowa, in which he blames the deepening U.S. involvement in the European war on Britain, Roosevelt, and Jews.

September 16: The Russian front at Kiev collapses in the face of intense German pressure, and some 500,000 Soviets surrender. Kiev will officially fall to the Germans in two days. • Mohammed Reza Pahlevi takes the Shah's throne of British-occupied Iran when his father, Reza Khan, abdicates. • In an effort to quell partisan violence in the Soviet Union, German field marshal Wilhelm Keitel orders his troops to randomly execute 100 Russian civilians every time a civilian kills a German soldier.

September 17: At least one day too late, the Red Army high command orders its men to retreat from the city of Kiev.

September 18: Already suffering high casualties, the captured Russian troops in the surrounded region of Kiev begin to be summarily executed by the Germans. The Soviet death toll in defense of Kiev will top 350,000. • Japanese military leaders are instructed to prepare their troops for operations in the Pacific.

September 20: The Soviet Union receives advance notice of a German attack on Moscow, thanks to Britain's success in capturing and decoding Enigma encryptions.

September 22: A Ukrainian militia squad does the Nazis' dirty work, murdering 28,000 Soviet Jews near the town of Vinnitsa.

U-boat torpedoes the *Kearny* On October 17, 1941, a U-boat torpedoed this destroyer, the USS *Kearny*, in the North Atlantic. The *Kearny* had gone to aid a slow convoy under wolf pack attack, but it became a target itself when it was silhouetted at night by the light of a torpedoed merchant ship and halted by passing traffic. The torpedo that hit its starboard side caused many casualties, including 11 deaths. A Navy Catalina (flying boat) dropped plasma to the ship by parachute. The *Kearny* returned to Iceland under its own steam, escorted by the USS *Greer*. The latter's inconclusive battle with *U-652* on September 4 had led to President Roosevelt's "shoot on sight" policy against vessels interfering with American shipping.

Britain dominates in Mediterranean Upon becoming Britain's prime minister in 1940, Winston Churchill defied his admirals and wielded his considerable naval expertise against the Axis powers in the eastern Mediterranean. Under his leadership, British aircraft destroyed Axis U-boats as they surfaced to recharge their batteries. British warships, such as the tiny corvette HMS *Daisy* (*pictured*), were also remarkably successful at destroying submarines. Commissioned in October 1941, the *Daisy*'s service was distinguished but short. The ship foundered on January 2, 1942, while en route from Alexandra to Tobruk.

Americans help out in Iceland American soldiers stationed in Iceland needed heavy protective clothing against the freezing weather. In July 1941—months before the U.S. would officially enter the war—President Roosevelt sent troops to relieve British forces in Iceland. Soon after the Nazi occupation of Denmark in 1940, the British had moved into Iceland in order to keep northern sea lanes open. When British forces were badly needed elsewhere, U.S. troops took over the defense of the small country.

U.S. loses its first naval vessel The USS *Reuben James*, a Clemson Class destroyer, was the first American naval vessel lost in World War II. It was one of five destroyers escorting a fast convoy when, about 600 miles west of Ireland on October 31, 1941, a torpedo from *U-552* struck it. The forepart of the ship was blown off as far back as the fourth of its characteristic four stacks. Only 45 of its crew of about 160 survived. Among the dead were all of the ship's officers, including the commanding officer, LCDR H. L. Edwards. This disaster prompted further amendments to the Neutrality Act.

The many uses of the M3 tank The M3 was the most important American light tank of the war, with more than 13,000 produced. First built in March 1941, it underwent numer-ous improvements. For example, the first model was riveted and the final was entirely welded. A gyrostabilizer was incorporated in 1941 to enable it to fire accurately while moving. The M3 was fast and mechanically reliable but lightly armored and armed. Allied armies employed it—thanks to Lend-Lease—in conditions ranging from the North African desert to Soviet snow and Pacific jungles. The tank was called the M3 or, unofficially, the Honey. Mine-exploder and flame-thrower versions were also made.

"Rats of Tobruk" In 1941, during the longest siege in British history, predominantly Australian troops defended the strategic Libyan seaport of Tobruk from forces led by German commander Erwin Rommel. William ("Lord Haw-Haw") Joyce, the British radio announcer who broadcast Nazi propaganda from Berlin, derisively described Tobruk's defenders as rats. Desperate but valiant Allied troops embraced the name, calling themselves the "Rats of Tobruk" as they tunneled to escape Axis bombing, launched daring and ruthless raids, and commandeered enemy weaponry, such as the antiaircraft gun pictured here.

1941

September 23: Nazis murder the residents of the village of Krasnaya Gora in retaliation for the killing of three German soldiers by Russian resistance fighters.

September 24: German U-boats enter the Mediterranean for the first time, via the Strait of Gibraltar.

September 27: The United States launches the *Patrick Henry*, the first of more than 2,700 so-called Liberty ships. These are relatively inexpensive, quickly constructed merchant ships used to ferry war materiel from the United States to Europe. • About 100,000 Japanese troops are trapped when 11 Chinese divisions cut their escape route, turning the tide in the battle for Changsha, China.

September 28–30: In the largest German mass murder of the war, 34,000 Russian Jews are ordered to the outskirts of Kiev by a resettlement order, corralled, marched to the edge of the Babi Yar ravine, and shot.

September 29: Hitler issues a directive ordering Leningrad razed to the ground. He claims that the welfare of the city's three million residents is a problem that cannot be solved.

October 1: More than 3,000 Jewish residents of Vilna, Lithuania, are murdered by Nazi occupation forces.

October 2: Hitler launches Operation Typhoon, a plan to send the *Wehrmacht* into the Soviet capital of Moscow. • With most of the Jews of Paris either dead or deported, the Nazi Gestapo turns its eye toward the destruction of synagogues.

October 3: In a brash and, it will soon become apparent, premature speech delivered at the Berlin *Sportpalast,* Hitler claims that Russia is "broken and will never rise again."

Udet blamed for *Luftwaffe*'s failings
Ernst Udet (*right*) was a gifted pilot, talented aircraft designer, and World War I flying ace for Germany (rated second only to Baron Manfred von Richthofen). In 1936 he became chief of the Technical Office of the Air Ministry and inspector-general of aircraft design, production, and inspection. However, his preoccupation with developing fighters, dive-

bombers, and light bombers reduced the *Luftwaffe*'s effective heavy bomber capability. Both Hitler and Göring blamed Udet for the *Luftwaffe*'s defeat in the Battle of Britain, and its later inability to combine effective defense against RAF bombers with full support for the German forces on the Eastern Front and in North Africa. Consequently, in a fit of depression, Udet committed suicide in November 1941.

Soviet citizens, industry relocate Operation Barbarossa gave the Germans control of 60 percent of the existing Soviet armaments industry, and up to 74 percent of its strategic resources and energy output. The Soviets needed to relocate much of their population and industry into the hinterland. More than 10 million people were evacuated or fled as refugees. In addition, 2,000-plus industrial plants were eventually reestablished in the Urals, Siberia, Kazakhstan, and other portions of Central Asia. Pictured is an electrochemical plant under construction at Chirchik, Uzbekistan. By late 1944, Soviet armaments production had more than doubled.

Misery and death in the Warsaw Ghetto In Poland's Warsaw Ghetto, starving children such as these were often reduced to begging and sometimes abandoned to die on the streets. The Nazis allowed very meager food rations and no medical supplies to the Jews whom they imprisoned inside the ghetto walls. In some cases, small, emaciated children squeezed through drainage gutters at night to scrounge in nearby neighborhoods for food and medicines. At the risk of their own lives, some non-Jewish Poles helped supply them. By July 1942, more than 100,000 Warsaw Ghetto Jews had died from hunger and epidemic diseases.

Frank's rule of terror in Poland A Nazi Party member from the outset—he took part in the 1923 Munich Beer Hall *Putsch* as a Stormtrooper— Hans Frank rose to become leader of the NSDAP legal division. He later became Bavarian minister of justice and also held other important ministerial posts. As governor-general of occupied Poland from 1939 to '45, he sought to destroy that country's national identity while using its natural resources, agriculture, industry, and manpower for the exclusive benefit of Germany. Frank's rule of Poland was characterized by terror, coercion, and the extermination of Poland's Jews. He was tried and hanged at Nuremberg in 1946.

No mercy for Russian civilians German soldiers empty this Russian home in order to search for weapons or partisans, or to requisition the house for winter quarters. Whatever the reason, the eventual fate of the family was undoubtedly grim. German soldiers had been indoctrinated by the Nazi ideologues to believe that the Russians were an ethnically subhuman race, whose Bolshevik/Communist ideology presented a potentially cataclysmic danger to the civilized Western world—and to Germany in particular. Therefore, Russians were of absolutely no significance. Accordingly, they were mistreated, used as forced labor, or killed.

Standby of German infantry In 1939 the Mauser 7.92mm Kar98K was the standard rifle of the German armed forces. Robust, accurate, and reliable, it was used extensively throughout the war. In 1941 the updated Mauser Gewehr 98/40 (pictured here with a sniper scope) entered service, and remained the German infantryman's standard weapon until the end of the war. A shorter, folding-stock carbine version, the Gewehr 33/40, was produced for parachute troops. All of the Type 98s were bolt-operated and had a five-round box magazine. A bayonet or grenade launcher could be fitted when required. Maximum effective range of the Gewehr, for most practical purposes, was 600 to 800 yards.

1941

October 3: Indian spiritual leader Mohandas Gandhi suggests that Indians should employ his passive resistance techniques to stymie the British war effort.

October 4: The United States and Great Britain agree to a regular monthly shipment of tanks and planes to the Soviet Union.

October 7: Some 17,000 Polish Jews from the town of Rovno are tortured and executed at the hands of the Nazi SS.

October 9: Claiming that adherence to the Neutrality Act is not possible when faced with the "unscrupulous ambitions of madmen," Roosevelt asks for congressional permission to arm the U.S. merchant fleet.

October 10: The vast majority of voters in the Grand Duchy of Luxembourg boycott a referendum calling for Germany's annexation of their small nation. • In a remarkable effort to maintain production during wartime, the Soviets continue a mass relocation of Moscow-area factories to locations in the East.

October 12–13: Nuremberg, Germany, withstands a large-scale, overnight assault by the RAF.

October 16: While Stalin remains, most Soviet officials flee Moscow, taking the body of a dead but well-preserved Lenin with them. The government relocates to the eastern city of Kuibyshev. • A massive defense perimeter, including more than 5,000 miles of trenches, is constructed around Moscow by a half-million Muscovites—mostly women, children, and old men. • Prince Konoe, prime minister of Japan, resigns. General Tojo Hideki will succeed him the following day.

Germans murder "hostile elements" The German Sixth Army, commanded by General Walter von Reichenau (a steadfast supporter of Hitler's war plans), captured Kharkov, Ukraine, on October 25, 1941. Thereafter, he ordered extreme punitive action taken against "hostile elements," such as Jews and Bolsheviks. Saboteurs were to be publicly hanged, such as these six men who allegedly had destroyed an explosives store. Soon, executions and hostage-takings numbered in the hundreds. However, such atrocities were of little consequence to Stalin—himself the leader of an equally repressive regime—other than for their propaganda value. Meanwhile, the opposition of those who might otherwise have welcomed the Germans was strengthened by such excesses.

Children fight for Russia Although surprised by Germany's invasion in June 1941, Soviet Russia speedily mobilized to fight what was generally recognized to be a war of survival—Russia's "Great Patriotic War." Men, women, and children were soon fully committed to the war effort. Here, children train with replica weapons with adult military instructors. In Moscow, children conducted street patrols and enforced air raid precautions. In the occupied areas, they gathered intelligence, carried messages, and fought alongside the partisans. Their actions prompted a German order that any child found on a railway line was to be shot.

Red Army POWs in German Hands

ABOUT 5.5 MILLION Red Army officers and soldiers were captured during the war, three-quarters of them in 1941. Their fate was bleak. By May 1945, approximately four million of these captured troops were dead.

Nazi dogma identified bolshevism as the ultimate evil and Russians as racially subhuman. This translated into an almost complete disregard by the Germans for their Russian POWs, other than as a source of slave labor. Indeed, the SS regularly executed Russian POWs upon their capture, thereby avoiding the administrative inconvenience and wasted resources necessary to escort and confine them. As a matter of German policy, Red Army political officers and NKVD soldiers were summarily executed, as were many ordinary Soviet military officers.

Red Army POWs who survived the first few days of capture faced endless marches and interminable rail travel—usually in sealed cattle wagons, but sometimes in open wagons even during winter—as well as disease, forced labor, and starvation. Those POW camps established specifically

Heinrich Himmler visiting a POW camp

for Russian prisoners were maintained at standards even lower than those of the main concentration camps.

The ill-fortune and misery of many of these Red Army POWs did not necessarily end in 1945. Stalin and the Soviet leadership subsequently condemned large numbers of them, as traitors, cowards, and/or collaborators. The Soviets executed some of them and imprisoned many.

The craft of sniping Sniping represented the ultimate professional challenge for an infantryman, as it required marksmanship and field-craft skills as well as initiative, judgment, and intelligence awareness. A single sniper—who targeted officers, other commanders, radio operators, and weapons specialists—could have a significantly detrimental impact upon an enemy's morale and operations. Here, a Soviet sniper steadies a Mosin 1891 rifle fitted with a telescopic sight. The Red Army also used female snipers. Although sniping was carried out by all sides, snipers risked being shot if caught, as the nature of their task often provoked exceptional anger among their opponents.

Grand mufti meets Hitler Grand Mufti Muhammed Amin al-Husseini (*left*)—an Islamic scholar, religious leader, and member of a powerful Palestinian clan—fought against Jewish immigration and the establishment of a Jewish state in the British Mandate of Palestine. In 1941 al-Husseini fled to Germany. Meeting with Hitler on November 28 (*seen here*) and other Nazi leaders, al-Husseini pushed to extend Germany's Jewish extermination program. Hitler promised him that all Jews in Palestine and elsewhere in the Middle East would be killed. Since Hitler intended to turn the area over to Mussolini, he would not announce support for Arab independence.

1941

October 17: The United States suffers its first military casualties when 11 sailors die aboard the torpedoed destroyer *Kearny*.

October 21: The Nazis retaliate for a series of attacks against Reich soldiers by Serbian partisans by massacring thousands of residents of Kragujevac.

October 23: Charles de Gaulle warns French partisans to stop attacking Germans, hoping that German reprisals will stop.

October 26–27: Some 115 bombers with the RAF attack Hamburg, Germany, during the overnight hours.

October 27: The Nazis test-drive a van designed to dispatch its occupants with engine exhaust. They will kill nearly 300 Polish Jews from Kalisz with this technique. • German *Einsatzkommandos* murder some 9,000 Lithuanian Jews, nearly half of whom are children.

October 30: Roosevelt extends a $1 billion loan to the Soviets under the provisions of the Lend-Lease Act. • After a month in which it rained incessantly, the Germans are forced to postpone their Moscow campaign while the ground dries out.

October 31: The Nazi SS commander in Estonia reports the successful extermination of essentially all Estonian Jews. • In a series of 45 strikes, the *Luftwaffe* "softens" the defenses of Moscow prior to a ground attack. • The United States loses its first ship in combat when the destroyer *Reuben James* sinks off the Icelandic coast, claiming the lives of 115 sailors.

November: Over the next month, some 11,000 Soviet civilians will starve to death during the Siege of Leningrad.

The tide turns at Rostov Despite the onset of October's mud and November's snow, panzers of Germany's Army Group South reached Russia's Don River on November 21, when Rostov fell. However, on November 30, Soviet Marshal Timoshenko's newly constituted Southwest Front counterattacked. Rostov was recaptured by Soviet troops (*pictured*), and the Germans were pushed back about 60 miles. Although not a catastrophic reversal, this was nevertheless Germany's first such enforced large withdrawal. It accompanied mounting German casualties, increasing logistic and maintenance problems, escalating partisan activity, and the full onset of Russia's winter. The Germans had not prepared for winter weather because they had assumed victory would be theirs within a few months.

Cossacks fight on both sides Cossacks, the warrior horsemen of the Russian Steppes, fought on both sides from 1941. Despite persecutions by the Soviet Communists in the 1920s and 1930s, some 100,000 served loyally within the Red Army. But many Cossacks, after being captured by the Germans, formed units within the German forces. In 1944 these units were combined to create a *Waffen-SS* cavalry corps. The Cossacks' legendary skills in irregular, counter-partisan, and guerrilla-style warfare enabled them to wreak havoc across the German and Soviet rear areas. In 1945, following their enforced repatriation to the Soviet Union by the Allies, Stalin inflicted savage retribution upon the thousands of Cossacks who had fought for the Germans.

General Tojo

IF ANY ONE FIGURE came to personify Japanese militarism in the Allied mind during World War II, it was Prime Minister Tojo Hideki. The son of an army general, Tojo attended the Japanese Military Academy. In subsequent years, he demonstrated bureaucratic abilities as a staff officer, rising to the rank of major general by 1935. His businesslike attitude earned him the nickname "The Razor."

Fervently nationalistic and militaristic, Tojo was named minister of war in 1940 and helped implement the right-wing policies that ultimately led to war with the United States. In 1941, backed by Japanese militarists, he was named prime minister by Emperor Hirohito. His power and influence were so strong that from Pearl Harbor to mid-1944, he seemed to be a virtual dictator. Tojo was often caricatured in Western media, and his bespectacled image came to symbolize perceived Japanese treachery and barbarism.

Tojo's reign ended with the string of Allied victories in the Pacific, culminating with the fall of Saipan in July 1944. Abandoned by his supporters, he was forced to resign and went into seclusion. Following Japan's surrender in 1945, Tojo shot himself in a failed suicide attempt. The Allies tried him as a war criminal, charging that the murder of millions of civilians had occurred under his authority. He was sentenced to death on November 12, 1948, and was executed by hanging on December 23, 1948.

"Inferior subhumans" The Nazis described homosexuals, prostitutes, criminals, beggars, the mentally or physically disabled, and anyone holding certain religious or political views as *Untermenschen,* meaning biologically inferior subhumans. They also considered all Jews, Slavs, Turks, Mongols, Gypsies, and those of African descent as *Untermenschen.* Seen here is the cover of *Der Untermensch*, a 52-page 1942 magazine edited by Heinrich Himmler that contrasts carefully selected images said to be of depraved *Untermenschen* with those of beautiful "Aryans." Warning that the *Untermenschen* would overrun civilized Europe, the Nazis claimed justification for military aggression, enslavement, and genocide.

Japanese negotiators Japanese ambassador Nomura Kichisaburo (*right*) appeared on the cover of *Time* on September 22, 1941. He was nicknamed the "Honorable Fire Extinguisher" due to his efforts to negotiate a peace agreement between Japan and the United States. Here, Nomura and Special Envoy Kurusu Saburo share a laugh during diplomatic talks days before the Pearl Harbor assault. They were unaware an attack had been planned when, in the afternoon on December 7, they presented Secretary of State Cordell Hull with what amounted to a declaration of war. Hull coldly informed them that the attack had already begun.

**Across the sea, corpses soaking in the water,
Across the mountains, corpses heaped upon the grass.
We shall die by the side of our lord.
We shall never come back.**

—VERSE FROM THE JAPANESE *MAN'YŌSHŪ* ANTHOLOGY OF POETRY, WHICH WAS POPULAR WITH JAPANESE SERVICEMEN

Japanese prepare for attack Crew members on a Japanese aircraft carrier cheer as their planes take off for Pearl Harbor on December 7, 1941. "As boys," one Zero fighter pilot later recalled, "we were told we should join the military when we grew up because that was the best way to bring honor to Japan." The plan to open war with the U.S. by attacking Pearl had been approved in mid-October. To train for the attack, mock-ups of U.S. warships were used by air squadrons to simulate level and dive-bombing on moving and fixed targets. All was ready by mid-November 1941.

Yamamoto spearheads Pearl attack Wounded in the Russo-Japanese War, Yamamoto Isokoru of Japan later spent considerable time in the United States. He studied at Harvard and the Naval War College and served as a naval attaché in Washington. As commander-in-chief of the Combined Fleet, Admiral Yamamoto opposed war with the U.S., saying, "I shall run wild for the first six months . . . but I have utterly no confidence for the second or third year." When war was decided in Tokyo, he insisted on replacing the Japanese plan for war with the attack on Pearl Harbor. Later, he saw his fears borne out at Midway and Guadalcanal. He was killed on April 18, 1943, when U.S. fighters ambushed his plane over Bougainville.

Japanese strike Ewa station first U.S. Marines armed with Springfield 03 rifles look skyward for Japanese planes at Ewa Marine Corps Air Station southwest of Pearl Harbor on December 7, 1941. Ewa came under air attack about two minutes before the main enemy raid struck Pearl Harbor. Eighteen to 24 enemy fighters descended to within 25 feet of the ground to strafe the base. They destroyed 33 out of 49 U.S. aircraft on the ground and damaged the remainder.

Attack on Pearl Harbor

A<small>T</small> 8.00 <small>A.M.</small> <small>ON</small> S<small>UNDAY</small>, December 7, 1941, nearly 200 Japanese carrier-borne aircraft attacked Pearl Harbor in Hawaii. On Battleship Row, 70 combatant ships and 24 auxiliary vessels of the United States Pacific Fleet, under Admiral Husband Kimmel, presented excellent targets for the Japanese "Val" dive-bombers and "Kate" torpedo-bombers. Four hundred Army, Navy, and Marine Corps aircraft, parked wing tip to wing tip on the three nearby airfields, were also easy prey for Japanese planes. Japanese commander Fuchida Mitsuo radioed back to the task force the code words for attack: *"To! To! To!"*

Although the possibility of an air attack on Pearl Harbor had been discussed for years, and although war with Japan was a distinct possibility as negotiations over China and Indochina faltered, the defenders were indeed surprised.

The USS *Shaw* exploding during the Pearl Harbor attack

Kimmel and Lieutenant General Walter Short, Hawaii's army commander, had considered an attack unlikely and strategically pointless. Nevertheless, the island's radar had detected the approaching enemy aircraft, and a Japanese submarine had been attacked outside the harbor, but these warnings went unheeded.

The first wave of the attack inflicted terrible damage to the airfields and to a half-dozen ships—most notably the *Arizona, Oklahoma,* and *California*—before departing at about 8:30 <small>A.M.</small> Thirty minutes later, another 170 aircraft attacked, concentrating on previously undamaged ships. This wave lost 20 planes to antiaircraft fire before its departure at 10 <small>A.M.</small> signaled the end of the raid. American casualties included 21 ships damaged or sunk (all but three would be salvaged) and 3,600 men killed or wounded. One hundred and eighty-eight aircraft were destroyed, and 159 were damaged.

Fortunately for the fleet, its especially precious ships, the aircraft carriers, had been away. The *Enterprise* and *Lexington* were delivering aircraft to Wake and Midway islands, and the *Saratoga* was being repaired on the West Coast. Moreover, the Japanese task force commander, Admiral Nagumo, had not sent in a third wave to destroy Hawaii's huge oil tanks (which held 140 million gallons of diesel oil)

and repair facilities. The attackers lost 29 aircraft (with a further 70 damaged) and five midget submarines.

Though the assault was a tactical success, strategically it was a disaster. President Roosevelt's depiction of it as an "unprovoked and dastardly attack" reflected the mood of the American public, which subsequently cast aside isolationism and pacifism. According to Roosevelt's critics, he allowed the attack to occur (in order to justify his desire to enter the war) by withholding warning information from Kimmel and Short. The balance of evidence still refutes this conspiracy theory as well as the arguments that Churchill withheld information about the imminent attack.

Pearl Harbor engendered a lasting desire to apportion blame. Afterward, Kimmel and Short were relieved of command and condemned by a commission of inquiry for dereliction of duty. Six more administrative inquiries followed.

The Pearl Harbor attack led to the merging of the aggressive wars of Japan and Germany and the involvement of the United States in a global war. The cry "Remember Pearl Harbor" resonated throughout the war, as well as in postwar American foreign policy.

1941

November 3: As tensions mount between the U.S. and Japan, American women and children leave Guam, Wake, and Midway Islands.

November 6: The U.S. National Academy of Sciences reviews the technology behind the invention of fissile nuclear weaponry and calls for the immediate development of the atomic bomb. • Japan's military command prepares for planned attacks throughout the East Indies and South Asia, including Thailand and the Philippines.

November 7: Stalin rallies his war-weary subjects with his inspirational "Mother Russia" speech, recalling the heroics of great Russians from years past.

November 9: Working off intercepted intelligence information, the Royal Navy destroys two Italian shipping convoys.

November 10: Underscoring his commitment to Britain's partnership with the United States, Churchill insists he will declare war "within the hour" if Japan and the United States engage forces.

November 14: The British aircraft carrier *Ark Royal* sinks two days after being torpedoed in a German U-boat attack. The crippled ship is making its way back to England from its post off the coast of Gibraltar when it finally goes down. • The beleagured city of Leningrad gets a lifeline with the first airlift of supplies.

November 17: Congress allows for the arming of merchant ships with its repeal of key sections of the Neutrality Act, a move that Roosevelt lobbied hard to achieve. • The Japanese high command signs off on Admiral Yamamoto's plan to bomb Pearl Harbor.

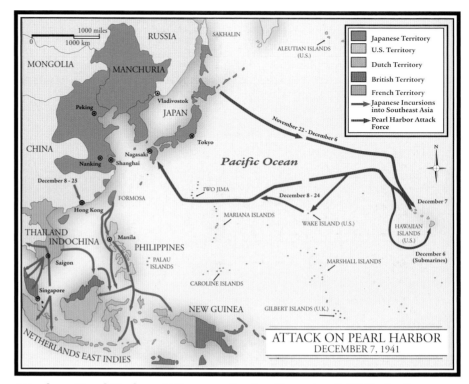

Attack on Pearl Harbor At 8 A.M. on Sunday, December 7, 1941, the first wave of 353 carrier-based Japanese bombers and other combat aircraft struck the U.S. Pacific Fleet's base in Hawaii. The U.S. naval and military garrison was almost completely surprised, and the devastation was extensive. Japan's dramatic entry into the Second World War was a remarkable strategic accomplishment, notwithstanding its political repercussions, the adverse propaganda, and the absence of the U.S. aircraft carriers from Hawaii that day.

Bombers assault U.S. battleships The U.S. battleships *West Virginia* and *Tennessee* (*both pictured*) were heavily damaged during the attack on Pearl Harbor. Seven torpedoes and two bombs struck the *West Virginia*, and two bombs hit the *Tennessee*. (Both ships were repaired and saw action before the end of the war.) Although the surprise attack on Pearl Harbor was a tactical victory for the Japanese, it was a long-term strategic defeat. In reflecting on the outcome of the attack, its primary planner, Admiral Yamamoto Isoroku, is said to have declared, "I fear all we have done is awaken a sleeping giant and fill him with a terrible resolve."

Zealous fury The men piloting the aircraft during the attack on Pearl Harbor had been trained in a culture in which loyalty unto death in the service of their emperor was a sacred principle. They were taught that America threatened the existence of Japan itself. The zeal that they brought to their mission is depicted in this cartoon, which was found in the wreckage of a Japanese aircraft after the attack. This drawing also included a phrase that translated to: "Listen! The voice of the moment of death. Wake up, you fools."

1,177 die in *Arizona* bombing The USS *Arizona*, whose wreckage is pictured, was commissioned by the Navy in October 1916. It was docked on "Battleship Row" in Pearl Harbor on December 7. Minutes after the attack began, the *Arizona* was hit by a 1,760-pound armor-piercing bomb. The explosive penetrated the deck and ignited more than a million pounds of gunpowder, tearing the ship apart and killing 1,177 of the crew. A sailor on another ship saw the Arizona "jump at least 15 or 20 feet... upwards in the water and sort of break in two."

HORRIFIED

WHEN THAT BIG BOMB blew up and they put the fire out, I looked down in that big hole that went down three or four decks. I saw men all blown up, men with no legs on, men burned to death, men drowned in oil, with oil coming out of their eyes and their mouth and their ears. You couldn't believe it was happening. You could see it in front of your eyes, but you couldn't believe it. Here it was, a beautiful day—a beautiful Sunday morning—and you see everything blowing up and ships sinking and men in the water. And you think, we're at peace with the world. This can't be happening.

—SEAMAN SECOND CLASS EDDIE JONES, USS *CALIFORNIA*

Volunteers come to the rescue On the morning of December 7, an alarm sounded across Oahu directing all civilian shipyard workers to report to Pearl Harbor, even as the battleships were still under attack. One group of civilians under the direction of Julio DeCastro, on board the USS *Oklahoma*, was credited with saving the lives of 32 crewmen trapped in the ship's hull. Many other civilians, both men and women, worked for hours fighting fires on the ships and docks. One civilian, George Walters, was cited for risking his life by running a crane up and down its tracks, shielding three battleships from enemy fire.

1941

November 17: Lewis Clark Grew, the U.S. ambassador to Japan, sends a message to U.S. secretary of state Cordell Hull. He emphasizes the need "for guarding against sudden military or naval actions by Japan in areas not at present involved in the China conflict."

November 18: Operation Crusader, the first British counteroffensive launched on the North African front, pits seven British divisions against 10 divisions of Axis soldiers.

November 19: In the biggest battle of the West African desert to date, British commandos raid Rommel's headquarters but fail to kill him as planned.

November 20: Japan issues an ultimatum to the United States, demanding American noninterference in Japanese relations in Indochina and China. Roosevelt will submit an equally unlikely program for peace in the Pacific.

November 24: Rommel makes one last unsuccessful attempt to outflank the British, while the Allies capture the key supply depot of Gambut, Libya. • Congress approves an expansion of the Lend-Lease Act to include French who are not living under Nazi rule.

November 25: The Axis renews the Anti-Comintern Pact for five years. Signatories include Italy, Japan, Spain, Croatia, Bulgaria, Romania, Hungary, Slovakia, Denmark, Finland, Manchukuo, and Japan's puppet government in Nanking. • Nearly 860 sailors die when the British battleship *Barham* sinks off the coast of Crete after being torpedoed by a German U-boat.

B-17s caught in line of fire On the morning of December 7, 12 unarmed B-17s were on a mission to the Philippines as part of the American effort to build up that area's defenses in the hope of deterring a Japanese attack. The planes' crew members planned to stop in Hawaii for refueling and the mounting of their guns. Chillingly, they did not realize that they were on a collision course with the Japanese attack force. The B-17s arrived at Oahu during the attack and had to dodge enemy and American antiaircraft fire. Miraculously, even though they were strafed by gunfire that wounded crew members, all of the B-17s landed intact except for the one pictured here. Although it split in half, its crew survived the landing.

Civilian casualties Joe McCabe and three other family members, all shipyard riggers, raced in McCabe's car to the harbor as Japanese attack planes flew overhead. An explosion suddenly riddled his car with shrapnel, killing three of the men and mortally wounding the fourth. By the end of the attack, 68 civilians had been killed and 35 wounded. Initial reports stated that the McCabe group had been killed by a Japanese bomb. It was later revealed, however, that the deaths were caused by an American antiaircraft shell. Further investigations showed that most of the civilian deaths and wounded were at the hands of Americans, not Japanese.

Miller's heroism

Admiral Chester Nimitz personally awarded Doris "Dorie" Miller with the Navy Cross on May 27, 1942, for his actions during the attack on Pearl Harbor. Miller was a mess attendant on the USS *West Virginia* the morning of the attack when he carried his mortally wounded captain to a safer spot on the ship. Although untrained, he proceeded to man a .50 caliber antiaircraft machine gun until ordered to abandon ship. He died in action almost two years after Pearl Harbor.

"above and beyond the call of duty"

DORIE MILLER
Received the Navy Cross at Pearl Harbor, May 27, 1942

Americans turn to their president Crowds began to form in front of the White House as soon as word of the attack on Pearl Harbor was announced. The men and women standing in this picture were not there to picket or demonstrate. They sought reassurance from President Roosevelt that the country was safe in his hands. Those who had supported isolationism now realized that America could not sit this war out. United States soil had been attacked and American men and women killed. They stood in front of the White House seeking both comfort and revenge.

FDR signs declaration of war On December 8, 1941, President Roosevelt made an impassioned speech to Congress calling for a declaration of war. His opening—"Yesterday, December 7, 1941, a date which will live in infamy..."—helped to stoke the American fever for revenge. FDR signed the declaration (*pictured*) in the Oval Office while surrounded by legislators and Cabinet members. Revisionist historians have claimed that Roosevelt had known about the attack and purposely withheld the information to provoke America's entry into the war. However, no evidence exists to support this assertion.

American men sign up Hundreds of thousands of Americans enlisted in the armed forces in the weeks after the United States declared war on Japan. This number included sports figures and movie stars. "Rapid" Robert Feller, star pitcher of the Cleveland Indians, enlisted in the Navy two days after Pearl Harbor was attacked. The young men in this picture line up outside a Navy recruiting station in Boston on December 8, 1941. Many enlisted in the Navy in order to avoid the Army.

1941

November 26: The Japanese Hawaii task force leaves the Kurile Islands, bound for Pearl Harbor, Hawaii. Later in the day, in a note to the Japanese ambassador, U.S. secretary of state Cordell Hull demands the complete withdrawal of all Japanese troops from China. Japanese prime minister Tojo will refer to this as "an ultimatum."

November 27: With the fall of Gondar, Ethiopia, the 350,000-man Italian army has been routed by about 20,000 Allied troops, marking the final stand of Italy in East Africa. • Believing that Japan is likely to attack within a matter of days, the United States military is placed on high alert.

December 1: In a unanimous vote, Japanese leaders officially endorse plans to enter the war against the United States.

December 4: Britain calls for unmarried women, ages 20 to 30, to serve in public service jobs, primarily on the home front.

December 5: At the end of a massive Russian campaign that has seen the elimination by death or injury of more than 750,000 Axis soldiers, Hitler calls for a temporary halt in the offensive. • In the interest of protecting wartime intelligence, U.S. naval facilities throughout Asia are ordered to destroy almost all documents and communications codes.

December 6: General Zhukov launches a successful counterattack around Moscow, pushing back the cold and starving German troops. It is the *Wehrmacht*'s first major defeat. • Roosevelt promises more than adequate funding for an atomic bomb research project.

Kimmel, Short held responsible for Pearl attack One week after Pearl Harbor, Admiral Husband Kimmel, commander-in-chief of the U.S. Pacific Fleet, was on the cover of *Time* magazine due to the investigation into who was at fault for the Navy and Army's lack of vigilance. Kimmel and Army Lieutenant General Walter Short were eventually found responsible for dereliction of duty. Both resigned, their careers ruined. Kimmel went to work for a private-sector military contractor, and Short accepted a position with the Ford Motor Co.

ADMIRAL KIMMEL, CINCUS
The enemy's first blow struck him.

Japan bombs naval yard in Philippines Flames rise from the Cavite Naval Yard in Luzon, Philippines, following a Japanese bombing raid on December 10, 1941. Japanese air superiority had been assured two days earlier when their planes caught much of the U.S. Far East Air Force, including a number of valuable B-17 bombers, on the ground at Clark Field. The Japanese followed with multiple landings on Luzon and later Mindanao. Deprived of his airpower and facing multiple enemy advances, U.S. general Douglas MacArthur abandoned plans to defend all of Luzon. On December 23, he ordered his forces to withdraw to the Bataan Peninsula for what would turn out to be their final stand.

The Philippines

HOME TO 17 MILLION PEOPLE in 1941, the Philippine Islands had been dominated by regional foreign powers since the third century A.D. European control arrived with the Spanish in the 1500s and lasted until 1898, when the islands were ceded to the United States following the Spanish-American War.

Possession of the Philippines placed the United States along crucial trade routes between Japan, China, and the oil- and mineral-rich regions to the south. Manila Bay on the island of Luzon was the finest natural harbor in the Far East.

During the 1930s, U.S. military planners correctly assumed that the islands would be a prime enemy objective in any war with Japan. U.S. defense plans, code-named "Orange," went through several versions over the years. They essentially called for American and Filipino forces to hold out against a Japanese invasion until the U.S. fleet could steam to the rescue. Anticipating this strategy, the Japanese called for attrition attacks on the U.S. fleet as it passed through imperial possessions in the central Pacific. Theoretically, the remainder of the American fleet would then be destroyed in battle off the Philippines.

By 1939, U.S. planners were backing away from Orange. Any war with Japan would clearly be part of a wider conflict, presumably involving Germany. The feasibility of projecting sufficient force 5,000 miles across the Pacific in the event of a two-front war was questionable at best. A new

American and Filipino soldiers in Luzon, Philippines

plan, Rainbow 5, conceded it might be necessary to abandon the Philippines. Meanwhile, Japanese plans also changed. In October 1941, Japan abandoned a reactive naval engagement in favor of an offensive strike against the U.S. Pacific Fleet at Pearl Harbor with a simultaneous invasion of the Philippines.

Rainbow 5 notwithstanding, the stunning Japanese success at Pearl Harbor on December 7, 1941, made relief of the Philippines a military impossibility. Not until October 1944 did U.S. forces finally return to wrest control of the islands from Japan.

Japanese sink British ships The battleship HMS *Prince of Wales* sinks on December 10, 1941, after coming under attack by Japanese dive-bomber and torpedo planes off Singapore. Caught without air cover, the battleship was easy prey after a torpedo disabled the rudder. Among the 327 killed was Admiral Sir Tom Phillips, the Far East Fleet commander. The obsolete battle cruiser *Repulse* was also sunk in the attack. Despite fears that design problems contributed to the disaster, the battleship's stronger hull actually allowed much of the crew to be rescued—in contrast to HMS *Repulse*, which took 513 men to the bottom.

1941

December 6: British sailor John Capes makes a miraculous escape from the submarine *Perseus*, which had been sunk by a mine. Despite injuries, he ascends from a depth of 170 feet and swims to the Greek coastline. • Britain declares war on Finland, at the request of the Soviet Union. • Citing his doubt that Japanese troops in Indochina are there for defensive purposes, Roosevelt asks Emperor Hirohito to withdraw his forces.

December 7: Hitler issues the "Night and Fog" decree, calling for the convenient disappearance of anyone who threatens the security of Nazi Germany. • Japanese planes attack American ships and planes at the U.S. base at Pearl Harbor, Hawaii. More than 2,300 American sailors and soldiers are killed.

December 8: Hitler acknowledges that the Soviet campaign will be neither quick nor easy. • Calling December 7 a "day that will live in infamy," Roosevelt calls for a congressional declaration of war on Japan. • Japanese troops occupy Shanghai, China, and capture a small U.S. garrison.

December 10: Britain's naval force is dealt a heavy blow when the Japanese sink the battleship *Prince of Wales* and the battle cruiser *Repulse*. • Guam quickly capitulates when overwhelmed by 6,000 Japanese troops.

December 11: Germany and Italy declare war on the United States. Congress responds by declaring war on those two nations.

December 13: The American policy of preventive internment is launched with the confinement of nearly 600 Japanese and 200 Germans.

Soviet-British alliance The Soviet Union began the war as a virtual ally of Germany, due to the Soviet-German nonaggression pact. But Operation Barbarossa changed this situation completely. The Kremlin rarely promoted publicly the contribution of its Anglo-U.S. allies to the defeat of Germany, as it directed most of its propaganda to self-promotion and to motivating the Russian people. Nevertheless, this 1941 poster recognizes Britain's involvement in the war. It was produced when the Soviet Union was particularly dependent upon receiving large quantities of Anglo-U.S. war materiel to fight the "Great Patriotic War."

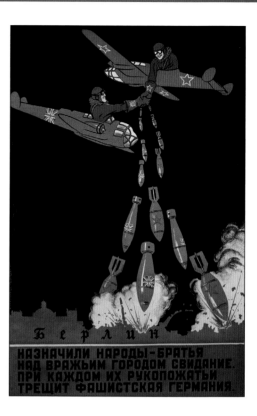

The siege of Leningrad The name "Leningrad" was of particular ideological significance to Hitler, and he ordered the obliteration of Leningrad and its people through bombing, shelling, starvation, and disease. He also forbade the acceptance of any surrender offer, if made. Field Marshal Leeb's Army Group North reached Leningrad on September 8, 1941, and began an 872-day German siege, during which close to a million of the city's citizens died. Here, a woman pulls the corpse of a child on a sleigh. Meanwhile, the survivors suffered almost unimaginable hardships, especially during the Russian winters. Bitter and often large-scale fighting raged about the city intermittently until January 27, 1944, when the much-weakened *Wehrmacht* was finally forced to withdraw in the face of a major Red Army offensive.

Allied Aid to Russia

IN JUNE 1941, the British stood alone in their fight against Germany. The United States had not yet entered the war, France had fallen to the Nazis a year earlier, and Italy had partnered with Germany in the fight to control Europe and North Africa. When the Nazis broke their alliance with the USSR by invading Russia on June 21, the British were quick to accept the Soviets as an ally in their fight against Germany. While many skeptics in Britain questioned the Soviet Union's intentions, they had little choice in their support. The Soviets provided much-needed assistance.

President Franklin Roosevelt also recognized the importance of nurturing the relationship with the USSR. The Lend-Lease Act, which authorized the U.S. to sell, exchange, or trade $50 billion in war materials to its Allies, did not include the USSR when it was passed in March 1941. It was not until November 7, 1941, that Congress finally declared the Soviets eligible to receive materials through the Lend-Lease Act.

British women selling flags to aid USSR

Almost $11 billion worth of war materials were shipped to the USSR during the war, including combat aircraft, tanks, trucks, and jeeps. These supplies were especially needed at the beginning of the war when the Soviets did not yet have the ability to manufacture sufficient amounts of war materials. The United States and Britain also gave food and clothing through the Russian War Relief and the Red Cross.

To avoid capture by German or Japanese troops, much of the Soviet aid was shipped via the Persian Gulf and Iran. Most of the remaining supplies were transported across the Pacific Ocean to Vladivostok and the North Atlantic to Murmansk.

When the end of the war was near, Soviet leader Joseph Stalin acknowledged the importance of Allied aid. "Lend-Lease," Stalin said, "is one of Franklin Roosevelt's most remarkable and vital achievements in the formation of the anti-Hitler alliance."

Leningrad's lifeline Although Leningrad was besieged by the Germans, Lake Ladoga to the northeast of Leningrad nevertheless provided a lifeline for the starving population and military resources for the city's defenders. In summer, boats could traverse the lake, while in winter it froze hard, enabling supply trucks to drive across it (*pictured*). Understandably, such hazardous activities were usually conducted by night, as they took place within range of German artillery and of the *Luftwaffe*'s bombers. The returning trucks carried evacuees—hundreds of thousands in 1942—although many died in the unheated vehicles.

STARVATION IN LENINGRAD

TO FILL THEIR EMPTY STOMACHS, to reduce the intense sufferings caused by hunger, people would look for incredible substitutes: they would try to catch crows or rooks, or any cat or dog that had still somehow survived; they would go through medicine chests in search of castor oil, hair oil, vaseline or glycerine; they would make soup or jelly out of carpenter's glue (scraped off wallpaper or broken-up furniture). But not all people in the enormous city had such supplementary sources of "food."

—HISTORIAN D. V. PAVLOV, ON CIVILIAN STARVATION DURING THE GERMAN SIEGE OF THE CITY, 1941

1941

December 16: Japanese troops land on Borneo in Southeast Asia.

December 17: Admiral Chester Nimitz is appointed commander of the U.S. Navy's Pacific Fleet.

December 19: Hitler himself becomes commander-in-chief of the German army, replacing Walther von Brauchitsch. • Amending the Selective Service Act, the U.S. Congress requires all men ages 18 to 64 to register. Those 20 to 44 are eligible for military service.

December 20: The soon-to-be legendary pilots of the U.S. Air Force Flying Tigers engage in their first combat mission, dominating their Japanese counterparts in the skies over Kunming, China.

December 22: The 23-day Arcadia Conference begins in Washington, D.C. The United States and Britain agree that defeat of Germany is their No. 1 objective. They also agree to combine military resources under one command.

December 23: With the United States officially among the world war belligerents, American military leaders hold their first joint war council with the British. They create the Combined Chiefs of Staff to craft Allied strategy. • The last American base in the Pacific between Hawaii and the Philippines is lost with the Japanese conquest of Wake Island. • American and Filipino officials evacuate Manila. • The Japanese take Jolo Island, the capital of the Philippines' Sulu province.

December 25: India's Congress Party offers its support to Britain, causing Mohandas Gandhi to resign his leadership post in protest. • Britain surrenders Hong Kong to Japan.

December 30: Most of Borneo falls to the Japanese.

Japan takes Hong Kong Japanese infantrymen engage in the fight for Hong Kong in December 1941. Though British strategists originally considered Hong Kong too isolated to defend, they hoped that a show of force in 1941 would deter Japanese aggression and preserve British control of the colony. This effort to save face proved to be a miscalculation. Elements of the Japanese 38th Division attacked on December 8. With the advantage of air and artillery superiority, veteran Japanese troops quickly overwhelmed the British defenders. Governor Sir Mark Young surrendered the colony on Christmas Day, 1941. Many Japanese atrocities followed.

Zhukov's winter counteroffensive In late November, the leading troops of Army Group Center's Second Panzer Division—many of them frostbitten, without proper winter clothing, short of fuel, and weakened by earlier fighting—halted within sight of the Kremlin's spires. Elsewhere, Army Groups South and North were already stalled. Then, on December 5, Marshal Zhukov launched his major counteroffensive, striking Army Group Center with the 17 armies of his Western Front. They pushed the Germans back 60 miles, thereby safeguarding Moscow. This painting romanticizes the Russians' wintertime efforts.

Marines defend Wake Island The 1942 film *Wake Island* commemorated America's defense of the tiny Pacific atoll in December 1941. Initially, just 450 U.S. Marines and a squadron of obsolete Wildcat fighters garrisoned Wake's valuable air base. The

Japanese attacked Wake with heavy air raids followed by an amphibious assault on December 11. Wake's coastal guns repulsed the fleet, and two Japanese destroyers were sunk. Sustained Japanese bombing followed. A U.S. relief force moved too slowly to reach Wake before the second Japanese attack on December 23. About 2,000 Japanese landed, supported by carrier-based aircraft and naval guns. The defenders resisted effectively, even counterattacking against immense odds, but were doomed when the relief force was recalled to Hawaii. Surrender followed.

Japan's potent Zero-sen When the Japanese naval air force became engaged in the conflict, first against China in 1937 and then in December 1941 against the Western allies, its opponents were shocked by the superior quality of its aircraft. Typical of these was the pictured Mitsubishi Zero-sen (Zeke), which entered service in 1940. A light, highly maneuverable, and well-armed fighter, the Zero outclassed Allied fighters in the Pacific Theater in 1941. It maintained its technological edge into 1942, when design weaknesses such as its light armor protection and non-self-sealing fuel tanks made it increasingly vulnerable to the new types of Allied fighters.

Germans unprepared for winter As autumn 1941 drew to a close on the Eastern Front, mud froze solid—as did most lubricating oils. Many vehicles, weapons, and equipment became useless. For Germans soldiers, winter clothing was not generally available, as the high command had confidently planned for Barbarossa to conclude within four months. Soldiers began to suffer respiratory diseases, and sentries literally froze to death. Frostbite and cold-burn injuries escalated in −40°F temperatures. Meanwhile, increasingly erratic deliveries of food, fuel, and ammunition via overextended supply lines affected operations and morale alike, while the campaign became ever more bitterly contested and brutal. Subsequently, the Russians launched their November–December offensives. For those German prisoners of war (*pictured*), unimaginable privations lay ahead.

Canadian escorts From September 1939, convoys left Nova Scotia for Great Britain every eight days. The escorts were usually comprised of a large British warship (*pictured*) and two Canadian destroyers. At about longitude 20°W, the escort group handed the convoy to escorts from Britain, then usually took a westbound convoy to Halifax. Though the Royal Canadian Navy began the war with just six destroyers and five minesweepers, it expanded to more than 40 times its original size and contributed immensely to the Battle of the Atlantic.

THE AXIS
SMASHES FORWARD

JANUARY 1942–JULY 1942

"The fruits of victory are tumbling into our mouths too quickly."

—Japanese Emperor Hirohito, April 29, 1942

On February 15, 1942, the British Empire suffered one of its most humiliating defeats. At 6:15 P.M., in a makeshift conference room in the Ford Motor Company factory in Singapore, General Arthur Percival surrendered the island to Lieutenant General Yamashita Tomoyuki. The Japanese made the island the headquarters of the Southern Army, which conquered Southeast Asia, and renamed Singapore "Shonan," meaning "Light of the South." Of the 50,000 white troops captured, 18,000 would die of disease and/or mistreatment before war's end.

The Japanese armed forces aimed to capture a broad area in the south. They would defend the perimeter while the rich resources of the region were incorporated into the Japanese war effort. Resistance was limited. In the Dutch East Indies, the 140,000-man colonial army was overwhelmed. The northern Philippines, with a mixed native and American force, was quickly overrun except for the Bataan Peninsula, where 100,000 soldiers and refugees were bottled up. The Japanese captured the peninsula in April. The American headquarters in the fortress of Corregidor, in Manila Bay, fell on May 6, 1942, after a fierce defense. By early June, nearly all American forces in the Philippines had surrendered. Further west, a Japanese force overran Burma and entered the capital, Rangoon, on March 8. A Japanese aircraft carrier

Japanese soldiers celebrate the fall of the Philippines—and the defeat of the U.S. and Filipino defenders. This image exemplified the militaristic mood of self-confidence that was pervasive throughout Japan in April 1942. However, the Japanese empire was already overextended, and its fortunes of war were about to change dramatically.

raided the northern Australian port of Darwin on February 19, and in April Japanese aircraft sank British shipping on the Indian coast.

This was the limit of Japanese expansion, though the assault had been so successful and rapid that senior commanders sought to capitalize on their advantage with further advances. In early May, a naval force sailed south to seize the southern peninsula of New Guinea while Admiral Yamamoto planned a mid-Pacific offensive. This was designed to destroy what was left of U.S. naval power in the ocean and cut off American aid to the South Pacific.

The prelude to the final Japanese assault was the seizure of Port Moresby

Japan's capture of the island fortress of Singapore in February 1942 shocked Britain and other European colonial powers. The unthinkable had happened: What had been generally regarded as a second-rate Asiatic power had comprehensively defeated and humiliated the military forces of one of the world's greatest empires.

in southern New Guinea. The task force that was dispatched south in early May was attacked by a small Allied force in the Coral Sea. The battle was a strategic setback for Yamamoto, who was obliged to abandon his plan to seize Port Moresby and isolate Australia. This was the first hint that Japanese expansion was nearing its limit. A month later, Yamamoto dispatched a huge task force to Midway Island, hoping to lure what was left of the U.S. Pacific Fleet to battle and then annihilate it. With a small force of carriers and sufficient secret intelligence on Japanese intentions, the Pacific Fleet commander, Admiral Chester Nimitz, planned a daring interception. As the Japanese carrier fleet neared Midway, it was attacked by American dive-bombers. Only a few of their bombs struck, but they sank all four fleet carriers. Yamamoto ordered a return to Japan. His plans had been frustrated by America's intelligence successes, astute leadership, combat skills, and luck.

Elsewhere, the global war remained balanced on a knife edge. China's long, drawn-out conflict with Japan had become a formal state of war on December 9, 1941, following Pearl Harbor. Although the Japanese army controlled much of eastern and northern China, Chinese hit-and-run tactics made it difficult for Japan to pacify and control even those areas under occupation. In May 1942, Japanese commanders embarked on a ruthless policy of pacification—"kill all, steal all, burn all"—to try to deter further Chinese resistance. Roughly 250,000 Chinese were killed in 1942.

In North Africa, British Empire forces based in Egypt had moved forward successfully across Libya against weak Italian resistance. But in January 1942, against an Axis force strengthened by a German corps under General Erwin

Rommel, the British Empire Forces began a long retreat back to Egypt. Tobruk fell to the Axis on June 21, and by the end of June Axis forces were a few miles from El Alamein, Egypt, within striking distance of the Suez Canal.

The British position at sea—in the Mediterranean and the Atlantic—remained precarious. In 1942 they lost 7.8 million tons of shipping. Britain was able to import only one-third of what it took in before the war. The Allies' persistent bombing of German naval installations and submarine building sites achieved almost nothing.

The most dangerous situation lay in the Soviet theater. With the successful defense of Moscow in December 1941, the Soviets launched further offensives, trying to find weak spots in the German line. In the south, the Red Army created a large salient in German defensive lines south of Kharkov. But when Stalin ordered the Red Army to capture the city in May 1942, the German front absorbed the attack and then encircled and annihilated the attackers. In the Crimea, the Germans repulsed a Soviet counteroffensive on the Kerch Peninsula. In July, they captured Sevastopol after an assault with the world's largest artillery piece: "Big Dora."

On July 4, 1942, German general Manstein's 11th Army captured Sevastopol. This followed a six-month siege, supported by intensive artillery bombardments. Here, a German infantryman gives food to a malnourished Russian child–one of the very many civilian survivors among the shell-shocked and exhausted population of this important Soviet bastion.

Germany's central ambition was the final defeat of the Soviet Union in 1942. Hitler planned to attack the less well-defended southern front toward the Volga River and the Caucasus oil fields. Their capture would give his forces huge new oil supplies and deny them to the enemy. On June 28, Germany launched "Operation Blue" with substantial success. The Soviet southern front retreated. So successful was the assault that Hitler divided the force in two. He sent the Sixth Army, under General Friedrich Paulus, to seize Stalingrad and cut the Soviet Union off from the resources of the south. By August, German forces had reached the oil city of Maikop and were advancing toward the rich oil fields around Grozny.

In midsummer 1942, the war was poised in the balance. The strategic dream of the Axis powers was to link up in the Middle East. They would seize the Suez Canal and the oil that lay beyond it from one side, and they would sweep down from the Caucasus on the other side. With Japan threatening India and the United States not yet fully armed, the ambition seemed less fantastic at the time than it now appears. Yet the summer of 1942 saw the high watermark of Axis aggrandizement. Over the next year, the Allies would find not just greater resources but also more effective ways of fighting. They were poised to reverse the long series of defeats that had until then littered their war effort.

1942

January: In a directive that is important for troop morale, British General Claude Auchinleck reminds his Eighth Army that Erwin "Desert Fox" Rommel is an ordinary, though successful general, and not an invincible, supernatural force.

January 1: The United Nations is born from an agreement among 26 Allied nations not to make separate peace with the signatories of the Tripartite Pact. • Auto dealerships across the United States close their doors after steel conservation measures force a moratorium on new car and truck sales. • Twenty-three Czech partisans are murdered by the Nazi occupation force on suspicion of sabotage.

January 2: The rampaging Japanese army occupies the Philippine capital of Manila.

January 3–12: China emerges victorious in a battle for Changsha, Hunan. The Chinese drive some 70,000 Japanese troops into full retreat.

January 4: New Japanese bases in Thailand are now operational.

January 6: Washington and London announce plans to station American troops in Britain to help further Allied military goals in Europe. • In a victory that is Britain's first against German troops in this war, the Eighth Army routs a division of Rommel's Panzer Corps, inflicting nearly 40,000 casualties.

January 10: The Japanese launch a propaganda war in the skies over the Philippines, dropping leaflets on Allied troops that press for their surrender.

January 11: Japan invades the Celebes Islands, part of the Dutch empire, and declares war on the Netherlands. • Japan continues its campaign of conquest with the seizure of the Malaysian capital of Kuala Lumpur.

Borneo falls to Japan Japanese infantry go on the assault in British Borneo. Mountainous and heavily jungled, with a limited network of roads, Borneo was strategically important due to its position on the main routes between Japan and Malaya. It also offered large supplies of oil and raw materials to the resource-starved Japanese (though for Japan to successfully transport oil along shipping lanes that would see increased Allied activity would be difficult). For the moment, though, the possibility of Japanese access to additional oil was unappealing to the Allies. British strategists had long realized that Borneo could not be held. Nevertheless, the only Allied ground unit on Borneo, an outnumbered Indian battalion of the 15th Punjab Regiment, managed to resist for 10 weeks before it was overwhelmed.

The Battle of Changsha A Chinese soldier mans a light machine gun during the Battle of Changsha. The Japanese offensive against the city began with 120,000 troops in late December 1941. The Chinese army resisted with 300,000 men, which harassed the Japanese advance and then established lines of defense in Changsha itself. The Japanese assault penetrated the city, but on January 1 the Chinese counterattacked, inflicting heavy casualties. Other Chinese units swept down from the mountains to sever Japanese supply lines. Suddenly finding themselves besieged, the Japanese began a costly retreat, finally reaching the safety of the Sinchiang River on January 15.

Japanese Military Culture

At the outbreak of the Pacific war, the Japanese armed forces combined modern technology—including ships and aircraft equal to or superior to their Allied equivalents—with a military spirit that remained feudal. Termed *Bushido* (The Way of the Warrior), that spirit gave rise to behavior that Allied soldiers found bewildering as well as barbarous and fanatical.

Based on peculiar perspectives on Confucianism and Zen Buddhism, *Bushido* demanded unquestioning loyalty and sacrifice. The Japanese soldiers' written code ordered them to keep in mind that duty was "weightier than a mountain," while death was "lighter

War vet practicing sword fighting

than a feather." Indeed, death was idealized as something to be welcomed. Thus, soldiers, sailors, and airmen willingly sacrificed themselves in *banzai* charges, *kamikaze* aircraft, and *kaiten* submarines.

Japan's leaders now believed surrender as unthinkable for Japanese and contemptible in enemies, thus justifying abominable treatment of prisoners after prior years of very decent treatment of prisoners (also attributed to *Bushido*). In keeping with the samurai tradition, they also revered the sword, which led to the beheading of their captives. The International Military Tribunal for the Far East blamed *Bushido* as a contributing factor in Japanese atrocities.

Atrocities were part of every major Japanese land operation, and were directed against both combatants and civilians. The demeaning training and disciplinary regimes in the Japanese services featured corporal punishment, and probably contributed to the brutality of their personnel. The Japanese army employed ruses that their enemies considered unacceptable, including wearing enemy uniforms, booby-trapping corpses, and feigning surrender in order to kill would-be captors.

The atrocities could be blamed on other reasons. The Japanese were fighting a losing war, combating insurgencies, and trying to survive amid starvation. However, the atrocities had begun when Japan was winning the war.

Japanese servicemen were repeatedly told that their martial spirit was superior to that of their materialistic enemies, who would eventually succumb. Initially, the combination of Japanese ferocity and skill was frighteningly successful. However, the ultimate defeat of the Japanese discredited their cultural prejudice.

Brazil linked to Nazi Germany U.S. undersecretary of state Sumner Welles, Brazilian foreign minister Oswaldo Aranha, and Brazilian dictator Getúlio Vargas *(left to right)* chat amiably during a 1942 conference. Despite the smiles, the United States had deep concerns about Brazilian policy in the years prior to World War II. Enamored of the German model, Vargas had dissolved Brazil's constitutional government in 1937 and strengthened trade links with Nazi Germany, creating alarm in U.S. political circles. Vargas cleverly played upon those fears to win economic concessions from the U.S. In 1942 Brazil finally came into the war on the Allied side. However, enemy agents and the large German population in South America provided pro-Axis pressure and cover for Axis communication facilities well into 1944.

1942

January 12: The Inter-Allied Conference meets in London and resolves to try Axis officials with war crimes at the end of the conflict.

January 13: The first 700 of 10,000 Polish Jews from the city of Lódź scheduled for "resettlement" are shipped to the newly established Chelmno death camp in Poland.
• The Germans launch Operation Drum Roll, a U-boat offensive along the American East Coast.

January 14: American and British war planners, meeting in Washington, D.C., agree to focus on Hitler's defeat before turning their attention to Japanese domination in the Pacific.
• Nearly 2,000 European companies with Axis interests are barred from doing business with any American entity, public or private. • The tanker *Norness*, flying Panamanian colors, is torpedoed off North Carolina's Cape Hatteras. It is the first ship attacked off the U.S. East Coast by a German U-boat.

January 20: At the Wannsee Conference in Berlin, the Nazis draw most German government agencies into the European portion of the "Final Solution" for the Jews. Reinhard Heydrich suggests that they should be worked to death, and those that don't succumb should be executed. • Facing a certain threat by Japan, Churchill calls on British troops to defend Singapore "to the death."

January 21: Rommel shocks his British foes by directing his *Afrika Korps* in a tactical about-face. He launches an offensive in Libya that will see him regain lost territory almost immediately.

January 22: The Soviets begin the evacuation of hundreds of thousands of people from the besieged city of Leningrad.

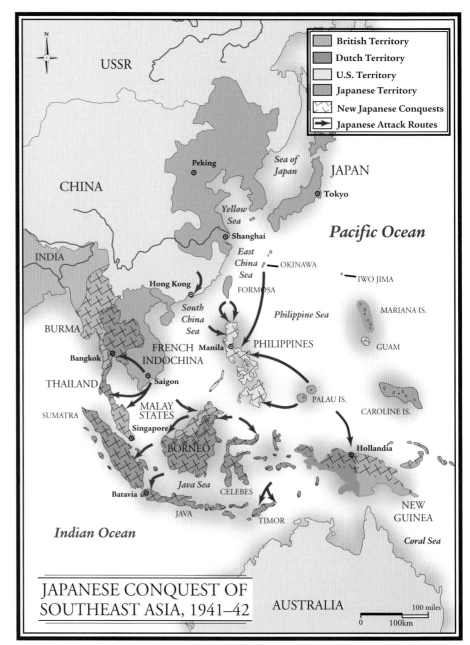

JAPANESE CONQUEST OF SOUTHEAST ASIA, 1941–42

A string of victories Soon after Pearl Harbor, Japanese forces invaded Thailand and Malaya. Landings also took place in the Philippines, North Borneo, and the Dutch East Indies. On December 26, the fall of Hong Kong ended an 18-day Japanese onslaught. During January 1942, Manila and Kuala Lumpur were occupied and the Solomon Islands invaded. From February to April, the British stronghold of Singapore fell, and Japanese landings were made at Bali, Mindanao, and Dutch New Guinea. Then, just as the overextended Japanese forces sought to consolidate their newly won territories, a series of U.S. victories from May to August—in the Coral Sea, at Midway, and at Guadalcanal—finally reversed the strategic situation.

The biting cartoons of Dr. Seuss A decade before he broke through as a famous children's book author, Dr. Seuss (Theodor Seuss Geisel) created more than 400 political cartoons for the liberal New York tabloid *PM* during the war. Primary targets for his biting caricatures were Hitler, Mussolini, conservative politicians, and isolationists. Dr. Seuss also condemned anti-black and anti-Semitic beliefs, but he targeted all Japanese as potential enemies of America. In this cartoon, which appeared in *PM* on February 13, 1942, he expressed the fear that most of the Japanese Americans on the Pacific coast were potential saboteurs. His cartoons contributed to the hysteria that led to the internment of Japanese Americans in 1942.

Italy routed at Tobruk In January 1942, the Italian garrison of Tobruk, Libya, fell to the Allied Western Desert Force. Some 25,000 prisoners, 208 guns, 23 tanks, 200 trucks, and a multiplicity of rations and supplies were captured—as was a guaranteed source of fresh water. The British also acquired a major port vital to their logistic plans. Meanwhile, the Italian navy suffered from defective operating concepts, underfunding, poor gunnery, and general mismanagement. Accordingly, the part-submerged remains of this Italian destroyer, sunk by the Royal Navy outside the harbor, symbolized the totality of the Italian defeat at Tobruk.

Germans freeze on Eastern Front German soldiers huddle around a fire during their first winter in Russia in 1941–42. Daytime temperatures were routinely −30°F. Although German morale generally held up remarkably well, the *Wehrmacht* high command was unprepared for campaigning in the Russian winter. Lubricants froze, and consequently vehicles and weapons refused to work. Many horses upon which the army—especially the artillery units—still depended died during the bitterly cold nights. Meanwhile, many infantry companies were quickly reduced to platoon strength due to their lack of winter clothing. The Red Army was much better prepared.

Australians ambush Japanese Trapped in a defile, Japanese troops are cut down near the Gemencheh Bridge near Gemas, Malaya. On January 14, 1942, A company of Australians ambushed Japanese bicycle-mounted troops who were passing through a cutting that led to the bridge on the Sungei Gemencheh River. Despite inflicting heavy casualties in their first major confrontation with the Japanese, the Australians were eventually forced to withdraw. The Japanese Fifth Division lost an estimated 1,000 men in the ambush and subsequent fighting closer to Gemas. The Australian 2/30th Battalion suffered just 81 casualties.

1942

January 23: Australia sends an urgent request for assistance from the Allies after a series of conquests in the Southwest Pacific brings the Japanese within a thousand miles of Australian territory.

January 24: U.S. Supreme Court justice Owen Roberts reports that inquests into culpability for the Japanese attack on Pearl Harbor reveal indifference and neglect on the part of Navy and Army commanders—Rear Admiral Husband Kimmel and Lieutenant General Walter Short.
• The first significant naval battle in the Pacific Theater, the Battle of Makassar Strait, ends with the Japanese losing four transport ships. Despite their losses, they will achieve their objective of securing the oil-rich port of Balikpapan, Borneo.

January 25: Thailand declares war on the United States and Great Britain.

January 26: The U.S. armed forces establish their British office in the capital city of London. • The Japanese gain a critical base with the capture of Rabaul, New Britain.

January 30: In a speech that leaves no doubt about one of Hitler's primary goals of the war, the *Führer* asserts that the conflict will end with the "complete annihilation of the Jews," calling them "the most evil universal enemy of all time."

February 1: The Reich institutes a policy of tobacco rationing in the Fatherland, allowing German women half a man's ration. • Nazi puppet Vidkun Quisling is named Norwegian premier for the second time. He will publicly accept his reappointment in a speech unapologetically delivered in German. • German U-boats adopt a new cipher called "Triton," meaning the Allies can no longer interpret their messages.

Evacuation of Singapore Women and children arrive in Britain after evacuating from Singapore. Confident of the impregnability of the fortress and fearful of creating a panic, British authorities waited too long to begin the mass evacuation of civilians. As defeat loomed, all available ships were hastily loaded with fleeing civilians. *The Empire Star*, designed to carry a small number of passengers, was crammed with 2,000 refugees. As coordination broke down, the evacuation became a debacle. Enemy planes attacked the fleeing ships and thousands of civilians drowned. Others survived drowning only to be murdered by Japanese troops as they struggled ashore on Bangka Island.

Australian survives Japanese massacre Sister Vivian Bullwinkel, an Australian Army nurse, was among the last 65 nurses evacuated from Singapore before it fell in February 1942. Their ship was sunk by Japanese aircraft off Bangka Island near Sumatra. Bullwinkel and a group of survivors struggled ashore and surrendered to Japanese soldiers, who bayoneted the men and shot the women. Miraculously, Bullwinkel survived a bullet to the side. She escaped into the jungle and eventually surrendered to Japanese sailors, from whom she concealed her wounds. She then endured three years of harsh imprisonment, attributing her survival to the friendship of fellow nurses and faith in Australia.

The Combined Chiefs of Staff

FOR THE ALLIES TO prosecute the war successfully, they needed to establish and maintain a sound working relationship between the national military staffs of the U.S. and Great Britain at the strategic level. To achieve this, the U.S. Joint Chiefs of Staff and the British Chiefs of Staff formed the Combined Chiefs of Staff in February 1942. Britain was represented in Washington by the British Joint Staff Mission.

The Combined Chiefs advised on, developed, modified, and directed Anglo-U.S. strategic policy on behalf of Churchill and Roosevelt. Heading the British mission was Field Marshal Sir John Dill (*pictured, seventh from left*), formerly chief of the British Imperial General Staff (CIGS). Although Dill's caution as CIGS chief had not endeared him to Churchill, his appointment to Washington proved to be a smart decision. There, working with his American colleagues, he was instrumental in circumventing or defusing numerous issues and policy differences that could have disrupted Anglo-U.S. relations. Foremost among these was the recurring U.S. pressure for an unrealistically early Anglo-U.S. "Second Front" invasion of France.

Combined Chiefs of Staff at the 1943 Quebec Conference

The gentlemanly Dill was lauded for his diplomacy, intellect, and achievements in Washington. He also formed a great personal friendship with U.S. general George Marshall, the U.S. Army chief of staff. When Dill died in post in 1944, he was accorded the unique honor of burial in the Arlington National Cemetery.

Britain's heartbreaking defeat
In a scene that has come to symbolize the end of an empire, British officers prepare to surrender Singapore to the Japanese. The loss of the "Gibraltar of the Far East" on February 15, 1942, ranks among the greatest defeats in British military history. The quick Japanese victory over a numerically superior force stunned the world, shattered British military power in the region, exposed the myth of Western superiority for all to see, and raised the hopes of nationalist movements chafing under colonial rule. Britain's colonial star went into decline and would never regain its former ascendancy.

1942

February 1: Japanese bases on the Gilbert and Marshall islands come under attack by more than 90 carrier-based U.S. warplanes.

February 4: In Egypt, British ambassador Sir Miles Lampson surrounds King Farouk's palace with Allied tanks to pressure the monarch into appointing a pro-British government. • Japan presses Britain to surrender control of Singapore, the crown jewel in the British Asian empire.

February 6: British and American officials meet in Washington, D.C., for the first conference of the Allied Combined Chiefs of Staff. • The United States counterattacks a reinforced Japanese force on the island of Luzon, Philippines.

February 7: A congressional call for $500 million in aid to the Nationalist Chinese gets Roosevelt's stamp of approval.

February 9: The Japanese capture Singapore's Tengah airfield, a vital supply link.

February 10: Axis sabotage is suspected when *Normandie*, the luxury French liner impounded in New York, catches fire and capsizes. No sabotage actually occurred.

February 11: London questions Vichy France's assertions of neutrality, revealing that France has supplied German forces in North Africa with more than 5,000 tons of fuel over the past three months.

February 11–13: The German navy humiliates the British with the perfect execution of Operation Cerberus, also known as the "Channel Dash." Unable to return from Brest, France, to their home ports via the British-controlled Atlantic route, the German battleships *Scharnhorst* and *Gneisenau* and the cruiser *Prinz Eugen* make an audacious escape up the English Channel.

The *Wehrmacht*'s youngest general Adolf Galland, probably the best-known *Luftwaffe* ace of the war, led a fighter group during the Battle of Britain that accounted for 103 aircraft "kills." By late 1941, he was commanding the *Luftwaffe* fighter arm. In late 1942, he became the *Wehrmacht*'s youngest general (age 31). Despite his youth, he consistently demonstrated impressive organizational and intellectual abilities. Galland's well-founded advocacy of using the *Luftwaffe* tactically rather than strategically was fully in line with the air-warfare policies of Göring and Hitler. He was dismissed in January 1945, and was later shot down and captured while commanding an Me 262 jet fighter squadron.

The Blenheim bombers The RAF's Bristol Blenheim bombers were the first RAF aircraft to make a bombing attack against German targets. These three-man-crewed light bombers flew at 225 mph to a range of 1,450 miles, carrying up to 1,350 pounds of bombs. Five machine guns were provided for self-defense. Fifteen RAF Blenheim squadrons were in service by 1939, with a much-improved "long-nose" Mark IV version introduced that year. Used for low-level daylight bombing raids in 1941–42, almost 600 of 1,012 RAF Blenheims were lost—403 to enemy action. They were finally withdrawn from service in late 1942, and were replaced progressively by Boston, Ventura, and Mitchell bombers.

The Siege of Malta

BRITAIN HAD HELD THE central Mediterranean island of Malta since the Napoleonic wars. Malta was already a vital naval base, as its aircraft commanded the sea lanes between Italy and North Africa. Britain had to hold Malta to win a Mediterranean war.

Shortly after Italy entered the war in June 1940, Malta came under bombing attack. At first, the island's only air defense was three Gladiator biplanes, named *Faith, Hope,* and *Charity*. The Germans joined the fighting in early 1941, and raids intensified in early '42. By April 1942, Malta had received twice the tonnage of bombs dropped on London during the entire Blitz. Nearly 1,500 civilians were killed.

With the island under siege, the Royal Navy deployed a high proportion of its strength to protect convoys headed for Malta in the face of heavy German and Italian air attack. In nine epic convoy battles, Axis warships, bombers, submarines, and E-boats attacked Allied merchant ships making the Malta run. Though starved, Malta survived. When Churchill came to suspect that the island's commander was considering a surrender, he replaced him with General Lord Gort, who would never surrender.

Meanwhile, Malta became the base for British naval and air force attacks on Axis convoys that tried to get supplies (especially fuel) to support Rommel's *Afrika Korps* in Libya and Egypt. Using "Ultra" intelligence (which gave precise

Grand Harbour, Malta, under air attack

details of ships and cargos), Malta-based submarines and bombers starved Rommel of vital supplies.

Why was Malta not invaded and taken? A German plan, Operation Hercules, was devised, but Hitler—having seen his airborne force badly hurt on Crete—refused to risk it again. The refusal to run this risk allowed British forces based on Malta to make a decisive contribution to the outcome of the war in the Mediterranean and North Africa.

In 1942 King George VI recognized the courage and endurance of Malta's civilians by awarding the island the George Cross, Britain's highest award for civilian gallantry.

Japan goes after Java's oil Clouds of smoke roil into the sky following an air raid on Surabaya, Java, in the Dutch East Indies (now Indonesia) in February 1942. The Japanese had long coveted the region's vast oil fields and refineries, and they moved to occupy Java soon after the fall of Singapore. An Allied attempt to turn away the Japanese invasion fleet failed in the seven-hour Battle of the Java Sea on February 27. Five Allied warships were sunk in the melee, while the Japanese lost only a single destroyer.

1942

February 13: After numerous delays, Hitler permanently cancels the German invasion of Britain, code-named Operation Sealion. • Japanese aviators inadvertently dive-bomb their own troops in a raid on the Bataan Peninsula in the Philippines.

February 14: The British government directs the RAF to begin a campaign that targets German civilians, shifting the focus away from exclusively bombing military and production facilities.

February 14–16: The Japanese score an important strategic victory with the seizure of the oil-rich island of Sumatra in the Dutch East Indies.

February 15: In a stunning defeat for the Empire, the British surrender Singapore to the Japanese, who will raise the rising sun flag over the governor's residence the following day.

February 19: The Canadian Parliament approves a resolution calling for a military draft. • In just one day, the unstoppable Japanese attack Bali, Mandalay, and Timor. They will install occupation forces in both Bali and Timor the following day.

February 20: Lieutenant Edward "Butch" O'Hare, Navy flying ace for whom Chicago's major airport will eventually be named, shoots down five Japanese bombers over a five-minute period.

February 22: The Allies launch a campaign against Japanese shipping when they seed the mouth of Burma's Rangoon River with 40 British magnetic mines dropped from USAAF B-24 bombers. • President Roosevelt reassigns General MacArthur, pulling him from his post in the Philippines and naming him commander of Allied forces in Australia.

Kondo among Japan's top commanders Vice Admiral Kondo Nobutake ranked among Japan's most outstanding fleet commanders in 1941 and '42. He led the naval forces that supported the invasion of Malaya, Java, and Singapore, and spearheaded the main "covering force" in the Battle of Midway. He later commanded the Second Fleet in the bitter—and ultimately unsuccessful—struggle to dominate the waters off Guadalcanal from August to November 1942. Following that defeat, he served as deputy commander of the Combined Fleet and briefly as commander following Admiral Yamamoto Isoroku's death in 1943. Kondo survived the war and died in 1953.

Kozo's revenge on California In the late 1930s, a Japanese tanker docked near the Ellwood oil field outside of Santa Barbara, California, for refueling. As its commander, Kozo Nishino, walked along a path from the pier, he slipped and fell on a prickly pear cactus. Several workers on a nearby oil rig laughed at Kozo's misfortune. Humiliated, he reportedly swore revenge. On February 23, 1942, a Japanese submarine fired several shells at an Ellwood oil rig. Although the shells did minimal damage (*pictured*), they raised the anxiety level of civilians anticipating a Japanese invasion. The skipper of the enemy submarine was none other than Kozo Nishino.

Allies scorch Rangoon before departing Smoke billows over Rangoon on March 6, 1942, as British forces prepare to abandon the city to the advancing Japanese. As Burma's capital and major port, Rangoon served as a major Allied supply point. Determined to leave nothing of value for the Japanese, the Allies evacuated the city and declared a general scorched-earth policy. Oil storage tanks, refineries, port installations, cars and trucks, stockpiles of tires, and even stocks of blankets and bed sheets were destroyed. The main power station was blown up on March 9 as the last defenders left. The Japanese entered the ravaged city the following day.

The bat bomb scheme In January 1942, dental surgeon Lytle Adams submitted a plan to the White House that, he claimed, would bring the blazing effects of war to Japanese civilians. Upon review, President Roosevelt released funds for testing. Adams's plan called for the delivery of a large number of bats carrying small incendiary bombs over enemy cities. The bombs

would be set to ignite after the bats took daylight refuge in surrounding buildings. Testing began in March 1943 with limited success. Approximately $2 million was spent on the project before it was scrapped in early 1944.

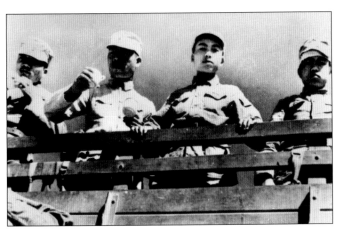

Chinese try to help in Burma Chinese troops arrive in Burma in early 1942 to join the British in the battle against invading Japanese. Concerned about the loss of their Lend-Lease supply routes, the Chinese offered assistance soon after Burma was invaded by the Japanese. The British accepted their help only after the Japanese had broken through toward Rangoon. By late February, two Chinese armies had joined the campaign, but they proved to be little match for the Japanese. The British withdrew to India and the Chinese units returned to China as best they could, some as an undisciplined mob of refugees.

Divided loyalties in Burma Burmese civilians trudge north to escape the advancing Japanese in March 1942. Many Burmese resented British colonial rule and supported the Japanese in hopes of obtaining independence. Others, particularly groups such as the Karen and Kachins, remained loyal to the British and organized resistance units to fight the Japanese. They suffered severely from both the Japanese and the puppet Burmese Independence Army. They later provided invaluable aid when the Allies recaptured Burma in 1944–45.

1942

February 23: In the first Japanese "attack" on the American mainland, a Japanese submarine surfaces at night off Ellwood, California, near Santa Barbara. It fires on an oil derrick, damaging a catwalk but little else. Much local panic follows for a few days.

February 26: Stalin makes the first of many requests to the American and British command to open a second European front against the Germans so as to relieve some of the pressure on the Red Army.

February 27: Japan launches an assault on the Andamans, a chain of islands on India's Bay of Bengal.

February 27–March 1: Ten Allied warships are sunk during the disastrous Battle of the Java Sea. With the Allies suffering one of the worst wartime defeats at sea, Japanese ships are left to roam Indonesian waters at will.

February 28: Pearl Harbor commanders Lieutenant General Walter Short and Rear Admiral Husband Kimmel retire. The U.S. military announces it will court-martial the two commanders at a later date.

March: The Allies lose 273 merchant vessels this month. • Desperate for metal to manufacture airplane engines, Germany begins to collect bronze and copper church bells for the smelter's fires.

March 2: The U.S. government bans all Japanese Americans from all of two and portions of three Pacific coastal states. • Nazis murder some 5,000 Jews in Minsk, Belorussia.

March 8: The Japanese take the Burmese capital of Rangoon.

March 9: The Japanese seize the Indonesian island of Java from the Dutch.

"No matter what I did, I was still in an artificial government-spawned community on the periphery of the real world. I was in a dismal, dreary camp surrounded by barbed wire in the middle of a stark, hard landscape that offered nothing to refresh the eye or heal the spirit."

—YOSHIKO UCHIDA, INTERNED AT THE TOPAZ CAMP IN UTAH

Japanese Americans report to camps In response to dire warnings from the military and rising panic among ordinary citizens, the U.S. government in February 1942 began evacuating people of Japanese ancestry from Pacific Coastal areas. About 8,000 Japanese Americans voluntarily left, and another 120,000—72,000 of whom were U.S. citizens—were forcibly relocated. Like the young people seen here, Japanese Americans were held under guard at assembly centers, where their baggage was inspected for forbidden items, such as cameras, shortwave radios, and guns. They were then bussed to camps east of the Sierra Nevada Mountains.

Life in the internment camps Japanese Americans were relocated into barracks such as these at Manzanar, California. Since the internees knew nothing about where they were being taken, most did not have suitable clothing for the extremes of heat and cold in their new locations. Each family was assigned a 20′×25′ living space, and they shared communal latrines and showers. Confinement to barbed-wire fenced camps that were overseen by armed guards and watchtowers was psychologically devastating to people who considered themselves good Americans.

Japanese Internment

IN FEBRUARY 1942, President Roosevelt signed Executive Order 9066, paving the way for the forcible removal of Japanese Americans from the West Coast. Fear and anger over the attack on Pearl Harbor and concerns about potential sabotage spurred FDR to take action. So did concerns about a Japanese landing as well as intercepted and decoded Japanese messages that pointed to instances of disloyalty.

About 110,000 people of Japanese descent, more than 60 percent of whom were American citizens, were relocated to 10 inland War Relocation Camps. Limited to taking only what they could carry, the internees lost homes, businesses, and personal possessions.

Camp life was spartan. At Manzanar, located in California's arid Owens Valley, about 10,000 internees lived in 100-foot-long barracks that were divided into six one-room apartments. Those who lived in each block of 14 barracks shared latrine, bath, and eating facilities—all behind barbed wire and under guard. While numbers of German and Italian aliens were also interned during the war, their detentions did not approach those of Japanese Americans in scope or severity.

Despite reason for resentment, substantial numbers of young Japanese Americans volunteered for U.S. military service. The Japanese American 442nd Regimental Combat

Children interned at Manzanar

Team fought in Italy and became the most highly decorated unit of its size in U.S. military history.

In 1988 President Ronald Reagan apologized on behalf of the government for the internment of Japanese Americans, which a federal commission had stated was the result of "race prejudice, war hysteria, and the failure of political leadership." Beginning in 1990, reparations were paid to surviving internees.

Canada interns Japanese An officer of the Royal Canadian Navy questions Japanese Canadian fishermen. When Canadians became afraid that fishermen of Japanese ancestry might be charting the Pacific coastline for the enemy, the government confiscated all Japanese fishing boats. In early 1942, Canada interned the nearly 23,000 Japanese Canadians who lived in British Columbia—about three quarters of whom were citizens—in 10 camps scattered throughout the nation. At first, men and women were incarcerated separately. Later, families were allowed to be together if the men agreed to fill labor shortages on sugar beet farms.

1942

March 10: Britain has already spent more than nine billion pounds on the war effort, more than was spent on the entire First World War.

March 11: The French Resistance blows up a Nazi troop train, killing about 250 German soldiers. • As compensation for their shipping losses to the Axis, Brazil seizes Axis property.

March 13: America enters the China-Burma-India theater with the arrival of U.S. Army Air Force airmen in Karachi, India.

March 14: Washington sets plans in motion to increase troop levels in Europe in preparation for an eventual attack on the heart of the Nazi Reich. • In response to the Japanese menace, the first contingent of American troops that will serve under General MacArthur lands in Australia.

March 17: General MacArthur assumes his new post as supreme commander of Allied forces in the southwest Pacific Theater. He lands in Darwin, Australia, a few days after his first group of men.

March 17–31: Some 20,000 prisoners, mostly Jews, are murdered in the new Belzec, Poland, death camp, which opened on March 13.

March 18: The American and British Combined Chiefs of Staff install Admiral Lord Louis Mountbatten as the chief of Combined Operations.

March 19: British home secretary Herbert Morrison accuses the London paper *The Daily Mirror* of "reckless indifference to the national interest" for its practice of publishing stories with an antiwar slant.

March 20: Japanese and Chinese troops clash along the Sittang River on the Burmese front.

Hu solicits U.S. support for China Known as "the father of the Chinese literary revolution," Hu Shih studied at Cornell University in 1910 and later at Columbia University. A noted philosopher and intellectual, he served as Chinese ambassador to the United States from 1938 to 1942. As ambassador, he successfully rallied U.S. sympathy and support for his nation's battle against the Japanese. He later served as a delegate to the San Francisco Conference, which established the United Nations. An outspoken advocate of democracy and human rights, Hu Shih relocated to Taiwan after the Chinese Revolution. He died of a heart attack in 1962.

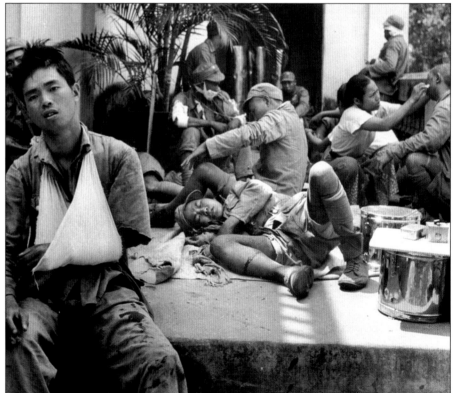

Chinese medical care Throughout the war, the Chinese struggled to adequately treat wounded and diseased troops and civilians. The relatively few available hospital facilities suffered from a lack of supplies and equipment, and a shortage of doctors. Conditions were better at the center seen here, a U.S. missionary hospital run by Dr. Gordon Seagrave and his nurses in the Namhkam Valley, Burma, off the Burma Road. Seagrave had been recruited by the U.S. military, and may have had intelligence duties as well as medical responsibilities.

The "Forces' Sweetheart" When war began, young British singer Vera Lynn was sure that her fledgling career was over. She volunteered for wartime duty, expecting to work in a factory or join the Army. To her surprise, Lynn was told that she would be more useful as an entertainer. Soon

dubbed the "Forces' Sweetheart," she became the most popular vocalist of her time, raising spirits on the war front and at home with her wide repertoire of wartime songs. "We'll Meet Again" was one of Vera Lynn's best-loved selections.

Britain's "land girls" The Women's Land Army (WLA) was formed in 1939 under its first director, Lady Gertrude Denman, and numbered 87,000 fully trained "land girls" by mid-1943. The organization's members worked in agriculture (*pictured*) and forestry, producing much of the vital food stocks and timber for wartime Britain. Although many land girls lived fairly well, either on the farms or in hostels, others endured an isolated and often rudimentary rural existence. In 1945 government parsimony denied the land girls postwar financial benefits.

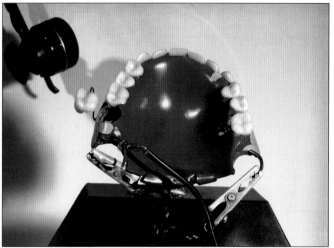

Resisters' innovations Active and passive resistance movements developed within most of German-occupied Europe. Inevitably, resisters attracted harsh reprisals, brutal interrogations, and summary executions. Many resisters utilized ingenious technical innovations—assassination weapons, booby traps, codes, sabotage explosives, and communications equipment. Such innovations were designed and provided by the British Special Operations Executive (SOE) or devised locally. One such Norwegian device was an intricately wired denture plate (*pictured*) that could receive radio broadcasts from London some 1,200 miles away.

The war's oldest aircraft carrier Launched in 1919, the HMS *Hermes* was the world's first purpose-built aircraft carrier. A relic by the time of World War II, the *Hermes* suffered from design problems that included a small hanger and instability at high seas. Even so, the carrier served the Allies in the southern Atlantic and off the coast of Africa. On April 9, 1942, it was destroyed by 70 Japanese attack aircraft near Ceylon. Shown sinking here (in a photograph taken by a Japanese pilot), it went down with 307 men.

1942

Spring: Construction begins at the Dugway Proving Ground in Utah. The U.S. Army constructs simulated Japanese and German towns in order to test the effects of incendiary bombs and other weapons.

March 22: British and American air force units are left exposed to assault as they beat a retreat after the Japanese capture of Burma's Magwe airfield. The loss of the strategic landing strip leaves the Allies unable to call for air support. • *Abwehr* (German intelligence) captain and double agent Paul Thummel, a British MI6 asset on the ground in Czechoslovakia, is arrested by the Nazis.

March 24: Japan launches an offensive against Bataan.

March 26: The Nazi government orders that all Jewish homes in Germany and the occupied territories must be identified as such. • Admiral Ernest King, commander-in-chief of the U.S. Fleet, becomes the highest-ranking officer in the Navy with his appointment as chief of Naval Operations.

March 28: Allies deliberately slam the HMS *Campbeltown* into the gates at the Normandy dock at St. Nazaire on the French Atlantic coast, the largest drydock in Nazi-occupied Europe and the only one large enough to handle the German battleship *Tirpitz*. Once past the gates, Allied commandoes sabotage the facility. • The first of 6,000 Parisian Jews designated for "resettlement" at Auschwitz are loaded onto a train and sent to that extermination camp.

March 31: India's Congress Party demands immediate independence from Britain. It rejects a British offer made the previous day that included Indian independence but only after the conclusion of the war.

Homma commands Philippines invasion
Japan's Homma Masaharu, whose 14th Army conquered the Philippines, was an unusual general. Highly intelligent, artistic, and familiar with Western ways through close contact with the British Army in World War I and India, he was said to lack samurai spirit. After experience in China, he was appointed to command the Philippines invasion. He planned meticulously and captured Manila quickly, but his failure to prevent American withdrawal to Bataan precluded victory within the allotted 50 days. His unimpressed superiors effectively ended his career by recalling him in August 1942. Arrested by U.S. troops in 1945 for war crimes in the Philippines, Homma was executed by firing squad in April 1946.

Bataan prisoners await grim fate Hands tied behind their backs, these three Americans were among 78,000 American and Filipino troops who went into captivity on Bataan on April 9, 1942. Their starving and diseased condition influenced Major General Edward King's decision to surrender, though he was unable to extract from the Japanese commanders a commitment to treat the prisoners compassionately. The Japanese decided to march the prisoners

to Camp O'Donnell, some 65 miles away. The tragedy that would follow is encapsulated in the story of these three, all of whom apparently died in captivity. James Gallagher (*right*) reportedly died on the day this photograph was taken.

TORMENT ON BATAAN

THE FIRST JAPANESE SOLDIER I came into contact with used sign language to ask if I had a cigarette....I had to tell him I did not have any cigarettes. He smiled and then a second later hit me in the face with the butt of his gun. Blood spurted from my nose and from a deep gash on my cheekbone. He laughed and said something that made all of his buddies laugh, too. He walked away from me and went to the GI on my right. He used the same sign language, and this time my buddy had cigarettes and offered him one. The Japanese soldier took the whole pack, and then he and his friends began beating my friend with rifle butts and cane-length pieces of bamboo until he could not stand. Then they left, laughing, laughing at the defeated and weak Americans.

—U.S. ARMY TANK CREWMAN LESTER TENNEY,
ON HIS EXPERIENCES FOLLOWING CAPTURE ON BATAAN

Japanese Atrocities

MANY THOUSANDS OF POWs and untold numbers of civilians died at the hands of the Japanese armed forces during World War II. They were victims of murder, disease, starvation, malnutrition, medical experiments, and overall neglect.

Though signatories to the 1929 Geneva Conventions, the Japanese in practice paid little heed to humanitarian restrictions. Prisoners were worked to death; would-be escapees were summarily beheaded; prisoners were denied routine medical care, food, and water; and prisoners were bayoneted or decapitated for sport. The death rate for prisoners of war in Japanese hands ranged between 30 and 50 percent.

The statistics become numbing. On the Bataan Death March in 1942, hundreds of American and thousands of Filipino prisoners died of exhaustion or were murdered. In a single year, 20,000 Allied POWs—one in three—died in forced labor on the Burma-Siam railroad. During the Rape of Nanking in 1937, tens of thousands of Chinese men, women, and children were systematically murdered. Thousands of other Asian women were enslaved as military prostitutes during the course of the war. The rape, torture, and murder of civilians by the Japanese military became almost routine.

A Japanese participant in the Guadalcanal campaign wrote of two POWs who were dissected alive. "It was very informative," he observed nonchalantly. An American survivor of the Bataan Death March recalled a Filipino couple

Japanese soldiers preparing to bayonet Chinese prisoners

who tried to give the marchers a bit of food. Japanese soldiers burned them alive. Another marcher began counting decapitated heads along the roadway but soon quit, fearing he would go insane.

A Japanese "research unit" known as Unit 731 used thousands of civilians and prisoners as human guinea pigs. Victims were infected with plague, gas gangrene, and anthrax. Their limbs were frozen in frostbite studies, and some were forced to drink mustard gas. Others were dissected alive in order to study their working organs.

Despite the magnitude of these crimes, only some of the perpetrators were ever brought to justice by the Allies.

The Bataan Death March The trek from Bataan to Camp O'Donnell became known as the Bataan Death March. Japanese plans for the march did not take into account the exhaustion, starvation, and illness of the prisoners, who were thus sure to die in large numbers. Added to this neglect was active Japanese persecution. Some senior Japanese officers so despised the prisoners that they wanted them killed en masse. Field officers beheaded many with their swords, and Japanese common soldiers willfully buried prisoners alive or set fire to civilians who sought to aid those suffering. No single factor adequately explains this brutality.

1942

April 1: Vital supplies reach the Soviets, as 14 of the 19 ships of the first Arctic convoy successfully make it to the Russian port of Murmansk.

April 3: Some 2,000 Burmese civilians die during a Japanese air raid on Mandalay.

April 4: Hitler orders the Baedeker raids. Named after a series of tourist guides, the raids will be specifically targeted to inflict maximum damage on Britain's most important historic sites.

April 6: Japanese troops land at Bougainville in the Solomon Islands.

April 7: The air raid sirens on Malta sound for the 2,000th time since the beginning of the war.

April 8: In one of the most intense air raids of the war, the RAF attacks Hamburg, Germany, with more than 270 bombers. • A new lifeline is opened to China with the inauguration of U.S. Air Ferry Command service over the Himalayan mountain range.

April 9: Soviet general Mikhail Yefremov takes his own life rather than suffer the shame of surrendering to the Germans.

April 10: Japanese troops land on Cebu Island, Philippines. • The atrocity that will become known as the Bataan Death March begins with the surrender of more than 78,000 exhausted and starving American and Filipino troops in the Bataan Peninsula. In an effort to get them to the nearest railhead, their Japanese captors will force-march the prisoners some 65 miles. Eleven thousand of the captives will be killed or will perish along the way.

April 11: The first 8,000-pound bomb is dropped on Essen, Germany, by a Halifax bomber. It is not known if the bomb reached its target or what damage it caused.

Program for the Week of April 13 to April 19, 1941

EVERY DAY

		6:00 A. M. — 4:50 P.M.			D J Z — 25 m	
		D J B — 19 m		3:30	12:30	News in English
				3:45	12:45	News in French
EST	PST			4:00	1:00	SILENT
A.M.	A.M.					
6:00	3:00	Call, Early Bird Concert			D Z D — 28 m	
6:30	3:30	News in English				
6:45	3:45	"Action Reports from the Front"		4:30	1:30	News in English
		(Monday, Wednesday, Friday)				
		Rieder Talk —			11:05 P.M. — 1:00 A.M.	
		(Tuesday, Thursday, Saturday)			D X P — 49 m	
7:00	4:00	Music				
8:00	5:00	News in German				
8:15	5:15	Music		11:05	8:05	Late Music
8:30	5:30	News in English		11:15	8:15	News in English
8:45	5:45	SILENT		11:30	8:30	Late Music Continued
11:30	8:30	News in English		Midnight		
11:45	8:45	SILENT		12:00	9:00	News in English
P.M.				A.M.		
12:30	9:30	News in English		12:15	9:15	Concert of Light Music by a Regional
12:45	9:45	SILENT				Broadcasting Orchestra
1:30	10:30	News in English		1:00	10:00	Sign Off until 6:00 A.M. (3:00 A.M. PST)

"Germany Calling" This program guide, titled "Germany Calling," lists German shortwave radio broadcasts to North America for April 13 through April 19, 1941. In addition to German versions of international news, the schedule included such programs as *America Asks—Germany Answers* (purported to be answers to questions from American listeners), *German Contributions to Making America,* and *From the German Heart,* as well as commentary from the infamous "Lord Haw-Haw."

The Baedeker Raids The 15th-century Old Boar's Head Inn in Norwich, England, was damaged (*pictured*) in an April 1942 *Luftwaffe* raid. Germany bombed the picturesque English towns of Exeter, Bath, Norwich, and York. Nazi propagandist Baron Gustav Braun von Sturm declared, "We shall go out and bomb every building in Britain marked with three stars in the [German-published] Baedeker [travel] guide." These Baedeker Raids on England—which included Canterbury and other nonstrategic historic sites—took lives and destroyed property. However, the heavy toll on the *Luftwaffe* revealed the German bombers' limitations.

The Flying Tigers The P-40 Tomahawk fighters were operated by the American Volunteer Group (AVG), more popularly known as the Flying Tigers. Commanded by Claire Chennault, the AVG was comprised of American military pilots who had "resigned" from the service in order to fly against the Japanese in China. In their first encounter on December 20, 1941, the AVG shot down three or possibly four Japanese bombers. Though their overall impact was limited, the AVG provided some deterrent to Japanese airpower over the next several months. The Flying Tigers were incorporated into the U.S. Army Air Force in 1942.

American Chennault helps Chiang A native of Louisiana, Claire Chennault learned to fly during World War I and remained in the service for two decades afterward. However, he was unpopular in the U.S. military because of his acerbic criticism of accepted fighter tactics, and he retired in 1937 with the rank of major. He then was hired by Chiang Kai-shek to revamp the Chinese air force, and he became a lifelong supporter of the Nationalist general. After the U.S. entered the war, Chennault was promoted to general and given command of the 14th Air Force.

Japanese bomb Australia On February 19, 1942, some 200 Japanese warplanes dropped more bombs than they had on Pearl Harbor in two waves of attacks on Port Darwin, Australia. They sank eight ships, devastated structures, and killed at least 243 people in a population of about 2,000. Here, an American Hudson bomber lies in the ruins of a hanger damaged in the raids. The unprepared Australian government reaffirmed its intention to rely on the American military rather than the British, and U.S. general Douglas MacArthur promptly established his headquarters in Australia.

Australia's able leader John Curtin of the Labor Party became prime minister of Australia in October 1941. Curtin was a pacifist before the war, and his cabinet was short on military experience. Nevertheless, the Pacific war enabled him to galvanize the nation in 1942–43. His insistence that

the Seventh Division be returned to Australia—and not Burma, as Churchill wanted—proved wise and saved Port Moresby when the Japanese tried to take it by a land assault. Curtin announced in December 1941 that Australia looked to America rather than Britain for support. He welcomed the appointment of General MacArthur as supreme commander of Allied Forces in the South West Pacific Area, and proved amenable to the American's direction. Against his party's traditions, Curtin promoted labor and military conscription. He died in office in July 1945.

Doolittle's Tokyo Raid

ON APRIL 18, 1942, 16 B-25 bombers lumbered off the deck of the American aircraft carrier *Hornet* and turned toward the Japanese coast, more than 600 miles away. Their top-secret mission: to carry out the first attack of the war on the enemy homeland.

Leading the raid was 45-year-old Lieutenant Colonel James Doolittle, a modest but highly capable officer who owned all the major aviation racing trophies of his day as well as a Ph.D. in aeronautical engineering from MIT. Doolittle's airmen were volunteers who knew only that they had signed on for a "dangerous secret mission." Details would be revealed after they were at sea. The bombers were fitted with extra fuel tanks, and the fliers practiced taking off from shortened runways intended to simulate a carrier flight deck. Since the B-25s were too cumbersome to land on a carrier, their missions would be one-way, with the bombers continuing on to secret airfields in China.

Doolittle intended to launch about 400 miles from the coast, but an encounter with a Japanese picket vessel 600 miles out forced an earlier departure. All 16 B-25s got airborne and bombed various military and industrial targets, most located in Tokyo, before fleeing toward China. Short on fuel due to the early launch, the crews of 15 planes either crash-landed or bailed out. One bomber landed in Vladivostok, Russia, where the five-man crew was interned.

Of the other 75 raiders, one man was killed bailing out, two drowned after crash-landing in the water, and eight

B-25 bombers aboard the USS *Hornet*

were captured by the Japanese. Three prisoners were executed. Another died of malnutrition while in captivity. The other fliers evaded the Japanese and found refuge with the Chinese Nationalists. Upon his return home, Doolittle was awarded the Medal of Honor.

While the material damage inflicted was minimal, the Doolittle Raid lifted Allied morale and stunned the Japanese, who had grown complacent with victory after victory. No longer could the Japanese pretend that the homeland was inviolate.

Doolittle prepares for raid Air crew members on the deck of the USS *Hornet* watch as Lieutenant Colonel James Doolittle wires a Japanese medal to a 500-pound bomb before the daring B-25 raid on Tokyo. A former racing and stunt pilot, Doolittle had been directed to look into the feasibility of flying medium bombers off an aircraft carrier to attack Japan. Doolittle worked out the takeoff requirements, weight limitations, and necessary fuel, and arranged for special equipment and training for the all-volunteer force. Eager to get into combat, he volunteered to personally lead the dangerous mission.

"I ran up to our roof and saw four American bombers flying in over the rooftops. They couldn't have been more than 100 feet off the ground. I looked down the street. All Tokyo seemed to be in panic...."

—RAMON MUNIZ LAVELLE, ARGENTINEAN COMMERCIAL ATTACHE TO TOKYO, ON THE DOOLITTLE RAID

Bombers take off from aircraft carrier A B-25 lumbers off the deck of the USS *Hornet* on its one-way bombing raid against Tokyo. The Army pilots had practiced short takeoffs from dry land, but none had ever tried it from a heaving carrier deck. The raiding force was comprised of 16 modified bombers, each carrying five crew members, four bombs, and extra fuel. An encounter with a Japanese picket boat forced the Doolittle Raiders to launch earlier than planned. Aided by a 50-mph headwind, all the B-25s got safely into the air, though many hung perilously close to the waves before gaining altitude.

Raid affects morale on both sides This aerial photo, snapped during the Doolittle Raid, reveals ships moored in Tokyo Bay. Most of the B-25s arrived over Tokyo just after noon on April 18. They targeted an oil tank farm, steel mill, and power plants. Other bombers hit targets in Yokohama and Yokosuku. All the B-25s survived the actual raid, except for one that crash-landed in China after it ran out of fuel. Though minimal damage was done to the targets, the harm to Japanese morale was immense. By contrast, the raid lifted American spirits, which had been at low ebb following a string of Allied military defeats.

Reprisals after the raid Chinese Nationalist leader Chiang Kai-shek had been reluctant to allow the U.S. bombers to land in China following the Doolittle Raid, fearing that harsh Japanese reprisals would result. Events proved him correct. Less than a month after the raid, the Japanese army launched the operation *Sei-Go*. Japan intended to seize Chinese airfields within range of the home islands and take vengeance on villages that aided the airmen. As many as 250,000 civilians were killed in the Chekiang and Kiangsu provinces during *Sei-Go*. Ying-Tan (*pictured*) was one of the cities that was razed.

1942

April 14: The U.S. Navy "kills" its first U-boat when *U-85* is attacked by the destroyer USS *Roper* in the Atlantic Ocean. • With Japanese forces closing in, British troops torch Burma's Yenangyaung oil fields to keep them out of Axis hands.

April 15: Sobibór, the newest Nazi extermination camp in Poland, opens its gates. • In an effort to minimize textile-industry labor, Britain bans the manufacture of lace on women's underwear, effective June 1.

April 16: German field marshal Gerd von Rundstedt is appointed commander-in-chief of the Atlantic Wall defenses. • Britain presents the strategically critical island of Malta with the George Cross, a medal given for valiant service to the Empire.

April 18: Japan is blindsided by a carrier-based bombing raid on Tokyo by 16 B-25 bombers from the USS *Hornet*.

April 20: The *Luftwaffe* destroys 30 Spitfire planes on the island of Malta.

April 21: General Henri Giraud, captured by the Nazis when they occupied his native France, makes a daring escape to Allied territory.

April 24: German authorities issue a decree prohibiting Jews from using public transportation of any kind.

April 26: Hitler is empowered to act outside the laws of the Reich in dealing with his subjects when the *Reichstag* confers on him the ultimate title of "supreme justice," among others.

April 29: Hitler and Mussolini meet to decide how to address internecine border bickering between Hungary and Romania. • Nazi saboteurs are suspected when an explosion in a Belgian chemical plant claims some 250 lives. • A critical link to China is lost when Japan's capture of Lashio, Burma, closes the Burma Road.

Allies deliver tanks to Soviets When Germany sent its powerful army against the USSR in June 1941, Russia dismantled and moved some of its arms factories away from highly endangered areas. That disrupted production, and by fall the nation was in urgent need of tanks and aircraft. Britain and the U.S. began supplying Russia with 400 tanks and 500 aircraft per month—numbers that would rise as the war progressed. Here, British Valentine and Matilda tanks are loaded onto a train for shipment to Russia via ship convoy through the Arctic.

Hess keeps the music playing When German air raids closed down British concert halls, internationally renowned English pianist Myra Hess organized hundreds of musicians to play lunchtime concerts at London's National Gallery. Even while bombs fell on London, Hess herself gave hugely popular performances of German composers, not merely defying Nazi violence but reminding audiences of the humanity of German culture. For her patriotic efforts, Hess was honored with the title Dame Commander of the British Empire (DBE) in 1941.

Jews deported to death camps In spring 1942, trains began transporting Jews from ghettos in Germany and its occupied nations to camps. Here, Jews board trains for deportation from the ghetto in Lódź, Poland, to the Chelmno extermination camp in Poland in April 1942 . On July 19, Heinrich Himmler accelerated the program, ordering that all Jews be "resettled" by the end of 1942—although the deportations would extend far beyond his deadline. In all, some 3,000 trains moved about three million people. Since this was only about 15 percent of the total trains that the Reich operated each day, the economic effect on Germany was manageable during the early years of the Holocaust.

A DEPORTATION OF JEWS

O N APPROACHING HRUBIESZOW, we became aware of an unusual commotion; big crowds were gathered on the platform. Unsuspecting, we alighted at the station. But we soon learned that the thousands herded there were Jews: men and women, old and young, children pressed among bundles of household effects; cries and shouts of the Germans.

Four stout, red-faced Germans, arms bare, gallop on horseback along the platform, ply their whips ceaselessly, treading whomever they find in their way, vent their wrath on mothers holding babies in their arms....

Suddenly a horrible scream of a woman is heard, followed by a shot. A woman with a baby in her arms keels over. She wanted to throw the baby over the fence, in the hope that it would be spared. But a moment later she and the baby are trodden to death by the horses' hooves. A deadly silence descends on the platform. I hold fast to the window-sill; I feel terribly dizzy.

—HAVA FOLLMAN, A YOUNG FUGITIVE FROM THE WARSAW GHETTO, DESCRIBING A SCENE AT HRUBIESZOW, POLAND, JUNE 1942

Germans prepare boys for war *Wenn die Soldaten durch die Stadt marschieren (When the Soldiers March Through Town)* was a hugely popular 1942 book of verses and pictures that portrayed children enraptured by German soldiers. The Nazi regime did more

than merely romanticize the military in children's eyes. Starting in 1936, preparation for military service became mandatory for boys. If he was deemed sufficiently fit and racially pure, a 10-year-old boy began his training and indoctrination in the *Deutsches Jungvolk* (German Youth). He then graduated to the paramilitary organization *Hitlerjugend* (Hitler Youth) at age 14.

Americans committed to stopping Hitler Adolf Hitler is hung in effigy in New York's Times Square on his birthday, April 20, 1942. Calls for isolationism had been loudly drowned out by this time. After the German declaration of war on the United States in December 1941, Americans committed themselves to stopping the spread of Nazi evil in Europe. Rallies such as this one expressed American sympathies and also boosted the sale of War Bonds, which helped finance the war effort on both fronts.

1942

April 30: By the end of the month, the squalor of the Warsaw Ghetto has claimed the lives of nearly 4,500 Polish Jews.

May 1: A strategic error by Britain allows the Japanese to take Mandalay by penetrating the Royal Army's exposed left flank.

May 2: Aid is promised to both Iran and Iraq under the provisions of the U.S. Lend-Lease Act.

May 4: The USAAF Flying Tigers shift their base of operations to Kunming, China, and out of Japanese-occupied Burma.

May 4–8: The Battle of the Coral Sea, the first carrier-to-carrier battle in history, results in a tactical Japanese victory, since they sink a major American carrier. But it marks a strategic Japanese reverse since the Japanese are unable to seize New Guinea and thus isolate Australia.

May 5: Nationalist Chinese general Chiang Kai-shek leads his troops in a major offensive against the Japanese occupation, striking seven key cities.

May 6: After 27 days of artillery barrage, the Americans surrender to the Japanese at Corregidor in the Philippines.

May 8: Japan's ability to produce fuel from its captured oil fields in the Dutch East Indies is seriously crippled when the ship carrying skilled production workers to the fields is sunk by an Allied torpedo.

May 10: Churchill sternly warns Germany against engaging in chemical warfare on the Russian front.

May 11: An Allied personnel transport ship is struck by a German U-boat that managed to make its way up Canada's St. Lawrence River undetected.

The Red Cross Blood Bank In February 1941, the American Red Cross began a blood donor service in anticipation of America's entrance into the war. By September 1945, the Red Cross had collected 13.4 million pints of blood from 6.6 million donors. The system for storing blood plasma was pioneered by African American physician Dr. Charles Drew, who was appointed the first director of the Red Cross Blood Bank. He resigned, however, when the organization excluded black blood donors. As the war progressed, the Red Cross began accepting "black blood" but restricted its use to black GIs.

German E-boats The German fast patrol and torpedo-carrying *Schnellboot* was dubbed "E-boat" by the Allies. The MTB and PT boats were the Anglo-U.S. equivalents. E-boats were used extensively in the English Channel and North Sea littoral region for raids on Allied shipping, routine patrols, clandestine operations, and rescue of downed aircrew. By 1944 about 40 E-boats were operating in the Channel area. One of their most significant successes was on April 28, 1944, when two flotillas attacked a D-Day landing exercise in the Channel off Slapton, Devon, sinking two LSTs and killing 749 men of the U.S. Fourth Infantry Division.

Germany's premier admiral In 1933 Admiral Erich Raeder became the architect of German naval rearmament. A committed Nazi, he planned to provide Germany with world-class surface and subsurface fleets by 1949. The outbreak of war in 1939 forestalled this aspiration. Nevertheless, he successfully oversaw the operations of the *Kriegsmarine* as its commander-in-chief until 1943. That

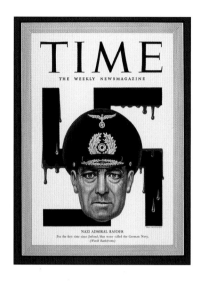

year, his friction with Hermann Göring over airpower priorities, and the increasing divergence of his maritime policy views from those of Hitler, resulted in his enforced retirement. Found guilty on three counts at Nuremberg, Raeder was sentenced to life imprisonment. He was released in 1955 due to ill health.

Massive warfare at Kharkov A group of German troops surrenders to Red Army soldiers near Kharkov, Ukraine, on May 4, 1942, following four relatively uneventful months near the city that the Germans had captured the previous October. Much more activity occurred in May around Kharkov, which Hitler had selected for the launch of the German spring offensive. Stalin ordered a major offensive there by Marshal Timoshenko's Southwest Front beginning May 12. Initially, Timoshenko's armies struck deep, with two tank corps pushing rapidly to seize Kharkov. But then, on May 17, the German Sixth and First Panzer armies counterattacked, trapping more than 250,000 Soviet troops and 1,200 tanks by May 28.

Corregidor's tunnel To make full use of Manila Harbor after the surrender of the American and Filipino troops on Bataan, the Japanese had to first take control of the nearby island of Corregidor, which the U.S. military occupied. Beneath the surface, the U.S. built the Malinta Tunnel, which housed headquarters, communications, service staff, refugees, and casualties. Reinforced concrete walls rendered Malinta Tunnel impervious to the bombardment that destroyed the island's above-ground defenses. However, as conditions worsened outside, crowding, vermin, odor, heat, dust, noise, and lack of water made conditions oppressive. To protect 1,000 wounded men and other defenseless occupants of the tunnel from slaughter, General Jonathan Wainwright surrendered.

Japan takes Corregidor At first, Japan struggled to capture Corregidor. Though supported by powerful artillery, the confident invaders landed in disorder on May 5, 1942. The cornered Americans, including Army and Navy personnel, fought back fiercely, inflicting hundreds of casualties. The Japanese ran dangerously short

of ammunition and landing craft, but the arrival of tanks and continuous artillery bombardment eventually proved decisive. On May 6, General Wainwright sought terms. Here, Japanese troops lower the U.S. flag on the island, although official sources say the American command had lowered it themselves before raising a white flag. General MacArthur had the U.S. flag raised on the same flagpole in 1945.

1942

May 12: Thirteen German transport planes go down in the Mediterranean after an RAF engagement off the coast of North Africa. • Overwhelming monsoon-induced mud brings operations in Southeast Asia to a standstill.

May 14: Not entirely trusting British guarantees to return Madagascar to France at war's end, General de Gaulle sends troops under his command to force the issue. • Congress establishes the U.S. Women's Army Auxiliary Corps.

May 15: Fuel rationing begins in 17 cities along the United States' eastern seaboard. • Chinese troops retreat into China and British troops retreat into India, officially completing Japan's occupation of Burma.

May 16: Roosevelt appeases the Soviets by releasing Earl Browder from federal prison. Browder, the leader of the Communist Party in the U.S., had served 14 months for passport violations.

May 20: Thanks to outstanding work by U.S. intelligence cryptologists, the Allies possess advance knowledge of a Japanese attack on Midway Island and a simultaneous diversionary attack on the Aleutians. The U.S. command responds by deploying a defensive force to Midway.

May 21: Hitler delays a planned invasion of Malta indefinitely, as he is afraid of losses to airborne troops after the experience on Crete. He opts to focus on the conquest of Egypt.

May 22: Mexico declares war against the Axis.

May 25: A small Japanese fleet steams out of Hokkaido en route to Alaska. The Japanese stage an attack on the Aleutians that they hope will draw attention away from the real target of Midway Island in the South Pacific.

Fighting in Madagascar British troops rush ashore from landing craft at Madagascar on May 5, 1942. Seizure of the Vichy French-controlled island was prompted by fears that Japanese long-range submarines might use it as a base to interdict Allied communication lines and shipping in the Indian Ocean. This was critical for supply lines to India, the Soviet Union, and the Middle East. Vichy forces, consisting mostly of Madagascan and Senegalese troops, offered more resistance to the operation than expected. Low-level fighting dragged on until November 5, when the Vichy commander finally surrendered.

Battle of the Coral Sea A wrecked Japanese plane floats in the water after being shot down during the Battle of the Coral Sea in May 1942. A major turning point in the Pacific war, the battle foiled a Japanese amphibious assault on New Guinea's Port Moresby, which could have led to the invasion of northern Australia. Fought by carrier aircraft, this was the first naval engagement in which the surface ships never sighted or directly fired on one another. The U.S. lost the carrier *Lexington*, and the *Yorktown* was badly damaged. The Japanese lost the small carrier *Shoho*, while *Shokaku* was severely damaged. Though a tactical victory for the Japanese, the Allies were the strategic winners because the Japanese invasion was aborted. It was Japan's first real setback of the war.

Alternative Japanese Strategy

By MARCH 1942, THE JAPANESE had achieved nearly all of their initial goals. Their ultimate objective—to establish an impenetrable defensive perimeter to secure their vast Southeast Asian conquests—was impossible to achieve given the length of the perimeter and the limitations on the size of forces available to defend it. Yet the scale of their successes and their failure to destroy the Pacific Fleet at Pearl Harbor made them reluctant to surrender the initiative by taking a defensive stance.

Admiral Yamamoto still sought the long-cherished decisive sea battle with the American fleet, which led to subsequent plans to invade Midway Island. However, squabbling strategists—infected by what one admiral called "victory disease"—diffused Japan's strength with additional forays in the Aleutians, the Indian Ocean, and the South Pacific. The setbacks that followed at the Coral Sea, Midway, Guadalcanal, and Papua allowed Japan's enemies to regroup and permanently gain the initiative. Given its inadequate resources, Japan had little chance of ultimate success.

Japan did have other strategic options in 1942, none of which came to fruition. One option was to attack Australia, but this effort was halted at the Battle of the Coral Sea. Another was to attack Hawaii, but this attempt was halted at the Battle of Midway. A third option was to attack Britain's lifeline in the Indian Ocean. Such an offensive likely would have cut off Britain's oil supplies, cost it India, eliminated the supply route to the Soviet Union across Iran, and had an impact in North Africa and the Caucasus. But by the beginning of 1943, all such discussion was academic, since Japan's war had become defensive.

The deadly Mosquito Operational from 1942, the RAF's De Havilland Mosquito fighter bomber is generally regarded as the most successful and versatile combat aircraft of the war. With its revolutionary lightweight, wood-based construction, the "Mossie" could fly at 408 mph up to 2,206 miles while carrying its two-man crew and a total bomb load of 5,000 pounds. A Mossie could fly to Berlin and back twice in one night to deliver its devastating 4,000-pound "Blockbuster" bombs. When configured as a fighter bomber, it had four 20mm cannons and four machine guns and could carry 1,000 pounds of bombs or eight rockets.

Harris promotes city bombing
Arthur Travers Harris, the head of the RAF Bomber Command, implemented area bombing—the indiscriminate destruction of cities instead of specific military targets. The British adopted this policy in winter 1942–43 after learning that their bombers could not hit specific targets. Harris believed that this tactic alone would destroy enemy morale and force Germany to surrender. His most controversial action was the bombing of Dresden on February 13, 1945, which caused a firestorm that killed tens of thousands of civilians. After the war, Harris grew bitter that his methods were increasingly criticized.

1942

May 27: The British Eighth Army shows off the American Grant M3 tank, its newest piece of high-tech weaponry, against Rommel's troops in Libya. • Damaged in the Battle of the Coral Sea, the carrier USS *Yorktown* returns to Pearl Harbor for repairs.

May 29: Effective today, all French Jews must wear the yellow Star of David badge. • Czech partisans sent from England attack the car carrying Bohemia and Moravia deputy *Reichsprotektor* Reinhard Heydrich, mortally wounding him.

May 30–31: Cologne, Germany is devastated by the first RAF raid to employ more than 1,000 bombers.

June: Eight German secret agents arrive via U-boat in the U.S., four in New York and four in Florida. They plan to destroy a cryolite factory in Philadelphia, but two of the members betray the operation to the FBI.

June 1: The *Luftwaffe* inflicts heavy damage on Canterbury, England.

June 2: More than 130 Czech citizens are murdered to avenge the attack on Reinhard Heydrich.

June 4: Reinhard Heydrich dies in Prague of an infection stemming from his injuries at the hands of Czech partisans.

June 4–6: The momentum of the Pacific war shifts to favor the Allies when they achieve a stunning victory at the Battle of Midway. The Japanese lose 3,500 men and four of their six largest aircraft carriers, permitting the Allies to go on the offensive.

June 5: Forty-nine civilians die in an accidental explosion at an Elmwood, Illinois, ordnance plant. • The United States formally declares war on Axis satellites Bulgaria, Romania, and Hungary, each of whom had declared war on the U.S. in December 1941.

The bombing of Cologne For 90 minutes on the night of May 30–31, 1942, the RAF dropped 1,445 tons of high explosives and 915 tons of incendiaries on Cologne, Germany, and its one million inhabitants, killing more than 500 and injuring more than 5,000. The docks and railways were destroyed, together with 36 factories and more than 3,000 homes. Some 45,000 people were left homeless. Of the 1,046 bombers involved, only 40 failed to return. This devastatingly successful raid was inspired by Air Chief Marshal "Bomber" Harris. It was designed to boost British morale, shatter German self-confidence, and impress Britain's allies.

Japanese subs attack Sydney area A shattered Japanese midget submarine is hoisted from the waters of Sydney Harbor following an attack on Allied shipping on the night of May 31, 1942. Three of the two-man midget subs, launched from standard submarines, participated in the attack. All were lost. One became tangled in an anti-torpedo net and blew itself up. The crew members of the second committed suicide after their sub was damaged in a depth-charge attack. The third sub fired two torpedoes, one of which sank a depot ship. Though never found, it too failed to return to the mother sub. One week later, a Japanese sub attacked the Sydney area, damaging houses but causing no serious injuries.

> ## "The more of this filth that is eliminated, the better for the security of the Reich."
>
> —German propaganda minister Joseph Goebbels, on the reprisals in Lidice following Heydrich's assassination

Reinhard Heydrich and the SD

FROM FALL 1941 TO SPRING 1942, Reinhard Heydrich was regarded as a potential successor to Hitler. He had played a key role in the development and implementation of the "Final Solution" to exterminate Europe's Jews—a policy enthusiastically expounded by him at the Wannsee Conference in January 1942.

Heydrich's time as one of the most powerful men in the Third Reich actually began in 1934 when he became head of the Gestapo, from which he shifted in 1936 to become chief of the *Sicherheitsdienst* (Security Service, SD). His assassination by Czech partisans in May 1942 reflected not only his personal status but also his new role as the German official in control of occupied Czechoslovakia.

Formed in 1932, the SD was the intelligence and security branch of the SS. Initially, the SS was responsible for the security of Hitler, other prominent Nazis, and the wider NSDAP organization. Later, it assumed responsibility for security throughout the Third Reich. The SD was the intelligence branch of the SS. It helped to implement Nazi policies concerning Jews, Communists, and other socially or politically "undesirable" groups, in parallel with traditional security and intelligence-gathering activities. The SD played a significant role in the *Einsatzgruppen*, which conducted counter-partisan operations. The *Einsatzgruppen* carried out many thousands of executions in German-occupied territories, and played a part in the clearance of Jewish ghettos in Eastern Europe.

Heydrich's assassination In September 1941, Reinhard Heydrich became the governor of German-occupied Bohemia and Moravia (today's Czech Republic). The overly confident governor often rode in an unescorted, open-roofed car. On May 27, 1942, two British-trained Czech resistance fighters successfully ambushed him in Prague, wounding him with a grenade. Seen here is the car in which he was attacked. After several days of agony, Heydrich died on June 4.

The destruction of Lidice The Nazis' most notorious retaliation for Reinhard Heydrich's assassination was the destruction of the Czech village of Lidice, suspected by Hitler of being a hotbed of anti-Nazi resistance. On June 10, 1942, German authorities rounded up the town's entire population. All males over 16 years of age—about 172 in number—were shot to death the next day. Many of Lidice's surviving women were sent to their deaths at the Ravensbrück concentration camp, while some children considered sufficiently "Aryan" were adopted by German families. All told, about 340 people from Lidice were murdered. This photograph of massacred men was taken before the Germans leveled Lidice's houses and buildings to the ground. The village was rebuilt after the war.

217

Battle of Midway

FLUSH WITH VICTORY in the spring of 1942, Japan turned its attention to tiny Midway Island, 1,100 miles northwest of Hawaii. Seizure of U.S.-held Midway would provide a useful outpost for the subsequent occupation of Hawaii. Furthermore, the operation was expected to bring out the U.S. Pacific Fleet, which could then be totally destroyed.

Commanded by Admiral Yamamoto Isoroku, the attacking force consisted of several groups and subgroups and included a secondary thrust into the Aleutian Islands of Alaska. The striking force, with four aircraft carriers, would hit Midway. The main body, which included a light carrier and three battleships—one of them the fearsome *Yamato* with its 18-inch guns—would follow. Other groups included battleships, cruisers, destroyers, and transports. When the U.S. fleet sortied from Hawaii, these groups were to close in and destroy the Americans in a complicated pincer movement.

There was one fatal flaw. U.S. cryptologists had broken the Japanese naval code and knew Yamamoto was coming.

Armed with details of the enemy plan, the Americans set a trap. When the Japanese arrived on June 4 and began their aerial attack on the island's defenders, the U.S. carriers *Yorktown*, *Enterprise*, and *Hornet* were waiting in ambush.

The Japanese suddenly found themselves under attack not only from land-based aircraft from Midway, but from torpedo bombers, dive-bombers, and fighters from U.S. carriers that they had not suspected were in the area. Initial attacks by the torpedo bombers, carried out by Americans flying obsolete aircraft, failed as whole squadrons were shot down. But the unrelenting pressure created openings for the carrier dive-bombers, which proceeded to sink Japanese aircraft carriers *Akagi*, *Kaga*, *Soryu*, and *Hiryu*. Stunned by these losses, Yamamoto ordered a withdrawal.

Midway cost the Americans the carrier *Yorktown*, a destroyer, 147 aircraft, and 307 dead. Yamamoto lost four carriers, a cruiser, 322 aircraft, and 3,500 dead, including irreplaceable air crews. Also lost forever was the once-overwhelming Japanese naval initiative in the Pacific.

A tide-turning triumph for the U.S. Many historians consider the Battle of Midway the most significant naval engagement of World War II. Fought from June 4 to 7, 1942, the battle turned back a Japanese attempt to seize Midway Atoll and destroy the U.S. fleet in a decisive confrontation. Armed with key intelligence on enemy plans, outnumbered U.S. forces mauled the Japanese. The Imperial Japanese Navy would never regain the superiority it had enjoyed over the first six months of the war.

Nimitz leads the Pacific Fleet Chester Nimitz entered the Naval Academy at the age of 15 in 1901 and graduated seventh in his class. President Roosevelt chose him to replace disgraced Admiral Husband Kimmel as commander-in-chief of the Pacific Fleet after Japan's surprise attack on Pearl Harbor. Nimitz's first task was to rebuild the Pacific Fleet, a job he accomplished swiftly. Within six months of the attack, Nimitz achieved a stunning victory over the Japanese at the Battle of Midway. The U.S. followed that triumph with a string of amphibious attacks, one island after another, until the Allies were at the doorstep of Japan in August 1945.

Japan's important aircraft carrier The Japanese aircraft carrier *Hiryu* takes evasive action while under attack by U.S. B-17 bombers during the Battle of Midway. Commissioned in 1939, the 20,250-ton carrier was involved in the raid on Pearl Harbor in December 1941 as well as in operations in the East Indies and Indian Ocean. At Midway, its planes heavily damaged the U.S. carrier *Yorktown* on June 4. Hours later, *Hiryu* was attacked by 13 dive-bombers from *Enterprise*. Struck by four bombs, it was abandoned when massive fires could not be brought under control. The *Hiryu* was subsequently scuttled by torpedoes from the destroyer *Makigumo*.

Yorktown **sunk at Midway** Smoke billows from the USS *Yorktown* following Japanese air attacks at Midway. The carrier survived three bomb hits and returned to action before coming under renewed attack by enemy torpedo planes. Struck by two torpedoes, the carrier lost headway and began listing to port. Fearing the carrier was about to capsize, the crew was ordered to abandon ship. Hours later, with the *Yorktown* still stubbornly afloat, efforts were underway to salvage the ship when a Japanese submarine sent two more torpedoes into the carrier. Mortally wounded, *Yorktown* sank in 3,000 fathoms the following morning.

The reliable Dauntless A U.S. Navy Douglas SBD Dauntless dive-bomber releases part of its payload. Considered obsolete when war broke out, the Dauntless was underpowered, slow, noisy, and fatiguing to fly over long distances. On the plus side, it handled well, could absorb considerable punishment,

and was very accurate. These attributes transformed the Dauntless into the mainstay of the U.S. Navy's air fleet from 1941 to 1943. In fact, it was credited with sinking more Japanese warships than any other U.S. aircraft type. At Midway alone, Dauntless dive-bombers sank four Japanese carriers and damaged two heavy cruisers.

Nagumo's star wanes Japanese vice admiral Nagumo Chuichi led the attack on Pearl Harbor and gained fame during the initial flood tide of Japanese victories in the Pacific. Since Nagumo's schooling was in surface tactics, many fellow officers had questioned his appointment as commander of the First Carrier Fleet

in April 1941, feeling he lacked familiarity with the naval air arm. Despite early successes, Nagumo fell out of favor after the loss of four carriers at Midway. He was eventually demoted to a series of less important posts. Assigned to the Marianas, he was trapped by the U.S. invasion of Saipan, and took his life on July 6, 1944.

1942

June 7: The *Chicago Tribune* states that the U.S. Navy had advance knowledge of the Midway strike. The article jeopardizes years of intelligence collection and cryptology work. • Japanese forces occupy the Aleutian islands of Attu and Kiska in the war's only Axis occupation in North America.

June 10: The entire Czechoslovakian village of Lidice is razed in reprisal for the killing of Reinhard Heydrich. More than 400 residents are driven from their homes; the men are executed while the women and children are sent to concentration camps.

June 11: The office of SS *Reichsführer* Heinrich Himmler calls for the transfer of some 100,000 Jews from occupied France to "relocation" camps. • German U-boats launch a mine-laying campaign in eastern U.S. coastal waters. • U.S. officials sign a new Lend-Lease agreement with Soviet ambassador Litvinov.

June 12: The oil-producing region around Ploesti, Romania, is strafed by U.S. Army Air Force B-24 bombers.

June 13: British troops suffer a major defeat at the hands of General Rommel when Lieutenant General Neil Ritchie orders an attack against a well-entrenched German Army in Libya.

June 15: The tanker *Robert C. Tuttle* runs aground on Virginia Beach after hitting a German mine, making it the first American ship lost to enemy mines at home.

June 18: A six-hour gun battle in a church ends with the deaths of seven Czech partisans who took part in the Heydrich assassination. • Bernard Robinson becomes the first African American U.S. naval officer (an ensign in the Reserves).

June 20: Roosevelt and Churchill agree to move forward with an invasion of the French colonies in northwest Africa.

The expanded role of the FBI
The Federal Bureau of Investigation (FBI) was established in 1908 and led by J. Edgar Hoover beginning in 1924. Primarily a crime-fighting agency during its early years, the FBI was authorized to investigate subversive organizations beginning in 1936. When war broke out in Europe in 1939, the FBI's role was expanded to include sabotage and espionage investigations. With the added responsibilities came an increase in agents, from 391 in 1933 to 3,000 in 1942 to 4,886 in 1944. Hoover publicized the successes of his department, increased the confidence of civilians, and expanded the FBI's responsibilities well beyond its prewar assignments.

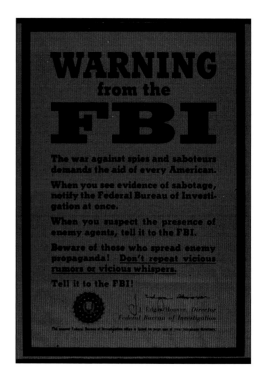

WARNING from the FBI

The war against spies and saboteurs demands the aid of every American.

When you see evidence of sabotage, notify the Federal Bureau of Investigation at once.

When you suspect the presence of enemy agents, tell it to the FBI.

Beware of those who spread enemy propaganda! Don't repeat vicious rumors or vicious whispers.

Tell it to the FBI!

J. Edgar Hoover, Director
Federal Bureau of Investigation

FBI captures German spies On August 8, 1942, six men, found guilty of espionage, were led individually to an electric chair in a District of Columbia jail. The condemned had been members of two four-man German teams sent to New York and Florida via submarine about two months earlier to disrupt the manufacture of war materials. The men had been chosen for the mission because they had lived in the U.S. before. Two of the men revealed the plan to the FBI before any acts of sabotage could be carried out, and thus had their death penalties commuted by President Roosevelt. Richard Quirin (*pictured*) was one of the executed.

Americans ration rubber, gas The U.S. Office of Price Administration (OPA) was created in August 1941 to stabilize prices and ration consumer goods. Rubber was the first item rationed, followed later by gasoline. Five priority levels were created for travel, ranging from A for pleasure driving to E for emergency vehicles. Any vehicle with an A sticker received only three to five gallons per week. The allocated amount increased with each level. Commuters (level B) were encouraged to carpool. Appeals to patriotism notwithstanding, many Americans elected not to follow Washington's program. New or nearly new tires were available to anyone who had the money to pay a black-marketeer. Trade in black market gasoline also was robust.

OWI's propaganda In June 1942, the U.S. government created the Office of War Information (OWI) to funnel information to the American media. The OWI soon concentrated on "selling" the war by manipulating pro-American sentiment and dehumanizing the enemy. For instance, the OWI sent story directives to pulp magazines, as illustrated by this set-up photo with its heavy implications of sexual threat. In addition, rigid guidelines restricted what could appear in movies. With the OWI controlling what the American public read, saw, and heard, relevant information about the war was laced with propaganda.

Hitchcock's *Saboteur* Not one instance of enemy sabotage occurred in the United States during the war—a testament, in part, to FBI vigilance. For the 1942 film *Saboteur*, however, director Alfred Hitchcock supposed that such a crime did take place. In the film, an innocent shipyard worker becomes a fugitive. Footage of the capsized troopship USS

Lafayette (formerly the French passenger liner *Normandie*) was used by Hitchcock to suggest sabotage. The real destruction of this ship, which occurred at New York's Pier 88 on February 9, 1942, was traced to a welder's spark.

1942

June 21: German General Rommel pushes east after conquering Tobruk, Libya. His troops capture supplies, along with 33,000 prisoners of war.

June 22: Fort Stevens, Oregon, escapes harm when it is shelled by the Japanese.

June 23: Rail-transported Parisian Jews are the first to go through the selection process for the Auschwitz gas chambers.

June 25: Roosevelt appoints Dwight Eisenhower to the post of U.S. Army chief in Europe.

June 26: The important U-boat base of Bremen, Germany, is in flames following a massive RAF attack.

July 1: Some 250 alien saboteurs are arrested in the U.S. when the FBI uncovers a plot to blow up the Pennsylvania Railroad.

July 4: After eight months, the Germans finally prevail in the Battle of Sevastopol, the site of the Soviets' main naval base on the Black Sea. Germany's 11th Army takes 90,000 Soviets as prisoners. • American bombers undertake their first independent raids of the war, attacking four German air bases in Dutch territory.

July 5: Russia yields the Crimea to Germany. • Britain angers Stalin by imposing a moratorium on convoys to northern Russia. This follows a devastating German attack that sank 23 of 33 Allied ships in a convoy on the Barents Sea.

July 7: The British send Nazi spies Jose Keys and Alphonse Timmerman to the gallows.

July 8: U.S. Pacific Fleet commander Admiral Nimitz orders the invasion of the strategically significant Solomon island of Guadalcanal. His aim is to take an airfield being built by the Japanese, who have seized this island.

Germany's railroad guns From 1937, the German manufacturer Krupp designed and built two enormous railroad guns: "Gustav" and "Dora." The guns were arguably vulnerable to air attack. However, the existence of Europe's extensive railroad system and the ability to utilize poor-quality and rapidly repaired rails generally validated the railroad gun concept. Eventually, Dora was test-fired in 1942. It was manned by 1,420 men commanded by a brigadier general. Subsequently, it was employed to good effect in the Crimea, where it fired 40 seven-ton shells almost 30 miles into Sevastopol in mid-1942. It later fired 30 rounds into Warsaw during the 1944 uprising. The Gustav was never used in action.

Yugoslav resistance
Moments before his death by hanging on June 22, 1942, Yugoslav partisan fighter Stjepan Filipovic shouts his defiance against his country's Nazi occupiers and his allegiance to the Yugoslav Communist Party. The Yugoslav partisans (officially the People's Liberation Army and Partisan Detachments of Yugoslavia) brought together an unlikely alliance of Balkan ethnic groups— including Croats and Serbs—through their commitment to communism. The partisans' cunning and courage (along with their sometimes savage brutality) and pressure from the advancing Red Army combined to free Yugoslavia from Nazi rule.

The "Mosquito Army" The Long Range Desert Group (originally the Long Range Patrol Group) was founded by Major Ralph Bagnold in 1940 to assist British military efforts in North Africa. Sometimes called the "Mosquito Army" and the "Libyan Taxi Service," the group's purpose was to disappear behind enemy lines in order to scout routes, gather intelligence, and launch raids. Members such as the ones pictured here sometimes spent weeks or even months on dangerous missions in oppressive desert heat. LRDG teams were so cunning and skillful that, as Bagnold observed, raids seemed to come from "a fourth dimension," leaving German and Italian forces baffled and paralyzed.

American POWs stick together American prisoners celebrate the Fourth of July in 1942 in the Malaybalay camp in Mindanao, Philippines. The Japanese regime in Malaybalay seems to have been relatively benign, but this gathering was against regulations and dangerous. At Malaybalay, rations were far better than at Davao, where by October the U.S. prisoners had been moved. Prisoners of war of all nations sought to maintain a sense of national unity and to find diversions from the boredom and suffering of imprisonment. Mutual support was crucial to survival.

Life's **valiant reporter** "The woman who had been torpedoed in the Mediterranean, strafed by the *Luftwaffe,* stranded on an Arctic island, bombarded in Moscow, and pulled out of the Chesapeake when her chopper crashed," wrote biographer Sean Callahan, "was known to the *Life* staff as 'Maggie the Indestructible.'" Margaret Bourke-White was a staff photographer for *Life* magazine during World War II, and she covered the war from its front lines in Italy, Russia, and Germany. Her book *Dear Fatherland, Rest Quietly* captures the atrocities of warfare, from the battlefield to Nazi death camps.

1942

July 9: Teenaged diarist Anne Frank goes into hiding along with her family and friends as the Nazis begin to purge Amsterdam of its Jewish population.

July 10: In a disturbing new facet of Nazi inhumanity, 100 female Auschwitz inmates are selected for medical experimentation.

July 11: RAF bombers fly to Danzig to bomb U-boat pens.

July 13: President Roosevelt approves the creation of the Office of Strategic Services (OSS), the forerunner to the Central Intelligence Agency.

July 15: In the first deportation of Holland's Jews, some 2,000 are sent to Auschwitz under the guise of being relocated to a German labor camp.
• Rommel must postpone his Egyptian offensive to assist two Italian divisions under Allied attack at El Alamein.

July 17: The United States begins its campaign to convince Britain to launch an invasion of mainland Europe in 1942. The British will resist, opting to build their strength for a major invasion at some unspecified future date.

July 19: The Germans attempt to limit French partisan violence by imposing a law calling for the slaughter and deportation of male family members of known "terrorists" that evade capture by Nazi authorities.

July 22: The Nazis open the Treblinka death camp outside of Warsaw, Poland. Like Belzec, Treblinka's mandate is exclusively extermination, not confinement and labor.

July 23: The German army captures some 240,000 Soviet troops at the fall of Rostov. • A German U-boat lays mines in the Mississippi River delta.

U.S. begins production of war goods Laborers in the Lockheed plant in Burbank, California, work on a B-17 Flying Fortress. One of the tasks facing President Roosevelt in the early days of the war was to dramatically shift the focus of American manufacturing from domestic to war goods. To oversee that process, the president called for the creation of the War Production Board, whose job would be to oversee the manufacture of war materials. The first decision of the board, which was formed in January 1942, was to ban the production of all cars and light trucks after that month. By the middle of the year, production of consumer durable goods decreased by 29 percent. America's shift to a wartime economy had begun.

U.S. materiel aids effort in Tobruk When German commander Erwin Rommel seized Tobruk, Libya, on June 21, 1942, the United States had barely joined active combat in the western hemisphere. Nevertheless, President Roosevelt immediately saw that the Allies in North Africa needed increased American materiel. With U.S. tanks and planes, such as the American-built Glenn Martin bombers seen here, British-led forces soon turned the tide against Rommel. But for the moment, Rommel ruled the desert.

Operation Magic

By 1941 American cryptanalysts had broken the Japanese "Purple" cipher, enabling them to read Tokyo's diplomatic traffic. Dubbed Operation Magic, this intelligence coup yielded a wealth of information regarding Japanese political aims.

Military codes, such as the Japanese navy's JN-25, proved more difficult to crack. Introduced in 1939, JN-25 remained in effect in various versions throughout the war. U.S. cryptanalysts broke the early version of JN-25, but a second version introduced in late 1940 remained largely unsolved until 1942.

The attack on Pearl Harbor prompted a determined Allied assault on enemy codes. By May 1942, about 40 percent of intercepted Japanese navy radio traffic was being deciphered, though only 10 to 15 percent of each message was readable. While Japanese code changes periodically shut off the flow of information, the U.S. advantage was incalculable. This advantage grew in early 1943 when cryptanalysts also managed to penetrate the Japanese army code.

Information from decrypts, code-named Ultra, provided intelligence on every aspect of the Japanese war effort: operations, ship sailings, troop movements and strategy, even the promotion of junior officers. Such information enabled the U.S. to ambush the Japanese fleet at Midway in June 1942—one of the greatest victories in the history of naval warfare. Foreknowledge of Admiral Yamamoto's planned visit to Bougainville in 1943 allowed

Headquarters of the Army cryptanalyst service in Virginia

U.S. fighter pilots to intercept his aircraft and send him to his death. Armed with enemy ship departures and schedules, U.S. submarines proceeded to destroy the Japanese merchant fleet, delivering a mortal blow to the enemy war effort. Reports from Japanese diplomats in Europe provided critical information on German defenses, new weapons, and other topics.

Incredibly, the Japanese never realized that the string of disasters and hemorrhaging ship losses were largely caused by the compromising of their codes. Like the Germans, each time they became suspicious, they decided that since they themselves could not break Allied machine codes, the Allies—who they deemed less intelligent—could not accomplish such a feat. As a result, U.S. code-breakers continued to "read Japanese mail" until the end of the war.

The Colt pistol
The Colt M1911 A1 semiautomatic pistol was widely used by American personnel in all branches of service during the war. The weapon, which could easily be assembled and

disassembled, featured a magazine that carried seven bullets. Its .45-caliber round had excellent stopping power at close range. In comparison to pistols used by servicemen of other countries, however, the M1911 was quite heavy and large. In order to meet the demand for the weapon during the war, nine different manufacturers were required, which posed problems with interchanging parts.

Americans fear German invasion Hitler was the subject of many propaganda posters, such as the one shown here. They often poked fun at his speeches, but underlying this humor lay a foundation of fear for those Americans who believed it possible for Germany and Japan to bring the war to North America. Their concern was not unfounded. Germany began to develop plans for an invasion of the United States

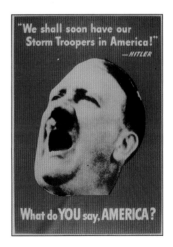

even before Hitler's declaration of war on the U.S. Some felt that Germany's invasion of Russia was just a staging ground for an attack on America.

1942

July 23: *Judenrat* president Adam Czerniakow, who is charged by the Nazis with delivering 6,000 Jews a day for "resettlement" from the Warsaw Ghetto on penalty of the death of his wife and some 100 other Jewish hostages, takes his own life. A day earlier, he was unable to convince the Nazis to spare the ghetto orphans from being sent to Treblinka as part of a mass deportation of Jewish children.

July 26: British minister of food Lord Woolton institutes a sweets and chocolate rationing program that allows a half pound for every man, woman, and child every four weeks.

July 27: Hamburg is once again bombarded by the RAF. This time, some 600 planes participate in the attack.

July 28: According to President Roosevelt, no less than four million Americans are serving in the military.

July 30: The First Battle of El Alamein in Egypt, fought mostly between British Commonwealth and German troops, ends in a stalemate, thereby halting the German advance. • With the Germans on the move on two separate Russian fronts, Stalin issues a directive forbidding retreat. • The U.S. Navy begins a reservist program for women called the Women Appointed for Voluntary Emergency Service, better known as WAVES.

July 31: The approaches to the harbor at Charleston, South Carolina, are mined by a German U-boat. • American planes bomb Japanese positions on Guadalcanal and Tulagi in the Solomon Islands. • A Nazi "scientific" organization calling itself the Institute for Practical Research in Military Science begins to collect corpses from the Oranienburg concentration camp in an effort to study Jewish skeletons.

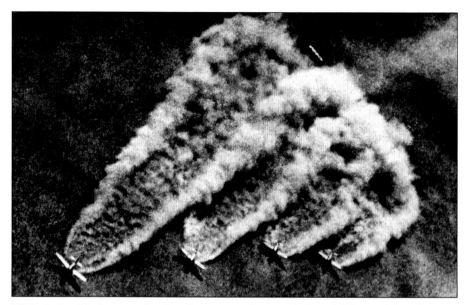

Hitler's bad judgment in the Caucasus Germany's insatiable need for oil-based products meant that the capture of the oil fields at Maikop, Baku, and Grozny remained a key strategic objective. Here, four German dive-bombers take off in the Caucasus. This strategy was ostensibly sound and could have succeeded. However, from mid-1942 German combat power in the Caucasus was dissipated by Hitler's ill-judged decisions to redirect forces to the competing operations at Leningrad, Moscow, and Stalingrad. Thus, the Caucasus advance lost momentum. Characteristically, Hitler blamed his generals for this failure.

The battle for Sevastopol The German campaign in the Crimea (a Ukrainian peninsula between the Black Sea and the Sea of Azov) focused on the capture of the strategically vital fortified city of Sevastopol. In a bid to prevent this, a series of landings by some 40,000 Soviet troops in December 1941 resulted in the temporary ejection of the Germans from parts of the peninsula. However, the better quality and training of General Erich von Manstein's forces eventually led to German victory, and by July the Soviets had been cleared away by the Germans. Although the peninsula battles delayed the fall of Sevastopol by about six months, it finally fell to a German assault in July 1942 (*pictured*).

Red Army greatly improved in '42 By the second summer of the "Great Patriotic War," the Red Army was finally experiencing a renaissance after its ignominious defeats of 1941. Previously, years of centralized political command and control had stultified operational effectiveness and emasculated the officer corps, but now various aspects of this policy were progressively relaxed or revised. Some 500,000 battle-proven, front-line soldiers were quickly trained as commanders, while new radio equipment reduced the army's traditional reliance on landline communications. Meanwhile, thousands of new artillery guns, rocket-launchers, tanks, trucks, assault guns, and automatic weapons at last began entering service.

БИТЬ ВРАГА ДО ПОЛНОГО ЕГО УНИЧТОЖЕНИЯ!

Postcards as propaganda Britain, Germany, Italy, and other nations used postcards as wartime propaganda tools. Some cards vilified the enemy, stirred patriotism, or celebrated victories. In other cases, postcards with faked origins and images were dropped into enemy countries to cause dissension among citizens. The Soviets faked dozens of German postcards with the message that soldiers had been lied to by Hitler and the only *Lebensraum* they would find in Russia would be their own graves. This 1942 Soviet postcard glorifies Russia's victory over German troops outside Moscow.

Russia's female flying aces The heavy losses of pilots sustained by the Soviet air force during Barbarossa were offset by the training and employing of hundreds of women as combat pilots. Marina Raskova, an already famous Russian aviator, organized three all-female air combat units. Another combat flying ace was Lilia Litvak, the "White Rose of Stalingrad," of the 586th Women's Fighter Regiment. Then there was Natalya Meklin (*pictured*) of the 588th

Women's Night Bomber Regiment (known to the Germans as the "Night Witches"). Meklin flew more than 800 night-bombing missions and was honored as a "Hero of the Soviet Union."

Britain's new "battle schools" The fall of France and the evacuation of the British Expeditionary Force from Dunkirk in June 1940 prompted significant changes in the organization and training of the British Army and Royal Marines, as Britain prepared for a protracted conflict. Based on the combat experience gained by many officers in France, realistic, imaginative, and physically demanding "battle schools" (*pictured*) were established. These schools supplanted the comprehensive but often predictable and inflexible training regime of the prewar period.

THE ALLIES STRIKE BACK

AUGUST 1942–JANUARY 1943

"We have thrown the national existence into the balance. There is no turning back now."

—German propaganda minister
Joseph Goebbels, regarding Stalingrad,
Das Reich, November 15, 1942

THE GERMAN ARMIES that moved relentlessly toward Stalingrad in summer 1942 were confronted with a bleak terrain. "A barren, naked, lifeless steppe," wrote Johann Wieder, who survived the conflict to write his memoirs, "without a bush, without a tree, for miles without a village." For a time, the advance appeared to be a repeat of the summer of 1941. The Sixth Army of General Friedrich Paulus pushed the Soviet forces in front of it. By August 19, they had reached the outskirts of Stalingrad. On August 23, the first formations reached the banks of the Volga River. Paulus promised Hitler that the city would fall within a few days.

In reality the attempt to seize Stalingrad turned into one of the epic battles of World War II. During the five months in which the battle for the city raged, the advance of the Axis powers was halted and crushed. By the time Paulus surrendered in early February 1943, the tide had begun to turn not just on the Eastern Front but also in the Middle East and the Pacific.

Following the Japanese defeat at Midway Island in June 1942, the Allies found it possible to begin the long and brutal campaign to dislodge Japan's forces from the string of islands they had occupied around the ocean perimeter of the Empire. This was a difficult and costly campaign for both sides. Men and equipment had to be transported over long oceanic supply lines, thousands of miles from the home countries, and in terrain where tropical heat and disease took a high toll on the combatants, as did some of the bitterest fighting of the war.

German troops surrender at Stalingrad in January 1943. The two *Waffen-SS* men in the foreground were probably executed summarily. The capitulation of General Paulus's Sixth Army finally exposed the disastrous consequences of Hitler's flawed and obsessive strategy in Russia, while also vividly demonstrating the ever increasing capability of the Soviet forces.

The first battles were fought in southern New Guinea and the Solomon Islands, deemed by Japanese planners to be areas in the new perimeter that needed to be consolidated. In New Guinea, Japanese forces attempted, by an overland campaign, to seize Port Moresby, which they had tried to secure three months earlier by sea. The battle against Australian and American forces continued for six months until finally, on January 22, 1943, the last Japanese troops were cleared from the central portion of the huge island.

American forces landed on Guadalcanal and Florida Island in the southern Solomons on August 7, 1942. There, against fierce resistance, they captured the port of Tulagi and the airfield on Guadalcanal. The U.S. needed six months to secure these modest gains against fierce resistance that was repeatedly reinforced. However, the American capacity to supply large numbers of planes and trained pilots slowly tilted the conflict toward the Americans. All Japanese efforts to destroy the tenuous American foothold were beaten off. At the end of December 1942, the Japanese high command decided to abandon the contest, having lost more than 20,000 men, 600 aircraft, and 15 warships in the attempt. Though Allied gains on New Guinea and in the Solomons had been modest, it was now clear to both sides that Japan was fully stretched by commitments in the Pacific and China, and lacked the capacity for further advance.

The bodies of dead Japanese soldiers float in the sea near Buna Mission, New Guinea, in January 1943. The victory achieved by the Seventh Australian Division and the 32nd U.S. Division followed almost two months of fighting. The ill-prepared and poorly equipped U.S. division suffered 90 percent casualties, mostly through sickness.

In the Middle East, German general Erwin Rommel advanced into Egypt and toward Palestine. However, this apparently disastrous position for the Allies was stabilized and then reversed. As in the Pacific, both sides were fighting far from the home base and at the end of supply routes, which were regularly threatened by submarine and air action. By autumn 1942, British Empire forces had succeeded in building up large reserves while Axis supplies were regularly interrupted by submarine action in the Mediterranean. North Africa mattered differently to each side as well. For Hitler, North Africa was a sideshow. For the Allies, it was a vital part of their global strategy; the Middle East and Mediterranean should not be abandoned to the Axis.

Nevertheless, Rommel had achieved a great deal. On August 31, 1942, he began a final offensive designed to bring him into Egypt and Palestine so that the Jews there could be killed before the area was turned over to Italy. Like the Japanese, he discovered that his overstretched resources had reached their limit. The British Eighth Army, which was dug in on a line near the small Egyptian city of El Alamein, absorbed Rommel's assault. On October 23, with overwhelming materiel advantage, a new British commander—General Bernard Montgomery—launched a counteroffensive. His 1,030 tanks proved too large an obstacle for the 500 or so Axis tanks that opposed him, and by November 4 Axis forces were in full retreat.

Montgomery did not cut off the Axis retreat, but by early February, Axis forces had been pushed back into Tunisia. Many of the Italian units were destroyed, and thousands of soldiers were taken prisoner. Once again, as in the Solomons, airpower had played a critical role in the Allies' success.

The change in fortunes owed something to the willingness of the Allies to collaborate. The three Axis powers made little attempt to coordinate their strategies, share economic resources, or divulge military or technical secrets. The Western Allies recognized earlier how important it was to share resources. They also understood how vital it was to mobilize their extensive manufacturing and scientific capacity as fully as possible to compensate for their lack of a large and experienced army.

A sign on the road to El Alamein, Egypt, in September 1942 warns of the threat posed by General Rommel's *Afrika Korps*. However, a month later British general Montgomery's victory at El Alamein changed the course of the war for the Allies, signaling what Churchill called "the end of the beginning."

The United States sent large amounts of food, raw materials, and equipment to Britain. So too did Canada, whose contribution is often overlooked. The Soviet Union was the beneficiary of a rich flow of resources from both North America and the British Empire, including a half-million vehicles and a million miles of telephone cable. The Soviets received few weapons, but the provision of food, manufactured products, and materials allowed the Soviet economy—which had lost around 60 percent of its capacity in 1941—to concentrate on the mass production of armaments.

The help was sourly acknowledged, because Stalin wanted his allies to launch a second front in 1942 to take the pressure off the Red Army. In August 1942, Winston Churchill flew to Moscow to discuss Allied strategy face-to-face. It was a difficult confrontation. Stalin implied that the British were simply afraid of the Germans. Churchill's furious rebuttal finally won over Stalin. He was told of Western plans for an expanded bombing campaign against German targets and of a still-secret operation, code-named "Torch," of Allied landings in northwest Africa, planned for November.

The invasion of North Africa began on November 8, 1942. Like operations in the Pacific, the American task force sailed the whole width of an ocean to reach the Moroccan coast on November 7. British forces landed at Oran and Algiers. After brief fighting with French colonial forces, the whole area was secured three days later. The Allied armies rushed toward Tunis to cut off the retreating Rommel. The Germans deployed enough forces into the pocket from Italy to create a stable front line, and the battle for Tunisia began in the last week of November.

In retaliation, Hitler ordered German forces to occupy the whole of Vichy France, which was absorbed into the German New Order. Jewish refugees who had managed to hide in the unoccupied zone were now pursued with a new vigor. As Axis forces found themselves pressed on all fronts, the mass murder of Jews reached its crescendo in the death camps at Auschwitz, Sobibór, Belzec, Chelmno, and Treblinka.

The gains in other theaters paled in comparison to the struggle that had engulfed the southern front in the Soviet Union. German expectations that the city of Stalingrad would quickly fall were frustrated by many factors: German forces had to be supplied along a single rail track into the battlefield. The destruction of the very large city by German bombers created the ideal conditions for a determined infantry defense. And most of the buildings were modern steel and concrete structures with bunkers and cellars beneath them, which meant that not even regular shelling and bombing could easily flatten what was left of the twisted structures.

Ideologically, Churchill and Stalin were diametrically opposed to each other. However, war had made them comrades in adversity. In mid-August 1942, at the First Moscow Conference, they met face-to-face for the first time. Despite their philosophical differences, they developed the unique personal relationship that subsequently ensured the Allied victory.

Into this wrecked landscape, the remnants of Soviet divisions retreated. They hid in the crumbled buildings and underground hiding places, attacking in small groups, often at night. Soviet sharpshooters pinned down German forces, which for most of the battle greatly outnumbered their opponents.

The commander in Stalingrad was a young Soviet general, Vasily Chuikov. The son of a peasant, Chuikov was robust and unflinching in the face of battle. His 62nd Army was scattered in pockets of what remained of the center of Stalingrad. It was supplied across the Volga River from the east bank, from which came waves of artillery and rocket fire, a stream of Soviet air attacks, and large numbers of soldiers. On several occasions, his weakened forces were close to collapse, but Paulus lacked the means to launch a knock-out blow. The last major German offensive, designed to sweep Chuikov's remaining troops into the river, began during the second week of November. On the 8th, Hitler told the party faithful in Munich that in days he would be "master of Stalingrad."

The swift retreat on the southern front had been a shock to Stalin, who was determined to hold the city which now bore his name. In mid-September, his deputy commander-in-chief, General Georgi Zhukov, worked with the army staff on a possible way out of the crisis. Rather than throw more troops into the Stalingrad pocket, he suggested building up massive reserves on the German flanks that could be used to cut the German line of advance and encircle Paulus's troops. As long as Chuikov could hold the city, the plan—Operation Uranus—would work.

Further north, Zhukov planned Operation Mars, another large assault on the German line. This operation would prevent any German reinforcement of the south and might unhinge the whole German front line in Russia. This was the first time Soviet commanders had been able to plan, with Stalin's approval, a large-scale counteroffensive. Preparations were made under the strictest secrecy.

On November 19, Soviet armies fell on the unprepared Axis forces. Because they lacked the forces to guard the flanks of their advance, the Germans had pushed their Romanian, Italian, and Hungarian allies to increase their commitment of troops to the Eastern Front. Since the Germans had failed to provide these troops with proper equipment, the Romanian front was torn apart and Paulus was encircled. German field marshal Erich von Manstein launched a counterattack to break the ring, but failed. Axis forces retreated back across the steppe. In the Caucasus, Soviet armies drove the southern German front back as well, though they failed to close off all avenues of escape. The success of Uranus masked the mixed fortunes of Operation Mars, in which the Red Army suffered very heavy casualties for virtually no strategic gain.

After another two months of bitter fighting, Paulus and his shrunken army of diseased, hungry, and frostbitten soldiers finally surrendered on February 2, 1943. The remnants of the remaining Axis forces in the north of the city surrendered two days later. Some 91,000 Axis soldiers were taken prisoner. This defeat, far more than the victories elsewhere, signified to the world that the Axis was not invincible.

Although romanticized, this French magazine illustration of the fighting at Stalingrad signified the particular importance of that battle and the Soviet victory to the wider Allied cause. After Stalingrad, a German strategic victory on the Eastern Front was unachievable.

1942

August: As many as 400,000 Jews will be murdered in occupied Europe during this month alone.

August 1: In an attempt to conserve oil for the war effort, President Roosevelt asks residents of the coal-rich states in the East to use that source of fuel instead of oil at every opportunity.

August 4: Auschwitz receives the first trainload of Jews from occupied Belgium to be designated for "resettlement."

August 7: Lieutenant General William "Strafer" Gott is killed by a German air assault in Egypt one day after reporting to his new post as commander of the British Eighth Army.
• For the first time, the United States seizes control of territory occupied by Japan when the 19,000-man First Marine Division lands on Guadalcanal and Tulagi.

August 8: The United States executes six of eight German spies caught after coming ashore in Florida and Long Island. Two are given life sentences instead of death sentences after testifying against their comrades.
• The day after a local victory on Guadalcanal, the Allies suffer a stunning setback offshore in the Battle of Savo Island, losing more than 1,000 sailors and four cruisers.

August 9: German operatives mark the ground near Long Island's Mitchell Field so that the important air base can be easily seen from the air. • In India, Mohandas Gandhi is arrested for impeding the war effort, three days after promising to engage his people in widespread civil disobedience if Britain continued to deny India immediate independence.

August 11: Vichy prime minister Pierre Laval claims that France will be liberated "when Germany wins the war."

Germans advance toward Stalingrad
During the first half of July 1942, German infantry and armored forces battled to the Don River near Voronezh (a key city in the supply line to Moscow), Rostov, and other towns. Soviet resistance was initially disorganized but determined, and it delayed the Germans' crossing of the Don *(pictured)* long enough to move Red troops away from danger of capture. By mid-month, Stalin realized that the ultimate objective of this German drive was Stalingrad. Soviet resistance stiffened accordingly.

Medical care on the Eastern Front German soldiers comfort a comrade whose arm has been blown off during fighting on the Eastern Front. In the early days of their invasion, wounded Germans could be treated and even evacuated by air. But as German forces penetrated deeper into Soviet territory, and as Red Army resistance increased, German soldiers found themselves cut off from medical care. Russian troops stationed in cities had rudimentary emergency services, sometimes with medicines supplied by Allied nations. However, the isolation and sheer ferocity of the battlefields meant that any soldier with an injury of this severity had little chance of survival.

Young members of the *Waffen-SS* These young men were members of the *Waffen-SS* (Armed-SS), the military arm of the larger German *Schutzstaffel* (SS; Protective Squadron). An elite combat group famous for fierceness and willingness to take casualties, the *Waffen-SS* was also notorious for atrocities perpetrated against civilians and prisoners of war. Initially, *Waffen-SS* members had to be at least 17½ years old, with experience in the Hitler Youth, but rules were relaxed as the German war effort became more desperate. The *Waffen-SS* saw action on the Polish, eastern French, and Balkan fronts, and troops numbered in the hundreds of thousands.

King commands U.S. Navy In December 1941, U.S. secretary of the Navy Frank Knox wrote, "Lord how I need him." He was referring to Admiral Ernest King (*pictured*), in whose hands Roosevelt placed the command of the Navy. Single-minded and uncompromising, King often clashed with General George Marshall (a fellow member of the Joint Chiefs of Staff) and later in the war with General Douglas MacArthur. King's creation of the antisubmarine command of the 10th Fleet was a major reason for American success in the Atlantic. At times, King felt that not enough attention was being paid to the Pacific Theater, and his ideas and plans were a significant reason for the success in that region.

Donovan creates the OSS "Espionage is not a nice thing, nor are the methods employed exemplary.... But we will turn terror against him—or we will cease to exist." This was William "Wild Bill" Donovan's mission statement in June 1942 for the overseas intelligence agency, the U.S. Office of Strategic Services (OSS), which he had been chosen to create and lead. Although members of different political parties, President Roosevelt and Donovan had been classmates in law school. Donovan had proven himself as a master of espionage when Roosevelt chose him as coordinator of information (COI) in July 1941. This led to Donovan being assigned the task of creating the OSS a year later. By the end of the war, he had 16,000 agents working behind enemy lines.

The "Woodpecker" The Allies called the Japanese Type 92 heavy machine gun the "Woodpecker" because of its distinctive sound. Introduced in 1932, its origins lay in the French Hotchkiss 6.5mm caliber machine gun and its 1914 Japanese copy, the Taisho 3. The 7.7mm caliber Type 92, distinguishable by its pistol grips, was a robust improvement on these older designs, but it had weaknesses. The 30-round horizontal ammunition strips limited its rate of fire to 450 rounds per minute. The gas-operated design required cartridges to be oiled before loading. At 122 pounds, it was heavy, requiring three men to move it while gripping carrying handles.

Amphibious Assault Doctrine

BY THE OPENING of the Pacific war, the Japanese had mastered the art of unopposed landings against undefended or lightly defended coastlines. This skill was repeatedly demonstrated on Southeast Asian coasts in the first few months of the Pacific war.

The Japanese, in fact, were the first practitioners of modern amphibious landings using purpose-built craft. In the initial Pacific campaigns, the hallmarks of Japan's highly effective amphibious doctrine were thorough planning, local air and naval superiority, and surprise, achieved notably through night landings. What the Japanese never developed was a capability in amphibious *assault,* such as that developed by the U.S. Marine Corps.

The disastrous Gallipoli campaign of 1915 largely discredited amphibious operations. But in the interwar years, the U.S. Marine Corps—looking for a distinctive role to justify its separate existence—decided to specialize in amphibious assault, coordinated landings in the face of a heavily defended shoreline. The Marine Corps Schools published a *Tentative Manual for Landing Operations* in 1934. In the remaining prewar years, the corps won some interservice support for its increasingly refined doctrine. Moreover, some actual landing craft were developed.

Guadalcanal marked the Pacific debut of U.S. amphibious forces. The Marine landing there was hastily planned and executed, and the failure to secure lines of communication might have been disastrous for inferior troops. General Douglas MacArthur in the South West Pacific Area and Admiral William Halsey in the South Pacific improved the doctrine through increasingly large and sophisticated operations, and the development of better and, especially, bigger vessels. Both leaders employed "leapfrogging": bypassing strongly defended outposts, which became isolated and strategically irrelevant. General Tojo later identified this amphibious strategy as a key factor in Japan's defeat.

Bypassing enemy forces was often impractical in the central Pacific, where routines had to be developed for attacking heavily fortified beaches where surprise was impossible. The bloody experience of Tarawa helped improve this doctrine, which involved preliminary bombardment of the enemy positions, for days or even weeks, then armored amphibians landing in daylight. By 1945 the routine was so effective that the Japanese gave up resisting the beach landings and instead tried to stop the attackers inland.

U.S. Marines conquer Tulagi
A crashed Japanese bomber floats off Tulagi. U.S. Marines invaded the small island, located just 20 miles north of Guadalcanal, on August 7, 1942, to secure its valuable harbor. The initial landing took the defenders—a detachment of the Third Kure Special Naval Landing Force—by surprise. The Japanese detachment radioed Rabaul, stating: "Enemy troop strength is overwhelming. We will defend to the last man." By August 8, the Marines had pushed the defenders into the southeastern part of the island, where they were annihilated. All but three of the 300-man garrison were killed.

Marines land on Guadalcanal American Marines storm ashore from a landing craft at Guadalcanal in August 1942. After U.S. Intelligence discovered a Japanese airfield under construction on Guadalcanal, the First Marine Division interrupted its training in Australia and hastily shipped out to seize the island. Planners saw the airfield as an unacceptable threat to supply lines to Australia and New Zealand and a possible preliminary to a renewed enemy advance to the south. The landing by more than 11,000 Marines took the 2,571 Japanese—mostly laborers working on the airfield—by surprise. Most of the enemy fled into the jungle as the Marines stormed ashore.

THE NOISE OF WAR

Here at Edson's C.P. [command post], I heard for the first time the tight woven noise of war. The constant fabric of the noise is rifle fire. Like a knife tearing into the fabric, every once in a while there would be a short burst of machine-gun fire. Forward we could hear bombs fumbling into the jungle, and the laughter of strafing P-39s. A mortar battery directly in front of us was doubly noisy, for its commander was an old-fashioned hollering Marine. But weirdest of all was the sound of our artillery shells passing overhead. At this angle, they gave off a soft, fluttery sound, like a man blowing through a keyhole.

—AMERICAN WAR CORRESPONDENT JOHN HERSEY, REPORTING FROM GUADALCANAL, 1942

America's first modern battleship The USS *North Carolina*, the first of the U.S. Navy's modern battleships, participated in the invasion of Guadalcanal in August 1942. Though damaged by a torpedo on September 15, it returned to action, participating in operations throughout the Pacific. Its role was to screen carriers from air and surface attack and use its big guns to soften enemy island defenses prior to amphibious assault. The *North Carolina* received 15 battle stars for service during the war, more than any other U.S. battleship. It was decommissioned in 1947.

Japanese navy fights back Crashed aircraft and the transport USS *George F. Elliott* burn off Guadalcanal on August 8, 1942, following an attack by Japanese bombers and torpedo planes. In the early morning hours of August 9, seven Japanese cruisers and a destroyer slipped past U.S. picket vessels in the darkness. In 32 minutes during this Battle of Savo Island, the Japanese sank four Allied heavy cruisers and a destroyer, killing 1,270 officers and men at virtually no loss to themselves.

1942

August 12: Churchill arrives in Moscow for a summit with Stalin, who will be disappointed with Churchill's assertion that U.S. and British forces will concentrate on driving Rommel out of North Africa rather than relieving the pressure on the Soviets with a second European front. • Japan goes on the offensive in China's Shantung Province, capitalizing on internal strife between Chinese Nationalist and Communist troops.

August 16: The United States Army Air Force (USAAF) sees its first action in the skies over Egypt, staging raids against Rommel's troops.

August 17: USAAF high-altitude "Flying Fortresses" attack Rouen, France, in the first all-American air raid of the war. • A contingent of Marine commandos known as Carlson's Raiders attacks Japanese units and a seaplane base on Makin Island, killing the entire Japanese garrison.

August 19: A racing pigeon named Tommy finds its way back to England from the Netherlands. It carries a message from the Dutch resistance that reveals the location of an important U-boat base.

August 20: With a portion of Guadalcanal in the hands of the Allies, 31 American fighters land safely on that island at Henderson Field.

August 21: The Nazi swastika is planted at the 18,500-foot summit of Mt. Elbrus in the Soviet Caucasus Mountains. • The Japanese suffer 800 casualties in an attempt to retake the airfield on Guadalcanal.

August 22: In the past two weeks, some 75,000 Jews from the Polish city of Lvov have been murdered at the Belzec death camp.

Japan's unwise assault Dead Japanese soldiers lie half-buried on an Ilu River sandbar after Colonel Ichiki Kiyono's ill-fated assault on Marines defending Henderson Field on Guadalcanal on August 20–21, 1942. Grossly underestimating the number of U.S. defenders, Ichiki ordered a frontal assault with only 900 men. Nearly 800 Japanese were killed by the dug-in Marines. It was a mistake Japanese commanders repeated throughout the campaign. First Marine Division commander General A. A. Vandegrift wisely kept his forces in a defensive posture to protect the valuable airfield, moving reinforcements to critical points as needed.

Anti-Japanese propaganda The U.S. Office of War Information (OWI) was created in June 1942 to consolidate the release of propaganda at home and overseas. It was common to use a stereotypical image of Japanese soldiers with slanted eyes engaged in evil acts. Here we see a frightening depiction of a Japanese soldier with very sharp features carrying, apparently, an American woman from a scene portraying hell. The message is that unless the Allies stopped the Japanese in the Pacific, horrors like this would happen in America.

Disaster at Dieppe

IN 1942 RAIDS BY British Combined Operations on the coast of occupied Europe intensified. Commando raids at Bruneval and St. Nazaire, France, showed the value of an aggressive strategy in anticipation of an eventual invasion and liberation.

For the summer of 1942, the Combined Operations (under Louis Mountbatten) and the Home Forces (under Bernard Montgomery) planned a powerful raid, 10 times the size of St. Nazaire, against the French port of Dieppe. The purpose of the raid remains unclear. It may have been to test the practicality of seizing a port, to alarm the Germans, to "blood" the untried Second Canadian Division, or to reassure the Soviet Union.

Montgomery wished to cancel the upcoming raid, but after he left to command the Eighth Army, Mountbatten revived the plan. On August 19, 1942, 5,000 Canadians, 1,000 British troops, and 50 U.S. Rangers landed. They were covered by 237 warships and 70 squadrons of medium bombers and fighters.

The scale of support did not guarantee success. Poor planning and intelligence compounded by bad luck turned the attack into a disaster. Photographic reconnaissance failed to find powerful German batteries, and the attackers had lost surprise when detected in the Channel. Only on the right flank, where commandos neutralized German batteries, were the landings successful. Shocked soldiers,

Canadian soldiers awaiting medical assistance near Dieppe

who had been safe in Britain the day before, were marched off into captivity.

The raid failed disastrously, with heavy losses. Fifty percent of the Canadians became casualties. The raid at least showed the difficulties of a cross-channel invasion, and it persuaded Operation Overlord's planners of the need to bring their own port with them. It also convinced the Germans to place their big guns near the ports.

Many Canadians never forgave Churchill for Dieppe, and debate continues over the necessity of a raid that was likely to fail.

War dogs The U.S. "K9 Corps" was created weeks after the U.S. entered the war. It initially accepted more than 30 breeds, but as the program progressed, the K9 Corps limited the breeds to German shepherds, Belgian sheepdogs, Doberman pinschers, farm collies, and giant schnauzers. To train each dog took from eight to 12 weeks. During the Battle of Guam in 1944, 25 Marine dogs were killed while serving as sentries, scouts, messengers, and on mine and booby-trap detection. America's allies and enemies also used dogs for these purposes. Germans primarily chose German shepherds and Doberman pinschers. Here, a sentry dog detects a nocturnal prowler.

1942

August 23: The fortifications around Stalingrad are beginning to succumb to the endless German onslaught, as some 600 *Luftwaffe* planes bomb the city.

August 25: The plane carrying the Duke of Kent (brother of King George VI) crashes in Scotland en route from Britain to Iceland. He becomes the first member of the modern Royal Family to die on active duty.

August 26: As many as a half-million German and Romanian soldiers attack the Red Army near Stalingrad.

August 28: The first of thousands of Japanese-launched incendiary balloon bombs fall on an Oregon forest.

September 2: British commandos raid a lighthouse off the Channel Islands (in the English Channel), seizing seven German operatives and secret codebooks.

September 3: Rommel's troops come under heavy Allied fire as they attempt an overnight retreat from Alam el Halfa in the North African desert.

September 5: Allied leaders determine that the invasion of northwest Africa, code-named Operation Torch, will include the landing of troops near Casablanca, Morocco, as well as Oran and Algiers, Algeria. ● Soviet air raids bring nightly blackouts to the Hungarian capital of Budapest.

September 8: In a national broadcast, Roosevelt characterizes the global conflict as "the toughest war of all time."

September 10: In a speech before the House of Commons, Churchill reports that troops have been sent to India to quell the revolutionary impetus of the Congress Party. ● Germany makes a renewed attempt to disrupt American East Coast shipping when a U-boat plants 12 mines in and around the Chesapeake Bay.

Soviets hold strong at Stalingrad Ferocious Soviet resistance at Stalingrad stalled the German military juggernaut that had smashed through Russia. Even though German bombardment had turned 80 percent of the city to burnt rubble and killed tens of thousands of civilians, the Soviets held fast—as depicted here by Leslie Illingworth. A longtime cartoonist for London's *Daily Mail*, Illingworth excelled at strong images that needed no words of explanation. His name was on the Nazis' death list, and a number of his cartoons were found in Hitler's bunker after the war.

Fighting among the rubble When German troops reached the suburbs of Stalingrad on August 23, 1942, they found little more than ruins. But German claims to victory were cut short by Russian soldiers and civilians fighting back from those remains. The war broke down into smaller battles in which, as a German general said, "The mile, as a measure of distance, was replaced by the yard...." Here, in the fall of 1942, Soviet soldiers fight the enemy in an area already devastated by warfare.

> "Those who have seen Stalingrad from the air in the moonlight say it might be an impressionist's concept of craters on the moon. But when the sun is full and bright, Stalingrad from the air seems to be a dazzling desert of rhinestones—a mirage caused by tons of scattered glass."

> —TIME-LIFE CORRESPONDENT RICHARD LAUTERBACH

Stalingrad resisters refuse to quit German soldiers enter a captured factory in Stalingrad, where they find little left to reward their victory. Even when the Germans had taken most of Stalingrad, they met strong resistance in the city's northern industrial areas. Factory workers joined militias, produced tanks and weapons (which they sometimes took into battle themselves), and repaired damaged Soviet tanks near or on the battlefield. Raging conflicts at the Red October steel factory, Dzerzhinsky tractor factory, and Barrikady gun factory lasted far beyond Nazi expectations.

SAVAGERY AT STALINGRAD

ON THE FLAT PLAIN were thousands of bodies, tossed like broken dolls onto the ground. Most were Russians, victims of German artillery and Stukas. At the height of the bombardment, Petrov saw a tiny figure, no more than three feet high, waving his arms wildly. Amazed, Petrov looked more closely and saw that it was the upper body of a Russian soldier. Beside it on the ground lay a pair of legs and hips, neatly severed by a shellburst.

The man was looking at Petrov and his mouth opened and closed, sucking air, trying to communicate one last time. Petrov gaped at the apparition until the arms stopped flailing, the mouth slackened and the eyes glazed. Somehow the soldier's torso remained upright and forlorn beside the rest of the body.

> —HISTORIAN WILLIAM CRAIG, DESCRIBING A MOMENT DURING THE BATTLE OF STALINGRAD, DECEMBER 1942

Soviets move factories Within a short time of the Germans' invasion of the USSR, they captured an area that contained 40 percent of the Soviets' population, 60 percent of the armament industries, and vast deposits of its natural resources. The Soviet leadership decided to move any major manufacturing plants not yet in German hands out of the enemy's reach, relocating them to the Ural, Volga, and Siberia regions. Plant workers were also shipped to these areas, even though they were unprepared for the severe weather and poor living conditions. Those industries that would remain closer to the Soviet cities were moved underground, as shown in this picture, to escape German bombers and artillery.

1942

September 10: Düsseldorf is in flames following an intense, one-hour RAF raid that dropped more than 100,000 firebombs on the German city.

September 12: The British liner *Laconia* is torpedoed and sunk off Ascension Island in the South Atlantic. To the horror of the attacking U-boat crew, some 1,500 Italian POWs are among the victims. The U-boat crew attempts to rescue the Italians but comes under heavy American aircraft fire, leading Germany to decide to repudiate a 1936 accord calling for the rescue of vanquished crews.

September 13: Operation Torch planning gets underway in London, with U.S. general Dwight Eisenhower in command. • Some 1,200 Japanese die in a desperate bid to wrest control of Guadalcanal's Henderson Field from the U.S. Marines. • All Vichy French men 18 to 50 years of age, and single women ages 20 to 35, are ordered to labor for the Reich's war machine.

September 14: The U.S. emerges victorious from the Battle of Bloody Ridge at Guadalcanal when a large Japanese contingent is forced into retreat by 11,000 U.S. Marines.

September 15: The carrier USS *Wasp* goes down in waters south of Guadalcanal after being torpedoed by a Japanese submarine.

September 18: The shipping lanes into Charleston, South Carolina, are mined by a German U-boat.

September 20: General Eisenhower and his military team decide to schedule Operation Torch, the invasion of the French protectorate of Morocco and the colony of Algeria, for November 8. • The situation in Stalingrad has so deteriorated that German and Soviet troops are engaging in house-to-house combat on the streets of the devastated city.

The *Enterprise* survives bombing A gun position lies in ruins after bombs struck the USS *Enterprise* on August 24, 1942. A veteran of Midway and the Doolittle Raid, the "Big E" survived thanks to efficient damage control. The carrier was struck again in the Battle of the Santa Cruz Islands, but went on to participate in the Naval Battle of Guadalcanal, the "Great Marianas Turkey Shoot," the Battle of Leyte Gulf, and numerous other engagements, receiving 20 battle stars for World War II service. Though struck by a *kamikaze* off Okinawa in May 1945, the *Enterprise* survived the war and was decommissioned in 1947.

Finland fights alongside Germany A Finnish combat patrol breaks into a Soviet position in 1942. Finland had lost some 16,000 square miles to a 1939–40 Russian onslaught known as the "Winter War." From 1941 to '44, in hopes of regaining that territory and perhaps more, Finland allied with Germany against Russia. Though they were dependent on Germany for food, fuel, and weapons, the Finns did not go along with most Nazi policies. They maintained a democratic government, kept armed forces from falling under German control, and did not persecute native Jews.

The Japanese Army's Fatal Flaw

THE JAPANESE ARMY had spent decades preparing for confrontation with the Soviet Union on the plains of Manchuria. The China war and the war in the Pacific brought not only different battle environments but different enemies—one the Japanese failed to fully understand.

In the Pacific, the Japanese war plan called for a wave of attacks on American, British, and Dutch forces throughout the Pacific. Planners anticipated a short, intense conflict that would end to their advantage with a negotiated peace. Little consideration was given to the possibility of failure or to contingency planning should Japan unexpectedly find itself involved in a protracted war.

This heady optimism was inherent in the very fiber of the Japanese army. Rank and file were certain that their "warrior spirit" would prevail over weak-willed Westerners, even if faced by superior numbers or firepower. Emphasis was largely on offensive action. The Japanese soldier— whether a general conducting a campaign or a private manning a machine gun—was expected to fulfill his duty or die in the attempt. To question orders was a shameful sign of weakness. Since failure was not allowable, there was little call for tactical flexibility or deviation from the plan once underway.

The result was disaster. Campaigns such as those in Guadalcanal and New Guinea were pressed long after they were lost. Japanese troops in the field launched attacks that followed failed plans and satisfied their warrior code but had little impact beyond their own destruction.

The absence of long-range programs such as army pilot rotation also began to bear bitter fruit as the war dragged on past expectations. Lack of search-and-rescue capability meant that highly trained pilots who went down with their planes were lost. As the small pool of experienced pilots died in combat, they were replaced by rookies who were easy game for enemy fighters.

In their failure to appreciate their enemy's resolve and their own flawed mind-set, the Japanese contributed to their own defeat.

Japanese repulsed on Papua New Guinea Two Japanese Type 95 Ha-Go light tanks are bogged down along a narrow jungle road following a failed amphibious assault at Milne Bay, Papua New Guinea. About 2,400 Japanese Special Naval Landing Force troops attacked the Australian base on August 25, 1942, intending to seize its strategically important airdrome. The Japanese light tanks inflicted severe casualties on an Australian infantry battalion. But Australian Kitty Hawk (Curtiss P40) ground attack aircraft retaliated with a vengeance, forcing enemy landing operations farther and farther from the air base. Encountering fierce resistance from a superior Australian force, the Japanese commander ordered a withdrawal on September 5.

Japanese airmen Japanese naval pilots in the Pacific were without equal at the start of 1942. Training was highly selective. Of 1,500 naval pilot applicants in early 1937, only 70 were accepted and only 25 graduated. The lengthy program required 260 to 400 hours of basic flight training, followed by gunnery, combat tactics, and carrier operations. This training regimen broke down in the latter months of 1942, as pilot losses soared in the battle for air supremacy over the Solomons. The qualitative edge dulled and then vanished as veteran Japanese pilots were killed and the vacuum was filled by hastily trained replacements.

1942

September 21: The women and children of Stalingrad are evacuated from the dying city. • Boeing Field in Seattle is the site of the maiden voyage of the Boeing B-29 Super-fortress, a high-altitude, long-range bomber.

September 24: Russian pilot Olga Yamschchikova becomes the first woman to record an aerial "kill" when she downs a German plane over Stalingrad.

September 25: Madagascar becomes controlled by British forces after Vichy governor general Armand Léon Annet refuses to accept peace terms and the British gain control of the island nation's main port.

September 29: The RAF's Eagle Squadrons, comprised of American pilots, are officially transferred to U.S. command.

September 30: In a speech delivered at the Berlin *Sportpalast*, Hitler mocks the Allies, calling them "military idiots."

October: Britain and the United States begin sending troop and materiel convoys to North Africa in preparation for Operation Torch. • Both Britain and the United States lower their military induction minimum age to 18.

October 1: Bell test pilot Robert M. Stanley puts the XP-59 Airacomet, the first U.S. jet, through its paces in the skies over the Mojave Desert. • The *Lisbon Maru*, a Japanese ship carrying 1,816 Allied prisoners of war, goes down with its human cargo when the USS *Grouper* torpedoes it and the Japanese crew seals the exits before abandoning ship.

October 2: The *Queen Mary*, sailing in an evasive zigzag pattern off the coast of Ireland, accidentally slices through its escort, the *Curacao*, which sinks, claiming 338 lives.

Japan firebombs Oregon On September 9, 1942, the Japanese submarine *I-25* surfaced off the coast of Oregon. The sub carried a Yoko-suka E14Y, a small, folding-wing seaplane type dubbed a "Glen." Not long after the aircraft was catapulted from the *I-25*'s deck, Chief Warrant Officer Fujita Nobuo and Petty Officer Okuda Shoji dropped two incendiary bombs on Mount Emily, near Brookings, Oregon. Their hope was to ignite colossal forest fires and create panic. However, the incendiaries had little effect. A Glen is depicted in this John Meeks painting, *The Last Act.*

Capa photographs the war The American public's window to World War II was provided by civilian photojournalists and military photographers whose work appeared in the illustrated news magazines of the day. Some, such as Hungarian-born Robert Capa (*pictured*), became famous. Capa first received acclaim for his coverage of the Spanish Civil War. During World War II, he worked for *Collier's* magazine and later for *Life*. He risked his life by jumping into Sicily with an airborne unit in 1943, and landed under fire at Normandy on June 6, 1944. Though Capa survived the war, he was killed while on assignment in Indochina in 1954.

Hitler ousts the respected List Competent field marshal Wilhelm List was commander-in-chief of Army Group A in the Caucasus in 1942 when Hitler unreasonably commanded him to push on to the Soviet city of Grozny and its nearby oil centers. Faced with fierce Russian resistance along a sprawling front, List failed to carry out the *Führer*'s orders. Hitler angrily relieved List of his command on September 9, creating a rift between himself and some of his highest officers.

The massive Tigers The Tiger I was Germany's most famous and feared tank. After its introduction on the Leningrad and Tunisian fronts in 1943, Allied soldiers' first instinct was to identify every enemy tank as a Tiger. This huge, fearsome weapon's 88mm gun could destroy any Allied tank at long range, and its armor was virtually impenetrable frontally. Its elite crews appreciated these qualities, but because it was underpowered and mechanically unreliable, they nicknamed it "furniture van." By war's end, the Henschel company had built about 1,350 Tigers.

Krupp arms the military Inspectors test shells at the Krupp munitions works in Germany. Krupp made an enormous contribution to rearming Germany before and during World War II. The firm supplied the Third Reich with staggering amounts of military hardware ranging from submarines to artillery. But Krupp's wartime profits came at a steep human cost. Some 100,000 slave laborers, about 23,000 of whom were prisoners of war, worked for Krupp under brutal conditions. After the war, the company's CEO, Alfried Krupp, was convicted of crimes against humanity.

Allied raids over Ruhr By late 1942, American assembly lines were able to build enough bombers and fighter planes to support the United States' entry into the air war over Europe. Allied commanders began formulating a plan for around-the-clock bombing over the industrial centers in the Ruhr area of western Germany. In this new campaign, the Royal Air Force continued its blanket bombing of German cities at night while American planes struck industrial centers that were important to the German war effort during the day. In this picture, American bombers fly over the Ruhr after an attack on a rubber factory.

1942

October 3: Wernher von Braun, the Nazi rocket scientist who will ultimately go to the U.S. after the war and become one of the greatest minds at NASA, sees Germany successfully launch one of his earliest creations, the A4 ballistic missile.

October 4: Underscoring the Nazi obsession with Jewish genocide that will eventually contribute to the fall of the Reich, *Reichsmarschall* Hermann Göring claims that the war is "not the Second World War, [but]...the War of the Races."

October 5: Nationalist Chinese leader Chiang Kai-shek calls for the withdrawal of all Soviet forces from Sinkiang Province.

October 7: In a concept that will develop into the Nuremberg Trials, Roosevelt says that the perpetrators of mass murder and other wartime atrocities will be judged at the conclusion of the war.

October 10: Citing the "splendid showing the Italians in America" have made during the war, U.S. attorney general Francis Biddle suspends the "enemy alien" status of some 600,000 resident Italian citizens.

October 11–12: The Allies have an open supply line to Guadalcanal in the wake of Japan's defeat in the Battle of Cape Esperance.

October 12: The RAF's new long-range Coastal Command Liberator sinks its first U-boat in the North Atlantic.

October 14: Guadalcanal's Henderson Field is badly damaged in a bombardment by the Japanese battleships *Kongo* and *Haruna*. • The Red Army manages to stand against yet another intense, five-division German attack in Stalingrad.

Ukrainian forced labor Delighted by the 1941 Nazi conquest of the Ukraine, Hermann Göring considered murdering all of the region's males over the age of 15 to make living space for the "master race." But German labor shortages soon persuaded Göring to work Ukrainians to death as slave laborers. As 1942 wore on, a small number of Ukrainians were enticed to come and work in "beautiful Germany." Many more were brought by forced deportations, such as the one seen here. Considered subhuman according to Nazi ideology, Ukrainian workers were starved and mistreated. Well more than 10 million Ukrainians are believed to have been killed from 1939 to 1945, many in Allied bombings.

France's Laval aligns with Germany "If the Germans are beaten, General de Gaulle will return," predicted Pierre Laval, prime minister of the Vichy government, in September 1942. "He will be supported by...the French people, and I shall be hanged." After the Germans invaded France in 1940, Laval was named vice premier in Philippe Pétain's Vichy government. Laval, convinced Germany would win the war, pressed for a German-French military alliance. Suspicious of his subordinate, Pétain had Laval dismissed, but Laval came back even stronger with the support of Germany and was named prime minister. When the Vichy government fell in 1945, Laval was shot by a firing squad—not hanged.

America's Aircraft Carriers

THE UNITED STATES ENTERED World War II in 1941 with seven fleet carriers. By war's end, those numbers had quadrupled; the aircraft carrier had replaced the battleship as the preeminent surface ship of the Navy.

Airpower played a key role in the naval campaign against Japan, and the aircraft carrier provided the means to deliver that power over the vast distances of the Pacific. To that end, U.S. carriers were built without heavy armor or big guns so that they could carry more planes and fuel, and to maximize their speed and mobility.

The Essex Class aircraft carrier, introduced in 1943, was a 27,000-ton, 32-knot vessel capable of operating 90 to 100 aircraft. The complement generally included a mix of fighters, torpedo bombers, and dive-bombers. The proportion of fighters increased from about 25 percent of the total to 75 percent by the end of the war.

Though loaded with antiaircraft guns, the carriers also relied on escort ships—destroyers, battleships, and cruisers—for protection against enemy air and surface attack. Defense was enhanced by the carriers' own fighter protection—known as Combat Air Patrol—which remained overhead to deal with enemy air attacks.

Naval officers eventually realized that three or four carriers organized into groups with supporting battleships, cruisers, and destroyers offered the best combination of offensive punch and defensive firepower. These Task Groups could operate independently or in combination as a Fast Carrier Task Force, which provided considerable flexibility.

A Hellcat taking off from the USS Lexington

Radar and combat information centers allowed the various ships and aircraft to coordinate offense and defense. These task groups benefited from a logistical supply system that made around-the-clock offensive air operations against land targets possible. This put the Japanese, who were capable only of quick raids, at a distinct disadvantage.

Despite the prominence of the aircraft carrier, only five carrier-to-carrier battles were fought during the entire war. Most carrier operations were conducted against shipping and island bases and in support of amphibious landings. Combining speed, mobility, and fearsome power, the Fast Carrier Task Forces made the island-hopping campaign of the Pacific war possible.

Japanese sink the USS Wasp

Mortally wounded, the carrier USS Wasp burns on September 15, 1942, after taking three torpedo hits from the Japanese submarine I-19. Commissioned in 1940, the Wasp was a smaller model of the larger Yorktown class carriers. Prior to the war, it engaged in Atlantic patrol duty and ferried RAF planes to Malta. Sent to the Pacific in June 1942, the Wasp participated in the Guadalcanal landings and later provided cover for resupply convoys to the Solomons. It was sunk by the I-19 southeast of San Cristobal Island while escorting troop transports to Guadalcanal.

1942

October 16: The supply line to the Burma front is crippled by a cyclone that claims 40,000 lives and devastates India.

October 18: Hitler issues a directive calling for the execution of all British commandos who fall into Nazi custody.

October 21: With defense expenses skyrocketing, Roosevelt signs legislation calling for an all-time high $9 billion tax bill.

October 23: The American M4 Sherman tank, equipped with high-explosive shells and capable of speeds up to 24 mph, makes its battlefield debut in the Second Battle of El Alamein in Egypt.

October 29: An overland military supply route to Alaska is opened with the completion of the 1,500-mile Alaska Military Highway through the Yukon Territory.

October 30: As a U-boat sinks, two British sailors rescue a German Enigma machine. Before they drown, the sailors pass it into Allied hands.

October 31: The cathedral city of Canterbury, England, suffers extensive damage in a retaliatory raid for the RAF bombing of the Italian city of Milan.

November 2: Operation Supercharge, a massive Allied attack on Rommel's line in Egypt, is successfully launched. Defeated Axis forces will retreat by November 4. • Some 100,000 Polish Jews from Bialystok and the surrounding area are marked for deportation to the Treblinka death camp. • Berlin's so-called Ancestral Heritage Institute, a quasi-scientific organization searching for biological "proof" of Jewish inferiority, obtains the corpses of 150 Jewish Bolsheviks for dissection.

Gypsies targeted for extermination Nazis classed the Sinti and Roma people—nomadic groups commonly called Gypsies—among the "inferior races." During the 1930s, Nazis arrested Gypsies, sterilizing some adults and making many children wards of the state. In December 1942, Himmler ordered the deportation of Gypsies and part-Gypsies to concentration camps. Scarce information on Sinti and Roma populations makes it hard to estimate how many were killed, but historians believe the number to be between 220,000 and 500,000. Seen here is a Gypsy couple at Belzec, a camp in eastern Poland built in 1942 to carry out the "Final Solution."

French town harbors Jews "Things had to be done, and we happened to be there to do them. It was the most natural thing in the world to help these people." This sentiment was shared by the citizens of Le Chambon-sur-Lignon, a small mountain town in southern France. Under the leadership of a local minister, Andre Trocme, and his wife, Magda, the citizens of the town began hiding Jews in their homes. A network of informants warned Trocme when searches of the town were to be made. Trocme encouraged a cousin, Daniel Trocme, to run a refugee house for children, but Daniel and his wards were discovered and shipped to the Majdanek concentration camp, where Daniel died. The townspeople saved nearly 5,000 lives.

Vital U.S. fighter plane
The Grumman F4F Wildcat was virtually the only Navy and Marine fighter that opposed the Japanese air force between Pearl Harbor and August 1943. The Wildcat was slow due to its small engine, but its large, square-cut, folding wings made it agile in battle. It was also more robust than its Japanese adversaries. It required only a short take-off, and the final model, the FM-2, was the standard fighter on U.S. escort carriers in 1945.

Hitler overextends his forces German troops advance in the Caucasus in October 1942. Hitler attempted to seize this oil-rich region while other German troops advanced on Stalingrad. His decision vastly overextended his forces; German men and tanks in the Caucasus quickly outpaced their supply lines. Moreover, they faced impossibly narrow roads and impenetrable walnut forests. In one pointless act, alpine troops scaled 19,500-foot Mount Elbrus and planted a German flag at the summit. Hitler raged at this, and in the end the Caucasus misadventure destroyed whatever respect he retained for his generals.

Oil fields burn in the Caucasus
With their eye on the region's oil reserves, the Germans began their ill-fated invasion of the Caucasus on June 28, 1942. In response, the Soviets, as they retreated, carried out the scorched-earth tactics that they had followed in 1941. When the advancing Germans captured the North Caucasus oil center of Maikop, they found themselves faced with the demoralizing spectacle of burning oil fields, such as the one pictured here in October 1942.

1942

November 5: General Eisenhower opens the operational headquarters for the Allied invasion of North Africa on the British island of Gibraltar.

November 6: Angling one more time for a second European Front, Stalin complains that the Soviets are dealing with the far greater Axis force while the British and Americans concentrate on the comparatively quiet North African front. • General MacArthur arrives in Port Moresby, the capital of Papua New Guinea, to supervise operations in that sphere of the Pacific Theater.

November 8: Allied forces land at their North African targets, with Algiers capitulating almost immediately. The U.S. and Britain plan to use occupied North Africa as a base for launching operations against Southern Europe. • Vichy France announces the severing of diplomatic ties with the United States following the invasion of French North Africa.

November 9: Units of the German and Italian armies occupy Tunisia without opposition by the French colonialists.

November 10: In a Mansion House speech covering Britain's victory over Rommel, Churchill famously quips, "This is not the end. It is not even the beginning of the end. But it is, perhaps, the end of the beginning." • All traffic into and out of one of the world's busiest ports ceases for two days when it is discovered that the Germans have mined the waters off New York Harbor.

November 11: Hitler ends the armistice between Free and Vichy France, occupying the entire country north of the Riviera. • The Moroccan city of Casablanca falls to the Allies.

House-to-house fighting The Soviet tactic of "hugging"—keeping their soldiers close to or even intermingled with the enemy—nullified Nazi air and artillery superiority. It reduced the war to house-to-house fighting, which the Germans called *Rattenkrieg* (rat war). In October 1942, a German officer wrote, "We have fought for fifteen days for a single house with mortars, grenades, machine-guns and bayonets." He added that the battlefront had become "a corridor between burnt-out rooms" or "a thin ceiling between two floors." Here, Soviet troops storm through smoking ruins toward an apartment block in Stalingrad.

Battle of the Santa Cruz Islands A Japanese torpedo plane approaches the battleship USS *South Dakota* during the Battle of the Santa Cruz Islands. The battle on October 25, 1942, stemmed from a Japanese plan to use carrier aircraft to support a ground attack on Henderson Field on Guadalcanal (which, along with the Santa Cruz Islands, was part of the Solomon Islands). The Santa Cruz engagement pitted two U.S. carriers and support ships against four Japanese carriers and their support. U.S. pilots damaged two enemy carriers and a cruiser, but the carrier USS *Hornet* and a destroyer were sunk in the exchange. The Japanese claimed a tactical victory, but their failure to crush U.S. naval forces in the Solomons left the strategic advantage with the Americans. Indeed, Japanese losses in precious first-line aircrews made the battle a far greater Japanese defeat than Midway.

The dependable P-40s The Curtiss P-40 won international fame in late 1941 when the "Flying Tigers," American-manned versions painted with shark teeth, fought the Japanese in China. P-40 fighters were built in the United States and flew with virtually every Allied air force. They proved valuable in France and with the RAF over the North African desert, and they shot down Japanese aircraft at Pearl Harbor in December 1941. Though not especially fast, they were stable and tough. More than 14,000 were built, and numerous versions and designations existed, including Hawk, Mohawk, Tomahawk, Kittyhawk, and, most commonly, Warhawk (*pictured*).

No-nonsense Marine Lieutenant General Lewis Burwell Puller was the most decorated Marine in U.S. history. He received five Navy Crosses, a decoration second only to the Medal of Honor. Nicknamed "Chesty" on account of his barrel chest, Puller was a gruff, no-nonsense warrior. Shown a new-model flamethrower, he is said to have growled, "Where do you put the bayonet?" Puller earned his third Navy Cross when his outnumbered battalion fought off a Japanese attempt to seize Henderson Field on the night of October 24–25, 1942, and he earned a fourth for the Cape Gloucester campaign. Puller earned his fifth Navy Cross for heroism during the Korean War. He retired in 1955.

The Persian Corridor The Soviet Union and the British government became allies following the German invasion of the USSR. The Soviets were in desperate need of supplies, but a secure supply line had to be opened. They chose the newly completed Trans-Iranian Railway as the Persian Corridor to open the supply line from the Persian Gulf to the Soviet Union. Necessary permissions were secured from Iraq and Iran to use the corridor. Once the United States entered the war, it sent troops to guard and maintain the railway.

1942

November 12–15: The United States loses nine ships and the Japanese lose five in the waters off Guadalcanal. This is one of the most ferocious naval battles of the war, and a tactical victory for the United States.

November 15: The cruiser USS *Juneau* sinks off Guadalcanal, claiming the lives of five Sullivan brothers of Waterloo, Iowa. Despite popular myth, no law or executive order inspired by the Sullivan tragedy is created that would prohibit family members from serving together. However, the practice is discouraged.

November 20: The RAF launches its most destructive raid against Italy in this war, devastating the northern industrial city of Turin. • In an address to the French people, Vichy prime minister Pierre Laval encourages the Vichy alliance with the Third Reich in the face of continued threats from "Jews and Communists."

November 22: In a stunning turnaround, some 270,000 soldiers of the German Sixth Army are surrounded by the Red Army in Stalingrad.

November 23: The U.S. Women's Coast Guard Reserve is established.

November 24: The Japanese begin construction of a new airfield at Munda, New Georgia, their new base of operations in the Solomon Islands.

November 25: The U.S. government selects a site in Los Alamos, New Mexico, to build a lab devoted to the development of the atomic bomb.

November 27: Citing betrayal by Vichy France, Hitler disbands the Vichy army.

November 28: Against the recommendation of Rommel, his accomplished general on the ground, Hitler insists that his beaten German forces fight to the death in the North African desert.

"As there wasn't time to dig graves the bodies were simply laid out and covered with sand. Near one with a rough wooden cross marked 'Unknown German' lay pieces of vertebrae."

—AMERICAN WAR CORRESPONDENT WALTER GRAEBNER, DESCRIBING THE FRONT DURING THE BRITISH OFFENSIVE AT EL ALAMEIN, NORTH AFRICA, FOR *LIFE* MAGAZINE, 1942

Rommel's desert retreat Allied soldiers watch two German vehicles go up in flames. On October 23, 1942, British lieutenant general Bernard Montgomery's Eighth Army struck Germany's *Afrika Korps* near the village of El Alamein, Egypt. After 12 days of desperate fighting against an army twice the size of his own, German general Erwin Rommel finally ordered his corps to retreat—in defiance of Hitler's command to fight until they won or died. In those 12 days, the Germans lost 12,000 men and 350 tanks. Rommel had no more than 80 tanks remaining for the 1,400-mile retreat through the desert to Tunisia, where he hoped to find reinforcements and supplies.

Operation Torch Allied forces make an amphibious landing near Algiers on November 8, 1942. Few American troops based in Europe had been under fire, and they did not know whether Vichy French defenders would resist the landings. Military considerations aside, Torch was tricky politically because Stalin was insisting that U.S. and British forces commit significant numbers of men to European combat with an invasion of France. Roosevelt and Churchill knew such an assault was not yet possible, and offered Torch as a substitute.

Higgins Boats and the Beaches

AMERICAN PLANS TO LIBERATE Europe depended on amphibious assaults. A shortage of landing craft hamstrung initial planning. General George Marshall eventually overcame the U.S. Navy's skepticism of the need for landing craft in Europe by threatening to make landing craft production an Army responsibility.

A classic problem of amphibious warfare was getting troops from ship to shore; from the large vessels in which they left port to the enemy-held beach. Andrew Higgins, a Louisiana boat builder, resolved this problem with his Higgins boat, which would evolve into the LCVP (Landing Craft, Vehicle, Personnel). Transported by ship, then released near the target area, the Higgins boat took troops to the beach and released them through bow ramps. More than 20,000 Higgins boats of many types were built. General Eisenhower later said: "If Higgins had not designed and built those LCVPs, we never could have landed over an open beach. The whole strategy of the war would have been different."

The 1942 landings in French North Africa involved more than 500 vessels and 65,000 men. The landing craft included early-model Higgins boats, some without ramps. However, British craft (largely makeshift) predominated.

The 1943 landings in Sicily and Italy were more sophisticated. Complex planning was required to ensure the optimum balance of men and materiel in each vessel; to coordinate air and naval support before, during, and after the landing; and to meet the logistical challenges of con-

Marines landing at Guadalcanal

solidating and swiftly expanding the beachhead. In both campaigns, amphibious forces made "end runs" to cut the enemy's lines of communication: successfully in Sicily, but without the desired outcome at Anzio.

The intricacy of amphibious operations peaked in the planning for D-Day (June 6, 1944), when more than 130,000 men hit five Normandy beaches. For months afterward, those beaches operated as ports. The last major amphibious landings in Europe—in southern France in August 1944—had typical outcomes: Formidable Axis defenses were virtually negated by Allied air and naval superiority. The troops reached shore with relatively few casualties.

French resist Torch invasion It took Roosevelt's intervention in July 1942 to resolve a serious dispute between U.S. and British military advisers. He sided with the British plan to invade North Africa in order to engage the Germans as soon as possible. French Morocco and Algeria were chosen as the sites for this attack since the Allies would face only French troops, who might let the Allies land unopposed. That is not how it turned out. After the November 8, 1942, landing, the French troops did defend the landing sites. Here, a British ship takes a hit not far from shore. Negotiations with the French troops' commander, Admiral François Darlan, were needed to end the fighting on November 10. Darlan was assassinated in December by a French monarchist.

1942

December 1: The United States institutes a gasoline-rationing program across the nation.

December 2: In a breakthrough that will make atomic weaponry a reality, University of Chicago physicists Enrico Fermi and Arthur Compton achieve the first nuclear chain reaction.

December 3: Attacking American bombers hamper the efforts of Japanese engineers to build an airfield on New Georgia in the Solomon Islands.

December 4: Long-range U.S. Liberator bombers sink ships in a raid on Naples, Italy.

December 5: The German hospital ship *Graz* sinks after being torpedoed off the coast of Libya.

December 7: More than 700 young German Edelweiss Pirates, a group formed in response to the rigidity of the Hitler Youth movement, are arrested by the Gestapo in Düsseldorf, Cologne, and several other cities. • The USS *New Jersey,* the largest battleship in the U.S. fleet, is launched from the Philadelphia Navy Shipyard on the first anniversary of the Japanese attack on Pearl Harbor.

December 8: Spanish dictator General Francisco Franco delivers a speech in Madrid. He defends his Axis alliance by claiming he'd rather be a Fascist than a Communist.

December 11: Hitler orders that the surrounded and besieged German Sixth Army may not retreat from Stalingrad.

December 13: The "Shark" Enigma code, which was especially difficult to crack due to its use of an extra rotor, is finally deciphered. This intelligence breakthrough allows the Allies to resume intercepting German communications to U-boats in the Atlantic.

The Flying Fortresses B-17 Flying Fortresses bomb Lae, New Guinea. Many B-17s were destroyed on the ground by Japanese attacks in the opening days of the war, and the heavy bombers that survived attempted to interdict enemy shipping, with mixed results. Pacific-based B-17s proved more useful in attacks against enemy bases in the island-hopping campaign that followed Midway. The B-17 was tough, though early models were vulnerable to attack from the rear. The "belly gunner" also faced a horrifying fate if the plane was forced to land without its landing gear.

Barbed-wire beaches on Hawaii Once a vacation retreat for the rich and famous, the Royal Hawaiian Hotel was leased by the U.S. Navy as a major rest and relaxation center for military personnel. The average stay was 10 days at $1 a day for officers and a quarter for enlisted men. Barbed wire in front of the Royal Hawaiian, as seen in this picture, stretched the length of Waikiki Beach. An air of suspicion existed across the rest of the Hawaiian Islands because approximately 118,000 civilians were of Japanese descent. Plans had been developed to evacuate 100,000 to the continental U.S., but when discussion ended, only about 1,000 were transferred.

African American Soldiers

IN APRIL 1944, nine African American soldiers were denied service at several establishments in Texas. As they left, "about two dozen German prisoners of war, with two American guards came to the station," remembered Corporal Rupert Trimmingham, one of the black soldiers. "They...had their meals served, talked, smoked, in fact had quite a swell time....I could not help but ask myself why they are treated better than we are?"

In the 1940s, the segregation of African Americans was not limited to civilian life. About 909,000 black Americans served in the Army during WWII, but most of these recruits were assigned to support details because military leaders questioned their ability to perform effectively in combat.

Two all-black infantry divisions, the 92nd and 93rd, were led by white officers, some of whom were openly racist. Morale was low in these units due to substandard facilities, poor training, low pay, and inferior commanders. The 93rd was shipped to the Pacific and showed promise in its first few fights. It was later split up, with its troops assigned to support positions.

The 92nd Division, nicknamed the Buffalo Division, had mixed success in Italy. By the end of fighting, the division had suffered about 22 percent casualties while earning about 12,000 decorations. Its erratic performance in the field, due primarily to ineffective leadership, damaged the division's reputation and reinforced the stereotype that African Americans were unfit for combat.

Fighter pilot Lieutenant Andrew D. Marshall (*left*)

Tuskegee, Alabama, became the training site for black pilots. The 99th Fighter Squadron and the 332nd Fighter Group were two of the units formed from its graduates. The 99th was inadequately trained when it was sent into combat, and its poor performance placed the Tuskegee program in jeopardy. Given a second chance, these airmen eventually proved themselves in combat. By the end of the war, almost 1,000 pilots had graduated from Tuskegee and earned more than 850 medals. The 332nd Fighter Group, nicknamed the "Red Tail Angels," earned fame as the only escort group that did not lose a bomber to the enemy.

The Sullivan brothers "I am writing to you in regards to a rumor going around that my five sons were killed in action in November," Alleta Sullivan began in a letter to the Bureau of Naval Personnel. Soon after she sent the letter, she learned that all five of her sons serving on the USS *Juneau* had not survived its sinking in November 1942. The War Department turned this tragedy into a propaganda piece by sending the boys' parents on a lecture tour across the United States and by having Mrs. Sullivan christen the USS *The Sullivans* on April 4, 1943. The tragedy led to a Navy policy that discouraged family members on the same ship.

1942

December 14: Despite an airlift of supplies, the German Sixth Army remains trapped, inadequately equipped, and under siege in Stalingrad. The airlift is hindered by the weather, the Red Air Force, and the need to use many transport planes to support Axis forces in Tunisia.

December 16: Hitler issues a directive that Germany is to be purged of Gypsies, and anyone with any amount of Gypsy blood is to be sent to "resettlement" camps in the East.

December 17: An Allied official makes the first public statement confirming the Nazi death camps when British foreign secretary Anthony Eden tells the House of Commons that Hitler has begun to make good on his threat to annihilate Europe's Jews. • Vichy admiral François Darlan announces that French ships and resources at North African ports will be at the disposal of the Allied cause.

December 22: A group of Jewish partisans sets off bombs in two Kraków cafés, killing 20 German army officers.

December 26: Former German prisoner of war general Henri Giraud succeeds Admiral Darlan as high commissioner for French North Africa following Darlan's assassination in Algiers two days earlier.

December 28: Despite the wartime alliance between the two nations, Roosevelt admonishes the Los Alamos science-research team against sharing atomic secrets with the British.

December 31: In the Barents Sea north of Norway, German ships attack a British convoy that is attempting to deliver materiel to the Soviet Union.

Soviets punish German POWs During the winter of 1941–42, and again the following winter (*pictured*), German mechanized transport, tanks, artillery, and aircraft froze up, while frostbite killed and maimed inadequately clothed soldiers. Since Hitler still banned retreat, capture must have seemed a better option to many Germans, including those surrendering here. However, the Soviets took revenge for the crimes that Germans had committed against civilians during the invasion. The Soviets executed some POWs and sent others to work camps, where many died of exposure, starvation, and overwork during forced labor. Nearly 500,000 of the more than three million prisoners taken by Russia died in captivity.

The "Moaning Minnie" Early during Operation Barbarossa, the *Wehrmacht* noted the efficacy of the Red Army's multibarrel rocket-launchers and quickly developed similar weapons, with the six-barrel, 150mm *Nebelwerfer* ("fog launcher"; *pictured*) entering service in 1942. Over a 10-second period, while operated by a four-man crew, it fired salvos of six projectiles up to 7,000 meters. Due to the heat and blast it produced, the *Nebelwerfer* was fired electrically from a position 10 meters away. With great trails of fire, smoke, and a whistling noise in flight, the weapon simultaneously inflicted destruction and had a deleterious psychological impact on the enemy. It was nicknamed "Moaning Minnie" by Allied troops.

Beasts of Burden

IN 1939 POLAND'S CAVALRY famously fought against the invading Germans. Both Germany and the Soviet Union used large cavalry forces on the broad steppes of Russia and the Ukraine, including Cossacks fighting on both sides. A Soviet cavalry corps once operated behind German lines for four months. Italian mounted cavalry had some success in Russia. Two cavalry divisions served in the *Waffen-SS*, and the German army formed more units later in the war.

Though the popular image of the *Wehrmacht* is of panzers, it remained dependent upon 5,000-plus horses in each infantry division for the war's duration. More than 600,000 animals drew German artillery and transport wagons in the advance into Russia. They suffered terribly, with 180,000 dying in the winter of 1941–42 alone. In July 1944 in France, British and Canadian troops in the Falaise Pocket saw the horrific effects of Allied air attacks on the congested horse-drawn transport of Panzer Group West.

While the U.S. Cavalry was mechanized by the end of 1941, the 26th Cavalry Regiment of the Philippine Scouts is said to have made the last American charge, on the Bataan Peninsula in January 1942. Britain mechanized its

Red Army calvaryman on the Eastern front

last cavalry division in Palestine in 1941, but the Burma Frontier Force made a suicidal charge against the Japanese at Toungoo in March 1942. The Japanese in turn used cavalry regiments in China and mule transport in the rugged terrain of New Guinea and Burma, as did their opponents there and in Italy.

German brutality in Russia A young woman from a village near Moscow is hanged by German troops in 1942. Although beaten and tortured, she gave her captors no information before her death. This photograph was found on the body of a German officer killed in action near Smolensk. The woman's defiance and the officer's grotesque souvenir both testify to a fierce

antipathy between Germans and Slavs—a loathing that helped make the Eastern Front a particularly brutal theater of operations.

Mythology as propaganda European nations drew on history, heroic legends, and mythology to build nationalism, inspire their citizens, and spur their militaries to action. This Soviet propaganda poster compares 1942 to 1242, the year when Russian prince Alexander Nevsky led his troops in a rout of German invaders. In Germany, Hitler presented his Third Reich as the succes-

sor to the Holy Roman Empire and claimed to be establishing the 1,000-year utopia predicted in millenarian stories. In Italy, Mussolini justified expansionism as the creation of a New Roman Empire.

1943

January: The German Sixth Army, trapped in Stalingrad, is in desperate need of food and supplies the men need to survive.

January 1: Americans' annual salaries are capped at $25,000, part of a short-lived plan designed to curb inflation. The law will be repealed within the year.

January 4: After forcing the Japanese to quit Guadalcanal, the U.S. Navy attacks Japan's new Solomon Islands base at Munda, New Georgia.

January 5: In an effort to put a stop to the Axis practice of seizing property and goods from occupied nations, 18 Allied nations agree that property transfers and similar business conducted under German or Italian occupation can be declared null and void at the discretion of the occupied government.

January 6: Ion Antonescu's forces detain and execute scores of disbanded Fascists after another attempt by the Iron Guard to wrest away control of Antonescu's Romanian government.

January 10: A Soviet force of nearly 300,000 men closes in on the surrounded German Sixth Army at Stalingrad following the refusal of German general Friedrich Paulus to negotiate a surrender.

January 11: The Chinese Nationalists form an official alliance with the United States and Britain. This comes two days after their Japanese-puppet counterparts in Nanking declared war against the Allies.

January 13: The Germans brutally suppress dissent in occupied Bulgaria, executing 36 anti-Nazi protestors in the capital of Sofia.

The French scuttle their warships When the Germans invaded France, they signed the armistice of 1940 with the Vichy government. This agreement stipulated that the French navy would disarm and remain in its ports, including Toulon. When the Germans learned that the fleet there was possibly on the verge of joining the Allies, they broke the armistice and attacked Toulon. Before the ships fell into the Nazis' hands, they were scuttled on November 27, 1942 (*pictured*). The sunken ships included three battleships, 15 destroyers, 13 torpedo boats, 12 submarines, and more than 80 additional vessels.

Nuclear breakthrough A number of scientists and dignitaries gathered together on December 2, 1942, on a platform next to a large oblong structure of bricks and wooden timbers. They were in a racquet court under the west stands of Stagg Field at the University of Chicago. Physicist Enrico Fermi closely monitored a set of instruments, and at 3:25 P.M. directed a colleague to withdraw a rod from the structure. For 28 minutes, Fermi and onlookers witnessed the first artificial self-sustaining nuclear chain reaction. The experiment produced only about ½ watt of controlled energy, but it was the first step in developing the atomic bomb.

Pyle chronicles the war Ernie Pyle's coverage of the war began in 1940 when he traveled from his home country, the U.S., to England to write stories of the London Blitz. In November 1942, he joined American troops in North Africa and beyond. His stories of GIs in combat brought the true experiences of sons and husbands to the families back home. In 1945 he wrote to his wife about the war: "I've been part of the misery and tragedy of it for so long that I feel if I left it, it would be like a soldier deserting." On April 18, 1945, Pyle was killed by a sniper on Ie Shima, an island west of Okinawa.

Temporary housing Mrs. Emma D. Gaw serves dinner to her husband, a worker at the Glenn Martin aircraft plant, in their trailer home in Middle River, Maryland. New or expanded war defense plants attracted tens of thousands of workers, creating a critical need for employee housing. The U.S. government eventually produced about two million dwelling units for workers nationwide, ranging from temporary economy units and trailers to dormitories and converted apartment buildings. Due to wartime shortages, temporary housing was constructed with materials that did not meet prewar standards.

British intern enemy aliens The British government's wartime policy of restricting or interning most enemy (German, Austrian, and Italian) aliens residing in Britain or arriving as refugees was unedifying and frequently unfair. However, it was an inevitable consequence due to the fear of spies, "fifth columnists" (subversive agents), and Nazi collaborators. Some 73,000 people were interned under military guard in temporary camps, partially constructed housing estates, and on the Isle of Man (including these internees), or they were deported to Canada and Australia. Such indiscriminate government action provoked a public outcry. By mid-1941, only 5,000 detainees remained in custody.

Wartime super-heroes Spy Smasher, an American comic book superhero introduced in 1940, beats up Axis leaders on the cover of a 1942 British edition. Comic book hero Captain America, clad in red, white, and blue, also achieved astound-

ing popularity for his anti-Axis adventures. Allied propaganda thrived in comic books, pulp novels, radio, and movies. Spy Smasher appeared in a movie serial in 1942, as did Captain America in 1944. Perhaps the most unlikely propaganda superhero was Sir Arthur Conan Doyle's Victorian detective, Sherlock Holmes. Played by an implausibly ageless Basil Rathbone, Holmes matched wits against the Nazis in a series of wartime movies.

1943

January 14: The RAF raids German U-boat ports at Lorient and Cherbourg in occupied France.

January 14–24: The Allied leadership meets in Casablanca, Morocco, to strategize the next phase of the global war. First priority is assigned to the defeat of the U-boats. In addition, Roosevelt and Churchill announce publicly that they will demand the unconditional surrender of the Axis countries.

January 15: Acting on assurances from Hermann Göring, Hitler calls for the daily delivery of 300 tons of supplies to the trapped Sixth Army in Stalingrad. While 300 tons would meet the needs of the men on the ground, it is far beyond what the *Luftwaffe* can accomplish.

January 16: For the first time in months, the RAF bombs Berlin.

January 18: After two and a half years, the siege of Leningrad comes to an end. With some 20,000 civilian deaths a day, relief has come too late for many of the city's residents. • The German army fields its new weapon, the Mark VI Tiger heavy tank, in a battle on the outskirts of the Tunisian capital of Tunis. • Realizing that the German concept of "resettlement" is a charade designed to lead them quietly to their deaths, the Jews of the Warsaw Ghetto fight back for the first time.

January 21: Dr. Nahum Goldmann, president of the World Jewish Congress in New York, receives a telegram from prisoners in the Warsaw Ghetto. They plead for aid and say, in part, that they are "poised at the brink of . . . annihilation" and that they "live with the awareness that in the most terrible days of our history you did not come to our aid."

Plotters and predictors
Seen at work is a plotter with the Women's Auxiliary Territorial Service, the women's branch of the British Army, in which women served in many capacities normally allocated to men. Working in Britain, plotters used radar to collect data about incoming enemy aircraft. Meanwhile, predictors stood on rooftops looking for planes. Together, their information was used to direct antiaircraft fire, vector fighter planes toward the German intruders, and alert the public to air raids.

Tanaka's claims to fame Rear Admiral Tanaka Raizo was the leading tactical commander of Japanese destroyer forces during the war. His finest hour came during the Battle of Tassafaronga off Guadalcanal on November 30, 1942, when his eight destroyers were ambushed by U.S. warships. Heavily outgunned, Tanaka sank one American cruiser and damaged three others with "Long Lance" torpedoes, while losing only a single destroyer. Tanaka also gained fame for his tenacious effort to resupply Japanese troops on Guadalcanal via the so-called "Tokyo Express." He was exiled to a shore command in 1943 because of his criticism of Japanese strategy and tactics in the Solomons.

Manstein's successes *Generalfeldmarschall* Erich von Manstein devised the *Sichelschnitt* (sickle-cut) plan that allowed troops to move past France's Maginot Line in 1940. Sent into Russia in late 1942 to rescue the trapped Sixth Army, Manstein fought through blizzards to within 30 miles of Stalingrad on December 19 before being stopped by the Red Army. Put in charge of Army Group South, Manstein halted the Red Army offensive and went on to capture Kharkov. A strong supporter of the Nazi Party, he accepted huge bribes from Hitler. However, the *Führer* relieved him of command in 1944.

Japanese Rivals: Army vs. Navy

THE EFFECTIVENESS OF THE Japanese military during the war was seriously diminished by the dissension—even outright hostility—between the Imperial Army and Imperial Navy. This conflict was rooted in a history of fierce competition for funding, endless battles for political influence, a fundamental difference in worldview, and disagreement on strategic policy.

Some Japanese naval officers tended to be more cosmopolitan in outlook, while most of the Army remained provincial and deeply conservative. Militarily, the Navy placed strategic emphasis on Southeast Asia, while the Army focused almost exclusively on China and Russia.

The Japanese command structure exacerbated interservice squabbling by allowing the two services to function as antagonistic equals. No authoritative joint command structure existed. Nor was there a meaningful recourse to a higher authority or method for resolving interservice differences.

The result was an almost pathological mutual mistrust. The services consistently failed to pool information, coordinate operations, or cooperate on the battlefield. With few exceptions, they did not share research, supplies, materiel, or resources, even when faced with disaster.

Squabbles could descend to astonishing pettiness. At the Mitsubishi factory at Nagoya, locked doors were put in place to conceal each service's contract work from the other. On a more serious level, some Army officers were not informed about the extent of the 1942 naval catastrophe at Midway until as late as 1945.

The outcome of this fratricidal relationship was inescapable: an impaired war effort and the speedier defeat of both services.

Americans listen in on Japanese An NBC technician mans a listening post in North Hollywood, California, monitoring shortwave radio broadcasts from the Far East. Numerous listening posts were maintained by American press associations, broadcasters, and government agencies—such as the Federal Communications Commission—to monitor foreign broadcasts. Though such broadcasts tended to be heavily laced with propaganda, they also provided clues about enemy intentions, policy changes, and other useful information.

FBI raids In 1936, as the Fascist movement gained momentum in Germany and the threat of war grew stronger in Europe, President Roosevelt believed that America would soon become a target for seditious activities. The role of the Federal Bureau of Investigation (FBI) was expanded to include the investigation of those types of treasonable schemes. In 1939 the FBI's responsibilities were again expanded to include sabotage and espionage investigations. Raiding homes of suspected subversives proved fruitful in the bureau's fight against terrorism in the states. This picture shows a cache of arms seized in the home of an enemy alien.

1943

January 21: Six teachers and 38 students, most under the age of seven, are killed when the *Luftwaffe* destroys the Catford Central School for Girls during a bombing raid of London.

January 22: Hitler refuses to consider the surrender of his forces at Stalingrad despite a desperate message from General Friedrich Paulus reporting dire conditions on the ground.

January 23: The British Eighth Army captures Tripoli, the capital of the Italian colony of Libya. • The United States seizes control of Kokumbona and Mount Austen, Japan's last two strongholds on Guadalcanal.

January 27: American bombers attack the critical port at Wilhelmshaven, Germany, causing extensive damage. It is the first air raid against Germany conducted exclusively by American forces.

January 29: Dr. Ernst Kaltenbrunner takes the post in Hitler's inner circle vacated by the assassinated Reinhard Heydrich. Kaltenbrunner will oversee the death camps, the *Einsatzgruppen*, the SS, and the Gestapo.

January 30: As Germans in Berlin gather to observe Hitler's 10th anniversary as *Führer*, RAF bombers sweep down over the city in their first daytime raid on the German capital. • The H2S bombing radar, a device that displays the contours of the ground below a bomber, is made operational by the RAF.

January 31: To Hitler's disgust, newly promoted field marshal Friedrich Paulus surrenders to the Red Army at Stalingrad. Hitler made the promotion because no field marshal in German history had surrendered.

U.S. in control of Guadalcanal
Rowdy American servicemen celebrate Christmas on Guadalcanal in a scene far removed from the perilous early days of the campaign. By January 1943, the Japanese conceded defeat and started to evacuate surviving troops from the island. As the war moved on, U.S. engineers transformed Guadalcanal into a

bustling rear-area base, complete with full amenities. The campaign had cost Japan nearly 25,000 dead, irreplaceable resources, and control of the central portion of the Solomon Islands. At a cost of approximately 1,600 Marines and soldiers killed, the U.S. had turned the tide of the ground war in the Pacific.

Summit in Casablanca President Franklin Roosevelt and Prime Minister Winston Churchill met in Casablanca, Morocco, from January 14 to 24, 1943. Because the strategy to defeat the Nazis was discussed, the Combined Chiefs of Staff also attended. The leaders agreed that the campaign against the U-boats must have the highest priority in 1943. They also agreed on a combined bomber offensive against Germany. A landing on Sicily was to follow the end of the fighting in Tunisia, and might in turn be followed by a landing in Italy. They also decided to make public their policy that the war against Germany, Italy, and Japan would end only with the unconditional surrender of those enemies.

Paulus surrenders In November 1942, surprise Soviet offensives isolated the German Sixth Army in Stalingrad, led by General Friedrich Paulus. Hitler refused to allow Paulus to break out while escape might have been possible, even though the German forces were not equipped with sufficient clothing, food, or medical supplies to withstand the Soviet winter. On January 30, 1943, the *Führer* promoted Paulus to *Generalfeldmarschall*, assuming that a man of such rank would either fight to the death or commit suicide rather than surrender. Paulus, hoping to save some of his men, is seen here surrendering to the Soviets on January 31.

The casualties of Stalingrad These German soldiers were taken captive by the Soviets following the surrender. The Battle of Stalingrad has been called the bloodiest battle in history. More than a million Germans and Soviets (combined) were killed, wounded, or captured. The 91,000 taken as Russian POWs were already exhausted, starving, and weakened by disease and untreated wounds. Only 6,000 of them would survive the overwork and malnutrition of Russian labor camps and return home after the war. Some of the 22 captive senior officers, including General Paulus, signed anti-Hitler statements that were used in Soviet propaganda broadcasts.

Montgomery despised, admired General Bernard "Monty" Montgomery, wearing his trademark beret with two badges, inspired conflicting emotions in others, ranging from fury to fierce loyalty. Montgomery was deeply disliked by many of his officers for the discipline he imposed on them, and deeply admired by his soldiers for the confidence he instilled in them. He was frequently at odds with other Allied generals. For example, his vain and boastful personality provoked legendary quarrels with the equally vain and boastful General Patton, and General Eisenhower considered him a limited strategist. Above all else, Monty was methodical, cautious, and reluctant to throw away the lives of his men—characteristics that made him slow but highly effective.

THE TIDE TURNS

FEBRUARY 1943–DECEMBER 1943

"How fortunate were the [German soldiers] who died in France and Poland. They could still believe in victory."

—Diary entry of German lieutenant Karl-Friedrich Brandt, Russia, summer 1943

ALLIED VICTORIES on Guadalcanal and at Stalingrad have to be put into perspective. In both cases, the overwhelming bulk of enemy armed forces remained undefeated. In each case, victory was geographically remote from the enemy heartland. The Allies understood that winning the war would be a long, drawn-out, and costly endeavor.

The turning points that are familiar to us now were less clear-cut at the time. In most cases, small victories were important in order to keep the Allied populations committed to an otherwise demoralizing and indecisive war. In February 1943, Hitler's propaganda minister, Joseph Goebbels, asked an audience in Berlin, "Do you want total war?" His audience clamored approval, but the mood among Germany's non-Nazi loyalists was somber and fearful. The changing expectations on both sides also played an important part in determining an outcome that was still more than two years away.

Just days before the German surrender at Stalingrad on January 31, 1943, Franklin Roosevelt and Winston Churchill met for a high-level conference in the Moroccan city of Casablanca, recently captured in Operation Torch. There they discussed the future direction of the war. They gave the European Theater priority, but they would not commit to an invasion of Northern Europe until the Atlantic could be made safe for the mass transport of men and supplies. While the naval struggle continued, they agreed, the two Western states would capitalize on success in North Africa by continuing a Mediterranean strategy against Mussolini's Italy. They would also maintain

The relentless Allied bombing campaign against the Axis in 1943 had a purpose beyond inflicting material damage on enemy infrastructure. The Combined Bomber Offensive was also intended as a substitute for a second front in the ground war, and to relieve pressure on the Red Army until the Allies could mount an invasion of Europe. Pictured are civilians killed in a bombing raid on Hamburg, Germany.

a relentless bombing campaign against the European Axis states to ease the pressure on the Red Army. This Combined Bomber Offensive was the Allies' substitute for a second front, which was deemed too risky in 1943.

At the final press briefing of the conference, Roosevelt—in agreement with Churchill—announced that the enemy states had only one option open to them: "unconditional surrender." Though secret contacts were occasionally made between individuals on both sides with a view to brokering an agreement, Roosevelt's public statement committed the Allies to a fight to the finish. No room was put aside for maneuver or compromise.

After a year in which the Allies lost 7.8 million tons of shipping, the submarine threat was expected to get worse during 1943. But a fortunate set of tactical changes tilted the balance in the Allies' favor. Most important was the adoption of new forms of radar on ships and aircraft as well as the transfer of adequate numbers of long-range planes to patrol the sea lanes. In May 1943, the German navy lost 41 submarines while Allied merchant vessel losses dropped sharply. Over the next two months, a further 54 submarines were sunk, prompting the German naval commander-in-chief, Admiral Karl Dönitz, to withdraw from the North Atlantic. The Allies' victory over the submarine menace was a critical one, for it made possible the full extension of American military and economic power into the European Theater.

Members of a German U-boat crew glumly contemplate their future as POWs after their submarine was depth-charged in the Atlantic. By May 1943, German U-boat losses were skyrocketing as Allied technological advances in antisubmarine warfare began to take their toll. Two months later, the German navy withdrew from the Atlantic battle.

That power was principally represented in the air in 1943. The Combined Bomber Offensive was officially launched as Operation Pointblank in June 1943, although British Bomber Command and the U.S. Eighth Air Force had begun around-the-clock bombing—the British by night, the Americans by day—from the winter of 1942–43. The offensive was aimed at the enemy's military-economic complex—the source of German airpower and the morale of the urban workforce.

Efforts to attack identifiable industrial or military targets could not be achieved with prevailing technology without a high cost to civilians. From July 24 to 28, a succession of attacks on the northern German port city of Hamburg resulted in the first "firestorm," which killed an estimated 40,000 people. Over the course of the war, more than 420,000 German civilians would die from the bombing attacks; a further 60,000 civilians would be killed in attacks on Italian cities. The bomb attacks immediately affected German strategy. The Germans established a large air defense sector. To do so, they had to withdraw valuable resources of manpower, artillery, shells, and aircraft from the military front line. There, German armies were forced to fight with shrinking air cover. Though military production continued to rise in Germany during 1943, the increase was much lower than it would have been otherwise. Bombing placed a ceiling on the German war effort and brought the war to bear directly on German and Italian society.

The Allies capitalized on these growing advantages. In North Africa, the Axis forces that were bottled up in Tunisia were slowly starved of supplies by Allied naval and air power in the Mediterranean. By May 13, when the battle was over, 275,000 Italian and German troops had surrendered. As had been decided at Casablanca, the Western Allies launched an attack on Sicily on July 9–10, 1943. During the capture of the island, Mussolini's regime was overthrown by the Fascist Grand Council and the monarchy. On September 3, an armistice was agreed upon, and on September 8, Italy surrendered.

A Russian T-34 tank rolls through a burning village during the Battle of Kursk in July 1943. Anticipating the German offensive, the Soviets absorbed the blow with a network of well-prepared defensive lines, then counterattacked. The counterblow drove the German army out of central and southern Russia and opened the way to victory in the East.

That same week, American and British Commonwealth forces landed in southern Italy against limited German resistance. However, German forces were reinforced as the battle took shape. Though Naples was liberated on October 1, Allied progress slowed in the difficult mountain terrain. By the end of 1943, the German army—which had formally occupied Italy as an enemy state—consolidated a strong line of defense, the Gustav Line, south of Rome.

The Allies' pressure at sea, in the air, and on the southern front made the Axis task in the Soviet Union more difficult. Following the collapse of the German assault on the Caucasus and Stalingrad, the Red Army became overly ambitious. After the Soviets pressed the German army back, a swift counteroffensive around Kharkov in early 1943 was a reminder that the huge German army remained a formidable foe. Hitler listened to the advice of his generals, who argued that in summer weather, with good preparation, they could smash a large part of the Soviet army in a single pitched battle. They chose a large salient that bulged into the German front line around the city of Kursk as their battleground.

Operation Citadel lacked the geographical scope of previous operations, but it became one of the largest set-piece battles of the whole war. It followed a classic German pattern: Two heavily armored pincers would close around the neck of the salient, trapping the Soviet armies in the salient and creating conditions for a possible drive into the areas behind Moscow. Manstein, who commanded the southern pincer, wanted to attack in April or May, before the Red Army had time to consolidate its position. But Hitler, in agreement with General Model (who commanded the northern pincer), ordered a delay until German forces were fully armed with a new generation of heavy tanks and guns—the Panthers and Tigers.

The Soviets, for the first time, guessed the German plan correctly. Stalin had to be persuaded by Georgi Zhukov and the General Staff that a posture of embedded defense was better strategy than seeking open battle against a powerful mobile enemy. Stalin accepted it only because the defensive stage was to be followed by a massive blow struck by Soviet reserves against the weakened and retreating German armies.

In May and June, a vast army of Soviet civilians turned the Kursk salient into a veritable fortress. Six separate defense lines were designed to absorb the expected shock of the German armored assault. The Red Army numbered 1.3 million, the Germans 900,000. Each side had approximately 2,000 aircraft and more than 2,500 tanks. On July 5, German forces began the attack. They made slow progress over the first week against determined Soviet resistance. Zhukov's plan worked, and for the first time in the two years of fighting on the Eastern Front,

President Franklin Roosevelt meets with Soviet foreign minister Vyacheslav Molotov in Tehran in November 1943. Though their situation was improving, the Soviets continued to suffer terrible losses in their single-front ground war against the Axis. Roosevelt promised that the Allies would open a second front in the spring of 1944 with an invasion of Europe.

a large-scale German campaign was held and then reversed without the crisis and retreat that had preceded other victories.

On July 13, Hitler canceled Operation Citadel after news of Allied landings in Italy. But at just the moment that German forces pulled back, the Soviet punch into the rear of the northern pincer was delivered. The German army had not expected a counterstroke of such size and ferocity. Over three months, they were pushed back across the whole area of southern and central Russia. On November 6, Russian forces reentered the Ukrainian capital of Kiev. The Battle of Kursk, more than any other single engagement of the war, unhinged the German war machine and opened the way to victory in the East.

In the midst of the euphoria of victory, Stalin traveled to the Iranian capital of Tehran for the first summit conference with his Western partners. The central issue was a second front in the West. Though Stalin now privately argued that his forces could finish the job without Western help, the Red Army continued to suffer a terrible level of loss that could not be sustained indefinitely in a single-front ground war. After two days of argument, in which Churchill tried to insist on a strengthened Mediterranean strategy at the expense of invasion, Roosevelt was able to promise Stalin an operation in the spring of 1944 that would bring American and British forces in strength into northwestern Europe. One witness recalled a sober, pale-faced Stalin replying, "I am satisfied with this decision."

In the atmosphere at Tehran, it was easy to forget that another war was being fought in Asia and the Pacific that was quite distinct from the conflict in Southern and Eastern Europe. There, it was still possible for the Japanese to attempt further expansion. In October 1943, the Japanese army undertook military operations in central China designed to erode the spread of Chinese communism. The Communist forces were led by Mao Zedong, who had devoted much of the Communist efforts to maintaining independence from the Chinese Nationalist army of Chiang Kai-shek.

In the Pacific Theater, the Japanese defeat on Guadalcanal was followed by a slow American advance through the Solomon Islands and a combined American and Australian campaign in New Guinea. Japanese air and naval strength could not match the United States' huge production programs. And though the Allies' move through the islands of the southern and central Pacific, code-named Operation Cartwheel, was slow and costly, it proved unstoppable. By the end of 1943, the central Solomons had been occupied and progress had been made on New Guinea. Japan's major base at Rabaul was bypassed.

Throughout the region, Japanese garrisons were left to themselves in strategically unimportant places, increasingly hungry and sick but supplied by submarines. In the rest of the Japanese empire of occupation, imperial rule was consolidated. Anticolonial and anti-European movements were encouraged. The Japanese encouraged the formation of the Indian National Army under the leadership of nationalist Subhash Chandra Bose, who recruited 18,000 Indian prisoners of war to the cause in Southeast Asia. They were tolerated only as long as they fought for the Japanese. For millions of others in the so-called Great East Asia Co-Prosperity Sphere, one form of domination had been exchanged for another. In China, more than 10 million people died during the course of the war with Japan in a conflict largely unnoticed by the rest of the world.

Chinese Nationalist troops march through a wrecked town in Hunan Province in late 1943. While Japanese troops in the Pacific were going on the defensive in the face of Allied advances, Japanese military forces in central China continued to mount powerful offensive operations in an effort to expand their influence over the region.

1943

February: Along several fronts in Tunisia, Allied forces clash with German units in heavy fighting. Germany's Mark VI tanks battle the Allies' Churchill and Sherman tanks.

February 3: Germans observe the first of three official days of mourning for the loss of the Sixth Army at Stalingrad. Of a force of about 270,000 men, nearly 150,000 were killed and 90,000 taken prisoner.

February 4: The RAF Bomber Command receives orders that the next phase of the German bombing campaign is to focus on the destruction of Germany's U-boat manufacturing capabilities. • American General Dwight D. Eisenhower assumes command of the Allies on the North African front. • The British Eighth Army, fresh from victory in Tripoli, rolls into Tunisia.

February 5: Mussolini relieves his son-in-law, Count Galeazzo Ciano, of his duties as Italy's foreign minister, reassigning him to the ambassadorship at the Vatican. *Il Duce* will appoint himself to fill the vacant ministry post.

February 8: The Russians retake Kursk, a vital operations base, from the German occupation force that has held the city for almost 14 months.

February 9: President Roosevelt orders a 48-hour minimum workweek in several U.S. industries that are key to the war effort. • After six months of desperation, disease, and brutal fighting, the U.S. declares Guadalcanal secure the day after the last Japanese soldier quietly evacuates the island.

February 10: Civilians evacuate the town of Lorient, France, site of an active German U-boat base, in the face of a heavy RAF bombing campaign.

Hundreds of thousands die at Treblinka Before Jews and other enemies of the Third Reich were exterminated at the Treblinka death camp in Poland, their shoes (and other possessions) were confiscated. This image alone suggests that a huge number of people met their fates at Treblinka. In fact, more than 700,000 Jews died at the camp, a death toll exceeded only at Auschwitz. Most of the victims came from such major ghettos as Warsaw (250,000 in the summer of 1942) and Bialystok, while others endured (or died during) long train rides from Czechoslovakia, Greece, and other countries. Deportations to Treblinka ended in May 1943.

Wretched conditions in New Guinea Australian infantrymen fight in New Guinea in this painting by Henry Hanke. The Japanese naval offensive toward Port Moresby in New Guinea in 1942 raised justified concerns that an invasion of Australia was imminent and prompted the recall of Australian troops from the Middle East. Australians shouldered the brunt of the early fighting in New Guinea, as significant numbers of U.S. troops were not available. Plagued by disease and constant rain—their movement limited to muddy footpaths over steep, jungle-choked mountains—soldiers on both sides suffered terrible hardships during the seven-month campaign.

Barbarism in the Pacific Frozen in a silent scream, the charred head of a Japanese soldier decorates a knocked-out tank like some macabre hood ornament. A disregard for the enemy's humanity was routine on both sides during the war, due to the racism and the sheer brutality of Pacific combat introduced by the Japanese. Death was no novelty, and there was little room for compassion in the struggle for survival on the battlefield. Most U.S. commanders discouraged displays such as this, but the use of skulls as decorations on vehicles and at island base camps—and the collection of gold teeth from enemy dead—remained fairly commonplace.

A warning to U.S. workers Allied propaganda typically portrayed the Japanese as nearsighted, bucktoothed caricatures or as monkeys, alternating between a subject of ridicule and an object of fear. This particular piece, probably made to be posted in U.S. defense plants, reminds workers that goldbricking hurts productivity and aids the enemy. It also links Japan to its Axis partner, Germany, through the subject's swastika collar medallion.

The "White Mouse" Nancy Wake used her position as wife of a wealthy French businessman to help the French Resistance. She served as courier, obtained false papers, bought an ambulance to aid fleeing refugees, and helped get some 1,000 escaped prisoners and downed Allied fliers out of France. By 1943 Wake—called the "White Mouse" because she was so hard to catch—topped the Gestapo's most-wanted list. She fled to Britain, was trained by the SOE (Special Operations Executive, a spy agency), and then parachuted back into France. There she served as liaison between London and the *Maquis,* and also led guerrilla raids.

Allies lose fewer merchant ships In February 1943, a triumphant German submarine crew watches its prey—a U.S. merchant ship—sink. During the early war years, Allied merchant ships in the Atlantic were destroyed faster than they could be built. But by May 1943, Allied shipping losses dropped sharply due to increased air protection, the relocation of some U.S. warships from the Pacific to the Atlantic, and tremendous progress in antisubmarine technologies. Even though enemy air attacks still could be devastating, Allied merchant ship losses in 1943 were half those of 1942.

1943

February 10: Mohandas Gandhi stops eating in protest of Britain's detention of India's independence-seeking Congress Party leaders. He vows to consume only diluted fruit juice for the next three weeks.

February 11: The Allied assault on the U-boat program continues with the first of a series of intense RAF raids on the German port of Wilhelmshaven.

February 14: The RAF launches a nighttime bombing raid against the northern Italian city of Milan. • The Allies suffer a setback in Tunisia, as the Axis drives back Allied forces with the capture of the city of Sidi Bou Zid.

February 15: A German panzer unit withdraws from the Russian city of Kharkov in defiance of an order from Hitler to stand against the Red Army. The Soviets will retake the city the next day.

February 16: Radio *Risorgi,* an anti-Mussolini radio show broadcast from Britain and staffed by Italian detainees, begins operation. • The Vichy French government institutes a mandatory labor program to which young adults must devote two years of their lives.

February 18: A prototype B-29 long-range bomber crashes into the Frye Packing Plant during a test-flight near Boeing's Seattle headquarters. The accident kills 31 people. • Madame Chiang Kai-shek makes a state visit to Washington. In a speech before Congress, she expresses confidence in a Japanese defeat.

February 21: The *Wehrmacht* attacks the Red Army in an attempt to retake the Russian city of Kharkov.

February 22: University of Munich students Christoph Probst and Hans and Sophie Scholl die at the guillotine for leading the "White Rose" anti-Nazi resistance movement.

Bomber gunners U.S. Army Air Force machine gunner Sergeant William Watts fires at enemy planes from a bomber over Europe in 1942. Almost 300,000 aerial gunners were trained during World War II—a substantially greater number than were trained as pilots, navigators, or bombardiers, and for good reason. A

bomber's very survival depended upon the gunners' skill at fending off enemy planes. Gunners also held the crew's most dangerous and physically disagreeable positions. They were unprotected by armor, and because of high altitudes, they sometimes had to endure temperatures as low as –60°F.

The bombing of Wilhelmshaven The German port city of Wilhelmshaven was bombed twice in 1943—once by the USAAF on January 27, and again by the RAF Bomber Command on February 11–12. These aerial reconnaissance images show Wilhelmshaven before and after the two bombings. The second, carried out at night, was especially challenging because of dense cloud cover. Planes equipped with the RAF's newly developed H2S ground-mapping radar located strategic targets, then illuminated them with parachute flares. A successful strike on a naval ammunition dump south of Wilhelmshaven caused widespread destruction of dockyards and the city.

Wartime Euphemisms

WORLD WAR II GENERATED many words that concealed rather than clarified meaning. Over the span of the war, numerous euphemisms were added to the languages of the belligerent nations.

The Japanese, for example, described their empire as the Greater East Asia Co-Prosperity Sphere, despite their ruthless exploitation of Southeast Asia's people. Japanese commanders used the word *tenshin* ("to advance in a different direction") rather than admit to retreat. After the war, the Japanese devised the term *comfort women* to conceal the reality of thousands of women coerced into military prostitution.

Many Allied euphemisms also carried propaganda meanings. *Lend-Lease* was neither a loan nor a lease, but a gift not expected to be repaid. Japanese Americans were interned in camps blandly called *relocation camps.* Psycho-logically wounded RAF airmen unable to continue flying were stigmatized for their *lack of moral fibre.* The air war also generated the term *precision bombing*—which was usually anything but. *De-housing workers* meant razing whole cities and killing their people.

The Nazis perfected the use of euphemisms. *Resettlement* in Poland meant the deportation of Poles to death camps. *Special duties* units exterminated Europe's Jews as part of the *Final Solution* to the *Jewish question.*

Correspondents on both sides talked glibly about *mopping up,* a phrase that got under the skin of American general Robert Eichelberger. "If there is another war," he stated, "I recommend that the military, and the correspondents, and everyone else concerned, drop the phrase 'mopping up' from their vocabularies. It is not a good enough phrase to die for."

The German defense of Tunisia German artillerymen fire at British aircraft in Tunisia. In January 1943, Allied troops were advancing on the German *Afrika Korps* in Tunisia from the southeast and northwest. This pincer movement threatened to trap German and Italian troops under the command of Field Marshal Erwin Rommel. He bought some time by striking uncoordinated British and American troops on February 20, driving the hapless Americans back through the Kasserine Pass in central Tunisia. In their first battle with the *Afrika Korps,* it was apparent that the untested Americans were not ready to face some of Germany's best troops. In the spring, the tide would turn.

Hitler and his generals Hitler and his generals study maps in February 1943. From the left are General Field Marshal Erich von Manstein, Adolf Hitler, General Theodor Busse, and General Field Marshal Ewald von Kleist. Hitler had made himself supreme military commander early in the Nazi reign. In December 1941, he became commander-in-chief of the German army. By 1943 devastating failures on the Eastern Front and in North Africa had convinced some German generals that they could save their nation only by getting rid of the *Führer.* However, a bomb placed on a plane carrying Hitler to Smolensk in March failed to go off, and several other attempts on the *Führer's* life also failed.

1943

February 22: The Bulgarian government authorizes the deportation of 11,000 Jews from the annex areas of Thrace and Macedonia. Most will die in the gas chambers of Treblinka.

February 25: The Allies enjoy 24-hour bombing capability with the implementation of a schedule that assigns daytime raids to the USAAF and nighttime bombing to the RAF.

February 27: Allied commandos sabotage the Vemork power plant, a German plant on Norwegian soil that produces heavy water used in atomic weapons research. Engineers will get the facility back on line by summer.

February 28: The Allies outline the ELKTON Plan, with the goal of seizing and occupying the southwest Pacific region of New Guinea, New Ireland, and New Britain.

March: Spring mud bogs down both the *Wehrmacht* and the Red Army on the Soviet front, leading to a relative (though temporary) peace. • The Nazis begin the deportation of Greek Jews from their zone of occupation. Most are bound for Auschwitz, though the fortunate ones escape to Palestine via Turkey and a small number are rescued by Spanish and Turkish diplomats.

March 1: The Polish government is put on notice that the eastern part of the country that was occupied by the Soviets following Germany's 1939 invasion will be incorporated into the Soviet Union. • The Allies convene the Atlantic Convoy Conference in Washington. They agree on a plan in which the U.S. Navy, the Royal Navy, and the Royal Canadian Navy will share the escort of convoys on the Atlantic.

March 2: Berlin threatens retaliation against New York and Washington after the most punishing Allied air raid to date on the German capital.

The Gestapo's new chief As head of the Austrian SS, Ernst Kaltenbrunner assisted in the 1938 German annexation of Austria, enforced anti-Jewish measures, and opened a death camp. In 1942 he replaced assassinated Gestapo chief Reinhard Heydrich, assuming responsibility for the Nazi "Final Solution" to the "Jewish question." Kaltenbrunner claimed ignorance of genocide when he was brought to trial at Nuremberg, but he was found guilty and hanged. More than 50 years later, his personal seal identifying him as head of the Nazi security police was discovered in an Alpine lake, where he had apparently tossed it before surrendering under a false name.

The White Rose From left to right are Hans Scholl, his sister Sophie, and Christoph Probst, students at the University of Munich who helped found the White Rose, a nonviolent resistance movement against the Nazi regime. Using a hand-operated mimeograph machine, the White Rose distributed thousands of leaflets eloquently denouncing Hitler's tyranny. On February 18, 1943, Sophie impetuously threw leaflets from the top of a university staircase, leading to the prompt arrest of the group's active members. On February 22, the same day as their conviction for treason, Hans, Sophie, and Probst bravely faced their deaths by guillotine.

Tresckow involved in Hitler murder plots "Hitler is not only the very enemy of Germany, but the enemy of the world." This sentiment was expressed by German major general Henning von Tresckow, chief of staff of the German Army Group Center. Although an officer, Tresckow hated Hitler and was a leader in the military resistance. An attempt to blow up Hitler in a plane in March 1943 was unsuccessful. Another attempt at a meeting in July 1944 also failed. Learning of this latest failure and realizing it could be traced back to him, Tresckow killed himself a day after the attempt.

Reprisals in Yugoslavia Serbia, Croatia, Slovenia, and other territories were joined together to create Yugoslavia in December 1918. From the beginning of its occupation in 1941, insurgents mounted stiff resistance against the German army. On October 16, 1941, rebels killed 10 Germans and wounded 26 in Serbia. In retaliation, the commander of German forces in Kragujevac reported on October 21, "For every dead German soldier, 100 residents have been executed, and for every wounded German soldier, 50 residents have been executed . . . all totaling 2,300." Thousands of other civilians were murdered by German troops. This Serbian partisan was hung from a lamppost in April 1943.

The Katyn massacre On April 13, 1943, German commanders announced over Berlin Radio that they had discovered a mass grave of 4,000 Polish officers in the Katyn Forest near Smolensk, Poland. They later discovered the number to be about 4,400 bodies, each shot in the back of the neck with his hands tied. The Germans accused the Soviet Union of carrying out these executions. The Soviet government denied the charge, accusing Germany of the killings. In 1944 an international commission determined that the killings took place in 1940 when Poland was under Soviet control.

The Coast Guard's contributions On April 17, 1943, U.S. Coast Guardsmen watch the explosion from a depth charge they have dropped on the German submarine *U-175*. Spotting the U-boat on sonar as it maneuvered to attack an Allied convoy in the mid-Atlantic, the Coast Guard Cutter *Spencer* took the submarine by surprise. Coast Guardsmen boarded the badly damaged submarine when it surfaced and rescued the surviving 41 German crewmen. In the Atlantic, the Coast Guard sank 13 U-boats and captured two Nazi surface ships. In the Pacific, they sank at least one Japanese submarine.

1943

March 2: In the wake of a devastating defeat at the hands of the Red Army, Mussolini pulls Italy's surviving troops from the Eastern front. • An Allied attack on a Japanese troop convoy en route to New Guinea culminates in the Battle of the Bismarck Sea. The Japanese will suffer heavy losses.

March 3: Nearly 180 Londoners die after a woman trips entering an Underground station serving as an air raid shelter. The crowd rushing to get under cover presses in and suffocates the fallen.

March 5: The RAF introduces its latest weapons technology, the OBOE navigation system, in an air raid over Essen, Germany, home of the Krupp plant. • The Reich war machine orders the Vichy government to deliver an additional 100,000 slave laborers. • The RAF conducts test-flights of the Gloster Meteor, its first fighter plane powered by a jet engine.

March 6: General George Patton assumes control of the U.S. Second Army Corps on the same day that German general Erwin Rommel loses his last North African battle. Rommel, accused of "pessimism" by the *Führer,* will be succeeded by General Jürgen von Arnim. • The Allies lose 13 supply ships when a North Atlantic convoy is attacked by German U-boats.

March 10: Congress moves to extend the Lend-Lease Act, which would allow the United States to continue to supply the Allies with war materials without any expectation of repayment.

March 13: Some 14,000 Jews are sent to Auschwitz and other death camps as the Nazis begin to shut down the Jewish ghetto in the Polish city of Kraków. • An attempt on Hitler's life fails when the chosen weapon, a bomb made of plastic explosives, fails to detonate.

Jews revolt in Warsaw Ghetto By late 1942, Jews in the Warsaw Ghetto realized that those among them who were deported usually went to death camps, not to labor camps as the Nazis had claimed. On January 9, 1943, SS chief Heinrich Himmler ordered that another 8,000 Jews from the ghetto be deported. On January 18, Warsaw resistance groups began fighting back with weapons smuggled in through the sewers. Ordered to quell the uprising, SS officer Jürgen Stroop (*center*) did so in April. He claimed to have caught or killed 56,065 Jews with a loss of only 15 Germans. *The Stroop Report* bragged that "the Warsaw Ghetto is no more."

Warsaw resisters go down fighting This photograph from *The Stroop Report* shows the Nazi roundup of civilians during the Warsaw Ghetto uprising. Many were shot where they were caught, their bodies left in the streets. Others were deported to death camps. Resistance members fought the Nazis with improvised explosive devices and whatever weapons they managed to acquire. The ghetto fighters held out to the end, often still shooting or exploding hidden grenades when captured. Some estimates count the dead and wounded Germans and their collaborators at 1,300, far more than Stroop claimed.

Nazi Death Camps

THE WORDS "*ARBEIT MACHT FREI*" ("Labor Liberates"), displayed prominently above the entrance of the camp at Auschwitz in Nazi-occupied Poland, exemplified the deceitfulness and hypocrisy of the Nazi regime. Auschwitz was a facility dedicated not to the liberation of its inmates but to their systematic extermination in accordance with the plan for a "Final Solution" of the "Jewish question."

Auschwitz was the most notorious of the Nazi death camps in Poland, whose overall purpose was the extermination of Europe's Jews, together with Gypsies, homosexuals, and many other groups considered socially, politically, or racially undesirable. Treblinka, Sobibór, Majdanek, Belzec, and Chelmno were the other main extermination camps, *aka* death camps (not to be confused with the concentration camps, which had primarily penal, economic, and slave-labor functions). These extermination camps were designed to kill on an industrialized scale, this being achieved most efficiently through the use of gas chambers. The resulting corpses were burned in purpose-built crematoriums.

The victims usually arrived at the death camps by rail, often after days traveling in sealed cattle wagons under the mistaken impression that they were being "resettled"—an illusion scrupulously maintained by the Nazi guards and camp staff until the very end. Europe's extensive rail network readily facilitated the mass movement of these people, with railway lines that often terminated at the very gates of the camps.

Jews at Auschwitz

On arrival, those chosen for immediate extermination—the aged, the infirm, children, and men and women deemed useless—were separated from those assessed as suitable for slave labor. Thereafter, those destined for immediate death were led to the camp "bathhouse," where they were ordered to store their personal effects and then strip to "shower" after their long journey. Any remaining illusions were finally shattered as the "bathhouse" doors were locked behind them. At that point, the deadly Zyklon B gas crystals were dropped into what was in reality the gas chamber, or carbon monoxide was pumped in. About four million people died in the extermination camps.

The Auschwitz complex Jews huddle together at Auschwitz. This German complex, built from 1940 to '42 outside the town of Oswiecim in southern Poland, included three concentration camps and 36 subcamps. Auschwitz I contained Polish political prisoners, Auschwitz II (Birkenau) was the extermination camp, and Auschwitz III was a forced-labor camp. Birkenau contained gas chambers and a crematorium that could dispose of 2,000 bodies at a time. Dr. Josef Mengele, wearing an immaculate white medical coat, often met incoming inmates and immediately chose who were to live and who were to die. He also chose subjects for his ghastly medical experiments.

1943

March 15: The Germans prevail in the Third Battle of Kharkov, the last major local victory for the Germans in the war.

March 16: Tired of having the burden of the entire Eastern Front placed on the shoulders of the Red Army, Stalin demands a second European front from the U.S. and Britain.

March 16–19: The Allies suffer serious losses when 21 merchant ships and a convoy escort are lost in a three-day battle with nearly 40 German U-boats.

March 18: General Henri Giraud, a French war hero and new leader of the Free French, restores full citizenship, rights, and property to French Jews. • The government of French Guiana aligns itself with the Free French, repudiating Vichy France.

March 20: Another attempt to assassinate Hitler, this time via suicide bomber, fails when Hitler leaves the vicinity before the bomb can be detonated.

March 22: The Nazis open a new, diabolically efficient death chamber at Auschwitz. Crematorium IV will allow the Nazis to drive their victims into an underground gas chamber equipped with a lift that conveys the corpses into the crematorium.

March 26: The U.S. Navy prevents Japan from reinforcing its troops on Alaska's Aleutian island of Attu, as it attacks and repels a Japanese naval convoy.

March 30: The suspension of Allied convoys to the Soviet port of Murmansk, due to very heavy ship losses, drives a wedge between the Soviet Union and its allies.

April 2: Hermann Göring orders every able-bodied man and woman in Germany to take part in anti-air raid civil defense, manning antiaircraft guns and partaking in similar duties.

Thousands killed in uprising The final battle in the Warsaw Ghetto began on April 19, 1943. Most resistance was quelled by April 23, and the uprising was over by May 16. About 13,000 Jews were shot, burnt alive, or gassed in their bunkers, and about 50,000 were sent to death camps. Here, a Polish man records the number of corpses stacked in a wheelbarrow. Obsessive Nazi record-keeping included detailed accounts of people's ancestry (to prove Aryan heritage or at least non-Jewish bloodlines), military service records, and tallies of prisoners and prisoner deaths—some of which would become useful to prosecutors during war-crimes trials.

Allied gains in North Africa In the fall of 1942, General Montgomery's Eighth Army inflicted a significant defeat upon General Rommel's *Afrika Korps* at El Alamein in Egypt. At last the tide of German successes had turned, as Alamein now opened the way for a general advance westward by the British. Simultaneously, Anglo-U.S. landings (Operation Torch) at Casablanca, Oran, and Algiers were largely unopposed by the Vichy French defenders. Tripoli fell on January 28, 1943, and in February the Allies entered Tunisia—where U.S. forces suffered a costly reverse at Kasserine Pass. However, the end was in sight, and the remaining Axis forces in North Africa surrendered on May 12.

The air war in North Africa A German Messerschmitt Me-109 is camouflaged to blend in with the African desert. Prior to February 1941, the fight for North Africa was waged between British and Italian forces. The arrival of German divisions commanded by General Erwin Rommel tipped the scales in Italy's favor. The equalizer for British troops was the superiority of its air force over the German *Luftwaffe*. Squadrons based in Malta and occupied areas of North Africa attacked German supply lines and supported ground troops across North Africa. The greatest threat to both Allied and Axis aircraft was the damage inflicted by sand and the torrid climate.

"I saw 50 Germans marching in good order toward Tunis with no guards at all. They had assembled themselves, were tramping to surrender."

—*TIME* CORRESPONDENT WILL LANG, ON THE ALLIED VICTORY AT TUNIS, MAY 1943

Allies prevail in North Africa On May 6, 1943, the Allies launched their last offensive against the Axis in North Africa. On May 13, the German and Italian troops in Tunisia surrendered. This was the first major success of the alliance between America and Britain. It was not only good for the morale on the home front, but it also took some pressure off President Roosevelt to turn the military's attention primarily to the fight in the Pacific. To promote this success, director Frank Capra prepared this 75-minute documentary of the North Africa campaign, beginning with Operation Torch and ending with the fall of Tunisia.

Armored cars From the outset, the main belligerents' armored forces included armored cars. Their primary roles were reconnaissance and scouting, so they needed to be faster and quieter than tanks, and to have a better range. Typically they had thin armor, light or nonexistent armament, and limited cross-country performance. This vehicle, a British Daimler, fires its two-pounder (40mm) gun near Tripoli in January 1943. Daimler armored cars performed well in the desert from their introduction in 1941. They served throughout the war, with nearly 2,700 produced.

1943

April 5: The German SS murders 4,000 Jews at the Ponar Woods near Vilna, Lithuania. • USAAF pilots staging a raid on a *Luftwaffe* facility in Antwerp, Belgium, miss their targets by more than a mile and kill more than 900 Belgian civilians. • The Allies launch their most intense air raid to date on both sides of the Mediterranean, hitting Axis targets in Italy and North Africa. • Japanese troops overrun British headquarters on the Mayu Peninsula in Burma.

April 7: A downcast Mussolini meets Hitler in Salzburg to discuss the string of recent Axis defeats and to lobby for a separate peace with the Soviet Union, but Hitler convinces him that their setbacks are temporary. • The British government releases the Keynes Plan, named for economist John Maynard Keynes, which calls for the establishment of a world bank.

April 12: Thousands of bodies—Polish army officers massacred by the Soviet secret police—are found in Russia's Katyn Forest. The grim discovery is seized upon by German propagandists and denied by the Soviets.

April 14: Joseph Stalin's oldest son, Yakov, dies in a German POW camp. Captured in 1941, he was offered back to Russia in a prisoner trade, but Stalin declined.

April 15: The Allies attack the important German manufacturing center of Stuttgart with aptly named bombs called "factory-smashers" and "block-busters." • The U.S. high command is reorganized, as General Patton is needed to plan the American portion of the invasion of Sicily. General Omar Bradley will take Patton's place as the commander of the U.S. Second Army Corps.

The Battle for Cassino Early in 1944, Axis-occupied Cassino, Italy, stood in the path of the Allied advance toward Rome. On February 15, Allied bombers destroyed the city's historical abbey of Monte Cassino (founded by St. Benedict in 529), on the assumption that it was occupied by Axis forces. After the bombing, German troops moved into the ruins and defended them. During the brutal months that followed, the Allies demolished Cassino, finally capturing the city in May. Here, victorious British and South African soldiers and engineers pose amid Cassino's ruins with a captured Nazi flag.

The king of Italy King Victor Emmanuel III decorates an officer for war service in 1944. Emmanuel became a figurehead sovereign after failing to oppose Benito Mussolini's rise to power. Not until 1943, after the Allied invasion of Sicily, did he order Mussolini's arrest, belatedly acknowledging widespread public disillusionment with the war. His actions came too late to save the monarchy. Widely despised, the king and his son went into exile in Egypt following the declaration of the Italian Republic in 1946.

The Dam Busters

ON MAY 16–17, 1943, the British Royal Air Force launched Operation Chastise. With a new type of bomb, the RAF attacked three dams (the Möhne, Eder, and Sorpe) that supplied water to the German industries of the Ruhr.

Invented by aeronautical engineer Barnes Wallis, the cylindrical "bouncing bomb" needed to be released precisely and at a very low level. The bomb needed to "skip" across the lake surface to slide down the dam wall and explode.

The bombs were delivered from specially modified Lancasters, which were crewed by experienced (and very brave) British and dominion airmen. A newly formed 617 Squadron, led by Wing Commander Guy Gibson, trained over the dams of England, perfecting the technique, which needed to be performed in the face of intense flak. Of the 19 attacking aircraft, eight were lost. Gibson received the Victoria Cross, while his crews were decorated and celebrated. The dams, however, were repaired within months.

The dam raids boosted British morale more than they damaged the German war effort. Perhaps the most signifi-

The Eder dam after it was bombed

cant result was the creation of the elite 617 Squadron, demonstrating the value of giving highly trained aircrew specialized weapons. Later, 617 Squadron achieved striking success in attacking industrial targets and railroad viaducts with "Tallboy" bombs and in sinking the last German battleship, the *Tirpitz,* in its Norwegian fjord.

Decorated dam busters "As great a warrior as this island ever produced," was the eulogy expressed by British air marshall Sir Arthur Harris on the death of Guy Gibson. Gibson (*fourth from left*) was 23 and had won the Distinguished Flying Cross by the time he was promoted to wing commander of the newly formed 617th Squadron. He led the 19 planes in his group on a mission to blow up dams in the Ruhr Valley on May 16, 1943. For his leadership and valor, Gibson was awarded the Victoria Cross, the highest British military award. His plane crashed in the Netherlands while on a mission on September 19, 1944.

Horton's ideas lead to success in Atlantic
Late in 1942, British admiral Sir Max Horton, commander-in-chief of the Western Approaches Command, changed antisubmarine strategy. He sent groups of fast "hunter-killer" ships away from their convoys to attack German U-boats, preventing the formation of "wolf packs." By spring 1943, those tactics had successfully reopened the North Atlantic to merchant and military ship-

ping. As a WWI submarine commander, Horton had responded to an admiral's assessment of all submariners as "un-English" and "pirates" by flying the "Jolly Roger" (skull and crossbones flag) after his sub sank two German ships. WWII British and Australian submariners took up the Jolly Roger as a signal of success.

1943

April 16: As Allied air raids against German U-boats continue unabated, France evacuates from several key ports all citizens who are not staffing critical war-related jobs.

April 18: In the midst of calls by the Polish government-in-exile for an investigation into the Katyn massacre, the Soviets attempt to save face by blaming the Nazi Gestapo. • The Allies shoot down 69 *Luftwaffe* planes en route to Tunisia into the Mediterranean in a 10-minute dogfight. The Allies lose just nine of their own planes in the process. • Japan's Admiral Yamamoto, commander in chief of the Japanese Combined Fleet and the mastermind behind the attack on Pearl Harbor, is shot down and killed over the Solomon Islands by American P-38 Lightnings.

April 19: A force of more that 2,000 SS men under General Jürgen Stroop, sent by SS chief Heinrich Himmler to empty the Warsaw Ghetto, are unexpectedly driven out by lightly armed Jewish residents.

April 21: Responding to rumors that the Japanese are executing American POWs, President Roosevelt promises to follow through with his plan to prosecute war criminals.

April 23: Hitler demands "utmost severity" from his SS troops in their suppression of the Warsaw Ghetto uprising. • The Allies establish a London-based command under British lieutenant general Frederick Morgan to plan an invasion of Axis-controlled Europe.

April 24: A U.S. Navy fleet departs San Francisco en route to Alaska's Aleutian Islands to reclaim the Japanese-occupied island of Attu.

April 25: Turncoat Chinese army commander Sun Tien-ying joins the Japanese.

Fears in the Aleutians Soldiers unload supplies during the invasion of Attu. The recapture of this remote, inhospitable island in the American Aleutian chain (off Alaska) cost the lives of 549 Americans from May 11 to 31, 1943. The operation was prompted by fears that the island—seized by the Japanese in June 1942—could serve as a base for air attacks on the U.S. mainland and threaten sea lanes between Seattle and the Soviet Union. Hindsight indicates that the invasion was driven as much by national pride and a determination to eject Japanese occupiers from American soil than by any overwhelming strategic concerns.

Japanese fight to the death on Attu A Japanese soldier who bound his own wounds and fought to the death lies sprawled in a defensive position on the island of Attu. The Japanese occupied Attu in June 1942. This operation was designed to divert American forces from the defense of Midway and

Hawaii. Since the Japanese expected to annex Alaska, a base in the Aleutians would have been a good place to start.

Chinese, Japanese battle in Burma Chinese soldiers battle Japanese units along the Salween River in Burma in June 1943. Spurred by American insistence, 16 Chinese divisions commanded by General Wei Li-Huang crossed the river on the night of May 11–12. Their mission was to trap enemy forces by seizing key terrain north and south of the Burma Road. Fierce Japanese resistance slowed the attack. Chinese forces to the south reached the outskirts of Lung-ling on the Burma Road in early June before a counterattack pushed them back. Lacking adequate supplies, the Chinese offensive finally stalled.

Stilwell commands Chinese in Burma U.S. lieutenant general Joseph Stilwell is pictured with Generalissimo and Madame Chiang Kai-shek. A prewar military attaché to China, Stilwell became U.S. commander of the resource-starved China-Burma-India theater in 1942. He nominally commanded Chinese forces in north Burma, from which he led survivors into India. "Vinegar Joe" bluntly described the 1942 Burma campaign as a "licking" that he wanted to reverse. In the Byzantine atmosphere of Chungking, the abrasive and cunning Stilwell alienated Chiang while seeking to improve the quality of U.S. aid and Chinese troops. The latter helped him win a crucial victory in northern Burma in August 1944, but Chiang persuaded Roosevelt to recall Stilwell that October.

Race riots rage in U.S.
Federal troops patrol Detroit in June 1943 after 34 people were killed in a race riot. Detroit defense industries had recruited African Americans from the South, but the city's segregation limited housing and services available to blacks. That month, riots broke out in Los Angeles when returning servicemen marched against Mexican American "Zoot Suiters." In August, another race riot erupted in New York City's West Harlem. The U.S. Army—itself accused of racial prejudice—intervened in all three conflicts. Concerned about possible protests from the southern wing of his party, President Roosevelt avoided comment on the riots.

1943

April 26: Angered by the investigation and accusations surrounding the Katyn massacre, Soviet officials sever diplomatic relations with Poland's government-in-exile. • A United States force reaches Alaska and begins its assault on the Japanese-held Aleutian island of Attu.

April 28–30: German panzer units attack Djebel Bou Aoukaz, Tunisia, in what will be Germany's last offensive armored maneuver in North Africa.

April 30: The British launch Operation Mincemeat by releasing a corpse—which is dressed as a British officer and carries falsified war plans—off the coast of Spain. The "plans," which indicate that the Allies will attack Greece and Sardinia, and not Sicily as long suspected, will successfully divert Axis defenses from several key fronts.

May: War shortages affect civilians on both sides of the Atlantic, as Canada introduces meat rationing while Germany further reduces the size of existing rations. • Due to improved Allied interception technology, Germany will lose a third of its U-boats out on patrol this month. This leads German admiral Karl Dönitz to implicitly concede an Allied victory in the Battle of the North Atlantic when he repositions his fleet to the south.

May 1: German and Italian forces retreat in Tunisia.

May 2: The war reaches Australian shores once more when Japanese aircraft pound the port city of Darwin in the Northern Territory.

May 7: A day after destroying Germany's 15th Panzer Division, the Allies score a major victory with the fall of the Tunisian capital of Tunis. Approximately 250,000 Axis soldiers will surrender in the upcoming days.

Eager to serve As a recruitment incentive, three young women declare their marital principles. Many American men who received deferments from the draft were embarrassed not to be in the military. However, a 4-F classification (physically, mentally, or morally unfit for service) could be based on something as intractable as color blindness. Others were deferred because their jobs were essential to the nation. Of some 10 million who received deferments, about 4.5 million appealed their classification.

U.S. bonds finance the war Treasury Department workers such as these received, checked, and counted a million Series E bonds daily, sealing them into packages of 4,000 for distribution. Sold at 75 percent of its face value, a "war bond" matured in 10 years to $25, $50, $75, $100, $200, $500, $1,000, or $10,000. War bonds were promoted on posters, in ads contributed by radio stations and print publications, at sports events, and via celebrity appearances. More than 85 million Americans (most of the population) spent a total of more than $185 billion on War Bonds —at a time when the median annual income was about $2,000. The bonds helped finance the war effort and took cash out of the economy to control inflation.

Nisei Troops

"BEFORE WORLD WAR II," U.S. admiral Chester Nimitz recalled, "I entertained some doubt as to the loyalty of American citizens of Japanese ancestry in the event of war with Japan. From my observations during World War II, I no longer have that doubt." The admiral's lack of trust in Japanese Americans had been shared by many at the beginning of the war.

Following the attack on Pearl Harbor, Japanese Americans were widely viewed as potential spies and saboteurs. Those of draft age were classified 4-C (enemy alien). Federal officials were more accepting of Nisei—second-generation Americans of Japanese descent—than of first-generation. After taking an oath of allegiance, the 100th Infantry Battalion, comprised of more than 1,400 Nisei, was activated. It fought in Italy in 1943, and suffered so many casualties that it was called the "Purple Heart Battalion."

In 1943 the 100th was assigned to the 442nd Regiment Combat Team, a segregated unit of Japanese Americans. The 442nd's motto was "Go for Broke." In 1944 the regiment saved the 141st Infantry Regiment, the "Lost Battalion" that had been surrounded by German forces in northern France. By the end of the war, the 442nd had suffered more casualties and won more medals than any other outfit of its size and length of service.

Color guard of the 442nd Regiment Combat Team

Japanese Americans also served the American armed forces in the Pacific Theater as interpreters. About 60 Nisei were being trained at the Military Intelligence Service Language School in San Francisco when Pearl Harbor was attacked. By war's end, 2,000 Nisei had served in Pacific combat zones as interpreters, interrogators, and translators. They earned the moniker "Yankee Samurai."

Nisei troops prove their mettle
Japanese American troops who comprised the all-volunteer 442nd Regiment Combat Team were drawn from Hawaii as well as from stateside internment camps. During basic training at Camp Shelby, Mississippi, mainland recruits labeled the rural Hawaiians "buddaheads," from the Japanese word *buta* (pig). The islanders shot back with "kotonks," from the sound of an empty coconut hitting the ground. Before tensions cooled, fights were common, and although the average Nisei was just 5'3" and 125 pounds, he proved himself as good in a scrap as he later did in battle.

1943

May 7: Japanese dominance on the Burma front continues unabated, as they handily capture Buthidaung from the Allies.

May 8: Operation Retribution, an Allied naval operation designed to prevent the Axis from safely retreating from the North African front, is staged in the Strait of Sicily. • British women ages 18 to 45 are now required to fill part-time national service jobs.

May 9: Three days after the Allies launch what will prove to be their last offensive against Axis positions in North Africa, several *Wehrmacht* units in North Africa surrender. All Axis forces in North Africa will officially surrender on May 12. • Concerned by an apparent increase in resistance activities among the Dutch, the German occupation force imposes martial law throughout the Netherlands. • The Allies score an intelligence coup when a German flight crew defects.

May 12: Thoroughly fooled by Operation Mincemeat, Hitler orders Axis reinforcements to Greece's Peloponnese while relaxing defenses on Sicily.

May 13: As a prelude to a full-scale assault in Sicily, the Allies attack Pantelleria, a small Italian island about 30 miles off the Tunisian coast and strategically located in the Strait of Sicily.

May 15: The Axis launches Operation Black in Yugoslavia, a military action designed to crush Josip Broz Tito's Communist partisans.

May 16–17: An RAF raid causes extensive damage to two of Germany's largest dams and important sources of hydroelectric power. Nearly 1,300 people die in the ensuing floods.

"Don't rush me. I'm going to enjoy this. It's the last meal I'll eat in this world."

—SOVIET TANK CREWMAN TO A COMRADE, MINUTES BEFORE THE MOMENTOUS TANK BATTLE AT KURSK, RUSSIA, EARLY JULY 1943

Million-man armies clash at Kursk Following its defeat at Stalingrad, the German Army formed a massive line of defense, with Leningrad to the north and Rostov in the south. It had a 118-miles-long and 75-miles-deep salient, with Kursk at its center. It was no surprise to the Soviets that the Nazis intended to attack them within the salient in an attempt to trap hundreds of thousands of Red troops. By the beginning of May 1943, more than a million Soviet soldiers and 3,600 tanks faced almost a million Germans with 2,700 tanks. Here, Soviet soldiers and tanks advance during the battle.

Fighting intensifies

Although the Germans had set May 4, 1943, as the date of the Kursk attack, it was delayed two months while they waited for new tanks to arrive. The battle opened early on July 5, when nearly 1,000 artillery pieces pummeled the German position. The barrage was answered by German guns and then the approach of German tanks—Tiger I, Panther, MK IV, and MK III—which penetrated 20 miles into the Soviet line on the 6th. As the Germans advanced, however, they were met with very stiff resistance. In this picture, a distraught German soldier sits with his battered artillery piece and a dead comrade.

Soviets halt German advance Soviet tanks, troops, and artillery stubbornly fought the advancing Germans, inflicting heavy casualties for each mile gained. As the Second SS Panzer Corps advanced on July 12 out of the town of Prokhorovka, it was met by the Soviet Fifth Guards Tank Army. About 1,200 tanks participated in this battle, the largest tank fight of the war. Although the Soviets suffered many more casualties than the Germans, the advance was halted. The Allied invasion of Sicily caused Hitler to order the Second SS Panzer Corps to Italy. Facing weakened resistance, the Soviets launched an offensive, which they would maintain until the end of the war.

UNSTOPPABLE CARNAGE

THEN IT HAPPENED. It was about six o'clock in the morning. Our tanks and our cavalry suddenly appeared and rushed straight into the thick of the two columns. What happened then is hard to describe. The Germans ran in all directions. And for the next four hours our tanks raced up and down the plain crushing them by the hundreds.... Hundreds and hundreds of cavalry were hacking at them with their sabers, and massacred the Fritzes as no one had ever been massacred by cavalry before. There was no time to take prisoners. It was a kind of carnage that nothing could stop till it was all over.

—RECOLLECTION OF THE FEBRUARY 17, 1943, SOVIET ROUT OF GERMAN FORCES IN THE KORSUN SALIENT, CENTRAL UKRAINE, BY RED ARMY MAJOR KAMPOV

Scorched-earth policies As the German Army pushed the Soviets through the Ukraine in 1941 and 1942, Stalin ordered his army and civilians to destroy anything that could be useful to the Germans, including industrial facilities, rail lines (*pictured*), communication lines, and shelter. The Germans practiced their own scorched-earth policy in 1943 and 1944 as they retreated through Russia and Europe. As his country was collapsing in March 1945, Hitler ordered his armaments minister, Albert Speer, to destroy any German resources not yet in Allied hands. Unknown to Hitler, Speer never carried out the order.

Ukrainian laborers Once the German army occupied the Ukraine, it attempted to attract large numbers of workers for German factories. Failing to supply the necessary number of workers voluntarily, the occupying troops began to ship large numbers of Ukrainians to Germany forcibly. Called *Ostarbeiter* (East workers), about three million were eventually deported to manufacture war supplies for the German army and other work. Many died from overwork and starvation while others were killed in Allied attacks on German factories. After the war, most workers were repatriated to the Ukraine, where many were killed or imprisoned by the Soviets on political grounds or because of purported collaboration.

1943

May 17: The British MI6 and the American Office of Strategic Services agree to share cipher intelligence. They also agree to the designation "Ultra" for all Axis code intelligence. • Allied ships traverse the Mediterranean unmolested by Axis ships for the first time since Italy entered the war, offering tangible proof that the Axis has quit North Africa.

May 19: Peter Dönitz, son of the German admiral, dies when his U-boat is sunk by the Allies.

May 19–20: The Allies heavily bomb Sicily and Sardinia as a precursor to their invasion of Italy.

May 22: The German Messerschmitt Me 262 jet plane reaches speeds of 520 mph in its inaugural test-flight, giving the *Luftwaffe* newfound optimism. • Stalin dissolves the Comintern in an effort to quell Allied concerns over Soviet ambitions of world domination.

May 23: The Allies attack Dortmund, Germany, with more than 800 planes, dropping more than 2,000 tons of bombs in what is the most intense air raid of the war to date. Nearly 700 civilians will lose their lives.

May 24: Dr. Josef Mengele becomes the camp doctor at Auschwitz. He will soon become infamous for conducting cruel and inhumane experiments on the prisoners. • Admiral Karl Dönitz recalls most of the German U-boats in the Atlantic after losing many of them to Allied aggression.

May 25: Roosevelt and Churchill conclude a successful summit in Washington, D.C. The meeting produces several strategic decisions regarding the continued prosecution of the war, most significantly setting the date for the invasion of France at May 1, 1944.

"It was not lust, but necessity, not depravity of the soul but the urge of the instinct to survive which led numerous women into the ranks of amateur prostitute...." —U.S. ARMY DOCTOR, NAPLES, ITALY, 1943

Sex and War

WAR NOTORIOUSLY DISRUPTS traditional morality, and such was the case during the biggest war of all. From female teenagers jitterbugging with British airmen in Alberta, to brothels condoned or organized by armies, to rapes committed with or without official knowledge, World War II affected sexual behavior across the globe.

The demands of war made millions of lonely, fearful men and women mobile. Many found solace in relations that were more accessible than they had been in peacetime, mixing at dances or in bars. Traditional moralists decried the spread of disease and out-of-wedlock pregnancies. (Military commanders regarded sexually transmitted

RAF officer with a French woman

diseases as an efficiency problem.) Propaganda stigmatized the "good-time girl" as dangerous, although many women felt liberated by wartime sex. Gays in the military found that service gave them unprecedented opportunities to discreetly meet other homosexuals.

In previous wars, armies in enemy territory had frequently, if tacitly, condoned rape. In this war, sex crimes involving people from Allied nations were often punished severely. However, some Allied forces (especially French colonial troops and New Zealand Maoris in Italy) gained a reputation for sexual brutality. Soviet troops in Germany used rape as a weapon of terror and revenge against literally millions of hapless German women in 1945.

When large numbers of well-paid servicemen arrived in impoverished countries, prostitution became rampant. The practice was common in Egypt, Italy, and India (especially around Calcutta), as well as in Germany after its defeat.

Axis soldiers generally raped without retribution, notably in Nanking, China, in 1937, where Japanese soldiers raped tens of thousands of Chinese women. The Japanese army operated officially sanctioned brothels, in which tens of thousands of Asian women, mainly from occupied Korea, were used, mostly against their will. In 2007, Japanese prime minister Abe Shinzo formally apologized for Japan's treatment of Asian "comfort women" during the war.

Allies invade Sicily

After the Axis defeat in North Africa, the Allies' next objective became the enemy's airfields and ports in Sicily. They also hoped that the fall of Sicily would force Italy out of the war. The plan called for American and Allied paratroopers to jump on the evening of July 9–10, followed the next morning by one of largest amphibious landings of the war with 160,000 British troops, 600 tanks, and 1,800 artillery pieces. These are two of the 26,000 Canadians who participated in the landing.

Allies ship materiel through Iran At the beginning of World War II, the Allies were aggravated by supposedly neutral Iran's coziness with Germany. On August 26, 1941, Britain and the Soviets invaded Iran, forcing Reza Shah to abdicate. The Allies then were free to move what ultimately amounted to more than five millions tons of materiel across Iran into Russia. The Soviet troops seen here operated horse-drawn wagons fitted with machine guns, as part of a joint Russo-British military exercise.

The adventures of Sad Sack Sergeant George Baker, a former Disney animator, points to his comic strip character Sad Sack, who debuted in the U.S. Army weekly *Yank* magazine in 1942. Sad Sack was a lowly, chinless U.S. Army private who, in the long tradition of service humor, was ever the butt of the humiliating absurdities of military life. During his three-and-a-half-year stint with *Yank,* Sad Sack haplessly toured every theater of World War II, always in pantomime. His postwar appearances in anthologies, newspaper strips, comic books, radio shows, and a movie brought him to an even larger audience.

American cargo ships This painting by American artist Thornton Oakley shows a U.S. cargo ship unloading scrap materials—indicating both Nazi and U.S. air force losses—to be recycled. In the background, more ships wait. Cargo ships carried food, ammunition, clothing, guns, and troops. These U.S. merchant vessels came in all sizes and were outfitted with cranes for loading and unloading. They were subject to destruction by mines, battleships, bombers, submarines, and *kamikaze* attacks. During the war, 733 cargo ships were lost and more than 5,000 U.S. merchant seamen were killed.

1943

May 29: Chinese forces arrest the progress of the Japanese army.

May 30: Almost 20 days after U.S. troops first landed on the Aleutian island of Attu, it is finally recaptured from the Japanese, who lose some 2,000 soldiers in the battle.

June 2: Pope Pius XII sends a pointed message to the Allies in which he implicitly condemns the routine targeting of civilians in "terror" bombing campaigns, although he has not commented on German bombing.

June 3: German mining operations sink *Halma,* a cargo ship sailing under the Panamanian flag, off the coast of Halifax, Nova Scotia. • French generals Charles de Gaulle and Henri Giraud join forces in Algiers to create the French Committee of National Liberation. Their organization will act as the French authority wherever the French empire exists beyond the reach of the Nazis. • The Michelin tire plant in Clermont-Ferrand, France, is sabotaged by the Resistance, costing the Reich some 300 tons of tires. • The plane carrying British serviceman Leslie Howard, the actor who played Ashley Wilkes in the screen version of Margaret Mitchell's *Gone With the Wind,* is shot down by Axis planes over the Bay of Biscay.

June 6: In a speech ironically delivered a year to the day prior to the Allied invasion of Normandy, General de Gaulle insists that France does not want assistance throwing off the Nazi yoke, claiming, "We intend to win our liberty ourselves."

June 7: The Axis discovers the "Comet Line," an underground network of safe houses established in 1940 to rescue Allies trapped behind enemy lines. The houses stretched from Belgium through France, Spain, and Gibraltar.

Indian faction sides with the Axis A one-time colleague of Mohandas Gandhi in the struggle for Indian independence, Subhash Chandra Bose chose a drastically different course from his pacifistic countryman by aligning with the Axis powers during World War II. In 1942 he created the Azad Hind Fauj, also called the Indian National Army, from 40,000 Indian men who had been taken prisoner by the Japanese. Bose's efforts to liberate India with Axis military backing ultimately failed. Here, Bose (*right*) reviews his army alongside Japanese prime minister Tojo Hideki in Singapore.

Allies slowed by intense heat, resistance Rough terrain and the stubborn resistance of German troops slowed the Allied advance across Sicily. Oppressive heat (100°F) also affected the advance. More than 10,000 Allied soldiers became sick with heat exhaustion and malaria. Those Allied troops who could still fight found that the enemy would not go down easily. The British capture of the town of Centuripe exemplified the intensity of combat. The British 78th Division launched its attack on the town on July 31, and needed four days of treacherous house-to-house fighting to finally capture it.

The Axis defense of Sicily Sicily was defended by some 300,000 Italian and 40,000 German troops with 50 tanks and 200 pieces of artillery. The Germans were formidable foes for the Allies, but the Italians were ill-equipped and badly trained, and had poor morale. German commanders realized that, given an opportunity, many Italians would surrender to the Allies. Lacking equipment and manpower to launch an effective counterstrike, Axis coastal troops encircled the island. In addition, German and Italian divisions were concentrated at the most likely Allied landing sites to prevent them from establishing a beachhead. Here, an Italian soldier mans a gun post on the coast.

Spaatz's many commands
American Carl Andrew "Tooey" Spaatz held U.S. and Allied commands, including the U.S. Eighth Air Force, the 12th in North Africa (1942), the U.S. 15th, the Royal Air Force in Italy, and the Allied North-

west African Air Force (1943). In 1943, finding himself bypassed by British Command communications, Spaatz set up his own network, known as "Redline." Lieutenant General Spaatz took charge of the U.S. Strategic Air Forces in Europe in January 1944, but his plans to defeat the *Luftwaffe* before the Normandy Invasion by striking German oil and aviation industries were blocked by more hesitant British commander Sir Trafford Leigh-Mallory. After lengthy deliberation, British air chief marshal Sir Arthur Tedder (Eisenhower's deputy) finally supported Spaatz's strategy.

Cunningham stars in Mediterranean British admiral Sir Andrew Browne Cunningham, the naval commander-in-chief in the Mediterranean, aggressively destroyed Italian warships and ran supplies to Malta. Using obsolete Swordfish aircraft, he mounted the first all-aircraft naval attack in history at Taranto in November 1940, cutting the Italian fleet in half. When Germany seized Crete in May 1941, Cunningham insisted on evacuating 16,500 trapped Allied troops in the face of heavy *Luftwaffe* opposition. He commanded the Naval Task Forces during Operation Torch—the November 1942 British-American invasion of French North Africa—under General Dwight Eisenhower, who praised Cunningham for his intelligence, devotion, and selflessness.

The power of the Browning The Browning automatic rifle (BAR), seen here on its bipod, was used by U.S. infantry throughout World War II. A lightweight, gas-operated weapon with a 20-round magazine, the WWII model of the Browning (unlike earlier versions) did not include a semi-automatic, single-fire option. Instead, it was solely automatic with an adjustable rate of fire. It therefore functioned more like a light machine gun than a traditional military rifle. Despite its drawbacks (including difficult cleaning, a tendency to overheat, and a recoil mechanism with a tendency for corrosion), the BAR was extremely useful for spreading heavy fire, and was standard at the squad level.

1943

June 8: Japanese military leaders order their troops to evacuate the Aleutian island of Kiska.

June 11: SS chief Heinrich Himmler orders the resettlement of all remaining Jews in occupied Poland from urban ghettos to death camps.

June 11–12: The RAF stages a massive air raid against Düsseldorf, Germany, bombing the city from some 800 planes.

June 13: Soviet director Mikhail Slutsky and 240 camera operators shoot *Day of War,* a documentary record of a day on the Russian front.
• Seventy-four die when the Germans drop antipersonnel bombs on Allied troops in a raid over Britain.

June 15: Germany conducts a test-flight of the first jet-powered bomber, the Arado Ar 234.

June 16: The U.S. enjoys a dramatic victory in the skies over Guadalcanal. An attacking Japanese force is mauled, losing 107 of 120 planes.

June 17: In an effort to reduce the number of collateral air-war casualties, the BBC warns civilians living near Axis factories to evacuate to safer ground.

June 18: The Allies "soften" Sicily with a pre-invasion bombing campaign.

June 20: For the first time, the Allies engage in "shuttle" bombing, hitting more than one target per bombing sortie and resting and refueling at remote bases between stops.

June 21: Heinrich Himmler orders the Jewish ghettos of occupied Russia emptied and their remaining occupants deported to the death camps.

June 22: The USAAF attacks the German Ruhr region in daylight for the first time, temporarily decommissioning a critical rubber factory.

"Nobody ever defended anything successfully. There is only attack and attack and attack some more."

—U.S. ARMY GENERAL GEORGE PATTON

The audacious General Patton
"All real Americans love the sting and clash of battle," declared General George Patton in an otherwise largely unprintable speech to soldiers in 1944. Profane, mystical, flamboyant, and audacious, Patton was undoubtedly America's most controversial general during World War II—especially when he slapped and verbally abused two shell-shocked soldiers for what he considered their cowardice. His skills as a tank commander, honed during World War I, proved valuable in North Africa in 1942—and in Sicily the following year. He showed his most dazzling leadership during the Battle of the Bulge of 1944–45, in which his Third Army's incredibly swift, bold movements drove back Germany's desperate last offensive on the Western Front.

Patton's troops liberate Palermo Still stung by the poor performance of American troops at Kasserine Pass in Tunisia earlier in 1943, General George Patton was determined to show the British the fighting skills of his men at Sicily. "This is a horse race in which the prestige of the U.S. Army is at stake," he wrote to General Troy Middleton, his 45th Division commander. "We must take Messina before the British." On July 22, Patton's men took Palermo, as seen in this picture, making it the first West European city to be liberated. Allied troops were greeted like this throughout Sicily.

Soviet Fighting Women

WOMEN SERVED IN THE FORCES of other Allied belligerents, but Soviet women were unique in their role as combatants. Between a half-million and one million Soviet women served in the armed forces or as partisans.

In 1943 women comprised eight percent of the Soviet armed forces. Although many female recruits served behind the front, up to half were at the front. One source puts the total there in 1945 at 246,000. Women soldiers fought as snipers, mortar crew members, tank drivers, artillery crew, and medics. They were given few if any sanitary and medical amenities.

Female aviators won particular acclaim. Marina Raskova, a celebrated prewar aviator, took the initiative in the creation of the all-female Aviation Group 122 in October 1941. It trained air and ground crews for three regiments—the 586th Fighter, 587th Bomber, and 588th Night Bomber. Among them, these units flew 30,000 combat missions and produced at least two aces, including Lilia Litviak. The 587th and 588th received the coveted "Guards" appellation as elite units.

Soviet soldiers with snow gear and skis

Other women served in mixed aviation regiments, and 33 Soviet female aviators received the title "Hero of the Soviet Union." So did some 57 other women. More than 100,000 women received one or more Soviet decorations. The nation regarded its use of women combatants as temporary. After the war, the women were rapidly demobilized, passing into historical obscurity.

Cavalry forces prove valuable In 1946 a U.S. *Intelligence Bulletin* reported, "Red Army cavalry units have proven the right of the almost legendary Cossack to remain part of the armed forces of the U.S.S.R." Mounted troops such as these could move through forests, swamps, and other terrain impassable by mechanized forces. They also could avoid air attacks by operating at night. Mounted troops sometimes flanked enemy units, staging surprise counterattacks and setting up roadblocks against retreats. The cavalry filled in gaps on the battlefield and covered Soviet withdrawals. Where needed, they dismounted and operated as infantry forces.

1943

June 24: African American troops and American military police engage in a gun battle in the streets of the village of Bamber Bridge, England, after the MPs attempted to detain the soldiers in a pub.

June 25: The ghettoized Jews of Czestochowa, Poland, are transported to Auschwitz after the SS crushes their resistance.

June 27: Following Jewish resistance, the ghetto at Lvov, Poland, is officially closed. Most of its 20,000 residents are en route to the Belzec or Auschwitz death camps. • The Allies attack the Greek mainland with a bombing raid. They target air facilities near Athens.

June 28: The air war continues in earnest, with Allied planes hitting such targets as Livorno, Italy, and Messina, Sicily.

June 30: The U.S. launches Operation Cartwheel in the Pacific, beginning in the central Solomon Islands. • As Washington closes the books on its fiscal year, it is revealed that a full 93 percent of the federal budget was allocated to national defense spending.

July 4: Prime Minister-in-Exile General Wladyslaw Sikorski and other members of Poland's ruling elite die when their plane crashes immediately after takeoff from the airport at Gibraltar. With the Soviet Union and Axis alike potentially benefiting from Sikorski's demise, there will be no shortage of conspiracy theories in the aftermath.

July 5: A German attack on Red forces at Kursk ends with a decisive Soviet victory. • Boise City, Oklahoma, is inadvertently bombed by a B-17 pilot who mistakes the lights on the town square for his training target.

The reliable, versatile P-38 The P-38 was designed to meet a 1936 U.S. Air Corps specification for a twin-engined interceptor. Lockheed's first military aircraft, the P-38 faced teething problems and went through numerous modifications before and after deliveries began in 1941. Ultimately, its reliability, exceptional range, and versatility compensated for its slightly inferior maneuverability. About 10,000 were built, including versions that carried rockets, lugged up to 4,000 pounds of bombs, and acted as ambulances and photographic aircraft. Lightnings, as the British and then Americans called them, saw action in North Africa, Europe, and the Pacific.

The Battle of Kolombangara Sailors examine the bow of the USS *Honolulu*, blasted by a Japanese torpedo in the Battle of Kolombangara. This cruiser and two others, as well as 10 destroyers, intercepted a Japanese naval force attempting to land reinforcements at the island on the night of July 12–13, 1943. U.S. commander Admiral W. L. Ainsworth relied on Radar to give him the advantage, but he failed to reckon with the lethal "Long Lance" torpedoes carried by Japanese destroyers. The Japanese lost the cruiser *Jintsu* to naval gunfire, but severely damaged all three Allied cruisers. The Japanese landed their reinforcements as planned.

Navajo code-talkers Navajo Indians radio a message during fighting in the Pacific. The Navajo code-talker teams were used to relay radio and phone messages in their native dialect during combat operations. The method was fast and indecipherable to enemy eavesdroppers. At the time of World War II, the Navajo language was understood by fewer than 30 non-Navajos. The code was never broken by the Japanese, and its security has been credited with contributing significantly to the seizure of Iwo Jima in 1945. Approximately 400 Navajo code-talkers served with the six U.S. Marine divisions during the war.

America's female pilots Shirley Slade, with the Women's Flying Training Detachment (WFTD), appears on the cover of *Life*. In August 1943, the WFTD merged with the Women's Auxiliary Ferrying Squadron (WAFS) to form the Women Air Force Service Pilots (WASP). The WASPs were American civilian pilots who freed male pilots for combat duty. Some, including Slade, were ferry pilots, transporting military aircraft from factories to embarkation ports and training bases. Others served as test pilots, trainers, and combat simulators. Despite their noncombat status, they faced real dangers. Of the 1,074 WASPs active during the war, 38 lost their lives.

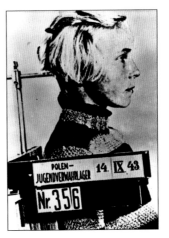

Polish kidnappings A Polish girl is chosen for inclusion in the Nazi *Heuaktion* (Hay Action) program. This program involved the kidnapping of "Germanic-looking" children and taking them to *Lebensborn* (source of life) institutions. Even though the Nazis considered Poles inferior, they took selected children with "Aryan" characteristics from their parents and raised them as Germans. Estimates of children kidnapped from Eastern countries run as high as 250,000. Only about 25,000 were returned to their families after the war. Some German families refused to give up the children, and some children refused to believe they were not originally German. Many children who did not adapt well were exterminated in concentration camps.

"War without mercy" This photograph was taken on Tulagi, near Guadalcanal in the Solomon Islands, in July 1943. Admiral William "Bull" Halsey commanded the South Pacific Area at that time. He galvanized the tired ground and naval American forces fighting in the Solomons, and led them to the signal victory at Guadalcanal. Halsey was unconventional, but his full-blooded hatred of the Japanese was not. The Pacific conflict has been called a "war without mercy." Allied troops' ruthlessness was prompted by prewar racism and personal experience of the extraordinary viciousness of their opponents.

1943

July 5–6: The light cruiser USS *Helena* is sunk in the overnight Battle of Kula Gulf. More than 150 of its sailors perish in the oil-slicked waters off the Solomon Islands.

July 7: The island of Malta, which suffered hundreds of punishing raids in the early days of the air war, receives word that Britain will grant it independence after the conclusion of hostilities.

July 8: Jean Moulin, the celebrated French Resistance leader, dies after weeks of torture at the hands of Klaus Barbie, the "Butcher of Lyon."

July 9: The USAAF and RAF drop paratroopers on Sicily. However, they are mistakenly dropped in an area too far remote from their destination to fulfill their mission of securing airfields for the imminent Allied invasion.

July 10: More than 150,000 Allied soldiers land on Sicily, catching the meager Axis defensive force completely by surprise.

July 12: Some 3,000 tanks clash in the Battle of Kursk, the largest tank battle in world history. Although the Soviets will lose more tanks than the Germans, they can replace them more quickly.

July 13: In a desperate bid to realign his forces, Hitler reallocates troops from the Russian front to reinforce the defense of Italy.

July 14: The Allies stage an intense bombing raid on the Sicilian city of Messina, which serves as the importation point for Axis troops and materiel.

July 15: The Japanese naval air force suffers a stunning defeat, losing 45 of 75 planes while knocking out only three U.S. aircraft in a daylight raid against the Allies in the Solomon Islands.

Kids contribute to war effort American youngsters participated enthusiastically in wartime "victory drives," collecting scrap metal, aluminum foil, rubber, and other materials that could be reused. Some pulled their wagons from door to door collecting old tools and appliances from their neighbors.

Here, boys pose on a scrap metal heap, displaying their finds along with a poster of the American flag. Kids also helped cultivate homegrown vegetables in community or family "victory gardens," and they took over jobs such as mixing yellow dye into the white butter substitute called oleomargarine.

The Stooges take on the *Führer* Because Hitler struck Americans as eccentric as well as intimidating, the *Führer* became ripe for parody. In a 1943 comedy short called *They Stooge to Conga*, the Three Stooges are inept handymen who stumble into a nest of German and Japanese agents. In short order, the boys impersonate Nazis, kick a few spies in the pants, and successfully foul up an Axis scheme to direct a German U-boat into New York Harbor. Moe Howard (*far right*) had lampooned Hitler, and the imaginary Axis nation of Moronica, in two earlier Stooges comedies, *You Nazty Spy!* (1940) and *I'll Never Heil Again* (1941).

BOMBS OVER HAMBURG

THERE WERE WALLS OF FLAME round them now. Suddenly into the square came a fire engine drawn by two startled horses. They swerved aside, and one of the terrified children rushed down a side street. The mother followed, leaving her boy behind. As the first child reached a burning house, some blazing wood fell near her, setting her clothes alight. The mother threw herself on top of the child to try and smother the flames, but as she did so the whole top floor of the house opposite crashed down on the two of them.

—HAMBURG RESIDENT ELSE WENDEL, RECALLING THE JULY 27, 1943, ALLIED BOMB RAID ON HAMBURG

Bombing raids devastate Hamburg The residents of Hamburg, Germany, had suffered through many British and American air raids since British planes began bombing runs in mid-November 1940. They were not prepared, however, for the payload that the Allies dropped on July 27–29, 1943. High-explosive and incendiary bombs dropped on those two nights unleashed firestorms that consumed nine square miles of the city in fire. The attacks killed more than 45,000 civilians and soldiers and left more than a million residents homeless.

Non-Germans join the *Waffen-SS* Beginning in 1942, Heinrich Himmler sought to expand the *Waffen-SS* by recruiting in other nations. The multinational forces, operating under German officers, included French, Danish, Flemish, Norwegian, Finnish, Dutch, and others. They even included Russians, Albanians, Hungarians, Ukrainians, and Bosnian Muslims—all of whom the Nazis generally classed as inferior *Untermenschen.* As many as 30 British citizens and about five Americans joined. Some volunteers supported Nazi ideas. Others, including the *Nederlanders* (Dutchmen) appealed to on this poster, could escape forced labor by becoming SS members.

America's secretary of war Following a distinguished career that included service as secretary of state under President Herbert Hoover, Henry L. Stimson was named secretary of war by President Roosevelt in 1940. A longtime critic of Japanese aggression, Stimson skillfully organized American industrial and economic might during the war years. He also directed the expansion of the Army to more than 10 million troops, and he was a key decision-maker on the atomic bomb project. At the same time, he expressed deep moral objections to the Allied bombing of civilian populations—particularly the fire-bombing of Japanese cities.

1943

July 16: In an Allied leaflet drop over Italy, President Roosevelt and Prime Minister Churchill ask the Italian people if they would like to "die for Mussolini and Hitler...or live for Italy and for civilization."

July 17: Hitler orders reinforcement of German forces to the Balkan States, believing the region will be the site of the Allies' next move.

July 19: Pope Pius XII offers to shelter Italians in Vatican City as the Allies drop more than 500 tons of munitions on strategic targets around Rome.

July 20: Reversing an earlier order, Roosevelt directs his Los Alamos team to share advances in atomic weapons research with America's British allies.

July 22: The Allies capture Palermo, the administrative seat of Sicily and the provincial capital.

July 25: Having lost the support of fellow politicians, his own military, and a majority of the Fascist Grand Council, Mussolini is ousted in a bloodless coup. • Naunita Harmon Carroll christens the destroyer escort *Harmon,* which is named for her late son. Leonard Roy Harmon, a hero of the Battle of Guadalcanal, is the first African American to be honored with a U.S. Navy ship. • Still thoroughly fooled by Operation Mincemeat, Hitler believes that the attack on Sicily is a diversion and sends Erwin Rommel, one of his better generals, to Greece. • Krupp steelworks in Essen, Germany, is put out of commission by a punishing air raid executed by more than 600 RAF bombers.

July 26: Pietro Badoglio, appointed by King Victor Emmanuel III to head the Italian government following the deposition of Mussolini, abolishes the Fascist political party.

The Marauder exceeds its reputation An engine of a B-26 Marauder is blown off by ground fire over the French city of Toulon. The American-made medium bomber was dubbed the "Widowmaker" after a number of disastrous early tests. Indeed, the plane was never popular with pilots, who jokingly claimed that it required half the state of Texas for take-off and glided like a flatiron. Nevertheless, it had the lowest loss record of any combat plane flown during WWII. In mid-1943, when the U.S. Ninth Air Force began serving a key tactical role in the European Theater, the Marauder was its primary bomber.

Fierce fighting on New Georgia Alert for Japanese snipers, GIs patrol a jungle track on New Georgia in the central Solomon Islands. The 43rd Infantry Division landed on New Georgia in July 1943 after U.S. intelligence learned that the Japanese were constructing an airfield on the island, at Munda. Enemy troop strength was greater than expected, and the offensive quickly bogged down. The Japanese sent in 4,000 reinforcements by sea via a convoy system dubbed the "Tokyo Express" to aid the 10,000 troops already on New Georgia. The battle settled into a slugfest, as the Americans also brought in reinforcements, including the 37th Infantry Division. The Allies finally occupied Munda on August 5.

German POWs in America

A S SOON AS THE 275,000 German and Italian members of the *Afrika Korps* surrendered at Tunisia in May 1943, Allied commanders faced a serious problem. They did not have the resources to sustain that many prisoners in North Africa. Allied leaders decided to transport the POWs to camps in the United States.

The first group of prisoners, arriving in the U.S. in August 1943, was transported to abandoned Civilian Conservation and military camps. Special camps were built in mid-America, far from the coasts and Canadian and Mexican borders. During the war, nearly 500,000 Axis prisoners were confined in 155 main POW camps or in more than 500 branch camps. In accordance with the Geneva Convention, these prisoners were put to work in nonmilitary jobs: logging, mining, harvesting crops, building roads, and other jobs important to the American economy.

The captives lived in comfortable barracks and were provided with basic necessities, such as food, clothing, and medical attention. If the jobs were outside the camp, the workers received pay enough to buy cigarettes or other items available in camp canteens. "When I was captured, I

German POWs in a saddle shop in Fort Carson, Colorado

weighed 128 pounds," one POW remembered years later. "After two years as an American POW, I weighed 185. I had gotten so fat you could no longer see my eyes." It was a stark contrast to the treatment of American POWs by their German captors.

Humane treatment for German POWs Axis soldiers imprisoned in America were treated much better than Allied prisoners in German and Japanese camps. A May 1945 *Newsweek* article noted that American POWs lost an unhealthy amount of weight during their confinement while Axis prisoners in America generally gained weight. Allied prisoners were often forced to march hundreds of miles when transferred from one German camp to another, while Germans were generally transported between camps by passenger trains. German prisoners also experienced freedoms that were not allowed to their Allied counterparts, such as saluting a Nazi flag at Camp Crossville, Tennessee (*pictured*).

1943

July 27–28: Some 20,000 German civilians die when an RAF raid on Hamburg ignites a series of deadly firestorms.

July 28: The U.S. continues to develop plans for an invasion of Kiska, unaware that the Japanese have secretly withdrawn from the Aleutian island.

August 1: The Americans hit Axis fuel supplies with a damaging air raid on the oil refineries in Ploesti, Romania.
• German troops begin to execute a plan to seize control of Italy in the wake of Mussolini's fall from power. The Germans infiltrate northern Italy and disarm Italian forces on Crete.
• With the occupation of Burma complete, the Japanese announce that Burma is henceforth independent, no longer a colony of Britain.
• Nazi propaganda minister Joseph Goebbels broadcasts an announcement on Berlin radio recommending the evacuation of all nonessential personnel. For many Germans in the capital city, this is the first admission that Berlin could be in jeopardy from heavy air raids.

August 2: An uprising at the Treblinka death camp leads to the deaths of 16 SS guards, while about 150 of the approximately 700 prisoners manage to escape in the melee.
• The Japanese destroyer *Amagiri* rams and sinks USS *PT-109*. Lieutenant John F. Kennedy and 10 of the 12 men under his command will survive the incident. Though Kennedy will be hailed by most for saving the crew, General MacArthur will be unimpressed with Kennedy and will question why the highly maneuverable PT boat was unable to evade the *Amagiri*.

August 4: About 150 Italian civilians die when the USAAF bombs the southern port of Naples.

GIs' favorite pinup girl
Far from home during World War II, American GIs found escape in the movies and image of actress, singer, and dancer Betty Grable. In 1943 the bubbly, accessible-seeming Grable was Hollywood's No. 1 star, and probably the highest-paid woman in America. In a publicity stunt engineered by her studio, 20th Century-Fox, her shapely legs were insured for $1 million. Servicemen voted her their favorite pinup girl, and her image decorated not just barracks walls but bomber jackets and aircraft. Even when Grable posed for pinups in bathing suits, she preserved her image as the wholesome "girl next door."

Raid on Ploesti By summer 1943, refineries in Ploesti, Romania (*pictured*), produced 60 percent of Germany's crude oil supply. The location was too far for bombers to reach from England, but the capture of Libya made such a raid possible. At dawn on August 1, 1943, 177 U.S. B-24 bombers flew out of Libya for a raid on Ploesti, one of the most heavily defended targets in Europe. Confusion after the lead navigators were shot down reduced the effectiveness of the raid. By the end, 54 bombers were lost. About 42 percent of the refineries' production capacity was lost, although they were rebuilt by the Germans within weeks.

Japanese demolish Kennedy's PT boat Naval lieutenant and future U.S. president John F. Kennedy rides aboard *PT-109* in the Southwest Pacific. Kennedy was at the helm in the early morning hours of August 2, 1943, when his PT boat (a motor torpedo boat) was rammed by the Japanese destroyer *Amagiri*. *PT-109* was sliced in half, and two crewmen were killed. Though Kennedy was later awarded the Navy and Marine Corps Medal for his actions following the sinking, some officers felt he should have been court-martialed for negligence. *PT-109* was the only PT boat in the war to be surprised and rammed by an enemy ship.

Vietnam's Ho helps the Allies Ho Chi Minh cooperated with the Allies during the war in hopes of obtaining Vietnamese independence from French rule. A fervent nationalist, Ho formed the Communist-dominated Viet Minh independence movement in 1941. Traveling to China in 1942 to

seek military assistance, he was arrested as a spy and spent 13 months in jail. Returning to Vietnam upon his release, he worked with the American Office of Strategic Services (OSS), rescuing Allied pilots shot down over Indochina and conducting operations against the Japanese. Despite his efforts, the U.S. government supported a return to French colonial rule after the war. Ho and his Communist forces would battle the United States in the Vietnam War.

The Nazis' portrayal of the Roosevelts In this 1943 German cartoon, President Franklin Roosevelt holds the war casualty list as Eleanor Roosevelt asks, "Have we lost many dollars, Delano?" The president replies, "Don't worry, Eleanor, we are paying only in human lives." Note the Star of David that Eleanor

Roosevelt wears and her exaggerated lips. Nazi propaganda frequently presented the Roosevelts as puppets of the Jews, and also made fun of the first lady's support of African American singer Marian Anderson.

FDR's vice president Henry Wallace was President Roosevelt's secretary of agriculture from 1933 to '40 and vice president from 1941 to '44. A committed anti-segregationist, he declared in a 1943 speech that America could not fight the Nazis abroad and condone racism at home. Wallace's vision of a postwar America included close relations with the Soviet Union. This position put him at odds with Roosevelt's successor to the presidency, the staunch Cold Warrior Harry Truman, who fired him from his cabinet post as secretary of commerce in 1946. Wallace made an unsuccessful run as the Progressive Party's presidential candidate in 1948.

1943

August 5: The Soviets recapture the city of Orel, Russia, from the Germans. • Sweden revokes the right of troop transit it had granted to the Germans at the beginning of the war. • A series of fierce battles concludes in the Pacific island chain of New Georgia, where the Japanese fled following their defeat on Guadalcanal. The Allies emerge victorious, capturing the airfield at Munda on New Georgia.

August 6–7: A small Japanese fleet attempting to resupply Japan's Solomon Islands base at Kolombangara is intercepted and badly damaged by a fleet of American destroyers.

August 9: In one of the first viable challenges to National Socialism in years, several German leaders form the Kreisau Circle, a resistance group calling for, among other things, the "acknowledgement of the inviolability of human dignity as the foundation for an order of peace and justice."

August 12: With Sicily all but lost to the Allies, Germany begins the successful withdrawal of a substantial portion of its reeling defensive force. Casualties include 32,000 Germans and 132,000 Italians. • More than 600 RAF bombers pummel Milan, Italy.

August 14: On orders from General Eisenhower, foul-tempered General George Patton apologizes to the two American soldiers he slapped in field hospitals after accusing them of malingering.

August 14–24: Allied leaders meet in Quebec for the Quadrant Conference, at which they hammer out details for the next phase of the war. It is decided that both the invasion of France and the occupation of Italy remain on the table. The invasion of France will take precedence.

Operation Strangle in Italy British general Bernard Montgomery (*left*) and American general Dwight Eisenhower study the Italian mainland. The lack of coordination between Allied commands in Sicily not only prolonged the fighting but also contributed to the escape of more than 100,000 Axis troops and thousands of vehicles across the Strait of Messina to the mainland. For several months, the Allied air force had been active in its own operation over Italy, Operation Strangle. The objective was to shut down the Axis supply lines throughout Italy. Rail facilities, railroads, and bridges were pounded from spring 1943 to 1944.

Battles for Kharkov Soviet tanks roll down a Kharkov street. Kharkov, the fifth largest Soviet city, was captured by the German Sixth Army on October 24, 1941. Soviet troops failed to recapture the city in May 1942. German defenders held off another Soviet attack in February 1943, but abandoned the city on the 16th when it was obvious they would be surrounded. Reinforced, these Germans mounted a counterattack in early March. Holding off Soviet attacks, the Germans retook the city on March 15. In the offensive thrust following their victory at Kursk, the Soviets drove German troops out of Kharkov for good in August.

Soviet Casualties

FOR THOSE WHO DOUBT that the principal scene of conflict of World War II was other than the Eastern Front, the Russian casualty figures settle the issue. During almost four years of total war fought across the unending vastness of the Russian Steppes, among the ruins of the Soviet Union's towns and cities, and through the devastation of Eastern Europe to the very heart of the Third Reich in Berlin, nearly nine million Red Army soldiers were killed and 18 million were wounded.

From October 1944 to May 1945 alone, the Red Army sustained 319,000 fatal casualties. Also, of more than 4.5 million Red Army prisoners captured by the *Wehrmacht*, only 1.8 million ultimately survived. Many of them were then persecuted by an unforgiving and suspicious Soviet regime. The wholesale destruction of Russian towns and villages during combat, and the reprisal operations and executions carried out by the SS and the *Wehrmacht* during an uncompromising counter-partisan campaign, resulted in at least 18 million Soviet civilian war dead. Altogether, some 26 million to 27 million Soviets died. In contrast, this was more than five times greater than the total German war dead incurred from 1939 to 1945.

Dead Soviet POWs

Corsican resistance From their mountainside position, a group of Corsican patriots fires upon occupation forces. When German and Italian troops occupied the French island of Corsica in the Mediterranean Sea, they were harried by highly effective resistance fighters. The tangled scrubby foliage on Corsica's mountainous terrain, called *maquis,* not only gave patriots a place to hide but also gave its name to the entire French resistance movement—the *Maquis.* On September 9, 1943, Corsicans rose up to participate in their liberation by the Free French and other Allies.

Italy's surrender When Italy surrendered in early September 1943, there was much celebration in America's Italian communities (such as this one in New York), for many had immigrated to escape Mussolini and his Fascist policies. Once Hitler learned of Italy's surrender, he ordered the German occupation of his onetime ally and the arrest of all Italian troops. More than 6,500 Italian soldiers were executed in Greece for allegedly resisting arrest. The Germans also removed 50,000 Allied prisoners from Italy and sent them and 268,000 Italian troops to labor camps in Germany.

1943

August 15: A 34,300-man Allied invasion force lands on Kiska, the last Japanese-occupied island in Alaska's Aleutians, only to discover it was abandoned weeks earlier.

August 16: The Nazis purge the Jewish ghetto at Bialystok, Poland, sending most of the remaining 25,000 inhabitants to the death camps at Majdanek and Treblinka.

August 17–18: Nearly 600 RAF bombers target the Nazis' rocket factories in Peenemünde on the German island of Usedom. • The Americans score a major victory over the Japanese on New Guinea when they ambush the airfield at Wewak and destroy an entire bombing formation of 150 planes.

August 18: *Luftwaffe* chief Hans Jeschonnek kills himself in despair over the failure of the *Luftwaffe* to defend Germany against the Allies. The Nazi command will lie about his cause of death to conceal their concerns about the status of the Reich.

August 22: Allied forces declare Kiska secure (and uninhabited) after a weeklong sweep of the island and a few friendly-fire casualties.

August 27: Germans and Italians clash in Ljubljana, Slovenia.

August 28: Bulgaria's King Boris III dies following an audience with Hitler, leading to rampant, though unproven, speculation that he was assassinated.

August 29: Washington puts Berlin on notice, saying it has become aware of German atrocities against Poles and that the perpetrators will pay for any war crimes when the day of reckoning arrives. • Following Nazi suppression of Danish civil rights and the arrest of King Christian X, the Danes sink most of their naval fleet to prevent it from falling into Nazi hands.

The Hellcats Despite its inelegant appearance and hasty development, the Grumman F6F Hellcat naval fighter contributed hugely to Allied victory. An improvement on the Wildcat, it proved superbly reliable and potent. Production figures reflected its effectiveness: 12,272 built from 1942, mainly in 1944 and 1945. Altogether, Hellcats destroyed some 6,000 enemy aircraft, most of which were Japanese. First sent into action in August 1943, Hellcats were usually carrier-borne and armed with six .5-inch machine guns. They could carry bombs, and ground-attack Hellcat aircraft employed rockets, notably at Iwo Jima and Okinawa. Night-fighter and reconnaissance versions also were made.

Student plans Mussolini's rescue German general Kurt Student (*right*), a pilot during World War I, pioneered the tactic of parachuting troops into battle. In 1940 Student's paratroops performed brilliantly in Norway, Belgium, and the Netherlands. The staggering casualties of Student's otherwise successful 1941 paratroop invasion of Crete caused Hitler to forbid any further major airborne operations. However, in 1943 Student planned a daring and successful hilltop rescue in September of the deposed and imprisoned Benito Mussolini. In 1944 his troops served as infantry in Italy, then in France after the invasion of Normandy.

Skorzeny's daring feats

After Italian king Victor Emmanuel stripped away Mussolini's power on July 25, 1943, he placed *Il Duce* under arrest and imprisoned him on the island of Ponza. After Mussolini was transferred to the mountain resort of Abruzzi a few months later, Hitler sent his best agent, Colonel Otto Skorzeny (*pictured*), and a commando unit to Italy in September 1943 to free Mussolini. Skorzeny's exploits later in the war included kidnapping Hungarian leader Miklos Horthy to prevent him from signing an armistice with the Soviets. Skorzeny also placed German agents in American uniforms behind Allied lines during the Battle of the Bulge.

The Hitler, Mussolini relationship As he reshaped Germany's government and society in the 1930s, Hitler turned to Benito Mussolini as a mentor for implementing his Fascist reforms. The war was not very old when Hitler realized that the Italian army could not be depended on to stop the Allied advances in the Mediterranean, but that did not affect his relationship with Mussolini. The situation changed, however, when *Il Duce* was deposed and imprisoned in July 1943. Hitler arranged for Mussolini's rescue and installed him as head of a puppet Fascist government. However, he no longer considered Mussolini a mentor or an equal.

Vilna resistance leader In the Vilna Ghetto, Lithuanian Jews in the *Fareinikte Partisaner Organizatzie* (FPO; United Partisan Organization) followed poet and resistance leader Abba Kovner's motto: "Let us not go like sheep to the slaughter." When the Nazis liquidated the Vilna Ghetto in September 1943—transferring its residents to death camps or killing them outright—Kovner helped FPO fighters escape into the Rudninkai Forest. For 10 months, he led the Jewish partisans in guerrilla attacks against the Nazis. Here, Kovner is pictured after the 1945 Soviet liberation of Vilna.

Polish women led to their deaths German security forces lead Polish women to their execution in the Palmiry Forest. The Nazis spread their plans for genocide throughout each occupied country, killing Jews, political opponents, and anyone else they believed was a threat or an inferior to the Aryan race. They often took pictures like this to denigrate victims as they were led to their deaths. German officers showed these to their troops in order to dehumanize the victims, making it easier for them to perform their gruesome assignments.

1943

September: The efficacy of Allied forces in India is jeopardized by a devastating famine in the Bengal province.

September 1: The U.S. military introduces its F6F Hellcat fighter during an attack on the Japanese base on Marcus Island.

September 2: The Polish government-in-exile publishes a report detailing atrocities against concentration camp inmates. The atrocities include bizarre medical experiments on healthy inmates at Ravensbrück and human skin "tanneries" at Dachau and Buchenwald.

September 3: A substantial Allied force lands in southern Italy and captures the town of Reggio in the province of Calabria. • Italy signs a treaty with American officials in Sicily, effectively surrendering to the Allies. The treaty will be kept secret for a time, both to aid Allied operations in Italy and prevent immediate Nazi reprisals against the Italian people.

September 6: For the first time in this war, Allied merchant ships are able to safely operate in Italy's Strait of Messina. • U.S. general Stilwell, Chiang Kai-shek's chief of staff, suggests that the Chinese Nationalists join forces with the Communists to defeat the Japanese. Chiang is disgusted by the suggestion and will ask the U.S. high command to recall Stilwell.

September 7: Corsicans take up arms against the Axis troops that have been occupying their French Mediterranean island. • Hitler permits his German troops, badly battered by the Red Army as they attempted to hold the Ukraine, to retreat to the Dnieper River.

Gruesome experiments at Ravensbrück During the course of the war, the Nazis built concentration camps throughout Europe. Ravensbrück, a camp primarily for women from many different nationalities, religions, and lifestyles, was located about 60 miles north of Berlin. As in most of the other camps, the Ravensbrück prisoners were required to do heavy labor or work in sweatshops making military supplies. Medical experiments were also conducted on helpless inmates. Two types were performed at Ravensbrück: testing the effects of sulfanilamide drugs on infected wounds, and studying the regeneration of bones, nerves, and muscles. This picture of Polish inmate Bogumila Babinska, smuggled out of the camp, shows the effect of four deep cuts on her thigh muscles.

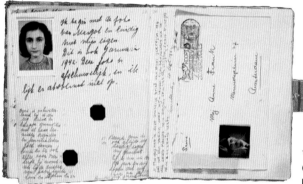

Anne Frank's diary
A German Jewish girl in Amsterdam, Anne Frank was given a diary for her 13th birthday on June 12, 1942. Three weeks later, her family went into hiding to escape deportation to a labor camp in Germany. Anne faithfully kept a diary during her two years in hiding. "It's a wonder I haven't abandoned all my ideals, they seem so absurd and impractical," Anne wrote less than a month before her arrest. "Yet I cling to them because I still believe, in spite of everything, that people are truly good at heart." Anne died at the Bergen-Belsen concentration camp in February or March 1945. *The Diary of Anne Frank* is one of the best-selling books of all time, with more than 25 million copies published.

Frick's fall from power Nazi Wilhelm Frick became Reich minister of the interior in 1933. He drafted anti-Jewish laws and other legislation that sent political foes to concentration camps. In 1943, after losing a power struggle with Heinrich Himmler, Frick was demoted to the ceremonial post of protector of Bohemia and Moravia. He refused to defend himself at the 1946 Nuremberg Trials, where he was found guilty and hanged. Frick's final words were "long live eternal Germany."

British Defeat in the Aegean Sea

IN 1912 ITALY SEIZED the 12 Dodecanese islands, located in the Aegean Sea, from Turkey. By 1940 Italian and German troops garrisoned the islands, just off the Turkish coast. Italy's surrender on September 8, 1943, prompted Winston Churchill to try to seize the islands so the Allies could strike at Germany's Balkan flank.

After British officers failed to incite the Italians to disarm the smaller German garrisons, Churchill ordered British infantry brigades and special-forces units to eight of the islands and the Greek Aegean Sea island of Samos. The Germans reacted swiftly. With naval and air forces already in the Aegean, they added reinforcements from Greece and Crete. These included *Luftwaffe* paratroops and a coastal raiding unit of the elite Brandenburg Division.

Airpower was crucial to the defeat of the scattered British garrisons. British (and South African) planes fought a losing fight against the *Luftwaffe* over the islands. By early October, the Germans had recaptured Cos. They seized Leros a month later and took Samos by late November.

German losses were minimal, while British casualties included more than 4,000 troops captured and the loss of more than a hundred aircraft. Losses also included four

RAF fighter striking a German flak vessel near Kalimnos, Dodecanese

cruisers and seven destroyers sunk or damaged (including several Greek ships). The hapless Italians and the islands' people (who had welcomed the British landings) suffered from German reprisals.

The venture exposed Allied tensions over a Mediterranean strategy. Churchill persisted in his aim, ignoring his generals' arguments against a campaign far from the nearest Allied bases (in Cyprus and Egypt). Eisenhower and other U.S. and British commanders saw the diversion from the Italian campaign as unjustified. The two-month campaign was the Allies' last defeat of the war.

Hitler's chief architect Albert Speer (*right*) watches a 1943 weapons demonstration with Hitler (*center*). Soon after joining the Nazi Party in 1931, Speer became the *Führer*'s chief urban architect. Speer designed monumental structures—such as the Nuremberg parade grounds—to exploit classical themes for Nazi spectacles. Appointed armaments minister in 1942 and given economic responsibilities in 1943, the ever-efficient Speer used concentration camp labor to increase war production, thus strengthening the economy. At the Nuremberg Trials, Speer professed both remorse and ignorance concerning the most inhumane Nazi practices. He kept a diary during his 20-year jail term and became a successful memoirist after his 1966 release.

1943

September 8: General Eisenhower announces Italy's surrender under Marshal Badoglio. Nazi officials characterize the act, undertaken by the new government under Badoglio, as treason.

September 9: The Allies land in Italy in full force, with the Americans establishing a beachhead near Salerno and the British landing on Italy's "heel." The city of Brindisi will fall to the British within two days, securing the region for the Allies. • Germany attacks the Allied base on the Arctic whaling island of Spitsbergen, causing considerable damage.

September 10: In answer to Italy's surrender, the German army captures Rome, taking control of the Eternal City from its former Axis partner.

September 12: Mussolini, under arrest at Abruzzi's Hotel Campo Imperatore, is freed in a dramatic raid by German troops, on Hitler's order.

September 13: The Allies' position at Salerno is in serious jeopardy, as several German divisions come within a few miles of completely repelling the Americans and British from their beachhead. • More than a month after the death of his predecessor, Lin Sen, Chiang Kai-shek is appointed president of Nationalist China.

September 15: Mussolini reorganizes Italy's National Fascist Party in an effort to regain power and restore ties to Hitler.

September 17: A depleted and heavily bombarded German force begins to withdraw from the Salerno beachhead as the Americans push inland to rendezvous with the British.

September 20: U.S. forces pushing in from Salerno in the west and British troops marching from Calabria in the southeast link up at Eboli, bisecting Italy with a solid Allied force.

B-17s pound factories Beginning in January 1943, Allied bombing runs focused on German wartime industries. The first mass-produced, four-engine heavy bombers were Boeing B-17s, known as Flying Fortresses. These heavily armed bombers were designed to be able to protect themselves, but a loss of one plane in every 10 was standard. This B-17, called *Virgin's Delight,* flies over the Focke-Wulf aircraft factory it has just hit at Marienburg, Germany. Although the Allies destroyed many German factories during 1943, the Nazis quickly compensated by stepping up production in others.

The mapmaking boom World War II revolutionized mapping. Aviation and aerial photography allowed the mapping of previously uncharted regions and much more detailed maps of known areas. Here, an Army Map Service Cartographer uses a Japanese map of a city to enter man-made works, such as factories and docks, on an Army chart. These will be potential bombing targets. By the end of the war, two U.S. armed forces agencies had reportedly produced approximately 650 million copies of 50,000 different maps.

"Mickey Mouse money"

Japanese authorities minted money, usually banknotes, for use in the territories they invaded. For example, they produced shillings and pounds for Singapore (where it was labeled "banana money") and centavos and pesos for the Philippines (where it was called "Mickey Mouse money"). Though supposedly at par with the existing local currencies, the occupation money was issued in

excessive amounts and quickly depreciated. The pre-invasion currencies tended to be hoarded. The Allies made propaganda versions of the currency with persuasive messages on the reverse side. After the Japanese defeat, the "occupation currency," or "invasion money," became worthless.

Beheadings Naval civil service officer Chikao Yasuno prepares to decapitate Sergeant Leonard George Siffleet, an Australian Army radioman caught operating behind Japanese lines in New Guinea. Siffleet and two comrades were beheaded on October 24, 1943, at Aitape after natives betrayed them to the Japanese. American troops found this film on the body of a dead Japanese during the invasion of Hollandia in 1944. The photo received wide publicity, reinforcing the perception that the Japanese were savages who gave no mercy and deserved none. Chikao was sentenced to hang after the war, but his sentence was later commuted to 10 years in prison.

The *Kempeitai* Members of the *Kempeitai* (Japanese military police) pose with British POWs. Though the *Kempeitai*'s authority over Japanese civilians was limited, the organization had free rein in the occupied territories, where harsh military justice prevailed. The *Kempeitai* dealt severely with anti-Japanese efforts in occupied territories. It was also responsible for travel permits, labor recruitment, rear area security, counterintelligence, operating POW camps, and providing "comfort women" to military brothels. Though the *Kempeitai* is sometimes equated with the Gestapo or secret police, that description is more accurately applied to the *Kempeitai*'s civilian counterpart, the *Tokkou keisatsu,* which combined criminal investigation and counterespionage functions.

1943

September 21: Japan leaves the central Solomon Islands to the Allies after losing 600 men in an unsuccessful bid to defend Arundel Island.

September 22: British submarine troops sabotage the *Tirpitz,* Germany's preeminent battleship, as it sits in port at Norway's *Altenfjord.* • Recognizing that a two-front war is straining the Reich's resources, Joseph Goebbels suggests that Hitler agree to a separate peace with the Soviets, but Hitler declines.

September 23: Mussolini announces the creation of the Salò Republic, in the Axis-controlled part of Italy beyond the scope of the Badoglio administration.

September 27: German troops abandon the Italian province of Foggia, with its strategically critical airstrips, to the Allies. • Chiang Kai-shek orders the execution of Chen Tu-hsiu, the founder of China's Communist Party.

October 1: The Allies occupy Naples, southern Italy's largest port city. It will become an important Allied naval and supply base. • The Nazis come up short in their effort to relocate Denmark's Jews, testimony to the character of the Danish people who have enabled their Jewish friends and neighbors to escape to Sweden. Most Danish Jews will survive the war.

October 3: Germany recaptures the British Aegean island of Kos. • Japanese troops complete their retreat from the Solomon island of Kolombangara.

October 4: More than 500 die on the ground when the USAAF and RAF join forces to keep bombs falling on Frankfurt day and night.

October 5: Germany incorporates the Istrian Peninsula, much of the Italian Alps, and the eastern Italian city of Trieste into the Reich.

Alternative fuel sources Due to wartime fuel shortages, alternative power sources were put to use in some European and South American countries. Seen here, the chauffeur of a "charcomobile" shows Brazilian women how to light the charcoal burner that powers their car. Although the charcoal-powered car took some time to get started and had poor acceleration and speed, its fuel supply could be regenerated by a simple stop to gather combustible materials. Brazilian army trucks were fitted with both charcoal burners and gasoline tanks—and with adjustable carburetors that could switch from one fuel to the other.

The Soviets' Yak fighters The Yak series of fighter planes was manufactured by the Soviet Union's Yakovlev company throughout World War II. Beginning with 1940's Yak-1, Yaks were regarded as among the war's finest aircraft. The Yak-3 (*pictured*) first saw service in 1944. Although it was manufactured in fewer numbers than the longer-range Yak-9 (which went into service in 1942, despite its higher designation number), the Yak-3 was widely favored by pilots for its strength, lightness, and maneuverability. At lower altitudes, it was considered superior to any of the *Luftwaffe*'s sophisticated fighters.

Josip Broz Tito

JOSIP BROZ TITO, secretary general of Yugoslavia's Communist Party, released a message to Yugoslavians as German tanks drove through their country. "You who are struggling and dying in this battle for independence," he declared. "Do not lose heart, close your ranks, and do not bow your heads under the heavy blows which you are suffering."

In Yugoslavia, the Communist Party had been persecuted by the government for years. In reaction, the party formed an underground to fight the government. It was, therefore, in the absence of an organized military resistance, ready to wage an underground campaign against the German invaders after the German invasion of the Soviet Union.

Tito, who became military commander of the partisans, called for the support of the Yugoslavian people with the slogan "Death to Fascism, Freedom to the People!" His forces fought a tough campaign against the Germans at the cost of thousands of lives. In the spring of 1943, Germans bombed his position. Tito dove for shelter behind a beech tree. He was saved from the blast of a German bomb by his dog, who had thrown himself across Tito's head.

The Soviet Union supported Tito's partisans throughout the war, and support from the British and Americans came in 1943. The Soviets entered Yugoslavia in April 1945 and backed his election as prime minister. Thus began his autonomous 35-year reign as the leader of Yugoslavia.

Yugoslavian women fight the Axis After the Axis powers seized Yugoslavia in 1941, Marshal Tito's Yugoslav Partisans proved themselves more capable of effective armed resistance than their rivals, the royalist Chechniks. By 1943 the Western Allies supported the Partisans over the Chechniks, despite misgivings about the Communist commitment of Tito's group. Some two million women (12 percent of Yugoslavia's prewar population) joined the Partisans in all capacities. Most of them were under 20 years of age. Many, like those pictured here, served in combat side by side with men.

Mountbatten named commander of SEAC
A great-grandson of Queen Victoria, the aristocratic Louis Mountbatten rose to military prominence during World War II as captain of the HMS *Kelly* and commander of the Fifth Destroyer Flotilla. He was appointed supreme Allied commander of the South East Asia Command (SEAC) in October 1943. In that post, which he held until 1946, he successfully directed international forces in the liberation of Burma and Singapore from the Japanese. After the war, Mountbatten became the last British viceroy of India, overseeing the independence of India and Pakistan from colonial rule.

1943

October 8: Civil war erupts in Greece when the country's pro- and anti-Communist factions face off.

October 10: A German U-boat lays mines at the eastern end of the Panama Canal. • The U.S. attacks the Axis-held islands of Crete and Rhodes with B-17 Flying Fortress bombers.

October 12: The Allies obtain permission to establish a convoy defense base on the Azores, an important island chain in the Atlantic that belongs to Portugal.

October 13: Italy joins the Allies when Premier Pietro Badoglio declares war on Hitler's Germany. • Yugoslavian partisans sabotage the Krupp steelworks in the city of Zeneca.

October 14: An uprising at the Nazis' Sobibór death camp claims the lives of 11 guards, while more than 100 prisoners manage to escape.

October 18: The Nazis begin the "resettlement" of Italian Jews to death camps in Poland. • The U.S. launches an air raid on the Japanese base on the northern Solomon island of Bougainville.

October 19: Some 5,000 seriously wounded German POWs and about the same number of British captives are heading home after the first British-German prisoner exchange of the war. • A civilian uprising in Jesselton, North Borneo, claims the lives of 40 occupying Japanese soldiers.

October 19–30: Allied foreign ministers meet in Moscow. They confirm the May 1944 date for the invasion of France, and agree that the Soviets will join the fight against the Japanese once the Germans are neutralized. They also announce plans for the postwar trials of war criminals. The Soviet Union promises to join a new international organization to keep the peace.

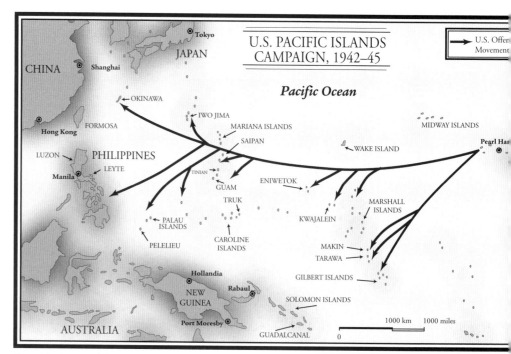

America's Pacific triumphs The turn of the strategic tide in the Pacific began in 1942 with the decisive U.S. naval victories at the Coral Sea (May) and Midway (June), followed by the successful operations on Guadalcanal from August. The subsequent "island-hopping" campaign concluded with the end of Japanese resistance on Okinawa on June 22, 1945. Other notable Allied successes during a consistently hard-fought series of amphibious landings and battles were Kokoda (1942); Bougainville (1943); Saipan, Guam, and Leyte Gulf (1944); and Iwo Jima and Corregidor (1945). Meanwhile, from November 1944, the capture of the Marianas enabled U.S. bombers to fly strategic missions against Japan—including the atomic bomb missions in August 1945.

"Sunny Jim" Vandegrift
General Alexander Archer Vandegrift, nicknamed "Sunny Jim" for his upbeat personality and courteous style, gained acclaim as the commander of the First Marine Division at Guadalcanal. Thrown into battle before his division was fully prepared, Vandegrift earned a Navy Cross for his landing on Guadalcanal and Tulagi. Later, his stubborn defense of Henderson Field stymied the Japanese and earned him a Medal of Honor. He later commanded the First Marine Amphibious Corps in the landings at Bougainville. On January 1, 1944, he was sworn in as the 18th commandant of the Marine Corps.

Americans land on Bougainville U.S. troops clamber into assault boats assembling for the landing on Bougainville, the largest of the Solomon Islands. Part of the effort to neutralize the Japanese base at Rabaul 220 miles away, the landing was spearheaded by the Third Marine Division on November 1, 1943, at Cape Torokina. Though the Japanese had some 17,000 troops on southern Bougainville alone, they had not considered swampy Cape Torokina a likely target, and the landing was lightly opposed. Work began on an airfield, and U.S. Army troops were brought ashore. Futile enemy attacks on the perimeter began immediately, the last occurring in March. Australian forces took over the fighting on the island until the Japanese surrendered in 1945.

Rookie GIs seize Makin U.S. Army troops in November 1943 view a wrecked Japanese seaplane in the lagoon at Makin Atoll, which was seized along with Tarawa as part of Operation Galvanic. The operation was a stepping-stone toward the more valuable Marshall Islands. Unlike Tarawa, which lay fewer than 100 miles to the south, Makin was not heavily fortified. Only about 300 of the 800-man garrison could be considered combat troops; the rest were mostly Korean laborers. Nevertheless, it took nearly 6,500 men from the rookie U.S. 27th Infantry Division more than three days to secure Makin.

Nasty fighting in the jungle American troops operate amid dead bodies on the island of Bougainville. Much of the fighting on Bougainville focused on efforts to dominate valuable high ground and the few trails that traversed the swampy terrain. Roadblocks, ambushes, and terrifying patrol encounters at point-blank range in the thick jungle were routine. Japanese machine gunners sheltered in well-concealed log and earthen bunkers had to be reduced one by one by infantrymen using hand grenades, small arms, and flamethrowers.

1943

October 20: The Allies take one step closer to Nuremberg with the establishment of a commission charged with the investigation of war crimes.

October 23: A brief uprising on the threshold of an Auschwitz gas chamber results in the death of a hated SS guard and the wounding of several others. The mutineers are then shot.

October 24: For the first time, the Allies stage an air raid on Axis targets from bases in the former Axis nation of Italy.

October 29: Dockworkers on England's Thames River go on strike, forcing soldiers to pick up the slack. • The U.S. Navy heavily mines the waters off French territory in Indochina.

October 31: The Red Army has cut the supply line and isolated some 150,000 German and Romanian troops in the Crimea.

November 2: The Battle of Empress Augusta Bay erupts when the U.S. Navy attacks a small Japanese fleet attempting to reinforce Bougainville, where the Marines landed the day before.

November 3: A massive force of 539 U.S. planes bombs the key German port of Wilhelmshaven. • The Red Army launches an offensive across the Dnieper River in a bid to retake Kiev from the Germans. • The Nazis purge the population of the Majdanek death camp, murdering some 17,000 Jews in a single day.

November 4: The United States begins to manufacture plutonium at a facility in Oak Ridge, Tennessee.

November 6: The Red Army recaptures Kiev from the Germans with relative ease. This third-largest Soviet city has been largely reduced to a smoldering ruin.

U.S. sinks merchant ships Its seagoing days at an end, the 7,000-ton Japanese transport *Kinugawa Maru* lies stranded on the Guadalcanal shore. Japan's merchant fleet was crucial for transporting raw materials to the home islands and for carrying supplies and reinforcements to the empire's far-flung outposts. As the war in the Pacific turned against Japan in 1943, U.S. planes and submarines began sinking Japanese merchant ships more quickly than they could be replaced. The mounting losses wreaked havoc on the Japanese war machine.

The dangers of carrier landings A crewman on the USS *Enterprise* scrambles to help the pilot of a burning F6F Hellcat, which crashed on the flight deck during operations off Makin Island. Flying on and off the heaving carrier decks was hazardous under the best of circumstances. One miscalculation could send the plane hurtling into the crash barrier at the end of the deck, or over the side. The process was also dangerous for the deck crews, known as "deck apes," who were exposed to everything from crash landings and spinning props to loose bombs. As one seaman remarked, "every landing was a potential casualty."

The mythical "gremlins" Faced with unexpected and seemingly inexplicable mechanical problems during WWII, RAF pilots added a supernatural, gnome-like creature to world folklore: the "gremlin." Perhaps more than semi-seriously, pilots discussed gremlins, their mischievous expertise, and methods of placating and controlling them. Gremlins were nothing but a myth. But like the one pictured on this book cover, they were said to often ride on wings, sometimes manipulating ailerons to tip the plane.

The coastwatchers Working on remote Pacific island locations, "coastwatchers" reported enemy activity and guided Allied attacks and guerrilla operations. They also rescued hundreds of civilians and Allied servicemen, including future U.S. president John F. Kennedy. White Australian, New Zealander, American, and Solomons Islands civilians provided most personnel, but they relied on natives as spies, guards, messengers, and laborers. Pictured is an islander at a New Georgia coastwatcher station.

The supreme commander General Douglas MacArthur was supreme commander of Allied forces in the South West Pacific Area during World War II. After commanding the futile defense of the Philippines in 1941–42, he escaped to lead the defense of Australia and later the recapture of New Guinea and the Philippines. MacArthur's personal attachment to the Philippines led

American planes clear "The Hump" American aircraft of the China National Aviation Corporation (CNAV) were able to fly over the Himalayas from China to India. After the Burma Road closed in 1942, such flights over "The Hump" were the only means of supplying the Chinese Nationalists. It was a 500-mile flight over 15,000-feet-high mountain ranges. In 1943 the pictured C-46 Commando replaced the C-47 as the main carrier. More than 1,000 C-46s took the journey, usually fully loaded. They battled severe turbulence, ice, and monsoonal storms. Unarmed, they risked air attack. CNAV aircraft made some 35,000 journeys over the Hump, carrying 71,000 tons in July 1945 alone.

him to insist on a speedy return to the islands, a course criticized by some strategists. During his southwest Pacific campaigns, MacArthur astutely bypassed heavily defended areas whenever possible, leapfrogging to strike where the enemy was weakest. He was a powerful personality—talented but also vain, imperious, a political machinist, and a shameless publicity seeker. During his career, he gained a reputation in the public mind as a military genius—a stature now in dispute among historians.

1943

November 9: General Charles de Gaulle is named president of the French Committee of National Liberation, the "Free French," in the wake of the resignation of General Henri Giraud.

November 11: Vichy police arrest 450 demonstrators in Grenoble, France, for rallying against the Nazis. • The Nazis running the Theresienstadt death camp torture some 47,000 Jews, forcing them to stand exposed for eight hours in a bitterly cold November rain.

November 12: Unaware of the Enigma breach, German admiral Karl Dönitz claims of the Allies: "He knows all our secrets." • Japanese bases in the Marshall and Gilbert islands come under heavy air assault by Allied planes. The attacks will continue on a daily basis.

November 14: A friendly-fired torpedo narrowly misses striking the battleship USS *Iowa*. President Roosevelt, en route to the Tehran Conference, is on board.

November 15: Effective immediately, all Gypsies in Germany are to be deported to death camps on the order of SS chief Heinrich Himmler. • The Nazis attempt to put a lid on sabotage by the nascent Italian resistance by taking some 2,000 of Milan's industrial workers hostage.

November 16: The Nazis round up another 2,000 Jews in the Netherlands and send them to Auschwitz. • The Germans effectively abandon their atomic bomb-building ambitions when the Allies launch another raid on the Vemork, Norway, heavy-water plant.

November 19: The Fog Investigation Dispersal Operation (FIDO) is employed for the first time by RAF officials hoping to enable landings in heavy British fog.

The Red Air Force Soviet pilot Victor Radkevich animatedly tells fellow fliers of his triumph over a German plane. On the first day of the 1941 German invasion of Russia, the *Luftwaffe* destroyed more than 1,000 largely outmoded Russian military aircraft—about 800 of them still on the ground. The next year, the Soviets began a huge buildup of air forces. Instead of British- and American-style long-range bombings intended to destroy enemy infrastructure and morale, the Red Air Force focused on supporting ground forces against the German invaders. By late 1943, the Soviets had achieved clear air superiority over the *Luftwaffe*.

German POWs face likely death These captured German troops were transferred to Soviet POW camps, many of which were in Siberia. In the camps, the prisoners received a harsh education in communism, and many died from overwork and malnutrition. Of the approximately 90,000 exhausted and starving German soldiers captured at the end of the fighting at Stalingrad, fewer than 6,000 returned to their homes.

German POWs in Soviet Hands

CONSIDERING GERMANY'S aggression toward the Soviet Union, it is not surprising that the Soviets treated German POWs without mercy. The Germans not only invaded Soviet territory, but the SS and *Wehrmacht* committed a litany of atrocities against those who Nazi leadership called Soviet *Untermenschen* (subhumans). Despite some isolated instances of Russian compassion, conditions in the POW camps were generally abysmal, with a daily death rate of one percent in the camp hospitals.

German POWs were often forced to build their own camps—but with underground earth bunkers rather than huts for accommodation. The bunkers regularly flooded in the spring and autumn. Suicide, disease, dysentery, summary execution, and death by freezing were all

German POWs in Stalingrad

commonplace. Even POWs who were fit when captured often succumbed to a below-starvation diet of unground millet and a punishing program of hard labor. POWs worked on major construction projects, such as the reconstruction of Stalingrad, hydroelectric schemes, and excavation of the Don-Volga canal.

In Soviet philosophy, man was just another material to be used to maximum effect and then discarded. In May 1945, the Soviets held nearly 1.5 million POWs in Germany alone. Several million more had already been transported to the Soviet Union to join the several hundred thousand German POWs captured earlier in the war. Of the POWs, two-thirds survived to return home to Germany. The final 9,626, who were sentenced for war crimes, were not released from the Soviet Union until 1955.

Bosnian Muslims support the Nazis In March 1942, the Mufti of Jerusalem, Haj Amin al-Husseini, said in a radio broadcast, "If, God forbid, America and her allies are victorious in this war...then the world will become hell." Al-Husseini helped recruit Bosnian Muslims into the *Waffen-SS* with assurances that Allah would never allow the Allies to win. Bosnian SS members and their German officers wore fez hats bearing the Nazi eagle, as seen in this photo of a 1943 meeting in Berlin.

SP guns Self-propelled (SP) guns, such as this U.S. Army 105mm howitzer, were guns mounted on tracked, turretless chassis that provided speedy, mobile fire support as required. Among the Western Allies, the U.S. led the development of SP guns and—for SP guns used in the anti-armor role—"tank destroyers." However, while the Anglo-U.S. forces generally utilized their SP guns as a more maneuverable form of conventional indirect-fire artillery, the German and Russian armies used SP guns primarily as direct-fire weapons—literally as "assault guns"—providing close support for infantry engaged in offensive operations.

The Tehran Conference Stalin, Roosevelt, and Churchill, The Big Three, met only twice during the war. The first time was in Tehran, Iran, from November 28 to December 1, 1943. For more than a year, Stalin had demanded the invasion of France to force Germany to shift resources to the West. In Tehran, Roosevelt and Churchill announced their decision to invade France in May 1944. Stalin agreed to simultaneously mount an aggressive offensive in the East. He also pressured his allies to accept some of his demands, including Soviet possession of the eastern part of postwar Poland and his veto on the plan to divide postwar Germany into five autonomous states. It also was determined that the Soviets would join the fight against Japan after Germany was defeated.

U.S. seizes Kwajalein, Roi-Namur Hit by antiaircraft fire, a Japanese torpedo bomber explodes during an attack off Kwajalein Island. The U.S. assaults on Kwajalein and nearby Roi-Namur, deep in the Marshall Islands chain, in February 1944 surprised the Japanese, who had committed more defensive effort to the outermost islands. The Fourth Marine Division seized Roi-Namur in two days, and the Seventh Infantry Division took Kwajalein in four. U.S. casualties were relatively light. Capture of the island air bases deprived the Japanese of a defensive shield and opened the way to the Carolines and Marianas, which were the true strategic springboards for any assault on Japan.

Japan defends Tarawa Draped with hand grenades and ammunition, a Marine pauses to drink from his canteen on December 6, 1943, during the fight for Tarawa. The Second Marine Division had fought in the Solomons, but the amphibious assault on tiny, heavily defended Tarawa was a new experience. Japanese rear admiral Shibasaki Keiji boasted that "a million Americans couldn't take Tarawa in a hundred years." Defenses included barbed wire, mines, tetrahedrons, nearly 500 pillboxes, light tanks, heavy machine guns, and eight-inch naval rifles. Thanks to the stubborn courage of individual Marines, Shibasaki was proven wrong, but the cost was high. More than 1,000 Americans were killed or went missing.

Shot down by the hundreds Dead Marines litter the beach following the 76-hour battle for Betio (at the southwest corner of Tarawa Atoll) and its strategically important airstrip. As the first large-scale test of U.S. amphibious doctrine against a strongly fortified enemy beach, the Tarawa assault was a costly learning experience. Preceded by an inadequate bombardment, hampered by a disastrously low tide, and lacking sufficient tracked vehicles to negotiate Betio's wide reef, Marines were shot down by the hundreds as they waded toward the heavily defended landing beaches. "It was a time of utmost savagery," wrote a witness. "I still don't know how they took the place."

Japanese choose suicide Trapped in their bunker on Tarawa, these two Japanese Special Naval Landing Force troops chose suicide over surrender. U.S. Marines would become accustomed to such tenacity in their march through the central Pacific. Typical of what was to come on Saipan, Guam, and Iwo Jima, the enemy garrison at Tarawa fought almost to the last man. Of the approximately 5,000 enemy personnel on Betio, 4,690 were killed. Of the 146 prisoners taken by U.S. Marines, virtually all were conscripted Korean laborers. Only 17 Japanese—all wounded—were captured.

CHARRED TO NOTHINGNESS

TWO MORE MARINES scaled the sea wall, one of them carrying a twin-cylindered tank strapped to his shoulders, the other holding the nozzle of the flamethrower. As another charge of TNT boomed inside the pillbox, causing smoke and dust to billow out, a khaki-clad figure ran out the side entrance. The flamethrower, waiting for him, caught him in its withering stream of intense fire. As soon as it touched him, the Jap flared up like a piece of celluloid. He was dead instantly but the bullets in his cartridge belt exploded for a full sixty seconds after he had been charred almost to nothingness.

—TIME-LIFE CORRESPONDENT ROBERT SHERROD, DESCRIBING A MOMENT DURING THE BATTLE FOR TARAWA, NOVEMBER 20, 1943

Spruance: low-key but successful Admiral Raymond Spruance led Task Force 16 with its two aircraft carriers at Midway in June 1942, playing a key role in that decisive engagement. As commander of the Fifth Fleet, he subsequently directed the operations to seize the Gilberts, Marshalls, Marianas, Iwo Jima, and Okinawa. He also commanded the force that defeated the Japanese carrier fleet in the Battle of the Philippine Sea in June 1944. Spruance succeeded Fleet Admiral Chester Nimitz as commander of the Pacific Fleet in late 1945. Described by historian Samuel Eliot Morison as "one of the greatest fighting and thinking admirals in American naval history," Spruance shunned publicity and never received much popular acclaim.

1943

November 19: Fourteen British sailors, survivors of the mine-sunk freighter *Penolver*, are rescued by the American freighter *DeLisle*. The *DeLisle* promptly strikes another mine, sending the British back into the Atlantic, where they are miraculously rescued for a second time.

November 20: U.S. forces battle fierce Japanese resistance as they land on the Gilbert islands of Makin and Tarawa.

November 21: In one of the most overpowering air raids in the history of warfare, Berlin comes under assault by 775 RAF planes.

November 22–26: At the Cairo Conference, Roosevelt, Churchill, and Chiang Kai-shek discuss strategy for the Burma front. They announce that all areas seized by Japan since 1894 will be returned to their former owners.

November 25: The Allies bomb Japanese positions in Rangoon, Burma.

November 28: Roosevelt, Churchill, and Stalin hold their first face-to-face meeting in Tehran, Iran. They restate their commitment to prepare for Operation Overlord, the invasion of France. • The Allies complete their conquest of the island of Tarawa. Some 4,600 Japanese and 1,100 Americans lose their lives in the battle.

December 2: The U.S. brings 15 noted atomic scientists to New Mexico to help build the bomb. • Facing a sharp decline in the number of miners working on the home front, British labor minister Ernest Bevin decrees that one of every 10 draftees will be sent to the coal mines instead of the front lines. • The southern Italian port of Bari is devastated by a German air raid. Nineteen ships are destroyed when bombs strike two shipboard ammunition stores.

Germans fight on in Italy Since the Casablanca Conference in January 1943, Churchill pushed for the invasion of Italy, the "soft underbelly of Europe." Roosevelt and his military advisers believed such an invasion would be an unwise distraction from preparation for the invasion of France. The third allied

partner, Stalin, was also against the Italian campaign. The fighting in Sicily had not yet started when discussions were renewed about Italy. It was finally decided not to stop the offensive momentum. British and Canadian troops invaded Italy on September 3 with little opposition. Before the second landing at Salerno on September 9, the troops learned that Italy had surrendered. German troops, however, stubbornly contested the Salerno landing and every inch of the Allied advance. Here, American troops prepare for an advance in December.

The Gustav Line To block the Allied advance, Field Marshal Albert Kesselring, the German commander in Italy, constructed defenses south of Rome. The Gustav Line was the most formidable of four lines of defense that extended across the Italian peninsula. The Gustav Line was a series of concrete bunkers and artillery positions on the rocky faces of mountains fronted by a no-man's-land of barbed wire and land mines. Allied infantry, airborne, and rangers fought stubbornly along this line, as seen here.

Clark fights the Nazis in Italy Capable but overly confident, General Mark Wayne Clark (*left*) was appointed commander of the U.S. Fifth Army in 1943. His September assignment, to land his troops in the port of Salerno and direct a portion of the invasion of Italy, seemed easy enough. Mussolini had already been removed from power, and the Italian government had surrendered to the Allies. But Clark and other Allied commanders failed to grasp Hitler's determination not to lose Italy. The Italian Campaign wore on bitterly at such places as Anzio and Monte Cassino until the Fifth Army entered Rome in June 1944. The Allied commanders finally accepted the surrender of Italy's last German defenders on May 2, 1945.

The Atlantic Wall From spring 1942 to 1944, Germany built fortifications along 3,000 miles of French and Belgian coastline. Called the *Atlantikwall* (Atlantic Wall), the defense system was designed by engineer Fritz Todt. Under the direction of Field Marshal Erwin Rommel, the wall was intended to protect Europe against seaborne Allied invasions. Defenses included 14,000 concrete bunkers armed with mortars, machine guns, and larger gun emplacements, such as this *Fernkampfbatterie* (distant battle battery). The beach and waters below were protected by antitank obstacles, steel "Belgian Gates" intended to damage landing craft, and six million mines.

Hitler's mistress Eva Braun, Hitler's longtime mistress, is pictured at the Berghof, the *Führer*'s Bavarian mountain home. Isolated from the political realities of the Third Reich and the war, Braun was permitted luxuries that Hitler denied to other German women, including makeup and the use of alcohol and tobacco. Although Hitler was said to become uncharacteristically lighthearted in her presence, he never publicly acknowledged their relationship, and Braun was reportedly lonely and unhappy. Hitler and Braun finally married in a civil ceremony on April 29, 1945, the day before they committed suicide together.

Food for Russian soldiers Red Army rations varied from adequate to nonexistent depending on the supply situation. Bread and soup were staples. A type of cabbage soup called *shchi* was common, as was *kasha,* which is boiled buckwheat. Supplements included macaroni, salted fish, tea, salt, lard or bacon fat, and whatever vegetables the soldier could forage. American Spam became a common source of meat. Bread and sausage were often issued prior to combat operations since they would last for days without spoiling.

1943

December 3: *Reichsmarshall* Hermann Göring orders an intensification of Germany's bombing campaign over Britain.

December 3–4: Some 1,000 civilian casualties result from an RAF raid on Leipzig, Germany.

December 3–7: Allied leaders return to the conference table at Cairo. They reach additional agreements about the prosecution of the war in the Pacific.

December 4: Josip Broz Tito is named head of a provisional Communist government in Yugoslavia. • The Japanese employ poison gas in an attack on the Chinese city of Changteh.

December 5: Some 350 die in a Japanese raid on the Indian port city of Calcutta.

December 8: Some Italian forces enter combat for the Allies, as the series of battles along Germany's Winter Line in Italy intensifies.

December 11: Germany loses nearly 140 planes in a dogfight in the skies over the Emden U-boat facility.

December 12: The Soviet Union and Czechoslovakia sign a mutual assistance treaty at the Kremlin. • Hitler sends General Rommel to mobilize forces along the French coast to prepare to defend against the anticipated Allied invasion.

December 14: Having experienced success against the Germans in bitterly cold Russian winters, the Red Army kicks off a new winter offensive against Hitler's troops in the western Soviet Union.

December 16: Three German POWs and their Soviet driver are tried in Kharkov for the deaths of tens of thousands of local civilians during the German occupation of Russia. They will hang on the 19th.

British fears of espionage When war began, the British worried about enemy agents operating from within their country. Thousands of Germans, Austrians, and Italians were arrested, questioned, and interned—or deported to Canada or Australia. Propaganda posters featuring slogans such as "Careless Talk Costs Lives" warned against spies in public places. This *Picture Post* magazine photograph, dated December 18, 1943, shows "What the Well-Dressed German Wears." Apparently, a Nazi spy (*left*) could be identified by his shabby, badly worn coat with broken buttons.

BBC and "V for Victory"
Tangye Lean, a BBC European Service radio commentator, broadcasts in 1943. During the war, the BBC transmitted information and propaganda in 45 languages, reaching every major European nation, North America, Iran, India, and Japan. Although the Nazis made listening to the BBC punishable by death, even German officials were among the millions of European fans. The BBC "V for Victory" campaign popularized the letter "V," its hand sign, and its Morse code signal (three dots and a dash). The opening bars of Beethoven's Fifth Symphony (replicating the code) became the European Service's call sign.

"[I] slapped three-eighths- or three-quarter-inch rivets by hand that no one else would do. I didn't have that kind of confidence as a kid growing up, because I didn't have that opportunity. Convair was the first time in my life that I had the chance to prove that I could do something, and I did."

—AMERICAN WAR WORKER RACHEL WRAY

Rosie the Riveter

"WE FELT SO RICH," recalled Helen Cabanis, a factory worker during the Second World War. "We had money to buy gasoline, we had tires to ride on, and we had a car that we could go places and do things." While their husbands, fathers, and sons were off to war, many women in America felt a sense of purpose and freedom that they had never experienced before. They were making a valuable contribution to the war effort and providing for their families without male assistance.

During the Depression, women had been discouraged from entering the workforce. Now they were sorely needed to fill the many factory vacancies due to the shortage of men on the home front. Government worked with corporate leaders to launch a propaganda campaign in the media to entice women to fill critical gaps in the workforce.

The image of "Rosie the Riveter," a confident, muscular woman in overalls, was created by the government to entice housewives and single women to help build warplanes. "Rosie" quickly became a familiar figure on the home front. She had her own song in 1942, was the subject of a popular painting by Norman Rockwell in 1943, and

A U.S. war worker

appeared in her own movie in 1944. Six million American women answered the call by 1945.

Women, however, were not appropriately rewarded for their sacrifice. Their salaries were less than half of their male coworkers', and at war's end, female workers were expected to give up their jobs and return to domestic life.

The speedy Mustang Although well armed, American B-17 Flying Fortress bombers were vulnerable targets for German fighters in 1943. One reason for the heavy casualties was the absence of Allied fighters with the range to accompany the B-17s to their targets. It was not until refined iterations of the P-51 Mustang fighter (*pictured*) arrived in late 1943 that the Allies had the planes to counter *Luftwaffe* attacks on the B-17s. The Mustang had an auxiliary fuel tank that could be dropped when empty to give the plane greater speed. Successful in dogfights, the Mustang was also effective in ground attacks.

Lancasters carry the load
Britain's Avro Lancaster bombers participated in every major night raid on Germany, and carried bigger loads and heavier bombs than any other aircraft in Europe. Approximately 7,300 of these bombers were constructed by war's end. Developed from the short-lived twin-engine Manchester bomber, the Lancaster went into immediate large-scale production after test-flights in early 1941. After their first raid in April 1942, these bombers made 156,000 sorties over Europe, dropping nearly 620,000 tons of bombs. Famous Lancaster attacks included the "dam buster" raids and the sinking of the battleship *Tirpitz*.

Soviets relocate their factories Beginning in 1941, trains that moved Red Army troops to the front also transported thousands of dismantled Russian factories and millions of skilled workers eastward to safer locations beyond the Ural Mountains. Rushed into production—often at considerable hardship to civilian workers—factories contributed to a surge in the Soviet manufacture of tanks and weapons during 1942–43. Stalin had saved Russia's manufacturing capability, which meant that in 1943 tanks and other equipment made up for the Red Army's manpower shortage.

Sexy Jane After cartoonist Norman Pett's wife, Jane, was asked to look after a "Count Fritz von Pumpernickel"—who turned out to be a dachshund—Pett started drawing cartoons and comic strips about Jane and Fritz. During WWII, Jane the cartoon character contributed to troop morale by shedding more and more clothes and finally appearing in the buff. The saucy, tremendously popular character was played by actress Christabel Leighton-Porter in a music-hall striptease act and in a movie.

Racial mixing A black man and white woman dance together at a London Club in 1943. Nearly 10 percent of the 1.5 million U.S. servicemen and servicewomen stationed in Britain were African Americans. As black journalist Roi Ottley reported in 1944, the British did not practice racial segregation "within the doors of the British Isles," and many British took offense at the efforts of some U.S. servicemen to impose segregation at British public events. Racial mixing, especially male-female pairings, sometimes drew violent responses from American Southerners in service.

Germany's "lucky ship" The German heavy cruiser *Prinz Eugen* (*pictured*) helped the *Bismarck* sink the HMS *Hood* on May 24, 1941, then managed to escape the British search that led to the *Bismarck*'s destruction on May 27. From February 11 to 13, 1942, the *Prinz Eugen* was among the ships that made the "Channel Dash," a daring retreat through the English Channel to German home bases. Late in 1944, it began patrolling the Baltic coast, where its crew bombarded Soviet troops and evacuated German refugees. Remembered by its crew as a "lucky ship," it was the only German heavy warship to remain operational at war's end.

The bombing of Berlin In a November 1943 letter to Winston Churchill concerning a planned bombing of Berlin, British air marshal Sir Arthur Harris stated, "It will cost Germany the war." The bombing of Germany's largest city began on November 18 and lasted until the end of March 1944. Although the attacks killed more than 10,000 civilians and left hundreds of thousands homeless, it failed to destroy the city or the morale of its citizens. In this image, bodies of citizens wait to be identified in a Berlin gymnasium decorated for Christmas.

1943

December 17: In gratitude for Chinese assistance in the Pacific Theater, President Roosevelt signs the repeal of the 1882 Chinese Exclusion Act and allows limited Chinese immigration to the United States.

December 22: One of the last remnants of the Warsaw Ghetto is wiped out when the SS murders more than 60 Jews discovered hiding in a basement in the Polish city.

December 24: General Eisenhower is promoted, receiving the title of Supreme Commander, Allied Expeditionary Force.

December 25: Having reached a stalemate on the Italian front, the Allies agree to a plan to send an amphibious force onto the beaches south of Rome.

December 26: Only 36 of a 1,900-man crew survive the Royal Navy's sinking of Germany's *Scharnhorst*. This ends the German interception of Allied convoys to Murmansk, a port city in northwest Russia.

December 28: Ortona, Italy, is finally in Allied hands after two weeks of violent clashes in the streets of the small city. The battle earned Ortona the nickname "Little Stalingrad." • Realizing that the Nazi war machine is short on labor and being undone by its own brutality, Heinrich Himmler orders labor camp commandants to reduce the death rate among their inmates.

December 29: The Red Army scores a dramatic victory along the line west of Kiev, forcing some 200,000 German troops back toward Poland.

December 30: The First U.S. Marines capture a strategically key airfield at Cape Gloucester on the South Pacific island of New Britain.

Americans battle malaria
Civilian quinine stocks are prepared in Washington, D.C., for shipment to troops in the Pacific. The Japanese occupation of South Pacific islands had cut off Allied sources of the anti-malarial drug. In 1943 General Douglas MacArthur complained, stating,

"This will be a long war if for every division I have facing the enemy, I must count on a second division in the hospital with malaria and a third division convalescing from this debilitating disease." MacArthur enforced anti-malarial measures, including mosquito netting, repellent, and the unpleasant quinine substitute, Atabrine. Even so, malaria killed thousands of U.S. troops in Africa and the South Pacific.

The logistics of ship loading Crammed with everything from stretchers to jeeps, an LST (landing ship tank) brings in materiel for the invasion of New Britain, a Pacific island. Despite the apparent clutter, Navy and Marine Corps logistics personnel transformed combat loading into an exact science. The least critical items were loaded aboard ship first, stowed deep in the holds. Priority items, such as ammunition, were loaded last so they could be made available more quickly during an assault. Special shore parties under the command of a beachmaster were responsible for unloading the ships, gathering supplies in organized dumps, and ensuring a smooth logistics flow as the battle developed.

Logistics and Distance

"I WANT TO TELL YOU from the Russian point of view," Soviet leader Joseph Stalin declared at the Tehran Conference in December 1943, "what the President and the United States have done to win the war. The most important things...are machines.... The United States... is a country of machines. Without the use of those machines...we would lose this war."

By 1943 the United States led all other countries in the production of military supplies. The success of the Allies in World War II was due not only to America's production capability, but its ability to place these materials into the hands of those who needed them most—the soldiers on the front lines. In the end, logistics won the war.

Realizing that they would have to fight a war on two fronts thousands of miles from their mainland, America's military leaders were determined to conquer Axis nations by creating and strengthening their supply lines across the Atlantic and Pacific oceans. America's strategy against the Japanese was to gradually push westward across the Pacific, seizing one enemy base after another. The U.S. not only wanted to drive ever closer to the Japanese mainland, but also provide the logistical support (fuel, ammunition, and food) necessary to keep its ships, aircraft, and infantry moving forward. The same strategy was followed in the

Army trucks on flatbed railroad cars in Virginia

European Theater. Ample supplies were assembled in Africa and England before the invasions of Sicily and France, respectively.

While the Allies grew stronger as the war progressed, the Germans and Japanese were steadily weakened. Their war plants were bombed, their number of workers decreased, and their supply lines were gradually strangled shut. The logistical strength of the Allied nations, with America as the chief contributor, was a decisive factor in the war's outcome.

The assault on Rabaul Marines push a jeep ashore from an LST (landing ship tank) at Cape Gloucester, New Britain. The operation in late 1943 formed part of Operation Cartwheel, the effort to isolate the Japanese bastion at Rabaul. Located on the northeastern tip of New Britain, Rabaul was a major air, naval, and staging facility for enemy operations in New Guinea and the Solomons. General MacArthur suggested a two-pronged assault on Rabaul from eastern New Guinea and the Solomon Islands, followed by invasion. Accompanied by a bombing campaign and raids by Admiral Bull Halsey's carrier forces, the preliminary operations so effectively neutralized Rabaul that an amphibious assault proved unnecessary.

Mortar combat on New Britain
Marines man an 81mm mortar in the fighting at Cape Gloucester, New Britain. Swampy terrain and thick rain forest severely hampered mobility on the island. Fighting was often at arm's length in heavy vegetation. Weighing 87 pounds and with a range of 4,000 yards, the 81mm mortar and its smaller counterpart, the 60mm mortar, provided close support both in offense and defense. Crews had to take care that the high angle shell had a clear upward path through the heavy jungle canopy.

Krueger the perfectionist As commander of the Sixth Army during the war, General Walter Krueger directed 21 successful amphibious operations in the southwest Pacific, including the seizures of Leyte and Luzon in the Philippines. A former enlisted man who rose through the ranks, Krueger was a hard-driving perfectionist. No detail, down to the condition of an infantryman's feet, was too small for his attention. Though sometimes ridiculed as "Molasses in January" for his cautious approach to battle, Krueger was the general whom MacArthur singled out to lead the ground assault on Kyushu, Japan, before the atomic bomb made the operation unnecessary.

PT boats American PT (patrol torpedo) boats cut through the water in this painting by Arthur Beaumont. Built of wood and only 80 feet long, the PT boats had a top speed of more than 41 knots and were heavily armed, with four Mark 8 torpedoes and a variety of automatic weapons. Crew size varied from 12 to 14. Originally designed to attack enemy warships, the radar-equipped PTs proved most effective in night actions against enemy barges and smaller vessels ferrying troops and supplies among the Pacific islands. Approximately 770 PTs were built during the course of the war.

Germany's *Scharnhorst* wreaks havoc Commissioned on January 7, 1939, the 31,000-ton German battleship *Scharnhorst* prowled the North Sea with its sister ship, *Gneisenau,* through 1939 and 1940. The ships sank the British armed merchant cruiser HMS *Rawalpindi* in late November 1939, covered the German invasion of Norway in spring 1940, and sank the British aircraft carrier HMS *Glorious* and two escorting destroyers on June 8, 1940. Repairs kept the *Scharnhorst* in dock through the rest of 1940, after which the sister ships broke into the Atlantic, where they sank 22 merchant ships.

No sympathy for slackers The U.S. War Production Board flooded manufacturing plants with posters designed to instill a sense of duty in workers. An employee who was slacking off or not on the job every day, six days a week, was accused of aiding the enemy. Although the system could absorb lazy or absent individual workers, the government wanted to head off the contagion of mass absences. On this poster, an idler is said to be "working for Hitler." On others, an idle machine was described as "an empty gun" that "may cost your pal's life."

The British sink the *Scharnhorst* Warned of the approach of the *Scharnhorst* after a German message was decoded, British ships sank the battleship on December 26, 1943, about 70 miles northeast of North Cape, Norway. Of the 1,968 men on the *Scharnhorst,* only 36 were rescued from the frigid sea. They were transferred to the battleship HMS *Duke of York* and arrived in England on January 1, 1944.

ALLIES STORM THE BEACHES

JANUARY 1944–JUNE 1944

"Your task will not be an easy one. Your enemy is well trained, well equipped, and battle hardened. He will fight savagely."

—GENERAL DWIGHT EISENHOWER,
JUST PRIOR TO THE D-DAY INVASION

O N JANUARY 27, 1944, the besieged Soviet city of Leningrad, where an estimated one million people had died from starvation, disease, and constant shelling, was finally fully freed from encirclement after almost 900 days. It was the end of a terrible epic of suffering in which the old had been sacrificed to save the young on the principle of Soviet doctrine that "he who does not work does not eat." Life in wartime Leningrad represented the idea of "total war" at its most intense. Every citizen was a potential victim. Everyone was obliged to do their utmost to defend the city. "We are all on death row," confided a nurse to her diary, "we just don't know who is next."

The year 1944 saw every combatant nation exert itself to the fullest extent. After three to four years of warfare, populations had become used to ceaseless rationing, travel restrictions, air-defense blackouts, and long hours in fields and factories. In Europe, approximately two-thirds of the countries' national product was diverted to war. Germany and the Soviet Union between them mobilized about 46 million men and women in the armed forces. These were levels of effort that few populations could sustain for long.

Total war necessitated the mass participation of women, who comprised 35 percent of the British and American workforce and more than 50 percent

The die is cast as U.S. infantrymen storm ashore under enemy machine gun fire at Normandy on June 6, 1944. After years of discussion, seemingly endless planning and preparation, and the assembly of hundreds of thousands of troops and countless tons of materiel, the Allies finally launched the long-awaited assault on Fortress Europe.

in Germany and the USSR. Only in the United States, whose geographical immunity freed the population from the more onerous restrictions, did the war produce an economic boom. The American economy alone could afford large armaments while maintaining reasonable living standards.

For the first six months of 1944, the pace of advance on land against the Axis slowed. Both sides knew that at some point Europe would be invaded from the west, and that this blow, if successful, would probably ensure the defeat of Germany and its European allies. But while preparations went ahead for the invasion of France, Allied forces engaged in prolonged and bitter fighting on other fronts.

In Italy, the German redoubt around the ancient monastery of Monte Cassino, perched high in the mountains, proved a firm barrier. On January 22, an Allied task force landed at Anzio, farther up the coast toward Rome, in the hope of outflanking the German line. But the beachhead was contained, and for five more months the front stalled. Only on May 18 did a fierce assault by a Polish unit fighting with the Allies secure Monte Cassino. This victory broke the German line. On June 4, American forces entered Rome. The German army retreated northward to a new defensive position, the Gothic Line, from Pisa to Rimini.

Russian soldiers celebrate the end of the 872-day siege of Leningrad in January 1944. Beyond this hard-fought victory, the siege of Russia itself was coming to an end in 1944. German forces went on the defensive, and the Soviets commenced their own inexorable advance toward the enemy homeland and Berlin.

In the Soviet Union, the momentum achieved after the Battle of Kursk (summer 1943) slowed. But in the winter of 1943–44, the Soviets advanced into the Ukraine against isolated counteroffensives from the German army. After six months, Soviet forces reached the Romanian and Hungarian borders. The Crimea was cleared, and on May 9 the Germans surrendered Sevastopol. Farther north, the Red Army reached the edge of the Baltic States and was poised for an assault on Poland.

In the central Pacific, the Americans' island-hopping campaign brought them control of the Gilbert Islands and Marshall Islands by February 1944. Moreover, landings along the coast of northern New Guinea isolated Japanese strongholds and brought the Philippines within striking distance. The Japanese carrier base at Truk in the Caroline Islands was neutralized by superior American airpower, and the advance on the Mariana Islands in June destroyed Japanese land-based airpower there.

When U.S. Marines landed on the Mariana island of Saipan on June 15, the Japanese fleet finally intervened. Admiral Ozawa Jisaburo led nine carriers and 450 aircraft against 15 American carriers and more than 900 aircraft. The Battle of the Philippine Sea was fought from June 19 to 20. By the end of it, the Japanese had lost the majority of their aircraft and withdrew. The 30,000-strong Japanese garrison on Saipan fought to the death, and by early July the island was in American hands. From the Marianas, it was possible to begin long-distance bombing of the Japanese homeland with the new B-29 Superfortress.

Throughout these months, the Allies' western strategy was dominated by preparation for Operation Overlord, the invasion of northwestern France by a combined American and British Commonwealth force. The planning and administration alone absorbed 300,000 people. A combined arms assault on a heavily defended coastline was an operation fraught with risk. The deadlock at Anzio and the cost of assaults in the Pacific against small but determined garrisons made it clear that a frontal attack on continental Europe across the Atlantic Wall defenses would be a costly and uncertain enterprise.

The attackers did have some clear advantages. Britain and the United States had overwhelming naval power, and after their victory in the Atlantic in 1943, they could maintain seaborne logistics without considerable difficulty. The Allies also had attained air superiority over Western Europe in February and March 1943. During the invasion, 12,000 aircraft would support Allied forces against only 170 serviceable German aircraft. The Allies also could choose the place and time of the invasion, as long as it could be concealed from the enemy.

The greatest success enjoyed by the Allies in the run-up to Overlord was in the field of disinformation. The extensive use of double agents, careful camouflage, and the strictest secrecy prevented the Germans from guessing the invasion point or the precise day. The German commander of the Atlantic Wall, Field Marshal Erwin Rommel, believed like most of the high command that the Allies would take the short route across the English Channel toward the Pas de Calais. Limited German forces were kept in Normandy, France, but it was always assumed that an attack there would be a feint.

U.S. general Dwight D. Eisenhower would decide the final date. He had been appointed the supreme commander of Allied forces due to his great skills as an organizer and diplomat, qualities he needed to the full in holding together his command team. General Marshall thus could be held in reserve in case the invasion failed and a second one had to be mounted. The Allies had appointed General Bernard Montgomery, who had already defeated

A welder at the Electric Boat Company in Groton, Connecticut, adjusts her goggles before getting to work in late 1943. This scene would have been unthinkable in the U.S. only two years before. However, total war brought many social changes, including the mass influx of women into jobs once considered the sole domain of men.

Rommel once, as their ground forces commander. In late May, the final battle plan was approved. Allied forces would attack in Normandy across five selected beaches. Once established, the bridgehead would be consolidated and then used as the launchpad for a breakout. The Allies would roll up the German front in France and push it back to the Rhine River.

The date for the invasion was fixed as early May, but postponed to June when more landing craft would be available. The weather in early June was so severe that German commanders relaxed. Rommel went back to Germany for his wife's birthday. Eisenhower set D-Day—military shorthand for the first

U.S. Marines ignore dead Japanese soldiers as they take the enemy under fire on Saipan in June 1944. More than 25,000 Japanese died on this island, and with them perished any lingering hopes of victory that the Japanese had. With the U.S. seizure of Saipan, the Japanese homeland was now within range of the American heavy bomber force.

day of any major operation—for June 5. But with no improvement in the weather by June 4, Eisenhower was faced with a difficult choice. At 9:45 P.M. on the 4th, he gathered his commanders to order the invasion for June 6. Though heavy rain continued outside, there was better meteorological news. Eisenhower said quietly, "OK, let's go," launching the largest seaborne invasion in history.

Twenty-seven hundred ships moved to position, and in the early hours of June 6 they approached the French coast. By the time German forces were alerted, the invasion was upon them. A colossal naval barrage and around-the-clock bombing reduced resistance on all but one beach, Omaha. There, U.S. forces faced stiff opposition from defenders who were dug in on high cliffs and had by chance avoided the worst of the bombardment. The American army did not have a foothold on Omaha until the evening. On the other beaches, rapid progress was made and a bridgehead a few miles wide and deep was carved out in the first hours. Within days, more than 300,000 soldiers and 54,000 vehicles went ashore, using prefabricated harbors known as "Mulberries" that had been towed in sections across the Channel.

Throughout June, the Allies made slow progress. U.S. forces cleared the Cotentin Peninsula further west, but the city of Caen—which was to be the hinge of the whole operation—remained in German hands. Relations between Eisenhower and Montgomery worsened. Historians to this day have argued that the British were too cautious in the face of fierce German resistance. Britain's chief concern was to avoid defeat at all costs. Most of the Anglo-American troops lacked battle experience, and the invasion was a steep learning curve. At no point in June could ultimate victory be taken for granted.

On July 1, Rommel began an assault on the British line with five panzer divisions, provoking the fiercest fighting of the campaign so far. American attempts to accelerate the breakout southward (code-named Operation Cobra) were slowed by the rapid redeployment of German armor.

The situation was made more awkward for the Western Allies by the rapid success of the Red Army in the East. Stalin had promised a renewed summer campaign to coincide with Overlord. The operation, code-named Bagration, was undertaken against the largest concentration of German forces in the East, Army Group Center. Bagration also was meticulously prepared, veiled in secrecy, and covered by a deception operation as successful as that in the West. Soviet forces moved into concealed positions, while partisan attacks disabled German communications and Soviet aircraft pounded German positions. On June 22, the full-scale operation was launched with devastating success. Within a week, Soviet forces broke through the German defensive line, captured tens of thousands of German soldiers, and advanced at a rate of up to 25 miles per day. Farther south, the Ukrainian campaign began again with assaults toward Lvov. Here, too, German defense crumbled. While the Western Allies were facing 15 German divisions, the Red Army engaged 228 German divisions across a 500-mile front.

German soldiers attempt to organize a defense at Warsaw in the summer of 1944. In June, while the Western Allies struggled to break out of the Normandy beachhead, the Red Army launched Operation Bagration. The Soviets swept forward on a 500-mile front against 228 German divisions, which proved unable to stem the tide.

Farther east, Japan launched a wide offensive across large tracts of central China. This was one of the last major offensives by the Axis powers, and it came at a time when Japanese fortunes in the central Pacific were waning. On April 18, the Japanese army began Operation *Ichi-Go* to destroy air bases that could be used by American aircraft to attack the Japanese mainland. The operation was also designed to open a continuous overland route (road and rail) between Manchuria and Singapore to facilitate the importation of strategic resources from Japanese conquests in the Southeast without interdiction from American submarines and aircraft.

On May 27, the Japanese launched a separate operation to capture the area of the middle Yangtze River. After six months of fighting, Japanese-held territory was consolidated into a single bloc. The campaign caused a growing rift between Chiang Kai-shek and the Americans, represented in China by General Joseph Stilwell. With the loss of air bases, there was little more that the Americans could achieve. Stilwell was recalled at Chiang's insistence, and the Chinese theater remained a contest between Nationalist, Communist, and Japanese forces over the future of Eastern Asia.

1944

January 1: American Louis Jordan and his Tympany Five hit No. 1 on the *Billboard* R&B charts with their song "Ration Blues."

January 3: Thousands of German troops die, and others are captured, as the Red Army invades Nazi-occupied Poland and sends Hitler's army into retreat.

January 4: The United States launches operations behind Axis lines, delivering weapons and supplies to anti-Nazi partisans in France, Italy, and the Low Countries.

January 7: In preparation for the invasion of France, Allied planes drop airborne operatives into the occupied country to help train their partisans in guerrilla tactics to support regular troops.

January 8: Count Ciano, Mussolini's one-time foreign minister, ambassador, and son-in-law, faces a tribunal for his role in the vote to oust *Il Duce*. His wife will escape to Switzerland the next day, but the count will die before a firing squad on January 11.

January 9: Churchill meets with Free French leader Charles de Gaulle to discuss the role the Free French will play in the Allied invasion of France.
• The Allies attack Cervaro and Monte Trocchio, Italy, in yet another effort to break through the defenses known as the German Winter Line. • Twenty-two civilians are murdered in Lyons, France, in reprisal for the assassination of two German soldiers by members of the French Resistance.

January 10: The waters off Burma are heavily mined by the RAF. This will ultimately bring a complete, though temporary, halt to Japanese shipping in the area.

Tojo's rise and fall Japanese prime minster Tojo Hideki reviews a regiment of Thai troops in January 1944. Disagreements within the Japanese supreme command over the conduct of the war prompted Tojo to name himself chief of Army General Staff in February. This unprecedented move brought the prime minister to the pinnacle of his power. His reign, however, was short-lived. Disaster followed disaster on the battlefield, culminating in mid-1944 with the fall of Saipan. Abandoned by his political backers, Tojo and his entire cabinet resigned on July 18, 1944. Once one of the most powerful men in Asia, Tojo went into seclusion.

Australians succeed in New Guinea Australian infantrymen engage the Japanese in New Guinea. From 1942 until about January 1944, Australian troops shouldered the brunt of the ground combat against the Japanese in New Guinea. In late 1943, the Australians drove the Japanese from Lae and Salamaua and then from the Huon Peninsula and the Ramu Valley. Defeated and starving, the Japanese 18th Army was sent into full retreat toward Wewak. About 35,000 Japanese died while the Australians lost fewer than 1,300.

Korea's forced laborers An Australian medic on New Guinea offers aid to Koreans who had been conscripted into forced labor by the Japanese. Koreans were only one of many nationalities tapped as slave labor by the Japanese Empire. Some were sent to work in Japanese factories and mines. Others were used as forced labor on engineering projects, as so-called "comfort women" in army brothels, and as soldiers with the Japanese military. As many as five million Koreans are thought to have been taken as forced workers. How many died from 1939 to 1946 will never be known, but the estimates run as high as one million.

A "souvenir" from New Guinea In May 1944, *Life* magazine featured this photo of Phoenix war worker Natalie Nickerson. She is writing a thank you note to her Navy boyfriend for sending her a Japanese soldier's skull as a war souvenir. Her "big, handsome Navy lieutenant" had collected the skull while fighting in New Guinea. He and 13 friends autographed the skull and inscribed it, "This is a good Jap—a dead one picked up on the New Guinea Beach." Natalie named the skull "Tojo" after Japanese prime minister Tojo Hideki.

French collaborators Even before the German invasion of France, part of the French population longed for a Fascist government similar to Franco's regime in Spain. Such people actually welcomed France's surrender to Germany in June 1940. During 1940–45, when France was ruled by the Germans and the pro-Nazi Vichy government, a low-level civil war was fought between the French Resistance and Nazi collaborators. In this 1944 photograph, French villagers, some of them armed, confront the woman in a dark dress and the man in a white shirt, both of whom deny having informed for the Nazis.

1944

January 11: Operation Pointblank, a direct Allied attack on the *Luftwaffe*, kicks off with a series of bombing raids against German aeronautic facilities.

January 14: The Allies bomb the Axis-aligned Bulgarian capital of Sofia.
• Roosevelt warns Nationalist Chinese leader Chiang Kai-shek that the United States will withhold lend-lease assistance if the Chinese do not send additional troops to the front. Chiang will reply by demanding a $1 billion loan in exchange for continued collaboration.

January 17: The British government denies an unfounded accusation in the Soviet media that it is negotiating peace with the Nazis. • Supreme Allied Commander Eisenhower taps General Omar Bradley to lead the U.S. First Army.

January 22: The Allies mount a massive surprise attack on German positions in south-central Italy, landing a 37,000-man force on the coast at Anzio.

January 24: Following Hitler's orders to hold it to the death, German forces harden their positions along the Gustav Line.

January 26: In a report detailing their "investigation" of the Katyn massacre, Soviet authorities issue a denial and blame the Germans. However, Katyn will prove to be one atrocity not attributable to the Nazis.

January 27: After 872 days, the siege of Leningrad finally ends. Close to a million Soviets died, mostly from starvation and bombings. • Churchill directs the British bomber command to prioritize the support of partisan guerrillas in occupied Europe, along with the destruction of the Axis war machine. • The U.S. government publishes a report detailing the horrors of the Bataan death march.

"The neutrons emitted from the gadget will diffuse through the air over a distance of 1 to 2 km, nearly independent of the energy release. Over this region, their intensity will be sufficient to kill a person."

—PHYSICIST HANS BETHE, LOS ALAMOS, NEW MEXICO, IN A MEMO ENTITLED "EXPECTED DAMAGE OF THE GADGET," 1943

Groves leads the Manhattan Project U.S. brigadier general Leslie Groves named the Manhattan Project and was a driving force behind the creation of the first atomic bomb. He chose the sites for research and materials production and put physicist J. Robert Oppenheimer in charge of the scientific laboratory. Groves was intelligent and highly organized, and although his arrogance offended some scientists, he worked well with Oppenheimer. Groves maintained high security at the Los Alamos, New Mexico, facility, having mail censored, long-distance calls monitored, travel restricted to within 100 miles, and contact with those on the outside limited.

Oppenheimer directs Los Alamos team The presence of brilliant American physicist J. Robert Oppenheimer attracted scientists from all over the world to the remote New Mexican desert to work on the Manhattan Project. Oppenheimer directed the scientific team headquartered at Los Alamos. Although he suffered from periods of depression, he personally helped resolve or control conflicts that inevitably rose among the diverse international group. He, like most Los Alamos scientists, was dedicated to ending war for all time. After atomic bombs were used at Hiroshima and Nagasaki, Oppenheimer was appalled at the civilian deaths. Following the war, as chief advisor of the United States Atomic Energy Commission, he lobbied for the international control of atomic energy.

The Manhattan Project

THE MANHATTAN PROJECT was America's effort to build the first atomic bombs. Ironically, nuclear fission was discovered in Germany in 1938. At the outbreak of war, Germany was the only nation with a military office dedicated to future applications of nuclear energy. However, American physicists recognized that fission's accompanying energy release had military potential.

Leó Szilárd, who fled Germany in 1933 and worked at Columbia University in New York City, conceived the possibility of a nuclear chain reaction. With Enrico Fermi, an Italian also at Columbia, he developed the first nuclear reactor in 1939. Albert Einstein, the world's most famous scientist, shared Szilárd's concern about German nuclear research, and on August 2, 1939, Einstein sent President Roosevelt a letter warning about the danger of a German atomic bomb. Consequently, Roosevelt established a committee of scientists to determine the feasibility of an American nuclear weapon.

Initial work proceeded at a leisurely pace. After Pearl Harbor, however, Roosevelt gave this project top priority. Eventually, $2 billion would be spent turning theory into reality. Roosevelt assigned the task to the Army Corps of Engineers. From September 1942, the project's commanding officer was Brigadier General Leslie Groves, whose practical know-how and determination were crucial.

Research had hitherto concentrated on achieving fission with the scarce uranium isotope U-235. But Ernest Lawrence made the significant discovery in 1942 that the more abundant U-238 could be converted into plutonium, which could also be made to undergo fission.

The name "Manhattan Project" derived from the Manhattan Engineer District, which initially managed the weapon's development. The project's facilities eventually spread across the country. There were four major locations: the basement of the University of Chicago's football stadium, where, with their reactor pile, Fermi and Arthur Compton produced the first uranium chain reaction; Hanford, Washington, where plutonium-producing reactors and chemical-separation plants operated; Oak Ridge, Tennessee, where a gaseous diffusion plant separated uranium-235 from uranium-238; and Los Alamos, New Mexico, where physicist J. Robert Oppenheimer headed a laboratory dedicated to designing and constructing atomic

Manhattan Project workers at a test site in Los Alamos

bombs. Although the 125,000 people involved in the project knew it was vital war work, very few knew its purpose.

Britain, where neutrons had been discovered, was allowed to share the research. It was in Britain that refugee scientists discovered the critical knowledge that not nearly as much fissionable material was needed as originally thought. Barred from this knowledge, the Soviet Union turned to espionage for information.

After Roosevelt's death, Truman was told of the atomic bomb. With German defeat imminent, he sought advice on how to use it against Japan. Truman, General Marshall, and Secretary of War Henry Stimson came to agree on a plan under which one atomic bomb would be dropped on a city to shock Japan into surrender. If that did not do it, a second one would be dropped to give the impression that the U.S. had a large supply. If Japan did not surrender, all bombs becoming available thereafter would be saved for use in support of the invasion of Kyushu (Operation Olympic), scheduled for November 1, 1945.

The first atomic weapon test took place on July 16, 1945, at Alamogordo, New Mexico. Staggeringly successful, it produced a blast equalling 15,000 to 20,000 tons of TNT. On July 24, Truman ordered preparations for use against Japan. The two bombs consequently dropped in August were products of the project. The first used uranium 235; the second, plutonium.

1944

January 29: More than 700 civilians die when U.S. bombers attack Frankfurt, Germany, with about 800 bombers. • The *Luftwaffe* takes another hit in a disastrous raid on Britain, losing 57 aircraft. • The U.S. begins an air campaign over the Marshall Islands to soften Japanese defenses prior to a ground-based assault.

January 30: The U.S. Army suffers a tremendous loss when an offensive against the Italian town of Cisterna turns into an ambush. Nearly two battalions of U.S. Army Rangers lose their lives.

February 1: Relaxed rationing rules in Britain allow for the return of pockets, pleats, buttons, and collars to men's suits.

February 2: The Americans obtain authorization to use Soviet air bases to rest and refuel during shuttle sorties. • One hundred Polish civilians are murdered by the Nazis in reprisal for the partisan killing of Franz Kutschera, the SS chief in charge of the Warsaw district.

February 3: The *Wehrmacht* is forced to divert valuable resources to rescue some 60,000 Eighth Army troops caught in a snare by the advancing Red Army within Soviet territory. • The U.S. Navy attacks Japanese soil for the first time, blasting the northern Japanese island of Paramushiro with ship-based artillery.

February 4: The United States loses nearly 150 troops while capturing the Marshall island of Kwajalein. The defeated Japanese fare far worse, losing nearly 5,000 soldiers.

February 5: Michel Hollard, the French Resistance leader who warned the British about Germany's V-bomb capabilities—enabling the Allies to destroy some related facilities—is captured by the Nazi Gestapo. He will survive the war.

The Los Alamos community In 1943 hundreds of families moved to the highly secret Los Alamos National Laboratory community in New Mexico, where the first atomic bomb was built. Isolated on primitive roads, fenced with barbed wire, and patrolled by mounted guards, the community was shut off from the outside world. Even so, young Princeton scientist Richard Feynman demonstrated security weaknesses by repeatedly sneaking out through holes in the fence and then walking back in through the gate to draw guards' attention to the flaws. Workers lived in simple housing (*pictured*), although those higher in the scientific hierarchy had proportionately better homes. Los Alamos residents worked hard and relaxed at movies, restaurants, and parties within the compound.

Italian groups resist German occupation After Italy's government surrendered to the Allies on September 8, 1943, a sprawling and spontaneous Italian resistance movement sprang up against German occupation. It consisted of a loose and sometimes quarrelsome network of Catholics, Jews, Communists, and other groups. Resistance took many forms, including strikes, noncooperation of Italian soldiers in the *Wehrmacht,* and partisan warfare. These Italians, pictured in Sicily, aided South African troops in locating German snipers. During 1944, resistance groups exasperated the Germans by establishing several provisional governments in northern Italy.

Operation Shingle The Allied invasion of Italy in September 1943 resulted in a stalemate as the Germans successfully defended the Gustav Line across Italy. The Allies launched Operation Shingle (so-called because it was expected to peel away German defenses like roof shingles) on January 22, 1944. Allied troops, such as the ones seen here, landed behind the Gustav Line a mere 35 miles from Rome. But the landing was not followed by an adequate Allied offensive, and the Battle of Anzio turned into a bitter four-month siege that was eerily reminiscent of World War I's paralyzing trench warfare.

Don't Let That Shadow Touch Them
Buy WAR BONDS

A stern warning After the surprise attack on Pearl Harbor, propaganda messages on the radio and on posters encouraged Americans to conserve particular materials and help fund the war. This poster of children about to be covered with the shadow of a swastika was typical of wartime propaganda. It attempted to convince everyone that the Axis threat was real and that the only way to stop it was through the purchase of war bonds.

Kesselring's strategy in Italy The military shrewdness of German field marshal Albert Kesselring (*left*), seen here at Anzio in February 1944, proved the bane of Allied hopes for an easy conquest of Italy. It was he who engineered the Gustav Line, a seemingly impassable barrier that thwarted an Allied advance upon Rome. Initially surprised by the January 1944 Allied landings of Operation Shingle, Kesselring quickly observed the inadequacy of the Allied offensive, then deftly mobilized German troops to pin down the invaders on the Anzio beachhead. Kesselring, who was especially adept at finding defensive advantages in Italy's landscape and weather, also ordered the killing of Italian civilians.

1944

February 7: The first U-boat outfitted with a *Schnorkel*, which allows delivery of outside air to the submerged ship, becomes operational.

February 8: The RAF drops the heaviest bomb of the war thus far, six tons, on the *Gnome-et-Rhone* aircraft engine manufacturing facility in Limoges, France.

February 9: Dr. George Bell, Bishop of Chichester, questions the necessity of bombing raids against German targets in a speech before the House of Lords. His concerns are rebuffed.

February 10: The Allies are told that Hungary might offer its unconditional surrender, provided that the Soviet Union is not represented at the ceremony.

February 10–11: Germany's prized battleship *Tirpitz* once again survives an attempt on its life, this time by the Soviet air force.

February 12: Wary of men in his own inner circle who would like to see him dead, Hitler merges the SD (political foreign intelligence organization) and the *Abwehr* (German military intelligence organization).

February 15: The historic monastery at Monte Cassino in Italy is bombed by the Allies in an effort to root the Germans from their strategically superior hilltop post. Though the monastery is destroyed, the Germans tenaciously hold the hill.

February 15–16: In the most intense raid to date, more than 800 Allied bombers rain destruction on Berlin.

February 15–20: New Zealand takes Green Island in the eastern Solomons, winning an important forward air base.

U.S. bombards Kwajalein GIs of the Seventh ("Hourglass") Division manhandle a gun forward during fighting on Kwajalein in the Marshall Islands. A model amphibious operation, the landing on February 1 was preceded by a naval, air, and artillery bombardment so intense that "the entire island looked as if it had been picked up to 20,000 feet and then dropped," said a witness. Initial U.S. casualties were light, but resistance stiffened on the third day. The island, with its valuable anchorage and airfield, was secured the following day. GI casualties included 142 killed and 854 wounded. Japanese casualties included 4,938 killed and 206 captured.

"Merrill's Marauders" In late 1943, 2,900 American servicemen responded to a presidential call for volunteers for hazardous duty. They formed a Special Forces unit (partly modeled on Orde Wingate's British "Chindits") to operate behind Japanese lines in Burma. "Merrill's Marauders"—named after their leader, Brigadier General Frank Merrill (*pictured*)—began disrupting Japanese communications and supply lines in February 1944. In five major engagements and many skirmishes, they defeated veteran Japanese soldiers, who greatly outnumbered them. The highly successful Marauders lost 700 men. Nearly that many, including Merrill, had to be hospitalized.

Enigma, Colossus, and Ultra

SIGNALS INTELLIGENCE—SIGINT—involved the interception, breaking, and interpretation of encoded radio transmissions. It played a vital part in the defeat of the Axis powers by allowing Roosevelt, Churchill, and senior Allied field commanders to make decisions based upon prior knowledge of enemy intentions and actions.

Before the war, the *Wehrmacht* had adopted an electromechanical encryption machine called "Enigma" for its strategic radio communications, and the Germans assumed that the Enigma system was entirely secure. Using material sold by a German to French intelligence, the Poles had broken the Enigma system and had shared their knowledge with the British and French in the summer of 1939.

Germans operating an Enigma machine

This meant that the Allied code-breakers already understood the operating system, which comprised a battery-powered keyboard with changeable internal settings. When the letter keys typed by the operator struck the machine's internal rotors, these revolved automatically to choose and apply substitute letters at random. Originally, the Enigma had three rotors, but a more secure four-rotor version was introduced for U-boats in 1942. However, without the rel-evant key, breaking the coded intercepts still depended upon thousands of hours of manual message analysis and mathematical calculations by the cryptanalysts.

In 1940 the top-secret SIGINT center at Bletchley Park, England, already possessed an early-type electromechanical computer that enabled much coded material to be read from the outset, albeit with varying success and often lengthy delays. Then, in December 1943, the Colossus 1 electronic computer became operational at Bletchley. It was followed in June 1944 by Colossus 2—the world's first programmable electronic digital computer. It had a limited capacity memory and a photoelectronic tape reading capability.

Eventually, numerous computers were used at Bletchley, together with several other code-breaking machines and more than 8,000 cryptanalysts. The vital intelligence gleaned from the Enigma intercepts was code-named "Ultra." Unknown to Hitler, the British successfully learned of his plans in North Africa through Enigma. They also learned the areas of Normandy where the Germans were likely to mount counterattacks after the D-Day invasion.

Raids devastate Japanese at Truk A Japanese "Jill" torpedo bomber attacks through a hail of antiaircraft fire during a U.S. carrier attack on Truk Island. As the principal Japanese fleet base in the Pacific, Truk was subjected to repeated U.S. carrier raids. One of the most devastating took place on February 17 and 18, 1944, in conjunction with the Marshall Islands operation. The attack destroyed 250 to 275 enemy aircraft and sank nearly 40 ships of various types. The raids so devastated enemy capabilities at Truk that Admiral Nimitz abandoned plans to invade the island with five U.S. divisions. The once potent enemy bastion was simply bypassed.

1944

February 16–17: Japan's Imperial Navy is forced to withdraw from Truk, its main base in the central Pacific, when Truk is subjected to a highly destructive assault by American carrier aircraft.

February 17: The Red Army accepts the surrender of nearly 20,000 German Eighth Army troops, who are among those trapped earlier in the month. However, most of the Germans, some 55,000, go down fighting. • The Americans capture another forward base in the Marshall Islands with the occupation of Bikini Atoll. The atoll will become famous in later years as the site of the first hydrogen bomb test.

February 18: Seventy members of the French Resistance, sitting on death row in Amiens Prison in Nazi-occupied France, escape when Allied bombs damage the walls of their cells.

February 20: A ferry laden with tanks of heavy water en route to German atomic research facilities is sunk by a Norwegian saboteur in the very deep waters of Lake Tinnsjö.

February 20–25: During "Big Week," the American air force in Britain forces the Germans to send up their fighters to protect their aircraft factories against a massive assault by bombers. The escorting Mustang fighters decimate German fighter strength.

February 22: Greek partisans sabotage a track used by German troop trains. As a result, a train plunges into a ravine, leading to the deaths of some 400 German soldiers. • Japanese prime minister General Tojo takes over as chief of the Japanese Army General Staff.

Soviet advances This grim picture of a slain soldier, mashed by military vehicles like "roadkill," hints at the savagery of the fighting on the Eastern Front. By early 1944, when this picture was probably taken, the Soviets had turned the tide against the Germans. On January 4, Axis forces were routed westward across the prewar Polish border. A month later, Soviet troops had advanced 100 miles into Poland. In the Ukraine, the port city of Odessa fell to the Soviets on April 10, and the Germans lost Sevastopol on May 9.

Kleist defies Hitler After participating in the invasions of Poland in 1939, France in 1940, and Yugoslavia in 1941, General Paul Ludwig Ewald von Kleist led his tanks across the Russian border on June 22, 1941. By September, he had played critical roles in astounding military successes, including the capture of much of the Ukraine. He was promoted to field marshal in 1943. But even Kleist's considerable prowess faltered before inexorable Soviet offensives. Never one of Hitler's yes-men, Kleist in 1944 defied the *Führer*'s orders by retreating across the Ukrainian territory he had earlier conquered. In March, Hitler permanently relieved him of command.

Göring's excesses By 1944 Nazi *Reichsmarschall* Hermann Göring, discredited by his *Luftwaffe*'s failures, was showing the ill effects of his devotion to sensual pleasures. His bloated girth, outlandish costumes, and erratic behavior made him a popular subject for cartoonists. (Even Germans referred to him as *"Der Dicke,"* meaning the "Fat One.") This caricature of a grossly fat Göring with a skull-like face is signed "Kukryniksy." The best known of Soviet cartoon signatures, Kukryniksy was actually a collective name used by collaborating artists Mikhail Kupriyanov, Porfiry Krylov, and Nikolai Sokolov.

Isolated Garrisons

JAPAN PLANNED TO PROTECT its Asian conquests with a chain of island garrisons. From the Aleutians in the north, through the central and southwest Pacific, through the Dutch East Indies to Burma, Japan held an enormous defensive perimeter with numerically inadequate forces.

Once the Japanese advance had been halted, Allied strategy was predicated on counteroffensives advancing eastward through the mid-Pacific and northward from Australia, leaving bypassed Japanese garrisons to wither on the vine. As a consequence, hundreds of thousands of Japanese troops held territory by 1944 that had neither offensive nor defensive value. Allied sea and air superiority meant that supplies could not reach them without great difficulty (often by submarines), and their redundant garrisons could not be switched to other fronts.

Even before this, Japanese forces in the Pacific faced severe shortages, largely because of rivalry within the Japanese system. For example, in the Dutch East Indies the army had trucks without tires, while on neighboring islands the navy had tires without trucks. Neither would swap. Japanese soldiers simply took food from local people. On New Britain, tens of thousands of civilian residents died, their gardens ransacked by starving soldiers.

At war's end, Allied forces gradually accepted the surrender of large garrisons, including 38,000 on Truk, 100,000 at Rabaul, and 40,000 in the Halmaheras. In the Solomons (where the first American counteroffensive had begun in mid-1942), more than 12,000 men remained, isolated and helpless. Japan's flawed strategy effectively neutered a half-million combatants.

U.S. fights on Bougainville American soldiers advance with a Sherman tank during the fighting on Bougainville in the Solomon Islands. After the initial landings on November 1, 1943, construction of an airstrip at Cape Torokina began immediately. Two other airfields were soon constructed to support the air campaign against Japanese-held Rabaul. U.S. Army troops under Major General Oscar Griswold relieved the Third Marine Division in December to expand the beachhead, protect the perimeter, and tend to the logistics of the newly established base. Army troops saw limited fighting until March 9, 1944, when the Japanese attacked in force. The GIs smashed the enemy assault, and the valuable airfields were never again threatened.

Americans seize Eniwetok Marines of the 22nd Regiment stay low during combat on Japanese-held Eniwetok. The U.S. seized the atoll on February 17–23, 1944, almost as an afterthought to the landings on Roi-Namur and Kwajalein. Those operations had gone so well that Admiral Chester Nimitz decided to capitalize on his good fortune and seize Eniwetok more than two months ahead of schedule. The atoll would serve as a base for future operations against Japanese-held Truk and the Caroline Islands. The 22nd Marines and the 106th Infantry quickly overcame the 3,500 Japanese defenders on Eniwetok and adjacent islands. Fewer than 350 Americans were killed in action.

1944

February 23: The Seventh Indian Division of the British 14th Army scores Britain's first military victory over the Japanese, at Sinzweya, Burma. • The Marianas see action for the first time during the war, as the Allies launch a series of air attacks against the Japanese on the islands of Guam, Saipan, Tinian, and Rota.

February 29: Ukrainian Red Army general Nikolai Vatutin is mortally wounded in an attack by Ukrainian nationalists who are fighting for a Ukraine independent of the Soviet Union. • American infantrymen invade the strategically important Admiralty Islands, north of New Guinea.

March 1: Germany announces that it has detained and enslaved some five million foreign nationals to fulfill the Reich's war-related labor needs.

March 2: More than 400 Italian civilians die on a cargo train when it stalls in a tunnel and asphyxiates them with fumes. The freight cars had become the only means of transportation in a country where all available resources are being devoted to the war effort. • Turkey pays for its stubborn neutrality with the loss of American lend-lease assistance.

March 3: The Allies reveal that the U.S., Britain, and Soviet Union will share equally in the war spoils of the Italian navy. • As many as six million workers in northern Italy strike in protest of deportations of Italians to German slave labor camps.

March 4: The Japanese authorities order schoolchildren as young as 12 to mobilize for the war effort.

March 6: Berlin is bombed by a U.S. force of nearly 700 bombers, but the Americans suffer the loss of 69 planes, a one-day record. • Chinese and American tank forces engage the remnants of a Japanese marine division at Burma's Tanai River.

Hitler's nephew Unknown to most Americans but watched very carefully by the FBI, William Patrick Hitler, the nephew of Adolf Hitler, lived with his mother in New York City during the war. He was the son of Hitler's half-brother, Alois, and Alois's Irish-born wife. William and his mother traveled to America for a lecture tour, and they stayed voluntarily there at the start of the war. His attempt to enter the American military in 1942 was stonewalled, but he eventually was sworn in to the Navy (*pictured*) in March 1944.

Allies' dual assaults in Italy The Allied landing at Anzio and the initial Allied assault on the Italian town of Cassino (*pictured*) both took place in January 1944. Allied leadership hoped that the Anzio landing would bypass the Germans' formidable Gustav Line and divert and weaken German defenses at Cassino, the key position on the line. The strategy failed, and fighting dragged on in both places. But in May, the Allies finally broke through both at Anzio and Cassino. Bombing raids left Cassino in ruins.

Britain's eccentric officer British major general Orde Wingate (*right*) confers with officers during his guerrilla campaign against Japanese forces in Burma. Eccentric, Wingate wore an alarm clock on his wrist and snacked on raw onions. He first demonstrated a flair for unconventional warfare while fighting Arab insurgents in Palestine. In 1941 he led a guerrilla unit against the Italians in Ethiopia, where his 1,700-man force eventually accepted the surrender of 20,000 enemy soldiers. In 1943 and 1944, he led a long-range penetration brigade, the famed "Chindits," against the Japanese in Burma. Wingate was killed in a plane crash on March 24, 1944.

Bose, INA fight against the British Indian nationalist Subhas Chandra Bose became commander-in-chief of the Indian National Army (INA). The INA allied itself with the Japanese during the war. A former president of the Indian National Congress, Bose rejected Mohandas Gandhi's nonviolent resistance to British colonial rule, declaring, "Give me blood and I shall give you freedom!" His 85,000-man INA fought alongside the Japanese in the defeats at Kohima and Imphal. They surrendered following the capitulation of Japan. Though official records claim Bose died in a plane crash in 1945, his actual fate remains uncertain.

Outlook bleak in Japan Osaka, Japan, suffers from the effects of Allied attacks *and* an earthquake. Despite a media brimming with upbeat "victory news," it was becoming clear by 1944 that the war was not going well for Japan. Shortages of food and clothing led to price controls and rationing, while defeats such as the loss of Saipan could not be concealed. Patriotic slogans—"Deny one's self and serve the nation"—proliferated in an effort to stiffen Japanese resolve. Despite their skepticism about the news, the general population was prepared to fight to the end.

Stigmatized veterans Japanese amputee war veterans climb sacred Mount Fuji in 1944. The popular Japanese rhetoric celebrating heroic death on the battlefield left wounded veterans in an uncomfortable situation when they returned home maimed but alive. An effort was made by the Military Protection Association, part of the Ministry of Welfare, to portray the war-wounded as *hakui yûshi* (heroes in white). Their presence was encouraged at patriotic rallies and other public events. Still, the unstated feeling that they had somehow failed to meet their obligation to seize victory or die was deeply ingrained and difficult to overcome.

1944

March 7: The British House of Commons debates whether popular singers, singing about the hardships of war on the BBC, damage morale on the front. • The gas chambers at Auschwitz-Birkenau claim more than 3,800 Jewish deportees from the Theresienstadt Ghetto.

March 11: In the first of what will be many trials of French "collaborators" (French men and women who aided and abetted the Nazis), Vichy interior minister Pierre Pucheu receives a guilty verdict and a death sentence.

March 12: Czechoslovakia's government-in-exile sends a message to Czech citizens back home to revolt against the occupying Nazis. • Britain suspends travel between England and Ireland two days after Ireland denies an Allied request to close down Axis consular offices that effectively serve as espionage operations for Axis nations.

March 14: In Germany, Wernher von Braun (a future NASA star) is detained temporarily for spending time and money on projects that have little to do with the imperialist aims of the Reich.

March 15: Responding to Hungary's recent flirtation with the Allies, German troops stage along the border, forewarning an invasion.

March 16: Oswald John Job, at age 59, becomes the oldest person to be executed under the terms of Britain's 1940 Treachery Act. Job had passed secrets to the Nazis in letters using invisible ink.

March 18: The RAF drops 3,000 tons of bombs on Frankfurt, Germany. A separate raid four days later will claim more than 1,000 civilian lives.

March 20: Germany occupies Hungary two days after Hitler gave his troops the order to march.

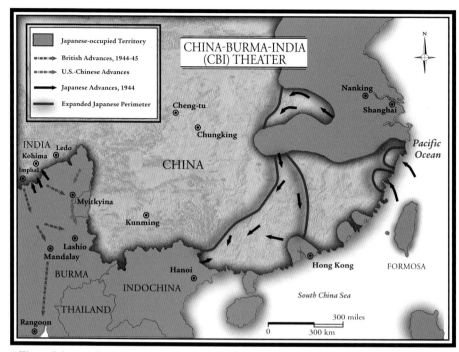

Allies ultimately prevail in Burma The fate of the China-Burma-India region was determined by the British 14th Army's successful Burma campaign (supported by U.S.-led Chinese Nationalist forces) from mid-1944, following its victories at Imphal and Kohima. The experienced and battle-hardened Japanese had initially enjoyed some successes against the British and Indian forces from 1942 to early 1944. However, Japan's overextended logistic support system finally frustrated its strategic plans. Mandalay was occupied by the Allies in March, and Rangoon fell in May. The Japanese forces in Burma eventually surrendered on August 28, 1945.

Allies advance in India, Burma
U.S. troops cross the Irrawaddy River in Burma. Alarmed by the buildup in Allied strength in late 1943, the Japanese launched an offensive against Imphal and Kohima in northeastern India in order to cut the railway that supplied "The Hump" airlift to China. After hard fighting, the Japanese conceded defeat by early July and retreated, having suffered 55,000 casualties. It was the largest Japanese defeat up to that time. Elsewhere, Chinese divisions commanded by General Joseph Stilwell were on the attack in the Ledo area of Burma, and in mid-April 1944 Chinese divisions mounted an attack on the Yunnan front. Hard-pressed, the Japanese retreated. By the time monsoon season arrived in 1944, the Allies were poised to recapture Burma.

Soviets storm into Belorussia A casualty of Operation Bagration lies by a German artillery piece in the Belorussian capital of Minsk. Launched on June 22, 1944, Bagration pitted 1.7 million Red Army troops against 800,000 Germans of Army Group Center in Belorussia. Enjoying overwhelming superiority in men and guns—including 24,000 artillery pieces—the Soviets were unstoppable. Minsk fell on July 3. In two months of fighting, the Red Army liberated most of Belorussia and drove into Poland. German Army Group Center was annihilated, with 300,000 dead, 250,000 wounded, and 120,000 captured. Soviet losses totaled 68,000 killed or missing and 110,000 wounded.

Sabotage by the French Resistance A train car sits atop the remains of an engine in Saône-et-Loire, France. Such acts of sabotage by the French Resistance were among the most effective tactics against German occupation. From January to September 1943, the number of attacks on railroads leaped from 130 each month to 530, greatly reducing German mobility in France. French factories used for German military production were also frequent targets. In addition to committing acts of violence and sabotage, the French Resistance also supplied intelligence to the Allied powers—information that proved especially crucial on D-Day.

Kaiser cranks out ships Known as the father of modern American shipbuilding, Henry Kaiser owned seven shipyards during the war. Using an assembly-line process, his yards could build a Liberty ship in five days, although most took two to three weeks. Kaiser began producing ships for the U.S. Maritime Commission in the 1930s. He expanded his production facilities with orders from England following the start of the war. In all, his shipyards built 1,490 vessels for the war effort.

Building Libertys Welders help build a Liberty ship in Henry Kaiser's Richmond, California, shipyard. Liberty ships were the workhorses of the war, carrying valuable military cargo to Allied forces across the Atlantic and Pacific. Eighteen shipyards across the U.S. built 2,751 Liberty ships during the war. While generally dependable, many Liberty ships suffered from structural defects, such as cracks in the decks and hulls. Nineteen split in half and sank during the war.

1944

March 24: The Chindits, a British special army force comprised of Indian nationals, are left rudderless after their leader, Major General Orde Wingate, dies in a plane crash over Burma. • The Nazis murder 336 Italian civilians to avenge a partisan attack that claimed the lives of 33 members of the SS who were marching through a narrow street in Rome.

March 25: Seventy-six Allied pilots escape from the German POW camp *Stalag Luft III,* outside of Berlin, via an expertly engineered underground tunnel.

March 26: Only one sailor survives to tell the story of the sinking of the *Tullibee,* a U.S. Navy submarine whose own torpedo struck the ship after following a circular trajectory after being fired.

March 27: The Nazi SS carries out a mass murder of the Jewish children of Kovno, Lithuania. No child younger than 13 is spared.

March 29: What will eventually become a massive flow of aid to war-torn Europe begins with a relative trickle when Washington allocates $1.35 billion to aid European refugees.

March 30–April 2: The Japanese suffer major equipment and supply losses when U.S. Navy ships bombard Japanese positions in the Caroline Islands.

March 31: In the worst RAF losses of the war, 95 bombers are lost in one night in an unsuccessful raid of Nuremberg, Germany. • Admiral Koga, commander of the Japanese Imperial Navy in succession to Yamamoto, is presumed dead after his plane disappears over the Philippines.

April 1: Neutral Switzerland loses 50 civilians in an accidental USAAF raid over Schaffhausen.

"There was a sudden whining overhead, then a dozen mortar shells erupted in the infantry above the road. Screams pierced the clouds of smoke and the valley suddenly was filled with crackling machine guns and rifles as the Germans poured their fire into the exposed men and machines."

—*LIFE* CORRESPONDENT WILL LANG, ON THE GERMAN DEFENSE OF THE GUSTAV LINE NEAR CASSINO AT ESPERIA, ITALY, MAY 1944

ENSA provides needed entertainment The British Entertainments National Service Association (ENSA) was similar to the American United Service Organizations (USO). ENSA musicians, actors, comedians, and singers performed in hotels, factories, theaters, and—as seen here—at war-effort work sites. ENSA performers also toured war fronts around the world. The organization presented more than 2.5 million shows to some 300 million British and Allied troops and civilian war workers. Although some British citizens liked to poke fun at the performances, ENSA entertainments were popular with their audiences.

The OPA controls prices Created in August 1941, the U.S. Office of Price Administration (OPA) was a governmental agency that controlled the prices and use of consumable goods. The agency had the power to place price ceilings on retail items. The OPA also oversaw the rationing of many frequently used items to ensure there were enough resources for the military. Rationed consumables included rubber products (such as tires), gasoline, sugar, shoes, and meat. Here, a man gets a ticket for "joy riding." When the war was over, rationing ended and price controls gradually disappeared. The OPA closed in 1947.

The Fight for Monte Cassino

IN JANUARY 1944, soon after the British and American landings at Anzio, Italy, General Mark Clark's Fifth Army ran up against the Gustav Line. Tenacious German defenders would prevent the Allies from taking Rome for a further five months. A key feature of the Gustav Line was the monastery of Monte Cassino, which overlooked the broad Liri Valley along which the Allies had to advance.

In four battles from January to May, American, French, New Zealander, Indian, and Polish troops battled for Monastery Hill, held mainly by German paratroops. The monastery, dating from the 6th century, was both a priceless treasure and a serious military obstacle, although the Germans did not at first actually occupy the monastery itself.

British and New Zealand commanders urged that the monastery be bombed. Though Clark disagreed, British commander Harold Alexander insisted. In mid-February, bombers destroyed the monastery. Cardinal Maglione later described the monastery's destruction as "gross stupidity"—on military as much as cultural grounds.

The attack killed hundreds of civilians, but no Germans. Moreover, it allowed the German paratroops to occupy the ruins as an even stronger fortress. They held the area against successive and costly attacks by Indian and New Zealander divisions in March.

Pressure mounted on the Allies to regain momentum in Italy. On May 11, Operation Diadem opened, backed by massive air support. It involved a coordinated offensive by

Ruins on Monte Cassino

Allied forces against the Gustav Line and out of the Anzio bridgehead.

The Poles, who had evaded German and Russian occupation to form Wladyslaw Anders's II Polish Corps, attacked on May 17 and at last took Monastery Hill. At the same time, Alphonse Juin's French Expeditionary Corps outflanked the Gustav Line in terrible mountain fighting in the neighboring Arunci Mountains. General Clark entered Rome on June 4, having fought what he called "the most grueling, the most harrowing, and in one respect the most tragic" battle of the Italian campaign. However, he unwisely allowed major German forces to escape to fight the Allies in northern Italy.

West Coast braces for attack
Half of all American military aircraft were produced in California. The oil industry thrived there, and millions of tons of cargo and munitions were shipped from West Coast ports. Citizens and military leaders constantly expected Japanese attacks. West Coast harbors were mined and guarded with mobile antiaircraft guns, radar, and searchlights. Sound detectors, such as those seen here near San Francisco, remained on guard in 1944 (even with radar in use), with military personnel still listening for enemy airplanes.

1944

April 2: Nazis murder 86 French civilians in reprisal for partisan aggression. • Soviet troops invade Romania, with a plan to recapture the oil-rich nation for the Allies.

April 3: With the Germans in control of Hungary, the Allies revoke their promise to spare the country and attack German positions in the capital of Budapest.

April 4: General Charles de Gaulle assumes leadership of the Free French army.

April 5: Allied aircraft again attack the Axis-controlled oil production and transport facilities of Ploesti, Romania.

April 6: In Britain, the dramatic increase in the number of wage-earning citizens leads the government to introduce pay-as-you-earn taxation, whereby an employer deducts a set amount from an employee's paycheck per pay period.

April 7: The Soviets decline a renewed Japanese offer to negotiate a separate peace between the Nazis and the Russians.

April 10: The Red Army reclaims Odessa, an important Soviet port on the Black Sea, from the retreating German army.

April 11: The RAF destroys the Gestapo's headquarters in The Hague, including files on individual Dutch nationals scheduled to be deported to the Nazi camps.

April 13: A massive Allied bombing raid hits German targets in Hungary and Yugoslavia, as well as in Germany proper.

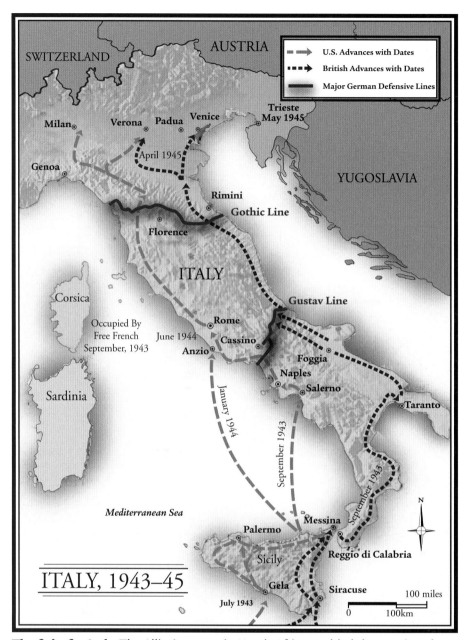

ITALY, 1943–45

The fight for Italy The Allies' success in North Africa enabled them to invade Sicily in July 1943 and Italy in September. But despite an Italian armistice on September 8, the Germans continued to fight on determinedly. Due to the impending Allied invasion of Northern Europe, the Italian campaign was consistently accorded a lower priority by the Allies, and consequently was often under-resourced. The strategic failure of the landing at Anzio exemplified this and other Allied deficiencies. Meanwhile, the German defense of Cassino was particularly tenacious. Nevertheless, the Allies advanced relentlessly northward, smashing through the Gustav Line and the Gothic Line. The Germans surrendered in Italy on May 2, 1945.

Eaker's plan American Ira Eaker, an infantryman during World War I, began training as a pilot in 1918. He won the Distinguished Flying Cross in 1929 for helping set a world flight endurance record. In 1942 he was named commander of the Eighth U.S. Army Air Force based in Britain, where he led the first U.S. bomber raid on Europe. A proponent of daylight precision bombing, he helped persuade Winston Churchill to launch the Combined Bomber Offensive (also known as the Eaker Plan), in which the Americans focused on daylight bombing and the Royal Air Force conducted night bombing. He was named commander-in-chief of the Allied Air Force in the Mediterranean in late 1943.

Romans hail American liberators Shortly before the June 4, 1944, liberation of Rome (*pictured*), the city had endured a week of Allied bombings that killed some 5,000 civilians. Even so, crowds of Romans grateful for an end to the Nazi occupation joyfully greeted the soldiers of U.S. general Mark Clark's Fifth Army, showering them with flowers. In his fireside chat of June 5, President Roosevelt reminded his listeners that Ancient Rome had once ruled the known world. "That, too, is significant," he said, "for the United Nations are determined that in the future no one city and no one race will be able to control the whole of the world."

Britain's WAAFs aid the war effort A member of the Women's Auxiliary Air Force (WAAF), the women's branch of the British RAF, tracks aircraft via radar in 1944. Although WAAFs did not fly planes (unlike their civilian female counterparts in the Air Transport Auxiliary), their duties centered around such vital matters as weather, radar, codes, reconnaissance, and intelligence. Beginning in 1944, many WAAFs served beyond the home front, including in Europe after the invasion of Normandy.

Pope hailed and criticized In 1943, *Time* magazine praised Pope Pius XII and the Catholic Church for "fighting totalitarianism more knowingly, devoutly, and authoritatively, and for a longer time, than any other organized power." However, even during his life, Pius's wartime policies were controversial. Despite his muted denunciations of Nazi

aggression and racial theories, the Vatican under his leadership remained officially neutral throughout the war. Pius also stirred criticism for not denouncing the Nazis' atrocities against the Jews. Members of the Church hierarchy, however, hid Jews in monasteries, convents, and the Vatican itself, saving thousands of Jewish lives.

1944

April 13: The Allies confront Sweden, which—despite increasing pressure from the international community—continues to supply the Nazis with ball bearings for their equipment and weapons. • Less than two months before the planned Allied invasion of France, American and British warplanes soften German defenses on the Normandy coast.

April 14: The Nazis deport the first trainload of Greek Jews from Athens. They are destined for the Auschwitz-Birkenau gas chambers. • At a Bombay port, nearly 1,000 people die, 20 ships are lost, and tens of thousands of tons of supplies are destroyed in a massive series of explosions that are triggered when a TNT-laden ship catches fire.

April 17: The Japanese initiate a major offensive, code-named *Ichi-Go,* against American and Chinese positions in China's Honan Province.

April 18–19: Nearly 1,400 French civilians die in Allied air raids over the province of Normandy.

April 19: The U.S. House of Representatives approves a one-year extension of the Lend-Lease Act.

April 20: The Allies are finally able to convince "neutral" Turkey to stop supplying the Axis with chrome for weapons and transport production.

April 24: The U.S. Department of War concludes that only through a ground invasion of the Japanese homeland will the Allies succeed in winning the war in the Pacific Theater.

April 25: U.S. general George Patton creates a buzz when he implies that the Allies have plans for world domination.

Americans capture a German sub Launched and commissioned in 1941, the German submarine *U-505* sank eight ships and survived more damage than any other German submarine during World War II. On June 4, 1944, depth charges from the USS *Chatelain* forced *U-505*'s crew to abandon ship, after which the sub was boarded and saved from sinking by U.S. sailors (*pictured*). Valuable documents and codebooks were taken from the submarine, which was then towed to the United States. This was the first enemy ship captured by the U.S. since 1815.

The bluff at Pas de Calais A German tank patrols the beaches of Pas de Calais, France, in the spring of 1944. The Germans had every reason to believe that the main impending Allied invasion would arrive in Pas de Calais—and not farther west in Normandy, as the Allies actually intended. After all, Pas de Calais was close to England and had excellent landing beaches. The Allies added to Germany's misapprehension through a number of ruses, including the creation of a phantom army group that was stationed directly across the channel from Calais and was led by U.S. general George Patton.

The Nazis' "model camp" The 18th century fortress of Terezin (*Theresienstadt* in German), Czechoslovakia, became a Nazi "model camp." To deceive Red Cross inspectors and other international visitors, Theresienstadt—which included a theater, café, and park—was filled with Jewish scholars, musicians, and artists who were encouraged to give public performances and exhibits. On Hitler's orders, actor Kurt Gerron directed a propaganda film, *The Führer Gives the Jews a City*, praising Theresienstadt. Of the 144,000 Jews sent there, about 33,000 died of starvation and epidemic diseases, and another 88,000 were deported to extermination camps.

Sauckel heads forced labor program In March 1942, Hitler put Nazi politician Fritz Sauckel in charge of acquiring manpower for the war effort. Sauckel pursued his duties with extraordinary cruelty, forcing war prisoners and citizens of occupied Eastern territories into brutal slave labor. In a memo, Sauckel ordered, "All the men must be fed, sheltered and treated in such a way as to exploit them to the highest possible extent at the lowest conceivable degree of expenditure." Sauckel's policies brought some five million workers to Germany, only about 200,000 of them voluntarily. After the war, he was convicted of crimes against humanity and hanged.

Tedder's bombers British air chief marshal Sir Arthur Tedder was appointed Eisenhower's deputy supreme commander for the invasion of Normandy. Tedder successfully carried out the Allies' "Transportation Plan," which involved bombing French railways to slow down Axis reinforcements during the Allied landing at Normandy on June 6, 1944. His tactic of using bombers to clear the way for advancing troops ("Tedder's Carpet") also proved effective at Normandy and elsewhere. In May 1945, he signed Germany's unconditional surrender on Eisenhower's behalf.

Sevastopol falls to the Soviets German soldiers go into captivity in the Crimean city of Sevastopol. On April 8, 1944, the Soviets launched a major offensive (500,000 troops) against the German 17th Army, which had been isolated in the Crimea since November. Outnumbered two to one and with their backs to the Black Sea, the Germans attempted to make a stand at Sevastopol. However, after being shattered by massive artillery barrages and relentless infantry attacks, the city fell on May 9. Of the 230,000 Axis troops originally trapped on the peninsula, about 150,000 escaped by sea. The rest were killed or captured.

1944

April 27: In the run-up to D-Day, British authorities ban all travel outside the country in an effort to put a stop to intelligence leaks about the invasion.

April 29: Disaster strikes a D-Day practice run when German naval forces attack an American training exercise, killing more than 600 troops. • Some 120 Japanese planes are destroyed as the Allies return to the key Japanese base of Truk to inflict further damage.

April 30: The first prefabricated, $2,200 home goes on display in London, in advance of Churchill's plan to use hundreds of thousands of these structures to house those left homeless by the war.

May 1944: The Soviets prevail in the Battle of the Crimea. The area is emptied of German and Romanian forces, tens of thousands of whom have been killed. • This month, for the first time since 1940, no British civilians will die in Axis air raids. • Japanese shipping is severely curtailed following Allied mining of the waters off Thailand and Burma.

May 2: Schoolteacher and crossword puzzle creator Leonard Dawe attracts the attention of the Allies when one of his puzzles, published in the *London Daily Telegraph,* contains the word *Utah.* Subsequent puzzles will include the words *Omaha* and *Overlord,* leading Allied security to suspect Dawe is leaking intelligence about the D-Day invasion. He is not doing so.

May 3: Spain's Fascist government under General Francisco Franco agrees to curtail supply shipments to Germany in exchange for an increase in oil shipments from the Allies.

May 4: The United States suspends the rationing program for most types and cuts of meat.

Disputes over area bombing Along with Arthur "Bomber" Harris, RAF chief of the air staff Sir Charles Portal (*pictured*) was a vigorous advocate of area bombing—destroying civilian populations instead of military targets. But Portal's thinking changed, putting him increasingly at odds with Harris. Over Harris's strong objections, Portal sided with Eisenhower's commitment to the "Transportation Plan" of bombing French railroads instead of German cities in preparation for D-Day. Portal grew increasingly skeptical of area bombing's military effectiveness, but was unable to restrain Harris from bombing city after city late in the war.

Ike greets troops before D-Day On June 5, 1944, General Dwight Eisenhower wrote a short note. "If any blame or fault attaches to the attempt," he wrote, "it is mine alone." Success was not guaranteed, and Eisenhower probably composed this message in advance of D-Day for fear that the proper words would not come to him if the invasion failed. Here, "Ike" visits the men of the 101st Airborne as they prepare for their drop. He asked their names and where they were from. Not long after, he watched as the planes carried his airborne troops into the night.

Bradley's men storm Omaha, Utah Due to his success in corps command during campaigns in North Africa and Sicily, General Omar Bradley was chosen by General Eisenhower as the First U.S. Army commander for the invasion of France. Eisenhower decided that Bradley's First Army, with its three corps, would land on the Omaha and Utah beaches in the first wave of the invasion of Normandy. Bradley watched the assaults from the USS *Augusta.* The landing at Utah met with relatively little opposition. Omaha, however, was heavily defended by German forces. After securing a beachhead on Omaha beach, Bradley's Operation Cobra, begun on July 25, 1944, tore a hole in German defenses.

General Eisenhower

"YOU ARE ABOUT TO EMBARK upon the Great Crusade," wrote General Dwight D. Eisenhower in his message to troops on June 5, 1944, the eve of D-Day. "The free men of the world are marching together to Victory!" Yet the responsibility for the success or failure of the invasion lay with Eisenhower alone. His years of study and experience had prepared him for this moment.

Eisenhower graduated in 1915 from West Point, where he gained a reputation as a motivator and natural leader. These were skills he sharpened during his years in the service. While some of his West Point classmates made names for themselves on European battlefields during World War I, Eisenhower was placed in command of the first American tank school at Camp Colt, on the historic battlefield of Gettysburg, Pennsylvania.

The army was dramatically reduced following the First World War, leaving limited command opportunities for Eisenhower and his fellow officers. During those quiet years, he excelled in his studies at the Army's senior military schools and colleges. As a result of his academic successes, he moved up the promotional ladder by filling staff positions, each one more important than the last.

Following the attack on Pearl Harbor, Chief of Staff General George Marshall called Eisenhower to Washington to serve as deputy chief of the War Plans Division. A series of promotions to command positions in the Mediterranean gave Eisenhower the opportunity to demonstrate his ability to work effectively with other Allied commanders. President Roosevelt named him supreme commander of the Allied Expeditionary Forces for the invasion of France because of his experience in North Africa and his political acumen, which was necessary when working with subordinates and politicians from several countries.

As commander of the Allied troops in Europe, Eisenhower was a master strategist. He led Allied troops off the beaches of Normandy to success and ultimate victory in Europe. Popular in America, "Ike" was elected U.S. president in 1952 and again in '56.

Aerial reconnaissance Photography provided essential intelligence to all belligerents. The RAF rapidly developed strategic reconnaissance (with fast, high-altitude, unarmed aircraft) and tactical reconnaissance (with low-flying armed fighters). Their photographs were interpreted with stereoscopic techniques, producing a 3-D image from two overlapping prints. By 1942 Allied aircraft could produce 1:10,000 scale photographs from 30,000 feet. The USAAF initially employed specially equipped bombers (such as the one pictured) for long-range reconnaissance, but it soon switched to adapted fighters. Aerial photography proved invaluable for assessing enemy defenses (notably for Operation Overlord), interfering with the production and use of the V-weapons, and planning strategic bombing.

D-Day

OPERATION OVERLORD, the Allied invasion of mainland Europe and the establishment of the second front long advocated by Stalin to relieve pressure on the Russians in the East, was the greatest amphibious landing operation in history. The invasion at Normandy, France, represented the culmination and fruition of an Allied planning process that had lasted more than two years.

A Normandy beach two days after D-Day

The deception measures taken to maintain Overlord's secrecy were almost as extensive as the main operation itself. The seaborne operation—Operation Neptune—was preceded by a large-scale airborne assault during the night of June 5–6 into the inland areas beyond and on the flanks of the landing beaches. This assault was carried out by 20,000 paratroopers and glider-borne infantry of the U.S. 82nd and 101st airborne divisions, and the British Sixth Airborne Division, flying in 1,087 transport aircraft and gliders.

With Allied airborne forces already in place (despite many paratroopers having landed far from their intended objectives during the night), the main seaborne landings began at 6:30 A.M. on D-Day. They were preceded by heavy air bombing and more than two hours of naval bombardment. Some 1,200 warships, 4,200 landing ships and landing craft, and 1,200 merchant ships were engaged off Normandy. Together they transported 185,000 men and 20,000 vehicles in the initial assault lift.

By last light on D-Day, from Varreville in the west to Ouistreham in the east, the U.S. First Army (under General Bradley) and British Second Army (General Dempsey), which together comprised General Montgomery's 21st Army Group, had gained a foothold at the five main landing beaches. These beaches were code-named "Utah" (U.S.), "Omaha" (U.S.), "Juno" (Canada), "Gold" (Britain), and "Sword" (Britain). At Omaha, however, this foothold proved somewhat tenuous for the first 24 hours.

On the Anglo-Canadian beaches, the "Funnies" of the British 79th Armored Division were used to particularly good effect. These were specialized armored vehicles specifically designed to breach the beach obstacles and defenses, and provide armored support on the beaches as soon as possible after landing. However, the U.S. commanders had declined to use these vehicles on their beaches.

Once safely ashore, the five U.S., British, and Canadian divisions—together with various independent brigades, U.S. Rangers, British Commandos, Free French, and other specialist units—quickly set about consolidating and exploiting the bridgeheads. Meanwhile, Hitler and the German high command believed that the main invasion was still to come at the Pas de Calais, with Normandy merely a diversion. The resultant uncertainty and delay in deploying the reserve panzer divisions held in readiness for this very task meant that by dawn on June 7 the only chance the Germans had possessed to repel the invasion was lost irretrievably. Hitler's "Atlantic Wall" had been breached.

About 4,500 Allied troops died on D-Day, 1,000 of whom were killed on "Bloody Omaha." The Allies were at last ashore in mainland Western Europe in strength, and the principal strategic aspiration of Roosevelt, Churchill, and Stalin had been realized. As a huge fleet of cargo- and troop-carrying vessels plied steadily from ports in England to the newly established beachheads and artificial "Mulberry" harbors, Allied strength in Normandy increased with each week that passed, and was soon unstoppable.

The five beaches Sword and Gold were code names for the beaches attacked by the British Second Army. Americans landed on Utah and Omaha. British troops landing at Sword met with very little resistance, sustaining 600 casualties. The Canadians attempting to land on Juno (*pictured*) met with greater resistance, suffering about 50 percent casualties in the first hour. But once over the sea wall, they faced less opposition. The British who attacked Gold faced some resistance, which decreased as they moved inland. Americans landing at Utah faced the least resistance, suffering only 200 casualties on D-Day. Omaha proved the toughest, as the terrain was best suited for defense. By the time the Americans advanced off the beach, they had left about 3,000 casualties behind.

Breaking through the wall To defend against an Allied invasion from Britain, the Germans constructed the Atlantic Wall—fortifications along the western coast of Europe. Obstructions were placed under water to tear holes in landing craft, and mines were seeded under the sand. Antitank barriers and walls of barbed wire were strategically placed along the beaches. The Omaha beach was raked by machine guns in pillboxes with overlapping fields of fire. Soldiers who made it to the barbed wire used Bangalore torpedoes—50-foot-long pipes (*pictured*) filled with 85 pounds of TNT—to blow holes through the wire wall.

Perilous advance Americans advance over a sea wall after landing on Utah beach. Allies met with the stiffest resistance on Juno and Omaha beaches. U.S. colonel George Taylor of the First Infantry Division tried to motivate his shell-shocked and fatigued men to advance off Omaha. "Two kinds of people are staying on this beach," he said, "the dead and those who are going to die." Once beyond the obstructions, troops advanced up the slopes to destroy pillboxes, from which machine gun and artillery fire rained down.

HELL BREAKS LOOSE

FINALLY THE GREEN LIGHT came on and we exited the plane. I honestly don't remember the opening shock. I remember the sky was being criss-crossed with tracer bullets and flak. The noise was terrible. I landed in water up to my chest. I saw one plane take a direct hit and explode in mid-air. Every man in that plane died a quick and merciful death. As it began to get lighter, all hell broke loose about three miles behind us. The navy had started bombarding the beaches.

—AMERICAN PARATROOPER ROBERT FLORY

1944

May 5: Ailing Indian Congress Party leader Mohandas Gandhi leaves prison nearly two years after his incarceration for impeding Britain's war effort.

May 6: Germany orders an additional 1,800 laborers from France to help staff the Mittelbau-Dora slave labor camp near Nordhausen, Germany. The workers are needed to step up production of the V-2 bombs that will terrorize Britain for much of the year.

May 8: Supreme Allied Commander Eisenhower confirms June 5 as the date for Operation Overlord, the invasion of France.

May 9: *Luftwaffe* installations on French soil are pounded by Allied aircraft in an attempt to render them harmless prior to D-Day. • On the Eastern Front, the Soviets recapture the Ukrainian city of Sevastopol.

May 10: President Roosevelt appoints James Forrestal secretary of the Navy following the death of Forrestal's predecessor, W. Franklin Knox.

May 12: The Allies engage in heated battles with German troops across much of Italy, and manage to make steady gains. • The Allies warn secondary Axis powers Romania, Hungary, and Bulgaria that they will suffer if they continue to stand with Germany. • A Free French tribunal finds Vichy Admiral Edmond Darian guilty of collaborating with the Nazis and sentences him to life imprisonment. • A joint U.S.-RAF aerial assault over Germany inflicts heavy damage on the *Luftwaffe* while wreaking havoc on several synthetic-oil production facilities.

May 13: The Allies finally break through the German Gustav Line, the western segment of the Winter Line, and begin their march northward through Italy.

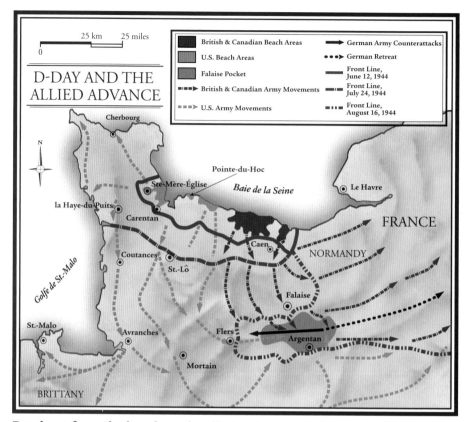

D-DAY AND THE ALLIED ADVANCE

	British & Canadian Beach Areas		German Army Counterattacks
	U.S. Beach Areas		German Retreat
	Falaise Pocket		Front Line, June 12, 1944
	British & Canadian Army Movements		Front Line, July 24, 1944
	U.S. Army Movements		Front Line, August 16, 1944

Breakout from the beaches The Allied seaborne and airborne landings in Normandy by General Montgomery's 21st Army Group on June 6, 1944, were the culmination of years of operational and logistic joint planning and preparation. Although the U.S. Fifth Corps landing on Omaha Beach at first encountered severe difficulties, Anglo-Canadian-U.S. success on the other four beaches—Utah, Gold, Juno, and Sword—was generally remarkable. Nevertheless, several first-day objectives—notably Caen—were subsequently secured only after weeks of hard fighting in the densely wooded countryside of northern France. The delayed Allied breakout meant that many German troops escaped encirclement in the Falaise Pocket.

News of the invasion At about 3:30 A.M. Eastern time in the U.S. on June 6, 1944, the following news was released: "Allied naval forces... began landing Allied armies this morning on the northern coast of France." This landing had been much anticipated in the Allied and Axis nations. Most Americans were anxious for news, as seen in this scene from New York City. President Roosevelt emphasized in a news conference that the invasion did not mean

the fighting was almost over. "You don't just walk to Berlin," he said, "and the sooner this country realizes that, the better." The Japanese ambassador in Berlin notified Tokyo that German headquarters told him there would be no counterattack in Normandy because the German army still awaited (erroneously) the invasion of "the main body, which the Allies [have] not yet landed."

Hedgerows impede progress "Too many hedges," an Allied unit reported. "Must go forward slowly . . . take one hedgerow at a time and clean it up." *Bocage* is French for mixed woodland and pasture separated by thick, high hedgerows, as shown in this photo. Cherbourg Peninsula's terrain proved excellent for defense, undermining America's advantage in air support, armor, and artillery. The hedgerows did not stop a tank, but the machine's underbelly—the weakest part of a tank's armor—was exposed to enemy antitank and bazooka fire as it reached the top of a hedgerow. Units from the U.S. First Army needed 17 days to travel seven miles toward Saint-Lô.

British seize Bayeux A British soldier fires a Bren gun over debris in Bayeux, France. Notice that censors have obscured his shoulder patch so his unit could not be identified. A member of the British 50th Division, he landed on Gold beach. The 50th came closer than any other Allied unit to its June 6 objective, as Bayeux was captured by the British the day after the landing. This soldier is using a Bren Gun—a light machine gun popular in the British Army during World War II. It used magazine- instead of belt-fed ammunition like other machine guns. One of the gun's benefits was that it fired the same ammunition as the standard British rifle, the bolt-action Lee Enfield.

Americans break through at Saint-Lô In mid-June 1944, the Germans' defense stiffened in the hedgerows of Normandy. The British advance stalled at Caen, which was defended by much of Germany's armor. However, the Germans had few tanks in the American sector at Saint-Lô, allowing U.S. forces to breach the German line there in early August. U.S. general George Patton's newly formed Third Army threat-ened to encircle the German force still deployed across Normandy. Hitler called for a retreat from Normandy on August 16, leaving 50,000 dead and about 200,000 captured. The Germans in this picture surrendered on June 9.

1944

May 13: Klaus Dönitz, son of the German *Kriegsmarine* commander, dies when the Allies sink the ship he is on.

May 15: The Nazis begin the process of deporting Hungarian Jews to labor and death camps with the assistance of the local Hungarian police. Ultimately, close to 440,000 will be deported, with about two-thirds ending their journey in the gas chambers of Auschwitz-Birkenau.

May 18: After four months of bloody battle and at a cost of some 20,000 lives, the Allies finally capture the ruined hilltop of the Monte Cassino monastery in Italy.

May 19: About 50 of the Allied POWs who escaped *Stalag Luft III* via an underground tunnel are executed after almost all who escaped were recaptured. About 20 are returned to the camp to serve as a warning to other inmates.

May 21: The Americans capture Wakde Island, off the north coast of Dutch New Guinea, two days after their initial landing. The conquest gives them an important forward base for their planned invasion of western New Guinea.

May 22: The North Atlantic island nation of Iceland declares itself independent of Denmark.

May 25: Josip Broz Tito, leader of the Communist Yugoslavian partisans, narrowly evades capture in a surprise German raid on his headquarters.

May 26: Nearly 5,500 French civilians die in Allied air raids over the southern part of the country.

May 29: *Luftwaffe* commander Hermann Göring admits that his fleet has yielded the skies over Europe to the Allies, telling Hitler "not a single *Luftwaffe* aircraft dares show itself."

Overlord a resounding success The Allies' successful invasion and subsequent landing of supplies surpassed everyone's expectations. Once the beaches were under Allied control, two prefabricated harbors, made of six miles of flexible steel roadway, were towed from England and constructed at Omaha (*pictured*) and Gold beaches. By the end of June, approximately 850,000 troops, 150,000 vehicles, and 570,000 tons of supplies had crossed the English Channel. Prime Minister Winston Churchill stated that Operation Overlord, the Normandy invasion, was "the most difficult and complicated operation ever to take place."

Massacre at Oradour-sur-Glane On June 10, 1944, a *Waffen-SS* battalion led by Adolf Diekmann surrounded the Vichy French town of Oradour-sur-Glane, where French informants had reported that the *Maquis* (resistance) was holding a German official for execution. The Nazis herded the town's men into barns and the women and children into a church. They then killed these local residents by arson and machine gun fire. After slaughtering 642 people, the Nazis burnt the entire town (*pictured*). The German official supposedly held there was never located.

American POWs in German Hands

THE FIRST AMERICANS to fall into German hands were airmen shot down during bombing raids of German war plants beginning in July 1942. It wasn't until the North African campaign in the early months of 1943 that large numbers of American infantry were captured. By the end of the war, more than 95,000 Americans had been imprisoned by Germans.

Before being shipped to their permanent POW camps, captured troops were sent to *Dulags*—temporary camps where prisoners were interrogated and processed. Rank and arm of service determined the type of camp a prisoner was sent to. Officers were transported to *Oflags,*

U.S. soldiers captured in Belgium

enlisted men to *Stalags,* and airmen to *Stalag Lufts.* While the mortality rate in German camps was far less than in those run by Japanese—four percent versus 40 percent—many

prisoners faced long hours of forced labor and became victims of disease and malnutrition.

One American survivor, George J. Davis, recalled the condition of a fellow prisoner after liberation: "U.S. Army doctors diagnosed Cress as suffering from seriously infected ulcerated lice sores, scabies, yellow jaundice, dysentery, and acute malnutrition. A prisoner could become a victim of each or all these diseases/sicknesses in only three months of captivity...."

Former prisoner Philip Miller wrote, "There was no freedom, no girls, insufficient food, poor clothing, poor quarters, no pay, dirt, loneliness, and endless monotony."

While some spent their time scheming to escape, "inertia kept most prisoners securely impounded," wrote author Lewis Carlson.

Remote-controlled tanks

British soldiers in France inspect three German "Goliaths." These small, remote-controlled tanks were loaded with TNT and designed to destroy such targets as bunkers, fortified positions, and full-scale tanks. Deployed in the Warsaw Uprising of 1944 and at the beaches of Anzio and Normandy, these devices were ingenious but not especially effective. They were controlled by lengths of three-wire electric cable, which a daring enemy soldier could simply cut with a shovel. Still, an unmolested Goliath could travel at a speed equal to a brisk walk, and the operator could detonate the charge at will.

1944

May 29: Tanks clash in the Pacific Theater for the first time when U.S. forces attempt to evict the Japanese from their strategically important airfield on the island of Biak. • The USS *Block Island,* a Bogue Class escort carrier, becomes the only American carrier to go down in the Atlantic when it is torpedoed by *U-549* in waters northeast of the Canary Islands.

May 30: The Nazis order all Germans to kill downed Allied airmen on sight.

June 1: The French Resistance is given its marching orders and alerted to the timing of the D-Day invasion when the BBC broadcasts Verlaine's poem *"Chanson d'Automne."* • The Ultra code-breakers at Britain's Bletchley Park press "Colossus"—a speedy, fully electronic Enigma deciphering machine—into service.

June 2: As the Allies approach Rome, appeals come in from all quarters to spare the ancient city the destruction wrought on much of the rest of Europe.

June 4: The Allies march on Rome, one day after Hitler orders his armies withdrawn. Though sporadic fighting occurs in the outskirts, the city center is spared. • A forecast of high winds and excessive cloud cover forces the postponement of D-Day by one day, to June 6. • The U.S. Navy captures *U-505,* an intact U-boat, off the coast of Africa.

June 5: Field Marshal Erwin Rommel leaves his post on the coast of France to travel to Germany to celebrate his wife's birthday. He will spend most of D-Day speeding back to the Normandy front. • Allied paratroopers land in France late in the evening as a prelude to the D-Day invasion.

Rockets constructed in Peenemünde On June 13, 1944, Germany launched the V-1 flying bomb at London for the first time. The "buzz bomb" was an unmanned, pulse-jet aircraft developed in Peenemünde (*pictured*), a town on a small German peninsula in the Baltic Sea. German scientists, under the direction of Wernher von Braun (later the father of the U.S. space program), also developed the V-2 ballistic missile, a pilotless aircraft that traveled at four times the speed of sound, making it invulnerable to antiaircraft and fighter fire. RAF bombers attacked Peenemünde on August 17–18, 1943, destroying much of the missile development site. However, production of these weapons continued there and at other locations.

The Fritz-X rocket Before and during World War II, the Germans researched rocket and missile technology. Even before German V-1 pilotless "buzz bombs" and V-2 ballistic missiles struck London and other cities in 1944–45, underground factories worked to complete a V-3 gun designed to fire long-range warheads. The Germans' "Fritz-X" missile (*pictured*) was the first successful radio-guided bomb. Fritz-X missiles sank the Italian battleship *Roma* and the British cruiser *Spartan,* and damaged other Allied warships.

Communication key to victory A Marine works a field telephone switchboard at a temporary command post on Mount Tapochau in the center of Saipan. Even command posts were unsafe on the island; 19 battalion commanders were killed or wounded. Tapochau, the island's highest point (1,554 feet), was a crucial objective from which Japanese observers had initially called down artillery fire on the beaches. Its capture by the Second Marine Division on June 25 without loss was a turning point. Despite a lack of radio batteries and occasional cut telephone lines, efficient American communications on Saipan contributed enormously to the complex invasion's eventual success.

Marines land on Saipan Invading the Mariana Islands, from which U.S. bombers could bomb Japan, was an immense logistical challenge. Some 535 combat ships and auxiliaries transported 127,571 troops to islands more than a thousand miles from the nearest U.S. base, Eniwetok. The Marianas were 3,500 miles from the troops' departure point, Pearl Harbor. Early on June 15, 1944, after Admiral Turner gave the go-ahead to the landing force, vessels such as this landing craft carried Marines to the key Mariana island, Saipan. More than 600 amphibious craft debarked two divisions on eight beaches on a four-mile front with no serious collisions. Some 8,000 Marines were landed in the first 20 minutes. Once the troops were ashore, they met fierce resistance.

U.S. troops face troublesome obstacles Saipan's terrain was much more diverse than the small, low-lying atolls of the Marines' and Army's recent campaigns. Mountains, tangled vegetation, cane fields, ravines, and caves (such as the one at left) all presented obstacles. The enemy usually proved difficult to locate, and fighting everywhere was at close quarters. Grenades, such as those being thrown here by Marines, proved invaluable. So did satchel charges and flamethrowers. U.S. naval dominance had prevented the Japanese from receiving the reinforcements and supplies needed to strengthen their defenses before the invasion. But the 30,000 Japanese defenders fought with characteristic determination for land that they considered strategically vital home territory.

1944

June 6: In an awesome show of military force, the Allies land on the coast of France. By the end of the day, German positions in Normandy will be bombarded with more than 175,000 troops, 600 warships, and nearly 10,000 bombers and other warplanes. By the end of the month, nearly a million Allies will be on French soil. • While the European Theater is heavily engaged on the beaches of Normandy, Allied Pacific Theater commanders set the date for a similar invasion of Japan for October 1 of the following year.

June 7: German troops detain King Leopold III of Belgium and transport him to Germany.

June 8: The beaten and depleted *Wehrmacht* retreats from coastal positions in eastern Italy.

June 9: For the first time, the Allies launch bombing missions on German positions from recaptured airfields on the French mainland.

June 10: The village of Oradour-sur-Glâne is destroyed, and 642 men, women, and children are slaughtered, by members of the *Waffen-SS* who are searching for a missing gold shipment and Major Helmut Kämpfe, kidnapped by French partisans. • Americans on the Normandy beaches code-named "Utah" and "Omaha" join forces and move inland.

June 11: The U.S. Navy deals a harsh blow to the Japanese, destroying more than 200 of their air fleet in an attack on bases in the Marianas.

June 12: Six days after the initial D-Day invasion, the Allies have cemented a solid offensive line along the Normandy beaches.

June 13: Hitler unleashes his long-promised "secret weapon" against England. Over the next 80 days, V-1 rocket bombs will kill 5,500 civilians and cause widespread destruction.

"Hell is on us."

—Japanese foreign minister Shigemitsu Mamoru, commenting on the Allies' capture of Saipan, June 1944

Japanese choose death over surrender The corpse of one of the 23,811 Japanese known to have died on Saipan leans back on a tree as if asleep. How he died is unknown, but he evaded the fate of thousands sealed in caves or charred beyond recognition. Perhaps he died in a night raid or a *banzai* charge. The last charge, on July 7, cost more than 3,000 Japanese lives. Perhaps this soldier committed suicide rather than surrender. Only 736 of the 30,000 defenders, including 438 Koreans, allowed themselves to be captured. As the garrison commander, General Saito, concluded before committing *hara-kiri,* "Whether we attack, or whether we stay where we are, there is only death."

Marines seek spiritual strength During the initial landings on Saipan, Marines listened as chaplains gave them a prayer and blessing over the ships' loudspeakers. Here, with the campaign in progress, an American pauses before a crucifix in a small cemetery. Of 71,034 officers and men committed to the invasion of the island, casualties amounted to 14,111, or about 20 percent. Nearly four times as many Marines became casualties on Saipan as on Tarawa. Navy chaplains, who supported the Marine Corps, moved between units from dawn till dusk, providing up to 14 services a day. They also performed burial services.

War Without Quarter

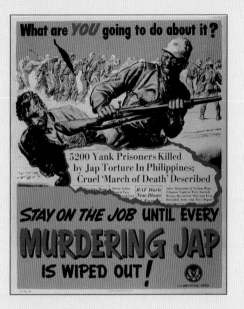

What are *YOU* going to do about it?

5200 Yank Prisoners Killed by Jap Torture In Philippines; Cruel 'March of Death' Described

STAY ON THE JOB UNTIL EVERY MURDERING JAP IS WIPED OUT!

THE FIGHTING IN THE Pacific Theater during World War II was unparalleled in its savagery. It was a no-quarter war with each side fervently dedicated to the total annihilation of the other. Fear, hatred, racism on both sides, and a mutual ignorance of each other's culture and society all contributed to a war without mercy.

For Americans, the surprise attack on Pearl Harbor on December 7, 1941, enraged the nation and roused an almost genocidal determination to exact revenge on the "treacherous Japs." Playing upon racist feelings, propagandists depicted the Japanese as subhumans, cruel and mindless tools of the emperor, "yellow monkeys" intent on world domination, and a rabid vermin that must be exterminated if civilization was to survive. Widespread reports of Japanese brutality in China even before the U.S. entered the war only reinforced these views.

Taught that surrender was a disgrace and that it was an honor to die for the emperor, Japanese soldiers would fight to the death under the most hopeless circumstances. They would booby-trap their own dead and wounded, feign surrender and then open fire, or execute prisoners out of hand—sometimes after torture. Westerners were viewed as barbarians, their concepts of mercy and surrender symptomatic of a weak and effete society undeserving of respectful treatment.

Japanese stubbornness in battle also led to a "kill or be killed" mindset among Allied soldiers. Expecting no quarter themselves, U.S. combat troops gave none. Few prisoners were taken even when the opportunity arose. Both sides shot pilots in parachutes and machine-gunned the survivors of sinking ships. Some U.S. troops became so hardened, they collected gold teeth from enemy corpses and mounted skulls on jeeps. One soldier even sent President Roosevelt a letter opener carved from a Japanese thigh bone (a gift that FDR declined). Admiral Bull Halsey declared that by war's end the Japanese language would be spoken only in hell.

Americans try to spare civilians
American forces on Saipan were ordered to avoid civilian casualties when attacking enemy-held caves. This image indicates the goodwill of most American troops towards civilians, even amid a quintessentially brutal battle. Also, it shows the fear with which civilians encountered servicemen whom the island's Japanese commander called "American devils." Propaganda that civilians would be tortured and killed prevented many from leaving their caves. Hundreds followed the lead of Japanese troops and committed suicide, most famously by leaping off cliffs at Marpi Point. Some vintage captions identify this pictured family as Chamorro, the Marianas' native population.

1944

June 14: Free French leader General Charles de Gaulle returns to France some four years after the Nazi occupation sent him into exile.

June 15: Operating out of Chinese bases, American B-29 long-range bombers attack the Japanese island of Kyushu, damaging a steel plant that is a key supplier for the imperial war effort.

June 19–20: The U.S. Navy deals a heavy blow to the Japanese, and their naval air fleet in particular, in the Battle of the Philippine Sea. U.S. losses are relatively small, while the incapacitated Japanese fleet is forced to retreat to Okinawa.

June 22: The Allies bomb the French city of Cherbourg after a warning, delivered a day prior to the occupying German force, is met with silence.
• President Roosevelt signs the GI Bill of Rights, a wide-ranging veterans benefits package that will become the catalyst for the "American dream" ideal of the 1950s. • Keeping an eye on the postwar prize, the Soviets establish a puppet Communist government in Chelm, Poland. The new body is called the Polish Committee of National Liberation.

June 27: The U.S. Army occupies the French city of Cherbourg two days after naval bombardments and street fighting began to engulf the city.

June 28: Philippe Henriot, the Vichy minister of information who was known as "the French Goebbels," is murdered in his bed by members of the French Resistance.

June 29: In a meeting with his top commanders at Berchtesgaden, Hitler refuses to listen to their bleak reports on the state of the war. They leave enthused by his comments.

Americans cripple Japanese carrier forces U.S. airman Ronald "Rip" Gift celebrates his survival following a night landing on the USS *Monterey* during the two-day Battle of the Philippine Sea (June 19–20, 1944). The "Get the carriers" exhortation on the ready room blackboard reflects the emphasis placed on aircraft carriers as priority targets. By mid-1944, U.S. carrier task forces were prowling the seas, striking enemy targets at will. By contrast, the Japanese navy was steadily

weakening. Losses of Japanese carriers, aircraft, and pilots during the Battle of the Philippine Sea were the final blows to Japanese hopes for naval dominance.

The GI Bill In June 1944, the U.S. Congress passed the Servicemen's Readjustment Act, more popularly known as the GI Bill of Rights. The House of Representatives had attempted to scale down the bill's provisions, but after much negotiation, the House finally passed it almost intact. The act was signed into law by President Roosevelt on June 22 (*pictured*). Two of its major provisions were low-interest home loans and educational benefits. The home loans, utilized by 2.4 million returning veterans, would help to develop America's suburban landscape and personal wealth. The educational provision would give colleges the financial boost to expand programs and enrollment. By 1951, 2.3 million GIs would attend colleges and universities of their choice, 3.5 million would receive educational training, and 3.4 million would take part in on-the-job training.

Battle of the Philippine Sea

THROWN ON THE DEFENSIVE in the Pacific by 1944, the Japanese navy pinned its hopes on a decisive fleet engagement to revive Japan's fading fortunes. Planners hoped to fight this decisive battle around the Palaus Islands and the Western Carolines, but the U.S. landings on Saipan on June 15 dictated otherwise. Combined Fleet commander Admiral Toyoda Soemu ordered the First Mobile Fleet to the Marianas.

Led by Vice Admiral Ozawa Jisaburo, the Japanese force was built around nine carriers. They would face 15 U.S. carriers, but Ozawa expected land-based aircraft from Guam and other island bases to reduce those odds before the naval engagement began. In fact, unbeknownst to Ozawa, U.S. carrier planes were neutralizing these land-based forces even as his fleet steamed into battle.

Believing erroneous Japanese claims that the U.S. fleet had already suffered serious losses from land-based air forces, Ozawa launched his carrier attack on June 19. More than 450 aircraft went after the U.S. Fifth Fleet, only to run into a buzz saw. Because the Japanese pilots were inexperienced, U.S. Grumman Hellcat fighters and massed antiaircraft fire wreaked havoc on the enemy. The Japanese lost 330 planes in the lopsided five-hour exchange, derisively dubbed the "Great Marianas Turkey Shoot" by American pilots. Also lost were the carriers *Taiho* and *Shokaku,* sunk

Contrails in the sky during the Battle of the Philippine Sea

by American submarines *Albacore* and *Cavalla.* The U.S. task force lost a total of 31 planes to all causes.

Left with about 100 aircraft, Ozawa withdrew. The next afternoon, operating at the far extent of their range, U.S. aircraft shot down 65 more Japanese planes, sank the carrier *Hiyo* and two oilers, and damaged two carriers and a battleship. About 80 U.S. planes were lost on the return when they ran out of gas and ditched or crashed, but more than half of the crew members were rescued.

The Battle of the Philippine Sea cost the Japanese 476 planes and about 450 pilots. The Japanese carrier air arm never recovered from this mortal blow.

THE ENEMY ABOVE

JAP PLANES ATTACKED our task force at 11 A.M. this morning, they attacked us from all directions. Jap planes were falling all around us and the sky was full of bursting shells, big puffs of smoke could be seen everywhere. Our ship was leading the rest of the ships, we were up front in the force, with some destroyers screening us. Bombs were falling very close to the ships, big sprays of water could be seen and Jap planes were splashing into the water. One Jap plane after dropping its load and with a charmed life flew through a hail of gunfire as it flew over many ships, but when it got to us we riddled it with shells, and sent it into the blue Pacific.

—JAMES J. FAHEY, USS *MONTPELIER,* ON THE BATTLE OF THE PHILIPPINE SEA

Children of the war
In June 1944, a British air raid warden holds a frightened child who is too young to remember peacetime. British youngsters were traumatized by bombing raids, separation from their families, and the deaths of parents. Some children were killed or wounded. "We sat there listening to German planes coming over the shelter

on their way to London and we then had to stay there until they came back," Margaret Hoffman later wrote about the 1944 air strikes. Hoffman had been three months old when Nazi bombs first fell on Britain.

HITLER'S FINAL GAMBLE

JULY 1944–JANUARY 1945

"You know, misery loves company. Well, we had plenty of misery and plenty of company."

—U.S. 106TH INFANTRY DIVISION VETERAN ED ROPER, RECALLING THE BATTLE OF THE BULGE

ON JULY 20, 1944, young German colonel Claus Schenk von Stauffenberg, a wounded veteran of the Tunisian campaign, attended Hitler's morning briefing at the Rastenberg headquarters in East Prussia while carrying a time bomb in a briefcase. He left the case under the heavy oak table at which Hitler was standing and found an excuse to leave. A few minutes later, the bomb exploded—but not before another officer, finding it in his way, had kicked the case farther under the table. The blast killed four of those present, but Hitler was shielded by the heavy table. He emerged alive and vengeful. Stauffenberg was executed that night in Berlin. Several thousand suspects were arrested and about 200 were executed in the weeks that followed.

The assassination attempt coincided with a sudden crisis in the German war effort. Until late July, the front in Normandy had held, though at high cost. Again and again, the Germans struggled to repulse the British effort to capture the French city of Caen. The effort denuded German troops and tanks from other parts of the front, which allowed American commanders to plan a breakout through the German line. After weeks of preparation and with overwhelming air support, U.S. general Omar Bradley launched Operation Cobra on July 25. For the first time, Western forces were able to develop

German soldiers advance past a knocked-out U.S. halftrack during the Battle of the Bulge in December 1944. Intended to divide the Western Allies, Hitler's ill-advised counteroffensive was halted and then thrown back with great losses of men and irreplaceable equipment. After the Bulge, Germany's defeat was clearly just a matter of months.

real mobility. The line was broken open, and Bradley—supported by notoriously belligerent general George Patton—drove the German army back toward Paris in a matter of weeks. On August 25, Paris was liberated, partly by the approaching armies and partly by the French Resistance, which staged a final revolt against German occupation.

A second landing in southern France began on August 15, and within two weeks the enemy was cleared from the rest of France, meaning the Allies stood on the frontiers of Germany. The Western Allies grew hopeful that Germany might be defeated before the onset of winter. But General Montgomery's airborne assault on the Dutch city of Arnhem in the middle of September (to make it possible to cross the Rhine River) was bloodily repulsed. German resistance stiffened in immediate defense of the home territory.

In the East, Soviet troops reached the German border on August 17. Finland sued for peace on September 2, and during the following month the Baltic States were occupied and reabsorbed into the Soviet bloc. Farther south, the Red Army made rapid progress after the destruction of German Army Group Center. Romania was occupied in August and switched to the Allied side. Bulgaria was occupied next, and by the end of October parts of Slovakia were also in Soviet hands. The Red Army stood on the boundaries of Hungary and Yugoslavia.

A French resistance fighter and an American officer engage German troops in a street battle in an unidentified French city. Resistance movements rose up against the German occupiers throughout Europe as Allied forces advanced from both the west and the east. Resistance fighters harassed German forces, aided Allied soldiers, and prepared for a new postwar political order.

The dramatic collapse of Axis resistance owed something to popular resistance both in the West and the East. In Yugoslavia, a large Communist army under the leadership of Joseph Tito played the major role in liberating Yugoslav territory. In Italy, partisans harried the retreating Germans and prepared for a new postwar order. In some cases, resistance was clearly anti-Soviet. In the Ukraine, a guerrilla war—fought by nationalists—tied down thousands of Soviet soldiers and security forces during 1944 and 1945 and slowed the move westward.

In Poland, the Home Army hoped to liberate its country before Soviet forces had time to construct a Communist state. On August 1, as the Red Army stood on the far side of the Vistula River, Polish nationalist forces in Warsaw staged an uprising against the German occupiers. The result was a savage response from the embattled German forces, which destroyed much of what remained of the city. The Red Army stayed where it was, and would not capture Warsaw until the start of the renewed campaign in January 1945.

In the Pacific, the Allies made rapid progress. Following the capture of Saipan, American forces retook Guam and opened the whole of the western Pacific to Allied forces. The Japanese again sought a decisive big battle as a key to saving what was left of their new empire. However, the American decision to reoccupy the Philippines exposed Japan's air forces to severe attack. When the Japanese main fleet was deployed to oppose the American landings on the Philippine island of Leyte, the force lacked adequate air cover. The encounter was the largest naval battle ever fought, involving 282 ships. In late October, three separate Japanese task forces were deployed to try to defeat the invasion. The result was a decisive victory for the U.S. Navy, as Japan lost 26 front-line warships. The invasion force landed on Leyte and cleared the island by the end of the year. Defeat of Japan was now only a matter of time.

The same could be said of Hitler's Germany, which was now surrounded on all sides by heavily armed enemies and subject to constant aerial bombardment. Yet Hitler still hoped for victory. From June, new "weapons of revenge"—the V-1 flying bomb and the V-2 ballistic missile—were launched against London. Hitler hoped that by holding or destroying ports in the West, combined with a renewed U-boat campaign with new types of submarines, Germany would deprive U.S. and British forces of replacements and supplies.

An American soldier guides B-29 bombers to their parking areas on the airfield at Eniwetok in the Marshall Islands in 1944. Though the air campaign against Japan was initially plagued with a multitude of tactical problems, U.S. bombers went on to lay waste to the enemy homeland and play a key role in the Allied victory.

In December 1944, Hitler ordered the German army and air force to use its scarce reserves for a daring counteroffensive in the West against American forces. The goal was to divide the Western Allies, seize the port of Antwerp, and force them to rethink their strategy. His commanders preferred a more limited offensive, but on December 16 Hitler unleashed Operation Autumn Mist.

In poor weather, which shielded the panzer armies from air attack, the Germans made rapid progress and carved out a salient 50 miles deep in the Ardennes. The Allies regrouped and counterattacked in what became known as the Battle of the Bulge. American resistance at St. Vith and Bastogne, Belgium, held up the German advance, and heavy counterstrikes drove German forces back to the German frontier. On January 8, Hitler pulled his battered army back. The loss of 600 tanks and 1,600 aircraft marked the defeat of the Ardennes offensive. Germany was now exposed to the grim finale of the European war that Hitler had launched six years before.

1944

July 3: The Red Army liberates Minsk, site of one of the largest wartime Jewish ghettos and the center of the Soviet resistance movement. • After nearly four months, the Battle of Imphal and Kohima in northeast India comes to an end. The Japanese have suffered nearly 55,000 casualties, including more than 30,000 deaths, in this campaign against the Allies.

July 6: German field marshal Gerd von Rundstedt, one of Hitler's top military officers, is replaced after painting a pessimistic picture of Germany's chance of success on the Western Front. • With the battle for Saipan all but lost to the Allies, Lieutenant General Saito Yoshitsugu and Vice Admiral Nagumo Chuichi commit suicide rather than face the shame of surrender.

July 8: Admiral Miklos Horthy, the Hungarian regent, orders an end to the deportations of Hungarian Jews to Auschwitz-Birkenau. His order will come too late for more than 400,000 men, women, and children.

July 9: American bandleader Glenn Miller performs the first of a series of concerts for troops in the European Theater. • The U.S. declares the island of Saipan secured after about 3,000 Japanese troops had died in a suicidal charge against a large contingent of American soldiers on July 7.

July 11: Tens of thousands of women and children evacuate London as the terrifying and destructive German V bombs continue to fall. • Washington formally recognizes the Free French government of General Charles de Gaulle.

July 12: The Nazis empty the so-called Jewish "family camp" at Auschwitz-Birkenau, sending 4,000 to the gas chambers.

Red Army overwhelming on Eastern Front At 5:00 A.M. on June 22, 1944, in Operation Bagration, roughly two million Soviet troops waited—to the east and south of Belorussia—as the Red Army fired thousands of guns for two hours. The main assault (*pictured*) of this Soviet offensive began the following day. The German army, with fewer than a million soldiers, was no match for the Soviets and their firepower. By the end of July, the Red Army reached the outskirts of Warsaw. In a little more than a month, the German army lost approximately 350,000 men, including 31 generals.

Housing for Britain's vets During the latter part of the war, Winston Churchill announced the Temporary Housing Programme, which would develop prefabricated houses for returning veterans, their families, and other civilians. In this May 1944 photo, British ex-serviceman Leonard Hickman and his family visit an all-steel, prefabricated "Churchill house." Other prefabs were made of timber, aluminum, or sandwiches of corrugated asbestos-cement panels filled with wood and wool insulation. The cost of prefabs, many of which were constructed by prisoners of war, averaged about £1,300. Though modest, the houses used space efficiently and gave each family such luxuries as a stove, a refrigerator, and a boiler.

Szenes tries to help Hungarian Jews In 1944 poet Hannah Szenes parachuted into Yugoslavia to help organize the rescue of Hungarian Jews. Born in Hungary, Szenes emigrated to Palestine, where she is seen here in her kibbutz garden. Szenes enlisted in the British Army in 1943 and was trained in Egypt. Soon after she was dropped into Yugoslavia, she was captured and tortured by the Germans. She gave up no information and was executed in November 1944. Earlier in the year, from May to July, German forces had deported more than 430,000 Hungarian Jews to Auschwitz, where more than 75 percent were killed on arrival.

Slim shines in Asia Intellectual, courageous, and practical, William Slim was a British army lieutenant in World War I and a brigadier by 1939. Following service in East Africa, Iraq, and Syria, Slim was promoted to lieutenant general in March 1942. He commanded Burcorps in the 900-mile retreat from Rangoon to India. In October 1943, Slim took over the newly created British-Indian14th Army, which in 1944 he led brilliantly in defeating Japanese attacks, notably at Imphal-Kohima (March to July). The Japanese suffered more than 50,000 casualties. In Operation Capital, "Uncle Bill" employed air supply, guerrilla tactics, and ingenious ruses, and recaptured Rangoon in early May 1945. Slim was arguably Britain's finest commander during the war.

Convalescence Medical care of American soldiers was always good, and it got better at the proper hospitals and convalescent centers that were set up as the Allies pushed deeper into Europe. Here, recuperating GI pals Bill Fernandez (*left*) and Mike Murphy enjoy some softball outside of Rome in the summer of 1944. Both had been wounded during the spring assault on Monte Cassino. The photo seems lighthearted, but both men knew that soon they would return to their unit, and more fighting.

French citizens punish collaborators In Marseilles, France, French civilians laugh as a woman—accused of collaborating with Germans—has her head shaved. Similar humiliations occurred all over France, as did more severe punishments of people thought to have collaborated with Nazis or the Vichy regime. Some Frenchmen who had volunteered as officers in the *Wehrmacht* or *Waffen-SS* were executed as traitors. Ordinary soldiers who joined the enemy were sent to prison or given the option of serving in the French Foreign Legion.

1944

July 14: In France, Bastille Day observances feature the public humiliation of French nationals who collaborated with the Nazis.

July 17: German troops are ordered to stand firm as the Red Army crosses into Poland. • German general Erwin Rommel is seriously injured in Normandy when an RAF plane strafes his car, fracturing his skull. • Port Chicago, California, suffers the worst homefront disaster of the war when 320 men die in a massive explosion involving two ammunition-laden ships. • Napalm, the incendiary weapon that will become infamous during the Vietnam War, is used by the U.S. in combat for the first time when Allied planes attack German positions on the ground near St.-Lô.

July 18: The disheartening, bloody Battle of the Hedgerows ends with the U.S. capture of the French town of St.-Lô. • On the heels of a string of military defeats, most recently the fall of Saipan, Tojo Hideki—the political and military leader of Japan—is forced to resign.

July 20: Hitler survives an assassination attempt by a member of his own inner circle, Colonel Claus von Stauffenberg. In retaliation, Stauffenberg and many other senior soldiers and officials will be executed.

July 21: U.S. Marine and Army divisions retake the island of Guam. Originally ceded to the U.S. by Spain in 1898, Guam was captured by the Japanese in 1941.

July 23: A Red Cross visit to the Nazis' Theresienstadt labor camp results in a favorable report due to a beautification program and a tightly controlled tour. The deportations to Auschwitz-Birkenau will resume shortly after the conclusion of the Red Cross visit.

The Port Chicago explosion At 10:18 P.M. on July 17, 1944, an explosion rocked the Port Chicago Naval Magazine in Concord, California. Black naval workers, untrained on how to handle munitions, had just finished loading more than 4,000 tons of explosives on the merchant ship *E. A. Bryan.* The blast killed 320 men and injured about 400. Three weeks after the explosion, 258 African Americans refused to return to work, protesting the dangerous conditions and the Navy's segregation policy. Two hundred and eight received bad-conduct discharges, and 50 were found guilty of mutiny and sentenced to prison. Those 50 received clemency in 1946.

Allied bombers clear St.-Lô Beyond Normandy's beaches, Allied tanks and infantry had to navigate narrow roads and hedgerows (matted earthen embankments hundreds of years old that divided the countryside into small fields). Each well-protected road and field became a deathtrap, and German defenses at the crossroads town of St.-Lô, France, blocked access to more open countryside. After hundreds of air strikes on St.-Lô by American and British bombers, U.S. forces fought their way into the almost totally devastated town on July 18. The civilian couple seen here walks through the ruins of St.-Lô.

German Opposition Groups

ONCE IN POWER, the Nazis encountered some continuing levels of opposition within Germany. This opposition developed into a resistance movement in 1938 and eventually evolved into a sophisticated conspiracy.

One such resistance group was *Weisse Rose* (White Rose)—an organization of students at the University of Munich. It was discovered and crushed in 1943, with about 80 arrests and the execution of three of its leaders, Christoph Probst and Hans and Sophie Scholl. Although two attempts on Hitler's life were carried out by army officers in 1943, the most significant attack occurred on July 20, 1944.

That morning, Colonel Claus Schenk von Stauffenberg secreted a powerful time bomb in the conference room of the *Führer*'s headquarters at Rastenburg, East Prussia. This

German resister Harro Schulze-Boysen

plot involved many senior *Wehrmacht* officers, diplomats, and former political leaders, who had planned not only Hitler's death but also to remove the Nazi government. Although the bomb exploded with devastating effect, killing four and wounding many, Hitler avoided serious injury. Hitler's rage and the retribution subsequently inflicted by the Gestapo upon the conspirators, their associates, and many others were ferocious. The key conspirators were tortured and later savagely executed at Plötzensee Prison in Berlin.

About 200 people were executed as a direct result of the July 1944 bomb plot, with many hundreds more consigned to concentration camps. The failure of the July Plot effectively ended any remaining resistance to Hitler, and strengthened the authority of the SS within Germany.

Hitler's would-be assassin

Claus Schenk von Stauffenberg's family and acquaintances included many who resisted Nazi rule. Stauffenberg chose a military career, but Operation Barbarossa and the mass murders at Auschwitz convinced him that Hitler must be stopped. After several aborted assassination attempts, Colonel Stauffenberg, on July 20, 1944, placed a briefcase of timed explosives beneath the table in Hitler's conference room, then left on a pretext. Convinced that Hitler had died in the blast, Stauffenberg flew to Berlin to organize a military coup against Nazi leaders. But Hitler was alive, and late on July 20 Stauffenberg was shot.

The *Führer* vows revenge Italian dictator Benito Mussolini (*left*) and Hitler examine the demolished conference room after the failed assassination attempt. Hitler's wounds were slight, although four men had been killed and others hurt. Historians speculate that someone moved the briefcase after Stauffenberg left, and that a massive wooden table leg had protected Hitler from the blast. A raging *Führer* had his Gestapo round up current suspects, various old adversaries, and their relatives. Hitler ordered some 5,000 people arrested, many tortured, and about 200 executed.

1944

July 24: The Red Army liberates the Majdanek death/concentration camp near Lublin, Poland. For much of the world, it is their first look at the horror of the Nazis' "Final Solution" for the Jews. • The Nazis introduce their distinctive "Heil Hitler" salute into German military protocol.

July 26: President Roosevelt meets with Admiral Nimitz and General MacArthur in Honolulu. They decide that the next course of action in the Pacific Theater will be an invasion of the Philippines.

July 29: Germany's Messerschmitt 163 fighter plane becomes the first jet plane to engage in combat operations.

July 30: Major General Mizukami Genzu performs *hara-kiri*, a form of ritualized suicide, after losing Myitkyina, Burma, to General Joseph Stilwell's Allied force.

July 31: Hitler promotes a last-ditch, total-war policy that will call on German troops and civilians to destroy everything in their wake as they retreat. • Heavy fighting develops between German and Soviet troops as the Red Army approaches the Polish capital of Warsaw.

August: In this month alone, some 67,000 Jews from Poland's Łódź Ghetto will die at Auschwitz-Birkenau.

August 1: With the Red Army on the outskirts of Warsaw, Polish resistance activity moves into high gear. • U.S. general George Patton leads his army on a charge to take the French province of Brittany. • Japanese resistance ends on the island of Tinian.

August 2: The *Kriegsmarine* attacks Allied shipping in the English Channel with manned torpedoes operated by frogmen.

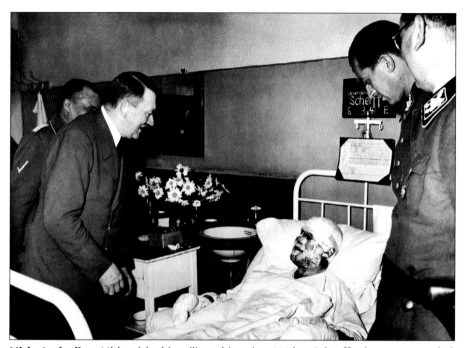

Hitler's decline Hitler visits his military historian, Walter Scherff, who was wounded in the July Plot explosion. Before the assassination attempt, a brooding Hitler had isolated himself at his Prussian *Wolfschanze* (Wolf's Lair) headquarters. After being attacked even there, the *Führer* descended into mental confusion, misanthropy, and hopes of yet winning the war. Although he was only slightly hurt by the blast, Hitler's physical health was also deteriorating. Some historians suspect that he had syphilis, while others cite Parkinson's disease. Many believe that Hitler's doctor exacerbated the dictator's decline with prescription amphetamines, opiates, and questionable quack "cures."

The fate of the conspirators Some German leaders realized early on that Hitler would destroy their country, but a series of assassination plans either failed or were abandoned. The July Plot was a desperate attempt that resulted in the destruction of the German resistance. General Erich Hoepner (*left*), an early opponent of Hitler, was arrested and tortured by the Gestapo, then executed by hanging. Colonel General Franz Halder (*center*)—not involved in the July Plot—was arrested when searches turned up letters and diaries that implicated him in earlier conspiracies. Halder was sent to a concentration camp but survived the war. Field Marshal Erwin von Witzleben (*right*) had been expected to take over command of the *Wehrmacht* after the coup, but was caught and hanged by piano wire.

Horrors of Nazi camps revealed As the Allies advanced on Germany from the east and west, they reached the Nazis' concentration camps and death camps, where most of the six million victims of the Holocaust perished. The Soviets became the first of the Allies to discover one of these scenes of horror when they entered the Majdanek concentration/death camp near Lublin, Poland, on July 23, 1944. Here, Russian soldiers and Polish civilians appear to be overcome by the sights and smells of death. Approximately 360,000 prisoners, mostly Jews, died at Majdanek from gas, hanging, starvation, disease, or overwork. The Red Army discovered only 500 inmates still alive at the camp.

HUMANS AS FERTILIZER

[T]HERE WAS A sloping plain, on which there grew acres and acres of cabbages. They were large luxuriant cabbages, covered with a layer of white dust. As I heard somebody explaining, "Layer of manure, then layer of ashes, that's the way it was done.... The SS men used to cart most of the ashes to their model farm, some distance away. A well-run farm; the SS men liked to eat these overgrown cabbages, and the prisoners ate those cabbages, too, although they knew that they would almost certainly be turned into cabbages themselves before long...."

—WAR CORRESPONDENT ALEXANDER WERTH, DESCRIBING ASHES OF GASSED AND CREMATED INMATES AT THE MAJDANEK CONCENTRATION/DEATH CAMP IN POLAND, JULY 1944

Marines face resistance at Guam Marines jump from an amphibious tractor on the island of Guam. The U.S. seized the island in July 1944 to secure additional airfields for the bombing campaign against Japan. With only 15 miles of potential landing beaches along Guam's west coast, the 18,500-man Japanese garrison knew where to concentrate its defenses and gave the attacking Marines a hot reception. The Third Marine Division landed on beaches swept by fire from the enemy-held high ground. To their right, the First Marine Provisional Brigade encountered easier terrain. However, it also ran into fierce resistance, including an enemy gun position that knocked out two dozen Marine AmTracs.

Fierce fighting on Guam Marine engineers blow up a series of Japanese dugouts during the fighting on Guam. Fierce Japanese resistance to the landings included a series of well-executed counterattacks intended to push the Americans back into the sea. In the Third Marine Division's zone, the struggle for the high ground behind the landing beaches lasted for days. The terrain included 100-foot precipices "that a trained cliff climber with line and spikes would have a hard time getting up," said one Marine.

1944

August 2: Despite relentless pressure from the Allies, Turkey refuses to join the battle against Nazi Germany.

August 4: After years of hiding in an Amsterdam attic, diarist Anne Frank and her family are betrayed to the German police. • The Germans retreat from Florence, the hub of the Italian Renaissance. Though the Germans destroy most of the bridges over the Arno River, which bisects the city, they spare the *Ponte Vecchio,* which dates to the 14th century.

August 9: With much of France under secure Allied control, General Eisenhower relocates his strategic headquarters to a Reims schoolhouse. • Officials with the Free French headquarters in Algiers, Algeria, announce the demise of Vichy France.

August 10: Hitler moves the entire 2,000-plane *Luftwaffe* force to Western Europe in a bid to challenge the power of the Allies' collective air strength. • The Japanese are crushed by American forces on Guam, leaving the U.S. with an additional solid forward base in the Marianas from which to bomb the Japanese mainland.

August 12: The Allies open an oil pipeline from Britain to France, greatly alleviating the crippling fuel shortages that had recently stalled offensive operations. It is nicknamed PLUTO, an acronym for Pipe Line Under the Ocean.

August 15: The Allies storm ashore in southern France in Operation Dragoon. • Audie Murphy, an American sharecropper's son who will be credited with 240 German kills and will become the most decorated soldier in American history, wipes out a force of Germans occupying a hill.

Dry docks The battleship *Idaho* is lifted out of the water in a floating dry dock at Guam. These repair platforms were constructed in sections in U.S. shipyards, towed to bases, and welded together on the spot. The dry dock was partially submerged to allow a damaged vessel to be towed into place. When water was pumped out of the dry dock's tanks, the whole structure rose, bringing its big passenger up with it. Dry docks carried their own power plants, storage areas, officer and crew quarters, and antiaircraft guns.

Marines secure Tinian Marine riflemen fire on the enemy during mop-up operations on Tinian. Marines had landed on the island on July 25, 1944. Located only three miles off Saipan, Tinian offered three valuable airfields for the bombing campaign against the Japanese home islands. The Marines made steady advances thanks in large part to Tinian's flat terrain, which allowed optimum use of U.S. tanks. Despite 9,000 Japanese defenders, the island was secured in nine days, five days ahead of schedule, at a cost of some 300 Marines killed and 1,600 wounded.

Mass suicide on Saipan Japanese civilians leap to their deaths from the cliffs at Marpi Point on northern Saipan. Recognizing that Saipan was lost, two Japanese commanders—Lieutenant General Saito Yoshitsugu and Vice Admiral Nagumo Chuichi—committed ritual suicide on July 6. Organized resistance effectively ended the following morning when thousands of Japanese troops perished in a final mass *banzai* attack. The subsequent U.S. advance to the northern end of the island cornered large numbers of terrified Japanese civilians. Convinced by their own propaganda that they would be tortured and murdered by Marines, hundreds of men, women, and children jumped to their deaths from the cliffs in spite of American efforts to dissuade them.

The Warsaw uprising Wearing a German uniform with a red and white armband, a Polish soldier fights from a Warsaw street barricade. On August 1, 1944, some 40,000 Polish Home Army soldiers, including 4,000 women, rose up against German occupiers. Although the Poles captured utilities and an SS food and military uniforms warehouse, Heinrich Himmler quickly sent in more troops and began aerial bombardments. Moscow withheld the help Poles had expected from Red Army troops just outside the city. One Polish patriot wrote, "We are waiting for you, red plague/To deliver us from black death."

Germans quash the revolt German occupiers hung Polish citizens daily and shot groups of captured soldiers and civilians. In Warsaw, 18,000 Polish soldiers and more than 150,000 civilians were killed during the uprising, which raged for 63 days. Little help came from the outside. Much of the Allies' air supply fell into German-held areas. By September, German panzer divisions and infantry had broken the Warsaw resistance. The Home Army surrendered on October 2, 1944, but only after guarantees that Geneva Conventions would be observed for both civilians and insurgents.

1944

August 18: President Roosevelt announces that he intends to send former war secretary Patrick Hurley to China in an effort to broker cooperation between the Nationalists and the Communists.

August 19: German field marshal Gunther von Kluge, wrongly suspected of involvement with the July 20 Hitler assassination attempt, kills himself. He was on his way home to Berlin two days after being replaced by Field Marshal Model as commander of the German army in the West.

August 20: Disaster befalls the German army in Romania, as the Romanians effectively switch sides at the same time that nearly a million Red Army soldiers march on the Axis satellite state.

August 21: The Dumbarton Oaks Conference is convened in a Washington, D.C., mansion of the same name. During the six-week international meeting, the framework of the United Nations will be largely agreed upon.

August 23: Romanian dictator Ion Antonescu is detained, as Romania's King Michael agrees to make peace with the Soviets.

August 24: The Nazis' sense of desperation is growing more apparent as Joseph Goebbels abolishes holidays, closes schools, and extends the work week, all in an effort to increase production for the war effort.

August 25: The Allies roll down the *Champs Elysées,* as Paris is liberated from the Nazis. • The SS murders more than 120 civilians in the French town of Maille as the Germans continue the practice of committing atrocities as they retreat.

August 26: The Axis satellite of Bulgaria announces that it is pulling out of the war and will no longer tolerate the staging of German offensive maneuvers from its soil.

Ford workforce short on housing When the Ford Motor Company located its Willow Run Bomber Plant in rural Michigan, prospective employees flooded the area. The Willow Run workforce would grow to 100,000, creating a demand for quick housing. This development near Willow Run promises "no red tape" for new tenants who put up $100. Although these new "modern homes" offered plumbing, heating, and other amenities, buildings such as trailers, barns, garages, stores, and at least one chicken coop were also used as living quarters. The Willow Run plant was extremely productive, turning out a bomber every 63 minutes.

Battle of the Falaise Pocket As the Battle of Normandy neared its end, the German Seventh Army and Fifth Panzer Army found themselves encircled by advancing British, French, Canadian, and American forces. The Germans' only escape route was the Falaise Pocket, an area in northern France. The pocket was held by the Polish First Armored Division, which fiercely fought the retreating Germans. The Battle of the Falaise Pocket raged from August 12 to 21, 1944, with many thousands of German soldiers killed and taken prisoner. Vast amounts of German materiel were destroyed, as this photograph shows. However, tens of thousands of Germans escaped to the Seine, partly because the Allies' fear of friendly fire among their converging forces prevented them from fully tightening their stranglehold.

Hitler's V-Weapons

ADOLF HITLER BELIEVED that Germany's *Vergeltungswaffen* (vengeance weapons; V-weapons) would ultimately force Britain to seek an armistice. The V-1 flying bomb was initially developed at Peenemünde, but following an RAF bombing raid in August 1943, the program was moved to Nordhausen. There, slave labor excavated factory and storage facilities deep within the Harz Mountains.

The V-1 carried a one-ton warhead 250 miles at 400 mph. From June 1944 to March 1945, 2,419 V-1s hit London, killing 6,184 people and injuring 17,981. Thousands died from V-1 attacks against Belgium. The V-2 was a sophisticated, electronically guided, supersonic ballistic missile that carried a one-ton warhead more than 200 miles. From September 1944 to April 1945, more than 1,100 V-2s hit Great Britain, killing 2,754 people and injuring 6,523. V-2s also killed 7,000 people in France, Belgium, Holland, and the Rhineland.

While V-1s could be shot down, deflected, or tangled by barrage balloons, there was no effective defense against the V-2s. Moreover, each of these V-weapons had a powerful psychological impact upon a population that already believed the end of the war was imminent.

A V-2 rocket (*left*) and destruction caused by a V-2 in Antwerp, Belgium (*right*)

The V-3s, the third type of vengeance weapons, were underground cannons that fired small shells enormous distances. Slave labor was employed to construct a vast underground emplacement for these guns on the French coast. However, this was destroyed by the RAF on July 6, 1944. The guns were moved to the southeast of Trier, where U.S. forces overran the site on February 26, 1945.

Finally, the V-4 was a multistage rocked called *Rhinbote*, of which a few were fired in the last months of the war. The Germans also made efforts to make a multistage missile to hit the United States, specifically New York City, possibly with a nuclear warhead.

Slaves construct the V-2s Slave laborers assemble V-2 rockets in the underground Mittelwerk factory near Nordhausen, Germany. About 60,000 prisoners from the nearby concentration camp Dora were put on the production line, and an estimated 10,000 to 20,000 died from overwork in those cold, damp tunnels. Some slaves fought back by sabotaging rockets—loosening screws, faking welds, urinating on wiring, or leaving out vital parts. Andrew Herskovits, put to work at age 14, said, "The punishment for sabotage was death by hanging—of course almost anything could be classified as sabotage." More than 200 suspects were hanged, and the bodies of some remained on cautionary display for days.

1944

August 26: On the *Führer's* orders, German forces begin their withdrawal from Greece. • Operating under the influence of the recently issued "lynch law" order, local residents in the German village of Russelsheim assault and murder the crew of a USAAF plane that crashed nearby.

August 30: The Red Army occupies the Romanian capital of Bucharest as well as the valuable oil fields of Ploesti.

September 2: General Eisenhower is forced to order his armies to stop for lack of fuel, giving Germany an opportunity to fortify its defenses. • The Soviet-Finnish War ends with the cessation of hostilities. A formal armistice will be signed on the 19th.

September 3: The British free the Belgian capital of Brussels from Nazi occupation.

September 5: In one of the quickest capitulations in the history of modern warfare, Bulgaria surrenders less than one day after a Soviet declaration of war. Bulgaria will declare war on Germany on the 7th.

September 6: The decline of the *Luftwaffe* enables Britain to stop enforcing a blackout for the first time in three years.

September 8: The next generation of V-weapons, the V-2, begin falling on London.

September 10: The mayor of Warsaw asks for Allied assistance as the city's partisans rise up against the Nazis. • Heinrich Himmler issues an order calling for the murders of the families of any deserting German military personnel.

September 11: More than 1,200 die when U.S. forces sink two Japanese prison ships containing thousands of Allied captives.

The Roosevelt-Truman relationship President Franklin Roosevelt chose Harry Truman as his running mate in 1944. Once elected, Truman had little contact with Roosevelt and was not a member of the president's inner circle of confidants who were developing America's end-of-war strategy, including the possible use of an atomic bomb. Roosevelt died 83 days after the start of his fourth term. Truman had to rely on Roosevelt's advisers to help him shape the policy that would lead the world to peace. Here, Truman and Roosevelt hold one of their infrequent dinner meetings.

The liberation of Paris Parisians cheer as Allied tanks roll past the *Arc de Triomphe*. On August 25, refusing to destroy the city as Hitler had ordered, German general Dietrich von Choltitz surrendered Paris to General Jacques-Philippe Leclerc and the Free French forces. French Communist Resistance fighters sought to take power, but Gaullist groups jockeyed into that position. French citizens hoped that Americans were bringing food, clothes, and gasoline, which had been in short supply during Nazi rule, but such items were also in short supply among the liberators.

Charles de Gaulle

BORN IN LILLE, FRANCE, in 1890, Charles de Gaulle excelled at Saint-Cyr Military Academy and served as an infantry officer from 1914 to '18. He not only was wounded three times, but he was held prisoner by the Germans from 1916 to '18. His interwar military career included fighting the Bolsheviks in Poland. He became an outspoken military theorist, supporting the unpopular position that France's army should be a professional, mobile, and mechanized elite, not a citizen force dependent on fixed defenses.

When Germany invaded France in May 1940, Colonel de Gaulle commanded France's new Fourth Armored Division, which he led in actions at Montcornet, Laon, and Abbeville. Reynaud appointed de Gaulle undersecretary of war on June 6. When Pétain took power 10 days later, de Gaulle escaped to England.

In a broadcast from London on June 18, 1940, de Gaulle urged his countrymen to continue fighting. Though later dubbed "the man of June 18," the new French leader was then little known. The forces at his disposal, ultimately called the Free French, were small. As a Catholic professional soldier, he was not a logical figurehead for the Left-dominated French Resistance. His natural constituency, the Right, was committed to Pétain.

De Gaulle also lacked political skill, but he had immense self-confidence and patriotic fervor. His diplomatic and martial efforts eventually brought recognition at home and alliance with the Resistance. De Gaulle depended on British backing, but he remained eternally suspicious of British intentions. His relations with Churchill and especially Roosevelt were difficult.

In 1943 de Gaulle became joint president of the French Committee of National Liberation (CFLN). He gradually dislodged his American-backed co-president, General Henri Giraud. He engineered the amalgamation of the Free French army and parts of the Vichy army of North Africa, thus enabling substantial French forces to contribute to France's liberation. On June 3, 1944, the CFLN was renamed the Provisional Government of the French Republic, which won recognition from the French population and later the Allies. On August 26, de Gaulle entered Paris to a rapturous welcome. The French hero would serve as president of the provisional government from September 1944 to January 1946.

The French Resistance Armed Resistance fighters maintain their guard during the liberation of Paris. The French Resistance included groups of students, Communists, liberals, anarchists, and Roman Catholics. Some organizations took orders from the British SOE (Special Operations Executive), some followed Charles de Gaulle, and others had different agendas, but all were anti-German. When the Allies approached Paris, Resistance cells organized strikes by police and other city workers. They fought skirmishes with German forces even after Choltitz surrendered. About 1,500 Resistance members and other civilians were killed during the fight for liberation.

1944

September 12: The RAF firebombs the central German city of Frankfurt. • Romania formally surrenders to the Allies. It agrees to take up arms against its former Axis partners in exchange for the postwar return of Transylvania to Romanian authority.

September 12–16: Churchill and Roosevelt meet in Quebec to discuss strategy in the Pacific Theater. They agree that a ground invasion of Japan will be necessary for victory.

September 15: One of the most laborious, hard-won battles of the Pacific war begins when the U.S. Marines land on the island of Peleliu. The Japanese will fiercely resist the American invaders for a month.

September 18: The United States and Britain airlift supplies to the Polish resistance in Warsaw. The Soviets, protective of their expansionist aims, are reluctant to prop up any Polish independence movement. The Soviets also refuse landing rights to U.S. and British planes in spite of appeals from Roosevelt and Churchill.

September 19: Female Nazi collaborators in the Dutch town of Nijmegen have their heads shaved and are publicly humiliated. • Churchill returns to Britain following a visit to Roosevelt's home in Hyde Park, New York. In their discussions, the two leaders agreed to fully share atomic research and to use the bomb only by mutual agreement.

September 21: A general strike called in Denmark to protest the deportation of nearly 200 Danes to Nazi concentration camps is violently suppressed by the Germans. • Japanese positions on Luzon, Philippines, come under intense aerial assault by a massive fleet of carrier-based U.S. warplanes.

September 22: Patton's Third Army is halted as supply lines are stretched to the breaking point.

"France seemed to wake again after being knocked out for five years."

—British general Alan Brooke, August 28, 1944

De Gaulle returns to Paris French general Charles de Gaulle makes a triumphant return to Paris on August 26, 1944. Ignoring sniper fire that sometimes scattered his admirers, the man who had led the Free French from exile in London walked down the *Champs Eleysées* and visited the *Cathédrale Notre Dame de Paris*. De

Gaulle moved back into his old office at the War Ministry and proclaimed the continuation of the Third Republic. He thus derailed an establishment of an Allied military government in France.

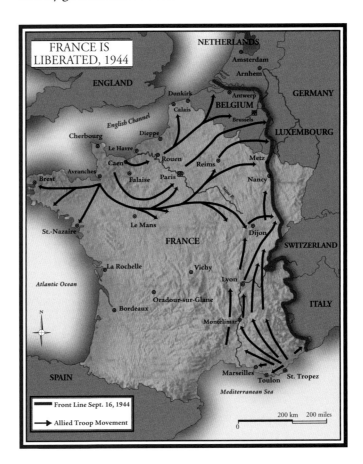

The liberation of France After several weeks of hard fighting among the hedgerows, woodland, and sunken lanes that dominated the post-D-Day Normandy battlefield, the Allied armor at last broke out of the beachheads and drove into France. Allied airpower was a major contributor to this. From July 25, U.S. forces (spearheaded by General Patton's Third Army) launched Operation Cobra, first striking west into Brittany, then south and east toward Paris. Simultaneously, the British Second Army and Canadian First Army struck east, across the Seine and into Belgium. Another Allied army landed in southern France in August. It drove quickly north to achieve a link-up and complete France's liberation.

Enemies still present in Paris Parisians who are gathered at the *Place de l'Etoile* to watch Allied forces march through the *Arc de Triomphe* dive to avoid sniper fire. Resistance forces had engaged in skirmishes with German occupiers for weeks before the liberation of Paris, and fighting within the city was not over yet. German soldiers and French Fascists were still shooting from the rooftops, interrupting celebrations and parades. French police, Resistance forces, and Allied soldiers fought back. The city was secured in a few days and quieted down after about a week.

U.S. Army hangs German civilians Enemy civilians who committed war crimes were not exempt from American military justice. On November 10, 1944, at Bruchsal Prison near Baden, Germany, the U.S. Army hanged five German noncombatants who murdered six American airmen the previous August. The crew had parachuted safely from their disabled aircraft near Ruesselsheim, only to be waylaid by angry locals. In a small irony, Bruchsal Prison had been favored by the Nazis as a place to guillotine or hang enemies of the state.

Mauldin's popular cartoons "More than anyone else, save only Ernie Pyle," Stephen Ambrose wrote in the introduction to a reissue of Bill Mauldin's book, *Up Front,* "he caught the trials and travails of the GI." Mauldin entered the war as an infantryman in the 45th Division and landed with his unit in Sicily and Italy. He began drawing cartoons in the 45th's newspaper, then transferred in 1944 to the *Stars & Stripes,* where his cartoons became popular in both the ranks and the States. His characters, Willie and Joe, came to represent the frustrations felt by all American GIs.

Political art To Hitler and other Nazi leaders, political art was a means of capturing the spirit of the Nazi Party for those in Germany—at that time and in the future. "No state," Hitler said, "lasts longer than the documents of its culture." This painting, *Auf Heimaturlaub* (*On Homeland Vacation*), portrays a German soldier returning to his home on leave and conveying exciting stories of victory on the front lines. The children pay close attention to their father—especially the boys, who long for the day they can fight for Germany.

1944

September 24: The U.S. releases the Morgenthau Plan, a postwar plan that proposes a total restructuring of the German economy to an agrarian footing.

September 25: Germany organizes the *Volkssturm,* a militia that drafts men as old as 60 and as young as 16.

September 26: Allied planes drop American paratroopers behind German lines in Italy to establish the same sort of resistance network that had been so successful in helping the Allies capture France.

September 27: The British suffer 1,200 deaths and lose some 6,600 more to German POW camps as they fail in their nine-day bid to secure a bridge over the Rhine in the Dutch town of Arnhem.

September 29: The Soviets fly their last sortie in support of the Warsaw resistance.

October 2: After two months of fierce urban warfare, the Germans crush the Polish resistance in Warsaw. As many as 250,000 Poles have died during the struggle. • The Allies break into the Siegfried Line, a defensive line running along Germany's western border. The breach is in the north, near Aachen, and it is there that U.S. troops will penetrate western Germany.

October 7: A group of *Sonderkommandos,* captive Jews whose lives are prolonged while they assist the Nazis with gas chamber and crematorium operations, attacks SS guards at Auschwitz. Though the revolt is quickly and violently quelled, they do kill several SS men and destroy their barracks, as well as Crematorium IV.

October 9–18: Churchill, Stalin, and U.S. ambassador William Averell Harriman meet in Moscow to discuss the postwar status of Poland and the Balkan States.

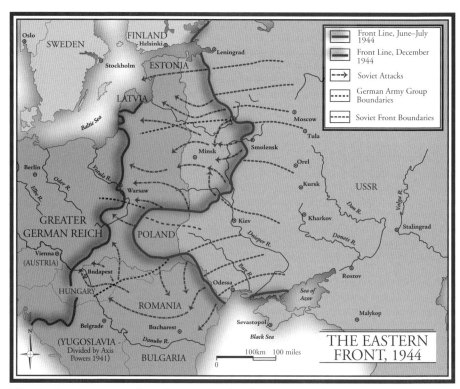

THE EASTERN FRONT, 1944

The Soviets' westward push Despite the disaster at Stalingrad in January 1943, the Germans subsequently halted a number of Soviet offensives, and even retook Kharkov in March. In July, however, their *Blitzkrieg*-style attacks at Kursk were effectively absorbed and defeated by the Red Army during the greatest tank battle of the war. The Russians then launched successful counteroffensives at Orel and Kharkov. These advances eventually paved the way for a devastating series of Soviet offensives across the whole Eastern Front beginning in June 1944. These included the destruction of Army Group Center in Belorussia and successes in the Ukraine, Poland, the Balkans, and Romania. By December, the Eastern Front no longer lay within the Russian homeland.

Russian Partisans As German forces stormed through Russia in 1941, pockets of resistance formed behind the German lines. By the end of 1941, anti-German resistance fighters (such as those pictured) began to come together, creating partisan units. Their mission was to cut or destroy supply and communication lines between the German troops and their supply bases. As their numbers

grew to the tens of thousands in 1943, partisans began to launch attacks on German units as the latter fled from the Red Army.

Russians begin to rebuild In the western Soviet Union, entire towns were razed during the war. But as soon as Russians regained their most important cities, they began restoring them. Here, Soviet soldiers rebuild a bridge that had been destroyed by retreating Germans. In Leningrad, the city was cleaned up and some museums reopened as early as 1944. The Crimean city of Sevastopol—named a "hero city" for its resistance to invasion—had to be rebuilt stone by stone. That same year, Russia began using German prisoners as forced labor in reconstruction work.

The drowning of Allied POWs British and Australian POWs are rescued by the submarine USS *Sealion II* following the sinking of the Japanese ship *Rakuyo Maru* in the China Sea. Crammed with 1,317 POWs from Singapore and unmarked with a red cross or any other indication that prisoners were on board, the *Rakuyo Maru* was torpedoed by *Sealion* on September 11, 1944. Japanese escort vessels rescued surviving crew members, but left most of the POWs to die in the water. Ninety-two POWs were picked up by U.S. submarines, but more than a thousand others died.

The Red Ball Express After Allied troops landed in Normandy in June 1944, they found that the railroads had been almost completely destroyed by their own bombers. Since transportation was needed to supply the Allied advance across Europe, the Red Ball Express was created. During the Red Ball's three-month history, starting in August, more than 6,000 trucks drove along a French highway loop restricted to military use. These vehicles carried more than 500,000 tons of food, fuel, and ammunition. Here, Corporal Charles H. Johnson waves on a Red Ball Express convoy near Alencon, France.

A top Canadian commander Henry Duncan Graham Crerar, commander of the First Canadian Army, reads a map while sitting on the wing strut of an observation plane. Although he had been an isolationist before the war, Crerar supervised the training of Canadian troops in 1941. By 1944 he was the leading Canadian field

commander in Northwest Europe, earning him a spot on the cover of *Time* magazine. *Time* reported that Crerar "drove his jeep from one command post to another—pausing to read reports with the avidity of a hungry wolf, to give orders in his quiet, precise, unbending manner."

1944

October 10: Japan's air forces are depleted further as 17 U.S. aircraft carriers launch a massive attack on Japanese installations on Okinawa.

October 13: Stalin once again assures his Allied partners that the Soviets will declare war on Japan, but he insists that he cannot spare the resources until the Allies gain Germany's unconditional surrender.

October 14: German general Erwin Rommel, suspected of having collaborated with the July 20 conspirators, swallows poison after being told by Hitler's chief of army personnel that unless he commits suicide, the Nazis will put him on trial and his family will lose its pension and an estate that had been given to him. The official party line will be that Rommel died of the wounds he suffered in the July RAF attack.

October 15: More than 2,200 Allied bombers pummel industrial cities in the Ruhr. • The Nazis detain Hungarian regent Admiral Horthy hours after he publicly requests peace terms from the Allies. Hungarian Nazi leader Major Ferenc Szálasi will take over the government.

October 18: Premier George Papandreou of Greece is restored to power four days after the last German soldier leaves the ancient capital of Athens. The Germans were driven out by Greek partisans and Allied forces. • Churchill rebuffs a request from Spanish dictator General Francisco Franco to align England and Spain against Communist Russia. • Reeling from losses at Leyte Gulf and elsewhere, the Japanese launch Operation *Sho-Go* (Victory) in a desperate bid to regain lost territory and protect the Japanese home islands.

October 20: In conjunction with Josip Broz Tito's Army of National Liberation, the Soviets liberate Belgrade, Yugoslavia, from the Germans.

Allies liberate concentration camp Two Allied soldiers examine an oven used to cremate victims at Herzogenbusch, a German concentration camp built outside the Dutch town of Vught. Jews began to be deported to Herzogenbosch in January 1943. While some were forced to work in local factories, others were temporarily held there before being sent to extermination camps in Germany. The camp eventually held more than 30,000 inmates, including Jews, political prisoners, and captured resistance fighters. By the time the camp was liberated in September 1944, about 13,000 had died there.

Red Army atrocities As Russia's Red Army raced into Germany from the east, officer leadership and troop discipline frequently broke down. In October 1944, units of Russia's 11th Guards Army rampaged through the East Prussian village of Nemmersdorf, nailing men to barns, raping women, and crushing the heads of infants. Russian atrocities of this sort prompted countless German civilians to make dangerous treks westward, in hopes of capture by relatively even-tempered American forces.

"If you didn't get to know them, you weren't as affected by their fates."

—87TH INFANTRY DIVISION VETERAN EUGENE KAPLAN, ON GREEN ARMY REPLACEMENTS

The Life of a Replacement

EVERY BELLIGERENT NATION confronted the question of how best to integrate replacements for casualties. The German and British armies generally sent each reinforcement to a unit raised in his home region, although this became less practical as the war intensified and casualties mounted. German and British replacements undertook basic training, then joined a reinforcement unit—such as a regiment or company—that would be integrated into a front-line unit.

The U.S. Army system was notoriously alienating. Individual soldiers were allocated from replacement depots ("repple depples") to replace casualties, who once recovered would frequently be sent not to their home units but wherever there was a gap. These processes fostered anonymity, neglect, and even contempt.

Reinforcements in all armies faced a difficult initiation and died in disproportionate numbers. Their initial training was often inadequate, so they required last-minute, front-line instruction. Such "green" recruits endangered their more experienced compatriots, who often left them to sink or swim. If they survived their first action and demonstrated willingness to contribute, they were usually accepted as comrades.

The need for new men grew in the second half of the war. Young reinforcements became the lifeblood of the Allied armies in 1944–45. The German and Soviet armies included many reinforcements from acquired or "liberated" territory. Many of these men were often conscripted against their will and thus were of dubious military value.

Operation Market Garden Allied tanks rumble across the bridge at Nijimegan during Operation Market Garden in September 1944. The brainchild of British general Bernard Montgomery, Market Garden was a bold but risky attempt to establish a bridgehead over the Rhine in southern Holland. Three airborne divisions were to seize key bridges at Eindhoven, Nijmegan, and Arnhem along a 64-mile route through Holland, opening the way for a lightning ground advance by the British XXX Corps. The gambit failed when the ground force was unable to meet its four-day timetable due to constricted terrain and unexpected German resistance. Isolated at Arnhem, the British First Airborne Division was destroyed after holding out for 10 days.

Allies enter Germany General Dwight Eisenhower's three army groups reached the German border in September 1944 with superior forces and firepower. However, they were slowed by acute gasoline and ammunition shortages, as well as by determined German troops. Many of the latter had dug in along the defensive Siegfried Line, which was newly rearmed, at Hitler's orders, with pillboxes, gun emplacements, tank traps, and other obstacles. To make matters worse, the American advance came during the wet season; daily cold rain turned the rough terrain to mud. By early October, when U.S. soldiers (*pictured*) drove into Germany, front-line American commanders realized that the German homeland would not be occupied quickly.

1944

October 20: American troops land on the island of Leyte in the Philippines and fulfill General MacArthur's promise to return to liberate the islands from the Japanese.

October 21: Aachen becomes the first German city to fall to the Allies, as desperately weakened German forces surrender.

October 23: Philippines president Sergio Osmeña is restored to office.

October 23–26: The Japanese navy suffers a resounding defeat as American forces dominate in the Battle of Leyte Gulf. The crowning loss for the Japanese is their super-battleship *Musashi,* which capsizes and sinks, costing the lives of more than 1,000 sailors.

October 25: SS *Reichsführer* Heinrich Himmler orders the destruction of the macabre Jewish skull collection at Berlin's so-called "Anatomical Institute." • Since it is no longer a member of the enemy Axis, Italy's diplomatic ties to the Allies are restored.

October 28: The Allies penetrate deep into German territory on General Eisenhower's orders. • U.S. major general Albert Wedemeyer replaces General Joseph Stilwell as commander in the Chinese theater. This comes 10 days after Stilwell is removed at the request of Nationalist leader Chiang Kai-shek. • The Soviets assume control of the Bulgarian armed forces, as Bulgaria capitulates to Russia. • The German army quits the small Adriatic nation of Albania. • The first of the soon-to-be-legendary *kamikaze* pilots commits suicide as he crashes his plane on the deck of the USS *Denver.*

October 30: The Auschwitz gas chambers are used for the last time, as one final transport of Jews—1,700 men, women, and children from the work camp at Theresienstadt—are murdered.

Casualties high at Aachen Two German prisoners of war, guarded by an American soldier, wait to be taken to a POW camp after the U.S. victory at Aachen. For seven days, fighting had raged from building to building and room to room, with enemy snipers on rooftops picking off scores of U.S. soldiers. While American tanks struggled through debris-strewn streets to dislodge defenders, German soldiers and civilians took to cellars and sewers. This strategically unimportant city cost each side some 5,000 casualties, and about 5,600 Germans were taken prisoner.

Jewish soldiers In May 1939, Great Britain decided to limit Jewish immigration into the British mandate of Palestine. This policy increased tensions between Zionists (Jews who strove for a Jewish homeland in Palestine) and Britain throughout World War II. However, faced with the hideous threat of Nazi Germany, thousands of Palestinian Jews—such as the ones seen here—volunteered for the British Army. That army's 5,000-member Jewish Brigade was created in September 1944. The British trained Jewish fighters in sabotage, demolition, and guerrilla warfare—techniques that, ironically, proved vital to the postwar Zionist resistance against British occupation.

Heavy Casualties in Hurtgen Forest

To THE SOUTH OF AACHEN, Germany, lies the densely wooded Hurtgen Forest. In 1944 it was heavily fortified by the Germans, and just to the southeast were the Roer dams. These dams were of considerable operational significance, for if breached by the Germans at a time of their own choosing, they could produce a major water obstacle to stall the Allied advance.

The German defense was centered on the village of Schmidt, and throughout the surrounding woodland were reinforced bunkers, snipers, mines, booby traps, dug-in antitank guns, and fixed line machine guns. It was a "green hell," within which the U.S. armor and artillery could do little to support the embattled infantrymen—many of them newly arrived replacements—who were drawn into the forest in ever-increasing numbers. Part of the formidable Siegfried Line defenses also ran through this damp, dark, freezing forest.

The bitter succession of battles fought in October and November by the Ninth, 28th, Eighth, Fourth, and First U.S. infantry divisions, under overall command of General Courtney Hodges's First U.S. Army within General Bradley's 12th U.S. Army Group, resulted in the most costly infantry fighting of the war in Northwest Europe for the U.S. forces. In early December, the Americans finally broke through the Hurtgen.

The excessive casualties sustained by some units in the Hurtgen were also attributable to poor preparation at divisional and regimental levels. Some U.S. troops lacked proper training and specialist equipment for close-country

U.S. infantrymen in the Hurtgen region

fighting. This type of combat was unlike the fast-flowing, mobile armored operations—with guaranteed air and artillery support on-call—to which the GIs had become all too accustomed ever since the breakout from Normandy four months earlier. Consequently, by early December, the Hurtgen combat had resulted in 24,000 U.S. battle casualties. A further 5,000 U.S. soldiers were noneffective due to trench foot, combat fatigue, and respiratory diseases.

Overall, American battle casualties in Northwest Europe that autumn totaled 57,000, not including 70,000 noncombat casualties. The Roer dams were finally captured on February 9, 1945, during a major new Anglo-U.S. offensive.

Germans plan the Ardennes campaign Hitler pores over plans for Germany's Ardennes campaign with staff members—from left to right, Reich Marshal Hermann Göring, Head of Security Police in France Helmut Knochen, two unidentified officials, and Chief of the Army General Staff Heinz Guderian. Hitler's irrational hope for the Ardennes attack, code-named *Wacht am Rhein* (Watch on the Rhine), was to seize the Belgian port of Antwerp (denying this vital port to the Allies) and to demoralize Britain and the U.S. into making peace separately from the Soviet Union. In an ideal outcome, Hitler would be free to shift forces to slow or halt the Soviet advance.

1944

November 3: The Japanese launch more than 9,000 hydrogen balloons with incendiaries attached, sending them on westerly winds to North America. Fewer than 300 of the balloons will reach their targets, but one is found and detonated in Oregon, killing a woman and five children.

November 5: German forces round up 200 Dutch citizens in the town of Heusden. The Germans barricade them inside the town hall and blow up the building, proving that they are as dangerous in retreat as they were on the offensive. • The Americans bomb Singapore.

November 7: Franklin Roosevelt wins his fourth consecutive term as U.S. president. • "Neutral" Switzerland's ties with Germany, coupled with its hostility toward communism, leaves Stalin disinclined to renew diplomatic ties. • Richard Sorge, a Soviet spy who kept Moscow apprised of Japanese war plans before his capture by the Japanese, is hanged in Tokyo.

November 8: The *Luftwaffe* loses one of its best when ace pilot Major Walter Nowotny crashes his Messerschmitt 262 over Germany.

November 10: The Japanese puppet government in Nanking, China, sees a change in leadership when Chen Kung-po succeeds a deceased Wang Ching-wei.

November 12: After many efforts to destroy the German battleship *Tirpitz*, the British finally succeed. Struck by at least two massive bombs, the great ship capsizes and goes under with most of its 1,900-man crew.

November 23: German holdings in the Alsace-Lorraine region of France are further reduced by the Allied capture of Strasbourg, the region's principal city.

Heavy casualties on Peleliu A helmeted Japanese skull calls attention to a warning sign ("Danger! Move Fast") on the island of Peleliu as the campaign winds down in October 1944. The First Marine Division had landed on Peleliu on September 15, despite indications that the original purpose of the campaign—to protect General MacArthur's flank in the push to the Philippines—was no longer necessary. Anticipating only a few days of battle, the Marines found themselves mired in bloody combat amid a maze of coral cliffs and caves. By the time the fighting ended in November, U.S. forces had suffered more than 9,500 casualties in exchange for an island that yielded little strategic benefit.

Lea's graphic paintings Tom Lea III (*left*) joined *Life* magazine as an artist-correspondent in 1940. His wartime paintings included subjects as varied as politicians and battlefield scenes. His graphic images of the fighting on Peleliu Island in 1944 became famous for their realism and horror, which were unlike anything he or any other American war artist had previously depicted. In *Two-Thousand Yard Stare* (*pictured*), he portrayed, he stated, a Marine "staring stiffly at nothing," whose "mind had crumbled in battle."

The "Ace of Aces" USAAF pilot Richard Bong, pictured center beside his P-38 Lightning, was the leading American ace during the war. In the Southwest Pacific in April 1944, Bong became the first American to pass Eddie Rickenbacker's World War I score of 26. After home leave, Bong returned to the Southwest Pacific in September 1944. Though ordered not to seek combat, he did. His "gallantry and intrepidity" in October and November earned him the Medal of Honor. Eventually reaching a total of 40 victories, the "Ace of Aces" died on August 6, 1945, the day of the Hiroshima bombing, while test-flying the new P-80.

Nose art The noses of many American bombers and fighters were decorated with sensual pictures of women. They were often modeled after the images of women in magazines, such as *Esquire*. Each plane's crew paid a professional or amateur artist, who was often a member of the crew or supporting staff at an air base. Some artists painted images of women that were too graphic for the tastes of commanding officers. In each instance, the crews were ordered to modify the artwork by painting over the offensive figures.

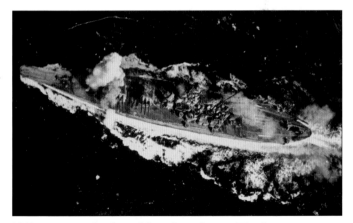

U.S. protects its beachhead on Leyte The Japanese battleship *Yamato* comes under bombing attack during the Second Battle of the Philippine Sea. The super-battleship sallied out as part of Operation Sho-1, an elaborate Japanese scheme to destroy the American beachhead on Leyte, Philippines. Though a diversion successfully drew away Admiral Bull Halsey's carriers, lack of Japanese airpower doomed Sho. A handful of U.S. destroyers, destroyer escorts, and the few available aircraft from escort carriers narrowly managed to turn the Japanese naval force away from the beachhead. "We had no air cover to repel the enemy, for whom it was pure offensive," observed a Japanese officer.

Attack on the *Princeton* Fires burn out of control on the aircraft carrier USS *Princeton* after a Japanese air attack. More than 60 land-based Japanese bombers and torpedo planes, escorted by 130 fighters, attacked U.S. naval forces covering the Leyte landings on October 24. Though these Japanese forces were decimated by U.S. fighters, one dive-bomber hit the *Princeton* with a 550-pound bomb that penetrated the flight deck. The crew abandoned ship as burning gasoline spread to parked aircraft and a munitions storage area. Damage-control parties remained to fight the conflagration, but hours later a massive explosion tore through the carrier, killing or wounding almost everyone still aboard.

1944

November 23: The Canadian Parliament approves a limited draft—a dramatic departure from what had been a strictly volunteer force. Some 16,000 additional Canadian troops will join the Allies.

November 24: Discouraged by the defeat of the Warsaw uprising and disgusted with Soviet manipulation of the Polish border, Premier in Exile Stanislaw Mikolajczyk resigns his post. • The United States attacks Tokyo with 111 B-29 long-range bombers. They operate out of forward bases on the recently occupied Mariana island of Saipan.

November 25: A German V-2 rocket levels a Woolworth department store in London. Of the more than 160 victims, many are children. • Several U.S. aircraft carriers are damaged by *kamikaze* attacks in the waters off the Philippine Islands.

November 26: As Soviet troops advance toward Auschwitz, Heinrich Himmler orders the complex of gas chambers and crematoria destroyed, along with the last of the *Sonderkommando* Jews, in an effort to hide evidence of Nazi atrocities.

November 27: A munitions dump explodes at Burton-on-Trent, England, killing 68 people and scores of animals. • Antwerp comes under heavy V-2 bomb attacks as the Allies finally open up shipping operations in the Belgian port. • The Chinese remain unable to unite for the common goal of battling Japan, and Chiang Kai-shek again refuses to share his stockpile of American weaponry with the Communists.

November 29: *Shinano*, a huge Japanese aircraft carrier commissioned earlier in the month, sinks after being torpedoed by the U.S. submarine *Archerfish*.

U.S. prevails on Leyte American troops regard the bodies of Japanese snipers on the Philippine island of Leyte. After two months of fighting, from October to December, U.S. forces secured the island as part of General MacArthur's promise to win back the Philippines. Nevertheless, Leyte was not an unqualified success. A flood of Japanese reinforcements prolonged the battle, and American casualties were higher than anticipated. But the Japanese fared worse. The naval engagements off Leyte effectively destroyed the remnants of the Japanese Navy, while the ground campaign consumed nearly 65,000 troops. In a last-gasp effort, Japanese paratroopers jumped on two U.S. airfields on Leyte on December 6. Despite creating considerable confusion, all were killed or driven off.

"MacArthur's Firefighter" General Robert Eichelberger steps up to the firing line near Buna Beach, New Guinea. Known as "MacArthur's Firefighter" for his skills as a battlefield problem solver, Eichelberger was one of the few U.S. generals who strove to maintain warm relations with the Australians. This foresight helped immeasurably when he was ordered to salvage the deteriorating situation at Buna in 1943. Subsequently named to command the Eighth Army, Eichelberger completed the seizure of Leyte in 1944, executed a series of amphibious operations in the Philippines, and defeated the Japanese on Mindanao. He later commanded the Eighth Army in the occupation of Japan.

Filipinos dismiss Japanese propaganda Filipino civilians examine a Japanese propaganda placard in Manila in October 1944. The message probably refers to an air battle off Taiwan in mid-October in which Japanese airmen claimed to have sunk 11 U.S. carriers and two battleships. In fact, no U.S. ships were lost. Such propaganda claims became less and less credible as the war turned against Japan. The Japanese propaganda machine had an especially difficult task in the pro-American Philippines, where clandestine radio reports kept the population abreast of Allied advances. "I Shall Return" graffiti showed up on everything from buses to brothels.

American submarines General Tojo stated that American submarines were a key factor in Japan's defeat. They sank nearly two-thirds of all the Japanese merchant tonnage that was destroyed and nearly one-third of all combatant ships that were sunk. Initially, they performed disappointingly because of defective torpedoes, overly cautious captains, and unimaginative strategic deployment. These deficiencies were overcome in 1943. The U.S. Navy lost 52 of its 288 submarines, but American sub crews rescued more than 500 downed U.S. airmen, including future president George H. W. Bush. Pictured is the USS *Wahoo*, a 1,525-ton *Gato*-class submarine.

Pacific fleets rely on the *New Jersey* With a speed of 33 knots, the battleship USS *New Jersey*—like all *Iowa*-class vessels—could keep up with aircraft carriers. It had less armor protection than comparable Japanese battleships, but its nine 16-inch guns were formidable. As the flagship of Admiral Spruance's Fifth Fleet in 1944, it screened aircraft carriers, destroyed enemy vessels and aircraft, and provided shore bombardment. The *New Jersey* supported operations in the Carolines, the Marshalls, the Palaus, New Guinea, the Marianas, the Philippines, and Formosa, and acted as flagship for the Fifth and Third fleets. Its service continued into 1945, notably at Okinawa.

Kamikaze **pilots** Early in the Pacific war, the Allies noted a Japanese willingness to die in battle. When Japan's strategic situation became dire, its leaders methodically exploited that enthusiasm. Vice Admiral Onishi Takijiro instigated aerial suicide attacks on enemy ships at Leyte Gulf in October 1944. The suicide units were called *"kamikaze,"* or "divine wind," after the 13th century typhoon that

smashed a Mongol invasion. *Kamikaze* attacks appealed to the Japanese command because they negated pilot inexperience and aircraft obsolescence, and reduced fuel consumption. Moreover, they could demoralize the Allies and demonstrate the supposed spiritual superiority of a freshly inspired Japan. There was no shortage of volunteers, such as the young pilot pictured here.

Carriers key to U.S. victory A *kamikaze* hits the USS *Essex* in November 1944. Accurate statistics concerning the *kamikaze* are elusive, but apparently between 2,500 and 5,000 Japanese suicide pilots were killed, at least 34 Allied vessels were sunk, and 288 to 368 vessels were damaged throughout the war. Whereas the *kamikaze* could not change the course of the war, the Essex-class carriers did. Prime Minister Tojo identified their ability to operate for months without entering harbor as critical in Japan's defeat. In the pictured attack, the *Essex* was damaged, 15 crew members were killed, and 44 were wounded. However, the ship was back in action some three weeks later.

British hunt down the *Tirpitz* The German battleship *Tirpitz* lurks in a Norwegian fjord, waiting to pounce on Allied shipping. A sister ship to the *Bismarck,* the *Tirpitz* was a serious threat, and the British were intent on destroying it. In 1943 X-class midget submarines—three-man subs carrying a mine on each side—placed timed explosive charges that disabled the ship. In April 1944, the repaired *Tirpitz* was again damaged by carrier-borne aircraft. Effective German defenses, including smoke screens, as well as cloudy weather protected the *Tirpitz* during several more air strikes. However, on November 12, the RAF bombed and finally sank the ship.

Japanese balloon bombs reach U.S. On May 5, 1945, a woman and five children were killed while moving a large balloon they discovered near Bly, Oregon. It was one of about 9,000 balloons that the Japanese launched in the direction of the United States from November 1944 to April 1945. Each was

33 feet in diameter and carried one 33-pound antipersonnel bomb and four incendiaries. They reached an altitude of 35,000 feet and traveled about 100 mph. Approximately 300 balloon bomb incidents were reported in the U.S. and Canada, but the deaths in Oregon were the only casualties. The balloon in this picture was discovered in Montana.

Nazi mind games Propaganda was used by both sides during the war to undermine the fighting spirit of the enemy. Late in the war, the Germans circulated fake copies of *Life* magazine to remind American soldiers of home and to play with their minds. These two pictures were the front and back of one of the "issues" of *Life*. This piece of propaganda was circulated by three German soldiers along various trails used by Americans. Two of the Germans were killed and the third captured. Members of the 91st Division, who saw the pamphlet, "agreed unanimously," wrote Bernie Smith, a member of the unit, "that the unholy wench who posed for the picture on the front is far more gruesome than the old gaffer on the reverse side."

The Superfortress
American-built B-29 Superfortresses take to the air. The most advanced bomber of its time, the Superfortress had a pressurized cabin, a central fire-control system, and remote-control machine gun turrets. The advanced design, complex manufacturing requirements, and rush to production created major reliability problems in the early aircraft. However, the long-range bomber ultimately became the mainstay of the air campaign against Japan.

Bombers fly over Tokyo Japanese soldiers man an air-defense machine gun on the roof of a Tokyo department store. Such improvised defenses were largely useless against the high-flying B-29 bombers that began to appear over the capital in 1944. The limited numbers of Japanese fighter planes were only slightly more effective. The U.S. 20th Bomber Command reported losing only 20 bombers to enemy fighters and five to antiaircraft fire in 1944. Within a year, the heavy bombers would be flying over Japan with near impunity, even dropping leaflets warning the populace of future targets.

1944

December 3: Unchecked fighting between Greek pro- and anti-Communist factions leads to civil war. • King George VI demobilizes Britain's Home Guard.

December 8: American air forces launch a lengthy offensive against Japanese positions on the island of Iwo Jima. They will spend more than two months softening the Japanese defenses prior to the ground assault.

December 10: Representatives of the Soviet Union and France meet in Moscow and sign a 20-year treaty of friendship and aid. • The Allies build the world's longest bridge, at 1,154 feet, across Burma's Chindwin River.

December 12: Nearly 500 civilians die in a V-2 strike on Antwerp's Rex Cinema.

December 13: More *kamikaze* attacks damage U.S. Navy warships in the Sulu Sea.

December 15: The plane carrying American bandleader Glenn Miller disappears after taking off from England in foul weather.

December 16: The Battle of the Bulge begins when the Germans orchestrate a huge strike against U.S. positions in Luxembourg's Ardennes Forest. • President Roosevelt promotes General Douglas MacArthur to the rank of five-star general.

December 17: Sixty-seven American POWs lose their lives in the Malmedy massacre when a German unit randomly opens fire on a group of 170 prisoners. No motive is apparent. • The 509th Composite Group assembles at a site in western Utah for a special high-speed, high-altitude bombing mission over Japan.

December 17–18: A massive typhoon envelops the U.S. Third Fleet. More than 700 lives are lost.

Japanese desperate for food In 1944 Japan's food shortages worsened. Wild dogs roamed Tokyo streets searching for food, but sometimes became food themselves. Here, civilians farm crops and raise animals in the Olympic Stadium, built for the canceled 1940 Games. By 1941 nearly all arable land—including golf courses—had been brought under cultivation, but Japan still imported most of its soybeans and sugar. Domestic rice crops and imports helped people fend off starvation until the last year of the war. In 1945 shortages engendered by strategic bombing and the submarine blockade led to mass flight to the countryside and suffering in the cities and towns.

The young Kachin Rangers In the Burma campaign, indigenous groups—such as the Kachin, Karen, and Chin peoples—assisted the Allies. The "Kachin Rangers" scouted and provided flank guard for the American Galahad force, known colloquially as "Merrill's Marauders." On May 17, 1944, Kachin and Chinese forces aided the Americans in capturing the Myitkina airstrip. This photograph, taken at the airstrip that month, reportedly shows a 10-year-old Chinese soldier waiting to be flown to China. However, at least one of these boys may be Kachin. The Kachin Rangers included young boys who often carried submachine guns and traditional swords. The boy at left wears a predominantly British uniform.

> "[W]hen we reached the point of heading directly into the wind, the propellers of three or four planes, still parked on the bow, began wind-milling at about 200 rpm and a few seconds later these planes were torn from their moorings and flung like chips over the side."
>
> —Captain A. G. Olney, Jr., USS *Altamaha* (light aircraft carrier)

Typhoon in the Philippines

On December 17, 1944, U.S. Task Force 38 was 300 miles away from its destination: Luzon, Philippines. As the ships prepared to refuel at the island of Mindoro, winds began to pick up. "A moderate cross swell and a wind varying from 20 to 30 knots made fueling difficult," Admiral William Halsey recounted in his autobiography. He was told by his staff aerologist that it was only a "tropical disturbance."

As the storm intensified, Halsey suspended refueling and ordered his ships to move away from the storm. It was no longer a "tropical disturbance" but a typhoon. On December 18, it was on a collision course with the task force. Many of Halsey's destroyers were very low on fuel, causing the ships to ride treacherously high on the sea. As the center of the typhoon passed close to the task force, hurricane-force winds buffeted massive waves against the helpless vessels. "Shortly after twelve o'clock...," an officer on the destroyer *Hull* later reported, "the wind velocity increased to an unbelievable high point which I estimated at 110 knots. The force of this wind laid the ship steadily over on her starboard side."

The USS *Langley* during the typhoon

When the storm passed, Halsey recounted, it had "swamped three destroyers, cost the lives of 790 men, wrecked some 200 planes, and damaged twenty-eight ships." Over the next three days, every able ship and plane searched desperately for survivors. Following the disaster, the worst the U.S. Navy had suffered in a storm since 1889, new weather stations and offices were established across the Pacific.

Civil war in Greece The liberation of Greece from Axis occupation in October 1944 did not bring peace to the country. EAM-ELAS (National Liberation Front-National Popular Liberation Army), the Communist-led resistance movement against Axis occupation, controlled about two-thirds of Greece by the time the Germans evacuated. The ELAS (the organization's military wing, *pictured*) refused Greece's postwar government's demands to disarm. This refusal led to violence in Athens between Greek guerrillas and British forces, including these paratroops from the Fifth Parachute Battalion, part of Britain's Second Parachute Brigade. Civil war continued to rage in Greece until 1949.

1944

December 18: The U.S. tries to put a lid on recent Japanese gains on the Chinese mainland by directing a series of B-29 raids against Japanese positions around Hangkow.

December 19: Some 130 Belgian civilians, accused of sheltering U.S. troops, are murdered by members of the Nazi Gestapo.

December 22: Surrounded with his 101st Airborne Division in the Battle of the Bulge, Brigadier General Anthony McAuliffe receives a surrender ultimatum from the Germans, to which he delivers his immortal reply: "Nuts." In later years, he would suggest that his actual reply was a stronger four-letter word.

December 23: The American soldiers at Bastogne, Belgium, receive desperately needed supplies and offensive reinforcement.

December 24: Members of the German *Sicherheitsdienst* avenge an attack by the Belgian resistance by murdering nearly all the young men in the village of Bande. One, Leon Praile, is able to escape. • More than 800 U.S. soldiers die when the *U-486* sinks the American troop transport *Leopoldville* in the English Channel.

December 26: U.S. tanks break through the German line and end the Bastogne siege as well as the Ardennes offensive. Though they initially had been victorious locally, German forces are greatly depleted.

December 29: Hungary declares war on its former ally Germany as Soviet tanks roll in and urban warfare engulfs the city of Budapest.

December 31: Some German soldiers caught impersonating U.S. troops behind Allied lines are executed by firing squad. • The Battle of Leyte ends with the Allies losing 3,500 men of a 200,000-man force. The Japanese lose 49,000 of a force of 55,000.

Production woes doom German jet The potential of Germany's highly capable Messerschmitt Me 262 jet fighter was squandered because of slow production of the Junkers Jumo 004 jet engine that powered it. It was not because, as is commonly held, Hitler insisted that the plane be utilized as a fighter-bomber rather than as a pure fighter. The 540-mph 262 (America's P-51 Mustang could reach 437 mph) did not see combat until July 1944, too late to affect the D-Day landings or the war's larger outcome. Although some 1,400 Me 262s were delivered, fewer than 300 saw combat. During the same period, Britain fielded perhaps 20 Gloster Meteor jet fighters, and Germany experimented with the *Komet,* a difficult-to-fly Messerschmitt rocket plane capable of speeds just shy of 600 mph.

The Women's Army Corps
Members of the U.S. Women's Army Corps (WAC) faced objections from military and civilian conservatives who did not believe that women should be in uniform. When WAC began in 1942 as a special unit of the U.S. Army, its members were the first women other than nurses to serve with the U.S. Army. More than 150,000 American women took this opportunity to contribute to the war effort, filling such important military and industrial positions as clerk, stenographer, telephone operator, scientific technician, teletype and cryptographic technician, and mechanic.

The Malmedy Massacre

ON SUNDAY, DECEMBER 17, 1944, shortly after the Germans launched their great offensive in the Ardennes, a number of American prisoners were shot by soldiers of the First SS-Panzer Regiment at Baugnez crossroads, close to the Belgian town of Malmedy. The true scale and circumstances of the Malmedy massacre remain controversial to this day. What is known is that of the 113 prisoners assembled in the field at Baugnez, 67 died there. Forty-six of them, some of whom were wounded, managed to escape the scene.

The massacre began when some of the Germans opened fire. Several survivors claim to have heard an order given. A storm of machine gun and rifle fire lasted for 15 minutes, and was followed by deliberate shots to finish off anyone still showing signs of life. These final murderous *coups de grâce* turned a possible "battle incident" into an indisputable atrocity that resonated throughout the American forces in Northwest Europe. It immediately prompted orders in some U.S. Army units to summarily shoot any SS prisoners they might capture.

Although those believed responsible for the massacre were later tried by a U.S. military tribunal, serious coercive and procedural irregularities by the prosecution eventually resulted in the commutation of all of the many death sentences. Those who had been imprisoned received early releases, and by 1960, all had been released.

GIs discovering the massacred POWs

GIs suffer in freezing weather The bodies of 67 American POWs lie in the Belgian snow, murdered on December 17, 1944, by a *Waffen-SS* unit under the command of SS major Joachim Peiper. Those who escaped the Malmedy massacre reported the cold-blooded killings, and word reached U.S. front-line troops quickly. Apparently in response, a December 21 written order from the U.S. 328th Infantry Regiment read: "No SS troops or paratroopers will be taken prisoner but will be shot on sight."

FACING DEATH AT MALMEDY

A BULLET WENT through the head of the man next to me. I lay tensely still, expecting the end. Could he see me breathing? Could I take a kick in the groin without wincing?...He was standing at my head. What was he doing? Time seemed to stand still. And then I heard him reloading his pistol in a deliberate manner...laughing and talking. A few odd steps before the reloading was finished and he was no longer so close to my head, then another shot a little farther away, and he had passed me up.

—U.S. ARMY FIRST LIEUTENANT VIRGIL T. LARY,
DESCRIBING THE INCIDENT AT MALMEDY

Attacks and counterattacks Hitler ordered a major offensive in the West in December 1944 because he believed that it would split the Anglo-U.S. alliance, frustrate the Allied advance, and ultimately precipitate a situation similar to Dunkirk. The German strategic objective was Antwerp, Belgium, and the main attack was launched against the Americans out of the dense, snow-covered forests of the Ardennes. Elite *Waffen-SS* and armored units spearheaded the assault, initially advancing rapidly against the surprised and demoralized GIs. However, the heroic defense of Bastogne by the U.S. 101st Airborne Division, overwhelming artillery and airpower, and decisive counterstrokes mounted by Patton and Montgomery finally restored the Allied situation by the end of December.

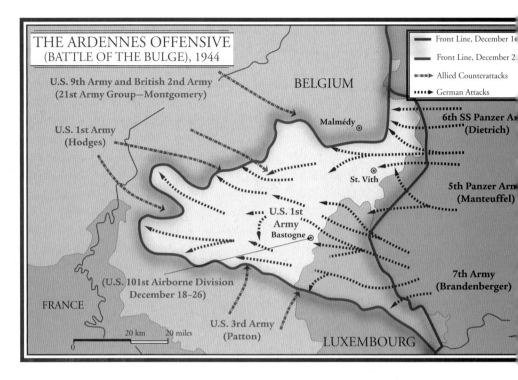

THE ARDENNES OFFENSIVE (BATTLE OF THE BULGE), 1944

Front Line, December 16
Front Line, December 2
Allied Counterattacks
German Attacks

U.S. 9th Army and British 2nd Army (21st Army Group—Montgomery)

BELGIUM

Malmédy

6th SS Panzer A (Dietrich)

U.S. 1st Army (Hodges)

St. Vith

5th Panzer Arm (Manteuffel)

U.S. 1st Army
Bastogne

(U.S. 101st Airborne Division December 18–26)

7th Army (Brandenberger)

FRANCE

20 km   20 miles
0

U.S. 3rd Army (Patton)

LUXEMBOURG

Battle of the Bulge On December 16, 1944, Germany began a massive attack in the Ardennes region of southern Belgium. The Germans forced a "bulge" in the faltering Allied advance, plunging surprised U.S. forces into some of the fiercest fighting they would endure in Europe. According to Kenneth Koyen, an officer in the Third Army, U.S. forces did not call the engagement the Battle of the Bulge in its early days, instead referring to it as the German Breakthrough. "The end and the outcome were not yet in view," recalled Koyen, "and the desperate German assault cast a chill over the battleground."

GIs die in frigid weather A Sherman tank rolls past another U.S. armored vehicle that has slid off an icy road in the Ardennes on December 20, 1944. Weather was the Allies' worst handicap during the first days of the Battle of the Bulge—and the Germans knew it. They deliberately began their attack when poor visibility restricted air support for U.S. ground forces. Most of the battle's staggering number of American casualties took place during the first three days. The coldest, snowiest weather that the rugged, mountainous forest had seen in memory took a serious toll on U.S. troops.

German infiltrators A German commando, captured wearing an American uniform during the Battle of the Bulge, prepares to face a firing squad. The surprise offensive was accompanied by an elite unit of English-speaking Germans trained to gather intelligence, conduct sabotage, and raise general havoc behind Allied lines. Small groups of these commandos, riding captured American jeeps and wearing GI uniforms, managed to penetrate U.S. lines in the early hours of the attack, causing great consternation. Considered spies, those unfortunate enough to be captured were shot.

Americans face numerous obstacles German forces took effective advantage of cloudy skies in the early stages of their surprise Ardennes offensive. Although American planes were able to take to the air when blue skies returned, that didn't automatically diminish the determination of German infantry, or the danger to American soldiers, including the GI seen here. A snowy landscape, coppices of trees that might conceal German troops and armor, loosely defined lines, the continuing cold—all of these took a toll on American troops as they regrouped to push the Germans back.

German forces depleted U.S. soldiers watch Allied and German planes battle on Christmas Day, 1944. The weather over Belgium had recently cleared, and Allied aircraft were finally able to support ground troops in a counterattack against the Germans. Hitler's belief that the Western Allies were weak and divided proved unfounded. Montgomery's British forces attacked from the north, Patton's U.S. Third Army attacked from the south, and American troops successfully defended the town of Bastogne. Beginning on January 8, the Germans retreated from the Ardennes. The Battle of the Bulge had been frightfully costly to all combatants. American casualties numbered about 81,000, and German casualties were between 60,000 and 100,000. But Germany's loss of men and materiel was irreparable.

1945

January: Germany begins to run out of fuel for its military. Tanks are abandoned where they stand.

January 1: The Soviet puppet Lublin committee assumes control of portions of Poland liberated by the Red Army. • The *Luftwaffe* launches a significant attack on Allied bases in France, Belgium, and the Netherlands, but it loses nearly half of its 800-strong air fleet.

January 2: British admiral Sir Bertram Ramsey, leader of Allied Naval forces during the Normandy invasion, dies in a plane crash after departing France for Belgium. • U.S. ships en route to Luzon from the Leyte Gulf come under vigorous attack by a fleet of Japanese *kamikaze* pilots.

January 3: Canada sends its first group of some 13,000 draftees to war in Europe, but many of them throw their rifles overboard in protest. • The U.S. Third Fleet loses 18 aircraft in raids on Okinawa, Formosa, and the Pescadores. Japan loses 12 ships and more than 100 aircraft.

January 5: Despite opposition from British and American authorities, Poland's Lublin government is recognized by the Soviet Union.

January 6: Allied attacks have whittled the number of Japanese aircraft on Luzon to 35—a reduction of about 115 in barely a month.

January 12: The Red Army stages a massive assault against Germany along the Eastern Front, sending more than a million troops to face a German force that is a fraction of that size.

January 14: The Japanese launch a counterattack against British forces at the Irrawaddy River in Burma. The Japanese will not be subdued for a month.

Fast but flawed World War II's only functional rocket plane, the Messerschmitt Me 163 *Komet* was first used as a fighter by the *Luftwaffe* in 1944. Its astonishing speed (a maximum of 596 mph) actually made it difficult for its pilots to target the era's much slower bombers. Also, its eight-minute powered flight time and 25-mile range were decided limitations. Moreover, the number of Me 163s destroyed in accidents greatly exceeded the number of enemy planes they shot down. Overall, the *Komet* was a fascinating experiment that appeared too late in the war to help the *Luftwaffe*.

The bastion of Bastogne Refugees evacuate the Belgian town of Bastogne in late 1944. When German armored forces began the push that became known as the Battle of the Bulge, many Belgians fled alongside the sparsely deployed American soldiers. But Americans were also headed *into* the battle. The U.S. 101st Airborne Division reached Bastogne—a junction where seven main roads converged—on December 19. German tanks surrounded the town, but the 101st, elements of the 10th Armored, and supporting units held Bastogne until fighting ended in January, preventing easy movement of German tanks along those roads.

Allies bomb Nuremberg Known for Hitler's elaborate prewar rallies and later as the site of the German war-crimes trials, Nuremberg was also an important manufacturing center for the German war effort. It became a target for Allied bombing raids, and on January 2, 1945, the center of the city—with its medieval architecture—was attacked by Allied bombers. The raid was so successful that most of the town's center was destroyed in less than an hour. This photograph captures the results of the attack. More than 1,800 residents of Nuremberg were killed and thousands were left homeless.

GI executed for desertion Private Eddie Slovik's unhappy life included several arrests during his youth, years before he was drafted into the U.S. Army. He arrived in France in August 1944 and deserted a few days later. After returning to his unit, he deserted again and refused to return to service. He was executed in France on January 31, 1945, making him the first American executed for desertion since the Civil War. Influenced by the high rate of desertion among U.S. soldiers, General Eisenhower had denied clemency for the young private.

Hitler inspects bomb damage—or does he? Though shaken and angered by Allied bomb attacks on German cities, Hitler rarely visited targeted areas. Nevertheless, London's *News Chronicle* ran this photograph in its January 31, 1945, edition, with a caption claiming that the *Führer* "is surveying ruins of a German town, the name of which is not disclosed." The paper overlooked (or ignored) the fact that Hitler stopped wearing the swastika armband as soon as the war began. The photo is almost certainly from an official visit to a prewar natural disaster or accident.

1945

January 15: Commercial shipping resumes in the English Channel for the first time in nearly five years.

January 16: Hitler moves both his residence and base of operations to the underground bunker at Berlin's Reich Chancellery.

January 17: The Red Army liberates the Polish capital of Warsaw.

January 18: Japanese stragglers at Peleliu attack U.S. ammunition dumps and the American air base.

January 19: The Germans retreat before the Red Army's advance through Poland. The Russians occupy the Polish cities of Tarnow, Lódź, and Kraków.

January 20: President Roosevelt is sworn in for his fourth term in office.

January 25: In the largest naval mining campaign of the Pacific war, the Allies seed the waters off Singapore and Indochina with nearly 370 mines.

January 26: The Soviet army liberates Auschwitz. They find nearly 3,000 inmates still in residence, with many near death.

January 27: The Japanese lose about 100 planes in U.S. counterattacks on Japanese air bases on Okinawa.

January 28: The Battle of the Bulge draws to a close as the last German soldiers are forced into retreat. • For the first time in nearly three years, supplies reach China over the Burma Road, which is newly reopened and renamed in honor of Allied general Stilwell.

January 30: With the Red Army less than 100 miles from Berlin, a defiant Hitler delivers his final radio address. • Seven thousand die when the German liner *Wilhelm Gustloff* is sunk by a Soviet submarine.

Americans liberated in the Philippines
Reduced to skin and bones by three years of captivity, American civilians Lee Rogers (*left*) and John C. Todd sit outside the gym at Santo Tomas University in Manila. They had been liberated by the U.S. First Cavalry Division on January 3, 1945. Santo Tomas was the primary internment center for American civilians following the fall of the Philippines, housing an average of about 4,000 internees. Though the

civilians at Santo Tomas and other camps suffered from food shortages and overcrowding, they endured less brutality than Allied military prisoners and even managed to set up a school for the children.

The indomitable *Hornet* Curtiss Helldivers fly over the USS *Hornet* (CV-12) in January 1945. This was the second American aircraft carrier of that name. The first (CV-8) had launched the Doolittle Raid, fought at Midway, and been sunk at the Battle of Santa Cruz in 1942. CV-12 was in continuous action for 16 months from 1943 to '45. It was attacked 59 times, but never hit. In contrast, its aircraft sank or damaged 1,269,710 tons of enemy shipping and destroyed 1,410 Japanese planes. The *Hornet* supported virtually every Pacific amphibious landing from March 1944, and contributed substantially to victory in the Battle of the Philippine Sea. In February 1945, it launched air strikes on Tokyo.

Nazi Medical Experiments

"**W**HEREVER A JOYOUS BIRD SINGS, he sings for another. Wherever a tiny star twinkles far away, it twinkles for another." This gentle poem was written by one of the most vicious German officers of the Second World War. Raised a Catholic, Dr. Josef Mengele, the "Angel of Death," was chief medical officer at Auschwitz.

Mengele was one of the first Germans seen by new arrivals as they entered Auschwitz. Dressed in an immaculate white medical coat, he decided who should live and who should die. Many of those chosen to live would become subjects of Mengele's merciless medical experiments. He was particularly interested in twins, engaging in such practices as injecting chloroform directly into twins' hearts to test comparative organ reactions. On more than one occasion, he took two healthy twins and joined them together to create Siamese twins. The majority of those who survived the experiments were eventually killed. The flesh on many corpses was boiled from bones, which were then sent to the Anthropological Museum in Berlin.

Mengele was not the only German physician who experimented on helpless prisoners. Also at Auschwitz, Dr. Horst Schumann exposed men's testicles to massive doses of X-rays before removing and examining them. Doctors Eduard Wirths and Carl Clauberg examined women's wombs after injections of toxic chemicals. These experiments were designed for the development of techniques of mass sterilization of people. Other physicians experi-

Prisoner remains at a Nazi anatomical institute in Stutthof

mented on prisoners at Buchenwald, Dachau, and other German concentration camps.

At the Nuremberg Trials following the war, 23 German physicians and scientists were tried from December 1946 to August 1947. Mengele was not included. He had escaped to South America, where he died in 1979.

The experiments conducted by the convicted doctors were grouped into 12 categories, including: high altitude, freezing, malaria, seawater, sterilization, and incendiary bomb. In each one, human subjects faced unnatural conditions that for most resulted in horrifying deaths. Of those physicians tried at Nuremberg, seven were acquitted, seven were sentenced to death, and nine were imprisoned.

Soviets liberate Auschwitz As the Red Army pushed westward in Poland, it arrived at the Auschwitz camp complex on January 27, 1945. "I saw the faces of the people we liberated," Soviet major Anatoly Shapiro recalled. "They went through hell." Nine days before the liberation, 60,000 prisoners had been marched from the Auschwitz complex to other camps out of the immediate reach of Soviet troops. About 7,000 inmates were left behind and freed. Here, Auschwitz survivors enthusiastically welcome their liberators. However, it was most likely staged a week or two after January 27, since the first group of troops to reach Auschwitz did not have cameras.

COLLAPSE OF THE THIRD REICH

FEBRUARY 1945–MAY 1945

> **"It is on this beautiful day that we celebrate the *Führer's* birthday and thank him, for he is the only reason why Germany is still alive today."**
>
> —JOSEPH GOEBBELS, AS SOVIET TROOPS STORMED THROUGH THE STREETS OF BERLIN, APRIL 26, 1945

ON THE AFTERNOON OF APRIL 12, 1945, U.S. president Franklin Roosevelt collapsed and died from a cerebral hemorrhage. Vice President Harry Truman was catapulted from relative obscurity to a world stage in which the United States had to oversee the final defeat of Germany and Japan and play a key part in the reconstruction of the postwar order.

Hitler interpreted Roosevelt's death as a miracle of deliverance. Locked away in his bunker in Berlin, the German leader played out grotesque fantasies of a final victory in which his enemies became divided and hostile—or tired of the terrible cost of subduing the German people. Hitler no longer saw the reality of his battered country. The heaviest bombing of the war reduced German cities to ruins one after the other—most notoriously the city of Dresden. From February 13 to 15, 30,000 people were killed there in Allied bombing. Germany could not sustain war production. In both west and east, German forces fought on fatalistically against hopeless odds.

By February 9, American troops had breached the Siegfried Line in western Germany, and by March 5 they had reached the Rhine River at Cologne. The Germans mounted little resistance, with only 26 poorly armed divisions. Meanwhile, 214 divisions tried to hold back the Red Army in eastern Germany. By May 4, the German forces in northern Germany, the Netherlands,

Soviet infantrymen charge past the corpse of a German soldier in house-to-house fighting for Berlin. The Soviet attack on the doomed German capital began on April 14, 1945. German resistance was fierce, but hopeless. Hitler killed himself on April 30, and the Berlin garrison surrendered two days later.

and Denmark surrendered to Montgomery's British Commonwealth armies. Farther south, Eisenhower swung the American advance away from the Rhine-Berlin axis toward southern Germany, where he feared the German army might make a final stand in a mountainous redoubt. Americans entered Austria in early May, by which time Axis forces in Italy had also surrendered. On April 28, Mussolini was captured by Italian partisans and killed.

Hitler survived him by just two days. Since January 1945, the Soviets had pushed relentlessly toward Berlin and Vienna. By February, a succession of rolling offensives brought the Red Army within striking distance of both capitals. In the south, Budapest was occupied by February 11 and the last Germans were driven out of Hungary by early April. Farther north, Zhukov's armies reached the Oder River by February 2, but for the next month fierce pockets of German resistance held up progress toward Berlin.

Hitler's chief of operations, General Alfred Jodl (*center*), flanked by Major Wilhelm Oxenius (*left*) and Admiral Hans-Georg von Friedeburg (*right*), formally surrenders the German armed forces to the Allies at General Eisenhower's headquarters in Reims, France, on May 7. Under Soviet insistence, a second surrender ceremony was held the next day on the outskirts of Berlin.

The plan for the final assault was approved by Stalin in early April, and a huge semicircle of Soviet forces was launched at Hitler's capital on April 16. The final battle cost both sides exceptional casualties, but Soviet progress was remorseless. Ten days after the start of the battle, the forces of General Chuikov—defender of Stalingrad two years prior—reached the center of Berlin. When on April 30 Hitler was told that there was no prospect of further defense, he said goodbye to his staff and commanders, retired to his bunker living room with Eva Braun—the mistress he had finally consented to marry the day before—and there poisoned and shot himself while she took poison. The bodies were incinerated in the garden of the Reich chancellery, where Soviet soldiers found charred remains a few days later.

Hitler's suicide heralded the end. On May 2, the battered remnants of the Berlin garrison surrendered. On May 7, Hitler's chief of operations, Alfred Jodl, signed the act of unconditional surrender in the early hours of the morning in Reims, France. The Soviet side wanted a more elaborate and symbolic ceremony, and a second surrender was staged in Berlin the following day. Though Victory in Europe (V-E) Day was celebrated on both sides of the Atlantic on May 8, German forces fighting a desperate last stand around Prague refused to give up until May 12.

In the Pacific, the U.S. planned its assault on Iwo Jima the previous October, when it became clear that the islands close to the Japanese homeland would make important staging posts for the eventual invasion. Both Iwo Jima and Okinawa were to be attacked and cleared as a preliminary step. On both islands, large Japanese garrisons—positioned in caves and foxholes—were ordered to resist to the last man. After a heavy bombardment, four U.S. divisions landed on Iwo Jima on February 19. Four weeks of savage fighting brought exceptionally high American losses, but almost the entire Japanese garrison, more than 20,000 men, was wiped out.

On April 1, 1945, a similar landing was undertaken on Okinawa. After the U.S. established secure lodgements ashore, another bitter struggle followed to clear the island. The U.S. naval task force was attacked for weeks by *kamikaze* suicide planes, which sank more than 30 ships. Some 12,500 U.S. servicemen were killed, but so were 110,000 Japanese. Resistance on Okinawa did not end until June 21. The intense combat indicated just how difficult a final battle for the home islands of Japan might prove to be.

A Japanese *kamikaze* pilot aims his aircraft at the USS *Missouri* in the waters off Okinawa on April 11, 1945. With the war clearly lost, the Japanese resorted to increasingly desperate measures in hopes of forcing a negotiated peace. Suicide planes sank 36 ships during the Okinawa campaign, but they could not halt the Allied juggernaut.

Before the capture of Iwo Jima, Stalin, Churchill, and Roosevelt met in conference together for the last time. In the Crimean city of Yalta, from February 4 to 11, Stalin repeated his earlier agreement that the Soviet Union would enter the war against Japan once Germany was defeated. In exchange, he was promised the Kurile Islands and the return of the Japanese half of Sakhalin Island. Agreement was also reached on creating a new Polish state.

Roosevelt, in poor health, was also determined to lay the foundation for a postwar world order in which the Soviet Union could participate. The result was a conference in San Francisco, California, that began on April 25, 1945. Participants laid the foundations for the United Nations organization, whose founding charter was signed on June 26. By that time, Roosevelt—whose vision the organization largely reflected—was dead.

Among the Western Allies, well more than a million people died during the war. The Soviet Union lost an estimated 27 million, Poland six million, and Germany more than five million. "What a terrible war," Stalin told Zhukov. "How many lives of our people it has carried away. There are probably very few families left who have not lost someone near to them. . . ."

1945

February: Peru, Lebanon, Turkey, Uruguay, Paraguay, Venezuela, Saudi Arabia, Syria, and Egypt join the Allies and declare war on Germany and Japan. Additionally, Iran will declare war against Japan this month. • Strong Japanese resistance slows the Allied advance throughout the Philippine Islands.

February 1: The USAAF launches a series of bombing raids on Iwo Jima, softening the island's Japanese defenses in preparation for a U.S. Marine ground assault.

February 4: Allied military leaders announce that they have cleared Belgium of all Axis forces.

February 4–11: Allied leaders Roosevelt, Churchill, and Stalin meet at Yalta (on the Crimean Peninsula) to plan the final phase of the war.

February 5: In Greece, recently liberated from the Axis yoke, Communist forces surrender their weapons to the new government.

February 6: Tens of thousands of German civilians flee Breslau before the westward advance of the Red Army.

February 9: The British 26th Indian Division captures Ramree Island, a strategically important Japanese base off the coast of Burma.

February 11: Reich officials remove Germany's 100-ton national gold reserve from Berlin and stash it in an Eisenach salt mine.

February 12: All German women between the ages of 16 and 60 are called up for service in the *Volkssturm,* the German people's army.

February 13: The German garrison at Budapest surrenders to the Red Army's Second Ukrainian Front. This follows a hard-won, 45-day battle in which 35,000 German prisoners of war were taken.

The Yalta Conference Roosevelt, Churchill, and Stalin (the Big Three) met for the second and last time from February 4 to 11, 1945, at Yalta on the Crimean Peninsula. Although Roosevelt was exhausted, Stalin refused to travel any farther west than Yalta. In negotiations for the fate of Germany and Eastern Europe, Stalin had the advantage since most of that area was already in Soviet hands. He was, therefore, able to violate the promises he made about free elections in Poland and democratic governments in the liberated states of Central and Southeastern Europe. The Soviet leader confirmed his prior promise to enter the war against Japan. Stalin also reduced his demand for all 16 Soviet republics to be represented in the United Nations to two: the Ukraine and Belorussia.

Allies firebomb Dresden The beautiful German city of Dresden was known as the "Florence of the Elbe" before it suffered a series of bombings in 1945. The heaviest of these were conducted by British and American aircraft from February 13 to 15. These bombings caused firestorms that destroyed much of the city and killed approximately 30,000 people. Outdoor temperatures reached as high as 2700°F, making it impossible for people to escape from their doomed homes. The military efficacy of the bombings has been questioned. Dresden was poorly defended from air attack at times, and its industries were mainly on its outskirts.

German A-bomb Research

THE THREAT OF A GERMAN atomic bomb provoked the initiation of and lent added urgency to the Manhattan Project. In August 1939, German-born refugee Albert Einstein warned President Roosevelt of the potential for a German bomb. The warnings by Einstein and others were alarmingly plausible because German scientists had been the first to discover nuclear fission, in 1938. Fortunately for the Allies, these fears proved unfounded. While the Germans established two teams to develop nuclear energy and the atomic bomb, the effort went virtually nowhere.

Multiple reasons contributed to this failure. A major setback occurred in 1941 when graphite was mistakenly ruled out as a possible moderator in creating a reaction. German scientists turned instead to heavy water (deuterium oxide), an expensive commodity that was in short supply and was reduced by attacks on the production facility in Norway. Reliance on an inefficient thermal diffusion method for isotope separation proved frustrating. German scientists also grossly miscalculated the quantity of material needed for a bomb. Failure was ensured by the German government's unwillingness to commit to the massive economic effort required for success. Top priority was assigned instead to the V-2 rocket program.

Latter-day reproduction of German nuclear reactor core

As Allied forces swept across Europe in 1944 and '45, a scientific intelligence unit called the "Alsos Mission" deduced that the German bomb program lagged at least two years behind the Allies'. German scientists had yet to even reach critical mass with a pile—which the Allies had done in 1942—and were not close to obtaining the bomb.

The fight for Manila Gutted buildings bear testimony to the Americans' struggle to capture Manila, Philippines, from the Japanese. General Yamashita Tomoyuki had decided to defend Manila, and Rear Admiral Iwabuchi Sanji implemented Yamashita's orders. U.S. troops arrived on February 3, 1945, to find the city held by about 21,000 Japanese naval and army personnel. Though General MacArthur initially placed restrictions on U.S. artillery and air support in hopes of avoiding serious damage to the "Pearl of the Orient," fanatical house-to-house resistance made such niceties impractical. The fighting lasted a month, and the city was largely destroyed.

Marines land on Iwo Jima U.S. Marines hug a sandy terrace under enemy mortar fire after landing on Iwo Jima on February 19, 1945. Americans hoped to seize the island, located only 660 miles south of Tokyo, to eliminate a source of interference with B-29 raids from Saipan. They also wanted to provide a refuge for crippled bombers on their way home from Japan. The Marines found that the three-day preliminary naval bombardment had done little damage to Iwo Jima's 21,000 defenders, who had literally moved underground into a maze of tunnels and shelters. Japanese gunners waited patiently until the U.S. beachhead was congested with successive landing waves. They then opened fire, inflicting severe casualties.

Nepalese warriors A Gurkha soldier brandishes his weapon of choice—the *kukri,* a curve-bladed knife. These natives of Nepal had served in the British Army since the beginning of the 19th century. During World War II, 40 battalions of Gurkhas fought in every theater of the war. Gurkha battalions attached to the British Eighth Army took part in the Italian campaign. They were feared by German troops for their ability to strike at any time and place, leaving their victims—often with their throats cut—as a sign of their presence.

Japanese troops embedded in rock A U.S. assault team warily clears a cave on Iwo Jima. Though dominated by 556-foot Mount Suribachi, the island's greatest defensive potential lay along a plateau two and a half miles to the north. General Kuribayashi Tadamichi located his best forces there among a nightmarish jumble of upheaved rock, gorges, caves, and ridges. The Japanese took full advantage of Iwo Jima's porous volcanic rock to burrow underground beyond the reach of U.S. heavy guns. Above ground, blockhouses with five-foot concrete walls and a multitude of pillboxes awaited U.S. Marines. These American forces had no alternative but to assault them one by one with flamethrowers and demolitions.

1945

February 24: Ahmed Maher Pasha, prime minister of Egypt, is assassinated on the floor of parliament, moments after reading a declaration of war against Japan and Germany.

February 26: In a daytime air raid, the USAAF drops 500,000 incendiary bombs on Berlin. British RAF units take over the attack after darkness falls. • U.S. forces capture Corregidor, leaving 5,000 Japanese troops dead and suffering 1,000 casualties.

March 1945: In a last-ditch effort to regain an upper hand in the air war, Germany forms its own suicide units, manned by some 300 volunteers. • With the exception of a few stragglers, the U.S. Navy has eliminated the enemy from shipping lanes throughout the central Pacific.

March 3: The Philippine capital of Manila is declared clear of Japanese forces.

March 4: The Finnish government in Helsinki declares war on Germany.

March 5: Continuing their advance into the German homeland, Allied troops march on Cologne. • Desperate for troops, the German army begins conscription of boys as young as 16.

March 6: Germany's Sixth Panzer Army launches Operation Spring Awakening against Soviet forces in Hungary in an effort to recapture the area between the Danube River and Lake Balaton. • In a move that leaves the Western Allies concerned about Communist expansion in postwar Europe, King Michael appoints a new, strongly pro-Communist Romanian government. • With Iwo Jima largely secure, the U.S. Air Force begins to use the island as a forward base.

March 7: Allied forces cross the Rhine River at Remagen and advance into central Germany, as German soldiers in the north capitulate in droves.

Savage combat on Iwo Jima The hand of one of Iwo Jima's 21,000 Japanese defenders lies half buried in the blasted rubble. Veteran *Time* magazine correspondent Robert Sherrod observed that the dead of both sides had one thing in common: "They had died with the greatest possible violence." Nowhere in the Pacific had he seen such badly mangled bodies. Sherrod described bodies cut in half, limbs lying 50 feet from the nearest body, and the strong smell of burning flesh.

Raising the flag Private First Class Jim Michels keeps watch as members of Company E, 28th Marines, raise the first flag on top of Mount Suribachi at about 10:30 A.M. on February 23, 1945. The 54″×28″ flag was hoisted aloft on a piece of discarded pipe after a Marine patrol, led by Lieutenant Harold Schrier, had scaled the height and engaged in a brief firefight with Japanese soldiers at the summit. Later that day, another patrol brought a larger, more visible flag up the mountain. The raising of the larger flag was photographed by Joe Rosenthal and became one of the most celebrated images of World War II.

The "Seabees" Bulldozer operators carve out an airstrip on Eniwetok following the island's seizure in early 1944. Naval construction battalions, the "Seabees," gained fame for their ability to construct airfields quickly and erect support facilities on captured islands. Army engineers performed similar feats in the Southwest Pacific. The speed with which these islands were seized and transformed into fleet and air bases—often within weeks—astonished the Japanese and facilitated the fast-paced U.S. advance across the Pacific. The Seabees, whose motto was "Can Do," boasted: "The difficult we do immediately; the impossible takes a little longer."

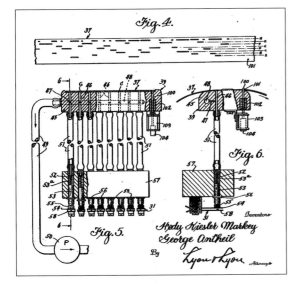

Lamarr's double life In 1933, 19-year-old Hedwig Kiesler (*pictured a decade later*) married Austrian munitions manufacturer Friedrich Mandl. Mandl sold munitions to Germany, where he and his wife socialized with Hitler. In addition to munitions sales, Mandl's company also conducted research on radio control systems. Hedwig, an actress, left her husband, changed her name to Hedy Lamarr, and moved to the U.S. in 1937. As a result of a casual conversation three years later with her neighbor, George Antheil, they invented the Secret Communication System (*diagram at left*) in 1941. The Allied system had many applications, such as torpedo control and the transmission of secret messages. All the while, Lamarr starred in major Hollywood productions.

Mexico aids the Allies Mexican Air Force planes patrol the coast near the U.S.-Mexican border. On May 21, 1942, the Mexican tanker *Faja de Oro* was sunk by a German submarine off Florida's Key West. Mexico declared war on Germany, Italy, and Japan the next day. The declaration of war came after Mexico had broken diplomatic relations with the Axis powers soon after the United States entered the war in December 1941. Besides contributing resources and manpower to the U.S. production of war materials, the Mexican Air Force engaged in battle in the Philippines, where the Aztec Eagle squadron saw combat. Of 31 pilots, five were killed in action.

1945

March 7: The Jewish Brigade, under the command of Brigadier General Ernest Benjamin, launches operations in Italy. • Josip Broz Tito consolidates the government of newly liberated Yugoslavia under his authority. • The Chinese 37th Division captures Lashio, Burma, the southwest terminus of the Burma Road.

March 8: Office of Strategic Services chief Allen Dulles opens cease-fire negotiations with SS commander Karl Wolff for a surrender of German forces in Italy. • More than 100 civilians die when a German V-2 rocket destroys London's Smithfield Market.

March 9–10: The deadliest air raid of the Pacific war claims the lives of 80,000 to 100,000 Japanese civilians when the U.S. attacks Tokyo with incendiary bombs.

March 10: Following the Allied breach of the Rhine, Hitler appoints Field Marshal Kesselring to replace Rundstedt as commander of German armies in the West. • Transylvania, the mountainous region in central Europe that has been occupied by Germany since early in the war, is restored to Romania. • President Roosevelt tells a Spanish delegation that the United States will be unable to supply aid to Spain as long as Franco remains in power. • The Japanese disarm and eject Vichy authorities and establish the "Empire of Annam" in French Indochina.

March 11: An RAF raid on Essen, Germany, halts production at the Krupp Works munitions plant.

March 13: The U.S. House of Representatives reauthorizes the Lend-Lease Act for the last time.

March 14: The RAF drops the 22,000-pound "Grand Slam," the largest bomb of the war to date, on Germany's Bielefeld railway viaduct.

Americans cross the Rhine On March 7, 1945, American Lieutenant Karl Timmerman led his company of the 27th Armored Infantry Battalion to the west end of the Ludendorff Bridge (*pictured*) near Remagen, Germany. Since this was the last bridge still spanning the Rhine, Timmerman halted and looked closely for explosives. An explosion did occur as Timmerman and his men advanced across, but, as the smoke settled, he saw that the bridge still stood. More than 8,000 Americans crossed within 24 hours, establishing the first bridgehead across the Rhine. When Hitler learned that the bridge had not been destroyed, he had four of the officers in charge of destroying it executed.

Wolff negotiates surrender Longtime chief of staff to Heinrich Himmler, *SS-Obergruppenführer* Karl Wolff (*second from left*) negotiated the surrender of German forces in northern Italy. In March 1945, Wolff met secretly with OSS official Allen Dulles in Switzerland. Wolff tried (in vain) to bargain for the relocation of German forces in Italy to the Russian front. In 1945 and again in 1962, Wolff—who denied any knowledge of extermination camps—was convicted in German courts for sending 300,000 Jews to Treblinka. He served one week the first time, and half of a 15-year sentence the second time.

Tokyo Burns

LATE IN THE PACIFIC WAR, U.S. leaders realized that conventional bombing missions over Japanese cities were having only a limited effect. To rectify the problem, General Curtis LeMay in 1945 implemented incendiary attacks. LeMay recognized that the wood and paper Japanese cities were highly vulnerable to fire. Such attacks also would have a greater impact on Japanese industry, much of which was dispersed in small shops.

The incendiary of choice had been developed by Standard Oil and DuPont in 1944. Only two inches in diameter and 20 inches long, these "fire sticks" were filled with jellied gasoline or napalm and weighed about six pounds. LeMay's plan called for B-29s to scatter thousands of these devices to create unmanageable fires.

On February 23–24, the U.S. launched its first fire raid on Tokyo, destroying one square mile of the city. This success was followed on the night of March 9–10, when more than 300 B-29s returned to drop 2,000 tons of incendiaries on the city. The resulting firestorm destroyed 16 square miles, incinerated as many as 100,000 Japanese people, and left a million people homeless in the most destructive

Tokyo after incendiary bomb attacks

attack of the war. The heat was so intense it literally boiled the water in canals.

Through June, continued low-level incendiary attacks on Japan devastated major portions of six large cities. By war's end, 66 cities had been largely reduced to ashes. An estimated 330,000 Japanese, mostly civilians, perished.

Americans firebomb Tokyo Gnarled trees and blackened walls testify to the effectiveness of the B-29 incendiary raids on Tokyo. Dissatisfied with the results of high-level bombing, the 20th Bomber Command turned to low-level nighttime incendiary attacks in March 1945. The first major Tokyo raid on March 9–10 killed up to 100,000 people and destroyed more than 267,000 buildings—about a quarter of the city's total. Over the next 10 days, B-29s torched a total of 32 square miles in Nagoya, Osaka, and Kobe. Losses among the bomber crews were light. Though some American officers questioned the morality of the attacks, the prevailing view was that the raids were appropriate retribution for Japanese atrocities, would destroy enemy industry, and would demonstrate to the Japanese population that further resistance was futile.

RAINING FIRE

ELSEWHERE, PEOPLE SOAKED themselves in the water barrels that stood in front of each house before setting off again. A litter of obstacles blocked their way; telegraph poles and the overhead trolley wires that formed a dense net around Tokyo fell in tangles across streets. In the dense smoke, where the wind was so hot it seared the lungs, people struggled, then burst into flames where they stood. The fiery air was blown down toward the ground and it was often the refugees' feet that began burning first; the men's puttees and the women's trousers caught fire and ignited the rest of their clothing.

—FRENCH REPORTER ROBERT GUILLAIN, DESCRIBING A FIREBOMB ATTACK ON TOKYO

1945

March 14–15: Thousands die in an American bombing raid on Japan's southern port city of Osaka.

March 16–17: American bombers attack Kobe, on the Japanese island of Honshu, inflicting several thousand casualties.

March 18: Nearly 30 Allied planes are lost in large-scale bombing runs over the German cities of Frankfurt and Berlin.

March 19: Hitler issues the "Nero Decree," a scorched-earth directive calling for the destruction of all German infrastructure presumed in danger of falling to the Allies. • The *Sarawak Maru*, the final surviving ship of a 21-vessel Japanese convoy, is sunk, illustrating Allied strength and Japanese isolation in Asian waters.
• Japanese *kamikaze* attacks on U.S. Task Force 58 damages American aircraft carriers *Essex, Wolf, Enterprise,* and *Franklin,* killing 832 on the *Franklin* alone.

March 20: Hitler appears in public for the last time. • The fiercely defended Burmese city of Mandalay is captured by Allied forces of the British 19th Indian Division.

March 21: More than 100 Danish civilians die when they become "collateral damage" in a British raid against Copenhagen's Gestapo headquarters. • Japanese piloted bombs make their debut against U.S. forces in the waters off Japan's home islands.

March 23: Charles de Gaulle announces that France will grant limited independence to Indochina at the conclusion of the war. • Allied forces from Britain, Canada, and the United States under General Bernard Montgomery launch Operation Plunder. They will cross the northern Rhine while protected by heavy air and artillery support.

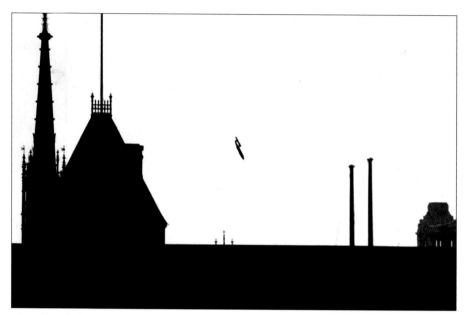

The dreaded V-weapons A V-1 descends on central London. German V-1s and V-2s were fired at targets in England, Belgium, and France (after liberation) and even within Germany. Although they could wreak extensive damage, neither type of rocket could be precisely aimed. The British put out false reports about hits, sometimes tricking the Germans into targeting less populated areas. The only defense against the more sophisticated V-2s was to take out their launchpads. The Allies struck bunkered sites in France, Belgium, and the Netherlands, although V-2s on truck-drawn mobile launchers proved hard to hit.

Americans land on Okinawa GIs of the U.S. 77th Infantry Division use spliced ladders to bridge a gulch during the fighting on Okinawa. Intending to seize a base for the invasion of Japan, the Americans landed on Okinawa on April 1, 1945. It was the largest invasion of the Pacific war. The Navy fired more than 100,000 shells in a weeklong bombardment of the landing beaches. This expenditure was largely wasted, since Japanese general Ushijima Mitsuru had decided to fight from prepared positions inland. The initial landings by four U.S. divisions were virtually unopposed, but progress stalled when U.S. forces encountered the main defenses across the southern end of the island.

Japanese defenders dig in A flamethrower tank clears Japanese snipers from caves on Okinawa. Dug deeply into Okinawa's ridges and escarpments, the Japanese were protected from even large-caliber artillery fire while taking a heavy toll of Americans who attacked in the open. By staying in their defenses, the Japanese intended to make U.S. troops pay dearly for every foot of ground while *kamikazes* battered the ships offshore. GIs and Marines countered with tanks and small-unit assaults. The latter included flamethrowers and demolitions to eradicate subterranean enemy positions—a tactic that became known as "blowtorch and corkscrew."

Inspecting the enemy Crewmen on the USS *New Jersey* watch a Japanese prisoner of war bathe before being issued GI clothing. The relative rarity of Japanese prisoners made them an object of curiosity among Allied servicemen—particularly those who were not directly engaged in infantry combat with enemy troops. Many U.S. servicemen were surprised to find that their enemy was not a superman, a monkey, or a slavering madman, but just an ordinary man much like themselves. Some even felt a degree of sympathy for their now helpless foe. This was not a sentiment shared by most front-line riflemen. With their personal safety in the balance, they had little room for curiosity or compassion for live Japanese.

Buried treasures As U.S. troops advanced through Central Germany in early April 1945, they learned from informants that the Nazis had moved gold and art treasures to a salt mine (*pictured*) in the town of Merkers. On April 7, American officers accompanied German mining officials to the main vault more than 2,000 feet below ground. Blocked by a large steel door, they blew a hole in the wall and entered a vault 75 feet wide, 150 feet long, and 12 feet high. It contained thousands of bags of gold, silver, and coins worth more than $520 million—as well as hundreds of pieces of jewelry and priceless art treasures that had been looted all over Europe.

1945

March 23: Task Force 58 launches air raids on the Japanese island of Okinawa in preparation for an eventual American landing.

March 24: The war in northern Burma comes to an end as the Chinese 50th Division meets the Chinese New First Army near Hsipaw, Burma.

March 26: The remainder of the Japanese force on Iwo Jima stages one final, suicidal attack against the U.S. forces that occupy the strategically critical island.

March 27: Soviet officials convene a meeting with anti-Communist Polish leaders under false pretenses. They will incarcerate the Poles and eliminate opposition to communism by Poland's government-in-exile. • Britain suffers an attack by the terrifying German V-2 rockets for the last time. • The U.S. begins a program of mining Japanese waters in an effort to completely blockade the home islands.

March 29: American troops occupy the German heartland city of Frankfurt am Main.

April 1945: The first helicopter rescue is achieved when a Sikorsky YR-4 is used to rescue Captain James Green, a U.S. Air Force pilot who crashed in the Burmese jungle.

April 1: More than 300,000 German soldiers are entrapped as the U.S. Army closes ranks around the economically critical Ruhr region. • Nazi propaganda chief Joseph Goebbels launches Radio *Werwolf* in an effort to bolster German resistance to Allied forces in portions of Germany occupied by Allies. • In an effort to ensure that all Japanese are available to assist the cause of victory, all schools in the nation are closed. • Some 60,000 U.S. troops land on the island of Okinawa, launching one of the bloodiest battles of the Pacific war.

Few African Americans honored
On April 5, 1945, Second Lieutenant Vernon Baker's company was pinned down while attacking a German position near Viareggio, Italy. Baker crawled forward and destroyed four machine gun nests, killing nine Germans. For this action, he was awarded the Congressional Medal of Honor. Since he was African American, however, it took the military 52 years to award it. More than 1.2 million African Americans served in the war, but few received battlefield decorations and none were awarded the Medal of Honor until January 13, 1997, when seven African Americans received it from President Bill Clinton. The 77-year-old Baker was the only one still living.

Americans mourn the death of FDR Residents of Washington, D.C., mourn the passing of President Franklin Delano Roosevelt, who died of a stroke in Georgia on April 12, 1945. Roosevelt, the only president elected four times, had pulled America out of the Great Depression and inspired his nation to victory in World War II. African Americans shared in the suffering of his loss: Through his Executive Order 8802, FDR had integrated the national defense program. Overseas, Churchill broke into tears when he relayed the news of Roosevelt's death in a speech to the House of Commons. Stalin, reportedly, was also moved by his ally's death.

"Boys, if you ever pray, pray for me now."

—Harry Truman, one day after being sworn in as president, April 13, 1945

Harry Truman

When Harry Truman ascended to the presidency in the spring of 1945, *Time* magazine decried his inexperience in high-level politics. Others worried that he would be too cautious and conservative in his decision-making. *Time* and others underestimated the new president, as Truman would soon make one of the most audacious decisions of the war.

Calling himself an "ordinary man," Truman hailed from Lamar, Missouri. He served in World War I, prospered as a farmer, and opened a haberdashery in Kansas City. As a Democrat, he was elected judge of a county court in 1922 and U.S. senator in 1934. President Franklin Roosevelt and party leaders chose Truman as the 1944 vice presidential candidate largely because he was "safe"—not controversial.

Truman was sworn in as president on April 12, 1945, following the death of Roosevelt, only 83 days after filling the office of vice president. Roosevelt had not taken his new vice president into his confidence, so one of Truman's first acts was to meet with the deceased president's advisers to catch up on matters of national security. Truman did not learn of the existence of the atomic bomb, or of Soviet espionage into the project, until the day he was sworn in.

After Japan did not adhere to the Allies' July 26 demand for unconditional surrender, this "ordinary man" had to make one of the most monumental decisions in world history. Following discussions with Secretary of War Henry Stimson and Army Chief of Staff General George Marshall, Truman agreed to drop an atomic bomb on a Japanese city in order to shock its leadership into surrender. No one doubted that the atomic bomb would kill a massive number of Japanese people. Truman justified its use by saying that the alternative to the atomic bomb—an Allied invasion—would result in far more deaths on both sides.

Truman unprepared for presidency
When Vice President Harry Truman was summoned to the White House on April 12, 1945, he was unaware of President Roosevelt's death. When he was sworn in as president, he was not well prepared for the responsibilities of the office since, during his three months as VP, he had little contact with Roosevelt. This picture of Truman, his wife, Bess, and their daughter, Margaret, was taken as he was sworn in as president that evening. The next day he told reporters, "When they told me what happened yesterday, I felt like the moon, the stars, and all the planets had fallen on me."

1945

April 3: The Red Army lays siege to the Slovak city of Bratislava in an effort to drive out German forces. The Soviets will liberate the city the following day. • Washington announces that General MacArthur and Admiral Nimitz will command land and sea forces, respectively, for the Allied invasion of Japan.

April 4: American troops liberate the Nazi concentration camp at Ohrdruf, Germany. Upon witnessing the carnage at the camp, a disgusted General Patton assembles local townspeople for a viewing.

April 5: Soviet foreign minister Molotov puts the Japanese on notice that the USSR does not intend to renew the 1941 nonaggression pact between the two nations. • The Japanese high command orders its entire Second Fleet to make a run against U.S. forces off Okinawa.

April 6: Yugoslavian forces under the government of Josip Broz Tito take control of the Bosnian capital of Sarajevo. • A fierce air and naval battle erupts off Okinawa. Japanese *kamikaze* pilots rain from the sky.

April 7: For the first time, the RAF launches bombing raids on Berlin from Allied bases in mainland Europe. • For the first time since the Allied capture of Iwo Jima, the island is successfully utilized as a base for operations against the Japanese home islands. • American planes engage the super-battleship *Yamato*, causing it to capsize in the East China Sea. Nearly 2,500 Japanese sailors die.

April 9: The German fortress at Königsberg falls to the Soviets. • Some 300 die when a bomb-laden Liberty ship explodes in the harbor at Bari, Italy. • The final offensive on the Italian front is launched by a multinational troop contingent that includes soldiers from Africa, Asia, Europe, and the Americas.

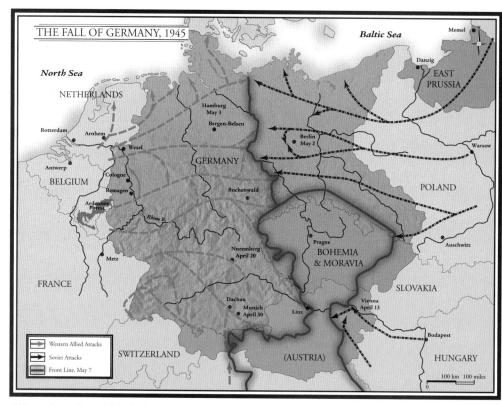

THE FALL OF GERMANY, 1945

Allies close in on both fronts Despite Allied setbacks at Arnhem in September 1944 and the Ardennes that December, the fate of the Third Reich was now inevitable. In the West, the Allies crossed the Rhine River in March 1945, with armored forces striking deep into Germany. In terms of scale and ferocity, the major fighting still raged on the Eastern Front, where the Red Army was rapidly overrunning Eastern Europe. Warsaw fell in January and Vienna in April. On April 16, 2.5 million Soviet troops, 6,250 armored vehicles, and 7,500 aircraft launched the great offensive toward Berlin, which ended at the *Reichstag* six weeks later.

Inouye's heroics On April 21, 1945, during combat near San Terenzo, Italy, U.S. Army second lieutenant Daniel Inouye was shot in the abdomen. He continued to lead his platoon while bleeding. After his right arm was shattered, he threw a grenade at the Germans with his left hand. Inouye earned the Distinguished Service Cross but spent 20 months in the hospital, where his right arm was removed. A review of the military records of the 442nd Regimental Combat Team, a Japanese American unit, 50 years later identified 20 members who were blocked, due to prejudice, from receiving the Congressional Medal of Honor. U.S. senator Inouye of Hawaii was among them. This infraction was rectified on June 21, 2000, when he and 19 others from the 442nd were awarded the medal.

> **"People died before my eyes, scarcely human, moaning skeletons, many of them gone mad. Bodies were just piled up. Many had gashed wounds and bullet marks and terrible sores."**
>
> —BBC European Service radio correspondent Patrick Gordon-Walker, in a broadcast to the U.S. from the Bergen-Belsen concentration camp in Germany, April 24, 1945

Liberation of the Camps

ON APRIL 15, 1945, BRITISH FORCES entered the Bergen-Belsen concentration camp near Celle, Germany. Troops already hardened by many months of campaigning were nevertheless appalled by the horrors that lay within.

During the following days, the soldiers buried 23,000 bodies on-site, necessarily employing bulldozers for this huge task after their initial use of the former SS guards proved totally inadequate. Meanwhile, 29,000 of the traumatized, diseased, and starving survivors were gradually evacuated. Following delousing and washing by co-opted German nurses, many inmates were treated by British military and civilian medical staff in the *Wehrmacht*'s large barracks complex at nearby Bergen-Hohne. However, several thousand of these people subsequently died.

Despite the camp's liberation, the daily death rate at Bergen-Belsen from April to May averaged about 450. As each hut was cleared, it was burned down in an attempt to stem the ever-present threat of typhus. In November, camp commandant Josef Kramer, SS wardress Irma Grese, and nine other Bergen-Belsen guards were sentenced to hang for their heinous crimes. In late April, at Dachau in southern Germany, General Patton's Third U.S. Army encountered similar results of the Third Reich's barbarous policies. It liberated what had been the very first of Germany's principal *Konzentrationslagers*. At Dachau, the young GIs were so incensed by what they found that they summarily executed many of the guards on-site, including members of the SS.

The Allies discovered more and more concentration camps, in which most of the living and dead prisoners were Jews. The Allied military authorities largely ignored instances of revenge beatings and killings of camp guards by those former prisoners still fit enough to carry out such action. Despite protestations of innocence and ignorance, many local German civilians were forced by the Allies to view the camps that existed close by. Civilians also were conscripted to bury the thousands of dead therein. Meanwhile, even greater horrors were emerging in Poland, as the advancing Red Army began to reveal the Nazis' extensive network of extermination camps.

Liberated Jews die by the hundreds
"They are Jews and are dying now at the rate of three hundred a day," British soldier Peter Coombs wrote after liberating the Bergen-Belsen concentration camp. A typhoid fever epidemic had been sweeping through the camp, claiming thousands of lives, including that of diarist Anne Frank, by the time British troops arrived on April 15, 1945. As this sign (and a nearby sign in German) declares, the liberators discovered more than 10,000 corpses throughout the camp. British troops forced captured guards to bury the diseased bodies without the use of protective gloves.

THIS IS THE SITE OF
THE INFAMOUS BELSEN CONCENTRATION CAMP
Liberated by the British on 15 April 1945.

10,000 UNBURIED DEAD WERE FOUND HERE.
ANOTHER 13,000 HAVE SINCE DIED.
ALL OF THEM VICTIMS OF THE
GERMAN NEW ORDER IN EUROPE.
AND AN EXAMPLE OF NAZI KULTUR.

1945

April 9: Former *Abwehr* chief Admiral Wilhelm Canaris is executed on the gallows at Germany's Flossenburg concentration camp.

April 10: American soldiers of the Ninth Army capture the central German city of Hanover.

April 11: Red Army troops of the Ukrainian army group penetrate the center of the Austrian capital of Vienna. It will fall to the Allies on the 13th. • The Russians liberate the notorious Buchenwald concentration camp. • American forces reach the southern German region of Bavaria, the birthplace of Hitler's Nazi Reich. • Japanese *kamikaze* pilots continue their barrage unabated off Okinawa, hitting the U.S. ships *Missouri* and *Enterprise*.

April 12: President Roosevelt dies suddenly after suffering a stroke at his Warm Springs, Georgia, vacation home. Vice President Harry Truman is sworn in as president.

April 13: The South American nation of Chile joins the Allies and declares war on Japan.

April 14: The Allies march through the center of encircled German troops in the Ruhr Pocket, taking prisoners and splitting the German ranks. • The Allies launch Operation Teardrop in an effort to locate German U-boats in the North Atlantic rumored to be carrying V-2 rockets to be used against New York City.

April 14–15: Japanese imperial loyalists crush an attempted coup by hard-line military officers who, convinced that Emperor Hirohito was on the brink of surrender, had decided to seize control.

April 15: The Bergen-Belsen concentration camp, with a survivor population of 40,000, is liberated by the British Army.

Civilians forced to bury camp victims On April 21, 1945, American troops of the 102nd Division ordered the males of the German town of Gardelegen to carry spades and white wooden crosses to a burned barn on the outskirts of their town. They were ordered to disinter and rebury the bodies of 1,016 prisoners who had been burned or shot by the Germans eight days earlier. Throughout occupied Germany, the Allies forced German civilians to confront the atrocities that took place in concentration camps short distances from their homes. Here, two women are forced to bury slave workers executed by German troops.

Prisoners finger SS guards Allied troops advanced so quickly across Germany that many SS guards in slave and concentration camps were unable to escape. Others chose to face the enemy instead of running away. Those guards who remained behind were immediately arrested once the Allies arrived. Liberated prisoners were asked to identify camp officials or brutal guards still in the camp. Other prisoners were taken to neighboring towns in an attempt to identify SS troopers who had abandoned their uniforms in an attempt to mingle with civilians. Here, a Soviet prisoner identifies a brutal guard at the Buchenwald concentration camp.

The Ruhr

A MAJOR PORTION OF Germany's coal, steel, and iron—all vital to the nation's war effort—was produced in the Ruhr, a region in western Germany. These industries were centered in Bochum, Dortmund, and Essen. Krupp of Essen was Germany's principal armaments manufacturer.

The Allies knew the importance of the Ruhr, so the area was subjected to intensive raids from the earliest days of the Allied strategic bombing offensive. Five years of bombing took a heavy toll, and by spring 1945 much of the Ruhr's industrial production ceased completely for protracted periods. Moreover, the destruction of canals and railroads meant that anything that was produced could not be out-loaded.

On February 22, 1945, in preparation for an Allied ground envelopment of the 320,000 German troops still manning their defensive positions in the Ruhr, the Allied air forces destroyed most of the area's remaining rail network. Then on March 11–12, the RAF dropped almost 1,000 tons of bombs on Essen and Dortmund. The RAF and USAAF also destroyed all the remaining road and rail bridges that provided access to the region. Before winter was over, the Third Reich's industrial heartland, its *Wehrmacht* defenders, and some four million civilians were effectively isolated within the Ruhr Pocket.

On March 25, the Second British Army, Ninth U.S. Army, and First Canadian Army of Field Marshal Mont-

U.S. troops in the Ruhr Valley, April 1945

gomery's 21st Army Group struck north and east of the Ruhr. In addition, General Bradley's 12th U.S. Army Group advanced eastward from the south, spearheaded by General Hodges' First U.S. Army and General Patton's Third U.S. Army. The Allied advance was rapid, and—despite a concerted German attempt to break out—soldiers of the First and Ninth U.S. armies linked up near Lippstadt on April 1. They thereby closed the Ruhr Pocket and neutralized the thousands of German troops trapped inside it.

Allies surround the Ruhr Pocket
As the Allies advanced into western Germany in 1945, General Eisenhower ordered U.S. and British forces to surround Germany's main industrial region, the Ruhr. On April 1, what came to be called the Ruhr Pocket was surrounded, along with millions of civilians and hundreds of thousands of German soldiers, including the prisoners seen here. During the course of the month, U.S. forces entered and seized the pocket. They found the "armory of the German Reich" reduced to ruins from Allied area bombing. The demoralized population faced years of grueling reconstruction.

1945

April 16: Hitler announces that he expects his officers to fight to the death. He orders summary execution for any officer who orders a retreat. • The German transport ship *Goya* is torpedoed. It goes down in the Baltic Sea with 6,200 Germans who had just been rescued from the Hela Peninsula. • The Allied air force announces that future operations over Germany will focus on cleanup rather than strategic targets, effectively ending the air war.

April 18: German field marshal Walter Model leads his remaining 225,000 troops, encircled in Germany's Ruhr, in mass surrender to the Allies. • Pulitzer Prize-winning Scripps-Howard columnist Ernie Pyle is felled by a Japanese sniper's bullet while reporting on the Battle of Okinawa.

April 20: The Allies capture Stuttgart and Nuremberg. They raise the U.S. flag over Nuremberg Stadium, the site of the Nazis' iconic political rallies.

April 23: Street-to-street fighting erupts in the German capital of Berlin as the Soviets storm the city. • *Reichsführer* Heinrich Himmler offers the Allies a conditional surrender, stipulating that he will not capitulate to a Soviet official. Allied officials will reject the offer.

April 24: Furious over Göring's play for power in the Reich's final days, Hitler orders the arrest of his former right-hand man.

April 25: Berlin is fully encircled by Belorussian and Ukrainian army groups of the Red Army. • Northern Italy continues to fall to the Allies. Verona and Parma are liberated, and citizens of Milan and Genoa rise up against their Nazi occupiers.

April 26: Marshal Philippe Pétain, former leader of Vichy France, is arrested and charged with collaborating with the Nazis.

Hitler Youth forced to fight Allies German soldier Hans-Georg Henke, age 15, cries after being captured by the U.S. Ninth Army in April 1945. On April 20, Hitler presented several 12-year-olds the Iron Cross for bravery in combat. After the ceremony, the boys returned to the front lines, joining youths and old men in battle against Soviets in the streets of Berlin. Three days after Hitler's presentation, Hitler Youth were chosen to defend bridges south of Berlin to be used by reinforcements that would never come. More than 5,000 boys fought the Soviets there, and when the fighting ended five days later, 4,500 Hitler Youth were dead or wounded.

Germans fear wrath of Red Army The Soviet Army entered Vienna, Austria, on April 13, 1945, and encircled Berlin on April 21. German civilians feared Soviet troops, who sought retribution for the atrocities inflicted on their homes and families by the Nazis. More than 100,000 women were raped in Berlin, and thousands of Germans took their own lives in Germany, Austria, and Poland. This photograph shows the aftermath of the murder-suicide of a National Socialist family in a Vienna park.

The Soviets reach Berlin Soviet troops encircled Berlin on April 21, 1945. With 2.5 million men, the Soviets faced one million German troops, including about 45,000 male youth and elderly. The Germans were also greatly outnumbered in artillery, tanks, and planes. "The amount of equipment deployed for the Berlin operation," a Soviet soldier remarked, "was so huge I simply cannot describe it and I was there." Enormous firepower was brought to bear, but the Soviets discovered that many forward German positions had been abandoned before the bombardment. The German command pulled troops tightly around Berlin for a final, doomed defense of the city.

DESPERATION IN BERLIN

WE LEFT THE CELLAR at longer and longer intervals and often we could not tell whether it was night or day. The Russians drew nearer; they advanced through the underground railway tunnels, armed with flame-throwers; their advance snipers had taken up positions quite near us; and their shots ricocheted off the houses opposite. Exhausted German soldiers would stumble in and beg for water—they were practically children. I remember one with a pale, quivering face who said, "We shall do it all right; we'll make our way to the north west yet." But his eyes belied his words and he looked at me despairingly. What he wanted to say was, "Hide me, give me shelter. I've had enough of it." I should have liked to help him; but neither of us dared to speak. Each might have shot the other as a "defeatist."

—BERLIN RESIDENT CLAUS FUHRMANN, DESCRIBING THE HOURS BEFORE THE SOVIET TAKEOVER OF THE CITY

Hitler's last birthday April 20, 1945, was Hitler's 56th birthday. The celebration in his underground headquarters, the *Führerbunker,* in the Reich Chancellery Park was very subdued. The Soviet Army was advancing toward Berlin, and Hitler knew that the end of his Third Reich was near. Later that day, Hitler left the bunker to decorate 20 Hitler Youth, most 12 to 15 years old, for bravery in combat, as seen in this picture. He then returned to the bunker in which he had lived since January 16, 1945. Protected by 16 feet of concrete and six feet of earth, Hitler's sanctuary protected him but did not mask the sounds of Soviet shells falling closer each day.

The death of Mussolini On April 25, 1945, Mussolini's puppet government in northern Italy dissolved, as Italian partisans and American forces ended German control of the region. Two days later, Mussolini and his mistress, Clara Petacci, were captured in the Italian village of Dongo while trying to flee to Switzerland. On the 28th, Mussolini, Petacci, and 15 aides were executed at *Giulino di Mezzegra*. The bodies were brought to the *Piazzale Loreto* in Milan on April 29. Six of them, including Mussolini and Petacci, were hung by the feet while a crowd of Italians spit on and beat the remains.

1945

April 27: Hitler sends one last message to his ally, Benito Mussolini. Defiant to the end, he asserts that "Bolshevism and the armies of Jewry...join their malignant forces...to precipitate chaos in our continent."

April 28: Italian partisans execute Benito Mussolini and his mistress, Clara Petacci.

April 29: Hitler and Eva Braun exchange wedding vows in Hitler's underground Berlin bunker. • General Vietinghoff, the German commander of Axis forces in Italy, signs documents surrendering to the Allies. • A U-boat wolf pack attacks Allied convoy RA-66 in the Arctic, in what will be the last convoy attack of the war.

April 30: The newly wed Hitlers commit suicide in the Berlin bunker. Joseph and Magda Goebbels follow suit, murdering their six children before taking their own lives. • Soviet forces capture the *Reichstag*. • The Dachau concentration camp is liberated as the Allies capture the Bavarian capital of Munich.

May 1: Admiral Karl Dönitz, Hitler's handpicked successor, establishes a government in Flensburg to control Germany following Hitler's suicide.

May 2: Some 490,000 German soldiers in Italy lay down their weapons, honoring the terms of the unconditional surrender signed by Vietinghoff three days earlier. • The British 26th Indian Division meets no Japanese resistance during an amphibious invasion of Rangoon, Burma.

May 3: Red Army units link up throughout Berlin as German resistance ends, completing the capture of the capital of the Third Reich. • Hamburg, Germany, and Innsbruck, Austria, fall to the Allies.

Reitsch flies to Hitler By 1945 German pilot Hanna Reitsch had received an Iron Cross and was one of the most accomplished fliers in the world. She had become a *Luftwaffe* test pilot in 1937 and flew several prototype planes and jets. In April 1945, Reitsch was a passenger when General Robert Ritter von Greim flew into beleaguered Berlin to meet with Hitler. Russian flak injured Greim's ankle, and Reitsch landed the plane in a rubble-strewn Berlin street near the *Führer's* bunker. When Hitler refused to fly to safety three days later, the plane, with Reitsch at the controls, took off amid a torrent of small arms and artillery fire. Reitsch was briefly interned after the war, and lived until 1979.

The fall of Berlin For 12 days, beginning on April 20, Stalin's troops fought through the streets of Berlin, one neighborhood at a time. Hitler ordered his Ninth and 12th armies to cut through the Soviet line and defend the city. But the Ninth was encircled and eventually decimated, and the 12th lacked the manpower or arms to attack the Soviets after holding up the Americans. The defense of Berlin was left to a disorganized band of soldiers as well as old men and boys of the Hitler Youth. They fought hard, inflicting 300,000 casualties on the Soviets.

Final Days in the *Führerbunker*

As Russian troops fought their way closer to Berlin, Hitler lived out the final days of the Third Reich within the *Führerbunker*. This massive two-level bunker complex was constructed some 22 feet below the Reich Chancellery. Some of the most senior Nazi political and military staff, with their SS guards and other administrative personnel, shared this space with their doomed leader.

In the world above, Germany had already lost the war to Allied forces, who demanded nothing less than unconditional surrender. The country was in ruins, its population displaced and traumatized. The once-invincible *Wehrmacht* was collapsing everywhere. However, in the surreal world of the *Führerbunker,* the Nazi leadership still conducted its business as usual.

Ever since the 1944 assassination attempt, Hitler's physical health had deteriorated. Moreover, his paranoia, irrationality, and impaired judgment had increased significantly. He now saw treachery and conspiracy everywhere—suspicions reinforced in late April 1945 by Hermann Göring's bid to usurp him, and by Himmler's attempt to negotiate with the Allies. Already Hitler had declared that Germany had proved itself unworthy of his genius, and therefore deserved defeat in its historic struggle.

In the twilight world of the bunker, gloomy fatalism prevailed. Its occupants indulged in alcohol and casual sex, knowing that each day might be their last. Above ground in Berlin, the madness persisted, as the SS continued executing deserters and any who counseled surrender.

On April 29, Hitler finally married Eva Braun, his mistress for some 15 years, and on April 30 they committed suicide together. Both bodies were subsequently burned just outside the bunker entrance. Joseph Goebbels and his wife, Magda, chose suicide after killing their six children. Several of the *Führerbunker* staff made desperate, last-minute bids to escape capture. Nevertheless, the end was inescapable, and on May 1 a blood-red Soviet victory banner at last flew above the *Reichstag* building.

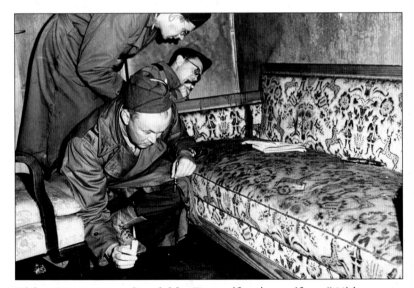

Hitler, Braun commit suicide "I myself and my wife . . ." Hitler wrote in his last will and testament on April 29, 1945, "choose death." Shortly after midnight on April 29, he married his mistress, Eva Braun. On the 30th, the two committed suicide, Eva from biting into a cyanide capsule and Hitler from cyanide and a shot under his chin, according to his valet, Heinz Linge. Their bodies were carried out of the bunker, doused with gasoline, partially burned, and then buried in a shallow bomb crater. The bodies were discovered by the Soviets, who performed an autopsy to confirm Hitler's identity. Here, war correspondents attached to the U.S. military examine blood stains in the bunker.

HITLER'S SUICIDE

The door to Hitler's room is still open at the end of the corridor. The men carrying the bodies had no hands free to close it. Eva's little revolver is lying on the table with a pink chiffon scarf beside it, and I see the brass case of the poison capsule glinting on the floor next to Frau Hitler's chair. It looks like an empty lipstick. There is blood on the blue-and-white upholstery of the bench where Hitler was sitting: Hitler's blood. I suddenly feel sick. The heavy smell of bitter almonds is nauseating. I instinctively reach for my own capsule. I'd like to throw it as far away as I can and leave this terrible bunker. One ought to be able to breathe clear, fresh air now, feel the wind and hear the trees rustling. But freedom, peace and calm are out of reach.

—Traudl Junge, Hitler's personal secretary, in her memoir, *Until the Final Hour*

1945

May 3: RAF planes attack and sink three German ships—the *Cap Arcona, Thielbek,* and *Deutschland.* Unknown to the RAF, these ships—under the direction of the Red Cross—are carrying rescued prisoners (mostly Jews) from German concentration camps. Some 8,000 lose their lives.

May 4: German troops surrender en masse throughout northern Germany and the Netherlands.

May 5: German and Allied officials meet in Reims, France, to reach agreement on the terms of Germany's capitulation. • The German army lays down its weapons throughout Bavaria. • American troops performing mop-up operations near Berchtesgaden capture Hans Frank, occupied Poland's Nazi governor general, who had established his headquarters in the city of Kraków. • U.S. forces liberate French and Austrian officials—including premiers Reynaud, Daladier, Blum, and Schuschnigg—from captivity in Austria. • Czech partisans rise up against the German occupation force in Prague. • A Japanese balloon bomb kills a woman and five children in Oregon, becoming the only such bomb of the war to induce casualties.

May 6: Admiral Lord Louis Mountbatten, supreme Allied commander of the Southeast Asia theater, announces that the Allied campaign in Burma has come to an end.

May 7: German general Alfred Jodl signs the formal surrender documents in Reims, France, as Germany surrenders unconditionally to the Allies. • The Red Army captures Breslau, Germany, after laying siege to the German garrison for 82 days. • *U-2336* sinks two merchant ships in the North Atlantic—the last U-boat "kills" of the war.

Germany's "secret leader" Martin Bormann, head of the Nazi *Parteikanzlei* (Chancellery), completely controlled personal access to the *Führer.* By manipulating Hitler, Bormann also affected Nazi Party directives, promotions, appointments, and finances. Present in the bunker during Hitler's final days, Bormann was a witness to the wedding of Hitler and Eva Braun. After that, he disappeared. Evidence indicates that he perished in Berlin while attempting to escape through heavy gunfire. After the war, Bormann was tried at Nuremberg *in absentia.* He was convicted and sentenced to death.

Americans skeptical of Hitler suicide This cover of *Time,* illustrated by Boris Artzybasheff, shows Hitler's face with a blood-red X over it. It appeared on the issue dated May 7, 1945, a week after the German leader's suicide. When word reached America that Hitler had taken his own life, the report was met with skepticism. In fact, the FBI conducted an extensive, 11-year investigation into whether the German leader faked his death. His suicide was confirmed in the 1960s by Russian journalist Lev Bezymenski. He reported that Soviets had performed an autopsy on corpses found buried in a shallow grave that were identified as belonging to Hitler, his wife, and their two dogs.

Traumatized soldiers At the front lines in Germany in 1945, a doctor gives a traumatized, exhausted American soldier a sedative. Throughout World War II, Allied forces were troubled by incidents of what is today called Combat Stress Reactions (CSRs). It was then referred to as "shell shock," "battle fatigue," or "war neurosis." The 1943 episode in which General Patton slapped two troubled soldiers in Sicily generated concern about the problem, and by 1944 a psychiatrist was assigned to each American division. The soldier seen here was sent to a rear hospital for psychological treatment.

1945

February 13–15: The Allies unleash a devastating attack on Dresden, Germany, killing more than 30,000 in a bombing raid that triggers intense firestorms.

February 16: Two battalions of U.S. forces invade the Philippine island of Corregidor by air and sea. They encounter fierce Japanese resistance. • Aircraft carriers attached to the U.S. Navy's Fifth Fleet, along with dozens of support ships, launch a series of air raids over Tokyo.

February 17: Some 170 U.S. Navy frogmen lose their lives in an ill-fated effort to thwart Japanese beach defenses on Iwo Jima.

February 18: General Ivan Chernyakhovsky, 39, one of the youngest Red Army generals to command a front during World War II, dies of wounds received in combat.

February 19: One of the bloodiest battles of the Pacific war ensues when 30,000 U.S. Marines storm the Japanese-held island of Iwo Jima.

February 20: Red Army troops advance on Berlin, Germany's capital and the heart of the Third Reich. • Allied troops breach the Siegfried Line in Germany and reach the banks of the Rhine River. • Twenty-three American aircraft are lost when some 1,500 bombers and fighters attack infrastructure targets in Nuremberg, Germany.

February 21: The Americans recapture the Philippine province of Bataan, site of the infamous Bataan death march three years earlier.

February 23: The USS *Henry Bacon* becomes the last Allied merchant ship to go down at the hands of the *Luftwaffe* when it is sunk in the Arctic Sea by German bombers. • The U.S. Marines capture Iwo Jima's Mount Suribachi and raise a foreign flag on Japanese soil.

Japanese kill Manila civilians The burned corpse of a Filipino civilian murdered by Japanese troops lies in a Manila street, his hands still tied behind his back. Trapped by U.S. forces and facing certain death, Japanese naval personnel in Manila ran amok, butchering and raping thousands of helpless civilians. "I saw the bodies of priests, women, children and babies that

had been bayoneted for sport... by a soldiery gone mad with blood lust in defeat," recalled Filipino editor Carlos Romulo. An estimated 100,000 civilians perished in what became known as the "Manila Massacre."

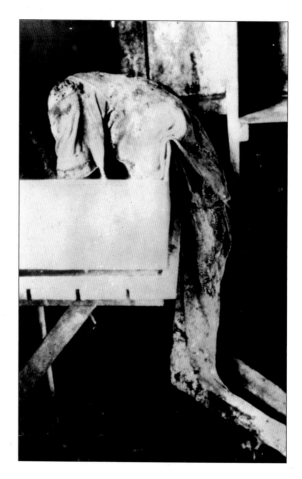

American POWs in Japanese hands Liberation came too late for this sick and malnourished American POW at the Davao Penal Colony on Mindanao in the Philippines. He died while trying to get a drink of water from a sink in the camp hospital. Of the approximately 25,000 U.S. troops captured during the war—most during the first months after Pearl Harbor—more than 10,000 died while in Japanese hands. Lack of adequate food and medical care, disease, forced labor, and outright murder all contributed to the toll. Japanese racism and a disdain for surrendered soldiers virtually ensured that the welfare of Allied POWs would remain a very low priority.

The liberation of Dachau A flat-bed truck hauls away bodies of prisoners who died at Dachau. Located near Munich, Germany, the Dachau concentration camp had been built in 1933 to confine political opponents of the Nazi movement, and in November 1938 11,000 Jewish prisoners were sent there. Dachau was used as a model for other concentration camps in Germany and Eastern Europe. In spring 1943, a crematorium with four ovens was put into use at the camp. Upon liberating Dachau on April 30, Americans discovered more than 30,000 prisoners and hundreds of unburied corpses. In its 12 years, more than 30,000 of Dachau's 200,000 prisoners died.

U.S. troops execute Dachau guards When Dachau was liberated on April 30, 1945, an unknown number of American GIs lined 16 SS camp guards against a coal yard wall in the adjacent SS training camp and executed them (*pictured*). Additional executions took place at Dachau's rail yard, at a guard tower, and at Würm creek. In all, 37 to 39 SS personnel were dispatched that day. These actions were "unauthorized" and did not reflect U.S. Army policy toward captured SS.

Dönitz named president of Germany In 1935 Hitler named German commodore Karl Dönitz (*center*) as the first commander-in-chief of U-boats. He advanced in rank and command until 1943, when he became grand admiral of the German Navy. When two of Hitler's highest lieutenants, Heinrich Himmler and Hermann Göring, betrayed him, Hitler named Dönitz as his successor with the title of president. The only part of the Reich not in Allied hands by the end of April was an area near Flensburg in northern Germany. Dönitz's government there was never acknowledged by the Allies and came to an end on May 23, 1945, when he was arrested by British troops.

1945

May 8: Victory in Europe (V-E) Day is declared as German troops continue to surrender to Allies throughout Europe. • Hermann Göring surrenders to Allied troops. He will become, along with Admiral Dönitz, the highest-ranking Nazi to face trial at Nuremberg.

May 9: Norwegian collaborator and infamous turncoat Vidkun Quisling turns himself in to the authorities in Oslo. • The Allies assume control of the German heavy cruiser *Prinz Eugen* in the port of Copenhagen, Denmark.

May 10: The U.S. high command announces that more than three million American troops stationed in Europe will soon be on their way home or to the Pacific Theater.

May 11: Australian troops capture Wewak from the Japanese, giving control of all of New Guinea's ports to the Allies.

May 12: Washington temporarily suspends Lend-Lease aid to the Soviet Union. • American Marines suffer heavy casualties as Japanese troops defend their positions on Okinawa's Sugar Loaf Hill.

May 14: Austrian self-determination returns to Vienna for the first time since the *Anschluss*. • The Allies discover a fortune in gold, currency, and looted art hidden by the Nazis in an Austrian salt mine. • USAAF B-29 bombers drop some 2,500 incendiary devices on the Japanese city of Nagoya.

Mid-May: The 1.2 million soldiers in German Army Group Center disband. Most will end up in U.S. or Soviet custody.

May 16: The Japanese cruiser *Haguro* goes down in the Malacca Strait after coming under attack by a small force of British destroyers.

Germany's rocket man Wernher von Braun, the civilian seen here with *Wehrmacht* officers at Pennemünde, Germany, had been steered (he said pressured) into the Nazi Party and the SS because of his genius with rocketry. While developing his V-2 rocket at Pennemünde, Braun visited the Mittlewerk facility, where enslaved laborers toiled and died under deplorable conditions. Fearing the Soviet forces who were approaching, Braun and his team surrendered to U.S. troops on May 3, 1945. In America's subsequent Operation Paperclip, 1,600 German scientists were sent to the U.S. to develop the space program. Following the 1969 moon landing, Braun became a hero in America.

Göring surrenders Brigadier General Robert Stack, assistant commander of the U.S. 36th Infantry Division, was handed an envelope on May 7, 1945, addressed to General Eisenhower. It was from Hermann Göring (*center*), who agreed to surrender if Eisenhower would work with him to reorganize Germany. Göring's request was refused, and he surrendered to the 36th Division the next day. Göring had incensed Hitler on April 23 by requesting that the *Führer,* who was trapped in a bunker in Berlin, name him as Hitler's successor. Accusing Göring of treason, Hitler ordered his arrest and considered ordering his execution.

The German surrender Field Marshal Wilhelm Keitel signs the ratified surrender terms for the German military on May 8, 1945. The terms included the unconditional surrender of all German armed forces, cessation of active operations, and surrender of all weapons and equipment to local Allied commanders. Though the document neglected to mention the civilian government, an Allied Control Council was subsequently formed with authority over all military and civilian agencies.

British celebrate V-E Day On May 8, 1945, the Allies celebrated Victory in Europe (V-E) Day. Here, Mrs. Pat Burgess of Palmers Green in North London waves a newspaper announcing Germany's surrender. She was one of more than a million Londoners who took to the streets to celebrate. They listened to an address by King George VI, cheered at exploding fireworks, and burned effigies of Hitler. In his speech that day, Winston Churchill somberly reminded the British that their rejoicing must be brief. "Japan, with all her treachery and greed, remains unsubdued," he said.

The American celebration Just as Londoners had done in Piccadilly Circus, New Yorkers packed Times Square on May 8, 1945, to celebrate V-E Day. By the end of the European phase of the war, the United States found itself a major player on the world stage, already assured leadership status in the soon-to-be-founded United Nations. However, America's V-E Day celebrations were dampened by the April 12 death of President Franklin Roosevelt, who had done so much to assure an Allied victory and the creation of the UN.

Plundered art After the war, U.S. soldiers find Édouard Manet's *In the Conservatory* among many other paintings hidden by the Nazis in a German salt mine. Hitler's regime began looting cultural objects upon its rise to power in 1933. As the Germans conquered much of Europe, they confiscated millions of artworks, many of them from Jewish owners. In Warsaw alone, a reported 13,512 paintings and 1,379 sculptures were stolen. A great number of artworks were returned to their rightful owners after the war, but many more were lost forever or became tangled in litigation.

1945

May 17: U.S. forces capture Manila's Ipo Dam following a three-day bombing campaign in which more than 100,000 gallons of napalm were dropped on Japanese positions.

May 18: An intense, 10-day battle on Okinawa ends when the U.S. Marines capture the hotly contested Sugar Loaf Hill.

May 19: Nazi functionary Dr. Alfred Rosenberg is captured. Rosenberg had promoted the belief in Aryan racial superiority and the need for German *Lebensraum* (living space).

May 21: A division between Britain's Labour and Conservative parties leads Churchill to call for general elections for the first time in a decade.

May 23: *Reichsführer* Heinrich Himmler commits suicide while in British custody. • Julius Streicher, the fanatical anti-Semitic publisher of the Nazi periodical *Der Stürmer,* is arrested in Bavaria. • Eisenhower orders the arrest of leaders of the German military and of the new Flensburg government headed by Admiral Dönitz. • The U.S. military leadership determines that Operation Olympic, the invasion of the Japanese mainland, will commence November 1.

May 27: Up to 200,000 Japanese troops are stranded when the Chinese reoccupy Nanning, cutting the Japanese supply route from Southeast Asia. • USAAF planes deliver the Chinese Sixth Army from Burma to China, marking the first airborne transport of an army in world history. • Japanese authorities close the crippled Japanese port of Tokyo.

May 28: British radio personality William Joyce ("Lord Haw-Haw") is captured by the Allies. • Shipping rules for wartime are abolished everywhere outside the Pacific. Merchant traffic is allowed to use navigation lights, and abandon convoys.

> ## "The Jap climbed suddenly and dived. It was all a matter of seconds. He came up the center of the flight deck, accurate as a homing plane, and abruptly all was lost in a confusion of smoke and flame."
>
> —Royal Navy seaman Michael Moynihan, describing a May 9, 1945, *kamikaze* attack

Kamikazes* strike the *Bunker Hill Wrecked aircraft litter the USS *Bunker Hill*'s flight deck after the carrier was struck by two *kamikazes* on May 11, 1945, off Okinawa. The first enemy plane careened through parked aircraft on the flight deck, igniting numerous fires while its 550-pound bomb exploded below decks. The second *kamikaze* hit near the base of the ship's aft deck. Fires were brought under control within five hours, but casualties totaled 346 dead and 246 wounded. The damage put the veteran carrier out of the war. It eventually returned to duty in September with the "Magic Carpet" fleet, transporting servicemen back to the States for discharge.

The liberation of the Channel Islands In July 1940, the Germans easily seized and occupied the British Channel Islands. Under Hitler's orders, the islands were heavily fortified and became the sites of slave labor camps for European prisoners of war. Ironically, the islanders' worst sufferings came after the Allied invasion of Normandy, when they were cut off from food and other supplies from Europe. The islands were not liberated until May 1945, after Germany's surrender. Here, elated civilians on one of the Channel Islands wait to greet British troops.

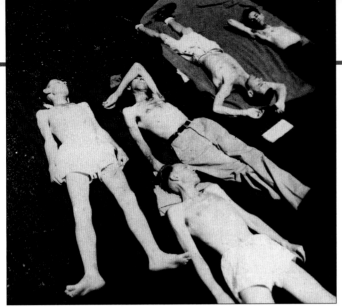

American starvation experiment Beginning in November 1944, Dr. Ancel Keys of the University of Minnesota worked with 36 conscientious objectors in the first study of the effects of semi-starvation. Receiving an average of about 1,500 calories a day from their fourth to 10th month of the yearlong experiment, the volunteers experienced significant changes in both their health and personalities. During the last three months, the men received from 2,000 to 3,000 calories daily, with the number increasing over time. It was learned that vitamins and proteins did not help on their own. The proper diet to nurse emaciated victims back to health consisted of about 4,000 calories a day.

Surrender leaflets This is one of millions of leaflets dropped among Japanese soldiers and civilians to encourage surrender. The *I Cease Resistance* phrasing was developed after it was discovered that Japanese soldiers were alienated by any mention of actual surrender. Leaflets were produced and printed by the Office of War

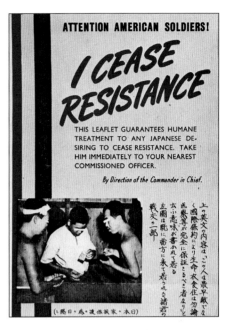

Information and by the Far Eastern Liaison Office and Psychological Warfare Branch in the South West Pacific Area command. Early efforts brought few surrenders, but results improved dramatically in 1945, both because of deteriorating Japanese morale and a growing willingness among Allied troops to take live prisoners.

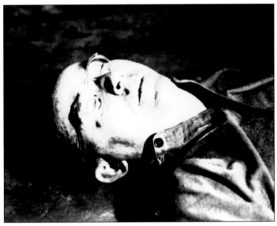

Himmler's final days On April 28, 1945, Hitler learned that his trusted lieutenant, Heinrich Himmler, had tried to negotiate the surrender of the German army to the Allies. Incensed, Hitler ordered Himmler's arrest. Following Hitler's suicide, the *Führer*'s successor, Grand Admiral Karl Dönitz, denounced Himmler. Hunted by Allied agents, Himmler disguised himself as a sergeant major and attempted to flee to Bavaria. Although he shaved his mustache and wore a patch over his left eye, he was arrested and eventually identified. To escape his trial and inevitable execution, he killed himself by swallowing a cyanide capsule on May 23, 1945.

Cologne takes a beating The Allied bombing of Cologne, Germany, began in March 1942. During the war, the city was attacked by air numerous times, primarily because it was a military, economic, and manufacturing center along the Rhine River. The most destructive of the raids occurred on the night of May 30–31, 1942, when more than 1,000 planes of the Royal Air Force dropped about 1,500 tons of explosives on the city in only 75 minutes. By war's end, more than 20,000 Cologne civilians had been killed or wounded and most of the city was destroyed, leaving tens of thousands of civilians homeless.

THE DEFEAT OF JAPAN

JUNE 1945–SEPTEMBER 1945

"Everything had disappeared. It was a stony waste littered with debris and twisted girders. The incandescent breath of the fire had swept away every obstacle and all that remained upright were one or two fragments of stone walls."

—AUTHOR MARCEL JUNOD, *WARRIORS WITHOUT WEAPONS*, DESCRIBING THE DEVASTATION IN HIROSHIMA

AFTER THE REPLACEMENT of Tojo Hideki as prime minister in July 1944 by General Koiso Kuniaki, the Japanese continued to adhere to their basic strategy. That was to fight so hard and inflict such heavy casualties on the Americans that the latter would be willing to settle for a peace in which Japan could retain some of its gains, would not be occupied or disarmed, and would not have its military or civilian leaders tried as war criminals. The Japanese government made an effort to persuade the Soviet Union to either mediate some sort of compromise or, alternatively, reverse alliances and join Japan in fighting the Western powers. A new prime minister, Admiral Suzuki Kantaro, saw these efforts fail; he did not grasp that this was because Stalin had decided to fight Japan, not his current allies.

By the summer of 1945, Japan's situation had become desperate. Allied aircraft and submarines had decimated its already inadequate merchant fleet. Oil and other raw materials could not be delivered by sea. The big reason for this was U.S. airpower. A year earlier, the American bomber force was built up on the conquered islands of the Marianas. From those islands, especially Tinian and Saipan, long-range B-29 bombers began to pound the home islands in the fall of 1944 and the winter of 1944–45. Under a new commander, Major General Curtis LeMay, the Americans shifted much of their effort from high-level aimed bombing with explosives to low-level area bombing with incendiaries.

A Japanese mother and child in traditional garb sit amid the ruins of Hiroshima four months after the atomic bomb devastated the city. Surrendering after two A-bomb attacks, Japan faced an uncertain future as it sought to rise from the physical and emotional ruin of an ill-conceived war.

The raid on Tokyo on March 9, 1945, was the first large incendiary raid. Some 16 square miles of the city were burned, more than 80,000 people were killed, and a million Japanese civilians were left homeless. Similar if somewhat smaller raids were mounted against other large Japanese cities in the following months. In addition, aircraft carriers brought additional planes to raid coastal cities, and land-based planes dropped mines in the main shipping lanes.

Major General Curtis LeMay (*second from left*), commanding general of the 21st Bomber Command, receives a first-hand report of a Superfortress raid against Nagoya, Japan, on March 26, 1945. LeMay's fire-bombing campaign laid waste to Japan's cities. All the while, Japanese military forces far from home suffered one defeat after another.

While havoc reigned on the home islands, the Japanese land forces in China and those forces still holding islands and parts of islands in the South and Southwest Pacific found themselves without many of the supplies they needed. The Americans and Australians launched one invasion after the other in the East Indies, and the British prepared to follow up on their reconquest of Burma with a landing on the coast of Malaya in order to retake Singapore.

The planning for an invasion of the Japanese home islands went forward; on June 18 President Truman gave his tentative approval of the landing on Kyushu (Operation Olympic). Both the final go-ahead for this assault, scheduled for November 1, and the subsequent landing on Tokyo Bay (Operation Coronet) scheduled for March 1, 1946, would have to come later. The bloody fighting that was still going on at Okinawa and elsewhere suggested that invasion of the home islands would result in huge casualties. The Pentagon ordered hundreds of thousands of Purple Hearts for wounded soldiers, and there was discussion of the possible need to draft nurses.

The collapse of Chinese military resistance in the summer of 1944 made it all the more imperative that Soviet forces attack the Japanese on the mainland of Asia and thereby prevent them from reinforcing the home islands. President Truman was greatly relieved when Stalin reiterated his promise to invade Manchuria three months after the defeat of Germany. By the time Stalin made his promise at the July 16–August 2 meeting of the three powers at Potsdam, Germany, large numbers of Red Army units and commanders were already on their way to the Soviet East Asian provinces.

At the meeting, Truman told Stalin that a powerful new weapon was now ready. Having been briefed on Soviet espionage discoveries about the atomic bomb project, the president thought Stalin might know what he was talking about. Regardless, he urged Truman to use the powerful weapon promptly. Just before the meeting, Truman had been informed that the first A-bomb test conducted in New Mexico had been successful. The project, initiated by Roosevelt years earlier, was now beginning to produce the first bombs.

At the conclusion of the Potsdam meeting, the Allies issued a special "Declaration" calling on Japan to surrender, but the threat was ignored. Therefore, Truman ordered that an atomic bomb be dropped on Hiroshima on August 6. The results were devastating, with close to 80,000 deaths.

In discussion with Secretary of War Henry Stimson and Army Chief of Staff George Marshall, Truman had decided that if the first bomb did not shock the Japanese into surrender, a second one would be dropped on another city. But if that did not persuade the Japanese to surrender, the bombs that later would become available would be saved for use in support of Operation Olympic. Since the bomb on Hiroshima did not prompt Japan to surrender, the second one was dropped on Nagasaki on August 9.

Anxious discussion took place inside the Japanese government, especially after Tokyo learned that the Soviet Union was joining Japan's enemies and invading Manchuria. Even after the second bomb was dropped, half of the Japanese leadership wanted to continue the war, hoping that the casualties that they expected to inflict on the Americans during landings at Kyushu would produce a change in American objectives. It was in the face of an evenly split group of leaders that Emperor Hirohito insisted that surrender was the only possible course. A coup attempt by those who wanted to continue fighting failed narrowly. The stage was set for a formal surrender, which was signed on the battleship *Missouri* on September 2.

Japan surrendered peacefully, and was not divided into zones of occupation the way Germany had been. Although western Honshu was under a British Commonwealth Occupation Force (BCOF), the home islands as a whole retained a Japanese administrative system that was under the supervision of an American occupation force and supreme commander (General Douglas MacArthur).

The Soviet Union, in addition to seizing the Kurile Islands, also took control of small islands off the coast of the northern home island of Hokkaido and removed the Japanese inhabitants. While Japan thus escaped the decades of partition that became Germany's fate, the Soviet action precluded the signing of a peace treaty between Russia and Japan.

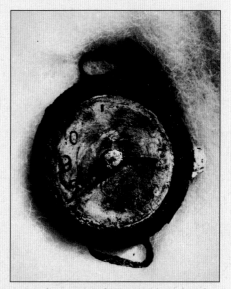

A watch remains frozen in time, marking the exact moment the atom bomb at Hiroshima changed the world forever. In one split second, the bomb ended one era and ushered in the atomic age with all of its ramifications for politics, culture, international relations, and the continued existence of humankind itself.

1945

June 1: As many as 700 of 40,000 Cossack troops who fought alongside the Nazis die when they resist British efforts to forcibly repatriate them to the Soviet Union. • Some 27 American P-51 Mustang fighters are lost to foul weather en route to an assault on Osaka, Japan.

June 5: Brazil, which had long been at war with Germany, declares war on Japan. • Nearly 500 U.S. B-29 bombers drop 3,000 tons of incendiaries on the Japanese city of Kobe. • A powerful typhoon strikes Okinawa, badly damaging more than 30 U.S. warships.

June 7: Norway's King Haakon returns to the throne of his liberated nation. • All German civilians living in the Western Allies' occupation zones are made to watch films of the concentration camps at Buchenwald and Bergen-Belsen. • Osaka suffers heavy damage as 400 American B-29 bombers rain terror on the Japanese city.

June 9: The RAF Vampire jet, boasting a maximum speed of more than 500 mph, is unveiled in Britain.

June 11: Czech police and civilians continue the process of driving ethnic Germans from the Czech Sudetenland into occupied Germany.

June 12: With a U.S. Marine victory on Okinawa's Oroku Peninsula a virtual certainty, Japanese troops on Okinawa commit suicide en masse.

June 13: The U.S. 24th Corps attacks Japanese-held caves on Okinawa with flamethrowers.

June 14: U.S. military leadership in the Pacific Theater receives orders from the Joint Chiefs of Staff to prepare for the invasion and occupation of Japan. • Former Nazi foreign minister Joachim von Ribbentrop is captured in Hamburg.

Soviet casualties Relatives greet a Russian soldier upon his return from the Great Patriotic War. This man was one of the lucky ones. Of the 30 million Soviets who fought in World War II, more than eight million died. Of the survivors, many returned to find that their families were among the 11.5 million civilians who perished in the conflict. According to Soviet records, military dead from 1941 to '45 totaled 8,668,400, including 500,000 missing in action. Another 1,283,300 were taken prisoner. Nearly 14 percent of the total population died, as compared to U.S. losses of 0.32 percent.

The "Beast" and "Bitch" of Belsen Irma Grese and Josef Kramer (*both pictured*) were two of many German concentration camp commanders and guards who faced postwar prosecution as war criminals. Kramer, commandant of the Bergen-Belsen camp, was called the "Beast of Belsen" by the inmates. He placed few controls over the activities of his guards, including Irma Grese, the most notorious of the female guards at all the camps. Grese had been transferred to Auschwitz at age 19. She was then sent in March 1945 to Bergen-Belsen, where she was known as "Bitch of Belsen" for torturing and murdering inmates. Kramer and Grese were tried with more than 40 other guards from the camp. Both were found guilty and were hanged for their war crimes on December 13, 1945.

Operation Downfall

PLANNING FOR OPERATION DOWNFALL, the invasion of Japan, began in earnest in early 1945 when strategists decided that a naval blockade alone probably would not bring about a timely Japanese surrender. Downfall called for two huge amphibious assaults, each dwarfing the Normandy landings of 1944. The first, code-named Olympic, would take place on November 1, 1945, when 14 divisions would land on three beaches on Kyushu, the southernmost of the Japanese home islands. Seizure of southern Kyushu was expected to take 90 days and would involve more than 427,000 Allied troops.

If the Japanese government failed to capitulate, phase two of Downfall, code-named Coronet, would take place on March 1, 1946. Coronet planners contemplated an assault over the Kanto Plain before Tokyo with as many as 23 divisions. Unlike Olympic, which drew on organizations already in the Pacific, Coronet would include a number of divisions redeployed from the European Theater.

Almost exclusively, Operation Downfall would be an American undertaking. Initially, planners counted on Russian forces to tie down potential Japanese reinforcements in Manchuria. Some British Commonwealth and French forces would be involved in Downfall, but their numbers would be small.

Planners, of course, worried about potential U.S. casualties. The Japanese had identified Kyushu as a likely invasion point and were pouring troops into the area. After the war, U.S. officials said American losses in Downfall might have totaled between 500,000 and one million men. Others felt such numbers were exaggerated. General Douglas MacArthur, who would have commanded the ground assault, estimated casualties for Olympic at about 56,000 dead, wounded, and missing over a period of 60 days. With Japan functioning with depleted resources, Coronet might have seen even fewer U.S. losses.

The atomic bombs ensured that those figures would remain historical speculation. Still, it was a near thing. Two American divisions from Europe, the 86th and 97th, were already arriving in the Pacific when the war ended, and Olympic was only three months away.

Operation Olympic An American pilot points out a target on a scale model of the Yokosuka naval base. Operation Olympic, the planned invasion of Kyushu on November 1, 1945, called for massive air attacks on the Japanese home islands. Hundreds of Navy fighters, dive-bombers, and torpedo planes were assigned to hit targets all over the island of Honshu in support of the operation. As Allied landing craft neared the beaches of Kyushu on November 1, waves of planes from no less than 66 aircraft carriers would bomb, rocket, and strafe enemy fortifications and troop concentrations along the beaches.

1945

June 17: Japanese Admiral Ota Minoru commits ritual suicide after U.S. troops breach Japan's final defense on Okinawa.

June 18: The USAAF launches a devastating series of air raids that target the civilian populations of major Japanese cities. •U.S. 10th Army commander General Simon Bolivar Buckner is felled by shrapnel while inspecting the Okinawan front line.

June 19: Manhattan honors General Eisenhower with a ticker tape parade upon his return to the United States following victory in Europe.

June 21: U.S. troops capture Aparri, the last Japanese port on the Philippine island of Luzon. However, substantial Japanese forces will continue the fight on Luzon until the August surrender.

June 22: The bloodiest battle of the Pacific war ends as American troops secure Okinawa following their hard-won victory over the Japanese.

June 24: General Zhukov rides a white horse into Red Square (while troops defile captured Nazi flags) as the Soviet Union celebrates victory over Germany.

June 26: Fifty nations sign the United Nations Charter in San Francisco.

June 27: Czechoslovakian Nazi puppet Emil Hacha, former president of the Bohemia-Moravia Protectorate, dies in a prison hospital before he can be tried for treason.

June 27: A *kamikaze* strike on the USS *Bunker Hill* claims the lives of 373 American sailors.

July 3: The Western Allies occupy the sectors of Berlin allocated to the Americans, British, and French by prior agreement with the Soviet Union.

Bombs devastate Osaka Desolation stretches as far as the eye can see after repeated B-29 incendiary raids on Osaka, which was Japan's second largest industrial city and the site of a military arsenal. The first incendiary raid on Osaka was conducted by 300 B-29s on the night of March 13, 1945. Within three hours, more than eight square miles of the city was in flames. The heat turbulence was so great that one B-29, *Thunderin' Loretta,* was flipped over on its back. On June 7, Osaka was hit by 400 B-29s. This was followed by another attack a week later. By then, there was little left to destroy.

Japanese children forced to work Former schoolgirls learn to use factory lathes as Japan tries to cope with manpower shortages late in the war. Women, prisoners of war, and forced laborers were all moved into the workforce in an effort to maintain production. As many as 3.4 million children exchanged their studies for hard manual labor in the factories. Work was proclaimed to be "equal education." Underfed and unskilled, the children were subjected to long hours under harsh conditions. "We worked twelve hours straight—no breaks except to go to the toilet which was outside the factory building," recalled one child laborer.

Heavy casualties on Okinawa A U.S. Marine takes aim with his submachine gun during an assault near Wana Ridge on Okinawa. Despite heavy casualties, the American divisions continued to batter the enemy defenses, transforming the terrain into a moonscape. Japanese resistance continued as General Ushijima Mitsuru's best units were gradually annihilated. Shuri fell in late May, and by mid-June the Japanese 32nd Army began to collapse. Ushijima committed suicide on June 22, and Japan lost 110,000 men in the battle. American dead totaled 12,281, making Okinawa the most costly Allied operation of the Pacific war—which did not bode well for the upcoming invasion of Japan.

Japan's rocket-powered weapon U.S. Marines examine an abandoned Japanese *Ohka* (Cherry Blossom) flying bomb at Okinawa's Yontan Airfield. Nicknamed *"Baka"* ("Fool") by the Allies, the rocket-propelled missile included a one-ton warhead. The weapon was designed to be launched from an aircraft and guided to its target—usually a ship—by a suicide pilot. The *Ohka* reached speeds of 650 mph in its rocket-assisted dive, making it virtually unstoppable on its final approach. Appearing late in the war, *Ohkas* are credited with sinking or damaging three ships beyond repair and significantly damaging three additional vessels.

Australians overtake Balikpapan Australian troops go ashore at Balikpapan on the southeast coast of Borneo in the last major amphibious assault of the Pacific war. The Seventh Australian Division landed in July 1945 to seize Balikpapan's port and oil fields. Outnumbered and outgunned, the Japanese offered stubborn resistance, but were eventually forced to retreat into the hills. Balikpapan cost the Australians 229 killed and 634 wounded. Japanese casualties totaled about 2,000. Conducted six weeks before Japan's surrender, the operation was later criticized as a waste of lives, although no one at the time could have realized that the war would end so abruptly.

1945

July 5: General MacArthur announces that forces under his command have succeeded in liberating the Philippines from Japanese rule. • John Curtin, Australia's wartime prime minister, dies of heart disease at age 60.

July 8: In what will prove to be the worst massacre at a POW camp in American history, guard Clarence Bertucci strafes a Utah tent city full of sleeping German prisoners with machine gun fire, killing eight. • RAF sergeant Simon Eden, son of British foreign secretary Anthony Eden, is listed as missing in action in Burma.

July 10: Tokyo's production and military facilities come under intense attack.

July 12: Britain honors Soviet general Zhukov and the Red Army in a ceremony at Berlin's Brandenburg Gate in occupied Germany.

July 13: Former Axis partner Italy declares war on Japan.

July 14: General Eisenhower officially dissolves the Supreme Headquarters Allied Expeditionary Force.

July 15: After more than 2,000 nights of mandatory blackouts, Britain turns on the lights.

July 16: Truman, Churchill, and Stalin meet near Berlin at the Potsdam Conference, at which they will issue a new public demand for Japan's surrender. • As Truman begins the summit at Potsdam, he receives word of the first successful detonation of an atomic bomb, at New Mexico's Alamogordo testing grounds.

July 19: In the largest B-29 bomb raid to date, 600 of the heavy bombers drop 4,000 tons of munitions on Japanese cities, including Choshi, Fukui, Hitachi, and Okazaki.

UNRRA administers DP camps The war was far from over in 1943. However, the leaders of 44 nations began to plan for rehabilitating the nations freed from Axis control and caring for the millions of displaced persons. On November 9, 1943, the United Nations Relief and Rehabilitation Administration (UNRRA) was formed to provide much-needed relief. After the war, the UNRRA administered hundreds of displaced-persons camps, primarily in Italy, Austria, and Germany. Here in July 1945, UNRRA volunteers give bread to survivors of a German concentration camp.

Germans lack food and shelter Children play on a tank in Berlin in 1945. When not playing, they searched for food to escape hunger. "There were G.I. mess halls," remembered American private George Stone, "where at the garbage pails where you scraped off your mess kit or plate, there were small children 3–4–5 years old with a little can or pail begging for the scrapings to take home to feed the family." The situation did not improve by that winter. "Thousands of shivering, tired Germans lugged their bundles of wood to cold, bombed houses," reported *Time* magazine in December 1945. "Hospitals were crowded. Because the patients were undernourished, many died."

The secret city A billboard at the top-secret Oak Ridge facility reminds workers of the need for silence. Located in a remote mountain area of central Tennessee, Oak Ridge was created in 1942 for work on the Manhattan Project. As headquarters for the entire atomic bomb project, Oak Ridge housed a graphite reactor and facilities for producing the fissionable uranium isotope 235. All the while, the government tried to keep the city secret. Though it grew to a population of 75,000, the city never appeared on any maps. Security was enhanced by geography, fences, armed guards, and a strict system of badges and passes.

Prostitution in Berlin To prevent black market activity, looting, and prostitution, Allied commanders made a futile attempt to prohibit soldiers from fraternizing with civilians in occupied Germany. It soon became apparent that violations of this order were unenforceable. Within six months of the fall of Berlin, more than 500,000 women turned to prostitution, many to provide for themselves and their families. One German official observed that even "nice girls of good families, good education and fine background have discovered their bodies afford the only real living." Incidents of venereal disease in Berlin more than doubled in the last six months of 1945.

Ex-*Wehrmacht* officer heads intelligence group Soon after the war in Europe ended, Major General Reinhard Gehlen, an intelligence officer in the German army, surrendered to the U.S. Army Counter Intelligence Corps. He negotiated his release and that of his colleagues from American POW camps in exchange for volumes of intelligence that his department, Foreign Forces—East, had collected on the

activities of the Soviet Union (but which proved mostly erroneous). Within a year, Gehlen became the head of a West German intelligence group that eventually would grow to more than 4,000 agents. He remained the leader of this group until he retired in 1968.

The Krupp empire In 1957 *Time* magazine stated that German manufacturer Alfried Krupp was "the wealthiest man in Europe—and perhaps in the world." Krupp rebuilt his industrial empire in less than six years after his release from prison, to which he had been sentenced in 1945 to 12 years as a war criminal. In his trial, it had been determined that his factories used slave laborers from concentration camps. Thousands of these laborers died due to poor rations, overwork, and deliberate killing. Krupp was released from prison early, and his property was returned, when Allied leaders decided that the steel produced by his factories was important for the stability of West Germany and the free world.

1945

July 23: The trial of Nazi collaborator Marshal Philippe Pétain begins at Paris' *Palais de Justice*.

July 24: The USAAF raids the densely populated Japanese cities of Osaka and Nagoya with some 600 B-29 bombers.

July 26: Truman, Attlee, and Stalin issue a statement from Potsdam warning the Japanese that they face "utter destruction" if they do not surrender unconditionally. Tokyo will reject the ultimatum within the week.
• The USS *Indianapolis* delivers critical atomic bomb components to the bombing base at Tinian. • The Labour Party takes power in Britain, forcing out Conservative Winston Churchill. He will be replaced at Potsdam by the new prime minister, Clement Attlee, on the 27th.

July 27: The USAAF drops some 600,000 leaflets over 11 Japanese cities, warning civilians of probable air raids.

July 28: More than a dozen people die when a B-25 bomber pilot becomes disoriented in heavy fog and crashes into New York's Empire State Building. • Japan's *kamikaze* pilots sink their last Allied ship, as the USS *Callaghan* goes down off Okinawa. • More than 13,000 Japanese troops die, either from hostile fire or drowning, in an attempt to retreat over Burma's Sittang River.

July 29–30: The USS *Indianapolis* goes down after being struck by two torpedoes fired from a Japanese submarine. A series of operational errors will delay rescue for days, by which time three-quarters of the crew will perish, many from shark attacks.

July 30: The Japanese government instructs its civilian population to collect acorns to stave off starvation.

The first atomic explosion On July 16, 1945, a plutonium-core nuclear bomb was raised to the top of a 65-foot-high steel tower in the New Mexican desert about 30 miles southeast of Socorro. The Trinity test began when the bomb, called "the gadget," was detonated on July 16 at 5:30 A.M. The scientists, watching 10 miles from the tower, had disagreed on what would happen following the detonation—from nothing to the end of the world. Instead it caused an explosion that was about the equivalent of 19 kilotons of TNT. The flash it created brightened the surrounding mountains and emitted a mushroom cloud about eight miles high.

The Potsdam Conference President Harry Truman had his first and only meeting with the other Allied leaders, Winston Churchill and Joseph Stalin, in Potsdam, Germany, from July 17 to August 2, 1945. Churchill left before the conference ended because his party had lost the British general election; he was replaced by Clement Attlee. The Potsdam agreements clarified major postwar issues for Germany and Poland. The Potsdam Declaration called for Japan to surrender unconditionally or face complete destruction.

The Occupation of Korea

ALTHOUGH JAPAN INVADED and annexed Korea in 1910, it wasn't until 1937 that Japan launched a campaign to assimilate Koreans into the Japanese culture. The occupiers forbade the use of the Korean language and the practice of Christianity, and they demanded that all names be converted to Japanese.

Not only did Japan confiscate cattle, crops, and other material resources during the course of the Pacific war, but they also forced about 2.5 million Korean civilians into labor camps. Nearly one million young Korean men were conscripted into the Japanese army and sent to work at mines, factories, and military bases stretching across the Pacific. Thousands of Korean women were forced into sexual slavery as "comfort women" for Japanese soldiers.

At the urging of U.S. president Harry Truman, the Soviet Union declared war on Japan on August 8, 1945. Included in the declaration of war was the Soviet promise of support for the independence of Korea. Its troops, however, entered the northern districts of the country only days later. The instrument of surrender that Japan signed on September 2, 1945, called for Japanese troops north of the 38th parallel in Korea to surrender to the USSR, while the

Residents of Seoul, Korea, greeting American troops

troops to the south were to surrender to the Americans. Korea was no longer in the grip of Japan, but the nation became two, split north and south, Communist and free. The Korean peninsula would quickly become a locus of grave international friction.

The sinking of the *Indianapolis* Medical personnel tend to sailors from the USS *Indianapolis* who survived days in the water after the heavy cruiser was sunk by a Japanese submarine. *Indianapolis,* returning after delivering atomic bomb parts to Tinian, went down in 12 minutes on July 30, 1945. Though the ship was overdue at Leyte, no alert was issued. The survivors were accidentally spotted by a patrol aircraft on August 2. Of the 1,196 crew members, all but 317 died, many of them killed by sharks. In a remarkable miscarriage of justice, the Navy placed blame for the disaster on the ship's captain, Charles McVay, charging him with "failing to zig-zag."

Hiroshima and Nagasaki

THE SELECTION OF POTENTIAL atomic bomb targets began even before the Trinity test bomb was detonated near Alamogordo, New Mexico, on July 16, 1945. The Target Committee at Los Alamos recommended Hiroshima as a likely target as early as May. By late July, the list of potential targets included four cities: Hiroshima, Kokura, Kyoto, and Niigata. Kyoto was later dropped from the list due to its significance as a cultural center. Nagasaki took Kyoto's place.

Hiroshima remained the primary target, followed by Kokura and Nagasaki. Each city had military facilities of some type. Hiroshima was a headquarters and logistics base; Kokura had a large munitions plant; Nagasaki had various arms factories.

Of equal importance, these sprawling urban areas did not require precision bomb drops and would vividly demonstrate the destructiveness of the new weapons. Civilian casualties were not an issue. This was total war, and civilian populations were considered a legitimate target in the effort to break Japan's will to fight.

A-bomb blast above Hiroshima

At 8:15 A.M. on August 6, 1945, the B-29 Superfortress *Enola Gay* dropped a U-235 bomb nicknamed "Little Boy" on the primary target, Hiroshima. The resulting blast instantly killed upwards of 80,000 people and damaged or destroyed 90 percent of the city's buildings.

Three days later, the B-29 *Bock's Car*, carrying the plutonium bomb "Fat Man," aborted over its primary target, Kokura, due to heavy cloud cover. *Bock's Car* proceeded to Nagasaki, its secondary target, and dropped the second atomic bomb of the war shortly after 11 A.M. About 25,000 people were instantly killed. On August 15, Japan capitulated.

The morality of the bombings has been passionately debated. Critics maintain that Japan was already near surrender; that the bombs were intended primarily as a warning to the Russians; and that racism was a motivating factor. Proponents argue that the bombings saved hundreds of thousands of American lives—and, in the long term, perhaps millions of Japanese as well—by forcing a speedy surrender.

Truman's approval
A handwritten note by President Harry Truman approves the wording of a statement he plans to issue after the first atomic bomb is dropped on Japan. Sent in reply to a cable from Secretary of War Henry Stimson, the message reads, "Release [the statement] when ready but not sooner than August 2." The Allies' demand for unconditional surrender, sent to Japan on July 26, 1945, was rejected. The U.S. had successfully tested an A-bomb in mid-July, so by the end of the month Truman knew that at least one of the two A-bombs that remained would be dropped on Japan, sooner rather than later.

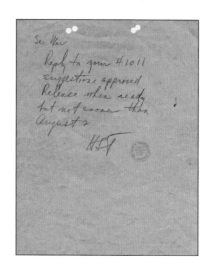

Tibbets in charge of A-bomb drop
Colonel Paul Tibbets stands by *Enola Gay*, the B-29 that carried the atomic bomb in the attack on Hiroshima. Tibbets spent months organizing and training the 509th Composite Group to meet the unique challenges of dropping atomic bombs, all with no assurance that the mission would actually take place. The successful bomb test in New Mexico in July 1945, followed by Japan's rejection of a demand for unconditional surrender, prompted President Truman to authorize use of the bomb.

"[H]e saw there were about twenty men, and they were all in exactly the same nightmarish state: their faces were wholly burned, their eyesockets were hollow, the fluid from their melted eyes had run down their cheeks."

—Journalist John Hersey, recounting what Father Wilhelm Kleinsorge (a German priest) had seen in Hiroshima

The Hiroshima blast Hiroshima is devastated following the atomic bomb attack by *Enola Gay* on August 6, 1945. The bomb detonated at 8:16 A.M., 1,900 feet above Shima Hospital. The fireball was so intense, it melted granite. The concussion obliterated virtually every building within two miles. A column of smoke and debris as high as Mount Everest rose into the sky. Upwards of 80,000 people were killed outright. Thousands would die later, many from radiation sickness. Nevertheless, the bombing probably saved lives elsewhere in Japan. Had the bomb not encouraged an end to the war, millions of Japanese might have died of starvation, of disease, in fire-bombing raids, and in efforts to resist a U.S. ground invasion of the home islands.

ATOMIC FIRE

BEYOND THE ZONE of utter death in which nothing remained alive, houses collapsed in a whirl of beams, bricks and girders. Up to about three miles from the center of the explosion lightly built houses were flattened as though they had been built of cardboard. Those who were inside were either killed or wounded. Those who managed to extricate themselves by some miracle found themselves surrounded by a ring of fire....

About half an hour after the explosion, whilst the sky all around Hiroshima was still cloudless, a fine rain began to fall on the town and went on for about five minutes. It was caused by the sudden rise of over-heated air to a great height, where it condensed and fell back as rain. Then a violent wind rose and the fires extended with terrible rapidity, because most Japanese houses are built only of timber and straw.

By the evening the fire began to die down and then it went out. There was nothing left to burn, Hiroshima had ceased to exist.

—Japanese journalist, as told to Marcel Junod of the Red Cross

How they died Stripped of flesh by the blast, the skeleton of a Hiroshima bombing victim lies in the rubble of a house next to an unbroken ceramic pot. Many of those exposed to the initial fireball were simply vaporized—some leaving only their silhouettes imprinted on walls or pavement. Others died of thermal burns,

from flying debris, in the collapse of buildings, or in the resulting fires. Japanese relief efforts began within days, as rice, wheat, sandals, and other necessities arrived. Medical care was less prompt, since many physicians had been killed or injured in the bombing. Thousands of victims succumbed within weeks to a mysterious illness later identified as radiation sickness. The Japanese government downplayed the carnage and expressed a determination to fight on.

1945

July 31: Former Vichy prime minister Pierre Laval surrenders in Austria.

August 2: Some 6,600 tons of bombs, a wartime high, are dropped overnight on several Japanese cities. The city of Toyama is almost totally destroyed.

August 3: The Allies emerge victorious from the Battle of the Breakthrough, bringing an end to all Japanese resistance in Burma. • The Allies tighten the noose around Japan as U.S. bombers complete their mining of Japan's major ports.

August 6: The United States drops an atomic bomb on Hiroshima, Japan, killing approximately 80,000 civilians. • A crash during an experimental jet test-flight claims the life of Major Richard Bong, the most successful American WWII flying ace (40 kills).

August 8: President Truman delivers a radio address in which he threatens to unleash more nuclear devastation on Japan. • The Soviet Union declares war against Japan.

August 9: With President Truman's signature, the United States becomes the first country to ratify the United Nations Charter. • Approximately 25,000 die as the U.S. drops a second atomic bomb, this one on Nagasaki, Japan.

August 11: The Japanese offer of surrender, delivered on August 10 and conditional on the continued sovereignty of Emperor Hirohito, is rejected by U.S. secretary of state James Byrnes.

August 12: Emperor Hirohito orders a divided Japanese government to surrender.

August 14: Washington orders the suspension of hostilities in Asia and the resumption of automobile production on the home front.

Americans killed by Hiroshima bomb
Sergeant Hugh Atkinson of Seattle was among an estimated 20 U.S. POWs killed in the atomic bomb blast at Hiroshima. Atkinson's B-24, *Lonesome Lady,* had been shot down on July 28, and he was imprisoned at Chugoko Military Police Headquarters near the epicenter of the blast. One account indicates that Atkinson survived the bombing and was later beaten to death. The possibility exists that some of the POWs were murdered before or after the atomic bomb attack. Two naval aviators who survived the initial explosion are known to have died of radiation sickness and beatings several days later.

The Nagasaki bomb
A workman stands next to "Fat Man," the atomic bomb dropped on Nagasaki on August 9, 1945. Unlike "Little Boy," the uranium bomb used against Hiroshima, Fat Man was an implosion-type weapon that employed plutonium. About 11 feet long and five feet in diameter, it was twice as wide as Little Boy. The new design resulted from the greater availability of plutonium and

the fact that the implosion method was less susceptible to accidental detonation than the simple "gun type" ignition used with Little Boy. The new design also yielded a greater blast.

The second A-bomb attack A mushroom cloud boils skyward over the industrial city of Nagasaki following the detonation of a plutonium bomb on August 9. The B-29 *Bock's Car,* piloted by Major Charles Sweeney, aborted an attack on Kokura due to heavy cloud cover and proceeded to Nagasaki, the secondary target. Finding a break in the clouds, he carried out the bombing shortly after 11 A.M. Heated controversy arose later over the necessity for the second bomb attack, but the mission was carried out because of the lack of reaction from the Japanese government following the Hiroshima bombing.

Results of the Nagasaki attack Pictured is ground zero in Nagasaki before and after the bombing. Though the city had good bomb shelters, many Japanese had become blasé about air raids and ignored the warning sirens on August 9. Due in part to the hilly topography, damage was confined to an area about 2.3 miles by 1.9 miles. Fire was limited by waterways. Some medical services survived, and even train service continued. The number of deaths was lower than at Hiroshima, with the Japanese government assessing the figure at 25,000. Ironically, Emperor Hirohito was at that very moment trying to decide how to end the war.

Japanese "bear the unbearable" A Japanese prisoner of war on Guam cries as he listens to Emperor Hirohito's radio broadcast announcing Japan's surrender. Hearing the voice of their "living god" for the first time, the populace strained to make out his message through the formal language and poor reception. "The war situation has developed

not necessarily to Japan's advantage," observed the Emperor. The Japanese people "must now bear the unbearable and endure the unendurable." Millions wept. Some military officers committed suicide, while others talked of continued resistance. But for many Japanese, beneath the grief and shock was also a sense of relief. The war was over.

Japan surrenders On August 14, 1945, the Japanese news agency Domei announced that the war was over. A crowd gathered before Emperor Hirohito's palace. People wept and bowed to the ground in disgrace, repeating "Forgive us, O Emperor, our efforts were not enough." Hirohito's subjects heard his voice for the first time ever the next day at noon, Tokyo time, when he formally announced the end of the

war and directed the Japanese people to cooperate with the Allied occupation. American newspapers splashed the news in very large type on their front pages on the 14th and 15th of August.

V-J Day celebration On August 15, more than two million people crowded into New York's Times Square anxiously awaiting word that the war with Japan was over. *The New York Times* agreed to keep its revolving news sign active until an announcement was made. Finally, at 7:03 P.M. Eastern Time, a message flashed across the *Times* sign stating, "Official—Truman Announces Japanese Surrender." The pent-up energy of the revelers exploded in a whirl of hysteria. Strangers hugged and kissed each other. This picture of a sailor kissing a nurse in Times Square is not the famous photograph taken by Alfred Eisenstaedt but one taken simultaneously by Navy photographer Victor Jorgensen.

1945

August 14: A coup attempt, in which a group of Japanese army officers tries to take the Imperial Palace and prevent surrender, fails.

August 15: Charles de Gaulle commutes the death sentence of Marshal Pétain (age 89) to life imprisonment. • The Allies celebrate Victory in Japan (V-J) Day. Meanwhile, Emperor Hirohito broadcasts a message to the Japanese people that he has agreed to unconditional surrender.

August 16: Underscoring the issues that will define the next great "war" of the 20th century, Winston Churchill delivers an address warning of an "iron curtain" descending across Europe.

August 18: Indian nationalist leader Subhas Chandra Bose dies when his plane crashes into the sea off Formosa.

August 21: Having accomplished what it set out to do, the United States brings the Lend-Lease aid program to a close.

August 23: Moscow announces that Japanese resistance has ended in the former Manchurian puppet state of Manchukuo. Manchuria is completely occupied by Soviet troops.

August 28: Indictments are handed down on Nazi war criminals, including Hermann Göring, Joachim von Ribbentrop, Rudolf Hess, and Martin Bormann.

August 30: U.S. Army and Marine forces arrive on the Japanese home islands to begin military occupation.

August 31: Truman writes British prime minister Clement Attlee, asking him to allow some 100,000 European Jews to immigrate to British-controlled Palestine. • General MacArthur becomes the first foreign authority in a millennium to assume power in Japan when he establishes the Supreme Allied Command in Tokyo.

"Tokyo was like a giant wake. It was like walking into a cemetery. The people wouldn't even look at us."

—NICK CARIDAS, U.S. ARMY

Tokyo in ruins Tokyo lies in ruins after Japan's surrender. By war's end, B-29 raids had transformed more than half of the city into a wasteland. With rice severely rationed, civilians were advised to supplement their diets with acorns and sawdust. In March, the cabbage ration was one leaf per person every three days. Hundreds of thousands were still homeless. Cooking and heating fuel had been in short supply for months. Malnutrition, malaria, and typhoid were widespread. The bombings did produce one surplus item: plenty of debris to use for kindling.

POWs are freed and fed American women prepare food after being freed from Japanese captivity in Manila, Philippines, in 1945. For most freed prisoners, liberation meant adequate food for the first time in years. Spam, cocoa, cigarettes, gum, and clothing were airdropped on prison camps throughout Asia, often accompanied by leaflets that warned: "Do not overeat." Within six weeks, most POWs were on their way home, although many would be plagued by health and psychological problems for the rest of their lives. Suicide, alcoholism, and depression were common.

The Soviet War Against Japan

UNTIL 1945, JAPAN AND THE Soviet Union held to their Neutrality Pact of April 1941. Had they not, each nation would have faced a two-front war. This agreement ended, however, due to the Soviet Union's interest in expansion in East Asia and pressure from the Soviets' Western Allies.

At the Yalta Conference in February 1945, Joseph Stalin promised Winston Churchill and Franklin Roosevelt that the Soviets would attack Japan within three months of the end of the war in Europe. Unaware of this, the Japanese government expected the Soviet Union either to mediate a compromised peace or to join Japan in war against the United States and Britain. Instead, on August 8 the Soviet Union declared war on Japan.

Russian soldiers in Korea

About two hours later, Marshal Vasilevsky unleashed three Soviet army groups against the Japanese in Korea and Manchukuo. Both the Kurile Islands and southern Sakhalin figured among their objectives. The Soviets mustered more than a million men to attack the Kwantung Army's 500,000 poorly trained and badly equipped troops. The Soviets also deployed some 5,000 tanks and 5,000 aircraft.

The Japanese army, fooled as to the attack's direction and timing, was overwhelmed in nine days of lightning assaults, panic, and massacre. More than 80,000 were killed, nearly 10 times the Soviet total. Some Japanese survivors fought until August 21, six days after Hirohito had announced the surrender. More than 500,000 Japanese prisoners in Manchuria and Korea were sent to Siberia.

Soviets battle Japanese in China

A Soviet soldier peers into a Japanese fort somewhere in China on August 23, 1945. American planners had originally thought that the Soviet entry into the war would be necessary to divert Japanese forces in China and Manchuria during the invasion of Japan's home islands. The Soviet Union's last-minute declaration of war on Japan on August 8 became more a political headache than a military benefit for the U.S. The Soviets saw intervention as an inexpensive way to reap the spoils of war in Japan's final hours. Faced with 1.6 million Soviet troops, Japanese forces in China collapsed. About 700,000 went into captivity.

1945

September 2: Japanese officials formally surrender to the Allies aboard the USS *Missouri* in Tokyo Bay. • Vietnamese nationalist leader Ho Chi Minh proclaims Vietnam's independence, despite the objections of the ruling French.

September 5: Iva Toguri D'Aquino, the Japanese American pro-Axis radio broadcaster known as Tokyo Rose, is arrested in Yokohama, Japan. • British authorities reoccupy Singapore.

September 7: The Allies stage a victory parade in occupied Berlin.

September 8: The United States stations troops in South Korea in accordance with an agreement between Washington and Moscow.

September 9: The repatriation of American troops begins with Operation Magic Carpet. • Some one million Japanese troops surrender to General Chiang Kai-shek in Nanking, China.

September 10: Former Norwegian premier Vidkun Quisling is found guilty of treason, for which he will be executed on October 24.

September 11: Former Japanese prime minister General Tojo Hideki shoots himself rather than submit to arrest by American troops. He survives, however, and will live in U.S. custody until his execution in 1948.

September 16: Britain reestablishes authority over its Hong Kong colony, as the Japanese garrison officially surrenders.

September 19: Britain's Labour government under Clement Attlee begins negotiations with India's Congress Party regarding Indian independence.

September 26: President Truman announces the equitable division of what is left of the German fleet between the three principal Allies.

Allies reeducate Germany's students
Rebuilding the German education system was one of the highest priorities for the Allies. In those sections of Germany and Berlin controlled by the U.S., Britain, and France, the emphasis was placed on reeducating youth—who had been raised for years on Fascist doctrines—in the fundamentals of democracy. In the

Soviet sectors, Marxist and Leninist principles were taught. The first step in the denazification process was to replace any teacher who was unwilling or unable to give up his or her Fascist beliefs. Before this new educational process could begin, however, students were required to turn in their Nazi-oriented textbooks (*pictured*).

Japan's surrender delegation Led by Foreign Minister Shigemitsu Mamoru (*with cane*) and Army Chief of Staff Umezu Yoshijiro (*to his left*), the Japanese delegation arrived aboard the USS *Missouri* in Tokyo Bay on September 2, 1945, to sign the instrument of surrender. Though the formal terms called for unconditional surrender, it had been inferred that the emperor would retain nominal authority. Umezu was present under duress; he agreed to participate only after a personal appeal by the emperor. Shigemitsu, who felt the war must end, viewed his assignment as "a painful but profitable task." Unsure of protocol, the 11-member delegation had been advised to put on a *shiran kao* (nonchalant face) during the proceedings. Civilians should remove their hats and bow, they were told. Military personnel should salute.

Japanese surprised by GIs' kindness A Japanese civilian watches curiously as elements of the U.S. 33rd Infantry Division come ashore during the occupation of Japan. Wild rumors prior to the American occupation told of rapes and looting. Women and valuables were hidden, and some factories issued poison capsules to female workers. Despite Japanese fears, American troops were generally well behaved, and the occupation proceeded smoothly. "We had images of glaring demons with horns sprouting from their heads," recalled Naokata Sasaki, a young student at the time. "We were disappointed, of course. No horns at all." To his surprise, the Americans seemed quite friendly and even gave the children chocolate.

The surrender ceremonies General Douglas MacArthur stands at the broadcast microphone as General Umezu signs the instrument of surrender on behalf of the Japanese Imperial Headquarters. Foreign Minister Shigemitsu signed on behalf of the emperor. MacArthur signed on behalf of the Allied powers, while Admiral Chester Nimitz signed for the United States. Those in attendance included representatives of all the Allied powers, as well as such military officers as Admiral William Halsey and Lieutenant General Jonathan Wainwright. The ceremony, broadcast worldwide, lasted only 23 minutes, ending at 9:25 A.M. Minutes later, hundreds of Navy fighters and Army B-29s roared overhead in a pre-arranged show of American military might.

MacArthur takes charge in Japan This widely circulated photograph of General Douglas MacArthur and Emperor Hirohito, taken on September 27, 1945, shocked the Japanese public, as it left little doubt as to who was now in charge of Japan. MacArthur successfully resisted efforts to put the defeated emperor on trial as a war criminal. He

Tokyo Rose Iva Toguri D'Aquino (*pictured*), a Japanese American woman, was trapped in Japan after the attack on Pearl Harbor. She found a job at Radio Tokyo and eventually became a broadcaster named Orphan Annie on an anti-American program called *The Zero Hour*. When she returned to the U.S. after the war, she was tried for treason. However, it became evident that no one "Tokyo Rose" had existed. It was a name created by American troops to signify a number of women who broadcast anti-American propaganda during the war. Nevertheless, D'Aquino was found guilty of eight counts of treason. She was sentenced to 10 years in prison, and was released after six years. President Gerald Ford pardoned her in 1977.

believed Hirohito would be of greater value as a symbol of continuity, as one who would discourage resistance to the occupation, and as an instrument to transform Japan into a democracy with a minimum of social upheaval. The emperor cooperated. He renounced his "divinity" and left MacArthur as the most powerful man in Japan.

AFTERMATH OF WAR

OCTOBER 1945–SEPTEMBER 1951

"The human animal and his emotions change not much from age to age. He must change now or he faces absolute and complete destruction, and maybe the insect age or an atmosphereless planet will succeed him."

—President Harry Truman,
DIARY ENTRY, 1946

THE END OF WORLD WAR II opened the way for the building of a new world order. It was a very different order from the one Germany, Italy, and Japan had envisioned when they divided the world into spheres of influence in the Tripartite Pact of September 1940.

In the first place, the war proved to be a victory for European communism, which only a few years before—as German forces bore down on Moscow—had seemed close to defeat. Yet it was also a victory for Western liberal capitalism, as the Western Allies set out to secure free economies and parliamentary politics in Western Europe after years of economic crisis and political authoritarianism.

One of the few issues on which the wartime Allies could agree was the International Tribunal, which put German leaders on trial at Nuremberg for crimes against peace and for crimes against humanity. The trial opened in November 1945. In October 1946, all but three of the 22 defendants were found guilty. The attempt to create a new framework of international law was compromised throughout by the knowledge that Stalin's Soviet Union was just as guilty of aggressive war and systematic violation of human rights. Nevertheless, the trials did promote a desire for a new international morality. In 1948 the United Nations agreed on a convention outlawing genocide. A year later, a new Geneva Convention established clear rules for the conduct of war. And in 1950, the European Convention on Human Rights was established to protect human rights and fundamental freedoms.

Children cling to the branches of a tree near Berlin's Brandenburg Gate in June 1948 as a U.S. cargo plane roars overhead. The plane bears food and supplies for the beleaguered city, which had been blockaded by the Soviets. The Allies won this early test of wills with Stalin, but the global struggle was just beginning.

On almost every other issue, the Soviets and the Western powers strongly disagreed. The future of Germany could not be settled, since neither side was prepared to see a reunited German state dominated by one of the two ideologies. In January 1947, the American and British zones of occupation were merged into Bizonia. Two years later, with the addition of the southern French zone, a separate West German state was created based on a democratic, federal constitution. Stalin blockaded Berlin in 1948, which was situated in the Soviet zone but was jointly administered by the four occupying

President Harry Truman signs the North Atlantic Treaty, which marked the beginning of NATO and the end of any lingering hopes that the Soviets and the West could collaborate constructively in the postwar world. Positions would only harden as each side suspiciously eyed the other over the so-called "iron curtain."

powers. Then, when the blockade proved ineffective (due to the Western Allies' airlift of supplies into the city), Stalin created a rival German Democratic Republic in the Soviet zone, run by a Communist-dominated regime. No formal treaty ending the war could be signed under these circumstances, and Germany remained partitioned.

The rest of the European continent was split between a capitalist west and a Communist east, divided by what Winston Churchill famously called an "iron curtain." When President Harry Truman announced in 1947 that the Western world would defend the right of free peoples everywhere who were "resisting subjugation," Stalin reluctantly accepted the division of the world into "two camps." In 1947, U.S. secretary of state George Marshall convened a conference in Paris to draw up plans for financial aid to the struggling economies of Europe. The Soviet delegation responded by walking out when it became clear that aid would be forthcoming only if the Soviet Union agreed to international scrutiny of its economic policy.

Over the next two years, Communist regimes were confirmed in all the states of Eastern Europe occupied by the Red Army. Political pluralism was ended in those states, and Stalinist economies and police systems were imposed. In Yugoslavia, Josip Broz Tito succeeded in establishing the only Communist state independent of Moscow. A savage civil war in Greece ended in 1949 with the defeat of the Communist insurgents. In Austria, a treaty allowed the creation of a nonaligned parliamentary state after 10 years of division into occupation zones.

In eastern Asia, the end of the war brought a long period of turmoil. In the European colonies occupied by Japan, liberation movements were established—some strongly Communist in outlook. In Indochina, Indonesia, and Malaya, wars were fought against the colonial powers as well as between rival factions. The messy aftermath of war precipitated the final crisis of the old European imperialism; by the early 1950s, most of Southeast Asia was independent. In Burma and India, Britain could not maintain its presence. India was divided into two states in 1947, India (Hindu) and Pakistan (Muslim), and Burma was granted independence a year later.

Japan was not restored to full sovereignty until after the San Francisco Treaty was signed on September 8, 1951. The emperor was retained, but the military was emasculated and a parliamentary regime had been installed. Japanese prewar possessions were divided up. Manchuria was restored to China in 1946 (though only after the Soviet Union had removed more than half the industrial equipment left behind by the Japanese). Taiwan was returned to Chinese control. Korea was occupied jointly by the Soviet Union and the United States, and two independent states—one Communist, one democratic—were established there in 1948.

News that Russia had successfully tested an atomic bomb in September 1949 shattered any complacency in the West about the seriousness of the so-called "Soviet threat." Soviet possession of the bomb brought military parity to the ideological struggle and initiated a different form of conflict, soon to be dubbed "the Cold War."

The most unstable area remained China, where the prewar conflict between Chiang Kai-shek's Nationalists and the Chinese Communists led by Mao Zedong was resumed on a large scale in 1945. After four years of warfare, the Nationalist forces were defeated and Chiang withdrew to the island of Taiwan. The People's Republic of China was declared in 1949, and a long program of rural reform and industrialization was set in motion. The victory of Chinese communism encouraged Stalin to allow the Communist regime in North Korea to embark on war against the South in the belief that America lacked the commitment for another military conflict.

The Korean War began on June 25, 1950, when the troops of Kim Il Sung crossed the 38th parallel, the agreed-upon border between the two states. By this stage, the international order had begun to solidify into two heavily armed camps. In 1949 the Soviet Union tested its first atomic bomb. That same year, the U.S. helped organize a defensive pact, the North Atlantic Treaty Organization (NATO), to link the major Western states together for possible armed action against the Communist threat. By 1951 Chinese forces were engaged in the Korean conflict, exacerbating concerns that another world war—this time with nuclear weapons—might become a reality. The optimism of 1945 had, in only half a decade, given way to renewed fears that international anarchy and violence might be the normal condition of the modern world.

1945-46

October 9, 1945: French collaborator Pierre Laval is sentenced to death in a French court.

October 24, 1945: The United Nations Charter is ratified by its five permanent members: the United States, Britain, France, China, and the Soviet Union.

November 13, 1945: Free French leader General Charles de Gaulle is named president of France's provisional government.

November 20, 1945: The Nuremberg Trials open. For the next 10 months, a tribunal comprised of Allied jurists will pass judgment on scores of Nazi war criminals.

December 6, 1945: The U.S. government commits to a multibillion-dollar loan to prop up the British economy.

1946: The U.S. government closes the camps in which some 120,000 ethnic Japanese in the American West had been incarcerated since 1942.

January 1, 1946: Emperor Hirohito addresses his subjects and tells them that he is not, contrary to popular belief, a divine being.

January 17, 1946: The United Nations Security Council convenes in London to agree on procedural rules for the international body.

January 24, 1946: The International Atomic Energy Commission is established to help regulate emerging nuclear weapons technology.

March 2, 1946: Nationalist leader Ho Chi Minh is elected president of Vietnam.

March 5, 1946: Winston Churchill delivers his seminal "iron curtain" speech at Missouri's Westminster College.

Coming home and readjusting The 1946 Academy Award for best picture went to *The Best Years of Our Lives,* which chronicled the return home of an Army Air Force officer, an infantry sergeant, and a sailor after the war. The film depicted the difficulties they and their families experienced during the readjustment. It was an accurate portrayal of what husbands and wives faced after years of separation. Not only had the GIs changed after two or more years overseas, but the experience had changed many wives and older children, who had taken on greater responsibilities in the absence of husbands and fathers. Many young children met their fathers for the first time, as was the case with the Deal family, pictured at La Guardia Airport in New York City.

Unease in Korea An American soldier chats with a female Russian officer in Korea in October 1945. Despite the outward show of friendliness, the mutual mistrust that would lead to the Cold War had already begun. Soviet troops poured into Japanese-occupied Korea well before U.S. forces were prepared to establish a presence there. U.S. leaders feared that the Russians would seize the entire peninsula and possibly move into Japan as well. An agreement was hastily reached that the Russians would stop at the 38th parallel, which roughly divided Korea in half. Much to Americans' relief, the Russians abided by the pact.

DP Camps

THE SUFFERING OF MILLIONS of Europeans did not end on May 7, 1945, the day Germany surrendered. More than 11 million displaced persons (DPs), freed from slave labor and concentration camps, were now alone, hundreds of miles from home. Many returned to their towns or cities by the end of 1945, but almost two million either had no home to return to or feared going home. In particular, Jews of Eastern Europe anticipated continued persecution should they return to their homelands.

To provide for the welfare of those remaining behind, DP camps were created throughout Germany. Initially, the accommodations in the camps were atrocious. "Housing conditions here [in Babenhausen] are horrible," repeated one displaced person. "They used to be stalls for the horses of the Third Reich; now they are homes for the surviving Jews. Jews did not want to leave the trains so as to have to move in here."

When President Harry Truman learned of the conditions in these camps, he delegated Earl Harrison, dean of the University of Pennsylvania Law School, to study this problem. Harrison visited 30 DP camps before issuing a report to the president. "Beyond knowing that they are no

German DPs preparing to leave Berlin, October 1945

longer in danger of the gas chambers, torture or other forms of violent death," Harrison wrote, they were left to "wonder and frequently ask what 'liberation' means." Eventually, life in the camps improved. All but one camp closed by 1952, and the last facility suspended operations in 1957.

The plight of displaced persons
During the winter of 1945–46, upwards of 20 million displaced persons either lived in camps or struggled to survive in all major cities of Europe. Those pictured here were among 150 people who walked from Poland to Berlin to find food and shelter. Reported *Life* magazine in its January 7, 1946, issue: "In Warsaw nearly 1 million live in holes in the ground." Vital resources were lacking in those countries most affected by the war. Stated *Life*: "[I]n Greece fuel supplies are terribly low because the Nazis, during their occupation, decimated the forests. In Italy the wheat harvest, which was a meager 3,450,000 million tons in 1944, fell to an unendurable 1,304,000 million tons in 1945."

1946-47

April 28, 1946: The International Military Tribunal for the Far East indicts Japanese war minister Tojo Hideki as a war criminal, charging him with 55 counts. He will be sentenced to death in November 1948.

July 1, 1946: The United States detonates a plutonium bomb, "Able," off Bikini Atoll, as part of Operation Crossroads, an effort to learn more about the power of the atomic bomb. A second detonation, code-named "Baker," will follow on the 25th.

July 4, 1946: Fueled by a false kidnapping allegation, a pogrom in Kielce, Poland, claims the lives of some 40 Jews.

July 16, 1946: Forty-three members of the *Waffen-SS* are sentenced to death for the December 1944 Malmedy massacre of American POWs during the Battle of the Bulge. They eventually will be released.

October 1, 1946: High-ranking Nazi officials, including Hermann Göring, Hans Frank, Joachim von Ribbentrop, and Arthur Seyss-Inquart, are sentenced to hang by the Allied court at Nuremberg. Göring will escape this fate by taking his own life shortly before his scheduled execution.

November 3, 1946: A new Japanese constitution, one that resolves that the nation will never again "be visited with the horrors of war through the action of government," is proclaimed by Emperor Hirohito.

December 31, 1946: Harry Truman issues a presidential proclamation declaring an official end to World War II.

February 17, 1947: The United States launches The Voice of America, a pro-West radio station, to broadcast to the Soviet Union and Eastern Europe.

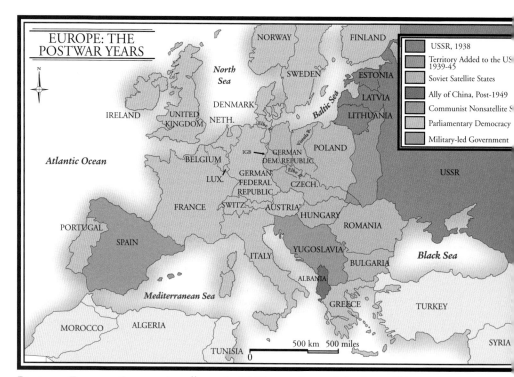

EUROPE: THE POSTWAR YEARS

Legend:
- USSR, 1938
- Territory Added to the US 1939-45
- Soviet Satellite States
- Ally of China, Post-1949
- Communist Nonsatellite S
- Parliamentary Democracy
- Military-led Government

Postwar Europe Germany's collapse in 1945 transformed the face of Europe. Millions became refugees as national boundaries were redrawn. Germany was partitioned into four zones of occupation. The Allied Zones merged into the Federal Republic of Germany in 1949, while the Soviet occupied zone became the German Democratic Republic. In the east, the Soviets expanded their borders at the expense of Germany, Finland, and Poland, and annexed the Baltic countries of Latvia, Estonia, and Lithuania. Communist states in the east soon arose to confront the western democracies.

German cities clean up, rebuild During the war, approximately 50 percent of Germany's infrastructure was destroyed. Dresden was one of the hardest hit cities. Eight square miles of Dresden, which had boasted some of the most beautiful baroque architecture in Europe, were destroyed when Allied bombers dropped more than 5,000 tons of high explosives and incendiary bombs on the city in February 1945. Following the war, the ruins were cleared and

replaced by modern structures. The *Dresden Frauenkirche,* a Lutheran church, was an exception, as its decaying ruins were left untouched. After the reunification of Germany, the church was restored for $175 million.

German children barter and beg Young children, such as this boy, sold or bartered whatever they could to survive on the streets of Berlin. Here the child, an orphan, attempts to trade his father's Iron Cross, earned for bravery in battle, for cigarettes. A black market developed in Berlin, with cigarettes, liquor, and chocolate as three

of the commodities most sought by Berliners from occupation troops. For many months after the war, German children roamed the streets scavenging or begging for food.

> The Sakawa is manned now by a Jap crew but a prize crew is preparing to board her soon and condition her for a trip to the Marshalls where she will be used in the Atom Bomb Tests.

A-bomb tests at Bikini The U.S. postwar nuclear tests at Bikini Atoll were designed to examine the effects of atomic bombs on naval vessels. Bikini's 167 inhabitants were forcibly relocated in early 1946, and 71 surplus and captured ships were anchored in the lagoon to serve as targets. Other targets included planes and 5,400 rats, goats, and pigs. Two separate atomic blasts in July 1946 sank some ships and left others heavily contaminated with radiation. Whatever the scientific gain, the highly public tests only exacerbated deteriorating relations between the U.S. and the Soviet Union.

Women vote in Japanese election Japanese women cast votes for the first time in their nation's history in what was perhaps the most visible sign of Japan's postwar political transformation. Frustrated by Japan's lack of progress with creating a new constitution, General Douglas MacArthur assigned the role to members of his own staff. The result was a constitution based more on British parliamentary rule than on the U.S. model. The document limited the emperor to a symbolic role and gave women the right to vote. Women reacted enthusiastically. In April 1946, millions of women voted in the election that gave Japan its first modern prime minister, Yoshida Shigeru.

Indians fight for independence Indian statesmen and National Congress Party leaders Jawaharlal Nehru (*left*) and Mohandas Gandhi (*right*) viewed World War II as an opportunity to shed the yoke of British colonialism and establish an independent India. Though the British governor-general used his own authority to bring India into the war in 1939, Indian leaders pushed for self-government in exchange for cooperation. In 1942 the British Cripps Mission instituted an interim government and promised full independence after the war. More than two million Indians eventually served on the Allied side during the war, and 24,000 were killed. When the war ended in 1945, Indians pressed for the independence that was promised. On August 15, 1947, power was finally transferred and India was declared a free nation.

1947-48

June 14, 1947: The Auschwitz-Birkenau Memorial and Museum opens its first permanent exhibition on the seventh anniversary of the arrival of the Nazi camp's first prisoners.

July 1947: In an article printed in the journal *Foreign Affairs,* senior U.S. State Department official George Kennan (under the alias "X") expresses his theory about containing Soviet Union expansion. This policy of containment will become the basis of the Truman Administration's foreign policy.

July 18, 1947: In an effort to stem the tide of Jewish nationalism in Britain's Palestinian mandate, the British navy sends the ship *President Warfield* and its 4,500 Jewish refugee passengers back to Germany.

November 29, 1947: UN Resolution 181, the partition plan for Palestine, is approved by the General Assembly. The Arab states thereupon invade the new Jewish state.

April 3, 1948: The Marshall Plan, which ultimately will provide more than $13 billion (U.S.) for the reconstruction of war-torn Europe, is signed into law by President Truman.

May 14, 1948: Britain's mandate to govern Palestine expires. Palestine is divided into the State of Israel and an Arab state. The Jewish National Council proclaims the independent State of Israel.

May 15, 1948: Egyptian, Syrian, and Jordanian forces invade the one-day-old State of Israel. Israel resists, and will soon go on the offensive.

June 25, 1948: President Truman signs the Displaced Persons Act, which will allow more than 200,000 European refugees to settle in the United States.

Jews and Palestine Jewish relations with Britain remained strong prior to the start of World War II, when the Jewish population in Palestine approached 400,000. The Arabs resented this immigration, and an uprising broke out throughout Palestine. To ensure that the Arabs did not side with the Axis nations, the British issued the White Paper of 1939, which limited the number of Jews who could immigrate to Palestine to 15,000 per year. This marked a death sentence for many European Jews attempting to escape the Holocaust. This photo of Jews hoisting the Star of David was taken in 1946. The White Paper was rescinded when the State of Israel was established in May 1948.

Bombing of the King David Hotel Driven to desperation by British stonewalling on the issue of a Jewish state, Jewish nationalist groups in Palestine campaigned to evict the British and establish the nation of Israel. On July 22, 1946, the *Irgun Tseva'i Le'ummi* (National Military Organization), founded by dissident Hagana members, blew up Jerusalem's King David Hotel (*pictured*), the headquarters of the British government and military in Palestine. Seventy-six Jews, Arabs, and British were killed, and dozens of people were injured. The *Irgun* subsequently claimed that sufficient warning to evacuate had been given; the British denied this. Regardless, the bombing hardened British resolve to block a Jewish state.

Far East War Crimes Trials

IN SPRING 1946, 55 COUNTS were brought against 28 Japanese political and military leaders in the International Military Tribunal for the Far East (IMTFE). Emperor Hirohito was not among those indicted. The trial was conducted in both English and Japanese, which prolonged proceedings. Defendants were permitted to choose their own counsel, call witnesses, and request evidence. The accused pleaded not guilty, and their lawyers unsuccessfully challenged the trial's legality.

The prosecution needed 192 days to present its case, and the defense lasted 225 days. More than 400 witnesses were involved in the trial. Chief prosecutor Joseph Keenan (an American) exhorted the judges to give the "sternest punishment known to law" to the 25 defendants still eligible for sentencing. He repeatedly urged that the verdict should deter future war, which the Allies considered a fundamental symbolic purpose of the trial. The defense argued that the war was based not on aggressive conspiracy, but on self-defense.

Judge William Webb (of Australia) announced the jurists' majority opinion in November 1948. All defendants were found guilty. Former prime minister Tojo Hideki, former foreign minister/prime minister Hirota Koki, and five generals were sentenced to death by hanging. Of the other

Tojo Hideki (*center, behind microphone*) during the trial

18 defendants, 16 received life imprisonment, one 20 years, and another seven years.

The judgment stated that the Japanese government had secretly ordered or willfully permitted atrocities in every theater of the war. All seven condemned to death were found guilty of conventional war crimes. They were executed on December 23, 1948, in Tokyo. Elsewhere in the East, thousands more Japanese were tried for conventional war crimes.

Life returns in Hiroshima
Women tend to gardens near newly built wooden barracks in Hiroshima in 1946, as the city takes the first struggling steps toward rebirth. Bomb survivors first built huts from scavenged materials. Three months later, with aid from the occupation government, construction began on wooden barracks to house the thousands of people returning to the city. Electricity, transportation, and other functions were gradually restored. Despite rumors that nothing would grow in Hiroshima for 75 years, gardens provided food with no immediate ill effects. Moreover, the health impact of lingering radiation proved less severe than many had feared.

1948-50

June 27, 1948: The United States, Britain, and France respond to the Soviet blockade of Berlin by effecting an airlift of supplies to the two million people in the city's western sector.

December 9, 1948: The United Nations General Assembly enacts the Convention on the Prevention and Punishment of the Crime of Genocide.

January 25, 1949: The trial of Axis Sally, who was a Nazi propagandist to American troops in Europe, begins in Washington, D.C.

April 4, 1949: The United States, Canada, and several Western European nations sign the North Atlantic Treaty, establishing the North Atlantic Treaty Organization (NATO).

May 1949: Realizing that their blockade of western Berlin has strengthened the resolve of the other Allies and led directly to the formation of NATO, the Soviets decide to lift it.

July 20, 1949: Israel signs the third of three armistice agreements, with Syria, to end the 1948 war. Agreements with Egypt, Lebanon, and Transjordan were signed earlier in the year.

August 29, 1949: The Soviet Union detonates an atomic bomb at its Kazakhstan test site.

October 1, 1949: In a resounding victory for China's Communist Party, Mao Zedong proclaims the People's Republic of China.

January 1950: The USSR and China recognize the Democratic Republic of Vietnam.

January 10, 1950: The Soviet delegate walks off the Security Council in disgust after the UN retains Nationalist China as the holder of China's Council seat.

22 tried for war crimes A total of 13 war crime trials against more than 200 persons were held in Nuremberg, Germany, from 1945 to 1949. The trial that received the most attention was the first, which involved 22 prominent Nazi leaders—all of whom were tried on one or more of four war-crime counts. Throughout the trial, Hermann Göring (*far left*) was a leader of the defendants, often dictating their responses to prosecution witnesses. Göring used his skills in manipulation to try to outwit the American prosecutor.

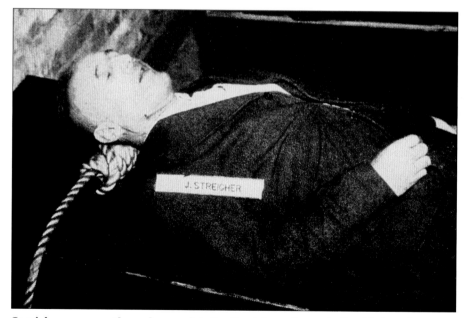

Streicher among those hanged Julius Streicher, pictured after his hanging, was the editor of *Der Stürmer,* the most popular anti-Semitic publication in Germany before and during the war. The June 1939 edition was a typical issue, depicting on the front page a "Jewish devil-snake" attacking a topless Aryan maiden. Streicher was one of the 22 defendants in the first Nuremberg trial—and among the 12 sentenced to death. He was the most defiant of those hanged, exclaiming "Heil Hitler" moments before his death on October 16, 1946.

> **"The wrongs which we seek to condemn and punish have been so calculated, so malignant, and so devastating that civilization cannot tolerate their being ignored because it cannot survive their being repeated."**
>
> —American chief prosecutor Judge Robert Jackson, Nuremberg War Crimes Tribunal

The Nuremberg Trials

FROM NOVEMBER 1945 TO OCTOBER 1946, the Allies imposed their judicial retribution upon those leading Nazis who had plunged the world into war in 1939—those who had inflicted unprecedented devastation, untold misery, and death on an industrial scale upon so many nations. Twenty-two prominent Nazis were tried for crimes against peace, crimes against humanity, and war crimes. It was considered poetic justice that the International Military Tribunal convened at Nuremberg—the city that had hosted spectacular party rallies during the Nazis' consolidation of power in the 1930s.

Judges and prosecutors were represented equally by the United States, Great Britain, France, and the Soviet Union. The accused Nazi leaders, military commanders, ministers, and other key figures are listed below, with sentence.

Illustration by Kukryniksky, a trio of Russian cartoonists

Martin Bormann (in absentia), deputy *Führer* (death)

Karl Dönitz, navy supreme commander (10 years)

Hans Frank, governor-general of Poland (death)

Wilhelm Frick, interior minister (death)

Hans Fritzsche, head of radio for the propaganda ministry (acquitted)

Walther Funk, president of the *Reichsbank* (life)

Hermann Göring, *Reichsmarschall* and head of the *Luftwaffe* (death)

Rudolf Hess, deputy *Führer* (life)

Alfred Jodl, chief of the *Wehrmacht* operations staff (death)

Ernst Kaltenbrunner, chief of the security police (death)

Wilhelm Keitel, chief of the *Wehrmacht* high command (death)

Constantin von Neurath, foreign minister and protector of Bohemia and Moravia (15 years)

Franz von Papen, chancellor of Germany (acquitted)

Erich Raeder, navy supreme commander (life)

Joachim von Ribbentrop, foreign minister (death)

Alfred Rosenberg, minister for occupied Soviet territory (death)

Fritz Sauckel, labor plenipotentiary (death)

Baldur von Schirach, Hitler Youth leader (20 years)

Hjalmar Schacht, economics minister (acquitted)

Arthur Seyss-Inquart, interior minister and governor of Austria, then commissioner for the Netherlands (death)

Albert Speer, armaments minister (20 years)

Julius Streicher, anti-Semitic publisher (death)

The tribunal also cited the Nazi leadership, the SS, the SD, and the Gestapo as criminal organizations. Robert Ley, head of the German labor front, was also indicted, but he committed suicide in prison before being brought to trial. The most prominent of those condemned cheated the hangman, as Göring committed suicide in his cell on October 15, 1946.

1950

January 12, 1950: A speech by Dean Acheson, U.S. secretary of state, is interpreted as implying that South Korea is not under the protection of the United States.

January 23, 1950: Israel's *Knesset* proclaims Jerusalem the capital of Israel.

January 25, 1950: U.S. government official Alger Hiss, an alleged Soviet spy who escaped a treason trial due to the expiration of the statute of limitations, is sentenced to five years for perjuring himself while under investigation.

January 27, 1950: Klaus Fuchs, a German who had helped the U.S. and Great Britain build atomic bombs, confesses to passing nuclear secrets to the Soviets.

February 9, 1950: In a speech in Wheeling, West Virginia, U.S. senator Joseph McCarthy (R–WI) asserts that Communists have infiltrated the State Department.

April 1950: Former Nazi scientist Wernher von Braun is appointed director of development operations of Redstone Arsenal's Army Ballistic Missile Agency in Huntsville, Alabama.

June 6, 1950: Supreme Commander of the Allied Powers Douglas MacArthur bans Communists from public service positions in Japanese government.

June 25, 1950: The Korean War begins as the army of Communist North Korea crosses the 38th parallel and storms toward Seoul, South Korea.

June 30, 1950: President Truman orders U.S. troops into Korea.

July 5, 1950: The Law of Return, which opens Israel to worldwide Jewish immigration, is passed by the Israeli *Knesset*.

Britain's postwar housing One major issue confronting the British Parliament was adequate shelter for those displaced by the war. Millions of housing units, including apartments and single homes, had been destroyed by German bombs, leaving large numbers of British citizens homeless. Many non-British victims of the war were also seeking shelter in Britain. Parliament passed the New Towns Act of 1946 and the Town and Country Planning Act in 1947. Single-family units were constructed. The aluminum, prefabricated houses shown in this photo were built in Cheltenham, outside of London, in 1946.

HOW TO CONTAIN THE SOVIETS

IT IS CLEAR THAT the United States cannot expect in the foreseeable future to enjoy political intimacy with the Soviet regime. It must continue to regard the Soviet Union as a rival, not a partner, in the political arena. It must continue to expect that Soviet policies will reflect no abstract love of peace and stability, no real faith in the possibility of a permanent happy coexistence of the Socialist and capitalist worlds, but rather a cautious, persistent pressure toward the disruption and weakening of all rival influence and rival power.

Balanced against this are the facts that Russia, as opposed to the Western world in general, is still by far the weaker party, that Soviet policy is highly flexible, and that Soviet society may well contain deficiencies which will eventually weaken its own total potential. This would of itself warrant the United States entering with reasonable confidence upon a policy of firm containment, designed to confront the Russians with unalterable counter-force at every point where they show signs of encroaching upon the interests of a peaceful and stable world.

—FROM "THE SOURCES OF SOVIET CONDUCT" BY "X" (GEORGE KENNAN, SENIOR STATE DEPARTMENT OFFICIAL), *FOREIGN AFFAIRS*, JULY 1947

The Marshall Plan

BY JUNE 1947, EUROPE HAD SUFFERED through a catastrophic war and one of its worst winters in history. Much of its industrial infrastructure had been destroyed. Major cities were still in ruins, and millions of people across Europe were homeless. There was little hope for a swift economic recovery. It became obvious to President Harry Truman that relief must reach these countries soon if they were to escape Soviet expansion.

In a commencement speech at Harvard University on June 5, 1947, Secretary of State George Marshall unveiled a plan to rebuild the nations of Europe, strengthen their economies, and reduce economic rivalry between them. Sixteen countries met in Paris in July 1947 to discuss the implementation of the Marshall Plan, officially called the European Recovery Program. Each of the 16 nations lobbied for a large piece of the aid package. They finally sent a request for $22 billion in aid

Secretary of State George Marshall

to Truman. In an attempt to ward off Republican opposition to the plan, Truman reduced the request to $17 billion in the bill he sent to Congress. After much debate by both sides of the House, Congress approved an appropriation of $5 billion for the first year and a total of more than $12 billion during the four-year life of the program.

The Soviets were extended an invitation to participate in the plan by the Allied leaders, but Joseph Stalin refused when he learned that it would require him to approve economic freedoms for Eastern European countries under postwar Soviet control. Stalin brought his opposition to the Marshall Plan to the United Nations. Finding few sympathetic ears, Stalin initiated the Molotov Plan, named after Soviet foreign minister Vyacheslav Molotov. This plan provided financial assistance to the Eastern European countries, which increased Soviet control.

Division and blockade Before the war ended, the Big Three Allied leaders signed an agreement to divide postwar Germany into four zones and Berlin into four sectors, each administered by an Allied nation, until Germany was eventually reunified. Berlin sat well within the Soviets' zone. Stalin did not agree with the other Allies' plan to rebuild Germany's economy. He therefore blocked access to the western sectors of Berlin on June 24, 1948. Truman rejected a plan to send trucks across the Soviet border because of the threat of war. Instead, the Allies airlifted supplies to West Berlin (*pictured*) until well after the blockade was revoked by Stalin in May 1949.

1950-51

August 1950: Operation Magic Carpet ends. It succeeds in airlifting 45,000 of the 46,000 Jews in Yemen to Israel, to escape religious persecution.

September 1950: The McCarran Internal Security Act, which calls for the registration of all Communist organizations, is passed by Congress over Truman's veto.

September 15, 1950: General MacArthur's X Corps lands on the Korean coast at Inchon and charges inland.

September 19, 1950: Communist Party members employed by the West German government are fired from their jobs.

December 1, 1950: President Truman creates the Federal Civil Defense Administration under the Office of Emergency Management.

March 13, 1951: Israel demands $1.5 billion in German war reparations to help pay for the post-Holocaust refugee crisis.

April 11, 1951: General Douglas MacArthur is relieved of his Korean command by President Truman. MacArthur's unauthorized threat to bring the war to China was in direct opposition to Truman's wishes.

May 1, 1951: The U.S. government-sponsored Radio Free Europe broadcasts for the first time, from Munich to Eastern Europe.

May 18, 1951: The United Nations moves to its new headquarters in New York City, on Manhattan's East Side.

September 8, 1951: Forty-nine nations sign the Japanese Peace Treaty in San Francisco, officially ending World War II and reestablishing Japanese sovereignty.

October 19, 1951: President Truman signs an act formally ending World War II.

WWII novelists Two of the greatest American novelists of World War II are James Jones and Norman Mailer, both of whom loosely based their stories on their own experiences. Jones completed a trilogy of highly acclaimed war novels: *From Here to Eternity, The Thin Red Line,* and *Whistle.* Mailer's first novel, *The Naked and the Dead* (1948), brought him international fame. It describes the tensions within an American infantry platoon as the soldiers face the terrors of battle on a South Pacific island.

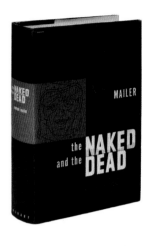

Mao, Communists take control in China Chairman Mao Zedong proclaims the founding of the People's Republic of China in Beijing on October 1, 1949. Support from the West was not enough to prop up Chiang Kai-shek's Kuomintang regime in the face of eight years of Japanese aggression, an economy ravaged by inflation, a devastated infrastructure, and a Communist movement that had gained new strength during the war. Two generations of civil war ended with a Kuomintang withdrawal to Taiwan, leaving the Communists in control of the mainland.

Rosenbergs executed for espionage The Jewish parents of two young boys were executed in New York City's Sing Sing Prison on June 19, 1953. They were Julius (*pictured*) and Ethel Rosenberg, and their crime was conspiracy to commit espionage. Julius, a leader in the Young Communist League in the 1930s, was first recruited by Russian agents in 1943. He recruited a number of other Americans, including Ethel's brother, David Greenglass. Julius and Greenglass provided the Russians with top-secret information, including details about the Manhattan Project. Greenglass, who was arrested in 1950, implicated Julius and Ethel, and the couple's conviction was based largely on his testimony. Years later, Greenglass confessed that he had lied about his sister's involvement to save the lives of his wife and himself.

Rebuilding Japan

FROM 1945 TO 1952, JAPAN CAME under Allied (effectively American) control, with General Douglas MacArthur serving as the Supreme Commander of the Allied Powers (SCAP). His administration was small but determined to fulfill its mission of demilitarizing and democratizing Japan while reestablishing a viable economy. The administration used the Japanese government and bureaucracy to enact those directives.

Demilitarization involved disbanding the empire, demobilizing the armed forces, dismantling armaments industries, bringing 25 war leaders to trial, and purging 200,000 wartime government officials. Essential to democratization was a new constitution, effective from May 1947. It renounced war and armed forces, while the emperor lost his divine status. Universal suffrage now elected a bicameral Diet.

Under the economic program of land reform, land was sold cheaply to tenants, who represented nearly half of all farmers. This program fostered economic growth. SCAP tried to break up the large corporations, but fewer than 30 of the originally targeted 1,200 were dissolved. However, antimonopoly and fair trading laws promoted industrial change. Some labor reform was enacted, such as independent labor unions, but in 1947–48 the Cold War brought a clampdown on burgeoning left-wing radicalism.

Social legislation benefited women, as the civil code announced equality between the sexes and equal inheritance rights. Coeducation became the norm, and education

Construction site in Tokyo, 1949

was democratized and generally improved at all levels. The reforms' fate was uncertain because it depended on the Japanese to implement the new policies. However, the population's genuine surprise at the benevolence of the occupiers and its desire for more freedom facilitated changes in Japanese lifestyles and mentality.

SCAP's efforts are a matter of historical controversy. Historians first depicted them as heroic and successful, but then "revisionists" attacked them as conservatism triumphing over reform. Recent accounts are more balanced.

The occupation formally ended on April 28, 1952, after Japan signed the Treaty of Peace with its wartime antagonists (except for the Soviet Union) on September 8, 1951. Firmly aligned with the West, Japan began a long, sustained period of economic growth.

The Korean War Exhausted U.S. Marines retreat after a surprise attack by Red Chinese hordes on the Korean Peninsula in December 1950. Separation of the peninsula into Allied and Soviet zones in 1945—a division opposed by Korean leaders—resulted in the creation of a Communist North and a nominally democratic South, each of which claimed national sovereignty. On June 25, 1950, thousands of North Korean troops poured across the 38th parallel intent on reuniting Korea by force. United Nations forces came to South Korea's defense, but the fighting dragged on into 1953 after Communist China entered on the North's side. An armistice finally reestablished the status quo, leaving the two hostile states still divided along the 38th parallel.

THE POSTWAR WORLD

OCTOBER 1951–TODAY

> **"Let's not talk about Communism. Communism was just an idea, just pie in the sky."**
>
> —RUSSIAN PRESIDENT BORIS YELTSIN

ON JUNE 21, 2000, U.S. president Bill Clinton awarded 20 Medals of Honor, most of them posthumously, to the Japanese American soldiers of the 442d Regimental Combat Team from World War II. This formal ceremony represented more than just overdue acknowledgment of the soldiers' bravery under fire. The award of the Medal of Honor was also a way of acknowledging that a wrong had been done to the Japanese American community in the crisis years of World War II, when 120,000 had been interned in American camps. The echoes of the Second World War have reverberated to the present in a myriad of different voices, and they can still be heard more than 60 years after its end.

The decades since the war have been among the most eventful in history, but they have not seen a repeat of the two cataclysmic conflicts that transformed Europe and Asia from 1914 to 1945. The absence of any major war between any of the states that fought the last war has been perhaps World War II's most enduring legacy. Although the Korean conflict provoked renewed anxieties about a Third World War, such a scenerio was averted. China, the Soviet Union, and the United States recognized that the stakes were too high. In 1953 a cease-fire was called, and the two Korean states found themselves back where they had started in 1950. South Korea went on to become one of the boom economies of the Pacific Rim, while North Korea became and remained a Communist dictatorship, impervious to the eventual collapse of world communism 40 years later.

Russian president Boris Yeltsin displays the old clenched fist of Communist solidarity at a funeral in August 1991. Ironically, by 1991 Communist solidarity was a thing of the past. The Soviet bloc had collapsed, the Berlin Wall had fallen, and the Soviet Union had dissolved. The separate republics demanded independence and adopted their own parliamentary systems.

The absence of general war did not mean the absence of crises and conflicts, many of which developed as a direct consequence of World War II and its aftermath. In Asia, the collapse of the colonial order brought about by Japanese aggression contributed to the rapid end of the old empires throughout the region. Nationalist revolt in the Dutch East Indies began in 1945 with a declaration of independence. After a violent anticolonial war, the Dutch were expelled and an independent Indonesia was established in 1949. In Malaya, Communist insurgency resulted in a prolonged anticolonial campaign that the British government fought with a mixture of brutality and concession. When the area won independence in 1957, communism had been defeated.

In French Indochina, the reverse happened. French colonial forces and the local French population responded to Communist insurgency with widespread violence. In 1954 French forces suffered a humiliating defeat at Dien Bien Phu and abandoned the whole region. Indochina was divided into the separate states of Laos, Cambodia, and Vietnam, with the last divided like Korea. North Vietnam became a Communist state led by veteran nationalist Ho Chi Minh, and South Vietnam became a pro-Western dictatorship backed by American aid. As in the case of Korea, the North soon began to put pressure on the southern area, and in 1957 it launched a full-scale guerrilla war. In 1960 Communist sympathizers in the South formed the National Liberation Front and provoked a civil war as well. The result was more than a decade of violence along the battle lines of the global Cold War. Only in 1975 did Laos, Cambodia, and South Vietnam finally become Communist states, putting an end to the long postwar crisis.

U.S. infantrymen fire on enemy troops somewhere along the South Vietnamese-Cambodian border in May 1970. The collapse of the French colonial regime in Indochina in the decade following World War II and the spread of the Communist movement in Asia led the United States into a lengthy—and ultimately futile—war of containment in Vietnam.

The rapid eclipse of the old imperial powers transformed the politics not only of Asia but of the Middle East and Africa as well. The end of the war led to the rapid disappearance of French and British influence throughout the Arab world. The mandated territories granted by the League of Nations after World War I were granted independence. These included Syria and Jordan in 1946 and Lebanon in 1943. The mandate in Palestine was liquidated, and a Jewish homeland—promised after World War I but never granted—was created in 1948: the State of Israel.

The realization of the full horrors of the genocide of the European Jews had led to growing demands for a Jewish state. British forces stood in the middle between Palestinian Arabs and Jewish settlers and immigrants, but a prolonged guerrilla conflict and growing American pressure forced the British to abandon the area. Israel was established by compelling Arab acquiescence, but the consequence has been six decades of violence. The surrounding Arab states fought Israel unsuccessfully in 1948 and again in 1967 and 1973.

In 1956 Israel found unlikely allies in Britain and France in the attempt to forcibly prevent the new nationalist regime of Egypt's Gamal Abdel Nasser from taking over the Suez Canal. The Suez crisis was the last flourish of old imperial Europe. American and Soviet pressure ended this European operation, making it finally evident that the long period of European hegemony that had dominated the wider world for two centuries was gone for good.

The unraveling of empire became complete with the independence of colonial Africa. The Allies had used African forces and resources extensively during the war. But Africa's nationalist and anticolonial forces—small before the war—increased during the years of fighting. In North Africa, the defeat of France in 1940 and the expulsion of Italy in 1942 undermined the credibility of Western imperialism and paved the way for independence. Libya became independent in 1951; Egypt followed in 1954 and Tunisia and Morocco in 1956. In Algeria, where an entrenched French settler community existed, there was strong resistance to withdrawal. A savage civil war broke out between French colonists, Islamic revolutionaries, and native nationalists. The French army fought the insurgency with considerable brutality, but after eight years of conflict, the new French president, Charles de Gaulle, accepted defeat. In 1962 the French army and French colonists abandoned Algeria for good.

Hungarian freedom fighters prepare to resist Russian forces in November 1956. The first stirrings of internal discontent with the Soviet domination of Eastern Europe surfaced in the early 1950s. In '56, the Soviets crushed the threat posed by the Hungarian Revolution with brute military force. Demands for reform in Czechoslovakia 12 years later were also answered by Soviet tanks.

In the rest of colonial Africa, independence was granted state by state in the 1950s and 1960s. Only in southern Africa did the colonial system persist. In southern Rhodesia, white settlers declared independence on their own behalf in 1965 and tried to suppress black demands for a democratic state and more equal distribution of land. Only in 1980, after another violent civil war, did the white settlers abandon the struggle and accept the new state of Zimbabwe. In the Portuguese colonies of Angola and Mozambique, an anticolonial war backed by Communist forces ended with Portuguese withdrawal and independence in 1975.

The last bastion of the old order was South Africa. Dominated by a powerful nationalist movement led by its predominantly Dutch settlers, South Africa was expelled from the British Commonwealth for embarking on a quasi-Fascist policy of race discrimination known as apartheid (separateness). The white minority kept a harsh grip on the rest of the population, including a fraction of white dissenters who opposed the regime. Cut off from the rest of the world by sanctions and moral pressure, the white regime finally conceded defeat in 1990 and proceeded to dismantle apartheid. In 1994 free elections brought victory for the African National Congress under its leader, Nelson Mandela, who recently had been released from a government prison. He became democratic South Africa's first president.

Contrasting with such upheavals, the situation in Europe stabilized in the 1950s and 1960s, though not without threat. In 1953 strikes and protests in East Germany produced the first internal reactions against the Sovietization of Eastern Europe. The hostility of the population was put down by units of the Red Army stationed there. When Hungarian nationalists and intellectuals staged an anti-Communist revolt in October 1956, the Soviet Union ordered troops from the Soviet bloc into Budapest to crush resistance. When similar demands for reform and openness developed in Czechoslovakia in the mid-1960s, the Soviet Union and other Warsaw Pact forces intervened. In 1968 tanks appeared in Prague and Communist orthodoxy was reinstated.

The Western states responded little to these internal Communist crises. However, the Cold War intensified when the status of independent West Berlin was once again threatened by the Soviet bloc. In 1961 the East German leader, Walter Ulbricht, ordered a solid frontier wall to be built across Berlin, dividing the capitalist west from the Communist east. The Berlin Wall came to symbolize the permanent division between the two different ways of life.

The Cold War marked the complete shift in the international balance of power, made possible by the rise of Soviet and American military and economic strength during World War II. The confrontation between the two camps was not entirely new, since the Soviet Union in the 1920s and 1930s had been feared by much of the West as the vanguard of a new social order. In the 1950s, however, the Soviet Union was perceived to be a much greater threat—not only a challenge to Western assumptions about personal free-

An angry Fidel Castro denounces the United States in 1962. U.S. officials became concerned in the early 1960s when Castro turned to the Soviet Union for support, and became greatly alarmed when the Soviets shipped ballistic missiles to the island nation in 1962. The aggressive act brought the two superpowers to the brink of war that October.

dom, but the center of a worldwide Communist web that menaced the established order throughout the developing world. The American government developed a strategy of "containment" designed to limit the spread of communism.

The strategy was supported by America's allies in NATO but opposed by a growing youth movement hostile to what was seen as a new form of imperialism, and anxious about the growing threat of nuclear war. The first major test for containment came in 1959 when Fidel Castro led a Communist-inspired revolt in Cuba. The new revolutionary regime was supported by the Soviet Union. When it became clear in 1962 that Castro was being supplied with Soviet missiles, Washington issued an ultimatum to the Soviet Union to remove them, and ordered a naval blockade of Cuba. The confrontation was one of the most dramatic episodes of the postwar period. At the final moment, Soviet leader Nikita Khrushchev ordered Soviet vessels bound for Cuba to turn back. U.S. president John F. Kennedy was saved from having to make a final decision for military action. A year later, Kennedy was assassinated; in 1964 Khrushchev was removed from office by his party colleagues.

The Cuban Missile Crisis was the closest the Cold War came to direct conflict between the two superpowers. The conflict was played out thereafter by proxy: one side or the other lending support to third-party states, engaging in espionage and covert operations, and arming and funding guerrilla movements and insurgencies. In 1964 the United States, led by President Lyndon Johnson, made the decision to commit troops and aircraft to the civil war in South Vietnam, and for 10 years the U.S. fought to contain the spread of communism in Southeast Asia. North Vietnam was supported by the Soviet Union. In 1975, following prolonged antiwar protests in the United States and Europe, the last American forces were withdrawn.

Four years later, the Soviet Union sent troops to fight in Afghanistan in support of the Communist regime, an intervention that lasted 10 years and cost the lives of thousands of Soviet soldiers. The United States provided aid and arms for the anti-Communist guerrilla movement. In 1989 the Soviet Union withdrew its forces. Both the Vietnam and Afghan wars were the longest periods of active fighting for both states since World War II. Both involved high casualties, considerable cost, and eventual defeat. Cold War by proxy proved deeply damaging to both of the superpowers that fought it.

Many explanations exist for why the Cold War never turned into open conflict. Memories of the horrors of World War II certainly played a part.

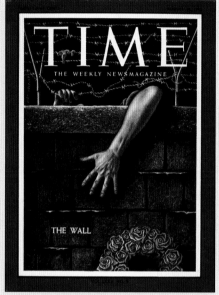

Constructed in 1961, the Berlin Wall bisecting the former German capital was a concrete manifestation of the ideological division between the capitalist West and the Communist East. Built by the Communists to keep people in, rather than out, it also became a powerful symbol of authoritarianism.

Most of the world's leaders in the 20 years after 1945 had experienced the war directly and understood its uncompromising and destructive nature. As the two superpowers produced increasingly destructive weapons, including the "superbomb" (hydrogen bomb) in 1952, they became increasingly fearful of an all-out war. They understood that nuclear weapons and, from the late 1950s, intercontinental missiles could produce terrible levels of mutual destruction.

The arms race was, however, an unstable element. In 1963 the two sides agreed to ban nuclear testing above ground. In 1968 the United States, the Soviet Union, Britain, and 59 other nations agreed on a nonproliferation treaty to prevent the spread of nuclear weapons. A year later, the first arms limitation talks (SALT I) began. The period of so-called détente that followed produced further agreements on reducing armaments.

In 1975 the Helsinki Accords were signed between 33 European states, the United States, and Canada. The agreements committed the signatories to accept the existing frontiers of

German neo-Nazi skinheads, on the march in Berlin in 2002, find themselves outnumbered by counterdemonstrators. Six decades after World War II, German democracy was a resounding success, the economy was healthy, and the nation was a respected partner of the Western powers. A demonstration by a few neo-Nazis inspired more disgust than alarm.

Europe, drawn up in the 1940s, and to promote human rights. In 1977 further agreement was reached in the Additional Protocols to the Geneva Convention, which defined more effective protection for civilians from the effects of war. In the 1980s, a new round of negotiations (START) was initiated by U.S. president Ronald Reagan, which led to more comprehensive arms limitation agreements by 1987.

One of the significant contributions to the long period of peace lies in the stabilization and revival of the international economy. Some of the rivalry and violence of the interwar years had been fueled by industrial and financial crisis, the closure of markets, and beggar-my-neighbor economic policies. From the 1940s to the 1970s, the developed world experienced an economic boom of unprecedented scale. The newly emancipated areas of Asia, the Middle East, and Africa stimulated the boom by demanding industrial products and supplying food and raw materials in return. The Soviet bloc also experienced high levels of planned industrial development.

The boom owed a great deal to international cooperation. In 1947 a General Agreement on Trade and Tariffs was signed, which freed world trade from the protectionist straitjacket of the 1930s. The World Bank and International Monetary Fund kept world currency and trading systems more open and flexible while modern industrial corporations developed more sophisticated and increasingly global operations. In Europe, major new trading blocs stimulated high levels of employment and trade. These blocs included the European Economic Community (forerunner of the European Union), founded in 1957, and the Communist COMECON organization, set up in 1949. Economic management, informed by improved macroeconomic theory, replaced the traditions of liberal free-market economics.

Among the most striking beneficiaries of the boom were Germany, Italy, and Japan. The three former Axis partners became major international economies, thoroughly integrated with the West and sharing access to international resources on equal terms. After 1945 there was never again talk of territorial "living space" as the answer to economic difficulties. Japan and Germany built into their new constitutions a prohibition on using their armed forces for any military activity outside their frontiers. When the economic boom slowed down in Germany in the 1980s and in Japan in the 1990s, there was no serious political backlash.

The fortunes of the Soviet Union took a different path. The victory of communism in 1945 assured the Soviet Union's domination of Eastern Europe for more than 40 years, but the international Communist movement was anything but united. Tito's Yugoslavia refused to be part of the Communist bloc in 1948. Instead, it embarked on a more flexible Communist experiment, with firmer links with the West and less rigid economic controls. In 1958 Soviet relations with Communist China deteriorated sharply at the moment when Mao launched the Great Leap Forward to modernize the Chinese economy. By 1960 there was an open rupture between the two powers. Albania and a number of Communist movements in the developing world followed Mao's lead, and the Communist world divided between allegiance to either Moscow or Beijing.

In Western Europe, Communist parties became increasingly critical of the crude authoritarianism of the Soviet model. By the 1980s, Communist nations were forced to adapt to the realities of the more prosperous West. In 1985 a new Soviet leader, Mikhail Gorbachev, embarked on a new policy of openness and restructuring (*glasnost* and *perestroika*) to try to introduce a

Sixty years after the end of World War II, the new face of China reflects a modern consumer lifestyle and booming economic growth. China, with a population of more than 1.3 billion, has taken its place among the great world powers of the 21st century.

reformed communism with greater economic freedoms. Reform in the Soviet Union encouraged other Soviet bloc populations to question the Communist system.

When in 1989 Gorbachev prompted the other Communist regimes to accept change, there was widespread upheaval. A non-Communist regime emerged in Poland in August 1989, and over the following four months every Soviet bloc regime collapsed. That fall the Berlin Wall was breached, and in 1990 the divided halves of Germany were united again in a single state. In 1990 the Soviet Union itself began to crumble as the separate republics demanded independence, and in 1991 the Union was scrapped. The Communist parties were at least nominally dissolved and parliamentary systems were adopted throughout the former Soviet bloc, bringing to an end a long era of European dictatorships. In Russia, Boris Yeltsin was elected president on June 12, 1991.

The problems faced by the world in the 1990s and the early 21st century were problems not inherited directly from World War II. Global warming and environmental crises, the rise of Islamic fundamentalism and the turmoil in the Middle East, and the emergence of China as an economic superpower were the products of the postwar transformation of the industrial and political landscape. The "war on terror," provoked by the destruction of the World Trade Center in New York City on September 11, 2001, is a war quite different from World War II.

This new war is set in an unfamiliar international setting in which, after the collapse of the Soviet bloc, there is only one major power, the United States. American defense spending is currently equal to the spending of the rest of the world combined, but the targets of American intervention have been failing states (Afghanistan and Iraq). The contest takes place on a global scale, and it combines the very latest electronic technology against primitive bomb attacks and ambushes. Yet this enormous technological and military gap has not produced the assurance of victory as it did in 1945.

Even today, the shadow of World War II remains thinly visible. On one level, the war generated myths that became embedded in popular culture. Images from the war enjoyed an iconographic status: St. Paul's cathedral

More than 10,000 people gather at the Holocaust Memorial Museum dedication in Washington, D.C., on April 22, 1993. They observed the lighting of the eternal flame in memory of the six million Jewish victims of the Holocaust. The museum not only commemorates the victims, but it serves as a sobering reminder—and a warning—of the dark side of "civilized" man.

standing amid the ruins of the Blitz, U.S. servicemen raising the American flag on Iwo Jima, and the portrait of German Jewish girl Anne Frank, perhaps the Holocaust's best-known victim. Memorials to the dead were still being erected more than 60 years after the end of the war.

Meanwhile, the idea of "victim" and "perpetrator" has assumed a fresh poignancy. There has been much discussion, for instance, of "comfort women," the war-time sex slaves of Japanese soldiers. Moreover, the significance and impact of strategic bombing on civilians in Germany and Japan has been debated. Other categories of victims were found among the forced labor force of the German and Japanese empires, and among the vast population of the Soviet concentration camps, which operated at the same time as Auschwitz and Dachau. The sense of right and wrong, which initially colored the popular view of the war, has become blurred.

In the West, the most enduring legacy of the war has been the memory of the Holocaust. No other single element of the war has recently attracted greater attention. In Washington, Berlin, London, and many other cities, museums dedicated to the Holocaust and to Jewish history have been founded within the last two decades. Stolen or confiscated Jewish assets have been tracked down, and a renewed effort of restitution has been set in motion. The memory of the Holocaust also keeps alive the historical image of Adolf Hitler. Although World War II was comprised of many different wars, which between them had many causes, it is the terrible war unleashed by Hitler against the Jewish people that remains the most grotesque and conspicuous legacy of the 1940s, the most violent and murderous decade of modern times.

INDEX

408, 416, 420, 421, *421*, 441–442, 448, 456, *456*
invasion of, 442
port closed, 438
postwar reconstruction, 475, *475*
Tokyo Express, 260, 298
Tokyo Rose, 458, 459, *459*
Tommy (racing pigeon), 238
Total war concept, 15–16, 331–332, 333, *333*
Toyama, Japan, 454
Toyoda Soemu, 369
Trans-Iranian Railway, 251
Transjordan, 470
Transportion Plan, 355, 356
Transylvania, 420
Treaty of Locarno (1925), 24, 36
Treaty of Peace (1951), 474, 475
Treaty of Versailles (1919), 18, *18*, 28, 34, 46
Treblinka (death camp), 224, 226, 232, 248, 270, *270*, 274, 277, 300, 304, 420
Tresckow, Henning von, 274, *274*
Trimmingham, Rupert, 255
Tripartite Pact (1940), 87, 114, 116, 118, 120, 132
Tripoli, Libya, 262
Triton code (German), 194
Triumph of the Will (movie), 35
Trocme, Andre, 248
Trocme, Daniel, 248
Trocme, Magda, 248
Truk Island, Battle of, 343, *343*, 344
Truman, Bess, 425, *425*
Truman, Harry, 425, *425*
    assumes presidency, 411, 428
    atomic bombs and, 339, 442–443, 452, 454, 461
    chosen as Roosevelt's running mate, 301
    Cold War and, 468, 472, 474
    communism in U.S. and, 474
    on defense of freedom, 462
    displaced persons camps and, 465
    invasion of Japan and, 442
    Korean War and, 472
    Potsdam Conference, 442–443, 448, 450, *450*
    reconstruction of postwar Europe, 468, 473
    Roosevelt and, 384, *384*
    World War II officially ended, 466, 474
Truman, Margaret, 425, *425*
T-34 tanks (Soviet Union), 155, *155*, 267, *267*
Tulagi, Solomon Islands, 230, 234, 236, *236*, 295, *295*
Tunisia, 123, 232, 250, 270, 273, *273*, 284, 479
Tunisian Victory (movie), 279, *279*
Turin, Italy, 252
Turing, Alan, 91, *91*
Turkey, 87, 128, 158, 274, 346, 354, 380, 414

Turkish Empire, 16, 17
Tuskegee Airmen, 255
Two-Thousand Yard Stare (Lea), 394, *394*
Type 95 Ha-Go light tanks (Japan), 243, *243*
Typhoons, 400, 401, *401*

U
Udet, Ernst, 168, *168*
U-48 (Germany, U-boat), 120, *120*
Ukraine
    Germans in, 344
        citizen collaborators, 162
        citizens fight, 155, *155*
        citizens forced to labor for, 246, *246*, 287, *287*
        citizens welcomed, 147, *147*
        Jews murdered in, 146, *146*, 166
    Red Army
        advances, 332, 335, 344
        atrocities by, 154
        citizens fight, 346, 372
Ulbricht, Walter, 480
Ultra intelligence, 197, 288, 364
Umezu Yoshijiro, 458, *458*, 459, *459*
Union of Soviet Socialist Republics (USSR). *See* Soviet Union.
United Nations
    convened, 464
    created, 151, 159, 163, 190, 382, 413, 414, 446, 454, 464
    genocide outlawed, 461, 470
    headquarters, 474
    Nationalist China (Taiwan) and, 470
    Palestine partition, 468
United Nations Declaration (1942), 151, 159
United Nations Relief and Rehabilitation (UNRRA), 448
United States
    aid to refugees, 350
    aircraft spotters, 89
    alliances and agreements, 144, 150, 158
    as Arsenal of Democracy, 96, 104, 110, 119, 124, 125, 128, 140, 142, *142*, 146, 150, 156, 167, *167*, 172, 178, 183, 212, 220, 231, 321, *321*, 338, 346, 354
    Atlantic defenses, 158, *158*
    atomic weapons, 320
        bombs dropped on Japan, *440*, 443, *443*, 452, *452*, 453, *453*, 454, *454*, 455, *455*
        Einstein and, 48
        limiting, 482
        Manhattan Project, 104, *104*, 252, 338, *338*, 339, *339*, 415, 448, 449, *449*, 450, *450*

plutonium, 134, 314, 466
    postwar tests, 467
    research shared by Americans and British, 386
    secrecy, 256, 298
    superbombs (hydrogen), 482
    Truman and, 442–443
    at University of Chicago, 258, *258*
    U.S. National Academy of Sciences, 176
    use of, 425
bases on British territory, 110
bombed by Japan, 198, *198*, 200, 222, 240, 244, 394, 398, *398*, 434
bombed by USAAF, 294
British children sent to, 157
cash and carry arms policy, 73
children in war effort, 296, *296*
Chinese Exclusion Act (1882) repealed, 326
communism in, 472, 474
conscription, 112, 118, *118*, 124, *124*, 137, *137*, 179, 184, 244, 284
consumer goods, 224
Cuban Missile Crisis, 481
D-Day news, 360, *360*
declaration of war against Japan, 153, 182
defense industries, 270, 271, *271*, 323, *323*, 327, 329, *329*, 349, *349*, 351, *351*
    explosions, 216, 376, *376*
    housing for workers, 258, *258*, 382, *382*
economy
    boom, 332
    defense spending, 44, 79, 104, 124, 294
    financing of war, 211, 248, 284, *284*, 341, *341*
    price controls, 350, *350*
    wage controls, 258
embargoes by, 46, 66, 68, 73, *73*, 76, 78, 106, 114, 126, 152, 156, *156*, 192
euphemisms used by, 273
fascism in, 51, *51*
FBI, 220, 261, 346
Finland and, 74
Free French government recognized, 374
French Indochina and, 107
German and Italian nationals in, 146, 182, 246
GI Bill of Rights, 368, *368*
Greenland protected by, 136
Hitler opposed to war with, 60
Holocaust memorials, 484, *484*
invasion fears, 225
invasion preparations, 351, *351*
isolationism in, 25–26, 41, *41*, 76, 98, 179
    America First Committee, 121, *121*
    Chicago Tribune, 76

Kennedy, Joseph, 121, *121*
Lindbergh, 41, *41*
Roosevelt and, 119
Japan
    commercial treaty with, 48
    embargo against, 104
    invasion of, 354, 366, 386, 442, 444
    talks with, 138, 178, 180
Japanese Americans
    in Army, 201, 285, *285*, 426, *426*, 477
    banned from West Coast, 200
    in Hawaii, 254
    interned, 182, 193, 200, *200*, 201, *201*, 464
Jews
    anti-Semitism against, 51, *51*, 166
    denied entry, 49, *49*, 126
    morale, *296*
        Doolittle raid, 208, 209
        movies, 115, *115*, 296, *296*
        rallies, 211, *211*
        Roosevelt and, 240
        Sad Sack, 289, *289*
        women and, 284, *284*
Neutrality Act, 26, 34, 44, 46, 66, 170, 176
neutrality declared, 58
postwar
    allows DPs in, 468
    atomic weapons program, 467, *467*, 482
    Cold War, 466, 468, 472, 474, *474*, 480–482
    containment policy, 472
    Korean War, 463, 472, 474, 475, *475*, 477
    loan to Britain, 464
    occupation of
        Germany, 462
        Japan, 443, 456, 459, *459*
        Korea, 458, 463
    reconstruction of Europe, 280, 473, 486
propaganda
    comic books, 259, *259*
    to encourage Japanese surrender, 439, *439*
    against Hitler, 225, *225*
    against Japanese, 367, *367*
    against Japanese Americans, 193, *193*
    magazines, 221, *221*
    movies, 115, *115*, 185, *185*, 221, *221*, 259, 279, *279*, 296, *296*
    Office of War Information, 221, *221*, 238, 439, *439*
    poster campaigns, 238, *238*, 329, *329*, 341, *341*
    tour by Mrs. Sullivan, 256
racism in, 212, 283, *283*
Radio Free Europe, 474
rationing, 190, 214, 221, *221*, 254, 350, 356

Acknowledgments

Page 35: Peter Herz quote from Introduction to *Voices from the Third Reich: An Oral History* by Johannes Stemhoff, et. al, Cambridge: De Capo Press, 1989.

Page 45: Quote from "Qualifying as a Leader" by Tominaga Shozo in *Japan at War: An Oral History* by Haruku Taya Cook and Theodore F. Cook, New York: The New Press, 1992.

Pages 55 and 57: Quotes from *Diary from the Years of Occupation (1939–1944)* by Zygmunt Klukowski and George Klukowski, Champaign: University of Illinois Press.

Page 157: Quote from "Cartons Family" transcript from http://www.bbc.co.uk/schoolradio/history/worldwar2audioclipslibrary_clip21.shtml.

Page 199: *The Bat Bomb.* Painting by Chris Fauver, originally commissioned by *Air Force* magazine. Reprinted with permission.

Page 244: *The Final Act.* Painting by John Meeks. Courtesy of www.subart.net. Used with permission.

Page 328: *Mosquito Boats 1941.* Painting by Arthur Beaumont, originally published in *National Geographic* magazine, September 1941. Courtesy of Arthur E. Beaumont II. Reproduced by permission.

Page 363: POW quotes from *We Were Each Other's Prisoners: An Oral History of World War II American and German Prisoners of War* by Lewis H. Carlson, Cambridge: Basic Books, 1997.

Page 394: *Two-Thousand Yard Stare.* Painting by Tom Lea. Courtesy of the Army Art Collection, U.S. Army Center of Military History. Reproduced by permission.

Page 399: "Life" and "Death" magazine covers. Courtesy of Ed Rouse and Herb Friedman. Used with permission.

Page 401: Quote from *Admiral Halsey's Story* by Admiral William F. Halsey and J. Bryan, III. Reprinted by permission.

Picture Credits

278 (top), 279 (top left), 280, 281 (bottom left), 282 (bottom), 283 (top right & bottom), 284 (top), 285 (bottom), 286, 288, 289 (top left & bottom left), 291 (top left, top right & bottom right), 292, 293 (top), 295 (top right), 296 (top), 298, 299 (bottom), 300, 301 (top left, bottom left & bottom right), 302 (top), 303 (bottom left & bottom right), 304 (bottom), 305 (top right & bottom right), 306 (center), 308 (top), 309 (top left), 311 (top & bottom left), 313 (top right), 315 (bottom left), 316, 317 (bottom right), 318 (top & center), 320 (top), 321 (top left), 322, 325 (top left), 327 (top), 329 (top), 332, 333, 334, 336 (top), 337, 338, 339, 340, 341 (top left & left center), 342 (bottom), 343, 345 (left), 346, 347, 349 (top right, bottom left & bottom right), 350, 351, 353, 356, 359 (bottom), 360 (bottom), 361 (bottom), 362, 363 (bottom), 364 (top), 365, 366, 367, 368 (bottom), 375 (top right & bottom right), 376 (bottom), 377 (bottom right), 378 (top), 381 (top & left center), 383 (top right), 384 (top), 385, 387 (top left & bottom left), 389 (bottom left & bottom right), 390 (top), 391 (left), 392 (top), 393 (bottom), 394 (bottom left), 395 (top left & bottom left), 396 (bottom), 397 (top left), 398 (top left), 399 (bottom), 400 (top), 401 (bottom), 402 (top), 403 (top right), 404 (right center), 405 (top left & top right), 407 (top), 408 (top), 410, 412, 415 (bottom), 416, 418 (bottom), 419 (right center & bottom), 421 (top), 422 (bottom), 423 (top), 425, 428 (bottom), 430 (top), 431 (bottom), 433, 434 (center & bottom), 435 (top), 436 (bottom), 437 (top right, bottom left & bottom right), 438 (bottom), 439 (top left), 440, 446 (bottom), 447 (top & bottom), 448, 449 (top left, bottom left & bottom right), 451 (top), 453 (bottom), 454 (center), 455 (top left), 456, 457 (top), 458 (top), 459 (top right, bottom left & bottom right), 460, 462, 463, 464, 465 (bottom), 466 (bottom), 467 (top left, bottom left & bottom right), 468 (bottom), 469, 470 (bottom), 472, 473 (top), 474 (center & bottom), 475, 476, 478, 479, 480, 481, 482, 483, 484, 485; Stock Montage, 119; Roger Viollet, 136 (top), 143 (bottom left), 248 (bottom); **The Granger Collection, New York:** 64 (bottom), 165 (right), 193 (top left), 439 (top right); Rue des Archives, 30 (bottom), 417 (right center); ullstein bild, 35 (top right), 53 (bottom), 67 (bottom), 137 (bottom), 148, 287 (right), 354 (bottom); **Harry S. Truman Library & Museum:** 391 (right), 405 (bottom), 450 (bottom), 452 (bottom left); **David Hogan Collection:** 131 (top right), 211 (right), 259 (bottom right), 315 (top left), 455 (top right); **The Image Works:** 184 (top); Topham, 72 (bottom); Roger Viollet, 386 (top); **Imperial War Museum:** 65 (bottom left), 87, 89 (top left), 98, 100 (bottom left), 102 (bottom), 103 (top), 106 (top), 112 (bottom), 113 (top left), 114 (top), 120 (top), 122 (bottom), 127 (bottom left), 128, 129 (top right & bottom left), 131 (bottom right), 133 (bottom), 135 (top), 147 (top left), 157 (bottom left), 163 (bottom right), 195 (top), 199 (bottom right), 212 (bottom), 215 (left), 260 (center), 263 (bottom), 272 (bottom left &

bottom right), 279 (bottom), 281 (bottom right), 290 (bottom), 291 (bottom left), 297 (top left), 307 (top), 311 (bottom right), 320 (bottom), 324 (right center), 325 (top right & bottom), 329 (left center), 336 (bottom), 355 (bottom left), 361 (center), 404 (left center); **Courtesy the office of Senator Daniel K. Inouye:** 6; **KPA:** HIP/National Archives, 78 (bottom); **Courtesy of Lancastria Association of Scotland:** Frank Clements, 102 (top); **Library and Archives Canada:** 201 (bottom); **Library of Congress:** 159 (top left), 259 (top right), 321 (bottom right), 323 (top), 384 (bottom), 398 (bottom right), 446 (top); **Lockheed California Co.:** 294 (top); **Loyal Edmonton Regiment Museum, Edmonton, Alberta:** 95 (bottom left); **Mary Evans Picture Library:** 234 (top); © **John Meeks 2004:** 244 (top); **National Archives, and Records Administration:** 108 (top), 114 (bottom), 124 (top), 140 (bottom), 142 (bottom), 143 (top left), 166 (top), 176 (bottom), 207 (top left), 209 (top right), 213 (bottom left), 225 (bottom right), 255, 258 (bottom), 266, 271 (bottom left), 272 (top), 275 (bottom), 283 (top left), 295 (top left), 297 (bottom), 313 (top left & bottom right), 314 (bottom), 318 (bottom), 319 (top), 326 (bottom), 327 (bottom), 328 (top), 329 (right center), 341 (right), 342 (top), 345 (right), 359 (top right), 367 (top), 379 (right center), 380, 389 (top right), 394 (top), 396 (top), 400 (bottom), 406 (bottom), 407 (center), 414 (top), 418 (top), 419 (top), 423 (bottom left & bottom right), 424 (bottom), 429 (bottom), 435 (center), 450 (top), 451 (bottom), 454 (bottom), 455 (bottom right), 459 (top left); **National Geographic Society:** 106 (bottom), 239 (bottom), 254 (top), 284 (bottom), 289 (bottom right), 308 (bottom), 309 (top right), 310 (top), 326 (top), 357 (bottom), 382 (top); **National Security Administration:** 143 (top right); **Naval Historical Center:** 92 (top), 167 (top right), 175, 178 (bottom), 198 (top), 208 (top), 218 (bottom left), 219 (top left & top right), 236, 237 (bottom left & bottom right), 242 (top), 247 (top), 250 (bottom), 282 (top), 294 (bottom), 295 (bottom left), 304 (top), 312 (bottom), 314 (top), 319 (bottom), 328 (right center), 354 (top), 368 (top), 369 (top), 376 (top), 395 (bottom right), 397 (top right & bottom), 398 (top right), 401 (top), 408 (bottom), 413, 417 (top), 438 (top); **NBCU Photo Bank:** 157 (top left), 261 (left); © **Northstar Gallery 2007:** 395 (top right); **Picture Alliance:** akg images, 95 (top left); 429 (top), 141 (bottom), 184 (top), 217 (bottom right), 228, 390 (bottom), 409 (bottom), 415 (top); dpa, 263 (top); 439 (bottom right); dpa/web, 444 (bottom); KPA/HIP/ National Archives, 216 (top); KPA/TopFoto, 139 (bottom right); **PIL Collection:** 27, 77 (top left), 163 (top right), 169 (bottom right), 185 (top left), 203 (top left), 221 (top right), 279 (top right), 296 (bottom), 323 (bottom); **popperfoto.com:** 188, 374 (bottom), 398 (bottom left), 428 (top); **Public Domain:** 260 (top), 309 (bottom), 364 (bottom); **RIA Novosti:** 183 (bottom), 227 (top right), 240 (bottom), 287

(top & bottom), 293 (bottom), 302 (bottom), 324 (left center), 349 (top left), 355 (bottom right), 388 (bottom), 389 (top left), 444 (top); **Robertstock.com:** 369 (bottom); **SGM Herb Friedman (Retired), Psywarrior.com:** 399 (top left & top right); **U.S. Patent and Trademark Office (USPTO):** 419 (left center); **ullstein bild:** 46 (bottom), 49 (top right), 54, 65 (bottom right), 71 (bottom left), 73 (bottom left), 84, 88 (bottom), 93 (top left), 105 (center), 107 (bottom left), 108 (bottom), 130, 155 (bottom right), 158 (bottom), 160 (bottom), 161 (top right), 168 (top), 169 (top left), 217 (bottom left), 242 (bottom), 260 (bottom), 263 (center), 264, 270 (top), 274 (bottom), 276 (top), 290 (top), 317 (top), 335, 355 (top left & top right), 377 (top), 378 (bottom right), 381 (right center), 382 (bottom), 432, 434 (top), 437 (top), 449 (top right), 473 (bottom); Archiv Gerstenberg, 52 (bottom), 57; Tita Binz, 378 (bottom left); Bunk, 414 (bottom); dpa, 281 (top); Voller Ernst, 303 (top), 310 (bottom), 430 (bottom); W. Frentz, 222 (top), 273 (right), 274 (top), 305 (top left), 307 (bottom), 321 (top right & bottom left), 344 (top), 378 (bottom center), 383 (top left & bottom); The Granger Collection, 67 (top); Grimm, 193 (bottom right); imagno, 39 (left center), 99 (top), 100 (bottom right), 155 (top); Kindermann, 66 (bottom); KPA/HIP Archive Collection, 63 (top); 197 (top), 375 (top left); KPA/HIP/Jewish Chronicle Ltd., 392 (bottom); LEONE, 95 (bottom right), 116 (bottom), 297 (right center), 358, 409 (top), 470 (top); Nowosti, 70 (top), 227 (top left), 374 (top), 431 (top left); pda, 436 (top); Stiftung, 377 (bottom left); SV-Bilderdienst, 41 (bottom), 77 (top right), 121 (bottom left), 129 (top left), 162 (bottom), 163 (top left), 164 (top), 189, 196 (top), 226 (bottom), 235 (top left), 246 (top), 256 (bottom), 267, 317 (bottom left); Roger Viollet, 101 (bottom); Tele Winkler, 295 (right center); Wittenstein, 274 (center); Wolff & Tritschler, 344 (center); Zitzow, 33 (bottom right); **United Kingdom Government:** 73 (top right); **United States Air Force:** 399 (center), 445; **United States Army Center of Military History:** Army Art Collection, 394 (bottom right); **United States Holocaust Memorial Museum Photo Archives:** 116 (top), 154 (top), 170 (top), 305 (bottom left); Robert Abrams, 211 (top); Julien Bryan, 56; Jerzy Ficowski, 248 (top); Anna Hassa Jarosky and Peter Hassa, 306 (top); Instytut Pamieci Narodowej, 65 (top left), 66 (top); KZ Gedenkstaette Dachau, 33 (bottom left); La Documentation Francaise, 246 (bottom); Muzej Revolucije Narodnosti Jugoslavije, 222 (bottom); National Archives and Records Administration, College Park, 72 (top); Jizchak Schwersenz, 49 (top left); Der Stuermer-Verlag, 45 (top right); **United States Marine Corps:** 251 (right center); **University of Kent, British Cartoon Archive, Templeman Library.:** 240 (top); **usmbooks.com:** 206 (top); **USS Arizona Memorial:** 174 (bottom); **Reproduced with the permission of West Dunbartonshire Council, Clydebank Central Library:** 132 (top); **www.calvin.edu/cas/gpa:** 301 (top right).